HULL IN THE EIGHTEENTH CENTURY

A Study in Economic and Social History

UNIVERSITY OF HULL PUBLICATIONS

HULL

in the Eighteenth Century

A STUDY IN ECONOMIC AND SOCIAL HISTORY

GORDON JACKSON

Published for the UNIVERSITY OF HULL *by*

OXFORD UNIVERSITY PRESS

LONDON NEW YORK TORONTO

1972

Oxford University Press, Ely House, London W.1

GLASGOW NEW YORK TORONTO MELBOURNE WELLINGTON
CAPE TOWN SALISBURY IBADAN NAIROBI DAR ES SALAAM LUSAKA ADDIS ABABA
BOMBAY CALCUTTA MADRAS KARACHI LAHORE DACCA
KUALA LUMPUR SINGAPORE HONG KONG TOKYO

ISBN 0 19 713415 7

Printed in Great Britain by
The Camelot Press Ltd., London and Southampton

For Hazel

PREFACE

Many books have been written about the Industrial Revolution, but little has been said about foreign and coastal trade and less about the individual ports of the British Isles. The object of this study is to emphasise the rôle of the ports in the Industrial Revolution by reconstructing the history of one of them, tracing in some detail the movement and direction of trade before and during the transformation of the seventeen-eighties, and the changes in mercantile, shipping and financial organisation that accompanied and facilitated that transformation. The story must be largely narrative rather than analytical in approach, partly because of the absence of comparative material for other ports, and partly because of the dearth of local information. Hull is not rich in manuscripts, especially of a personal nature. There are plenty of institutional records, both in Hull and London, but few merchants', shipowners' or industrialists' papers to put flesh on the dry bones of official reports and statistics. I have been forced to rely heavily on Customs records, with local colour added, where possible, from Corporation records and the surviving merchant, bank and Dock Company papers. It follows that many of the most obvious questions cannot be answered. Little, for instance, is known about the growth of Hull industry or about the accumulation of merchant capital, and nothing is known about the relative profitability of mercantile and local industrial capital or about the relationship between merchants and shipowning. In general I have refrained from guessing about such things as a rising or falling standard of living, and report the known facts and reasonable conclusions in the hope that a pattern of port life may emerge as the history of all the British ports comes to be written in the next decade. It is inevitable that some of my conclusions will have to be modified as comparative information becomes available, or as more local sources are discovered, but it is doubtful if the major premise will be undermined: that Hull played an extremely important part in the economic development of central England.

I have tried, while setting Hull in its national context, to present a picture of the town itself of its interlocking economic

PREFACE

Many books have been written about the Industrial Revolution, but little has been said about foreign and coastal trade and less about the individual ports of the British Isles. The object of this study is to emphasise the rôle of the ports in the Industrial Revolution by reconstructing the history of one of them, tracing in some detail the movement and direction of trade before and during the transformation of the seventeen-eighties, and the changes in mercantile, shipping and financial organisation that accompanied and facilitated that transformation. The story must be largely narrative rather than analytical in approach, partly because of the absence of comparative material for other ports, and partly because of the dearth of local information. Hull is not rich in manuscripts, especially of a personal nature. There are plenty of institutional records, both in Hull and London, but few merchant, shipowner or industrialist papers to put flesh on the dry bones of official reports and statistics. I have been forced to rely heavily on Customs records, with local colour added, where possible, from Corporation records and the surviving merchant, bank and Dock Company papers. It follows that many of the most obvious questions cannot be answered. Little, for instance, is known about the growth of Hull industry or about the accumulation of merchant capital, and nothing is known about the relative profitability of mercantile and local industrial capital or about the relationship between freight rates and shipowning. In general I have refrained from guessing about such things as a rising or falling standard of living, and report the known facts and reasonable conclusions in the hope that a pattern of port life may emerge as the history of all the British ports comes to be written in the next decade. It is inevitable that some of my conclusions will have to be modified as comparative information becomes available or as more local sources are discovered, but it is doubtful if the major premise will be undermined: that Hull played an extremely important part in the economic development of central England.

I have tried, while setting Hull in its national context, to present a picture of the town itself: of its interlocking economic sectors, of the merchants who dominated its economic, social and political life, and of the people who lived and died within its walls. The result may, I hope, be of interest to local as well as economic historians, and I should be delighted if it gives pleasure to the people of Hull among whom I spent many happy years.

I must record my gratitude to the many people who have helped me during the twelve years of intermittent research that have gone into this book. I am, of course, deeply indebted to those who allowed me to use their records, and to the institutions in whose libraries or record rooms I have been privileged to work: the Corporation of Kingston-upon-Hull, Hull Trinity House, Wilberforce House and Hull University Library; H.M. Customs Library (King's Beam House) and the Hull, Goole and Grimsby Custom Houses; the Public Record Office, British Museum and Institute of Historical Research; Sheffield Central Library, the East Riding Record Office (Beverley), the Lincolnshire Archives Office (Lincoln) and Scunthorpe Museum Library. The Hull City Librarian and his staff have been of the greatest possible assistance to me in making available microfilms and rare books from their local history collection. Mr. R. F. Parrott, lately the Corporation's Record Clerk, guided me through the mass of papers in the Guildhall, and my understanding of the problems surrounding the building of the first and second docks owes much to the late Mr. G. D. Lloyd, sometime Chief Dock Engineer, whose private office was placed at my disposal for several weeks while I read through all the surviving Dock Company Records (now in the British Transport Archives). Mrs. Doris Harrison-Broadley, Colonel Rupert Alec-Smith and the Managers of Barclay's Bank and the National Provincial Bank, Hull, allowed me to use letters and ledgers in their possession, and Mr. E. Ingram shared with me his knowledge of the Maisters and their surviving papers.

I am grateful also to the many teachers, colleagues and friends who have advised and encouraged me. Professor A. G. Dickens, Mr. F. W. Brooks and Mr. K. MacMahon were especially helpful in the early stages when I could draw on their great knowledge of local history, and I have gained much from conversations with Mr. Ingram, Mr. W. Foot-Walker, Mr. B. F. Duckham and Mr. R. C. Craig. Mr. MacMahon and Mr. Parrott have read parts of the manuscript, and I owe many of the revisions to the criticism of my colleagues, Professor S. G. E. Lythe, Dr. J. Butt, Mr. Duckham,

Dr. J. H. Treble and Dr. J. T. Ward. Above all I must thank Professor Ralph Davis, who introduced me to economic history, infected me with his love of trade and shipping history, supervised my Ph.D. thesis, and finally read some of the present book, which is based partly on that thesis. Finally I must thank my wife who has helped with the laborious tasks of reading microfilms and checking the manuscript, and my children for the patience with which they have awaited its conclusion.

The University of Strathclyde, GORDON JACKSON
1971

CONTENTS

CONTENTS

ILLUSTRATIONS

PLATES

MAPS

TABLES

APPENDICES

ABBREVIATIONS

Add. MS.	Additional Manuscript
BB	Bench Book (Hull Corporation Records)
BM	British Museum
BPP	*British Parliamentary Papers*
BT	Board of Trade Papers
BTA	British Transport Archives
c.	Long hundred (of 120 units)
c.	*circa*
CO	Colonial Office Papers
DDHB	Harrison Broadley Papers, County Record Office, Beverley
DNB	*Dictionary of National Biography*
Econ. Hist. Rev.	*Economic History Review*
Gent	Gent, T., *History of . . . Hull* (1735)
GH	Hull Corporation Records, Guildhall, Hull
Hadley	Hadley, G., *History of . . . Hull* (1788)
HCRL	Hull Central Reference Library
HCLB, B–C	Hull Customs Letter Books, Board to Collector
HCLB, C–B	Hull Customs Letter Books, Collector to Board
HDC	Hull Dock Company Papers
HUL	Hull University Library
IIA	Inrollment of Indentures of Apprenticeship; *GH*
KBH	Custom's Library, King's Beam House
LAO	Lincolnshire Archives Office, Lincoln
n.a.	not available
PRO	Public Record Office
Sheahan	Sheahan, J. J., *History of . . . Hull* (1864)
SCRL	Sheffield Central Reference Library
Strother	Strother's Journal, 1784, *BM* Egerton 2479
Tickell	Tickell, J., *History of . . . Hull* (1798)
WH	Wilberforce House Library
Woolley	Woolley, W., *Statutes Relating to . . . Hull* (1830)
WSS	W. Spencer-Stanhope Papers, *SCRL*
WWM	Wentworth Woodhouse Muniments, *SCRL*

I. INTRODUCTION

Hull is today one of the major British seaports. Every year she receives some three or four thousand ships, with a total net registered tonnage of six millions. The figure is low compared with other major ports, since Hull has little share in regular liner traffic or national distribution trades, but by value of trade she has few rivals and only two superiors: Liverpool and London. She cannot approach their eminence as international centres, but she prospers as a great regional port, with an emphasis on trade with northern Europe. The old traditional cargoes that will be noted in this study are still much in evidence, though not always going in the same direction as they used to do. The basic exports are cloth, yarns and machinery; the principal imports are foodstuffs, oil-seeds, iron ore and—most valuable of all—raw wool. Acre upon acre of the waterfront is covered by stacks of timber, the second most valuable import; and the centre of the old town is given over to the fruit and vegetable trades. The port stretches for almost seven miles along the muddy banks of the Humber, a memorial, for the most part, to the great transport revolution of the nineteenth century, when railways, steamships and telegraph combined to accelerate and concentrate the flow of trade. To the far west are the fish docks of the eighteen-eighties, with their streams of trawlers from the North Sea and the Arctic. To the far east are the latest development: the tanker-milking jetties of Salt End. In the middle, the old haven of the river Hull, once the only safe anchorage on the Humber, has lost its romance. Barges rest lazily on the silt where ocean-going vessels jostled for room, and the warehouses are interspersed with factories—and museums. The first dock is reclaimed as a public concourse, its gaunt warehouses trapped between court and college; the second and third docks, by their desolation, persuade the casual observer that Hull's trade must be sick indeed. The slough of yesteryear, they await the sweep of some gigantic wind of change.

The old town died before the docks that ringed it. Part of it is now occupied by offices and shops, part by the fruit trade; and between the two is a no-man's land where the aroma of apples and onions is drowned by the stink of decay. This is the town with which we are concerned; this was eighteenth-century Hull, smaller even than the present 'old town', since Humber Street marked the southern limits before land was reclaimed at the end of our period. Bounded on the south and east by water, and on the north and west by walls, it had a perimeter of little more than eight thousand feet. Its very smallness helped to create an atmosphere of activity and prosperity: 'in proportion to the dimensions of it,' wrote Defoe,[1] 'I believe there is more business done in Hull than in any town of its bigness in Europe.' It was, he thought, 'exceeding close built, and should a fire ever be its fate it might suffer deeply on that account; 'tis extraordinary populous, even to an inconvenience, having really no room to extend itself by building.' 'The town is not large, but very populous', wrote another visitor,[2] in 1717, though how many inhabitants made a town 'extraordinary populous', no one undertook to discover with any degree of accuracy. The population was, in fact, small at the beginning of our period. Various estimates for tax and church purposes in the seventeenth century would seem to indicate a population of around six or seven thousand in the undeveloped port of *c.* 1700–40. It is likely that numbers grew by immigration during the periods of trade growth in the forties[3] and sixties, giving perhaps thirteen or fourteen thousand in 1770[4]—a pattern which is supported, to some extent, by the irregular trend in poor rate assessments (Appendix 36). The greatest growth, as elsewhere, came with the great trade boom after 1780: by 1792, when the first local census was taken, there were 22,286 inhabitants, and 29,516 at the 1801 census. Both the number of households and the number of inhabitants had grown fourfold during the century, though chiefly towards the end, when Hull began the physical expansion that was to carry her through to the present day.

In describing the town, its trade and its people in the eighteenth century we shall, in fact, be considering the foundations on which

[1] D. Defoe, *A Tour through England and Wales* (Everyman ed., 1928), II, p. 242.

[2] H. Hare to J. Hare, 23 Dec 1717, *BM* Lansdowne MSS., 981, f. 140.

[3] The congestion within the walls in the 1740s, with resultant rising house prices, is reported in R. Hobman to R. Sykes, 7 May 1746, Sykes Deeds, *East Riding Record Office.*

[4] The Society for Literary Information, which took the 1792 census, estimated (by constant birth ratio) that the population should have been 12,964 in 1767 and 15,678 in 1777, but their estimates are of doubtful validity and are almost certainly too high, rather than too low.

Hull's prosperity in modern times was firmly based. For the great transformation of the nineteenth century rested on a comparatively greater transformation in the eighteenth. In 1700 Hull was closer in character to her past than to her future. In 1800 she was showing unmistakably those features of her economy that the railways and the steamships merely emphasised; only fish and coal remained to be added in the nineteenth century.

Hull was not always prosperous. Indeed, when our period opens she was a relative newcomer to the ranks of successful ports. If she now began to spread her wings, it was after two and a half centuries of hibernation during which optimism was less well founded than despair.[1] Like so many east coast ports, Hull owed her mediaeval greatness to the wool trade. She was well placed, near the vast sheep runs of Lincolnshire and Yorkshire, and at the height of the trade she was shipping something like a fifth of the total national exportation. No doubt York merchants played their part, perhaps those of Barton-on-Humber and Grimsby too, but the leading men were Hull men. The De la Poles, with greater fortune but less publicity than Alderman Whittington, became the greatest merchants in the land and moved as near to the Crown as any merchants have ever done. They left before the sunset of their trade. Hull's prosperity was too narrowly based and she declined, in company with the other wool ports, when the English textile industry rose to prominence towards the end of the Middle Ages. By 1528 Hull's wool trade was a nostalgic memory:

THE EXPORTATION OF RAW WOOL FROM HULL[2]

	(*sacks*)
1300/01–1309/10	59,363
1350/51–1359/60	57,643
1400/01–1409/10	33,494
1450/51–1459/60	11,487
1500/01–1509/10	3,599

[1] Three theses cover the period before 1700: W. R. Jones, 'The History of the Port of Hull to the End of the Fourteenth Century' (M.A., Wales, 1944), B. Hall, 'The Trade of Newcastle and the North East Coast' (M.A., London, 1934), and W. J. Davies, 'The Town and Trade of Hull, 1600–1700' (M.A., Wales, 1937). The best introduction is R. Davis, *The Trade and Shipping of Hull, 1500–1700* (East Yorks Local Hist. Soc., 1964).

[2] Figures calculated from tables in E. M. Carus-Wilson & O. Coleman, *England's Export Trade, 1275–1547* (1963), pp. 40–71.

Cloth had long ago replaced wool as the major English export. In the early days of the trade Hull—or rather York—had played a prominent part, sharing with London the bulk of the cloth going to the Baltic and the Low Countries.[1] Exports from Hull rose fourfold between 1370 and 1390, when only London, Bristol and Southampton shipped more cloth, but the promise of prosperity was not fulfilled.[2] Yorkshire cloth was not yet sufficiently important to save Hull, and her merchants found great and growing difficulty in establishing new trading connexions in the Low Countries, where London merchants had long had a virtual monopoly in everything except raw wool. The lion's share of the northern cloth trade was taken by the Hansards and other foreigners, who tended to ship through London, thus emphasising one of the chief features of the trade: its immense and increasing concentration on London, to the detriment of the outports. Hull settled down to a steady 2,500 cloths per annum (with the occasional boom period) until about 1510, when for a time the trade almost ceased.

Local merchants were no more successful in the far north than in the south. The Icelandic trade was founded, in the teeth of Danish and Hanseatic opposition, when Hull seamen found their way to Iceland, 'by nedle and by stone', in the fourteen-twenties.[3] The island enjoyed an abundance of fish, but its isolation encouraged piracy—in which Hull men played their part. For a time the Mayor and Corporation traded in a grand civic venture, until fishing, trading and raiding died away in the fourteen-seventies in a chaos of violence, intrigue and government decrees. Cabot's discoveries in Newfoundland were welcomed as giving relief from the necessity of visiting Iceland, and Hull lost all interest until recent times.

The Hansards were also a major obstacle to Baltic trade, and in the fourteen-seventies they appear to have strengthened their position in Hull itself.[4] Finally they removed themselves entirely from Hull in the fifteen-thirties, and redoubled their efforts to keep Hull ships and York merchants out of the Hanse towns of northern Germany. They were more or less successful. By the mid-sixteenth

[1] E. M. Carus-Wilson, *Medieval Merchant Venturers* (2nd ed., 1967), p. 259.

[2] See cloth export tables in Carus–Wilson & Coleman, pp. 75–88.

[3] E. M. Carus-Wilson, p. 112. Navigators discovered 'North' in cloudy weather by rubbing a needle with a lodestone and floating it on cork or wood.

[4] E. Power & M. M. Postan, *Studies in English Trade in the Fifteenth Century* (1933 and 1951), p. 137.

century the situation in Hull was desperate. The town was a mere shadow of its former glory—little more, in truth, than a transshipment centre for York. Most of the merchants were York merchants; most of the ships were foreign-owned. An analysis of the lists of burgesses in the fifteenth century Bench Books revealed that Hull 'was predominantly a city of seamen rather than of merchants',[1] and as late as 1639 the decay of the town was being attributed to the fact that Hull merchants resided elsewhere and the town was inhabited by sailors and lightermen.[2]

Hull might well have died in 1550 and gone down in history as another Hedon or Grimsby, noted only for her huge parish church and her two M.P.s.[3] In fact the phoenix was already stirring. A new trade rose from the embers of the old. The Low Countries and Germany might be lost for the moment, but the eastern Baltic and Russia were opening up to English merchants. Here the men of Hull found a ready market for the coarse West Riding cloths. There were at least four Hull men in the Russia Company in 1580,[4] and young Gregory Watson (of York) had been sent out to Narva to be 'one of the cheife factores ther for all the stragling marchauntes of Yorke and Hull in that Trade'.[5] The final revocation of the Hanse privileges early in the reign of Elizabeth opened the way for direct trading with Danzig, while the troubles of the Dutch enabled Hull to penetrate their old monopoly in the western Baltic and, for a time, in whaling. By the fifteen-sixties Hull was facing up to London and her ships were gathering in force at the Antwerp staple and trading—illegally—with Amsterdam. Twenty years later they were ranging freely along the Low Countries coastline and into the Baltic.[6] In 1575 Hull merchants were presenting to the Crown 'Sertaine causes of the decay of the traffique in Kyngston vpon

[1] Carus-Wilson, p. 114.

[2] *Calendar of State Papers Domestic, 1638–9*, p. 333. In 1554 the Corporation of York had confessed: 'wee have no shipps nor marryners belonging the Citie of York, but onely lightners that carryes our merchaundyses duly betwixt Hull and York; for truthe is when we make adventure beyond see we freght somme of the sayd shippes, aither of Hull, Newcastell or some other place'; quoted in B. F. Duckham, *The Yorkshire Ouse* (1967), p. 40.

[3] Hedon and Grimsby had the added disadvantage that their Havens were liable to silting.

[4] T. S. Willan, *The Early History of the Russia Company, 1553–1603* (1956), p. 76.

[5] ibid., p. 86.

[6] T. S. Willan, *Studies in Elizabethan Foreign Trade* (1959), pp. 60–1.

hull' and complaining that London was engrossing the country's trade,[1] but by now London merchants in their turn were complaining of outport activity in the Baltic: 'Wee had come to a good markett yf wee had come hyther in tyme', wrote one London factor, from Danzig, in 1559, 'but that there came 2 shipps of Hull and one of Newcastell which hindred oure markett. The Danskers desire not oure clothes nowe. . . .'[2]

It was not cloth alone that raised hopes in High Street. The developments in the woollen, linen and metal industries that led Professor Nef to write of the 'first Industrial Revolution' demanded raw materials from overseas. Timber, iron and flax were brought in, first from Holland and then directly from Norway, Sweden and Prussia. The miscellaneous cargoes were also beginning to arrive from Amsterdam: groceries, pots and pans, paper and glass, alum, oil and madder. By the end of the century Hull could look back on a generation of modest—if unspectacular—growth. She had more than survived; she entered the new century weak compared with London, but strong compared with the other outports. In 1594–5 she was, if Customs receipts mean anything, the fourth port in the kingdom.[3]

Hull's progress in the forty years after 1600 was slower than in the previous quarter-century. Peace between the Dutch and Spanish in 1609 had an adverse effect on her Baltic trade, though the decline was, to some extent, offset by the expansion of trade with Amster-

[1] R. H. Tawney & E. Power, *Tudor Economic Documents* (3 vols, 1924 and 1951), ii, 49–50. They listed: 1. 'the falce makinge of our northerne Clothe'; 2. 'the greatest parte of the trade for lead is taken from the towne' (being handled 'in the Ryver above'); 3. the London-based Companies 'maketh ordenances oftentymes beneficiall to themselves, but yett to others in the contrye the same ordenances is verye often hurtfull'; 4. 'by meanes of the sayd Companies . . . all the whole trade of merchandize is in a maner brought to the Citie of London, whereby all the welthye chapmen and the best clothyers are drawen to london, and other portes hath in a maner no trafficque, but falleth to great decay, the smart whereof we feele in our port of Kingston vpon hull'; and 5. the high Customs duties and piracy that 'so discourageth and impoverisheth the auncient and welthy marchantes that they gyve theyre trade of merchandize cleane over, and draweth them selves into the contrye, unto smaller charge and more quyetnes; whereby our poort is vnfurnyshed of menne of abylitie and of grave councell to maynteine the same . . .'.

[2] Quoted in G. D. Ramsay, *English Overseas Trade during the Centuries of Emergence* (1957), p. 97n.

[3] Willan, *Elizabethan Foreign Trade*, p. 71.

dam, which was in turn aided by the removal of the cloth staple in 1620. The more valuable dozens, particularly, went to Holland rather than to the Baltic. By the outbreak of the Civil War Hull had taken the Yorkshire cloth trade from London, and with it the potential for future development,[1] while the Navigation Laws of 1651 and 1660 finally removed the Dutch from the carrying trade and opened the way for direct Hull trade with the whole Baltic. For the first time there was real and lasting encouragement for local shipping: 53 per cent of the ships entering the port in 1567 had been foreign-owned, and 49 per cent in 1609; by 1687 88 per cent were English-owned. Despite the ups and downs of the Civil War, a significant pattern of trade was well established by 1660: Yorkshire cloth and other manufactured goods were exported to Holland and Germany, and to a lesser extent to the eastern Baltic, while bulky raw materials were imported from Scandinavia and the Baltic, miscellaneous goods from Holland and Germany, and wine and fruit from France and Spain. So far as the employment of foreign-going shipping was concerned, the northern trade was a vital encouragement:[2]

NUMBER OF SHIPS ENTERING HULL FROM ABROAD

From	*1567*	*1609*	*1637*	*1687*
Low Countries	41	30	36	21
Germany	0	4	6	4
France	16	10	35	19
Spain	4	1	0	0
Total Western Europe	61	45	77	44
Norway	3	16	29	59
Sweden	0	0	7	16
Eastern Baltic	14	33	32	16
Northern Baltic	4	0	0	18
White Sea and Arctic	4	4	1	0
Total Northern Europe	25	53	69	109
Scotland	43	19	6	0
America	0	0	0	1
GRAND TOTAL	129	117	152	154

[1] See R. Davis, pp. 21–3.

[2] These and the previous figures are from R. Davis, p. 24.

There were a number of features of the new trades that enabled Hull to break free from York just as York/Hull had broken free from London and the Hanse. Firstly, the search for raw materials and new markets in the Baltic led to the factorage system, and though the first known factor—Watson—was a York man, all the later factors—starting with Maister in Helsingore *c.* 1636—were Hull men, intent on diverting the maximum amount of trade through their fathers and brothers in Hull. Secondly, the growing imbalance of trade in the Baltic destroyed the barter system on which it was originally based. The supercargo, buying goods in return for cargoes delivered in the Baltic, gave way to the bill of exchange on Amsterdam. Exports to the Low Countries—or to London—paid for imports from the Baltic at least by 1660, and the greatest benefits were felt by those merchants with the closest links both with the Baltic and with Amsterdam—namely the rising merchant houses of Hull. The greatest of them came to dominate the Baltic trade to the virtual exclusion of York, while the cloth export trade was beginning to by-pass York and go through Hull houses as the centre of the cloth industry moved southwestwards from York. The merchants of York, not unnaturally, blamed their downfall on an unkind fate: 'trading here decreased', they told Charles I, 'and that principally by reason of some hindrances in the River, and the greatnesse of Shipps now in use. . . .'[1] Whatever the cause the result was the same: at the beginning of our period trade through Hull was largely Hull's own trade. She was no longer the handmaiden of York. A group of important and experienced Hull merchants were initiating and organising an increasingly complex trade. They employed the ships, paid the bills, and accumulated the profits for investment in yet more ships and trade. 'They have a very handsome exchange here,' wrote Defoe,[2] 'where the merchants meet as at London, and, I assure you, it is wonderfully filled, and that with a confluence of real merchants, and many foreigners, and several from the country. . . .' The heads would nod in gratified approval when the men of High Street learned that they were 'real merchants'.

Hull welcomed the Glorious Revolution because it brought peace, but it was the contemporary Commercial Revolution that brought prosperity. The national economy was changing in ways and places that suited Hull, and she found herself in a commanding position

[1] Quoted in Duckham, p. 49. [2] Defoe, II, p. 244.

on one of the chief commercial arteries of the country. The greatest movements were, of course, in colonial trade, of which Hull had no part, but she benefited indirectly from the growing national prosperity, and more obviously through her coastal trade. Lead had always been important; now it was joined by corn and other foodstuffs for the booming population of the capital. Coal was the major import coastwise, from Scotland and then from Newcastle, but the seventeenth century saw the beginning of wool importation and of the trade in colonial goods and other luxuries from London.

The movements in trade and local shipping following the Civil War laid the foundations for future development. Hull's trade in the eighteenth century was for the most part an extension and elaboration of trades already existing in 1700. The chief factors determining changes in direction and intensity were to be the demand for new and more raw materials in the hinterland, and the opening of new markets in the Baltic. Changes when they came were chiefly within the sphere of influence that Hull had already marked out for herself. She remained the chief connexion between northern England and northern Europe, but she made little headway elsewhere.

Potential greatness must not, of course, be confused with actual greatness. In 1700 Hull was a very minor port, despite the progress of the last half-century. By national—or rather, London—standards she was irrelevant. A bar across the Hull would have made almost no difference to the progress of the largest part of British trade at that time, despite the misguided willingness of Defoe to liken Hull to 'Hamburgh or Dantzick, or Rotterdam, or any of the second rate cities abroad, which are famed for their commerce'. Hull's great importance lay in her service to a particular region of national trade. She grew as that region developed. The sages of 1700 knew full well that if the past belonged to the De la Poles and the wool trade, the future belonged to the Wilberforces and the Baltic trade. But not even the wisest among them could have foretold the immense changes that would come over the hinterland, and Hull, in the next hundred years.

II. THE HINTERLAND

The rise of Hull was linked inseparably with the development of the vast hinterland served by the navigable rivers—and later the canals—flowing into the Humber. It was no accident, as Professor Willan pointed out,[1] that the great English commercial centres were river ports and sea ports combined; the inland waterways were every bit as important to Hull as the high seas, the agent in Bawtry or Sheffield as vital as the factor in Memel or Amsterdam. At the beginning of the eighteenth century Hull was already well supplied with exportable goods from the hinterland, and raw materials formed a large part of her imports. But industry—and consequently the trade of Hull—was not expanding very rapidly. Industrial techniques were primitive, large scale production was discouraged by sluggish demand, and grave obstacles faced the inland transport of bulky goods. Prosperity came with that quickening of economic activity, in the second half of the century, which is usually called the Industrial Revolution. It was not the product merely—or even chiefly—of technological change, but an amalgam of industrial and commercial advance. At one and the same time it encouraged and depended upon financial and mercantile reorganisation, the building of canals, docks and fleets, and the exploitation of markets and sources of raw materials at home and abroad. Especially, so far as Hull's hinterland was concerned, was it bound up with the general economic development of northern Europe. Whatever the peculiar circumstances that encouraged economic growth in Britain,[2] rather than France or Holland, the fact remains that the Industrial Revolution would have been impossible without a positive response from the outside world—in the consumption of cloth or ironmongery, or the production of flax, tar or sugar. Britain did not develop in isolation, but as a complementary—albeit

[1] T. S. Willan, *River Navigation in England, 1600–1750* (Oxford, 1936, reprinted Cass, 1964), p. 1.

[2] For a useful summary, see R. M. Hartwell, 'The Causes of the Industrial Revolution. An Essay in Methodology', *Econ. Hist. Rev.*, 2nd ser., XVIII, 164.

unique—part of the international economy, subject to the myriad influences of supply and demand. As a growing population produced more and demanded more, the flow of goods in and out of Britain, and round the coast, increased, and began to respond dramatically to changes in the demand schedule. Astride the flow were the ports, controlling it and controlled by it. The development of central England was thus of vital interest to merchant and 'industrialist' alike, and improved inland communications were, as the Hull Bench said in support of the Fazeley canal in 1782, 'a means of extending Trade and Commerce between the said Port of Hull, and the Northern Kingdoms of Europe . . .'.[1]

'The exportations', said the Hull Dock Company in 1793, 'consist of Woollen Cloths, Cottons, Hardware, and a variety of other valuable goods, manufactured at Leeds, Wakefield, Huddersfield, Manchester, Sheffield, Birmingham, &c. which are brought down to Hull in River Vessels'.[2] Before discussing the foreign and coastal trades of Hull it would be appropriate to consider briefly these regions and industries upon which Hull's trade was ultimately dependent.

The chief component of Hull's export trade was undoubtedly Yorkshire woollen cloth, which relied heavily on the foreign market.[3] It was a rare ship indeed that sailed from the Humber without at least a few packs on board, drawn for the most part from the complex of small manufacturers clustered round the leading wool and cloth markets. As the production of cloth rose (the average of both broad and narrow cloth more than doubled between 1775–9 and 1795–9,)[4] so the volume of goods flowing to and from Hull grew larger and more varied. Colliery- and forge-owners and

[1] BB ix, 580.

[2] *An Address of the Dock Company at Kingston-upon-Hull to the Merchants Shipowners and Others, Concerned in the Trade and Shipping of the Port*, 15 Feb 1793.

[3] Contemporaries in 1772 and 1781 estimated that 72 or 73 per cent of West Riding cloth was exported, slightly more, perhaps, than the national average; R. G. Wilson, 'Transport Dues as Indices of Economic Growth, 1775–1820', *Econ. Hist. Rev.*, 2nd ser., XIX (1966), 122.

[4] Broad cloth averaged 3·2 million yards 1775–9 and 7·8 for 1795–9; narrow cloth averaged 2·6 and 5·5 million yards. Based on J. Bischoff, *A Comprehensive History of the Woollen and Worsted Manufacturers* (1842), vol. II, Appendix 4.

merchants dealing in articles of common consumption benefited no less than woollen manufacturers from the construction of the navigations. The Aire and Calder reached Wakefield and Leeds in the early years of the century, and was extended by the Calder-Hebble Navigation to Salterhebble Bridge (for Halifax) and Sowerby Bridge (to take in an important kersey area) by about 1766. The whole navigation was ruined by flooding in 1767, but was restored and vastly improved in the seventies.[1]

Despite high freight rates,[2] the navigations encouraged the movement of coal to the east coast, iron to the forges of Leeds, groceries and luxuries—fast becoming necessities—to all the main towns, and, of course, the materials of cloth production: dyes and mordants, oil and tallow, wood for looms, wire for combs, and wool brought coastwise into Hull. The receipts of the Aire and Calder Navigation Company may, in fact, be taken as a rough indicator of economic growth in the woollen region. Dr. Wilson has shown that the dues of the Company roughly doubled in the last quarter of the century.[3] While Hull was obviously not concerned in all the goods paying dues, the figures show a close approximation to indices available in Hull itself, and the relationship between Hull and Leeds was very strong until the early nineties, when the new trans-Pennine canals began to siphon off some of the trade destined for America.

The rising town of Selby was, after the opening of the Selby canal in 1778, the key to the whole Aire & Calder system, and, at the end of the century, the gateway to the Huddersfield and Rochdale canals which linked Hull with Lancashire.[4] The building of the

[1] Halifax was not reached by water as early as 1740, as stated by H. Heaton, *The Yorkshire Woollen and Worsted Industries* (Oxford, 2nd ed. 1965), pp. 403–4. See B. F. Duckham, 'John Smeaton and the Calder & Hebble Navigation', *Journal of the Railway and Canal Historical Society*, X (1964), 19–25.

The beginning of the Aire & Calder Navigation is dealt with fully by R. W. Unwin, 'The Aire and Calder Navigation', *Bradford Antiquary*, XLII (1964), 53.

[2] 1*s*. 6*d*. per cwt. from Hull to Huddersfield, 1*s*. to Wakefield at the end of the century; advertisement in *Hull Advertiser*, 30 Sep 1797.

[3] R. G. Wilson, p. 117, Table 3. Receipts averaged £43,513 for the years 1775–9 and £83,378 for 1795–9.

[4] The Leeds–Liverpool canal, officially opened in Leeds in 1774, was not in fact completed until the early nineteenth century, and was of only limited value to Hull in our period. For Selby see B. F. Duckham, 'Selby and the

quays at Selby in the seventies heralded a boom in its trans-shipment trade as the various navigations encouraged the development of their regions. In 1800 it handled no less than 369,780 tons of goods (including coal), and Hull merchants were—as was the way of merchants—needlessly worried about Selby's ambitious plans. They looked askance at the coasters calling at Hull only for formal Customs procedures, and, fearing the worst, resolutely opposed the establishment of a Custom House at Selby.

The value of woollen exports was great, and far-reaching changes were taking place in the woollen industry towards the end of the century, but the attention of contemporaries and historians alike has always been focused on the birth of the Lancashire cloth trade. The manufacture of 'cottons', which for legal and technical reasons were made partly of linen at least until the seventies,[1] grew steadily, though relatively slowly, during the first three quarters of the century. Rapid expansion began in the last quarter, with the application of machinery and the creation of the 'mill' by Arkwright and his imitators. Although the cheaper, lighter cottons went principally to the colonies, cotton velvets found their best market in Europe,[2] and there was a regular exportation of Manchester cloth through Hull by the time of the French wars. Hull was, according to Manchester petitioners for a convoy to Hamburg in 1795, the 'key through which our manufactures can alone find a passage . . . [to] . . . Germany, Switzerland and Italy'.[3]

The finished cloth, much of which was consumed in Britain or exported through Liverpool, was probably less valuable to Hull than the raw materials consumed by the cloth industry. Already by 1750 Hull was the principal market for linen yarn, besieged by

Aire & Calder Navigation, 1774–1826', *Journal of Transport History*, VII, 2 (1965), 87–95.

[1] A heavy excise duty hampered the production of pure cotton cloth in an attempt to protect woollen manufacturers. An Act of 1736 allowed material with linen warp and cotton weft to be made, paying only 3*d*. per yard excise, but in any case cotton warps were considered inferior before the invention of Arkwright's spinning machinery. See R. S. Fitton and A. P. Wadsworth, *The Strutts and the Arkwrights, 1758–1830* (Manchester, 1958), pp. 68–75.

[2] A. P. Wadsworth and J. de L. Mann, *The Cotton Trade and Industrial Lancashire, 1600–1780* (Manchester, 1931), chaps. iv, vii, *passim*.

[3] Proceedings of the Manchester Commercial Society, 3 Feb 1795, op. cit. A. Redford, *Manchester Merchants and Foreign Trade, 1794–1858* (Manchester, 1934), p. 32.

Manchester merchants and their agents, whether it was young Robert Robinson buying six hundred *shocks* at a time[1], or Mr. Greatrex, who 'wanted to have bought what was in Town'.[2] In 1757 the Mayor requested protection for Hull ships approaching the Sound,[3]

> several of which will have very valuable cargoes being entirely loaded with Linnen Yarn. that should any accident happen to them, the Disappointment would greatly prejudice the Linnen manufacture and prove a heavy loss to the concerned; who also desire me to present the necessity of having the Yarn early home for the Bleaching Season. . . .

To a lesser extent Hull was also an importer of cotton wool, in the early days when it still came from the Mediterranean, and King Cotton had not yet conquered America: 'imports into Hull', Wadsworth and Mann wrote of cotton from the east, 'were much greater than those into Liverpool, but until the bumper year of 1787 they were insignificant in comparison with the quantity coming to London'.[4] The Strutts, admittedly not a Lancashire firm, purchased more of their cotton through London than through Liverpool in the nineties (and probably earlier),[5] and much of this London cotton found its way inland via the coastal route to Hull.

So long as navigable rivers rather than trunk canals were the principal mode of transport, the route from London to Manchester was either via Liverpool or via Hull and Wakefield, Doncaster or Rotherham. Some goods in the early days went up the Trent and by road from Wilden Ferry, although after the opening of the Don Navigation in the middle of the century linen yarn was sent to Tinsley, 'which is generally Reckoned the most Expeditious way of Sending goods from Hull to Manchester . . .'.[6] There was, however, every incentive towards the end of the century for Manchester merchants to ship through Liverpool wherever possible:

[1] *WH* 59/58/47, Letters from Joseph Pease, Hull, to Robert Robinson, Manchester, 1752–3, *passim.* Robinson's cousins, the Philips of Tean, also imported through Hull; Wadsworth & Mann, pp. 294–5.

[2] *WH* 59/58/47; J. Pease to R. Robinson, 1 Mar 1752.

[3] William Hall, Mayor and Chairman of Hull Convoy Committee to Lords Commissioners of the Admiralty, 2 Apr 1757; *GH* Minute Book of the Hull Committee for Convoys, 1757–82.

[4] Wadsworth & Mann, p. 190.

[5] Fitton & Wadsworth, p. 272.

[6] *WH* 59/58/47, J. Pease to R. Robinson, 10 Apr 1753.

freight on the Bridgewater canal was *7s. 2d.* per ton (*10s. 6d.* for cloth) when freight to Hull along the Aire and Calder was *50s.*[1]

The second major influence on Hull's development came from the iron industry of the Sheffield–Rotherham region, producing an infinite variety of knives, scissors, razors, files and edged tools, iron stoves and grates, rails and heavy cast goods. Hull imported the vast amount of foreign iron consumed by the industry, and was the chief outlet for its products, although Liverpool was beginning to catch up at the end of the century with the opening up of the American market.[2] Hull merchants financed the exportation of ironmongery, and 'regularly gave long credits to the Sheffield manufacturers, and thus shared the capitalistic responsibilities of the trade'.[3]

The long and arduous haul to and from Sheffield by way of the Trent and Idle involved at least twenty miles of land travel,[4] and the Don was too shallow for transport above Doncaster, which made that town, in the words of one hopeful son, 'the Metropolis, being the centre of the navigation between Hull and the high country'.[5] Gainsborough and Bawtry remained the transshipment ports while landowners and merchants haggled over the Don. The fury of the Humber made some doubt the possibility of a single navigation to Sheffield, 'not expecting to see such great shipping at Doncaster without drowning the country, or such small ones at Hull without drowning themselves',[6] but the navigation was eventually finished to Tinsley in 1751, despite the interested opposition of Gainsborough and Bawtry.[7] The value of the new Don

[1] Liverpool rates from T. S. Ashton, *An Economic History of England: The Eighteenth Century* (London, 1955), p. 88. Hull rates from the *Hull Advertiser*, 30 Sep 1797. Return frieght to Manchester was *10s.* per ton cheaper, no doubt reflecting the lower value of the goods concerned.

[2] P. C. Garlick, 'The Sheffield Cutlery and Allied Trades and Their Markets in the Eighteenth and Nineteenth Centuries' (unpublished M.A. Thesis, Sheffield, 1951), chap. 5 (x) *passim.*

[3] G. I. H. Lloyd, *The Cutlery Trades* (London, 1913), p. 329.

[4] ibid., p. 334.

[5] Daniel Baker to Joseph Mellish, 28 Nov 1722, quoted in T. S. Willan, *The Early History of the Don Navigation* (Manchester, 1965), p. 71.

[6] Same to same, 26 Nov 1722, ibid., p. 65.

[7] For a general account of the Don Navigation see the excellent introduction, Willan, pp. 1–40.

was immediately obvious, and Samuel Walker was probably not alone in shifting to the canal bank: 'although S. Walker, the year before, thought himself so well settled, begun to see the disadvantage of being so far from the navigable river, and with a deal of trouble prevailed to have a beginning at Masborough, near Rotherham, where he built a casting-house. . . .'[1]

The novelty of industrial goods should not be allowed to obscure the more mundane traffic. The Don navigation was supported in 1704 by London and Barnsley merchants because it was expected to cheapen the cost of transporting corn,[2] and at the end of the century at least one Lincolnshire farmer thought it worth while to invest in an iron barge for transporting sheep to Rotherham market.[3] By 1770 fish was being sent regularly up the Don to Newbridge and thence by cart to Sheffield when Thomas Lowther, 'Fish Carrier of Sheffield', 'found to his surprise the boat was loaded with fourteen half Ankers of Foreign Spiritous Liquors'.[4] The Customs Riders were less surprised than he was, and his protestations of innocence were addressed from Hull Gaol.

With the exception of the Yorkshire rivers (Aire, Calder, Don and Ouse, Derwent and Ure) and the Lincolnshire Ancholme, almost all the navigations feeding and fed by Hull formed a gigantic network centred on the Trent, which flowed for almost two hundred miles through central England. The River Trent, as opponents of the Don Navigation well knew,[5]

is a great and antient navigable river, and employs above 70 vessels (at this time as many more) some of 150 tun and upwards to Gainsborough and Stockwith from thence the goods are conveyed in small vessels to Lincoln, Newark, Nottingham, Derby and other adjacent places, and also to Bawtry . . . and so carried further into the west of Yorkshire and Derbyshire by land carriage, and return constantly with lead &c. which is the sole ballast that enables those ships to be cheap in their freight and quick in their returns to and from London and all remote parts to which great quantities of cheese, nails, iron, copper &c. from Cheshire, Staffordshire, Derbyshire and other parts are conveyed.

[1] Quoted in A. H. John, *The Walker Family, 1741–1893* (London, 1951), p. 2.

[2] Willan, *River Navigation*, p. 137.

[3] A. Young, *General View of the Agriculture of Lincolnshire* (1799), p. 406.

[4] HCLB, C–B, 6 Mar 1770.

[5] 'Reasons against the Bill for making the River Dun in the county of York navigable', op. cit. Willan, *The Early History*, p. 101.

> Great quantities of corn are brought out of Yorkshire, Lincolnshire and Nottinghamshire besides several other commodities, and shipped off at Gainsborough and Stockwith for London and other parts, there being a constant conveniency of shipping by reason of the great quantities of lead &c., without which those ships can bring no corn (lead being the only ballast at Gainsborough and Stockwith) either so cheap quick or safe as they do now. . . .

As the petitioners against the Don navigation made clear, Stockwith, Bawtry and Gainsborough were the nodal points of river traffic. Bawtry was, at the time of Defoe's tour, 'the centre of all the exportation of this part of the country, especially for heavy goods, which they bring down hither from all the adjacent countries . . .',[1] but it lost its Sheffield trade with the opening of the Don and was eventually ruined by the Chesterfield–Stockwith canal (1777). Nor did Stockwith survive as an important river port, its trade increasingly attracted across to Gainsborough, the last safe navigable point for ocean-going ships. Gainsborough thus became the great trans-shipment centre, one of the greatest of inland ports, always threatening to become a legal port in its own right, but not succeeding till it was too late;[2] condemned, to the chagrin of its merchants, to the inferior—though lucrative—role of intermediary between Hull and the shallower reaches of the river.[3] Its warehouses groaned under the weight of goods awaiting shipment by Henshalls, or some other river carrier; and Hull merchants stockpiled in Gainsborough to save a day or two on deliveries to Burton or Birmingham. In the first quarter of the century the Maisters' cargoes usually went via Dempster & Co. of Bawtry or Richard Turpin, James Wharton, (. .) Haines and Mrs. Wells of Gainsborough. 'Sold Mr. Jn Hall', reads a typical entry in their Day Book, 'and sent per Jn Thompson to Mrs. Wells of Gainsborough to go by way of Newark.'[4] Haines at least was still employed by the Maisters twenty years later, when

[1] D. Defoe, *A Tour Through England and Wales* (Everyman ed., 1928), II, p. 181. By heavy goods Defoe meant lead, 'wrought iron and edge-tools' from Hallamshire, and millstones, the latter 'carryed by sea to Hull, and to London, and even to Holland also'.

[2] Gainsborough became a port in 1841. In 1848 the Sheffield and Great Grimsby Junction Railway reached the new railway port of Grimsby, and Gainsborough's fate was sealed.

[3] For a recent account of Gainsborough's rôle, see I. S. Beckwith, 'The River Trade of Gainsborough', in *Lincolnshire History and Archaeology*, II, 1967.

[4] *HUL* Maister Day Book, 1 Sep 1714.

he forwarded three tons of Stockholm iron to Robert Watkin in Birmingham.[1] Towards the end of the century Wray & Hollingsworth of Hull maintained a similar agency—Robert Flower & Sons, who had a numbered stock of timber from which they drew to order: 'all the Timber of that mark is put together', Robert Flower wrote on one occasion, 'so you will please to send me the numbers you would have me send to C & B' [Calfract & Co. of Newark].[2] Other Hull merchants also drew from Flower's stock, as he reported to Wray & Hollingsworth in September 1791: 'As under you have the Numbers of the Timber delivered to the Order of Hall & Robinson, Hull'.[3]

Gainsborough was, geographically, the best placed of the Trent river ports, but it was certainly not the most ambitious. Further along the river was Nottingham, which tried desperately in the first quarter of the century to engross the entire trade of the upper reaches of the Trent. Defoe found the river there navigable for 'vessels or barges of great burthen, by which all their heavy and bulky goods are brought from the Humber, and even from Hull . . .'.[4] In return went 'lead, coal, wood, corn; as also cheese in great quantities, from Warwickshire and Staffordshire'. Unfortunately Nottingham attempted to remain the last navigable point on the Trent. The Corporation resolutely opposed all efforts to improve the navigation of the river, and at one time chained the bridge to prevent the passage of river craft along that part of the river to Burton-on-Trent which had been partially improved following the Act of 1699.[5] Nevertheless, Derby was able to break Nottingham's monopoly when an Act was obtained in 1720 for the Derwent navigation, although it was not until the eighties that the Derby coalfield was effectively tapped by the Erewash canal. To the south of the Trent, Loughborough was reached in 1766 by the Soar navigation, which was extended by canal to Leicester by 1797; Grantham was connected with the Trent by canal in 1793.

The travellers and publicists of the early eighteenth century were as impressed by the volume of lead moving along the Trent as

[1] Maister Letters, April 1738. I am grateful to Mr. Rupert Alec-Smith of Winestead, Yorks, the owner of these letters, for allowing me access to them.

[2] *HCRL* L.12869, Wray & Hollingsworth Letter Books, 2 Mar 1791.

[3] ibid., 13 Sep 1791.

[4] Defoe, II, p. 145.

[5] T. S. Willan, *River Navigation*, pp. 42–5.

they were by the caverns from which it came. It was almost always disposed of through Hull, collected in Wirksworth or Chesterfield and despatched through Bawtry or Stockwith, and later down the Chesterfield canal. Towards the end of the century the firm of John Barker & Company, with concessions in Grassington, Knaresborough, Skipton, Winster, Edensor and Castleton, send lead to Hull 'with all imaginable expedition',[1] and allowed it to accumulate in their agent's hands when the trade was bad, 'that it may be ready when a demand comes, and that the accounts may be made up and the workmen etc. paid what is due to them'.[2] But lead was already losing its significance. Other bulky goods were filling the barges, and the tourist's attention was now directed to the most recent Derbyshire phenomenon, the cotton mill. The hosiery manufacture of Derby, Nottingham and Leicester had already been rejuvenated by Jedediah Strutt's Rib machine when he entered into partnership with Richard Arkwright (*c.* 1770) to produce the empire of mills at Cromford, Bakewell and Wirksworth, Matlock, Belper and Derby.[3] Here for the first time true cotton cloth was made, and Hull was provided with an increasing supply of exports (both hosiery and cloth) and a new market for raw materials.

The river Trent also served, indirectly, the land-locked region of the Birmingham light metal industries. At the beginning of the century Birmingham was changing from the manufacture of 'rude' goods to locks, buttons, buckles, trinkets, candlesticks, guns and other brass and iron articles which, according to advertisements appearing in *Aris's Birmingham Gazette*, were usually shipped out through Hull, often to London. In the nineties, however, the European trade declined relatively in favour of the more important American market,[4] and Liverpool took Hull's place in the export trade, although it had no other advantage over Hull; they were roughly the same distance from Birmingham, and freight rates were the same—30*s.* per ton to both.[5]

The iron used in Birmingham came originally from Staffordshire,

[1] John Barker to Jacob Bailey, 29 May 1791, Barker Papers, *SCRL* Bagshawe 494.

[2] Jn. Barker to Jacob Bailey, 15 Jul 1789.

[3] Fitton and Wadsworth, *passim.*

[4] Attwood's Evidence, *Minutes of Evidence against the Orders in Council; Journal of the House of Commons*, April 1812, p. 3.

[5] See Advertisements in *Aris's Birmingham Gazette*, 28 Mar 1774.

but the quantity produced there had long since ceased to be sufficient and Swedish iron was imported via the Trent. 'Their trades . . .', said Birmingham supporters of the Derwent navigation, 'do chiefly consist in Steel and Iron and other ponderous commodities and the charges of land carriage is so great that it is a discouragement to those trades which by this navigation will be improved and the said charge lessened.'[1] How the Birmingham manufacturers hoped to benefit from the Derwent navigation is far from clear, unless they were thinking of the removal of obstacles, natural and human, in the Trent around Nottingham. Goods to and from Birmingham usually went to the final navigable point at Burton-on-Trent, which had built up a considerable trade to the west and south. In 1744, for example, Samuel Lloyd was advised that some iron had arrived in Hull and asked to make an offer 'for a sortable parcell at Burton',[2] and many years later another manufacturer, William Whitehouse, testified that his father 'bought the foreign bars at Burton-upon-Trent, before the Birmingham Canal was made, and brought them by land carriage to Birmingham'.[3] The canal, which met the Coventry-Trent canal near Tamworth and the Trent-Seven canal at Wolverhampton, reduced the travel time to less than a fortnight and the cost, at 1*s.* 6*d.* per cwt. was sixpence cheaper than the old route via Burton.

The last industrial region of importance to Hull, although to a lesser extent than those already mentioned, was the light metal and pottery region of Staffordshire. Clay and flints had to be imported—the former usually (though not entirely) through Liverpool and the latter through Hull—and pottery was exported, though the quantity was not great before the opening of the canals. 'The villages of Burslem, Stoke, Hanley Green, Lane-delf and Lane-end', wrote one pamphleteer in support of the Liverpool–Hull canal scheme in 1765,[4]

> are employed in the manufacturing of various kinds of stone and earthen-wares, which are carried, at a great expence, to all parts of the kingdom, and exported to our islands and colonies in America,

[1] *Journal of the House of Commons*, X, p. 410.

[2] Nathaniel to Henry Maister, 8 Dec 1744, Maister Letters.

[3] Evidence of William Whitehouse, *Minutes of Evidence against the Orders in Council*, p. 24.

[4] Anon., *A View of the Advantages of Inland Navigation between the Ports of Liverpool and Hull, 1765*, *BM* B.504, pp. 28–9.

and to almost every part of Europe: but the ware which is sent to Hull is now carried by land upwards of thirty miles, to Willington; and that for Liverpool twenty miles, to Winsford.

The development of the industry was greatly encouraged by the opening of the Grand Trunk Canal (finished in 1777), running from the Bridgewater canal to Shardlow on the Trent, and huge quantities of pottery began to arrive in Hull in the last quarter of the century.

The opening of trans-Pennine canals was not, as we have already seen, pure gain to Hull. True, the hinterland was extended; but so was that of Liverpool, and where the two overlapped a struggle for trade began which was now based less on the availability of inland transport than on the facilities offered by the ports. While in absolute terms the transatlantic trade of Hull increased, Liverpool's massive lead was confirmed.

So far mention has been made of goods sent to and from the major industries served by Hull, but there was also an infinite variety of miscellaneous goods—some in large quantities, some in small—coming from or going to a multitude of widely scattered places. Lime and stone, for example, were, after coal, the chief items by tonnage carried on the Chesterfield canal in the eighties.[1] They were followed closely by corn, lead and timber. Corn, cheese and other foodstuffs for the Hull or London market came from many places; in return wine, spirits and the more exotic imports went everywhere. This was especially true of the immediate hinterland to the north and south of Hull. The East Riding and Lincolnshire were almost entirely agricultural, with few centres of population demanding or producing goods on a large scale. Trials for coal in both countries produced nothing, and attempts to burn shale ended in disappointment;[2] an attempt at woollen manufacture (complete with 'fire-engine') on the Lincolnshire Wolds was, when Arthur Young visited Lincolnshire, 'all now gone and done with',[3] and proposals to establish cotton mills in Hull came to nothing.[4] Nevertheless, both counties had a considerable distributive trade

[1] Abstract of Tonnage, 1777–89; Chesterfield Canal MSS., *SCRL* Jackson MS1255.

[2] For Lincs see Lord Yarborough to George Tennyson, 6 Feb 1801, *LAO* 2 TdE/H/1/23. For Yorks see letters (*passim*) Cary Elwes to George Prissick (his Agent), especially 24 Apr 1759, *LAO* Cary Elwes Letter Book, 1758–82.

[3] A. Young, *General View . . .*, p. 407.

[4] L. Jopson, Rotterdam, to Joseph Pease, Hull, 6 Aug 1743, *WH* 59/58/49.

through York, Selby and Beverley, and Barton-upon-Humber, Brigg, Grimsby and Gainsborough, as well as the villages along the Ouse, Derwent, Hull, Ancholme and Trent. Although York was rapidly losing its overseas trade in the early eighteenth century, the Ouse remained a flourishing highway for less ambitious merchants.[1] In 1698 the mariners and watermen of the Ouse had claimed that they possessed:[2]

> several vessels of good burthen which are consistently employed in carrying great quantities of woollen manufactures, lead, butter, corn, rape-seed, tallow and several other commodities, the product of this and the adjacent country, to Hull, London, Newcastle, and several parts beyond the seas, from whence they bring all sorts of merchandise and sea-coals for supplying the city of York and the adjacent counties by the river Ouse. . . .

The woollen trade was gradually lost to the Aire and Calder, but the rest remained and grew. Hull was sufficiently impressed by the potential of the Ouse to petition in 1767 in favour of its extension, by the Ure navigation to Ripon and Boroughbridge.[3] The Malton region was linked to Hull by Lord Rockingham's Derwent Navigation, completed in 1723 but of no great importance till the second half of the century. By 1793 it was estimated to be carrying 50,000 quarters of corn per annum.[4]

To the south of Hull, the wool producing region of the Lincolnshire Wolds was tapped more efficiently by the Louth Navigation, built by John Grundy in the sixties, while the canalisation of the Ancholme, begun in 1765 and remodelled by John Rennie in the nineties, eased access to Brigg, surrounded by vast rabbit warrens until enclosure and improvement made it the centre of an equally extensive area of rich farm land. Derelict warehouses on the Ancholme, as on any of the navigations, bear witness to a flourishing trade which, according to Crutwell in 1801, regularly employed

[1] For an excellent account of the Ouse trade, see B. F. Duckham, *The Yorkshire Ouse* (1967), chap. 4.

[2] *Historical Manuscripts Commission* (*MSS. of House of Lords*), vol. iii, n.s. 1697–9, p. 210.

[3] *Journal of the House of Commons*, xxxi, pp. 68–9. Hull petitioned in favour of two other extensions (the Swale to Bedale and the Cod Beck to Northallerton) but these were apparently never completed. I owe this, and the previous reference to Mr B. F. Duckham.

[4] For the Derwent see B. F. Duckham, 'The Fitzwilliams and the Navigation of the Yorkshire Derwent', *Northern History*, II (1957), p. 45.

'about fifteen sloops, of forty tons each'.[1] Merchants engaged in local miscellaneous trade were to be found in all the market towns: the Dawsons in Bawtry, Etheringtons in Gainsborough, Claytons in Grimsby, Neves in Louth. When Christopher Clayton cast his account on Christmas Day 1752 he had 227 debtors in 62 places, chiefly Lincolnshire villages, and he was by no means unique in the range or extent of his business.[2]

Few merchant papers have survived to illustrate the nature of inland trade. Fortunately the only major source—the two letter books of Wray & Hollingsworth—is concerned mainly with timber, by far the most important of the general items of trade. Wray & Hollingsworth sent deals, raff, logs, staves and other forms of timber to customers in Leeds, Huddersfield, Barnsley, Sheffield, Nottingham, Derby, Leicester, Loughborough, Birmingham and a multitude of less important places. Much of the timber was used for the extensive building which took place under the stimulus of an increasing population and expanding economy; plaster laths went to Keighley and scaffolding poles to Leeds; a customer in Nottingham was described as an 'Architect',[3] and one in Ripon called himself a 'Chimney Doctor'.[4] In Birmingham they had some two dozen customers and one agent—William Suffolk. The most notable of their customers, Richard Arkwright, may have used his timber for machine building at Cromford,[5] while J. Jackson of Stafford ordered 'Raven Ducks' 'such as you think most suitable for Waggoners Tracks . . .'.[6] Wray & Hollingsworth also dealt in feathers, tallow, hides and iron—chiefly 'old iron'. The latter was sent, together with small quantities of Russian iron (Tswordishoff's), to Butler & Beecroft of Kirkstall Forge, Maude, Dade & Company of Leeds, Short, Willetts & Company of Wednesbury Forge, to West Bromwich Forge, to James Cam of Sheffield, Gelsthorpe & Wright of Nottingham, Beach, Warwick & Leonard of Birmingham (Weeford Mill) and Blessard of Bradford.[7] Great as were the ramifications of

[1] C. Crutwell, *Tour Thro' the Whole Island* (1801), V, 54.

[2] Abstract of Ledger Showing Debts Due to Christopher Clayton, *LAO* TdE/G/3/4.

[3] Wray & Hollingsworth Letter Books, 20 Jan 1795.

[4] ibid., 6 Jan 1795.

[5] ibid., 19 May 1791.

[6] ibid., 2 Nov 1791.

[7] Examples of letters from these firms (there is no index) are: 14 Sep 1791, 12 Mar 1795, 24 Nov 1791, 3 Dec 1791, 12 Mar 1795, 17 May 1791, 5 May 1791, 18 May 1791 respectively.

their business, they were probably typical of a score of other firms dealing in a dozen other commodities, with a vast network of business connexions between Hull and every part of central England, from Ripon to Loughborough, Chester to Grimsby.

Almost all the goods imported and exported through Hull spent part of their journey on the navigations, and the tonnage inland must have been related in some measure to the seaborne tonnage. It follows that the capacity of keels and barges (allowing for repeated voyages) must have been roughly equal to the capacity of the ships entering and leaving Hull in the foreign and coasting trades. Unfortunately we know very little about the huge fleet of river craft that must have been involved. Trinity House surveyors in 1698 thought that 'the number of Vessells, Keeles and boats belonging to Knottingley and other places upon the Aire may be abot 30 from 30 Tunns downwards, the bigest of which may now goe up to Knottingley . . .'.[1] Similarly the Ouse was reckoned to have '8 or 10 Vessells from 60 to 80 Tunns which use the sea & . . . some 20 or 30 smaller vessells & Keeles from 20 to 40 Tunns which use the Inland trade . . .'.[2] None sailed on the Wharfe, only a couple of feet deep in places, and only a couple of 20 to 30 tons and a few open boats on the Derwent. Twenty years later it was estimated that seventy or more vessels were employed on the Trent below Gainsborough, and the number was growing fast. One source reckons that 'a sett of Boats more then usually was imployed on the River Trent';[3] another speaks of a hundred per cent increase.[4] The situation above Gainsborough is obscure. In the early years of the century a frustrating wrangle took place as the Undertaker for the Trent Improvements and a boatmaster 'agreed to ingross the whole Navigation to their own Boats'.[5] They failed, as others failed, partly because of determined opposition, but partly also because of the bewildering complexity of inland trade.

Inland transport was, nevertheless, big business. As the navigations ramified, and the volume of goods increased, so the boat companies emerged, gradually maturing into the universal carriers of the eighteenth century. At one end of the scale was William

[1] R. A. Unwin, p. 84. [2] ibid., p. 83.
[3] Quoted in Willan, *Inland Navigation*, p. 128.
[4] Quoted in Willan, *The Early History*, p. 101.
[5] Quoted in Willan, *Inland Navigation*, p. 116.

Blow of Grimsby, typical of the small men with one or two boats, who started his packet service to Hull in the forties, and incidentally introduced Methodism to the port.[1] At the other end was the Burton Boat Company, with no less than twenty barges on the Trent between Burton and Gainsborough in the seventies, offering carriage at two pence per ton per mile.[2] The greatest carrier of all, Hugh Henshall of Stone, Staffordshire, carried no less than 23,000 tons of goods on the Trent in 1790.[3]

Detailed information becomes available for the first time at the end of the century, when an unknown person drew up a Register of Ships in the Inland Navigation,[4] possibly based on the Hull Shipping Registers, now lost. Altogether there were 420 vessels with an aggregate of 17,763 tons permanently engaged in the inland navigation from Hull. Of these, twenty-two, totalling *c.* 550 tons, were Humber ferries, and twenty-nine, totalling 1,057 tons, were lighters sailing to Spurn and Paull—presumably Humber Pilot or ballast boats. Of the remaining 16,156 tons, 2,751 sailed on the Don to the Yorkshire iron district, including 821 tons to Rotherham and 561 to Tinsley. The Aire and Calder trade, involving a longer route as well as a greater volume, required 7,455 tons, Leeds alone accounting for 3,352 tons and Wakefield for 1,906. Gainsborough and Stockwith, with a fairly fast turn round, are reckoned to have 2,213 tons, and the Ouse at least 1,442. Even these figures would appear to be incomplete.[5] They do not attempt to gauge the volume of foreign and coasting vessels that regularly sailed up to York, Selby, Stockwith and Gainsborough. Nor do they include vessels on the navigations above Gainsborough and the other transshipment centres, and vessels which did not regularly visit Hull.[6] The full story will probably never be known; suffice it to say that the inland sloop and keel were as important in the early part of the industrial revolution as the railway train was in the later part.

[1] W. H. Thompson, *Early Chapters in Hull Methodism, 1746–1800* (Hull, 1895), pp. 14–15.

[2] See advertisements in *Aris's Birmingham Gazette*, 7 Feb 1774.

[3] A. C. Wood, 'The History of Trade and Transport on the River Trent', *Thoroton Soc.*, LIV, 1950.

[4] *GH* MS M.445.

[5] They do not, for example, include the Hull-Brigg sloops noted by Crutwell.

[6] We know that thirty-five vessels were active on the Derwent, although only two were engaged in *regular* trips to Hull in 1793 (Duckham, 'Fitzwilliams and . . . the Derwent', p. 50).

III. FOREIGN TRADE

1. THE IMPORT TRADE, 1700–1760

i. SCANDINAVIA AND THE BALTIC

The goods demanded by Hull's developing industrial hinterland were, with few exceptions, obtainable from the Baltic and northern Europe, and it was natural that Hull merchants should be more deeply concerned with this region than with any other. Indeed, their interest at the beginning of the century can be defined with greater precision: the Dutch and German trade was extremely valuable; the Russian trade a novelty, well worth an adventure; but their fortunes were firmly based on the predominant trade with Norway and Sweden.

Norway, with its vast forests and ample water power, was the principal source of wood. Thirty or forty ships per annum made the fast crossing to one or other of the smaller fjord ports, there to search for deals, battens, masts and spars. Deals, which required no further sawing before being sent inland, were the most common form of wood arriving at the beginning of the century. Almost 1,500c.[1] were imported in 1702, and the number gradually rose during the century. There was, however, a limit to the amount of wood Norway could supply without permanently damaging her forests, and merchants were forced to compete for cargoes as their factors moved inland to secure the best quality wood before it reached the ports.[2] As early as 1719 one disappointed factor was bewailing the fact that there was not a single port where the supply was 'answerable to the demand'; ships not returning to Hull in ballast would have to wait a month or two, and 'at last be obliged to take any trash, and at most extravagant rates . . .'.[3] Realising that the situa-

[1] In this chapter the old 'hundred' of 120 will be denoted by the letter c.

[2] See H. S. K. Kent, 'Anglo-Norwegian Timber Trade in the Eighteenth Century', *Econ. Hist. Rev.*, 2nd Series, VIII (1955). The total imported into England declined slightly between 1700 and 1790, although the total imported through the outports remained fairly steady.

[3] Colletts & Leuch of Christiania, to Samuel Dawson of Bawtry, 29 May 1719; *SCRL* Tibbitts MSS, 516—14.

tion was unlikely to improve, Hull merchants followed the lead of London and began to search for alternative supplies. They turned eastwards. Although ships from Norway reached a peak, at fifty-four, in 1751, she had begun to lose her predominance, and the pattern of Hull's trade slowly changed. While the total import of deals trebled between the sample years 1717 and 1768 (from 1,070c. to 2,804c.), the number of ships arriving from Norway actually declined slightly, from thirty-three to twenty-eight.

From Sweden there came, in the words of Joshua Gee, 'near two thirds of the iron wrought up or consumed in the kingdom . . .'.[1] It was high grade, malleable iron, produced from the finest ores under stringent control. It enjoyed an enviable reputation as the best iron in the world, the only iron fit for steelmaking. Of the various kinds, *Oregrund* was held in highest regard in Hull. It was, according to a Swedish visitor to Hull in the early fifties, 'contracted for and sold here . . . to none other than a few people having steel furnaces in Sheffield'.[2] English iron was unsuitable for their purpose, and it was not until the end of the century that the adoption of the Cort process raised the status of the native product and placed the Swedish trade in jeopardy. The amount of iron imported in 1702 was 2,356 tons, and this probably represents the normal amount for peace time. The Northern wars and the prohibition of trade with Sweden in 1717 reduced the total to 353 tons for that year, but it was back to 2,481 tons in 1728.[3] Thereafter there was a slow rise, to 3,914 tons in 1737, although the total for 1751 was slightly lower, at 3,772 tons. The importance of the Swedish iron trade to Hull is evident from the number of ships engaged in it: thirty-two in 1728, forty-nine in 1737, and forty-seven in 1758, when they formed a quarter of all the ships entering the port. Several merchant houses considered it worth their while to maintain branches in Scandinavia, and a number of firms built up a very great business on the basis of Swedish iron. The best known, Sykes and

[1] Joshua Gee, *The Trade and Navigation of Great Britain* (1731), p. 17.

[2] Reinhold Angerstein, quoted in K. G. Hildebrand, 'Foreign Markets for Swedish Iron in the Eighteenth Century', *Scandinavian Econ. Hist. Rev.*, VI, i (1958), p. 29.

[3] The total national importation for 1717 was reduced to 1,428 tons. T. S. Ashton, *Iron and Steel in the Industrial Revolution* (1924), p. 111*n*. Some attempt was made to fill the gap with 'Germany' iron (which may have been Swedish in origin) from Holland; William Pease, Amsterdam, to Joseph Pease, Hull, 17 Dec 1717, *WH* 59/58/43.

Son, imported over 1,500 tons between June 1747 and January 1748 in their own ships, apart from any they may have received in shared cargoes, which were the general rule.[1]

The only other Scandinavian commodity worthy of notice was tar. The quantity imported was never very great—1,156 barrels in 1702, 960 in 1728. It came mostly from Bergen and Stockholm, and the trade was dominated by a handful of the leading merchant houses, such as Mowlds, Broadleys and Maisters; the latter sold no less than 500 barrels of tar and 800 of pitch in 1714.[2] The trade was seriously hampered by the Swedish tar producers, and both the navy and mercantile marine were gravely concerned at the inadequacy of supplies. The result was the first Naval Stores Act of 1705, which granted a bounty of £4 per ton on Plantation tar. By the middle of the century pitch and tar were conspicuously absent from Hull's trade with Europe; they now came exclusively from America.

Several hundred miles, and a week or two's sailing to the east of Stockholm lay Sweden's immediate neighbour, Russia. Despite her tremendous trading potential, and the activities of the Muscovy Company, she was little known to the west. At the beginning of the century she was, with the exception of the icy north, landlocked. St. Petersburg, founded in 1703 by Peter the Great as his link with Europe, was of little importance as a trading centre for a quarter of a century or more. Only two ships arrived in Hull from there in 1717, not more than a dozen in 1758. It was the Northern War that heralded the beginning of Anglo-Russian trade, when Russia acquired, in 1720, those Swedish territories that had previously barred her way to the sea—territories with which England already had a considerable trade. In the first half of the century St. Petersburg was less important than Narva and Riga which served, through well established commercial connexions, the forests, mines and fields of both Poland and Russia. Riga, lying at the mouth of the Polish river Dvina, reputedly had the best hemp, flax and masts in the world, and it was the English government's desire to secure a friendly supply of these basic naval stores that led to the Anglo-Russian Commercial treaty in 1734.[3] By securing better conditions

[1] HCLB, C–B, 28 Jan 1748/9. [2] Maister Day Book, *passim*.

[3] The best account is D. K. Reading, *The Anglo-Russian Commercial Treaty of 1734* (Yale, 1938), pp. 18–19. The treaty reflected both the fear of Scan-

for English merchants in Russia the treaty stimulated trade in general, and the number of ships arriving in Hull from Russia rose significantly from nineteen in 1728 to thirty-eight in 1737.

Trade with Poland and Prussia was concentrated almost entirely on the ports of Danzig and Konigsberg, and neither showed any sign of rivalling the great Russian ports. Apart from 1728, a corn importation year when thirty-one ships arrived from Danzig, it is doubtful if the number exceeded a dozen per annum. Nor did the Prussian trade expand until the second half of the century.

Goods imported from Russia, Poland and Prussia fall into three main categories: wood, hemp and flax, and iron. As we have seen, Hull merchants concentrated almost entirely on good quality Norwegian deals in the early part of the century, ignoring the rough-sawn timber that was already coming in considerable quantities to other English ports. Not until the demand for wood soared in the forties did they turn to the forests of the eastern Baltic. Between 1737 and 1751 the volume of imported timber rose from 25 to 1,343 loads, and it continued to grow. More important, initially, were the masts and spars required by Hull's own shipbuilding industry. The masts, mostly small ones, numbered approximately fifty in 1717 and a hundred in each of the other sample years. Spars fluctuated considerably—210 in 1702, 24 in 1728, 558 in 1737—depending not only on general movements in the economy of shipping, but also on such mundane variables as the weather and the ability of masters and crews. While the larger trees under canvas were transformed into the most majestic of sights, the smaller ones—the uffers—were consigned to the builder's yard, there to become the scaffolding for the rebuilding of England. The largest number in the sample years—31,000—occurred in 1737; the decline in later years may be due to their longevity or to the beginning of systematic forestry in England and Scotland. The middling trees were sawn into staves in the mills along the Haaf, or in Riga and Memel, and became the universal containers of the eighteenth century.

The second group of imports was based on the great hemp and flax production of northern Europe. The spread of these, and other 'industrial' crops in England was hampered, and eventually stopped, by the general emphasis on the more valuable food and

dinavian monopoly, and the failure of the bounty Acts to stimulate effective Colonial competition. It was also another mercantilist blow against Holland, which dominated the Russian trade before 1734; ibid, p. 31.

wool crops. It was easier for merchants to find supplies overseas than at home. Naval and merchant shipping relied heavily on foreign hemp for rope and canvas, and the expansion of the shipping industry in the early years of the century is reflected in the rapid increase in the importation of 'rough' hemp. From less than a thousand hundredweights in 1702, it rose to 5,601 cwt. in 1728 and 27,685 cwt. in 1751, the highest figure for our sample years.

The rising importation of flax, from 1,677 cwt. in 1702 to 17,302 cwt. in 1728 and 32,938 cwt. in 1751, is indicative of the flourishing state of the English linen industry, which was beginning to master the complicated finishing processes that had long made Haarlem the centre of the European fine linen trade. English spun flax was not, however, suitable for fine cloth, and the best quality yarn was generally imported from the older centres of linen production for the 'Linsey Woolsey Manufactures at Kiderminster, Manchester &c'.[1] Raw Dutch linen yarn came from Amsterdam, Rotterdam and Hamburg, Spruce linen yarn from Konigsberg. Raw Dutch was the more important in the first forty years of the century, rising rapidly in volume from 37,544 lb. in 1702 to 233,912 lb. in 1717 and, despite a setback in the twenties and thirties, from 274,641 lb. in 1751 to 839,274 lb. in 1758. Spruce linen yarn, which accounted for 37 per cent of yarn imports in 1737, rapidly overtook Raw Dutch as merchants turned eastwards for increased supplies. By 1751 it stood at 418,863 lb., 60·4 per cent of the total. The best of it, from Braunsburg and Konigsberg, was the Ermland yarn so highly prized in Manchester.

British linen was no longer 'Bumpkin ware',[2] but the techniques of mass production were as yet unknown, and it was still necessary to import huge, and growing, quantities of linen cloth from Holland, Germany and Russia: 'such is the exceeding Consumption of Linen here', thought Defoe, 'that it seems as if all the World were not able to supply us. . .'[3] The Baltic certainly tried. Some thirty different types of linen were imported in the middle of the century, although only Narrow linen and Spruce canvas were of any consequence.[4] The quantity of Narrow Holland was never great, and

[1] D. Defoe, *A Plan of the English Commerce* (1730 ed.), p. 214.

[2] See C. Wilson, *England's Apprenticeship* (1966), pp. 197–8.

[3] D. Defoe, *A Plan . . .*, p. 207.

[4] They included four sorts of 'canvas' and ten sorts of 'linen', together with small quantities of lawns, ducks, oilcloth, drillings, ticks, barras,

by the middle of the century Hull's Customs officials had ceased to count it by the *hundred* ells. Narrow German became fairly common in the twenties, and reached about 700c. ells in 1751; but by far the most important was Narrow Russian—Narrow Muscovy until the twenties—which increased from 17c. ells in 1717 to 1,352c. in 1750.[1] Spruce canvas was of no great moment at the beginning of the century, although it was the principal cloth imported in 1702; by 1717 the quantity had risen to 2,399c. ells, and the total in 1751 was 8,437c. ells. Altogether the total canvas imported rose from 185c. ells in 1702 to 12,418c. in 1750, and linens rose from 29c. to 1,910c.

The third basic commodity was Russian iron. It began to supplement Swedish supplies when the new Siberian mines were exploited in the early twenties, and serious trade was stimulated by the Anglo-Russian treaty.[2] Most of it went to London. Hull merchants showed little interest at first, importing only 50 tons in 1737 and 286 in 1751. They regarded it as something of a novelty, and doubted its suitability for their market. When, for example, Samuel Mowld offered iron to Samuel Shore of Sheffield, in 1744, a rival, Nathaniel Maister, was 'a little suspicious he will let him have his Rushia iron cheap in order to induce him to give a better price for the Sweeds'.[3] The merchants were, of necessity, drawn towards Russian iron, which partly accounts for the fifty per cent increase in iron imports between 1751 and 1758 at a time when Swedish iron, relying on limited charcoal supplies, had reached the point of optimal production beyond which prices would begin to soar.[4]

Finally there were a number of miscellaneous imports from the Baltic. Linseed was, in some ways, the most interesting, since it was the basis for the Hull seed-crushing and paint industries. The quantity of seed imported in 1728 and 1737 was not great, but by 1751 it had reached 30,000 bushels. Madder, a red dye, was imported at the rate of 500 cwt. per annum until 1751, when it advanced to a little over 2,000 cwt. Pearl ash, potash and weed

tabling and towelling. By far the most important of the miscellaneous linens was Russian napkining, which averaged 11,659 yards for the years 1750–4 and 17,646 yards for 1763–5.

[1] The figures for 1750 from HCLB, C–B, 4 Sep 1766.

[2] See D. K. Reading, *passim.*

[3] Nathanial Maister to Henry Maister, 8 Dec 1744; Maister Letters.

[4] See E. F. Söderlund, 'The Impact of the British Industrial Revolution on the Swedish Iron Industry', in L. S. Pressnell (ed.), *Studies in the Industrial Revolution* (1960).

ash (all potassium carbonate) came in fluctuating quantities from all places where vegetable matter could be burned—110,598 lb. in 1717, 60,101 in 1751. It may have been consumed locally, for it was chiefly imported by merchants with direct interests in soap manufacture. Juniper berries for the gin distilleries and spruce beer were imported from Danzig, mats for lining ships from Riga, and twine from almost all the ports of the Baltic.

Perhaps the best idea of the over-all progress of the Baltic trade is to be gained from the number of vessels declaring Hull as their origin or destination when paying tolls at the Sound. Although some masters were vague and declared 'England', by far the majority gave a particular port. A clear trend is shown by using five-yearly averages. In the first quarter of the century there were about twenty ships per annum, except in the worst years of war. The first major rise, to over forty per annum, came in the twenties; the second, to over sixty, came in the fifties; and the third, to about a hundred per annum, after 1765:[1]

SHIPS PASSING THROUGH THE SOUND, FROM AND TO HULL: FIVE-YEARLY AVERAGES, 1695–1783

	EASTWARDS		WESTWARDS	
	With Cargo	*In Ballast*	*With Cargo*	*In Ballast*
1695–1700	23·4	13·4	23·2	0·2
1700–4	17·6	8·8	18·0	0·4
1705–9	8·4	3·2	8·4	
1710–14	23·4	8·8	24·2	0·2
1715–19	18·6	7·0	18·0	0·4
1720–4	28·4	10·0	28·4	0·6
1725–9	42·6	27·8	43·0	
1730–4	40·8	19·4	40·2	
1735–9	48·4	21·2	46·6	0·4
1740–4	46·6	22·8	46·6	0·6
1745–9	48·6	20·8	46·8	0·2
1750–4	62·2	23·8	61·8	0·2
1755–9	65·8	24·6	64·0	0·6
1760–4	59·2	27·2	59·4	0·2
1765–9	91·2	43·6	90·8	
1770–4	105·4	57·6	102·6	0·2
1775–9	128·0	74·2	125·2	0·2
1780–3	107·6	50·4	106·0	

[1] N. Bang and K. Korst, *Tabeller over Skibsfart og Varetransport Gennem Øresund, 1661–1783* (Copenhagen, 1930), pp. 225–70.

The great volume of the import trade (ships westwards) compared with the export trade (ships eastwards) is shown by the large proportion of ships entering the Baltic in ballast—48 per cent of the total.

ii. GERMANY AND HOLLAND

Hull's close connexion with the Baltic tends to obscure the importance of the trade with Holland and the German ports on the North Sea. Bremen and Hamburg traded with the whole of northern Germany, making it unnecessary for Hull to have direct communications with the Baltic to the west of Danzig, while Holland supplied processed raw materials, especially yarn and wooden and metal goods, which she had originally acquired through her extensive carrying trade. She was, until the end of the eighteenth century, 'a Magazine or Collection of all the Products and Manufactures of the World . . .',[1] where Hull merchants could obtain exotic goods from countries with which they had no direct trade. In the time of Defoe it was frankly admitted that nutmegs, cloves and mace came 'from the Indies by way of Holland and (as it happens) no other way'.[2] Any inconvenience resulting from the Mercantilist system was circumvented by special licences which Hull merchants could usually secure.[3]

While no one would deny that Amsterdam was, in 1700, 'the staple market about which international trade and finance revolved',[4] enough has been said already to show that, for Hull at least, direct trade with the Baltic was carried on from an early date, and was never channelled through Holland to the extent suggested by Professor Wilson in his study of Anglo-Dutch commerce.[5] The pattern was not one of Baltic goods replacing goods from Holland, but one of expansion in basic commodities not generally obtained from Holland. Since the dominant theme was expansion in Baltic trade, it follows that Dutch trade declined in relative importance. So far as shipping is concerned, 22 per cent of total

[1] J. Gee, p. 191. [2] D. Defoe, *A Plan*, p. 217.

[3] Nor were licences always necessary in advance. One man had a cargo of spice worth £659 from Antwerp seized for lack of licence, but the money was returned on petition. *Calendar of Treasury Books and Papers, 1741*, pp. 509 and 560.

[4] C. Wilson, *Anglo-Dutch Commerce and Finance in the Eighteenth Century* (1941) p. 4. [5] ibid., pp. 6, 17.

entries came from Holland in 1699, 27 per cent in 1728 and only 11 per cent in 1751. There was, however, no absolute decline in the number of ships, which fluctuated in the thirties for the first three-quarters of the century. The number of ships from Bremen and Hamburg also remained fairly steady, accounting for approximately nine per cent of the total entries in 1717, 1751 and 1758.

Holland was justly famous as the source of fine linen, both Narrow Holland and Narrow German, and of Vitry canvas. But, as we have seen, a modest rise in western linen was completely overshadowed by eastern linen. By 1750 Russian linen was ten times as common as German, and Holland linen had virtually ceased to arrive. Vitry canvas was similarly eclipsed by Spruce canvas. Apart from Raw Dutch linen yarn, which grew in volume, the only bulky commodity to arrive from north-west Europe was wood in various stages of manufacture. Staves in many sizes came from Hamburg and Bremen in greater quantities than from any other ports, while Holland provided an assortment of oars, kits, tubs, scoops, stoops, shovels, spouts, pipes and laths. Both Germany and Holland sent the wainscot boards that found their way into many of the richer houses of eastern England (16,053 inches in 1737, 39,813 in 1751), while Holland was the chief source of intricate goods, such as children's toys, chairs and the plain and lacquered tables demanded by the new fashion of tea drinking. At the other end of the scale, Holland provided a number of coaches in the early years of the century, and at least a couple of fire engines, which the Corporation put into service in the first decade. More surprising, perhaps, is the fact that the Yorkshire textile industry, so jealous in preventing the exportation of its tools, was itself dependent to some degree on Dutch spinning wheels, 2,631 of which were imported in 1751.

The metals and metal goods were the product of the high quality —though small scale—metallurgical industries of Holland and Germany, which were superior to those of Britain at the turn of the century. Holland had indeed preceded England as the chief market for Swedish iron, and both Holland and Germany were justly famed for the 'Long German' steel which Hull obtained from Hamburg and Amsterdam. The small quantities involved—the maximum for our sample years was 668 cwt. in 1728—reflected the limited use made of steel at this time, while the decline in the trade was due to the ability of Huntsman's successors to satisfy the market. Copper and brass followed a pattern similar to steel: small quantities, probably increasing in the first quarter of the century, and then declining as English industries developed. The same was true of manufactured goods, such as brass and iron wire, 'battry' and 'Mettle prepared for battry', chimney backs, and various pieces of equipment for the kitchen. The change in the tin plate trade is particularly noticeable. Defoe listed tin plates with linen and paper as the only commodities obtained entirely by importation,[1] and imports were certainly growing at the beginning of the century, reaching 170,450 pieces in 1717. Then the trade declined, and by the middle of the century Hull was exporting tin plates. The longest surviving items were those requiring the greatest skill in manufacture. Copper plates for engravers were imported long after copper pots had ceased; cocks, taps and various special equipment were imported by Hull's oil interest in the fifties because English equipment was found wanting; and whaling irons were still being imported as late as 1768.

Metal of any kind was valuable, and iron was rarely thrown away. When its day was done, it was broken up, casked, and shipped over to Hull to be mixed with the best quality English ores. It consisted chiefly of old hammer heads and military equipment. It is one of the neglected facts of history that the widespread use of iron equipment in warfare, besides encouraging the iron-masters, produced a horde of scavengers who gleaned battlefields for anything that could be melted down in Sheffield or Leeds. Nor was all the equipment useless: in June 1750 the Maisters, who regularly dealt in old iron, had 789 cannon balls and 24 shells confiscated by the Customs officers because they were 'capable of being made use of in a military way'.[2]

Of the miscellaneous imports from Holland a few deserve special mention. Paper and pasteboard were almost a Dutch monopoly in the days before the development of the English paper industry, and fine quality writing and printing paper, and bound ledgers, were imported well into the second half of the century. At the same time the rise of the English industry required an increasing importation of 'linen rags fit only for paper making'. Printed books and, occasionally, printer's type also came from Holland, as did writing slates, quill pens and ink. Cloth produced in Holland and Germany was, as we have seen, of little importance compared with that from other areas, but they were the chief source of many of the dyes and other chemicals used in the finishing of cloth. Smalts, a blue dye made

[1] D. Defoe, *A Plan*, p. 77.

[2] HCLB, C–B, Jun 1750.

from powdered cobalt glass, increased from 4,879 lb. in 1717 to 24,530 lb. in 1751, and there were small quantities of yellow ochre, vermilion, indigo, amber, arsenic (a green dye) and other colours. Chemicals included aquafortis, lignum vitae, cantharides, mercury sublimate, quicksilver and antimonum crudens. Finally there were all kinds of drugs, spices and other goods from the Mediterranean;[1] whale oil and bone from the Dutch whaling industry, long before the British industry developed; and, to supplement lightweight but valuable cargoes, dogstones, paving stones, marble and gravestones.

iii. SOUTHERN EUROPE

Trade with France was insignificant, even in peacetime. No ships at all arrive in 1717, one in 1728, seven in both 1737 and 1751, and none again in 1758. Hull merchants made little effort to establish permanent trading connexions, preferring to obtain French goods through Holland or London. The chief exceptions were wine, brandy and linseed from the great wine port of Bordeaux, which sent nine of the fourteen ships entering from France in 1737 and 1751. Dried and fresh fruit and a few luxuries such as books and fine cloth attracted a little attention, but there were no potentially great trades.

A few more ships, though never more than six, went to Antwerp, Bruges and Ostend in the Austrian Netherlands, for oriental produce brought there by the Ostend Company and its successors. The trade never developed, for political conditions were difficult and, as Gee pointed out, 'the Dutch having the Command of the Mouth of the Scheldt, do thereby secure to themselves in a great Measure the Passage of Goods to and from Flanders through Holland . . .'.[2] As a result France and Flanders together sent only three per cent of the ships entering in 1717, 1728 and 1751, and they tended to be small ships.

The only remaining area in Europe from which Hull drew imports was the Iberian peninsula. Portugal and Spain provided most of the wine imported at Hull, in anything from half-a-dozen to a dozen ships per annum. The total quantity of wine from all sources was between 200,000 and 300,000 gallons per annum in the first half of the century, and of this roughly two-thirds was Spanish or Portuguese, mostly from the ports of Lisbon and Oporto. In 1728,

[1] For example, large numbers of Italian kid-skins were imported from Hamburg—over 21,000 in 1751.

[2] J. Gee, p. 21.

for example, the total from Portugal was 171,075 gallons, compared with 36,748 gallons from Spain and 1,788 gallons from the Rhineland. Ten years later the total importation was approximately 300,000 gallons and the emphasis had changed slightly. Of the 65 ships carrying wine to Hull in 1737, 23 were from Lisbon and Oporto, 17 from Malaga, 7 from Rotterdam, 5 from Hamburg, 2 from Rouen and 1 each from St. Ubes, Bordeaux, Dunkirk, Seville, Gibraltar and Genoa.

The wine ships almost invariably carried supplementary cargoes. Those from Portugal brought oil and most of the cork used in Hull or re-exported to the Baltic, and those from Spain brought fruit, olives, oil, nuts and anchovies. Oranges and lemons were particularly sought after, although the number appears to have been declining—*c.* 400,000 in 1717, *c.* 250,000 in 1728, *c.* 125,000 in 1751—as supplies began to arrive from London. Both countries sent dyestuffs, including sumack (a yellow dye, used in tanning), indigo and orpiment (arsenic trisulphide, a yellow dye).

Imports from Portugal and Spain were remarkably steady in the first half of the century. With the exception of the year 1737, when fourteen ships arrived from Spain, the number from there was two or three per annum, and those from Portugal fluctuated from five to twelve.[1] Similarly the wine import was fairly steady: 171,075 gallons from Portugal in 1717 and an average of 164,043 gallons for the years 1753–5.[2]

iv. AMERICA

The American trade was quite distinct from that with Europe, chiefly because it was dominated by specialist merchants in a port where specialisation was rare. Nor was the trade of any great significance. The long voyages involved, and the reluctance of Hull merchants to stray far from the Baltic, encouraged the coastal trade in American goods at the expense of direct trade with America. A ship from there was a rarity until the forties, and the two or three a year which did arrive were no advance on the number in the sixteen-eighties.[3] Undoubtedly the chief reason for the lack of

[1] The large Spanish total for 1737 may represent an attempt to secure the maximum number of cargoes before the inevitable war broke out. Some Hull seamen were already refusing to sail to Spain.

[2] HCLB, C–B, 21 Mar 1756.

[3] W. J. Davies, 'The Town and Trade of Hull, 1600–1700' (unpub. M.A. thesis, Cardiff, 1937), p. 119.

interest among Hull merchants was the difficulty of obtaining in America goods which could be obtained with greater speed and ease —and less risk and cost—from Europe.[1] Why go to America for iron, staves, indigo, turpentine or tar? All these things came in small quantities, but their chief value was as ballast for the basic commodity, tobacco. Previously ships had had to wait for full loading, 'whilst the worms were eating out their bottoms'.[2]

The importation of tobacco appears to have been irregular until 1743, when 57,631 lb. arrived. Once started, the trade expanded rapidly, to 859,256 lb. in 1748, and throughout the period 1742–58 imports rose and fell in a wave-like motion which averaged out at 432,451 lb. per annum.[3] Tobacco provided a useful re-export to pay for imported iron and wood, and of the 6,919,221 lb. imported between 1742 and 1758, no less than 2,300,491 lb. were exported to the Baltic.

The importatian of tar was partly due to the desire to find a source of supply outside the Baltic, which might be closed by an enemy, and partly to the financial incentive of the bounty on naval stores which the government gave to encourage the trade.[4] In 1752 the Customs reported that Plantation tar was frequently made use of in the manufacture of pitch, 'especially when foreign tar is scarce',[5] and some merchants appear to have deserted the Baltic for the American trade. Hamilton & Company was one of the best examples, importing 3,821 barrels of Plantation tar in 1750 and 4,791 in 1751, principally from Hampton and Brunswick in North Carolina.[6] The bounty was certainly worth considering. Two merchants, William Welfitt and Peter Hodgson, received £348 each for 'bounty on naval stores per *Virginia Packett*' in February 1759, and they received a further £251 and £152 respectively for other cargoes.[7]

Apart from tobacco, the only commodities that might, from the point of view of Hull, be regarded as peculiarly American were rice and train oil. Rice came from no other region with which Hull

[1] The freight on timber, for example, was three times the freight from the Baltic, and was an impossible burden until the Napoleonic war; R. G. Albion, *Forests and Sea Power* (Cambridge, Mass., 1926), p. 152. A major problem was the lack of stockpiles, which increased the period of loading.

[2] J. Gee, p. 207.

[3] HCLB, C–B, Feb 1759.

[4] 2 George II, c. 35, s3.

[5] HCLB, C–B, 26 Feb 1752.

[6] HCLB, C–B, Mar 1752.

[7] See their Accounts, Pease Bank Ledgers, Barclay's Bank, Hull.

traded, and supplies from Carolina were a welcome addition to foreign trade. Whale oil and whale fin were obtainable from Holland, but with the development of the great Nantucket whaling industry Hull merchants turned to Rhode Island as their natural source. The oil trade with Rhode Island was, in fact, an important step towards the establishment of Hull's own whaling industry, when merchants such as Hamilton, hitherto content to trade with intermediaries, began to send their ships direct to the Greenland Fishery.

It would be reasonably true to say that Hull obtained most of its tar and whale oil from America in the second quarter of the century. Of the rest of the goods none was more than supplementary. So far as Hull was concerned, America did not become the all-embracing supplier of the Mercantilists' dream. Even tobacco and sugar, the greatest American crops, came not from America but from London.

2. THE IMPORT TRADE, 1760–1800

i. SCANDINAVIA AND THE BALTIC

Northern Europe remained the chief concern of Hull merchants in the second half of the eighteenth century, despite the growth of hitherto insignificant trades, such as those with America, France or Italy. There was, however, a noticeable shift of emphasis, as the centre of interest moved from the western to the eastern Baltic, following changes in the trade in iron, wood and other raw materials.

The trend eastwards was first obvious in the wood trade. The importation of deals, the basic building wood, rose steadily, from 2,804c. in 1758 to 3,224c. in 1783, and then doubled in the late eighties to an average of 5,782c. for the years 1790–2. But, as we saw earlier, Norway lost its predominance in the wood trade before the middle of the century, and the increase was accounted for largely by deals from Russia, especially St. Petersburg. Hull rapidly assumed a dominating position in her new trade: in 1790–4 she took 40 per cent of the deals sent from St. Petersburg to England, and 43 per cent for the years 1795–1804.[1] Since Britain was the major consumer of St. Petersburg deals, Hull was in fact taking 40 per cent of the total exportion in the years 1795–1804. Hull also stepped up its importation of rough sawn timber. England as a whole had imported large quantities in the first half of the century, chiefly from Norway,[2]

[1] Calculated from J. J. Oddy, *European Commerce* (London, 1805), p. 123.
[2] H. S. K. Kent, p. 63.

but Hull showed little enthusiasm for timber before 1750. Then, quite suddenly, Hull merchants plunged into the trade. Between 1758 and 1768 the importation soared from 1,135 to 8,260 loads; by 1790 it was 30,515 loads, and the average for 1790–2 was 20,917. In common with other trades, timber was down at the turn of the century, averaging only 17,895 loads for the years 1799–1802, although it had recovered to 33,849 loads in 1802.

Another 'new' wood swelling the total importation was Russian oak, which began to arrive in quantity at a time when the old English forests were practically exhausted. From 123 loads in 1768, it rose to an average of 629 loads for 1790–2 and 1,065 for 1799–1802. In the older types of semi-processed wood there was little change, except for staves and masts. Staves were naturally in great demand for the casks and barrels in which practically everything, including ironmongery, was shipped. In the early years of the century the supply of casks was so short that the Peases (and presumably other merchants) had used their international connexions to hunt out second-hand sugar casks for use in the oil trade.[1] The importation of staves had then been about a thousand hundreds per annum; by 1790–2 it averaged 3,408c. and 3,817c. in 1799–1802. The trade in masts experienced a tremendous boom, from about a hundred per annum before 1783 to an average of 969 for 1790–2 and 843 for 1799–1802. Never before had such intensive mercantile and naval building coincided, and the importers of masts, like the importers of tar, appear to have benefited from the removal of the bounty on American produce which had previously favoured the west coast and London merchants with long-established trans-atlantic connections.

While St. Petersburg eventually became the chief source of deals, the wood trade as a whole was dominated by Memel, Riga, Narva and, latterly, Archangel. Trade with the great Prussian port of Memel, which began to tap the forests of Prince Radziwill after the Seven Years' War,[2] increased at a faster rate than that with any other Baltic port except St. Petersburg itself. From less than half-a-dozen per annum in the first half of the century, the number of ships entering from Memel had risen to twenty-two in 1768 and fifty-seven in 1796. Although the number from Riga and Narva

[1] Robert Pease, Amsterdam, to Joseph Pease, Hull, 25 Oct 1713; *WH* 59/58/43.

[2] J. J. Oddy, pp. 220–1.

did not increase so much (in fact both places sent fewer ships to Hull in 1796 than in 1737), the exploitation of new Russian forests provided an alternative flow of timber during the French Revolutionary war through the northern ports of Onega and Archangel, the latter sending fifteen ships to Hull in 1796.[1]

The importation of iron, like that of timber, increased rapidly in the last twenty years of the century. Between 1758 and 1783 the total rose by about a third; between 1783 and 1791 it doubled, to stand at 15,263 tons, although the average for 1790–2 was slightly lower, at 12,525 tons. The Armed Neutrality of the North ruined the trade in 1801, when imports were less than two thousand tons, but the average for the years 1799–1802 did not fall below 8,848 tons, despite appreciable increases in the price of imported iron in the nineties.[2] As with timber, it was Russia that was mainly responsible for meeting the additional demands made on Hull merchants by their developing industrial hinterland. As late as 1750–9 Russian iron formed only 28 per cent of the total British importation; by 1780–9 it had risen to 63 per cent.[3] In Hull Russian iron had reached 48 per cent by 1768, but available evidence suggests thas the percentage rose no further. Indeed, one of the distinctive features of the national iron trade was the growing importance of Hull as a consumer of Swedish iron. Professor K. G. Hildebrand has shown from the Stockholm Port Books that the average amount of iron exported to Hull in the early thirties was 980 tons, compared with 5,700 tons sent to London and 1,200 to Bristol.[4] Then, with the development of the Sheffield region, a gradual change began. By 1785–94 Hull was receiving 2,890 tons per annum from Stockholm, while London, which had a heavy consumption of iron, but not particularly for steel making, was down to 4,360 tons. Bristol, previously the second largest consumer of Stockholm iron, now received only 690 tons per annum. The Russian and Swedish trade together raised Hull to a position of pre-eminence among the Outports in the last quarter of the century. She was taking, on average, about 20 per cent of the total national importation

[1] Ships engaged in the northern wood trade tended to be very large. See p. 134.

[2] Russian iron rose from *c.* £13–£15 10*s.* in 1795 to £23–£26 10*s.* in 1798; Ashton, *Iron and Steel*, p. 146.

[3] K. G. Hildebrand, 'Foreign Markets for Swedish Iron', p. 10.

[4] ibid., p. 25.

from St. Petersburg, and about a quarter of the total from all sources.

Hull's position in the iron trade is well known. Less well known is her similar position in the flax and yarn trades. The importation of flax, already expanding rapidly in the first half of the century, doubled between 1758 and 1783, when 45,734 cwt. arrived, and the new linen industry of the Knaresborough and Barnsley areas was almost entirely dependent upon Hull. The opening of Marshalls flax mill in Leeds in 1788 marks the first successful attempt to mass-produce high quality yarn in England, and as a result the importation of flax doubled again by the end of the century, with Marshalls taking anything up to a third of the total arriving in Hull.[1] Similarly, it was Marshalls' experiments with tow spinning, perfected *c.* 1791, that sent up the volume of imported tow from an average of 2,921 cwt. for 1790–2 to 9,517 cwt. for 1799–1802.[2]

The importation of linen yarn, also increasing rapidly in the forties, rose about eightfold between 1751 and 1783. By the early nineties Hull was importing more than the rest of the English ports together, with the bulk of supplies for the linen industry coming not, as often supposed, from Ireland via Liverpool, but from Prussia via Hull. The average quantity for 1791–3, for example, was 4,681,616 lb., which represents no less than 73 per cent of the national total from the continent, and 57 per cent of the total from all sources.[3] Of this, perhaps a third came from Hamburg and Amsterdam in the last quarter of the century. Raw Dutch linen yarn maintained its lead until the middle of the century, and then lost ground to Spruce linen yarn, which was almost exactly double the quantity of Raw Dutch in 1783.[4] Hull was Prussia's best customer for high quality yarn, taking 112,145 of the 123,653 shock of Ermland yarn exported

[1] W. G. Rimmer, *Marshalls of Leeds, Flax Spinners, 1788–1886* (Cambridge, 1960), pp. 76–7.

[2] ibid., pp. 32–3.

[3] The general figures for 1790–1807 do not include flax and yarn returns. Yarn figures for 1791–3 are to be found in HCLB C–B, 10 Feb 1794, and national figures in *PRO* BT6/230.

[4] For a time Raw Dutch increased at a faster rate than Spruce. Taking 1751 as the base year, the increase was as follows:

	1751	*1758*	*1768*	*1783*
Raw Dutch	100	327	748	670
Spruce	100	239	295	857

from the Braunsburg-Elbing-Konigsberg complex of ports in 1804.[1] 'A ship or two generally winter here', Oddy said of Konigsberg, 'for the purpose of taking the Ermland yarn early to Hull, for the manufacturers at Manchester.'[2] Competition for the best quality, especially in the first ships, was at times fierce, and the representatives of Manchester merchants in Hull scrambled for 'first refusals'.[3]

The developments that encouraged the timber, iron, flax and yarn trades, also spelled the doom of the linen trade. The famous linens of Haarlem no longer came to Hull, and not even the Peases, with their cousin Clifford's estate in that town, could be persuaded to touch them. The lure of Manchester was too great. They acquired a new set of cousins there and invested in cotton factories. A minute share in the national linen trade was a natural concomitant of Hull's huge share in the raw materials for linen production. If Dutch and German linens were the first to be hit by British industrialisation, the great Russian factories, originated by Peter the Great to capture the British market, soon began to feel the draught. After reaching a peak of 15,213c. ells in 1754, a catastrophic decline took place during the Seven Years' War and the trade never fully recovered. In 1783 the total importation was only 8,605c. ells, of which 5,408c. were Spruce Canvas, and the figures at the end of the century show a fluctuating total that never exceeded this.

The trade in hemp developed more slowly than the trade in flax, and the total imported in 1783—26,974 cwt.—was only about 50 per cent higher than in 1737. The demand for hemp, as for masts, was stimulated by mercantile—and, later, naval—developments, and it follows that for hemp, as for most things, the eighties were a period of intense activity. By 1790–2 the average had reached 49,091 cwt. (64,897 cwt. in the best year) although there was little further expansion and the average for 1799–1802 was only fractionally better.

The miscellaneous trades with the eastern Baltic continued to expand in the second half of the century (potash, for example, doubled between 1758 and 1783), but the most noticeable development was in animal products. They ranged from feathers for beds—

[1] J. J. Oddy, p. 237.

[2] ibid., p. 231.

[3] For example, see J. Pease, Hull, to Robert Robinson, Manchester, 1752–3, *passim*; *WH* 59/58/43.

450 cwt. in 1792—to bristles, which doubled in quantity from 17,240 doz. lb. in 1790–2 to 34,884 doz. lb. in 1799–1802, while the by-products of the slaughter house—horns and tallow from St. Petersburg—made a welcome appearance on the English market. Far more important, however, were hides and skins.[1] The growing demand for leather—for clothing, upholstery, bookbinding and industrial purposes—soon exceeded the British production of hides, and the great tanneries of Hull and Beverley were forced to seek their supplies overseas.[2] Importation grew rapidly, to average 18,913 hides for the years 1790–2, and 22,500 at the turn of the century. The number of skins was considerably greater. They averaged about 50,000 per annum towards the end of the century and reached 141,243 in 1800.[3]

The tremendous growth in the volume of goods from Russia and Prussia is reflected in the number of ships entering Hull. Those from Russia—thirty to forty in the middle of the century—rose rapidly after the Seven Years' War to over a hundred in the early eighties, one hundred and sixty-six in 1796 and one hundred and eighty-nine in 1803. For at least the last twenty years of the century, Hull was the principal outport in the Russian trade, second only to London. Prussian trade involved between thirty and forty ships per annum until the eighties, when the number rose rapidly to sixty-eight in 1783 and eighty-two in 1790. After remaining fairly steady in the nineties, Prussian ships exceeded Russian ones for a time during the war, when Russian trade was sacrificed by Czar Paul in his attempt to gain the friendship of Napoleon. Of all the Baltic ports, St. Petersburg was now pre-eminent; Peter the Great's dream had materialised. From about a dozen a year in the fifties, the ships arriving from the Russian capital grew to twenty-eight in 1768, the largest number for a single port, Then, after a few years of fairly steady development, the boom came in the eighties, pushing the total up to one hundred and three in 1796, no less than 23 per cent of the total number of ships entering the port. Even in the harsh conditions

[1] Hides came from the larger animals such as horses and cattle; skins came from sheep, pigs and goats.

[2] The importance of the Hull tanneries may, in fact, be due to their location at the place of importation.

[3] Unfortunately, the Customs classification is 'skins and fur', so we cannot be sure that the entire importation was for the tanneries. It is, however, certain that coney skins were not involved, since they were always counted by the dozen. Seal skins were included.

at the turn of the century, the number did not drop below thirty-three, though the trade was very seriously affected by war conditions in 1804:[1]

SHIPS ENTERING FROM ST. PETERSBURG, 1789–1804

1789	74	*1793*	123	*1797*	75	*1801*	93
1790	72	*1794*	75	*1798*	110	*1802*	59
1791	109	*1795*	101	*1799*	33	*1803*	110
1792	110	*1796*	136	*1800*	52	*1804*	21

ii. GERMANY AND HOLLAND

After Russia and Prussia, the most important region was still Germany and Holland, which remained the chief source of manufactured goods, dyestuffs and luxuries, as well as the principal market for exports. The number of ships entering from Germany and Holland conformed closely with the general shipping pattern: they accounted for 22 per cent of total ships arriving in both 1758 and 1790. Those from Germany increased slightly in the late sixties, and then remained steady until they suddenly doubled in the nineties, to seventy-four in 1796. 'No sooner', said Oddy, 'had the French entered Holland, than at once the commerce of Europe flew to Hamburg, which became the focus and central point, through which the trade of the European continent passed to Great Britain. . . .'[2] Ships had reached 116 by 1802, the year before the Napoleonic fury broke upon Germany and brought trade to a halt. Shipping from Holland remained roughly the same for the first three-quarters of the century, between 30 and 40 per annum, and it was not until the late eighties that the number began to rise, to just over 60 in 1789, although it was brought down again by war at the end of the century.

The goods imported were, with a few exceptions, the same as during the earlier period, although quantities naturally increased. Among the dyestuffs, for example, madder trebled, from 1,900 cwt. in 1758 to 6,095 cwt. in 1783, and smalts increased from 44,579 lb. in 1758 to 226,206 lb. in 1783, although the quantity then went down, to average 125,616 lb. for 1790–2 and 93,315 lb. for 1799–1802. Other dyes included potassium dioxide, arsenic trisulphide (orpiment), arsenic trioxide and lampblack, while 'Saccharum Saturni' (lead acetate), was both a mordant used in dyeing and the basis of

[1] J. J. Oddy, p. 123. [2] ibid., p. 415.

the innumerable cures for the Itch—31,620 lb. of it were imported in 1783.

Perhaps the most interesting of the newer imports from Holland and Germany was cotton wool. It was grown, of course, in the eastern Mediterranean, with which Hull had only a tiny trade, and was obtained via the entrepôt trades of Rotterdam, Amsterdam and Hamburg. We do not know when the trade began, but in 1783 the quantity was 409,604 lb., about half the total English import from this source.[1] Unfortunately for Hull, Smyrna had long since ceased to be important as a source of cotton, and Hull had little share—or interest—in the West Indian trade. Hull's average importation at the end of the century was not much more than half a million pounds, compared with the national total of over fifty million pounds. An older branch of trade, but one in which significant developments were taking place, was that in food and drink. As Britain ceased to provide all her own food towards the end of the century, large quantities of wheat, rye, barley, beans and peas began to flow in, together with beef, pork, bacon and butter. In 1796, when a temporary bounty was placed on imports, the total of wheat was 22,621 quarters,[2] and two years later groceries amounted to 10,568 cwt. The total amount of spirits arriving will never be known, but the amount of Geneva passing under the eyes of the Customs leapt forward, from about a thousand gallons in 1764 to an average of seventy-five thousand for the period 1790–2 and one hundred and sixty-five thousand (22 per cent of the national total) for 1799–1802.[3] The craze for gin was obviously not confined to London, nor, for that matter, was the love of Rhenish Hock, which increased in quantity from less than two thousand gallons in 1764 to over fifty thousand gallons in 1798.[4]

iii. SOUTHERN EUROPE

The volume of imports from France, Flanders, Spain, Portugal and Italy remained small compared with that from northern Europe.

[1] In 1785, for e.g., 2,113 bags arrived in Hull compared with 1,800 in London and 4,382 for the whole country; *BM* Add. MS 38,347, f. 206. A table of 'Cotton wool aired from Quarantine ships, 1791–99' is in HCLB, C-B 10 May 1800. The quarantine requirements (six weeks between arrival and landing) was one of the chief obstacles to an expansion of this trade.

[2] Figures compiled from periodic reports, HCLB, C–B, 1796, *passim.*

[3] Figures for 1764 from HCLB, C–B, 4 Sep 1766.

[4] Figures for 1798 from HCLB, C–B, 1 Jun 1799.

A very few ships, still no more than three or four a year, came from the Austrian Netherlands, and trade was generally discouraged by the unhappy political conditions. In 1784 the Hull diarist, Strother, recorded[1] that a Captain Rosindale,

who during the last war commanded a Privateer of twenty guns, is now preparing a ship . . . , desiring to go and open the Scheldt to Antwerp which the Dutch and Emperor are nearly disputing about and it is expected the fort of Lille will fire at him. Rosindale says he will hoist the English flag at every mast head and swagger by the fort, let them fire as fast as they will at him.

Strother did not record Rosindale's fate, but the trade certainly improved in the eighties, and the number of ships trebled, to fifteen in 1790, before dying out again during the war. The goods imported were mainly corn, linseed, spices from the Antwerp entrepôt, and brandy.

War rarely caused a complete cessation of trade with France as it did with Flanders, chiefly because the desire to trade with France increased as the century progressed. Ways were found of circumventing official barriers, and trading relations took a turn for the better after the American Revolutionary War confirmed France's temporary exit from the imperial field. Thus the general trade boom of the eighties was reinforced by the Eden treaty of 1786, and between them they produced the fastest rate of increase for any country outside the Baltic area. As Adam Smith could have told them, it was not until the politicians stopped fighting to extend trade, that trade really began to expand between the chief rivals. By 1789 the number of ships from France had reached forty-six, but the trade had no time to settle into a routine before war again brought a decline. While it lasted, the trade was mostly in brandy, wine,[2] linseed, dried and fresh fruit, as it had always been; books, furniture and luxury goods appear to have increased in quantity; and there was an interesting trade in religious articles, such as the 'wooden painted image of a woman with a child in her arms (supposed) intended for the use of a Roman Catholic', which was seized because it had not been reported inwards to the Customs.[3] Rosaries and

[1] Strother, f. 24, 24 Sep 1784.

[2] In the period 10 May–17 Aug 1787 France provided 15 per cent of the total wine importation at Hull, plus 71,275 gallons of brandy; HCLB, C–B, 22 Aug 1787.

[3] HCLB, C–B, 4 Dec 1764.

crucifixes were often confiscated, including the largest single shipment—boxes of bones and other relics brought by Professor Kempler, when the English College of Liège fled from the French in 1794.[1]

The number of ships from Portugal remained steady, at about twelve per annum, until the end of the century, and slightly fewer came from Spain. Together they accounted for only four per cent of total arrivals in both 1758 and 1790, although the numbers were rising in the nineties, to thirty-seven for both countries in 1803. The amount of wine imported (from all sources) also rose appreciably, from an average of 873 tuns for 1750–4 to 981 tuns for 1763–5, 1,011 tuns for 1777–81 and 2,566 tuns for 1799–1802.[2] The wine was accompanied, as one might expect, by an increasing quantity of Portuguese cork. In 1783 1,500 cwt. were imported—two and a half times the 1737 figure—and by 1800 it amounted to 2,387 cwt. The trade in fruit and chemicals also grew and expanded. Oranges and lemons were joined by olive oil, and by onion and clover seed as the Agrarian Revolution progressed. The range of chemicals, dyes and medicines—sumack, indigo, orpiment—was extended to include barilla (3,454 cwt. in 1783), saltpetre, isinglass, copperas (iron sulphate), salphera, cream of tartar, and 'antimonum crudens'. The trade in tarras—a volcanic rock for making cement—is further proof of Hull's response to the demands of the expanding building industry.

Regular trade with Italy was a new venture in the second half of the century. Cargoes consisted chiefly of Mediterranean fruits, oil, lemon juice, liquorice, currants and other luxury foodstuffs, and the *objets d'art* that were beginning to grace the home of aristocrat and merchant alike. Typical of the entries from Italy were 'boxes belonging to Mr Weddell' which 'appear to contain only busts, statues and other curiosities in stone and marble' and which, by order of the Commissioners of Customs, were not to be opened because of the risk of damage, but accompanied to Weddell's house and examined there.[3] Building stone and marble was also imported; the Hull dock, for instance, was strengthened with concrete made of

[1] HCLB, C–B, 23 Aug 1794 and HCLB, B–C, 26 Sep 1794.

[2] Figures for 1750–65 and 1777–81 from HCLB, C–B, 4 Sep 1766 and 18 Mar 1782 respectively.

[3] HCLB, B–C, 27 Sep 1765. William Weddell, of Newby, Yorks., was M.P. for Hull, 1766–74.

crushed Pozzellana stone, which was brought from Civita Vecchia and Leghorn. The Italian trade was certainly attractive enough in the last decade for a special firm to be founded in 1793, known as 'Ships of Richard Terry and Company in the Italian trade'.[1] Four merchants joined together and bought three ships, the *Salerno*, the *Arno* and the *Neptune*, at a cost of £5,565. But this may have been only a consolidation of existing interests, for the trade does not appear to have increased as a result of it. Hull's interest in the rest of the Mediterranean was minimal, and there were no arrivals in our sample years. A few ships in other years did, however, bring cotton wool from Smyrna and wool and currants from Zante and Cephalonia, and at the end of the century at least one firm—Todd & Popple—were members of the Levant Company.[2] We hear of intense competition in the trade, which led Todd & Popple to move to Grimsby, where importation lists were not published,[3] but unfortunately no details are available.

iv. AMERICA

Serious trade with America was, as we saw earlier, only just beginning in the middle of the century. The number of ships arriving from America grew rapidly, and stood at twenty-four in 1768, but Hull was unable to break into the well established trade of Liverpool, and the average number of arrivals was only eight for the years 1786–91.[4] Not until the end of our period was there an appreciable rise in the number of ships arriving—to thirty-two in 1803—but this was almost certainly due to war conditions in the Baltic, when increasing prices made it worth while to import from the United States. The nearness of the Baltic remained the chief stumbling block to American trade and, with the exception of tobacco and rice, Hull imported little from America which was in any way unique. Typical cargoes in the seventies, as in the fifties, consisted of tar and timber from North and South Carolina, imported chiefly for the

[1] Information from their banking account, Smiths & Thompson's Ledgers, National Provincial Bank, Hull.

[2] *KBH* Customs 94/21; Board's Orders, 11 Jun 1811.

[3] *BTA* GHN/1/2; Grimsby Haven Company Papers, 5 Feb 1824. Todd & Popple threatened to return the bulk of their business back to Hull when it was proposed to publish Grimsby import lists in 1824.

[4] HCLB, C–B, 14 Aug 1792. 38 per cent of the ships came from North Carolina.

sake of the bounty.[1] The trade in whale oil, which appeared promising in the middle of the century, declined after the oppressive Act of 1766 placed a duty on American oil at the same time as British whalers were receiving a bounty. Another trade with little prospect of rapid expansion was that in Plantation pig iron. Some of it was actually re-exported to Europe—ten tons of Maryland iron, worth £300, was sent to Ostend in 1783—but there was little chance of American iron competing with the Swedish or Russian product. After the connexion with America was severed, the Baltic resumed its paramount position in the timber and tar trades, and little was left except tobacco, which continued to be imported directly from America. In 1784 Benjamin Blaydes Thompson asked the Members of Parliament for Hull to see that Hull was included among the places permitted to import tobacco 'without advancing the old Subsidy'... 'as some American business is likely to be introduced into the Port of Hull'.[2] American business there certainly was, but the amount of tobacco imported at the end of the century—an average of 596,756 lb. for 1790–2 and 427,729 lb. for 1799–1802—was no improvement on the position in the middle of the century. It seems clear that Hull failed to capture much of the internal market for tobacco and, while the total importation remained fairly steady, the amount re-exported rose from 33 per cent in the middle of the century to an average of 40 per cent for 1790–2 and 75 per cent for 1799–1802. At the same time Hull was handling little more than one per cent of the total English tobacco importation, and the total American trade involved only about three per cent of the ships entering Hull.

Little need be said about trade with areas not already mentioned. The most lucrative trades of all, those with the East and West

[1] For e.g., the *Two Brothers*, arriving from Roanoke, N. Carolina, in October 1775, carried 15 brls of pitch, 774 of Common tar, 245 of Green tar, 239 of turpentine, 90c. barrel staves and 15c. hogshead staves, 2,000 feet of pine plank, and 70 lb. of beeswax; HCLB, C–B, Oct 1775. In 1770 the Hull merchants interested in naval stores presented a memorial to the Commissioners for Trade & Plantations objecting to any alteration in the bounties, 'praying that no steps may be taken for such alteration without their being heard thereupon'; *Journal of Commissioners for Trade and Plantations, 1770*, Vol. 77, p. 172.

[2] Note in letter, B. B. Thompson to W. Spencer-Stanhope, 20 Jun 1784, WSS 1784.

Indies, remained closed to the merchants of Hull. An occasional shipment of sugar from Barbados or Jamaica—two ships in 1788 and 1789, three in 1790—is all that we find in the records. Hull produced no nabobs or West India princes, no sugar interest or slavers. The monopoly of the East India Company effectively excluded Hull interests,[1] while participation in the Plantation trade involved the slave trade, with which Hull had nothing to do. There is no clear evidence that Hull merchants rejected the slave trade on moral grounds, but the general atmosphere was certainly hostile to it, long before Wilberforce and the Thorntons started their campaign: if available records present the full picture, no slave ship ever cleared from the port of Hull. A more cynical view would probably attribute Hull's exclusion from the West Indian trade to its geographical disadvantages, and its hostility to slavery to its jealousy of Liverpool.

3. THE EXPORT TRADE, 1700–1760

The export trade was totally different in character from the import trade. Most obviously, it was smaller in volume, with many ships leaving the port in ballast. The goods involved were different (there was only a tiny entrepôt trade) and, whereas imports came more or less from specific areas (Swedish iron, Russian hemp, Portuguese wine, etc.), particular exports did not go to particular countries. With few exceptions all the goods exported from Hull went to all the countries with which Hull traded, and the entries in the Port Books Outwards are monotonously regular, irrespective of destination. In the early years of the century the export trade revolved around lead and cloth, chiefly the latter: 'take our English Woollen Manufacture,' said Defoe, 'and go where you will you find it; 'tis in every Country, in every Market, in every trading Place; and 'tis received, valued, and made use of, nay, called for and wanted everywhere.'[2] Other goods came to prominence as the century progressed, though none of them came close to rivalling cloth.

The raw material producers that figure so prominently in the

[1] Hull men could join the East India Company as shareholders, but all trade passed through London. The monopoly on Indian trade, strongly attacked by the outports, did not end until 1813.

[2] D. Defoe, *A Plan*, p. 181.

import trade at the beginning of our period were not necessarily the best markets for exports. They were poor and largely undeveloped countries, insignificant as consumers of English industrial goods. Norway and Sweden are good examples. Their consumption of cloth, leather goods, lead, bricks, and luxuries, employing a third of the ships clearing from Hull in 1728, was declining rapidly in volume, and after the middle of the century was of little importance. Trade with Denmark was, if anything, worse. Nothing was produced there which was valued in Hull, and the reverse would also seem to be true.[1] The relatively unimportant trade, chiefly in lead and leather to Elsinore, declined—six ships in 1728, four in 1737, one in 1751—and finally ceased, except in wartime, when Denmark acted as a useful entrepôt for trade with enemy territory. The decline in exports to Scandinavia was probably connected with the ending of the permanent Hull factories in the middle of the century; certainly many of the cargoes sent there by the Maisters and Broadleys, for example, were consigned to Hull factors.[2]

If the volume of exports to the western Baltic declined, the reverse is true of the eastern and south-eastern Baltic. The number of ships sailing to Russia, Poland and Prussia increased as those bound for Norway and Sweden decreased, partly because of the rise of St. Petersburg and its market, demanding an ever-increasing supply of woollen and iron goods. Here was a perfect example of a flourishing import trade stimulating a foreign economy which in turn demanded English manufactured goods. The number of ships clearing for Russia doubled in the second quarter of the century, until in 1758 they amounted to one-fifth of all ships leaving Hull in freight. Those sailing to the southern Baltic were usually fewer in number but they carried the same type of cargoes, for distribution far into the hinterland of Poland and Germany.

The general pattern of trade with Scandinavia and the Baltic was of a large volume of relatively low valued imports and a smaller volume of relatively high valued exports. The trade with Germany and Holland was quite different. Except for the year 1728, when an abnormally large number of ships—forty-eight—arrived from Rotterdam, the number of ships engaged in the export trade to Germany and Holland exceeded the number in the import trade. Moreover, the trade in both directions was in finished products. Holland had no raw materials and Germany only staves and linen

[1] J. Gee, p. 23. [2] See p. 121.

yarn; both countries were suppliers of valuable cargoes, and consequently in a position to take a larger proportion of Hull's exports than the raw material suppliers. Much of the cloth, lead, hose and other goods shipped from Hull found their way to Amsterdam, Rotterdam, Hamburg and Bremen, and through these ports to the hinterland of Germany via the Rhine, and the great fairs of Frankfurt-on-Main, Frankfurt-on-Oder and Leipzig. Defoe was duly impressed, and spoke of

> The incredible Vent for the woollen Manufacture of *England*, which is now actually in *Holland*, as well at *Rotterdam* as at *Amsterdam*; and from thence it is sent to all the Provinces and Counties of *Germany*; which, as I have said above, is said to amount to above two Millions Sterling per annum.[1]

He might have added that goods were re-exported to Baltic countries and to areas with which Hull had little or no direct contact.

The export trade to the remaining countries of Europe was negligible compared with that to the north. At the best of times not more than half-a-dozen ships went to France each year, although the merchants were probably less satisfied with this situation than the theorists such as Gee, who thought that 'France, above all other Nations, is the worst for England to trade with: It produces most Things necessary for life, and wants very little either for Luxury or Convenience. . . .'[2] Poor trade probably owed as much to the machinations of politicians as to the incompetence of merchants, or the self-sufficiency of France.

Spain and Portugal between them received about the same number of ships as France. At the beginning of the century Portugal was the chief market for leather, and she also received important shipments of lead and kerseys, the latter destined for the empire of Brazil.[3] But it was not until the second half of the century that southern Europe began to receive fairly large shipments of goods from Hull. Hull had not yet assumed a rôle of any importance in the English economy, and trade with the south of Europe was still very much a matter for the southern ports. The same might be said of

[1] D. Defoe, *A Plan*, p. 163. There was, he said, 'Not a capital City in the Empire, but you may find the Shops of the Tradesmen stored with *English* cloth, as far as the Navigation of the Elb, the Oder, or the Weissel can convey them,' ibid., p. 184.

[2] J. Gee, p. 19.

[3] H. E. S. Fisher, 'Anglo-Portuguese Trade, 1700–1770', *Econ. Hist. Rev.*, 2nd ser., XVI (1963), pp. 226–9.

Hull's exports to Britain's own empire in America; they hardly merit mention.

If Hull's export trade did not expand greatly during the first half of the century, it was chiefly because there was little progress in the woollen cloth trade. The exportation of cloths had been expanding rapidly in the last quarter of the seventeenth century, and 27,335 dozens, 53,868 kerseys and 16,376 bayes were exported in 1700. The removal of duties in that year[1] encouraged cloth exports, and two years later the dozens had risen to 45,833 and bayes to 46,487, while kerseys had more or less reached their peak, at 108,267.[2] There was very little increase in the volume of cloth after this date, but there was a very noticeable change in the type of cloth exported, which would in turn have an effect upon the value of the trade:

THE EXPORTATION OF CLOTH FROM HULL 1672–1783

	1672	*1682*	*1700*	*1702*	*1717*
Dozens	17,057	27,656	27,335	45,833	28,990
Kerseys	19,245	34,399	53,868	108,267	68,474
Bayes	4,030	12,221	16,376	46,487	31,114
	1728	*1737*	*1758*	*1768*	*1783*
Dozens	40,022	76,157	69,728	122,710	163,710
Kerseys	40,297	37,083	33,378	33,399	13,340
Bayes	22,076	52,221	44,040	70,232	134,600
Plains			914	1,880	15,520
Shalloons			18,400	28,956	17,810
Stuffs			45	50,485	57,877
Cotton Velvets			20	8,352	236,834

The continued rise in dozens and bayes was offset by the steady decline of the kersey, the cheap coarse cloth which could not withstand the competition of linen and was rapidly going out of fashion. By 1737 dozens were up to 76,157, but kerseys were down to 37,083, and twenty years later they numbered only 33,378.[3] Between the failure of the kersey trade, and the full flowering of the dozens trade, there was an hiatus that lasted until the general expansion of trade in the second half of the century. Nor were the New Draperies,

[1] 11 and 12 William III, c. 20.

[2] Figures for 1672, 1682, and 1700 from W. J. Davies, *passim.*

[3] The importation of kerseys into Russia was prohibited in 1718, when attempts were made to establish a Russian woollen industry; D. K. Reading, pp. 52–3.

especially those produced in Norfolk and the West Country, of great importance to Hull in the first half of the century. Of the serges, stuffs, plains, shalloons, cottons and cotton velvets exported, only plains, shalloons and stuffs were of significance, and they were all of interest rather as heralds of things to come than as actual articles of trade. Plains, for instance, began with 4 in 1717, and had reached no more than 3,105 twenty years later; shalloons, which were made around Halifax, provided the largest numbers, reaching 18,400 in 1758.

Compared with cloth, the other items exported from Hull were of little importance at the beginning of the century, and the only commodities in which there was a noticeable increase during the first half of the century were hose, lead, ironmongery, earthenware, linseed cakes and ale. Worsted hose were in great demand in Europe and America, and the trade grew very rapidly with the development of the Nottingham hosiery industry, from 4,448 dozen pairs in 1702 to 47,850 dozen pairs in 1737. Our figure in the middle of the century shows a decline, which may be related to a considerable drop in Portuguese imports of hose,[1] but the trade recovered in the second half of the century. Linseed cakes, on the other hand, were a by-product of one of Hull's own industries, and the trade in cakes grew as the demand for linseed oil grew, from 145,700 in 1717 to 407,000 in 1737.[2] There was a similar increase in the amount of ale exported, from 3,338 gallons in 1728 to 14,533 gallons in 1737. By the middle of the century Burton alone provided 740 barrels (31,744 galls), but there was no great success in the trade until the development of the canals in the seventies.[3] Earthenware, which was usually of extremely low value, began to leave Hull in the thirties, a few thousand pieces a year; by the fifties half-a-million a year was common, but again transport difficulties hampered expansion. Bricks, too, were exported in large, though fluctuating, numbers, but with both bricks and earthenware large numbers mean little; their chief value was as saleable ballast.

For the trade in lead and ironmongery, the twenties and thirties

[1] H. E. S. Fisher, p. 229.

[2] They were used among other things, for foddering the Dutch army in 1747; Herman Strings, Amsterdam, to J. Pease, Hull, 1 Sep 1747, *WH* 59/58/41.

[3] P. Mathias, pp. 175–6.

mark a quickening of activity. Lead and lead shot, which had fluctuated around 2,000 tons per annum, rose to 2,732 tons in 1737, and by 1758 had reached 3,347 tons, while the very important red lead, which had risen from 1,848 cwt. in 1717 to 11,623 cwt. in 1728, continued to increase steadily in quantity till it stood at 24,322 cwt. in 1758. The exportation of white lead—the product of another Hull industry—also began in the thirties, but was still comparatively unimportant in the middle of the century. The greatest increase of all, as might be expected, was in manufactured iron goods. The amount exported early in the century was negligible—not much more than a ton in 1702 and six tons fifteen years later. By 1728, however, the total had shot up to 89 tons, and with the growth of the Sheffield iron industry the amount rose rapidly to 203 tons in 1737 and 904 tons in 1758.[1]

The only commodity not fitting into the general pattern of trade was corn, which was both imported and exported, depending on the vicissitudes of Nature. Hull, like everywhere else, had its times of scarcity. The Hull historian, Gent, recorded that in 1727:[2]

> Even Beans were sold, in the West Riding at 40 shillings a quarter; and Corn would have been miserably dear, had not his Majesty, in Commiseration to his poorer Subjects been so gracious, as to take off the Duty of Foreign Grain: Hereupon, in our Distress, we were supply'd with ship loads, from Italy, Flanders, Poland, and other distant parts, to the unspeakable Comfort of many house keepers. . . .

But 1727 was not typical of the first half of the century. Developments taking place in agriculture resulted in an increasing surplus of wheat, and national exportation had reached almost a million quarters in 1750, before the decline began as an expanding population turned a net export of wheat into a net import. On the whole, then, Hull was an exporter of grain, obtained from the Vale of York and from the area around Doncaster. The chief markets were Hamburg, Amsterdam, Rotterdam and Lisbon, although later in the century it also went to Bremen, Leghorn and Oporto. The quantity, of course, fluctuated wildly: 10,123 quarters of wheat in 1702, 977 quarters in 1717, and none in the years 1728, 1737 and

[1] Ironmongery was unfortunately classified only by weight in the Customs records.

[2] Gent, p. 196.

1758.[1] Barley was important in our sample years only in 1737, when 23,080 quarters were exported.

4. THE EXPORT TRADE, 1760–1800

The universal distribution of goods throughout Hull's export markets was, if anything, accentuated in the later part of the eighteenth century. There appears to have been only one exception to prove the rule: kerseys were, at least by the eighties, exported only to Spain, Portugal and the Mediterranean. Kerseys apart, the chief difference between regional trades lay in quantity rather than quality, and the simplest way of making a rough comparison is to count the number of ships clearing from Hull.[2]

The trade to Norway and Sweden continued on its downward trend, and played a negligible part in Hull's total export trade, involving only four ships in both 1790 and 1802. On the other hand the trade to the eastern Baltic continued to grow by leaps and bounds. In 1717 and 1728 Russia, Poland and Prussia between them had received about 12 per cent of the ships clearing from Hull, but by 1758 their share had risen to 32 per cent. The number of ships bound for Russia had roughly trebled in the first expansion of the export trade in the late forties, from nine in 1737 to twenty-six in 1758, and thereafter remained fairly steady, with a slight decline in the sixties, before doubling in the eighties to about fifty per annum. Of these, a large proportion were destined for St. Petersburg—82 per cent in 1768—although the proportion declined as ships began to go to such ports as Archangel and Onega in freight in the eighties, and only 60 per cent of the Russian-bound ships went to St. Petersburg in 1783.

There was virtually no change in the volume of trade with Poland, except, perhaps, for a slight rise in the middle of the century. The port of Danzig was a distribution centre for manufactured goods, and as such had the distinction of being the only Baltic port for which the

[1] Unfortunately our sample years coincide with the nadir of the corn cycle, which occurred towards the end of each decade, except in 1738–9 (when it was delayed till 1740) and 1748. Britain was a net importer of wheat in 1728, 1758, and 1768.

[2] There were, however, differences in the average size of ships in different trades (see p. 134). In general the trades with the most ships also had the largest ships, so that the difference in volume of trade was greater than appears from a consideration of numbers alone.

number of ships engaged in the import trade did not greatly exceed those in the export trade; the number in both directions, at least in 1737 and 1790, was roughly the same. The number sailing to Prussia, in contrast, increased rapidly in the sixties, from four in 1758 to sixteen in 1766, and, although it remained steady for a time, it had reached forty-two in 1783, before falling again to twenty in 1790.

The Baltic countries as a whole remained less important in the export trade than in the import trade. Germany and Holland maintained their position as the chief market for manufactured goods, receiving 53 per cent of the ships clearing in 1717, 47 per cent in 1758 and 52 per cent in 1802, although there had been a slight decline in position in the sixties and seventies, when Russia, Poland and Prussia between them received a few more ships than Germany and Holland. The rise of the trade with Hamburg was, indeed, the most noticeable feature of the last quarter of the century. Between 1790 and 1802 the number of ships clearing for Germany (i.e. Hamburg and Bremen) rose from forty-five to one hundred and four, 31 per cent of total clearances, compared with 21 per cent bound for Holland and 14 per cent for Russia. Hamburg was undoubtedly the most important single port to which goods were sent during the French Revolutionary wars, or, for that matter, during any troubled time. In 1780, for instance, the Hull Convoy Committee requested a convoy to escort ships across the North Sea 'loaded with British Manufactures to a very large amount . . . part of these cargoes were intended for the Frankfurt Easter Fair, others to be sent by neutral ships now loading at Hamburg for Fairs in Italy. . . .'[1]

The rise of Hamburg as an entrepôt, especially in wartime, helps to explain the otherwise bewildering number of ships bound for Denmark and Norway in 1803 and 1804. Until the end of the century only one or two ships per annum had sailed to the Norwegian part of the kingdom and none to Denmark; but in 1803 the number going to Denmark—rather than Norway—rose suddenly to thirty-six, and in 1804 it was eighty-one. Similarly, the number of ships bound for Prussia rose from twelve in 1802 to eighty-two in 1804. Such was the effect of the invasion of Hanover (May 1803) and the seizure of Cuxhaven by the French, which reduced and

[1] *GH* Minute Book of the Committee for Convoys (1757–82), March 1780.

finally halted the trade with Hamburg. The ports might be changed, but the trade continued.

Another interesting feature at the end of the century was the volume of exports to France following the 1786 Eden treaty. In the years of Anglo-French bitterness the number of ships clearing for France had rarely exceeded half-a-dozen per annum. Now the merchants, relieved of political pressures, rushed into the new trade, and in 1790 no fewer than forty ships sailed for France. They were, however, small ships, and their number, while clearly indicating the expansion of French trade, may not be used to compare France with other markets; for although they represent 16 per cent of the ships, they account for only 7 per cent of the tonnage. In any case, there was an almost immediate collapse of the trade when the French Revolution broke out, and only half-a-dozen ships sailed for France again in 1802.

There was no major change in the remaining areas, at least until the last decade of the century. The number of ships sailing to Flanders in 1789 was the same as it had been in 1717, and only slightly more than in the sixties. Those bound for Spain and Portugal, after remaining roughly the same throughout most of the century, doubled between 1790 and 1802; while those bound for Italy rose very slightly between 1770 and 1790. Finally, ships sailing to the United States were the same in 1789 and 1790 as they had been in 1768 and 1769, although here again there was a rise between 1790 and 1802, when nineteen ships cleared. The trade had developed from practically nothing in the first half of the century, and an average of nine ships cleared in the years 1766–72, but Hull failed as an exportation port for the American trade as the manufacturers of the Midlands gravitated towards Liverpool. What trade there was, was due mainly to Sheffield ironmongery and Leeds cloth, chiefly the latter. For Leeds merchants Hull was the only outlet until the end of the century; in 1770 it was recorded in the *Leeds Intelligencer* that 'The account of the inhabitants of New York having agreed to the importation of goods from England, was received here by our American merchants with great pleasure; since when, great quantities of cloth have been sent to Hull, in order to be shipped for the above place.'[1] The *Intelligencer* and the *Leeds Mercury* carried many advertisements of ships 'Laid on' for America, but at least one of them implies that trade was not

[1] *Leeds Intelligencer*, 21 Aug 1770.

sufficiently brisk to create competition for freight: 'The Good Brigg *Cornelia*', for New York, offered to wait 'till the latter end of July, if timely notice is given that she is likely to get loaded . . .'.[1]

The second half of the century witnessed a tremendous expansion in the volume of exported goods out of all proportion to the increase in the number of ships, chiefly because cargoes were much bigger. In many cases ships were packed tight with goods, whereas before they had often sailed half-empty, and ships were increasing in size as the century progressed. Thus, in 1783, a typical cargo sent to Hamburg by William Williamson, the biggest exporter in Hull, contained: 1,200 single dozens, 1,600 broad bayes, 130 shalloons, 4,000 cotton velvets (which alone were worth £20,000), 30 tuns of ale, 600 cwt. of red lead, 180 cwt. of British Roman Vitriol, 300 tons of ironmongery and 40,000 pieces of 'iron plates tinned'.

The predominance of cloth in Williamson's cargo reflects its position in general. In almost every branch of textiles there was progress, as Old and New draperies combined in quantities exceeding the highest hopes of the merchants and the worst fears of the Dock Company. The older types of woollen cloth continued to be important; the number of dozens rose slowly to 163,710 in 1783, and the number of bayes began to expand fairly quickly after 1758, and stood at 134,600 in 1783. On the other hand, the kersey trade was almost over; by 1783 the number was down to 13,340 pieces, a sorry figure compared with the 100,000 of 1702. The newer types of cloth, made by the West Riding and Lancashire linen-'cotton'-industry, increased at a phenomenal rate. The total number of cotton velvets exported in 1758 was only twenty, and ten years later only 8,352 pieces, still an insignificant part of the total cloth trade. By 1783, however, almost 250,000 pieces of cotton velvet were exported, containing 6,832,240 yards. Anything up to 4,000 pieces were exported at a time, and they figured in practically every cargo leaving the port. Of the other new cloths, stuffs increased from 45 in 1758 to 50,485 in 1768, and then remained about 50,000 for the rest of the century, standing at 57,877 in 1783. Some silk and printed stuffs were exported, but they were relatively unimportant. Plains increased at a much slower rate, from 914 in 1758 to 1,880 in 1768 and 15,520 in 1783, while the number of shalloons, after rising

[1] *Leeds Intelligencer*, 11 Jun 1765. There were regular advertisements in the early seventies offering both freight and passage to North America.

from 18,400 in 1758 to 28,956 in 1768, declined again to 17,810 in 1783.

After seeing the expansion of the cloth trade, it comes as something of a surprise to discover that the exportation of woollen hose in 1768 was only a fifth of what it had been in 1737. Admittedly 1768 was a year of depression in the British export trade, and the number of Hull ships clearing for America and Germany was reduced, but the decline in hose was greater, proportionately, than in most things, and the total in 1783—a good year for exports—was still only 45,510 dozen pairs, compared with 47,850 dozen pairs in 1737. Quite remarkable, from the point of view of expansion, was the trade in worsted garters, of which 200 dozen gross were exported in 1768. They were either very popular or very fragile, for the total in 1783 had gone up to 47,600 dozen gross—a gross of garters for every pair of stockings exported, and a total of slightly more than 82,250,000. Men's felt hats also increased considerably in quantity in the last thirty years of the century. Only negligible quantities were exported until the sixties, and the total in 1768 was only 500 dozen: by 1783 they had reached 23,200 dozen, valued at approximately £1,800 per thousand dozen.

The most important branch of trade, after cloth, was in metal and metal goods. Lead, which for centuries had been one of the principal articles (by weight) exported from Hull, had reached its peak by the middle of the century, at 3,347 tons in 1758, and by 1783 it was down to 2,074 tons. There was nothing disastrous about this decline, which was more than offset by developments in the red and white lead trade. The amount of red lead exported in 1737, 1758, and 1768 was approximately 20,000 cwt., but by 1783 it had increased to 81,119 cwt. White lead was not easily made, and the quantity exported in 1758 was only 735 cwt. The development of the 'Dutch' process—probably introduced into Hull by Joseph Pease[1]—led to a very rapid increase in output, and by 1783 exports had reached 12,903 cwt. Far more important for British industry was the trade in manufactured iron ware from the forges of Sheffield, Birmingham and Leeds. From the very small beginning in the first half of the century, the volume of ironmongery doubled between 1758 and 1768, and again between 1768 and 1783, when the total exported was 4,676 tons. Ironmongery was joined by two new articles towards

[1] See p. 193.

the end of the century: iron plates and tinned plates. By 1783 the quantity of iron plates had reached 12,750 cwt., while the number of tinned plates, presumably from the Rotherham area of Yorks,[1] rose at a phenomenal rate, from 3,375 in 1758 to half a million in 1768 and five and a half million in 1783, when Britain was beginning to capture the European market.

If metal goods owed much, pottery owed everything to the canals and navigations. The enthusiasm of Wedgwood and his friends for water traffic to Hull and Liverpool was amply rewarded by the volume of pottery flowing to Hull; in 1783 the total exported was no less than thirteen and a quarter million pieces.

Pottery, like cloth and iron goods, was evidence of the growing industrialisation of Britain, and it was this industrialisation, with its related demographic changes, that brought about a revolution in the corn trade. The exportation of wheat reached a peak—at 34,269 quarters—in 1761, and then declined more rapidly than can be accounted for by the normal fluctuations in the trade. In 1766 only 3,754 quarters were exported, and the total was lower in the seventies, when importation began. Although some corn was still exported, imports generally exceeded exports in the last quarter of the century. Between 1775, when 30,143 quarters were imported, and 1783, when 28,158 quarters were imported, the total exported was only 3,130 quarters. The last large export was over 31,000 quarters in 1792 (the best year for national exports since 1764),[2] but war and bad harvests made importation essential, and only 582 quarters were exported in the years 1794–9 (see Appendix 6).

It should, however, be remembered that in the corn trade the full influence of market conditions was tempered by the policy of protecting British farmers by preventing the importation of cheap corn and granting bounties on exportation.[3] Between 1780 and 1790, for instance, Hull was legally open for the importation of wheat at low duty only in the periods January–October 1783 and April–November 1789.[4] It follows that importation did not necessarily begin as soon as exportation ceased, although some slight encour-

[1] W. E. Minchinton, *The British Tinplate Industry* (1957), p. 17.

[2] T. S. Ashton, *Economic Fluctuations*, Table 3, p. 183.

[3] The Corn Bounty Act (I William & Mary, c. 12) granted five shillings per quarter when the price fell below 48 shillings, if exportation took place in English ships.

[4] HCLB, C–B, 10 Mar 1791.

agement to importation was given in 1773, when the price at which duty was removed was reduced from eighty shillings to forty-eight. A new law, in 1791, increased protection by raising the price for duty to fifty-four shillings, but it had little effect because of bad harvests, when it was suspended. The position was so bad in 1796 that a bounty was actually placed on imported corn,[1] and over 37,000 quarters arrived in Hull from Konigsberg, Danzig and Hamburg, as part of the biggest importation of wheat that Britain had ever seen.

When the exportation of corn came to an end, Hull had no major export trade left which was not connected with cloth or metal. The remaining trades were miscellaneous, and more interesting than important, with the possible exception of ale, which was to be found in practically every cargo leaving Hull, usually in quantities of between ten and twenty tuns. It was particularly valuable as a ballast cargo which had the added advantage of being in wide demand in the Baltic and northern Europe, some of it going as far inland as Galicia, three hundred miles south of Danzig. The brewers of Burton-on-Trent, as well as Hull, kept their eyes on the export trade, and approximately 90 per cent of the export beer brewed in Burton went out through Hull; Wilson's alone sent 122 tuns in 1750 and 1,837 tuns in 1775.[2] The total quantity exported through Hull rose very rapidly in the second half of the century, from 57½ tuns in 1758 to 4,953 tuns in 1783—enough for over ten million pints.

The infant chemical industry was represented by 12,520 cwt. of copper sulphate and 2,018 cwt. of iron sulphate—'copperas'—in 1783, while the 649 cwt. of alum presumably came from the ancient mines of Mulgrate Castle, near Whitby. There were also a few hundred tons of common salt, but Hull did not have the great reserves which Liverpool found so useful in its 'triangular' and European trades.[3] Most of the other commodities were the produce of Hull's own industries, ranging from the 43 lasts of pitch to 29,412 gross of corks; from a few hundredweights of glue to 5,000 gross of

[1] 36 Geo. III, c. 21. Only in exceptionally bad years was importation encouraged; usually the most that could be expected was an embargo on exportation, as in September 1765; HCLB, B–C, 26 Sep 1765.

[2] P. Mathias, p. 176.

[3] See T. C. Barker, 'Lancashire Coal, Cheshire Salt and the Rise of Liverpool', *Transactions of the Historical Society of Lancashire and Cheshire*, ciii, 1951. Hull had a coastwise importation of salt.

tobacco pipes; from 35 tons of whale oil to a few hundred tons of rud. A few tons of nails presumably originated in Derbyshire, the 105,000 fruit trees and twenty hampers of flowering shrubs—sent to Lisbon—possibly came from the East Riding, while the four Bird Organs will probably remain a mystery for ever. Finally there were the horses and coaches. There were no horses exported in 1758, but the trade appears to have started before the middle of the century. It expanded rapidly after the end of the war in 1763.[1] By 1766 the number had reached 129, and the average for the rest of the century was probably about a hundred per annum. They went mostly to Germany and Holland, but unfortunately we have no means of knowing what kind of horses they were. Both hunters and race horses were common in the East Riding and Lincolnshire, and these would seem the most likely candidates. The exportation of coaches was a reversal of the situation earlier in the century, when coaches were imported. Exports in 1783 included two coaches, one of them sent to Narva, one Post Charriot, two Post Chaises and three Phaetons. English coaches became quite fashionable in France, especially after the Eden treaty.

5. THE GENERAL DEVELOPMENT OF TRADE

Having discussed in detail the various components of Hull's trade, we may consider its general development, indicating the periods of progress and, where possible, the relative position of Hull as one of the major English ports.

The expansion of Hull's trade took place in three distinct phases following the three major wars (Austrian Succession, 1739–48; Seven Years', 1756–63; American Revolution, 1778–83), and follows very closely the national pattern of trade as shown by Mrs. Schumpeter and Professor Ashton.[2] There are no reliable figures to show the *value* of trade in the eighteenth century, but a rough idea of the *volume* of trade can be obtained from the tonnage of shipping entering and leaving the port.[3] Ships entering Hull in freight during

[1] Besides occasional horses (worth *c.* £30 each) the Peases also exported oxen to Holland—42 in July 1747; Joseph Pease, Hull, to Robert Pease, Amsterdam, 29 July 1747, *WH* 59/58/47.

[2] T. S. Ashton, *Fluctuations*, Chap. 6; E. B. Schumpeter, *English Overseas Trade Statistics*, *passim.*

[3] See Table in Appendix 9.

the first quarter of the century remained fairly steady, at roughly 11,000 tons per annum and it was not until after *c.* 1730 that there were any signs of increasing activity. By 1737 the total had reached 19,000 tons, but further progress was halted by the war which began officially in 1739; shipping was reduced to 11,328 tons in 1744, and, although it rose again at the end of the war, the few years of peace were not sufficient for it to rise much above 20,000 tons.

The second period of expansion commenced with the return of peace, in 1763. Within two years the volume of shipping inwards had risen to over 30,000 tons, and in 1767 it exceeded 40,000 tons. For the next fifteen years it fluctuated between 40,000 and 52,000 tons, before finally being reduced again by the American war. The twenty years following the war were the most momentous the port had yet seen. In 1787 shipping inwards stood at 92,120 tons, by 1792 it had risen to 135,000 tons, where it remained for the rest of the century.

There was no direct relationship—or even similarity—between the movement of import and export tonnages. The volume of ships clearing from Hull in freight remained at approximately 8,000 to 9,000 tons during the whole of the first half of the century; indeed, the tonnage in the second decade was higher than at any other time before the middle of the century, when the first phase of expansion in the export trade began. By 1751 shipping outwards was over 15,000 tons, only to be reduced almost immediately by the war, to a little over 12,000 tons in 1758. There was no sudden increase following the Seven Years' War as there was in the import trade; the total shipping outwards in 1765 was only 0·8 per cent greater than in 1751, whereas shipping inwards had risen by 44 per cent. There was a slow growth to 18,000 tons in 1769 and 23,000 tons in 1779, but the second period of expansion did not begin until after the American war. Between 1781 and 1787 the total more than doubled, to stand at 46,107 tons in 1787, and over 51,000 tons in the remaining years of the century. Even if we allow for an 'increase' in the size of British ships with the introduction of measured tonnage, the increase in tonnage clearing was still considerable.

The evidence of general trade movements contained in the tonnage figures is corroborated by the lists of imports and exports. All the principal imports—cloth, flax, hemp, yarn, timber and iron —arrived in relatively small quantities in the first quarter of the century. There was, of course, some increase in the volume of goods, particularly of flax, but the most noticeable increase came in the thirties, when cloth, hemp and yarn trebled in quantity, flax doubled, and deals and iron rose by more than 50 per cent. In the second phase of expansion, in the middle of the century, increases are particularly noticeable in yarn, timber (as distinct from deals) and iron, while in the third phase flax, hemp, yarn, timber, tar and tow all figured prominently.

The increase in the volume of exports in the first half of the century is hardly noticeable. Woollen cloths appear to have been declining until the thirties, when dozens and bayes rose (although kerseys continued to decline), and the newer cloths, which were to become so important later, had not yet appeared in any great number. Lead remained about the same, and ironmongery was still not of very great moment. The first phase of expansion was the product of a reinvigorated woollen cloth trade coinciding with the beginnings of the trade in shalloons and stuffs and, later, in cotton velvets. Red and white lead became increasingly important, and the growth of ironmongery, tinned plates and earthenware is most noticeable. The rise in the volume of exports between the sample years 1768 and 1783 is impressive. The older cloths continued to increase, but the most spectacular feature was the boom in cotton velvets. Indeed, cloth of one sort or another played such a predominant part in Hull's export trade that it alone would be sufficient to account for a good deal of the prosperity at the end of the century.

The general pattern of development shows unmistakably the well-known boom of the eighties. It also shows the preceding period as one of intensive commercial activity, stretching back to the seventeenth century and periodically gaining momentum as a new set of favourable factors emerge. This period was, not only for Hull, the essential forerunner of later developments. During it were built up the commercial, financial and shipping connexions upon which Industrial Revolution was based.

The various developments in Hull's trade are impressive, but difficult to interpret. There is, in any local study, a danger of losing that sense of national perspective which alone gives meaning and proportion to local statistics. To assess the importance of Hull in the national economy we must compare it with the other major ports; but such comparison is hampered by a general lack of information. There are no easily available records of the value or volume of goods passing through individual ports for most of our period, and, with the notable exception of Professor Minchinton's work on Bristol,[1] no detailed investigation of a major port in this period has yet been published.

In the absence of other figures, it is possible to class ports according to the tonnage of shipping frequenting them, although certain qualifications are necessary. From a straightforward classification by tonnage, Hull appears as the least important of the major outports in the import trade in the early years of the eighteenth century. But she was also the fastest growing port, passing Newcastle and Whitehaven by 1751 and Bristol by at least 1772, when Hull was ranked as the third outport. In the export trade Hull's position was poor until the boom in the eighties. In 1709 only 5,780 tons cleared, compared with 12,636 tons from Liverpool and 40,076 from Newcastle, the leading port. Nor had Hull's position altered by 1790, when she was still at the bottom of the list, with 51,060 tons, compared with Liverpool's 237,884 tons and Whitehaven's 230,562 tons:

RELATIONSHIP BETWEEN THE MAJOR PORTS: TONNAGES INWARDS AND OUTWARDS, 1709–90[2]

Port	*1709*	*1730*	*1751*	*1772*	*1790*
(i) TONNAGE INWARDS					
Bristol	19,817	29,034	30,433	38,707	70,668
Liverpool	14,574	18,070	31,713	76,613	241,117
Whitehaven	9,945	15,147	10,765	33,000	34,838
Newcastle	7,757	14,441	21,705	21,472	35,364
Hull	8,090	12,440	23,598	44,419	95,962
London	n.a.	n.a.	234,369	382,348	553,722
(ii) TONNAGE OUTWARDS					
Bristol	21,199	24,585	27,299	35,714	63,734
Liverpool	12,636	19,058	33,693	92,973	237,884
Whitehaven	24,644	45,213	113,155	193,416	230,562
Newcastle	40,076	46,337	57,852	73,409	96,620
Hull	5,780	8,168	15,994	18,361	51,060
London	n.a.	n.a.	173,843	246,509	322,895

While the *volume* of trade is obviously important to the shipowners, wharfingers and dockers, the prosperity of a port must ultimately be

[1] W. E. Minchinton (ed.), *The Trade of Bristol in the Eighteenth Century* (Bristol Records Soc., 1957).

[2] Figures for 1709–72 from *BM* Add. MS 11256; for 1790 from *PRO* Customs 17/12.

based on the *value* of its trade; and here Hull was almost certainly ahead of all but Bristol and Liverpool. Tonnage figures alone over-emphasise the coal ports—Newcastle, Sunderland and Whitehaven—to the detriment of ports handling valuable but compact industrial products. So far as Customs receipts were concerned, Hull paid an average of £136,789 on imports for the years 1789–90, compared with £33,107 paid by Newcastle and £6,691 by Whitehaven.[1] Sunderland paid only £4,579 in 1790, the year in which she was credited with a dubious 105,314 tons inwards! One further qualification might be made: foreign trade in the eighteenth century included trade with Ireland, so that Whitehaven's—and to a lesser extent Liverpool's—tonnage includes ships which were not, strictly speaking, engaged in *foreign* trade.[2]

It seems reasonable to class Hull as the third outport in 1790, but the tremendous lead of Liverpool and Bristol must be stressed: Hull was not yet in the same class. Already Bristol's tonnage inwards was less than Hull's, but her Custom House returned £334,197 on imports for the years 1789–90, almost two-and-a-half times as much as Hull's. In only three major bulk commodities did Bristol's share of the national importation exceed Hull's; but they were, significantly, tobacco, sugar and wine. Liverpool's lead was even greater, in tonnage, value of goods, and Customs receipts. In 1790 her tonnage inwards was two-and-a-half times Hull's, her tonnage outwards four-and-a-half times Hull's; in the transatlantic trade she had no equal.

Even the greatest of outports were insignificant when compared with London, which completely dominated English trade. As the capital city and financial centre, London attracted a large and wealthy population which thrived on trade, and supported not only a great international trade, but also the coastal trade, which was strongly influenced by London's demand for fuel and food. Shipping figures for London were notoriously difficult to collect, and none exist before 1751, when the total tonnage inwards was estimated at 234,369 tons, ten times as much as Hull's, and twice as much as all the major outports together. In the eighties, and no doubt earlier, London's tonnage inwards was roughly equal to all the outports, great and small, put together, London having 338,826 tons in 1781,

[1] Customs receipts from *PRO* Customs 17/11–12.

[2] See J. E. Williams, 'Whitehaven in the Eighteenth Century', *Econ. Hist. Rev.*, 2nd Ser., VIII (1956).

and the outports 313,066.[1] But with developments in the eighties the emphasis of trade began to swing northwards, and in 1790 London's total was slightly less than that of the six major ports, and only six times Hull's total. London never dominated the export trade to the same extent, simply because goods brought into England were distributed from London via the coastal trade, whereas exports were more often sent directly overseas from the nearest outport.

Our comparisons are sufficient to remind us that though Hull was a great port, it was far from the greatest. They should not, however, be allowed to obscure the fact that Hull was, in her restricted sphere, unsurpassed among the outports. In the years 1790–2 she was handling 26 per cent of the national importation of iron, 15 per cent of the deals, 21 per cent of the tar, 11 per cent of the hemp, 40 per cent of the tow and 20 per cent of the wainscot logs. She was also, rather surprisingly, importing 7 per cent of the wine—a figure exceeded only by Bristol—and 9 per cent of the Brandy and Geneva. In the Russian trade in general she was second only to London. But the possibilities for rapid expansion were, given existing conditions, severely limited. Hull had concentrated, for a variety of reasons, on trade between its hinterland and the Continent of Europe, whereas the chief feature of trade in the eighteenth century was the development of the great intercourse with America and the East. Europe declined in importance, sending 53 per cent of the goods imported into England (by value) in 1700, 44 per cent in 1750 and 31 per cent in 1800. In the export trade the decline was more severe, from 78 per cent in 1700 to 63 per cent in 1750 and 45 per cent in 1800. Those ports which engaged in the American and Irish trade clearly had an advantage over those which did not.[2]

The narrowness of Hull's trade had a further drawback: there was virtually no entrepôt trade, except in tobacco and cork. Almost all the imports went into the hinterland, almost all the exports came from it; little was imported that was not first demanded, and little was exported that could not easily be obtained. Hull merchants did not trade for the sake of trade, and were not interested in making Hull into a great commercial centre like Hamburg, Amsterdam or London, partly because they had come to rely—perhaps too heavily—on those centres rather than on direct trade.

It is easier to say that Hull had little transatlantic trade than it is

[1] *BM* Add. MS. 38, 345, fol. 214.

[2] E. B. Schumpeter, pp. 17–18.

to explain why this should be so. We can only guess, and in so doing risk overlooking some at least of the many personal, local and national factors determining the pattern of trade. Geographical factors may have had some influence, although there is no direct evidence to support this popular view. In the early eighteenth century the rôle of a port was not determined solely by its position on the east or west coast, but by the historical precedents which led merchants to seek profit in one trade rather than another. Liverpool was a transatlantic port, and Hull a Baltic port, long before the canals gave them a geographical advantage in their respective trades. Trade is the product of experience, connexion and trust; success breeds success, and once a flow of trade has been established the current tends to suck in the minor streams, until it reaches a stage where it cannot easily be diverted. By the middle of the eighteenth century it was too late for Hull to turn her eyes westwards, as some few merchants tried to do. Hull merchants were excluded from the East Indies, through no fault of their own, by the monopoly of the East India Company; but there is little evidence that they ever tried to develop the transatlantic connexions necessary for participation in the more lucrative trades. This is partly a matter of capital: the African and West Indian trades produced profits which could be ploughed back in further profitable, though hazardous, adventures. It is also a matter of initiative. There was, in fact, little incentive to develop transatlantic trade. American products could be obtained more easily, and with less risk or capital outlay, from London or, occasionally, Amsterdam. We may also, perhaps, detect the absence in Hull of that spirit of adventure which one imagines was present in Bristol and Liverpool. Hull merchants were, on the whole, concerned only with steady, reliable trade. They were not unscrupulous, if the small number of privateers fitted out is anything to go by, and, as we have already noted, the atmosphere in Hull was alien to the slave trade upon which the transatlantic trade was partly dependent.

Whatever Hull's shortcomings, compared with the other major ports, she provided an invaluable link between the industrial areas of Yorkshire and the Midlands and the outside world. Her merchants, by providing raw materials and disposing of manufactured goods, aided and encouraged the process of industrialisation. They deserve to be remembered for the vital rôle they played in the Industrial Revolution.

IV. THE COASTAL TRADE

1. GENERAL DEVELOPMENT

Foreign trade, though vital to the national economy, was only part of mercantile activity, and care must be taken to avoid over-emphasising trade which can be easily measured at the expense of that which cannot.[1] Coastal trade, still the only adequate form of long-distance 'internal' transport, was both supplementary and complementary to it. British and foreign goods alike made the coastal run, and direct contact with foreign producers and consumers was not essential. An embryonic national market already existed in 1700, and London's position as the national entrepôt was assured.

No one who studies the coastal trade can fail to be impressed by its tremendous volume, whether measured in goods, ships, or Port Book pages. The river Hull, like most harbours, was alive with a constant bustle of small coasters and river craft, reinforced from time to time by a foreign-going vessel earning its keep between

[1] Foreign trade statistics were analysed and presented to Parliament and, whatever their value, preserved for posterity. Coastal statistics were not generally analysed. While the Port Books last—until the eighties—the problem is not lack of information but too much of it in an unsystematic mass. Unfortunately the Port Books were discontinued just when they were beginning to throw light on the rôle of the coastal trade in the Industrial Revolution, and no detailed records replaced them. As a result the coastal trade has not received the attention merited by its economic importance, the only major work being Professor T. S. Willan's *The English Coastal Trade, 1600–1750* (1938).

The following reconstruction of the trade was compiled from a detailed examination of the Coastal Port Books for 1706 and 1775, and a partial examination of those for 1702, 1728, 1737, 1758, 1768 and 1783. The years 1706 and 1775 were chosen for their availability and legibility rather than their economic significance. The Coastal Port Books are, on the whole, in much worse condition than the Foreign ones (of which three copies were kept), and it is common to find that only one of the two volumes per annum is now available or legible. The number of detailed examinations was restricted by the nature of the work involved; Coastal Books are two or three times as long as Foreign ones and infinitely more difficult to study because of the vastly greater variety of goods in a multitude of smaller parcels. (For the *PRO* call numbers, see Appendix 39.)

voyages. No creek was without its diminutive tramp, but the activities of coasters were concentrated on the major ports, where they easily outnumbered their grander foreign-going cousins. According to the rudimentary statistics of the Customs, the number of coasters 'belonging' to Hull in the first three-quarters of the century was about the same as the number of foreign-going vessels. But coasters made far more voyages in a year, and a better guide to relative volume is the tonnage of ships entering and leaving the port. Figures available for the years 1766–72 show that, on average, coasters entering Hull were 353 tons more than foreign-going vessels. There was a far greater difference in ships clearing, with foreign-going vessels averaging only 43 per cent of the coastal tonnage:[1]

COASTAL AND FOREIGN-GOING TONNAGES, 1766–72

	INWARDS		OUTWARDS	
Date	*Coastal*	*Foreign*	*Coastal*	*Foreign*
1766	39,438	31,750	36,062	16,610
1767	37,091	42,006	37,798	16,267
1768	38,921	40,790	40,902	17,207
1769	41,300	40,631	44,239	18,191
1770	42,867	46,475	40,634	19,797
1771	46,766	43,991	40,424	18,675
1772	47,162	45,434	48,084	18,361
Average	41,935	41,582	41,163	17,872

Unfortunately the tonnage figures for 1768–72 are of doubtful validity, since they consistently understate the true tonnage using the port.[2] One thing is, however, clear: the relationship between the foreign and coastal tonnage remained the same when ships were counted at measured tonnage after 1786. The figure of *c.* 100,000 tons per annum for 1789–91 may be taken as a reasonably accurate statement of the volume of Hull's coastal trade at that time.[3]

Her position as the natural link between the metropolis and central England guaranteed to Hull a leading position in the national

[1] Figures from *GH* Port Dues Box, loose paper.

[2] For example, the *number* of coasters clearing increased by 60 per cent between 1768 and 1789, whereas the *tonnage* rose by 150 per cent, which is too much to be accounted for by increases in the size of ships.

[3] Figures from *PRO* Customs 17, *passim.* In 1796, coasters entering Hull were more or less the same as in 1791 (1,484 ships and 122,672 tons), but the total clearing had improved noticeably (1,354 ships and 114,165 tons).

COASTAL AND FOREIGN-GOING VESSELS AND TONNAGES, 1789–91

	INWARDS				OUTWARDS			
	Coastal		*Foreign*		*Coastal*		*Foreign*	
	No.	*Tons*	*No.*	*Tons*	*No.*	*Tons*	*No.*	*Tons*
1789	1200	101,103	455	89,019	1232	102,587	293	51,335
1790	1334	100,156	494	95,962	1299	104,746	302	51,060
1791	1459	123,523	591	115,019	1122	92,829	316	53,042
Average	1331	108,261	513	100,000	1218	100,054	304	51,812

coastal trade, at least in the second half of the century. Although comparative shipping figures are not yet easily available for most of our period, those for 1789–91 reveal Hull as a leading coastwise importer: more coasters entered Hull in 1791 than any other outport. Her coastwise exports were also very great, and exceeded those of most ports, but, despite the great value of industrial products, their volume was completely overshadowed by the coastwise exports of the coal giants of the north:[1]

COASTAL TONNAGE ENTERING AND LEAVING THE MAJOR PORTS, AVERAGE FOR 1789–91

	INWARDS	OUTWARDS
Bristol	96,359	67,059
Hull	108,261	100,054
Liverpool	106,997	104,158
Newcastle	117,816	817,684
Sunderland	33,815	518,179
London	929,326	784,883

Hull's coastal trade was not, at first, extensive. No more than a dozen places were involved in the early years of the century: Newcastle, Sunderland, Stockton and Seaton, Whitby and Bridlington, Boston, Lynn, Yarmouth, Burnham and Clay. London was incomparably the most important, and no ship ventured further. By 1728 the number of ports had risen to thirty-one. They were still mostly along the east coast, but Poole, Southampton, Exeter and Bristol were now within range. Scottish ports do not appear to have been contacted regularly until the thirties, although by 1768 there were twelve among the forty-nine ports visited that year. Hull now traded with the whole British coastline but continued to concentrate on the east coast, and the inclusion of many new places

[1] *PRO* Customs 17/11–13.

did not alter the fact that the bulk of trade was always with a small number of ports with which links were already firmly established in 1700.

2. THE IMPORT TRADE: RAW MATERIALS AND LUXURIES

The coastal trade, like the foreign trade, is most conveniently studied by separating imports from exports. Although for the most part the same ports were involved, the goods were generally different, and there was a growing number of ports concerned only in the import or the export trade.

Within the import trade there were three broad, but not exclusive, divisions: the raw materials trade, centred at first on Newcastle and Sunderland and concerned mainly with coal; the trade with the east coast wool and corn ports; and the dominant general trade with London. Ten ports accounted for almost the entire trade in 1703–4, and although the number of ports increased fairly rapidly, the newcomers made no significant inroads until the sixties:[1]

THE CHIEF PORTS OF ORIGIN OF COASTERS ENTERING HULL

	1703/4	*1706*	*1728*	*1737*	*1758*	*1768*	*1775*	*1783*	*1796*
London	93	80	179	190	226	307	387	327	553
Newcastle	59	42	111	94	59	44	51	43	53
Sunderland	58	71	138	129	45	28	26	17	29
Whitby	0	0	0	0	20	15	20	31	50
Grimsby	5	3	13	11	22	33	44	25	24
Lynn	16	12	72	45	56	74	77	93	136
Wells	0	0	30	13	13	20	14	24	34
Yarmouth	2	3	26	25	27	35	39	31	79
Ipswich	3	0	5	11	6	22	37	14	15
Bo'ness/Leith	0	0	0	1	9	26	26	32	38
As % of total entries:	*97*	*96*	*90*	*92*	*87*	*83*	*80*	*79*	*75*
Total entries:	244	219	635	567	553	729	903	803	1346

Most of the places from which raw materials came might adequately be described as one-commodity ports. They provided the raw materials, whether of animal, mineral or vegetable origin, but were not conveniently situated for supplying general goods to the

[1] For ships entering and clearing coastwise, see Appendix 12.

Hull market. There were perhaps a dozen of them in the early years of the century. In 1706, for example, only salt came from Berwick and salt and coal from Cullercoats, Seaton and Sunderland; wool came from Grimsby and Colchester; Fuller's earth from Rochester; and tobacco pipe clay from Poole.

As the hinterland developed, the list of raw material ports grew longer. The 1775 Port Book recorded at least twenty-six places, and there would no doubt be many more if account were to be taken of small ports which happened not to trade with Hull in that year. One or two places were simply new suppliers of old commodities: Exeter, for instance, joined Poole as a supplier of clay, and between them they sent 2,800 tons. Others filled new needs. Poole, besides its clay, sent train oil to augment the produce of Hull's own whaling fleet. The growing iron industry encouraged the importation of iron ore from Campbelltown and Ulverston. The flourishing soap industry of Hull relied heavily on kelp supplies from Aberdeen and Kirkwall, and it seems that the producers of the Western Isles had Hull in mind when they shipped their kelp over to Oban for coastal distribution.[1] Flint, for the potteries as well as for domestic use, came from Newhaven; and almost the entire importation of the blue dyestuff, woad, came from Saltfleet in Lincolnshire, where its cultivation was described and deplored by Arthur Young. Dunbar and Lerwick became fish suppliers; Roebuck & Garbett's works at Prestonpans became the principal source of vitriol, exported in large quantities from Hull to the continent in the last quarter of the century; and Greenock was important as a source of tar, presumably of American origin and therefore only available until the Revolution. Plymouth sent tiling stones, Montrose sent paving stones, and slate came from Easdale, Lancaster, Ulverston and Whitehaven.

There were two commodities falling only partially into the category we have been considering: wool and coal. The hinterland had long since ceased to produce the huge quantity of wool demanded by the Yorkshire woollen cloth industry, and coastwise importation was very considerable, rising from 1,478 cwt. in

[1] Hull was one of the leading English consumers of Scottish kelp; M. Gray, *The Highland Economy, 1750–1850* (1957), p. 129. Kelp from Tiree, for example, was sold to Mr. H. Stevenson of Oban 'who sold it to Liverpool, Hull and Clyde'; E. R. Cregean (ed.), *Argyle Estate Instructions, 1771–1805* (Scottish History Society, 1964), pp. 21–2.

1706 to 11,823 in 1728, 27,806 in 1737, an average of 29,439 cwt. for the years 1748–54[1] and 61,363 in 1775. During the troubled period of the American war the total was down to 41,831 cwt. for 1782, but there is every reason to suppose that the coastwise importation continued to grow towards the end of the century. Some of this wool came from places that shipped nothing else—from Aldborough, Blakeney, Dover, Rye and Grimsby. Most of them sent only small quantities, but the ancient wool port of Grimsby—a port before Hull—was the leading outport in the trade. Its shipments increased in number from five in 1703–4 to twenty-two in 1758 and forty-three in 1781; by weight they rose from 377 cwt. in 1706 to 8,232 in 1775, helped no doubt by the building of the Louth Navigation. The bulk of the wool, however, came from ports which also had other interests, discussed below: Ipswich, Lynn, Newcastle, Wells, Yarmouth and Leith. Above all there was, as in every other trade, London. It was the principal source of British Raw Wool for most of the century, collecting supplies from the whole of southern England, with which Hull found it generally unnecessary to have direct contact: 46 per cent of the total importation came from London in 1775, 45 per cent in 1782.[2]

The inclusion of Newcastle among the wool suppliers illustrates the way in which Hull relied on her for more than coal. Sea coal was the chief item, by volume, in the British coastal trade. It was the life blood of modern Britain. It made urban life possible, if at times unbearable; it warmed the politicians and journalists who consequently looked upon it with favour; and—in some eyes its greatest merit—it supported that great nursery of seamen on which the empire was supposedly based. The huge fleet of colliers—growing faster than that in any other trade, coastal or foreign—were received eagerly in all the ports and creeks of Britain. In all, that is, except Hull. A mere two thousand chalders were imported in 1706, roughly 5,500 in 1728. Importation through Hull was never of great importance. In any other region Hull's network of navigable rivers would have served to distribute sea coal; here they tapped a coalfield potentially richer even than that in the north. Already by the fifties it was producing 800,000 tons per annum, and Hull had begun to receive coal down the Aire and Calder at least as early as Defoe's *Tour*. Supplies from Sunderland and Newcastle dwindled to

[1] BB ix, 239. [2] Based on the 1782 Port Books.

a little over a thousand chalders in the eighties,[1] and most of that was for re-exportation to Europe and America. At the same time the contemporary Hull historian, Tickell, estimated the amount of coal coming down the Aire and Calder 'for the use of the town' at 30,000 tons per annum.[2]

Hull was clearly not dependent on the coastal trade for coal, and as its volume contracted, so the number of ships entering from the north shrank gradually, from 245 in 1728 to 110 in 1758, and further as the century progressed (see Appendix 12). Moreover, coal was losing its predominance in the remaining cargoes, and at least by the middle of the century it was no longer the principal commodity from the north. Salt was always a rival, and hardly a ship arrived without it. But again the quantity did not increase greatly, partly because the hinterland could draw its supplies from Cheshire and partly because Hull began to import salt direct from Liverpool; Newcastle and Seaton sent 592 tons in 1706 and 609 tons in 1775. The same pattern holds good for wines and spirits, imported coastwise in large quantities: more came from the north at the beginning of the century than at the end. Nor were the northern pastures—producing a constant flow of hides (in their hundreds) and horns and bones (in tens of thousands)—able to compete effectively in Hull. On the other hand Newcastle, Sunderland and Stockton between them produced the bulk of the tow, old rope and rags imported coastwise.

To some extent the industries of the north supplemented those of Hull's hinterland, and the most significant imports were manufactured goods. English steel—several tons at a time—was imported before Huntsman had perfected his crucible process, and, although there was none in the sample year 1775, small quantities were constantly arriving. Iron pots and pans came in fair number, there was plenty of ironmongery and old iron, copper, brass and pewter, while imports of 'wrought and cast iron and steel' exceeded those from any other place except Carron. In 1775 eleven casks of 'edge tools' from Newcastle were listed separately, as was one 'cast metal oven' and one 'pott' from Stockton. Both places, with Sunderland, were regular suppliers of 'Ships Anchors' and also, needless to say, of grindstones.

Two further products stand out as being more or less peculiar to the northern trade: paper and glass. Hull was a net exporter of paper, but imported 61 tons and 250 bundles in 1775, chiefly from

[1] HCLB, C–B, 27 Jul 1789. [2] Tickell, p. 872.

Sunderland. The glass came almost entirely from Newcastle, in increasing quantities and at least eight different containers: 150 cases and 366 firkins in 1706, and 1,312 cases, crates and chests, 335 boxes and 61 hogsheads in 1775. Newcastle was also the chief supplier of glass bottles: 1,847 dozen in 1706 and 6,236 dozen in 1775.

The remaining—and, with Newcastle, the most important—ports with which Hull dealt, were general trade ports. They supplied a miscellany of local products and were entrepôts for European and colonial goods. Bristol, Liverpool, and Glasgow ought in theory to have led the way, sending on the products of their great colonial trades. In fact they did not. Bristol rarely sent ships, and the cargoes that can be traced are less obviously of colonial origin than might have been expected. Apart from small quantities of sugar, molasses and exotic wood, they consisted of local produce: West Country foodstuffs and cider, English steel and pig iron, Bristol Water and salt. There was no tobacco in the only ship to arrive in 1775; most of its hold was taken up with 9,000 gallons of 'British' and 13,000 gallons of 'Compound' spirits.

Liverpool traders were far more common than Bristol traders—ten to one in 1775. But again the cargoes were hardly romantic: a hundred tons of assorted hardwoods, 68 cwt. of currants, a cask of palm oil, two barrels of sugar and 233 gallons of rum were the total of 'foreign' goods. Most of the cargoes consisted of salt, making a total for the year of 51,241 bushels. The Liverpool whaling industry supplied the superior sperm oil; and Liverpool was a minor source of tar and turpentine, presumably of colonial origin.

Trade with the east coast was infinitely more important than that with the west. Every port, large or small, sent a ship at some time to Hull. The smallest were places like Wainfleet in Lincolnshire—hardly a port at all—which sent oats, sheepskins and horns, bones and 'sheeps foot oil'; Alloa, which sent a few hundred yards of camblets and small quantities of brandy and geneva; and Dundee, with small quantities of Scottish salmon and linen and imported wines. The medium range of ports included Berwick, Whitby, Scarborough, Bridlington, Boston, Spalding, Wisbech and Ipswich. The largest were Bo'ness, Leith, Yarmouth and Lynn.

The ports might be grouped more naturally by type than by size, The Scottish ports were different from the rest, firstly because, unlike the English east coast ports, they supplied colonial goods, and secondly because they were the outlets for an industrial region similar to that developing in Hull's own hinterland. The range of goods was consequently wider than that from most outports, corn being the only notable absentee (although Berwick sent barley in 1775).

The Forth had no advantage over the Humber when it came to colonial trade; they were both on the wrong side of the island. But the completion of the major part of the Forth–Clyde canal in 1774 gave that speedy connexion with the west coast for which the merchants of Leith and Bo'ness had struggled for generations.[1] Tobacco was the most significant and valuable commodity. Bo'ness alone sent 416,785 lb. in 1775, and Leith and Berwick together sent another 32,854 lb. Other entrepôt goods in that year included 2,225 lb. of tea, 3,045 gallons of imported spirits, and 2,065 gallons of wine from Germany, France, Spain, Portugal, Minorca and Madeira. Rum came from the distilleries of the north in small quantities, but there was almost no demand in Hull for whisky; only 2,264 gallons were imported in the ten years ending in July 1799.[2]

Linen was the chief industrial product of Scotland, and, after tobacco, the most attractive article in the Scottish trade. By the middle of the century large quantities were augmenting supplies from northern Europe. Roughly a hundred thousand yards arrived from Bo'ness and Leith in 1775, made up of 36,785 yards of 'British' linen, 9,000 of 'white linen drapery', 16,292 of printed linen, 20,300 of diaper, and 10,810 of lawns. There were also muslins, tablecloths, thousands of printed handkerchiefs and pairs of thread stockings, 3,571 lb. of thread and 12,660 spindles of linen yarn.

Scotland's Industrial Revolution was not confined to linen. Her ironfounders and forgers were as competent as their Yorkshire rivals, and there was a regular trade in their products. Seven and a quarter tons of steel, and 185 tons of cast and wrought iron were sent down in 1775; an impressive volume and variety of goods, but a mere token of what might have been.[3] The Carron Company established its Hull agency in the early sixties in an attempt to break into the

[1] See J. Lindsey, *The Canals of Scotland* (1968), pp. 24–6.

[2] HCLB, C–B, 18 Jul 1799.

[3] Wrought and cast iron are, of course, vastly different things, but they were lumped together—and sometimes with steel as well—so that the quantities of each cannot now be disentangled.

trade of the Yorkshire ironmasters, but competition was great and their venture was not entirely successful.[1]

The remaining goods from Bo'ness and Leith were the product of a variety of skills and trades, most of them in small quantities: coal, flint and saltpetre, vitriol, turps and tar, leather, old cordage and tow, sheepskins, horns and shoes, tin plates and printer's type. Not the least interesting were the shipments of books, from the learned printers of Edinburgh, entered in the Port Books by the hundredweight!

The English east coast ports could not match the new industrial goods of Bo'ness and Leith. Their prosperity was based, as it had been for centuries, on the produce of the land and the sea. The smaller ports to the north of the Humber were much less important than those to the south, for they sent neither corn nor wool. Whitby's weightiest contribution was alum, from the Mulgrave Castle estate; her most valuable was whalebone—13,130 lb. in 1775—for which Hull had an insatiable demand. She supplied whale oil too, and dried, pickled and salt fish. Like every port of any size she sent a few hundred gallons of wine, and there were the inevitable horns and bones, and old iron, copper, brass and pewter. For one shipment alone, in 1775, was she unique among outports: three casks of sulphur.

Scarborough's shipments were more or less the same as Whitby's—on a smaller scale and without the alum, but with paper and spa water instead. Bridlington's shipments were, by comparison, insignificant, consisting chiefly of malt and small quantities of ale.

It was from East Anglia that Hull attracted the most ships by the middle of the century—between a fifth and a quarter of all ships entering. Ipswich, Lynn and Yarmouth—in that order—were, after Grimsby, the chief outports supplying wool. Between them they sent 15,922 cwt. in 1775, 27 per cent of the total from all sources, while East Anglia as a whole accounted for 30 per cent of the total. In 1782, with wool imports down by a third, East Anglia still accounted for 27 per cent of the total.

Corn was the other leading commodity from East Anglia, but the

[1] R. H. Campbell, *The Carron Company* (1961), pp. 110–15. The Agents were Spence & King, the leading Hull ironmongers. For the Scottish end of the coastal trade, see H. Hamilton, *An Economic History of Scotland in the Eighteenth Century* (1963), especially Chap. VIII.

trade was naturally erratic. At one time Hull might be importing corn—chiefly from Lynn and Yarmouth—as in 1728, when 16,808 quarters arrived, 1732 when only 5,509 quarters were imported, or 1735 when 6,113 quarters came from Lynn alone.[1] At another time she was exporting in large quantities, both coastwise and to the continent. Sometimes there was both importation and exportation in the same year. This was the case in 1775, when Hull was a net exporter, but continued to import, presumably in reduced quantities, from East Anglia. Ipswich, Lynn and Yarmouth sent 1,105 quarters of wheat, 6,264 of barley and 2,712 of rye in that year. The same thing is true of peas—Hull exported twice as much as the 552 quarters she imported from Ipswich, Lynn and Yarmouth—but not, apparently, of beans, of which 2,815 quarters were imported and only 53 quarters exported (to London).

The East Anglian and Wash ports were the only source of a variety of seed crops destined for agriculture or the oil industry. Cabbage, clover, turnip, mustard and garlic seed came from Boston, Ipswich, Lynn and Yarmouth. For the oil seeds—hemp, rape and linseed—the Fens were the best source, with cargoes coming principally from Boston, Spalding, Lynn and Wisbech. Hull merchants bought the standing crops and secured refined oil in Lynn, but again supplies were determined by harvest conditions, and there was heavy competition from Baltic producers. Very little seed was, in fact, imported coastwise in 1775, and exports of linseed to Lynn exceeded imports from there.

Yarmouth had always been a great fishing centre and she was, needless to say, the principal supplier of herring to the Hull market. When the time came, during the Napoleonic war, for Hull to consider establishing a fishing fleet, it was from their Yarmouth friends that the Hull merchants sought estimates and advice. Yarmouth was also, with Ipswich, a supplier of cheese; it must have been of some quality, for both places received huge shipments from Hull and they were the only ports to send significant quantities in return. Finally, East Anglia and the Fens were the orchards from which Hull drew fresh fruit, in fair quantities but difficult, from the miscellaneous containers, to measure.

Lynn and Yarmouth were both considerable ports and, as we might expect, they sent entrepôt goods to Hull. Their wine shipments, particularly, exceeded those from any other outport. They

[1] T. S. Willan, p. 80.

were chiefly of Portuguese and Spanish origin, secured in exchange for the fish exported to Catholic Europe. Yarmouth also sent cork, and both of them sent small quantities of metal. Yarmouth sent a couple of tons of unclassified bar iron in 1775, while Lynn sent ten tons of Russian iron and, rather surprisingly, 22 cwt. of Long German steel. East Anglia imported a variety of agricultural and other ironmongery, but had little use for broken metal, with the result that Lynn and Yarmouth were also the leading shippers of old iron, brass and copper to Hull.

The east coast trade was great, but the London trade was vital. Of huge volume and incalculable value, it was the unknown and largely unacknowledged complement of Hull's one-sided foreign trade. Hull is often accused of being a Baltic port, a poor relation of the colonial trade ports. To some extent this is true,[1] but East and West Indian goods did not appear by magic in Leeds or Sheffield. They went, like the Swedish iron and the Russian flax, up the navigations. For if young Alfred Tennyson ever stood on his grandfather's staith in High Street he would have seen the 'argosies of magic sail . . . dropping down their costly bales';[2] argosies disguised, that is, as the humble ships of the coastal run.

It cannot be emphasised too strongly that Hull had a great trade in East and West Indian goods, for this branch of trade alters completely the pattern that emerged from the overseas Port Books. At the same time it must be acknowledged that Hull was dependent upon London in the most valuable eighteenth century growth trades, and that, so far as we can tell, the hinterland was supplied with American and oriental produce less by Hull merchants than by London merchants, who had direct postal contact with their customers in the inland towns. This deficiency in Hull had not been rectified by the end of our period, and its cost to the town, in terms of lost prestige and wealth, was, like the value of the trade, enormous. Had circumstances been different, had Hull established her own West Indian and American trades, had she been allowed access to the East, then she would have enjoyed the profits of those trades, rather than the wharfinger fees that were her lot. Her merchants and shipowners would certainly have been richer;

[1] The East Indies trade was closed to *all* ports except London.

[2] 'Locksley Hall'; George Tennyson, a leading member of the Grimsby Haven Company, owned the staith occupied by Alderman B. B. Thompson.

perhaps they paid the penalty for their reluctance to adventure.

It was not the foreign trade alone that was attracted by the magnetic force of the London market. The coastal trade, as we have already noted, was channelled through London. The Peases, for instance, had regular dealings with friends in Bristol and their relations in Ireland, but their goods always went via London. It was simpler, with London standing between the East and South coast, for cargoes to be assembled and shipped from there.

The growing volume of trade with London, and its relative importance as an employer of shipping and labour—though not, of course, its relative value—may be roughly gauged from the shipping figures. Hull received 97 coasters from London in the year ending Midsummer 1704, and 80 in the year 1706, 38 and 37 per cent respectively of the total number of coasters entering the port. The percentage changed very little in the next seventy years, if our sample years are truly representative, chiefly because the declining coal trade was offset by the rising East Anglian and Scottish trades. But the number of vessels had doubled by 1728, when war troubles were over, and rose by a quarter between 1728 and 1758. The coastal trade shared the expansion of trade after 1763; 387 vessels arrived from London in 1775, at least 553 in 1796:

COASTERS ENTERING FROM AND CLEARING FOR LONDON

	1703/4		*1706*		*1728*		*1737*		*1758*	
	IN	OUT	IN	OUT	IN	OUT	IN	OUT	IN	OUT
LONDON	93	310	80	185	179	150	190	208	226	318
BRITAIN	244	467	219	262	635	215	567	503	553	733
London as % of Britain	*38*	*66*	*37*	*71*	*28*	*70*	*34*	*41*	*41*	*43*

	1768		*1775*		*1782*		*1796*	
	IN	OUT	IN	OUT	IN	OUT	IN	OUT
LONDON	307	327	387	386	327	382	553	578
BRITAIN	729	747	903	892	803	1041	1346	1300
London as % of Britain	*42*	*44*	*43*	*43*	*41*	*37*	*41*	*44*

London's ascendancy is not fully revealed in the *number* of coasters trading. There is, for instance, some evidence that ships engaged on the London run were larger than those employed elsewhere, and certainly, in 1798, larger vessels owned in Hull and used on the

London run made more voyages per annum than smaller vessels.[1] Many of the cargoes from the outports—including coal shipments—were small in comparison with cargoes from London, and they were, for the most part, restricted to a small range of goods. Thus the London cargoes represent almost the entire coastwise importation of a great variety of the most valuable commodities (see Appendix 15).

Tobacco was the prize of the trade. As early as 1706 Hull imported 448,469 lb. from London and, despite the development of a more important direct trade with America, coastwise importation continued throughout the century. In 1775 leaf and cut tobacco amounted to 715,574 lb.—with another 16,898 lb. classified separately as 'Manufactured tobacco'—and 61,887 lb. of stalks. Although Hull had, by now, its own snuff mills, it was still found necessary to import 73,000 lb. of snuff, a notable advance on the 224 lb. of 1706.

If tobacco was the most valuable commodity, the greatest single consumer of shipping space inwards was sugar, rising from 767 tons in 1706 to 9,389 tons in 1775. Molasses was also imported in fairly large quantities for Hull's own distilleries, together with such things as boilers and sugar moulds—though the latter came chiefly from Liverpool. Assorted groceries were always important in the coastal trade, but particularisation is prevented, for the early part of the century, by the habit of lumping goods together as 'other groceries'. Raisins and currants amounted to 101 tons and 72 tons respectively in 1706, and oranges were a mere 227 chests. Nor was there much in the way of spices: a couple of tons of ginger and six hundredweight of pepper.

The 1775 Port Book presents a completely different picture. Quantities, of course, were far greater, and many items were classified which had been absent in 1706. The most valuable new item was tea—153,986 lb. compared with only 3,794 lb. of coffee and 10,251 lb. of cocoa. Pepper had risen phenomenally, to 30,941 lb. and ginger to 38,178 lb. Raisins were no longer entered by weight alone, but currants stood at 257 tons. Prunes and figs, nutmegs and almonds flooded in for the grocers of Yorkshire and, despite direct imports in the foreign trade, there was a considerable supply of oranges and lemons, Spanish juice and rice. The London coastal entrepôt trade no doubt accounted for the pork, beef, pickled cod,

[1] 'A list of Coasting Vessels, belonging to this Port, that used the Port of London in 1798.' HCLB, C–B, 1 Aug 1799.

wheat and hops that were imported, while the great breweries of the metropolis provided well over 300,000 gallons of beer.

Of wine there was every imaginable kind, led by Portuguese and Spanish, but not in quantities that could be regarded as significant: Hull was her own wine importer, and the total coastal importation for 1775 was not noticeably greater than that for 1706. The same thing was true of geneva, but certainly not of the other, British made, spirits. Rum, not found in the 1706 Book, stood at 110,071 gallons in 1775, and 'British' spirits rose from 17,633 gallons to 108,349.

The London trade was also a most valuable source of manufactured goods and raw materials, both foreign and British. Scottish and Baltic linen cloth was particularly common among cargoes: approximately 10,588 yards and 37,562 ells in 1706, and 149,609 yards and 30,851 ells in 1775. Small quantities of linen yarn and flax were imported, together with cotton wool, and London was, as we have seen, the principal source of British raw wool, and also of animal skins, hides and horns, tallow and grease. Oil, tar and turps were very important, and there were chemicals and dyestuffs of all kinds for the cloth mills, tanneries, soaperies and potteries: barilla and potash, madder and sumack, Fuller's earth and alum, blue, copperas, indigo, ochre, umber and woad. Fifteen different kinds of exotic and dye woods appeared in 1775, ranging from the humble valonia for the inkmakers to sandal wood, from bar wood to ebony.

Metals, too, were included: copper, brass, tin, pewter, and goods made from them, a few hundredweight of ironmongery and, in 1706, 23 tons of foreign iron. Manufactured items were never significant, and steel imports were neligible in 1775, but there was a fairly brisk trade in other metals in the second half of the century. All the tin and copper imported coastwise came via London, and, in 1775, foreign supplies of iron were augmented by 785 tons of English pig iron, 340 tons of Plantatation pig iron, and 440 tons of Russian iron.

The London trade was saved from endless monotony by an impressive and intriguing array of miscellaneous goods, some industrial, some frankly luxurious. Everything went by the coastal route: wigs, gold buttons, dress patterns and clothes; books, *objets d'art*, spinets and harpsichords; wallpaper, marble fireplaces and brass fenders. There was a regular procession of aristocratic carriages, wisely committed to the sea rather than the road, and furniture took the same route. The Grimstons shipped their pictures,[1] the Claytons of Grimsby their furniture and personal clothing;[2] and when Sir Charles Sheffield sold Buckingham House to the Crown in 1763 he distributed some of the contents between his Lincolnshire and Yorkshire houses in the same way.[3] Cargoes in 1775 included a box of watches and jewellery, tortoiseshell, silver knives and forks, many boxes of copper coin, several tons of silversmiths' sweepings, a tea urn, and 200 oz. of silver plate. There was '1 case containing a charriott', one 'Garden carriage', camel hair and sea cow teeth, artificial stone and a 'pewter worm', 'sham cocoa' and regimental clothing, a church bell, a 'stationer's cutting press', flambeaux, warming pans, 'Chymical Preparations' and '1 chest containing the Modell of a Ship'.

3. COASTAL EXPORTS: FOOD AND MANUFACTURES

The coastal export trade was roughly similar in pattern to the import trade. The same ports were involved, for the most part, and the trades grew in the same way until the eighties, when an increasing demand for raw materials and luxuries quickened the pace of the import trade.

Cargoes went to less than a dozen places in the early years of the century, and of these only London, Lynn and Newcastle were of any real significance. London was again dominant, even more so than in the import trade. Seven out of every ten coasters clearing in our early sample years were bound for London, and the volume and value of London-bound cargoes surpassed all others throughout the century. A major expansion in the trade appears to have taken place between the sample years 1728 and 1737, both in the number of ports and the number of ships, which more than doubled, to 503, with the beginning of a massive distribution trade along the east coast. Not until the thirties was London's proportion of the trade reduced, to just over 40 per cent, where it remained for the rest of the sample years.

[1] E. Ingram, *Leaves from a Family Tree* (1951), p. 50.

[2] Wm. Hathorne, London, to Christopher Clayton, 28 Jul 1758; *LAO* 2Td' E/G/1/6.

[3] Sir Charles Sheffield's Account Bk, 1763, *passim*; Sheffield MSS, Scunthorpe Museum.

There was no uniform increase in the trade. Although ships went to all parts of Britain, the bulk of them continued to go to very few places: to Newcastle and Sunderland in the north; to Whitby and Scarborough in Yorkshire; and to Lynn, Yarmouth and Wisbech in East Anglia. There was only one notable newcomer: Bo'ness/Leith began to trade with Hull in the middle of the century. During none of the sample years did these nine places (including London) receive less than 77 per cent of the coasters clearing from Hull:

COASTERS CLEARING FOR THE LEADING PORTS

For	*1703/4*	*1706*	*1728*	*1737*	*1758*	*1768*	*1775*	*1783*	*1796*
London	310	185	150	208	318	327	386	382	578
Newcastle	27	22	5	75	86	47	52	85	80
Sunderland	8	1	4	66	61	24	18	40	36
Whitby	14	8	2	18	42	41	76*	103	81
Scarborough/ Bridlington	5	3	1	23	24	22	27*	32	13
Lynn	35	8	14	39	41	58	62	87	96
Yarmouth	7	5	9	12	15	33	34	36	53
Wisbech	29	19	2	2	15	17	11	28	89
Bo'ness	0	0	0	1	18	25	27	56	40
As % of total	*93*	*96*	*87*	*88*	*84*	*93*	*77*	*82*	*82*
Total ships clearing	467	262	215	503	733	747	895	1041	1300

* Excludes ships calling on their way northwards.

The remaining 42 places in 1783 averaged only five shipments each (see Appendix 16), and in some cases, particularly in the Scottish trade, they were obviously small commissions—or speculations—undertaken by masters whose main concern was bringing goods to Hull. The only ship that left for Frazerburgh in 1775 carried 1,000 barrel staves, and the one clearing for Burnham carried 15 quarters of barley, 100 ridge tiles, 20 bunches of fir laths and 280 lb. of tallow candles.

Harvest conditions had an important effect on the number of coasters entering and leaving Hull, for foodstuffs, chiefly for London—or, in bad years, from East Anglia—played a large part in the coastal trade. The hinterland of Hull, as readers of Defoe were well aware, was one of the richest and most extensive agricultural areas on which the capital depended for the support of its population. Despite tales of pre-enclosure subsistence farming, corn surpluses were produced with the Newcastle or London markets in mind, and the commonest container passing through Hull was always the firkin—the butter-barrel. Oats was the leading corn export, followed by wheat and barley, in different proportions according to the harvests. Corn exports in 1683–84 amounted to 22,537 quarters, of which 12,180 were wheat. But the total exported was only 16,850 quarters in 1706 (of which only 330 was wheat) and 7,824 quarters in 1728 (of which 630 was wheat). In the latter year over 14,000 quarters were in fact imported, chiefly from Lynn, and there was also a heavy importation from Danzig. These were occasional setbacks; the general trend was upwards, reinforced by the agrarian changes in Yorkshire, Lincolnshire, and the Vale of Trent. For the seven years, 1780–6, the average exportation of corn had reached no less than 103,048 quarters, of which 17,349 was wheat and 84,606 was oats.[1] A closer look at the annual figures reveals the fluctuations in volume that made life difficult for the coastal shipping interest, and incidentally reveals that 1783, in the middle of a run of exportation years, was a net wheat importation year:

HULL'S COASTAL CORN TRADE, 1780–86

Exports	*1780*	*1781*	*1782*	*1783*	*1784*	*1785*	*1786*
Wheat	14,397	37,640	35,925	6,478	12,723	8,126	6,057
Barley	385	4,030	305	261	1,817	220	631
Oats	105,707	85,724	114,545	52,814	62,746	108,586	62,125
Imports							
Wheat	1	0	344	17,255	516	0	0
Barley	0	0	525	6,596	82	2,213	20
Oats	84	0	50	2,465	996	8	337

There was less fluctuation in the trade in butter and cheese, the former restricted almost entirely to London and the latter involving practically every port with which Hull traded. Almost 22,000 firkins of butter were exported in 1706, 32,000 in 1728, and 60,000 in 1775. In the early years of the century the cheese went to Lynn, Wells, Yarmouth, Newcastle and London: 862 tons in 1706 and 1,471 tons in 1731–2. By 1775 it went to twenty-one places (though not always in large quantities); 3,525 tons were involved, a tribute to the quality of 'Cheshire', and a reminder that cheese, like beer and ale, already had a national market. Beer, as we saw, was imported from London. Ale from the hinterland was sent in return, *c.* 35,000 gallons in 1775.

[1] HCLB, C–B, *passim.*

There were many miscellaneous foodstuffs exported. Malt and beans were both approaching 10,000 quarters in 1706, although Hull was a net importer in 1775. Peas were just over a thousand quarters in 1775, mustard flour went to a number of places, and 14,309 lb. of pimento went to London. There were regular, though small, shipments of crab claws, caviar, ketchup and honey, tongues, sturgeon and herring. Bacon and ham was always very important, though usually unclassified by weight; in 1775 there were 1,216 hogsheads, 12 casks, 6 barrels and 34 parcels sent down to London, together with at least 237 casks of pork. There were small quantities of mushrooms in the early part of the century, and 1,248 bottles and 2 hampers in 1775; and at least in 1728 there were eggs going coastwise, though none appeared in 1775.

Many coasters leaving Hull in the second half of the century carried nothing but potatoes. Few were exported in 1706, and only ten tons in 1728. By 1775 they were sent in large numbers to the north and by the fleet-load to London: 62,271 sacks, 44,772 bushels and 408 tons. The total exportation in that year amounted to 67,795 sacks, 52,002 bushels and 468 tons, representing by far the largest single employer of coastal shipping leaving Hull.

The coastal food trade was not confined to goods produced in the hinterland and exported mostly to London. As the century progressed Hull grew in status as the supplier of wines and provisions to many of the east coast ports. Just over 9,000 gallons of spirits, 31,500 gallons of red and white port wine and 5,300 gallons of Spanish wine were distributed along the east coast in 1775. Tobacco had already appeared in small quantities—7,448 lb.—in 1706, and it increased as more ports were brought within Hull's trading system. Twenty ports took 52,571 lb. of tobacco in 1775, and fourteen of them took 24,459 lb. of snuff. Rather surprisingly, 12,607 lb. were also sent down to London, passing on the way some of the 70,000 lb. that came from there. Again personal taste and easy transport were combining to create a national market in what might be regarded as a local product.

The 'provision' trade was limited in extent and volume. Although sugar went to fourteen places in 1775, only 1,100 cwt. was involved, and the currants, raisins, rice and spices went in very small quantities indeed. The ports involved were mostly within easy reach: Bridlington, Wainfleet, Saltfleet, Mumby Chapel, Boston and Spalding. Their shipments were a rag-bag of everything Hull ever sent anywhere; their entries in the Port Book the most tedious and inconsequential of any.

The Agrarian Revolution involved more than crops and flocks. As coastal timber was ravaged by the shipbuilding industry, landowners began a policy of afforestation of poor land, and merchants went ever further inland in their search for oak. It came from Selby down the Ouse, and from the Midlands down the Trent, its importance attested by Fisher in 1763:[1] 'The numerous ports of North Yarmouth, Hull, Scarborough, Stockton, Whitby, Sunderland, Newcastle and all the North Coast of Scotland, are supplied chiefly, I am informed, from the Humber and Trent.' He could have extended his list to include Harwich, London and, in wartime, the Royal dockyard at Chatham. In 1706 oak timber had gone only to the northern shipbuilding ports of Newcastle, Sunderland, Scarborough and Whitby, and to London—560 tons altogether. By 1775 it went to nineteen places, nine of them in Scotland. A total of 3,181 tons of timber was involved, of which 822 tons went to London and 1,226 tons to Whitby. With the oak went 871 tons of bark for the tanneries—a third of it to Scotland—and a few tons of ash. Newcastle and Sunderland also received semi-manufactured goods: 860 waggon wheels in 1702, 962 in 1706; 16 tons and 800 waggon rails (presumably wooden) and 200 oak sleepers in 1728; 2 bundles of 'shafts' and 17 tons of cribwood—for lining mine shafts—in the first half of 1758; and so on.

Imported wood played little part in the coastal trade. A few *hundred* deals went to Scarborough, Whitby and Yarmouth in 1706, and the addition of Blakeney, Saltfleet, Wainfleet and the other 'adjacent' ports made little difference in 1775. Wood was the sort of bulky commodity that ports got for themselves when they could, and all but a minute fraction of Hull's deals, battens, laths, uffers, staves and timber went into the hinterland. This was less true of the other goods from the Baltic. Flax and hemp went to most places, with the largest shipment of flax in 1775 going to Liverpool. Raw Dutch linen yarn went particularly to Stockton and Bo'ness; smalts and pearl ash went to London and Newcastle; and tar and pitch—3,573 and 3,198 barrels respectively—again went to most places, but chiefly to London, Lynn, Newcastle, Spalding, Sunderland and Yarmouth. The same places, together with Stockton and Whitby, were the main recipients of Russian and Swedish iron, of which 768

[1] R. Fisher, *Hearts of Oak* (1763), p. 38.

tons went coastwise in 1775. The only notable foreign cloth was Spruce canvas; just over a quarter of a million ells were exported in 1775, the bulk of it to London, Ipswich, Lynn and Yarmouth.

Native raw materials were recognised and listed by Defoe and mentioned in practically every canal petition. Lead was the best known, but exports, both foreign and coastal, were already declining in Defoe's time: 5,579 tons had been exported coastwise in 1683–4, 3,688 tons in 1703–4 and 2,654 tons in 1706. The decline continued in 1728 and 1731–2, when the total was down to 1,830 tons, and little more than 2,500 tons were exported in 1775. As in the foreign trade, the decline was offset by the rising exportation of processed lead. Lead shot went up from 26 cwt. in 1706 to about 700 cwt. in 1775, and lead sheets had become common, going chiefly to London. Red lead roughly doubled between 1706 and 1775 (from *c.* 5,300 to 11,100 cwt.), and white lead went up from one firkin to 37 barrels and 141 casks.

Lead was eventually joined by inland coal, 712 chalders of it in 1775, destined for Aldborough, Boston, Bridlington, Wisbech, Wells and London. Flagstones went to all the east coast ports, but particularly to London, which received 3,832 tons in 1775. Several hundred tons of plaster went to the same places, and a great deal of shipping space was taken up by 156,400 bricks and 926,300 pantiles, destined principally for East Anglia. Whiting, lime and limestone came in fairly small quantities from the Wolds, and millstones and hundreds of thousands of sythestones from the Pennines.

Manufacturing goods exported coastwise were drawn from the whole range of industrial production in Hull and her hinterland. English iron was exported from the beginning, and the quantity was growing slowly from *c.* 170 tons in 1683–4 to 260 in 1706 and 430 in 1731–2. About half of it usually went to London, and a quarter each to Newcastle and East Anglia. There was also anything from ten to thirty tons of steel per annum, again chiefly for London. Nails went almost everywhere, in rapidly increasing quantities, but 'ironmongery' had not yet made any significant contribution to the export trade. There was none in 1706, and very little in 1728. There were, however, a number of notable iron commodities listed individually: anvils and 58 tons of iron shot were sent down to London in 1706, while Yarmouth received a ton of 'English iron potts and bushes for waggons'.

The mid century witnessed a rapid expansion in the trade in

metals and metal goods. Steel, though still imported in small quantities from Scotland, was now a regular feature of the London trade: 105 tons, 759 bundles and 41 bars were exported in 1775. Iron, too, had risen in quantity, though it is not always easy to distinguish the different sorts. There were 30 tons and 65 bars of 'English iron' in 1775, 70 tons of English pig iron (most of which went to Liverpool), 407 tons and 366 bundles of 'English manufactured iron', and 350 tons of wrought and cast iron, 267 bundles of iron plates and 265 bundles of 'rolled iron'. But the most significant development was in 'ironmongery', included in practically every cargo leaving the port in 1775: 5,254 casks, 432 boxes, 491 trusses, 284 baskets, 1,529 parcels, 96 packs and 104 hampers. What it all was we shall never know.

Some iron goods were distinguished from the general run of ironmongery, chiefly, perhaps, because of their size. Iron fenders were sent to Portsmouth in 1775, 115 bundles of iron hoops and 12 iron axle trees to Ipswich, iron pots to Boston, Newhaven, Ipswich and Wainfleet, and 9 tons, 20 casks and 1,400 bundles and rings of iron wire to London. Chimney backs, grates and stoves became common, many of them from the works of Newton Chambers of Chapeltown. A typical shipment, sent to Lynn in 1799, consisted of '2 arched stoves, 4 full Pantheon stoves, 1 Pyramid stove, 3 Mortars & Pestles, Sad Irons and 1 Digester'.[1] Edge tools were also now to be found in almost every ship leaving the port: hay-knives and flay-knives, saws and sickles, and 15,000 scythes—many for East Anglia but again chiefly for London. There were anvils, hammers, files and 661 dozen shovels and spades. Nails, above all, left in a constant stream and went everywhere: 31,321 bags and 298 casks in 1775, a considerable advance on the 4,416 bags and 167 tons of 1728.

Although Betty Beecroft at Kirkstall in the eighties might be content to scrape along with nail rods, shovels, industrial screws and the paraphernalia of the kitchen,[2] the Walkers of Rotherham had long ago founded their fame and fortune on engines of war. Their products, exported in their own name at Hull, went to London and the royal arsenals and dockyards, especially in wartime. No fewer than 7,460 guns, ranging from three to thirty-two pounders,

[1] Newton Chambers & Co. Ltd., Archives. I am grateful to Mr. R. C. Burgin for drawing my attention to papers relating to the Company's extensive trade through Hull in the eighteenth century.

[2] R. Butler, *The History of Kirkstall Forge* (1945), *passim.*

went coastwise during the American Revolutionary War, reaching a peak, as production expanded, in 1782.[1]

GUNS EXPORTED COASTWISE, 1776–82

	Size : pounders							
	3	*4*	*6*	*9*	*12*	*18*	*24*	*32*
1776	40	1	116	8	0	9	28	35
1777	267	65	174	36	0	0	80	31
1778	0	0	0	54	30	32	32	31
1779	117	182	193	198	97	134	78	24
1780	0	100	281	313	322	208	131	1
1781	0	13	150	530	311	434	254	60
1782	15	535	411	149	56	549	312	233

With them went small quantities of iron shot, and nearly ten thousand shells.

Of the remaining manufactured goods, earthenware had been of some slight significance in 1706, when 319 crates were exported, but with the development of inland waterways the coastal exportation grew enormously; in 1775 the total was 12,957 crates, 265 hogsheads, 53 casks and 3,252 pieces. The trade in woollen cloth underwent a similar expansion. By comparison with the foreign trade, the coastal trade had been negligible at the beginning of the century. In 1775, however, 1,955 bales, 346 packs and 165 trusses went coastwise. Manchester cloth had also made its appearance and amounted to 77 bales, 147 packs and 252 trusses. Cloth exports to Lynn, Yarmouth and Wells were classified as 'Manchester and Woollen Drapery', and these accounted for a further 1,061 packs, 1,120 trusses and 63 boxes. The new trade was clearly of great value and growing volume, but its growth in the vital period after 1783 cannot be followed.

Of the local industries, soapmaking probably made the greatest contribution to the coastal trade. Led by Pead, Lee & Company, the soapers sent out 147,761 lb. of hard soap and 1,156 firkins and 2,234 half-firkins of soft soap, chiefly to Newcastle, Sunderland, Whitby, Scarborough and Boston. Hull was, however, a net importer of soap, with supplies from London more than four times as great as total exports. Nor did the seed-oil industry provide very heavy exports in 1775. With only a few hundred casks of linseed and rape oil exported, the industry was clearly selling its production to

[1] HCLB, C–B, 7 Jan 1793.

the hinterland. The same is true of the infant whaling industry, at least in 1775. Hull exported oil and bone to Newcastle, Sunderland, Boston, Lynn and London, but she was still a net coastwise importer of oil and rough spermaceti. Spermaceti candles, on the other hand, were only exported—well over 20,000 lb. in 1775, together with a generous quantity of tallow candles and tallow. Local tanneries sent many hides and skins to London, and the boneyards provided glue. Paint was to be found in many cargoes in the second half of the century, but the quantities were never very great before 1800.

Finally there were the miscellaneous goods. Ploughs and corn machines went to East Anglia; stocking frames to Scotland; brushes, in uncountable confusion, everywhere. 'A malt mill and wheel'—and a bureau and church bells—went to Boston, bundles of screws and a 'Baggage waggon' to Ipswich. Lynn received '1 ram alive', while Mumby Chapel got 6 dozen bottles of the infamous Godfrey's Cordial—opium water—with which Lincolnshire farm hands forgot their sorrows and kept their infants quiet. Nearby Saltfleet had the variety known as 'Daffy's Elixir'. To Sunderland went compasses and cabin stoves, fishing leaps to Aberdeen and curtain rods to Wells.

The coastal trade was, then, an integral part of the trade passing through Hull. It carried a fair proportion of the produce of the hinterland, supplied raw materials and luxuries, and employed shipping and seamen. But since it was more properly part of internal transport, and since direct communication often existed between producers and consumers, it is justifiable to question the extent of Hull's true involvement in the trade. Hull merchants were less predominant; 'foreigners' appear in the Port Books and coasters made long trips into the hinterland. In the period October 1789–90, 395 sailed up to Selby, 196 to Thorne, 45 to York and 15 to Stockwith; how many of them called at Hull for more than the formal Customs clearance is not recorded. At the beginning of the century Defoe had spoken of men in Leeds 'who buy to send to London; either by Commissions from London, or they give commissions to factors and warehousekeepers in London to sell for them. . . .' The majority of lead shipments in the first quarter of the century were accounted for by inland merchants, particularly the two firms of Leadbetter and Wigfall of Gainsborough and Stockwith, who used their own vessels. Coasters were often owned upriver. A check in the second half of 1703 revealed 65 'of Hull', 48 'of Stockwith', 16 'of Gainsborough', 2 'of Selby' and 1 'of York'.

Such evidence is only part of the story. The ascription of ships to inland towns and the naming of inland merchants is, to say the least, misleading. Ships were built and owned in the hinterland until well into the nineteenth century, but this did not necessarily mean that they traded regularly, or even at all, from the place of ownership. Moreover, the ships which started upriver may still have completed their cargo in Hull. Shared cargoes are in fact hidden in the Customs records. Every merchant is named in the Overseas Port Books; only the first merchant in the Coastal Books. It is more than likely that a ship 'of Gainsborough' would be entered in the name of a lead merchant simply because the Customs officers usually entered lead first in both foreign and coastal cargoes. It is significant that as lead declined in importance, the leading names in the Coastal Port Books become those of Hull merchants and wharfingers.

There is no doubt that the inland ports played a great part in the coastal trade, or that Hull interests were less important than in the foreign trade. But it should at least be noted that the rôle of the inland merchant *may* have been exaggerated, especially for the second half of the century when ships were growing larger and cargoes more diverse. There is no way of knowing how much capital and credit was put into the trade by inland merchants, or how much profit was lost by Hull merchants. But the important thing for the national economy was not the organisation of the trade; it was the fact that goods were moving into and out of the hinterland.

V. MERCHANTS AND THE ORGANISATION OF TRADE

'that glorious Head of Commerce, called *the Merchant*'
DEFOE

1. THE MERCHANTS

The trade of Hull, like that of most places, was controlled by an oligarchy of two or three dozen great merchant houses, which between them handled the bulk of the goods passing through the port. Below them, envying, fighting and trying to join them, was a fluctuating number of smaller firms, some the giants of tomorrow, others doomed to failure on the way. The total number of merchants is easily discovered, but for our purpose it is of little importance; the size, rather than the number of firms calls for attention. Of one hundred and sixteen merchants shipping outwards in 1702, ninety-four made fewer than 10 shipments and a considerable number made only one or two. The remaining twenty-two were the real Hull merchants. Eleven of them made between 10 and 20 shipments, four made between 20 and 40, and seven made more than 40. The greatest was William Crowle with 85 individual shipments, closely followed by John Thornton with 80; next came Philip Wilkinson with 68, and then Daniel Hoare with 48. A similar pattern emerges for leading goods exported. Of the kerseys in 1702 (108,267), Crowle accounted for 26 per cent and Thornton for 25 per cent. Of the lead, 56 per cent was exported by four men: Crowle (13 per cent), Thornton (11), Wilkinson (20) and John Beilby (12). For imports the names were different; individual merchants were unlikely to lead over the whole range of goods handled by the port. The Maisters, Sykes, Mowlds, Somerscales and Broadleys were now the leaders, but again the general pattern was little different. Nor did the passage of time have much effect. Of the total iron imported in 1751, 87 per cent was handled by ten merchants, and 59 per cent by the top two—Thomas Mowld (31 per cent) and Richard & Joseph Sykes (28 per cent). In the last quarter of 1768 four men received 77 per cent of the imported iron, while the Mowld share was pushed up by his nephews and heirs, Joseph & William Williamson, to no less than 33 per cent of the total. Williamsons already had their own import and export trade and, with 35 of the 174 shipments outwards in the third quarter of 1783, they were undoubtedly the most important firm in eighteenth century Hull.

The merchant community was not static. Although the number of firms did not grow as fast as trade, there was some growth, and as the century progressed there were greater opportunities for rapid advancement, especially in new ventures. Many leading firms at the end of the century had begun during the trade boom in the forties and fifties, and many flourishing in 1700 had died away. Unfortunately, in the absence of business archives the beginning or end of most firms cannot now be traced. All that can be said of them is that at a particular time they were flourishing, and we are reminded of the words of Defoe: 'the Merchant is no more to be followed in his Adventures, than a Maze or Labyrinth is to be traced out without a Clue.'[1]

Many of the principal firms in the first half of the century were merchant dynasties whose origin is lost, and whose survival is one of the most remarkable features of the merchant community in Hull. Their rise to prominence can be traced in the lists of Mayors, Chamberlains and Sheriffs, who were drawn from the leading merchant families. The Beilbys first held office in 1591, the Scotts in 1595, the Mowlds in 1597, the Fields in 1603, the Blaydes in 1611, the Carlills in 1616, the Popples in 1621, the Maisters in 1637, the Peases in 1639, the Crowles and Wilkinsons in 1657, the Thorntons in 1694 and the Broadleys in 1696. Of these, the Beilbys, Scotts, Mowlds, Crowles, Wilkinsons and Carlills are known to have survived into the third quarter of the eighteenth century, while Blaydes, Popples, Maisters, Peases, Thorntons and Broadleys were still active in the nineteenth. The Somerscales lasted from the mid-seventeenth century to the late eighteenth, and the Wilberforces, Sykes, Haworths, Booths and Boyes from the mid-seventeenth to the nineteenth century. Sons followed fathers, and brothers shared in firms, for generation after generation. It was expected of them. If there was no son the son-in-law was recruited, and failing that the nephews. Grandsons were carefully nurtured, and Richard Howard, the tar merchant, went so far as to create a reversionary interest for his.[2] Orphans were by tradition apprenticed to other leading

[1] D. Defoe, *A Plan . . .*, p. vii.
[2] Will of Richard Howard, 31 Dec 1779, DDHB/45/78.

merchants in an attempt to keep the line going, and widows were expected to hold the fort during minorities.[1] Thus Stephenson & Fearnley, and Eggingtons—one of the leading Greenland houses—were both controlled for a time by widows. Benjamin Blaydes Thompson bequeathed the bulk of his capital to be continued as 'Widow Thompson & Sons' and £9,000 to be spent on his children's education, but realistically provided that if it was thought best the firm might be wound up and the capital invested in government securities.[2]

Eventually there came a break in a seemingly endless succession. Towards the end of the century it was not unknown for a son, born in luxury and a stranger to the counting house, to retire on the family fortune. But it was more common, after 1750, for a family to take in a managing partner who eventually took over. William Wilberforce, for example, was very much the junior sleeping partner in Wilberforce & Smiths in the nineties. Some men, like Sir Henry Etherington, Sir Samuel Standidge and Alderman Christopher Scott passed into honourable retirement leaving no issue or—more usually—no sons, and others left minors of unproven ability. Old Joseph Pease was faced with this dilemma when his son died in 1770, and he himself was beginning to fail. 'I wonder . . .', his cousin wrote, 'you do not take your son [-in-law] Jopson in partnership with you. . . .' It would be a pity if the business went to strangers, 'and your Grandson being still young not much can be said of his capacity and inclination to Continew that affair.'[3] Pease refused to take Jopson, who failed in more ventures than any self-respecting Pease was allowed to do, and the gamble paid off in the end. One or two houses did not cease to trade, but moved their chief centre of interest out of Hull. The Henworths, Porters and Thorntons moved part of their business to London and the senior branch of the Thorleys moved to Narva. Finally, some went the humiliating way of Sill & Bridges or Alderman Daniel Hoare, whose family had

[1] Apprenticed orphans included Samuel and Thomas Mowld, Samuel Waller, John Somerscales, Richard Williamson and Isaac Howard; *GH* IIA, *passim.* In common with merchants in other places (except Liverpool), Hull merchants were not generally apprenticed, either to their fathers or to other merchants. Freedom, with political and financial benefits, was secured through paternity, and (with occasional exceptions) only relatives without paternity rights were taken in formal apprenticeship.

[2] Will of Alderman B. B. Thompson, 26 Aug 1799, DDHB/52/382.

[3] Isaac Clifford, Haarlem, to J. Pease, 14 Sep 1771, *WH* 59/58/138.

played such an honourable rôle in seventeenth century Hull; his business failed, and he was only saved by the Corporation, which paid his creditors out of respect for him. His son Richard, who ran the London end of the business, was more successful, but never returned to Hull.

i. MERCHANT RECRUITMENT

Some merchants came from merchant stock, but were not originally Hull men. The Somerscales, leading timber importers in the first half of the century, came from trade in Grimsby, and the Wilberforces came from Beverley. The Sykes were established in Leeds long before the brothers William and Daniel settled in Hull in the mid-seventeenth century; William Cookson also came from Leeds, and Samuel Wright came from Nottingham.[1] One or two came—or returned—from America, like Nathaniel Flemyng 'of Hampton but now of Kingston-upon-Hull', and the unfortunate John Storr.[2] Surprisingly few came from Europe, and only two are known to have succeeded. The first was Brandström & Küsel's, a Swedish house which flourished towards the end of the century, but was never entirely at home and tried to move to Grimsby in 1796.[3] The second was Pease's.

The Peases were an old Hull family, but at the beginning of the eighteenth century they were outside the Hull business community. Robert Pease, born in Hull in 1643, emigrated to Holland for religious reasons in 1663, and remained there for the rest of his life. In 1670 he married Esther Clifford, and put the seal on a commercial, financial and family connexion that lasted for a century. The new Pease house in Hull was created as a subsidiary of the main Amsterdam house for Joseph, the third son, who was posted to Hull in

[1] William Cookson, son of William Cookson, merchant of Leeds, was apprenticed to William Mowld in 1726, and Samuel Wright, son of Ichabod Wright of Nottingham, was apprenticed to George Thompson in 1745. IIA, 1720–65, Nos. 232 and 1018.

[2] 'Mr. John Storr who is a Native and freeman of this place but for many years past hath been a Merchant in America and for his steady Attachment to Government hath had his effects confiscated and person banished from thence and being at present without any kind of support I have peculiarly to request you'l give him every Assistance in procuring him a hearing or temporary relief from the American Commissioners.' Benjamin Metcalf to W. S. Stanhope, 30 Jan 1786, WSS 1786.

[3] Gordon Jackson, *Grimsby and the Haven Company* (1971), p. 35.

1708 just as his brother, George, had been sent to Ireland. 'To give to him [William, the third brother, kept in Amsterdam] and you a stock to begin to trade with I can't,' wrote Robert when Joseph spoke of marriage, 'nor have I given anything to your Brother George but have helpt him into business, & is in as good a way as ever I was to live well . . . and after the same manner I would endeavour to help you and your Brother as you must doe one another to get into business. . . .'[1] Joseph received a commission on the business he transacted, which as late as 1722 was described as 'your Commission or rather yearly Salary . . .'.[2] He managed to conceal the true position from his rivals in Hull, and in 1716 his father noted that he had told his future father-in-law 'as a secret not to be divulged how the business you manage for mee how farr it concernes you, which before hee thought was wholly your own, yet notwithstanding I find hee is willing to give you his daughter . . .'.[3] Robert gave him nothing but his blessing, and that with mixed feelings. Since times were bad—they always were!— 'I can't offer to give you anything as I readily would if had it, & this will much impair my esteem & Credit & . . . I & your mother are much concerned (things being thus) how you will be able Creditably to maintain a wife. . . .' Since Joseph had little capital of his own the dowry of £300 was very welcome. In typical fashion he drew on his father-in-law for £558, 'which is farr more than you can want for my acct', said his father.[4] Well Joseph knew it! He was a genius at assembling credit, forever balancing accounts without involving his own money. Good will and family connexions helped him in the early days. 'One cannot bee So Sharp and Strict with young marryed people, then with old Establisht houwses', Isaac Clifford wrote in 1730.[5] Cliffords allowed him to draw heavily until 1735, when they called a halt: 'your Engaging So deep with other peoples monny who can demand their Capitals together at one moment would cause your Entire ruin and shame of your Family . . . we must go open harted with you and tell you plain, that well not come under further Acceptance, for if you cannot keep yourself in bands others will be

[1] R. Pease, Amsterdam, to J. Pease, 1 Dec 1713, *WH* 59/58/43.

[2] W. Pease, Amsterdam, to J. Pease, 26 May 1722, *WH* 59/58/44.

[3] R. Pease, Amsterdam, to J. Pease, 24 Nov 1716, *WH* 59/58/43.

[4] R. Pease to J. Pease, 23 Nov 1717, ibid.

[5] I. Clifford, Amsterdam, to J. Pease, 28 Mar 1730, *WH* 59/58/46. Clifford's phrase was unfortunate; Joseph's wife had died in February 1728.

forced to do it. . . .'[1] Three years later it was his brother's turn to complain: 'Those damned bills of yours & the method you prescribe for their payment have so many years & still do vex me more than all my other buisnes & Correspondence, which I have so long been weary of & proved a Considerable loss to me, . . . but what care you for that, if you but gett mony at my Cost. . . .'[2]

The capital and credit that Joseph Pease assembled was invested in trade, shipowning, underwriting and whaling. He is best remembered as the founder of Hull's oldest bank, but he preferred to think of himself as an industrialist. His interests covered oil-seed crushing, white lead, whiting, soap and paint making, cotton spinning and, through his son-in-law, distilling and copper mining. He was, as we shall see later, one of the great entrepreneurs of the eighteenth century.

A most important training ground for new merchants was the counting house of the old established firms. If it is generally believed that country gentry passed their days in the idle pursuit of pleasure, it is also believed that merchants were permanently incarcerated in sombre counting houses. Nothing could be further from the truth. The major part of any merchant's administration, at least by 1750, was undertaken by the chief clerk, and great responsibility passed into the hands of men like Richard Terry, who started his business career as book-keeper to Samuel Watson, sometime partner of the Wilberforces and Thorntons. The leading clerks had the responsibility and experience, but not the creditworthiness. If that could be acquired they might succeed. Some worked for, borrowed, embezzled or married money; others, like Huntingdon & Company's clerk in the eighties, were simply not the stuff of which merchants were made. Mr. Storm, it was said, had a double advantage: 'the first he is Bookkeeper to Mr. Huntingdon and the second he has the advantage of selling his Master's liquors [retail] for which he receives a great profit.'[3] But when Storm's chance came —a period in Ancona—he 'had no opinion of going to a foreign country being one of those persons whom the sight of any difficulty discourages and condemns any novelty; rather delighting in an indolent life, ignorant of men and manners'. Social mobility was probably easier in a mercantile community than elsewhere, but

[1] I. Clifford to J. Pease, 22 Nov 1735, *WH* 59/58/46.
[2] W. Pease, Amsterdam, to J. Pease, 7 Jan 1738, *WH* 59/58/44.
[3] Strother, ff. 59–60.

more than ordinary drive and initiative—and good fortune—were required to ensure success.

The easiest rise came with the blessing of a grateful master. Legacies were common, ranging from the £100 left by Samuel Dawson to Richard Terry[1] to the £1,000 left by Joseph Williamson to John Wilson, 'now in the Accompting house of my brother William Williamson'.[2] Better still was a partnership, especially if the line failed or a minority was imminent. It was Thomas Harrison, sometime clerk, who ran—and almost ruined—the house of Pease after the death of old Joseph Pease in 1773. It was twenty years before Joseph Robinson Pease discovered that Harrison had been systematically using the Pease fortune for his own benefit. 'No sooner was my Grand Father your old master laid in his Grave,' he wrote, when the secret came out during the 1793 financial crisis, 'but you sought by every possible means to throw my property intrusted to your care into your Brother's hands, your system was to keep me as much as possible in the Dark. . . .'[3] In a world where so much depended on integrity Pease was not the last to discover the danger of relying too heavily on the service of the clerk or junior partner.

Young William Wilberforce was better served by Thomas Thompson, without doubt the greatest of the clerks. Wilberforce & Smiths was a firm to be reckoned with, according to the Collector of Customs, 'three of the partners being in Parliament'.[4] But its prestige in the world of commerce in the momentous twenty years at the end of the eighteenth century was due almost entirely to Thompson's astute business mind, before he, too, entered Parliament. The son of a farmer from Swine in Holderness, he came like so many to make his fortune in Hull. Unlike the many he had an extraordinary capacity for business which did not go unobserved by old William Wilberforce or Abel Smith.[5] For a time after Wilberforce's death Abel ran the business from his London office, and then put Thompson in full charge on a salary of £500. In 1784 he became the manager of the bank (Smiths & Thompson's) which the Smiths

[1] Will of Samuel Watson, 1773–8, DDHB/62/11.

[2] Will of Joseph Williamson, 24 Mar 1784, DDHB/28/91. John Wilson had been with Williamsons in Sweden.

[3] Copy, J. R. Pease to T. Harrison, n.d. (but 1795), *WH* 59/58/45. See also J. R. Pease to Harrison, 10 May 1795, *WH* 59/58/51.

[4] HCLB, C–B, 11 Feb 1791.

[5] Thompson's arrival in Hull may not have been entirely fortuitous. The Wilberforces owned a small amount of land in Swine.

opened in Hull, and three years later they lent him the money to buy his partnership in Wilberforce & Smiths. In 1802, when he was about fifty, he put his income at £3,700 per annum, and five years later he became the first Methodist preacher to enter the House of Commons.

Another obvious training ground was the sea itself. Master mariners were admirably placed for building up extensive overseas connexions. More often than not they held a share in the ship—or group of ships—which they sailed, and trading by masters was common. Many, of course, found that navigating a ship, with a little trade on the side, was all they could rise to; but for a few the future held out glittering prospects. It was said of Francis Bine that he was 'Master of a ship, but during the last war [American Revolutionary war] was very fortunate in Freighting ships from England to Ostend and from thence to various foreign ports, by which trade he acquired an immense fortune, it is thought not less than £20,000. At the conclusion of the war he commenced Merchant and Sugar-boiler having bought the New Sugar House in Wincolmlee.'[1] Not without envy, perhaps, did the members of the old established houses view Hull's only two knights, Etherington and Standidge. Sir Henry Etherington, Bt., was the son of a merchant who began as a master mariner and appears several times in ships carrying goods for the Maisters in the period 1713–23. By the thirties he was shipping goods on his own account, and his business expanded sufficiently for him to be elected Chamberlain in 1736, Sheriff in 1742 and Mayor in 1747 and 1758, the year in which his son became Sheriff. Henry Etherington junior, at one time a master for his father, became Mayor in 1769 and 1785, and was undoubtedly the most respected man in Hull in the last quarter of the century.

Sir Henry was respected but, except for his eccentricities, he was soon forgotten. Alderman Sir Samuel Standidge, on the other hand, grew in stature with the passage of time, his image boosted by the inaccurate gossip of Sheahan. He was given all the elements of the traditional fairy-tale: he was the son of a second marriage turned away by his father with nothing but a trite declaration that 'Samuel had brains enough to work his own way'; he created, single-handed it would seem, Hull's spectacular whaling industry; he was knighted in Russia and in England; and he died worth £76,000.[2] Standidge first appears in surviving records at the age of

[1] Strother, f. 27. [2] Sheahan, p. 728.

nineteen, as mate, and later master, of ships for Christopher Scott in the transatlantic run. 'But by successful merchandise', said another local historian, 'he rapidly accumulated a large fortune.'[1] The 130-acre New York farm in Preston (Holderness) was reputedly purchased—and named—by him out of the profits of a single voyage to America. But men did not become mates at nineteen, or carry on successful merchandise, without capital and friends. Like many of the rising stars, Standidge owed his prosperity to the range of his activities, rather than to a commanding position in any one of them. In the seventies and eighties he was variously described as master mariner, merchant, shipowner, shipbuilder and, of course, gentleman.

Finally, a small number of merchants came—by way of apprenticeship—from outside the mercantile community, chiefly from country gentry stock. Charles Healey, for example, was a younger son of the lord of the manor of Frodingham (Lincolnshire), who owned much of the land on which the town of Scunthorpe now stands. He arrived in Hull at the end of the seventeenth century with a thousand pounds, and made good.[2] The family's link with trade was strengthened in 1709 when his elder brother married the daughter of his friend, Alderman John Rogers.[3] Charles Healey remained in Hull all his life, so content with his lot that when he inherited the family estate in 1750 he promptly sold it to a younger brother for twenty pounds.[4] Another important house with roots—albeit short ones—in Lindsey was that of De la Pryme, Huguenot refugees from Ypres who had settled down with Vermuyden on drained land in the Isle of Axholme.[5] Francis De la Pryme came to Hull in the early eighteenth century and again rose rapidly in fortune, no doubt aided by the marriage of his sister to Hugh Blaydes, the foremost Hull shipbuilder. He became Mayor in 1749.

It is impossible to trace exactly the interaction of town and

[1] G. Poulson, *The History . . . of Holderness* (2 vols., 1840–1), ii, p. 495.

[2] His father left the family estate to the eldest son, John, on condition that he paid £800 to each of the other five children (Will of Chas. Healey, 1698/9, *LAO* Sheffield 45/10). In fact £1,000 was paid, and Charles Healey of Hull received a further £200 for Quitclaim of right in 1710 (Sheffield 45/17).

[3] *LAO* Sheffield 45/14.

[4] *LAO* Sheffield 45/28.

[5] For the De la Pryme family see Diary of Abraham De la Pryme, *BM* Lansdowne MSS., 890, printed as vol. 54 (1869) of the *Surtees Society*.

country, the arrival of gentry sons and money, and the incidence of success and failure. The only way of checking the arrival of 'gentry' merchants is through the Corporation's Inrollment of Indentures of Apprenticeships, available from 1720. Altogether twenty-one sons of gentlemen, nine esquire's sons and one knight's son were apprenticed to Hull merchants between 1720 and 1799, a third of them to four merchants—Alderman William Wilberforce, Alderman Samuel Watson, Richard Sykes and William Thornton. Most of them came from Yorkshire, Lincolnshire and Nottinghamshire, but there were a few from further afield: Walter Hickson came from Staffordshire,[1] Thomas Charlesworth from Derbyshire,[2] Thomas Vere Jones from Norfolk,[3] and Edward Campion from Sussex.[4] Although some of them disappeared without trace, a handful reached the top rank. William Welfitt was Hull's leading tobacco merchant in the middle of the century,[5] and John Jarratt was a leading oil merchant.[6] By no means least were three men from Nottingham: Walter Edge,[7] Abel Smith[8] and Gardiner Eggington.[9]

It would be an exaggeration to describe the majority of these men as anything more than minor gentry. The landed aristocracy showed no interest in Hull, which was not the kind of port where huge fortunes could be quickly made. Men like William Monson, son of Lord Monson of South Carlton, and Richard Carter of Redbourne (Lincs.) went not to Hull but to London, India or the West Indies, as, indeed, a number of Hull men did towards the end of the century. Even among minor gentry Hull's attractiveness was limited, and declined steadily. The thirties and forties were the

[1] IIA, 1720–65, No. 337.
[2] ibid., No. 244.
[3] IIA, 1766–87, No. 1022.
[4] IIA, 1720–65, No. 1780.
[5] Son of William Welfitt of Laceby, Lincs.; apprenticed to Richard Thompson in 1734, ibid., No. 579.
[6] Son of Henry Jarratt of Beverley; apprenticed to Alderman William Mowld, 1739, ibid., No. 720. His firm later became Jarratt & Coates, with extensive interests in oil milling and whaling.
[7] Son of Richard Edge; apprenticed to Alderman Leonard Collings, 1725, ibid., No. 186. Partner in Hamilton & Edge, leading tar and general American merchants.
[8] Son of Abel Smith; apprenticed to Alderman William Wilberforce, 1732, ibid., No. 512. Partner in Wilberforce & Smiths, thus linking the Hull merchant house and the Nottingham bank.
[9] Son of Robert Eggington; apprenticed after his death to William Thornton, 1747, ibid., No. 1088. Egingtons were eventually one of the greatest oil and whaling houses.

years of greatest inflow; thereafter newcomers were increasingly rare. Nineteen boys arrived between 1730 and 1749, only eleven between 1750 and 1799.

There were very few apprentices who were not of merchant or gentry origin. Not more than two dozen were enrolled between 1720 and 1799, from diverse backgrounds ranging from fellmonger and brassfounder to mariner and labourer.[1] Some no doubt had financial backing, but only one was obviously successful: Robert Thorley, son of a yeoman of Etton (E. Yorks.), who later became the partner of his master, Thomas Broadley.[2] The majority were probably little more than cheap office labour, to become a merchant's clerk the most they could justifiably expect.[3] The official apprenticeship system was no highway for extensive social mobility.

ii. MERCHANT CAPITAL

Whatever their origins, all merchants needed capital. Indeed, the great merchant was the one whose sound mercantile judgement was supported by an equal ability to concentrate his own and other people's money at the right moment. If any great merchant tramped into eighteenth century Hull with his cat, he did not advertise the fact, and 'Rags to Riches in one generation' is little more than a comforting myth.

[1] They came from the following occupational backgrounds: Yeoman (2), victualler (2), schoolmaster (2), fellmonger, cloth-dresser, land-surveyor, grocer, brassfounder, innholder, house-carpenter, joiner, ship-carpenter, painter, mariner (4), husbandman, labourer, and 'a poor boy of this town'. They were heavily concentrated in the fifties and sixties, perhaps as gentry recruits fell away. By 1770 apprenticeship had ceased to be common, and only eighteen boys, from all backgrounds, were registered between 1770 and 1799.

[2] He was later a partner in Thorley, Bolton & Co. of Hull and Narva, and spent the end of his life as a principal merchant and banker (Thorley, Ouchterloney & Co.) in Narva. He was the largest single sharehholder in the Hull Dock Company.

[3] Greater and more precise use has not been made of Apprenticeship returns because of grave difficulties of interpretation. There is no clear indication of the actual duties of master or apprentice in many cases, and we cannot always distinguish which of the master's various occupations are to be followed by the boy. Thus some of the poor boys apprenticed to merchants were almost certainly destined for service in whalers and other ships, and shipowner apprentices must be discounted altogether because they were too often—but not always—cheap labour.

Capital came from a variety of sources. The most obvious was 'ancient riches'—the family fortune preserved in the merchant house with the devotion lavished by landowners on their entail. It was locked up in ships and goods, land and investments, and helped to determine a firm's creditworthiness in Amsterdam. It was supplemented at the appropriate time by a dowry, though a daughter in the house would reverse the flow. When Joseph Pease chose a wife with only £300 he was told in no uncertain terms that 'you would much undervalue yourselfe & family . . . when as some time ago as I have heard you might very likely had a young widow with £800 . . .'.[1] Then the uncles and aunts—especially the latter—were expected to assist. It is true that merchants divided their fortunes in legacies to children, but those legacies usually remained in the family and were taken only as interest. In this way Joseph Pease had the use of at least £8,400 bequeathed by his sister and brother to his daughters.[2] Once a merchant had a reputation it was common for money to be left in his hands, at least in the days before banks were well established. William Pease had £5,000 at 3 per cent from 'Cousin Simkinson' until his death in 1747, when it was transferred to Joseph at 5 per cent,[3] and aunt Abigail Pease had £750 in her chest, which she offered to the family at 4 per cent in 1751.[4] Sometimes annuities were sold. Joseph Pease offered his son-in-law one at 10 per cent in 1752,[5] and Thomas Broadley gave £90 per annum for £1,102 in 1756.[6]

Merchants could also borrow from fellow merchants—who thereby spread their risks—or from landowners. Hugh Mason had £1,000 from John Thornton in 1728[7] and John Green had a similar sum from Simon Horner in 1790,[8] while Henry Etherington's business—or estate—may have owed much to the £10,000 he borrowed from Joseph Pease in 1775.[9] The Maisters, on the other hand, raised £2,500 from Cliffords, their Amsterdam agents, in

[1] R. Pease, Amsterdam, to J. Pease, 14 Jul 1716, *WH* 59/58/43.

[2] See will of J. Pease, 27 June 1755, *WH* 59/58/63.

[3] R. Pease, (*son* of J. Pease), Amsterdam, to J. Pease, 18 Aug 1747, *WH* 59/59/39.

[4] R. Pease to J. Pease, 8 Sep 1752, ibid.

[5] L. Jopson, York, to J. Pease, 5 May 1752, *WH* 59/58/49.

[6] DDHB/20/45–7. [7] DDHB/45/58. [8] DDHB/6/26.

[9] See bank books of J. and J. R. Pease, 1772–83, *WH* 59/58/108–9. Interest was also received on £7,000 lent to John Lee & Co., £500 to Ann Bateman and £350 to Thomas Westerdell, the Harbour Master.

1731.[1] They also borrowed from landowners, their friends the Grimstons of Grimston Garth. The largest recorded loan was one of £11,000 which Charles Pool secured in 1755 from Charles Pelham, Yorkshire and Lincolnshire landowner and M.P. for Beverley.[2]

The merchant partnership was an excellent way of consolidating experience and capital, and there was a definite trend away from the family business in the middle of the century. The growing complexity of the commercial world, where the rich survived and the very rich grew richer, led to a union of Williamsons with Waller, Maisters with Rennard and Parker, Stephensons with Fearnley, Terry with Wright and so on. Thomas Broadley & Company, founded in 1749, was no doubt typical of the many.[3] Broadley contributed two-thirds and Robert Thorley one-third of the (unnamed) capital. Henceforth they were to have no financial dealings outside the partnership, except that Broadley might insure ships and merchandise, and Thorley might deal in malt. Of the profits, Broadley was to have £50 a month and Thorley £25 a month, with a proportional distribution of the annual surplus. Broadley was clearly to run the firm, since he held the books, cash and goods, but Thorley had the safeguard that the partnership was automatically dissolved if by 'losses or accidents in Trade the joint stock of the said parties shall be diminished or lessened one fourth part'. In 1754 they became equal partners with £6,000 each, but the partnership was dissolved in 1757 or 1758, perhaps when Thorley went to Narva.

As time passed the raising of money and organisation of firms became a good deal more sophisticated. Nowhere is this illustrated better than in the case of Sykes & Co. and Wilberforce & Smiths. The Sykes seem always to have traded alone until the eighties. The Wilberforces, on the other hand, soon became involved in partnerships. In the 1737 Port Book their name is linked with the Thorntons —who originally owned Wilberforce House and the staith in High Street—and the Watsons. At a later date their connexion with the Nottingham Smiths brought a welcome influx of capital and fresh blood. There was, in the boom conditions of the eighties, no wiser choice for investment than the Wilberforces, already specialising heavily in the Russian trade, and Sykes, for long a leading Swedish house.

[1] *WH* Maister Accounts, *passim*.
[2] DDHB/20/113.
[3] For the partnership agreement, see DDHB/58/3–5.

In 1787 both firms underwent a financial overhaul.[1] The partners in Wilberforce & Smiths—William Wilberforce, Robert Smith, Samuel Smith and Thomas Thompson—each paid £2,062. 10*s*. into the newly constituted capital of the firm. But what is more interesting is the fact that Joseph and John Sykes were also admitted as partners, subscribing no less than 45 per cent of the total of £15,000. So far as Sykes & Co. was concerned the position was reversed. On the same day the partners also paid the first instalment of £4,812. 10*s*. each into Sykes, so that the Sykes became the largest shareholding group in Wilberforce & Smiths and Wilberforce, the Smiths and Thompson actually had a larger amount of capital invested in Sykes & Co. than in their own firm. Ten years later Wilberforce, the Smiths and Thompson reduced their holding in their own firm slightly to allow the Sykes to take a 50 per cent share, and in return they provided 50 per cent of the capital of Sykes & Co. which was now increased to £60,000.

These interrelated partnerships were obviously held by the Smiths and Wilberforce simply as financial investments, and they were expected to yield an appropriate profit. This they did. Starting with 4 per cent in 1787–90, Wilberforce & Smiths' dividend had risen to 33⅓ per cent in 1794 and 20 per cent for the years 1796–8. Sykes & Co. also started with 4 per cent, but their dividend rose more slowly, to 9 per cent in 1792 and 36½ per cent in 1799. Total dividends for the twelve years 1788–99 were approximately 145 per cent for Wilberforce & Smiths and 160 per cent for Sykes & Co.: £21,592 and £80,448 respectively. Unfortunately we have no information for other firms, but there is no reason to suppose that Williamson & Waller or Dixon & Moxon, for example, were any different. The sleeping partnerships may have been typical—they were certainly typical of the shipowning and whaling firms—although the degree of interdependence may be exceptional.

For success in trade—in raising credit, capital and customers—much dependend on connexion; and the best connexion was the family compact. When Robert Pease stressed that "wee keep entirely together to help one another . . .',[2] he was simply voicing the generally accepted view; that is what relations were for. Whether or not a marriage cemented an existing relationship, it was expected to lead

[1] Details from their accounts in Smiths & Thompson's Ledgers.

[2] R. Pease, Amsterdam, to J. Pease, 1 Dec 1713; *WH* 59/58/43.

to closer union between the parent houses: to a partnership or trading alliance; to a trustworthy factorage abroad; or simply to the recommendations that meant so much to an eighteenth-century merchant. Parental pressure was not the only—or chief—pressure. Endogamy was a natural result of the limited choice of socially acceptable partners in a relatively small and isolated community.

It is difficult to do more than slight justice to the complicated pattern of interrelationship between the great merchant houses (see Appendix 23). Two men must serve as examples for the rest: Alderman Henry Broadley and Robert Thornton. Both of Henry Broadley's grandfathers—Alderman Thomas Broadley and Alderman Robert Carlisle—were leading merchants. His wife's father was John Jarratt, oil merchant, and her maternal grandfather was the Robert Thorley who had been in partnership with Broadley. Henry's son, John Broadley, married Anne Elizabeth, daughter of Alderman William Osborne, the greatest timber merchant at the end of the century. Robert Thortnton's immediate connexions were as impressive. His sister married Alderman William Wilberforce and his son married the daughter and heiress of Alderman Samuel Watson. One of his daughters married William Wilberforce junior, and another married Alderman John Porter, in turn related by marriage to Alderman Sir Henry Etherington. Thorntons, Porters and Wilberforces were perhaps the most powerful Russian merchants in Britain, with at least seven members of their various firms in Parliament in the eighties.

iii. MERCHANT INVESTMENT: STOCKS AND LAND

All merchants wished at some time or other to invest money outside their normal trading activities, if only as a matter of safety. Their trading assets might be highly liquid, but they were also highly vulnerable. 'God knows where this will end . . .', wrote William Pease when the bankruptcies started in Amsterdam in 1720 and he found himself with 30,000 guilders to cover debts of 300,000.[1] There was security, Joseph could have told him, in an oil mill and a ship or two! The merchant, unlike the industrialist, did not need heavy fixed capital. His assets were his business contacts rather than buildings and equipment, and though he needed to have capital behind him, the system of credit was such that he need never show it over the counter. Consequently there was a growing dis-

[1] W. Pease, Amsterdam, to J. Pease, 25 Oct 1720, *WH* 59/58/44.

tinction between the business and private finances of individual merchants, especially after the development of the extra-family partnership, when the amount of capital involved in the house was fixed. When the banks opened, many business accounts contained only the financial transactions of the firm. Every halfpenny of profit was withdrawn—as it had been by Broadley & Thorley—for distribution to the partners. Only a small—sometimes dangerously small—balance remained, and sudden emergencies were covered by overdrafts. As a result, private fortunes were no longer immediately affected by the vicissitudes of trade.

In the absence of any great local demand for capital investment in the early years of the century, merchants had little choice but to invest in government and other stocks—including South Sea, which the Maisters bought at 349. Stocks remained popular. Joseph Pease invested in 4 per cents for his grandsons in the fifties;[1] and Thomas Thompson had £20,000 and John Staniforth had £14,000 in the 3 per cents in the nineties.[2] Opportunities for local investment increased with the growth of the town in the second half of the century. On the one hand there was the dock and related works, an expanding merchant marine, and local industry. On the other there was the physical expansion of the town. An increasing population—almost doubling in the last quarter of the century—encouraged speculation in house building. New streets to the north of the dock were developed in the eighties, and suburbs were spreading beyond the old walls. The Wilberforces, Maisters, Broadleys and Thorleys owned land all over the town, while half the land sold by the Dock Company for housing was bought by three men: Richard Howard, Richard Moxon and J. R. Pease. Finally, the Corporation raised loans—up to £1,000, at 5 per cent—to cover the gap between income and expenditure, which was increasing with the development of local government.

Some merchants were interested in investment outside Hull, particularly in inland transport. The Peases, as usual, led the field. In the nineties J. R. Pease had £6,000 in the Calder-Hebble Navigation (of which he was the second largest shareholder), £3,800 in the Driffield Navigation, an unknown amount in the

[1] Certificates for £5,000 are in *WH* 59/58/81.

[2] Thompson's account in Smiths & Thompson's Ledgers. The bank's customers between them had over £200,000 in the 3 per cents alone in January 1799.

Rochdale Canal, £385 in the Anlaby Turnpike and £240 in the Beverley Turnpike.[1]

Land was probably the chief interest outside commerce. No merchant of any consequence was without his seat or estate, large or small, in the East Riding or Lincolnshire. Little information is at present available about individual estates or the total land owned by Hull merchants at any particular time, but it is clear that three types of holdings, with different purposes, must be recognised.

Firstly there was the seat, the symbol of gentility, with its park or home farm. For many this was the sum of their territorial ambitions. Secondly there was short-term investment land, which provided temporary security for money accumulating for future business transactions. The age of Enclosure and agricultural improvement was particularly favourable for short-term investment, and small parcels, more or less independent of their estates, changed hands at remarkable speed, often with quite large increments in value. The Sykes, for example, bought land in Melton and Ferriby for £4,500 in 1769 and sold it to Joseph Williamson for £7,750 in 1772.[2] Eight years later Williamson used it to raise £4,000 from Samuel Smith, the banker.[3] Similarly, Thomas Broadley bought land for £800 in June 1771 and sold it for £960 less than a year later.[4] This short-term ownership was particularly common inside the town of Hull itself, where property or closes might be held for years or months, whether as assets or building speculations. Thomas Bridges bought a property in Manor Alley from Leonard Collings for £135 in March 1747, and sold it eight months later to Charles Pool for £140.[5]

The third type was the permanent family estate, giving a more secure—though less lucrative—base for the family fortune than trade. The distinction between the second and third categories is fine and they must inevitably overlap. It seems on available evidence that the larger an estate and the further from Hull, the more permanent it was likely to be. Some families, like the Maisters, developed a compact estate based on their country seat. Henry Maister inherited his Winestead property and his son (also Henry)

[1] A series of calculations of Pease's income are in *WH* 59/58/45.

[2] DDHB/28/64–9.

[3] DDHB/28/89.

[4] DDHB/28/29–33. It was sold to Joseph Williamson, who eventually sold it back to the Broadleys.

[5] DDHB/20/109–10.

received land in Owstwick, Burton Pidsea and Bempton from his mother's family, the Tymperons. Between them the Henries also purchased land in Ottringham, Weeton, Welwick, Skeffling, Patrington and Woodall. In general, however, the acquisition of land tended to be haphazard, with merchants investing in widely scattered parcels of land that were difficult to administer efficiently or effectively. Sir Henry Etherington held land in Paull in Holderness, and in Hatfield (of which he was Lord) in the Isle of Axholme. The known Wilberforce lands were situated in Coniston, to the north-east of Hull, Riplingham—where they had four or five hundred acres—to the west of Hull, and Wintringham in Lincolnshire. George Crowle also bought land in Lincolnshire, again without producing any seemingly logical pattern. Land which he bought for £21,500 from the bankrupt Duke of Newcastle in 1751[1] was scattered around the Lincolnshire villages of Irby-on-Humber, Hatcliffe and Gunnerby, and another estate which the Crowles acquired, in Wootton, was more than ten miles to the north of Irby.

Some of the merchant estates were large. The Maister lands in Welwick and Skeffling had a rental of £500 at the end of the century and their Winestead and Patrington land was worth over £100,000.[2] Robert Smith owned the whole of Humberstone in Lincolnshire and at least 400 acres of Wintringham—'one of the richest soils in England', according to Arthur Young, who thought him a model landlord.[3] The estate was, in fact, administered by Thomas Thompson, who developed his ideas of 'three acres and a cow', which he later propounded as President of the Board of Agriculture, during his rides through the villages in which he put them into operation. The greatest estates were those of the Sykes and the Broadleys, the largest and sixth largest respectively in nineteenth-century East Yorkshire. The core of the Sledmere estate came to Richard Sykes through his wife, the daughter of Alderman Mark Kirkby, and the estate was expanded out of the accumulated resources of two of Hull's leading merchant houses, aided, perhaps, by a fortunate 'gentry' marriage, with the Tatton family. For many years after the

[1] *LAO* Emeris 33/5. Crowle may have had a bargain; the land had previously been mortgaged for £31,000.

[2] I am deeply indebted to Mr. Edward Ingram for information about the Maister estates.

[3] Young, *Agriculture of Lincs.*, p. 37.

death of Richard Sykes the family business was run by his eldest son, Richard, and his third son (by a second marriage), Joseph. When Richard Sykes Junior died without issue the estate passed to the second brother, the Rev. Mark Sykes, and the estate and merchant house parted company.[1] Trading remained in the blood, however, and Mark's son, Sir Christopher, set up a bank—the East Riding Bank—towards the end of the century.

The Broadleys were the most inveterate land buyers among the merchants who remained in Hull throughout the century. Indeed, much of our information about merchants' land is available because sooner or later it was bought by the Broadleys and the deeds preserved in the magnificent collection now in the East Riding Record Office. They bought regularly—though often in small parcels—throughout the century, with purchases ranging from the 400 acres and sheepwalk in Hesleskugh Grange which cost them £1,800 in 1717[2] to the Hull Sacking factory which cost £8,000 in 1812.[3] They bought from other Hull merchants, sometimes for immediate resale, sometimes for permanent holding. Andrew Perrott's estate was purchased in 1776,[4] part of James Hamilton's in 1771,[5] Joseph Outram's after his death in 1780,[6] and Charles Pool's tithes of Sutton and Drypool in 1802.[7] Other land, most probably the bulk of it, they bought from 'outsiders': three oxgangs in Sigglesthorne for £200 in 1739,[8] 207 acres in Hollym (and a garden in Churchside, Hull) for £3,600 in 1768,[9] a small estate for £11,800 in 1793 from Napier Christie Burton of Upper Brook Street, London,[10] and so on. Eventually the estate reached almost 15,000 acres.

Although much research remains to be done on merchant landownership we may, perhaps, hazard a tentative conclusion that few Hull merchants moved from staith to estate *in the eighteenth century*. Mr. Dawn, 'Steward to Sir Christopher Sykes, Sir Henry Etherington, Colonel Maister, and several of the Hull Merchants' reported

[1] Created a baronet, 1783, chiefly on the initiative of his second son, Christopher, who had considerable political influence in the East Riding. His eldest son, Richard, was apprenticed to Joseph Sykes in 1759, but did not survive to join the family firm; IIA, 1720–65, No. 1904.

[2] DDHB/38/20. [3] DDHB/29/110–13. [4] DDHB/1/39–47.

[5] DDHB/28/29. This particular property was sold to Joseph Williamson less than a year later for an increased price; DDHB/28/33.

[6] DDHB/29/144. [7] DDHB/45/131. [8] DDHB/41/4.

[9] DDHB/37/26. [10] DDHB/45/164.

twice a week to his masters in Hull in the eighties.[1] Whatever the future held for them, merchant families were, with a few exceptions, still merchants. Land was not bought as the end product of trade, but as a means of investment that served trade. We cannot identify landowning as a separate, distinct function of merchants; it was an integral part of their total economic activity, and had been since time immemorial. They certainly did not buy land for a high return on their capital —trade and industry paid higher. Nor did they buy gentility by the acre. They may have seen a quick profit in agricultural improvement or urban growth: but above all they bought safety and insured the future. Safety, that is, for the capital that backed their trade, and must be unaffected by fluctuations in the business world. It may be significant that the people interested in large estates—the Sykes, Broadleys and Smiths—were also bankers, but even here there can be no dogmatism. J. R. Pease was also a banker but, despite the house at Hesslewood, he was no landowner; only 16 per cent of his income in 1796 came from land.[2] Many Hull merchants agreed with the Peases, that there were better things to do with money than buy land. It would suit the popular view of merchant land purchasing if there was a single metamorphosis, a single merchant who voluntarily retired from trade and henceforth drew the bulk of his income from land. We can find no such person. This does not mean that there was no one; but it would be more instructive to look to the great changes that took place in the early nineteenth century than to search the hidden depths of the eighteenth.

2. INLAND AGENTS

The merchants in the eighteenth century were in a seller's market, especially when the great boom got under way in the last quarter. The demand for their services was intense, and their profits corres-

[1] Mrs. N. M. Greame, Sewerby, to W. S. Stanhope, 15 Apr 1784, WSS 1784.

[2] Calculated from a rough survey of J. R. Pease's income, dated 12 Dec 1796; *WH* 59/58/45. His income in this year was low compared with others which do not specify landed income. (It excluded investments in government stock which he is known to have held, and perhaps excluded income from the bank.) It is possible that the bulk of Pease's land was his urban estate: he had invested over £20,000 in building on the the dock estate in the eighties, including this own magnificent town house in Charlotte Street.

pondingly high. But trading was a highly personal venture, and much depended on the character and reputation of a merchant, and on his ability to recruit and retain correspondents at home as well as abroad. It was here that the old established firms, with their existing suppliers and customers, scored heavily over the newcomers. The Sykes supplied Huntsman's and the Maisters supplied Shore's with Swedish iron for steelmaking from the beginning. Any merchant wishing to break into such an established relationship would have to provide a more attractive bargain based on an advantageous factorage, and this was virtually impossible. The hope of new merchants lay in new trades and new connexions. So the Peases built up their pioneering oil trade and made headway in the yarn trade because it was new and they had their own interests and relations in Manchester.

Once a correspondence had begun, matters were relatively simple. The merchants advised possible customers of goods that might interest them, and customers wrote to their regular merchant —or one recommended to them—for goods from stock or to order. Sometimes the fulfilment of an order was left to the discretion of the merchant: 'I would have them [ravenducks] pretty good therefore will leave it to you to send such as you think most suitable for Waggoners Tracks . . .', wrote one of Wray & Hollingsworth's regular customers.[1] Others were not so trusting. 'We never give orders', Worthingtons said, of staves, 'until they are arrived in Hull.'[2] In the yarn trade, where there was fierce competition for the early cargoes, merchants were instructed to buy, if possible before arrival, a certain quantity or value, whichever was the smaller. (Sometimes, when the price rose more than expected, they refused to buy without specific price instructions from their correspondents.)

In the second half of the century connexions with inland correspondents were strengthened by the growing tendency to employ commercial travellers. Young Robert Pease was despatched into the country as soon as he reached manhood. He visited customers in Halifax, Leeds, and Bristol, viewed fields of standing oil-seed in Wisbech, and periodically visited Ireland. Similarly, in 1785, John Stephenson sent his nephew 'upon a Circuit among my Correspondents in Derbyshire and in the West Riding of Yorkshire', but apparently thought little of his potential and tried to get him a

[1] Wray & Hollingsworth Letter Books, 2 Nov 1791.
[2] ibid., 9 Jul 1791.

government sinecure.[1] In the nineties Wray & Hollingsworth had at least one traveller, who ventured as far afield as Chester in his search for orders. 'We have an offer from your Traveller made to one of our partners at Rotherham . . .', wrote John Green & Co. of Hunslett Brewery, Leeds,[2] and John Aked of Bradford wrote to say: 'I gave an order to your Rider, when at Bradford, for a loading of Timber, and he informed me, it would be in Hull about the middle of this month. . . .'[3]

Although accounts were usually settled by bills of exchange, the travellers soon began to collect money as well as orders. Money owing to Wray & Hollingsworth, wrote Jeremiah Gascoigne of Rotherham, would be 'ready for your Traveller, Mr. Wharing at the time he come to Rotherham',[4] and William Thakeray of Harrogate excused a delay in payment with the excuse: 'Should have remited a Draught sooner, but I expected to have been cald upon for the money. . . .'[5]

Besides their traveller, Wray & Hollingsworth also had an appointed agent—William Suffolk—in Birmingham, where they had many customers. He sold goods, received orders and money, and 'paid Burton Boat Co. their Freight Account . . .'. A regular account of his business was sent to the Hull office and bills were sent to individual customers from there. William Osbourne had a similar agency in Grimsby in the same period.

There is little detailed information showing how goods produced in the hinterland found their way to Hull. In the case of manufactured goods, it was becoming common in the second half of the century for the manufacturer to have his own correspondents or travellers abroad, and to negotiate directly with his customers. Consequently all that was required in Hull was a merchant to handle the physical side of the shipment, and the manufacturer found the merchant rather than the merchant finding the manufacturer. Occasionally the foreign merchant came to England in search of goods. A Mr. Visser of Amsterdam, it was said in 1743, 'is now at Leeds, but will be for Hull Shortly, & give orders himself about shipping his packs . . .'.[6] Other manufactured goods were delivered to the merchant by the manufacturer. The Leeds Pottery, for

[1] J. Stephenson to W. S. Stanhope, 16 Mar 1785, WSS 1785.
[2] Wray & Hollingsworth Letter Books, 18 Apr 1795.
[3] ibid., 10 Jul 1791. [4] ibid., 21 Mar 1795. [5] ibid., 11 Oct 1791.
[6] L. Jopson, Amsterdam, to Robert Pease, Hull, 9 Jul 1743, *WH* 59/58/49.

example, were sending circular advertisements and order forms to Hull merchants towards the end of the century, and some firms were sending representatives to Hull to attract orders. Manchester Riders appeared in the eighties, and probably earlier, but we know nothing of their activities. It was obviously important for Manchester and other new manufacturers to secure outlets for their goods. Robert Robinson of Manchester sent his pattern book to Joseph Pease in 1753, only to find that at this late date Hull had still made little headway in the cotton goods trade. 'I have no Corespondance to Recommend you too,' Pease told him, 'in your Way of Manchester Wares for foreign parts, or to get you any Commissions for from London, which could wish I had. . . .'[1] The pattern books were sent on to Pease's friends in Amsterdam, and this seemed the easiest outlet for Hull merchants to pursue. Dutch merchants bought cloth in Manchester for their African trade, with Hull merchants acting for the two parties.[2] For the woollen cloth, and later the Manchester cloth trade, is seems most probably that deliveries were sent to Hull merchants as a result of long standing commercial agreements, and that firms like Williamsons, who occasionally sent out £20,000 worth of Manchester cloth in a single shipment, had permanent contracts, whether on the manufacturer's or the merchant's initiative.

The position of the Hull merchant was, then, less important in the export trade in manufactured goods than it was in the import trade in raw materials. In 1791, when opposing the introduction of new Customs fees, the Committee of Trade protested that '. . . our Correspondents, who provide the various manufactured Goods sent to our Address, only for us to forward, do not acquaint us with the contents of such package'.[3] While this system of trading was probably not as common as the Committee would have had the Customs men believe, the fact remains that it was thought to be a plausible excuse. Advertisements for foreign sailings began to appear in inland Newspapers such as the *Leeds Intelligencer*, and in some cases the Hull merchant became little more than a glorified shipbroker. One of the very few freight agreements to have survived was 'Between Christopher Brelin of the Swedish Brigg *Union* now

[1] J. Pease, Hull, to Robert Robinson, Manchester, 25 Mar 1753, *WH* 59/58/47.

[2] See, for example, *WH* 59/58/48 *passim.*

[3] *GH* Minutes of the Committee of Trade, 13 Aug 1791.

laying at Grimsby . . . and John Voase of . . . Hull, Merchant for and on behalf of Messrs. Roberts, Hodgson & Roberts of Sheffield . . . Merchants'.[1] Another agreement, between the master of the Danish ship *Anna of Altona* and Messrs. John & Samuel Lees of Halifax makes no mention at all of a Hull merchant.

Hull merchants were well aware of the attempts of some inland merchants to dispense with their services, and even—if allowed—to by-pass Hull altogether. Some of the inland 'ports' maintained their mediaeval trade until well into the eighteenth century, and one or two actually gained ground before the increasing size of ships put a stop to their ambition. There was constant friction throughout the century between the Corporations of York and Hull over the right of York merchants to exemption from tolls and, in some cases, from by-laws.[2] Bawtry, Stockwith, Gainsborough and Selby—the latter increasingly in the last quarter of the century—had their own merchants. Samuel Dawson was, perhaps, a typical example. Although he lived in Bawtry (at the beginning of the century), his Day Book reads almost the same as the Maisters'. The only difference between their trade and his was that his goods were received by Hull wharfingers, or sent inland by the masters of the ships concerned.

The inland merchant is a fascinating figure, but by no means was he a serious threat to Hull, with its established connexions and the only Custom House. The easiest weapon to hand, in moments of anxiety, was the law. In 1784 the Hull Committee of Trade reported to the Customs that they knew of 'Vessels passing this port up to a place called Selby above 40 miles up this river, and there taking in various cargoes, which they brought down here and cleared at this Custom House coastwise for Yarmouth; where they were permitted to clear out for abroad without delivering and unloading their cargoes. . . .'[3]

The Customs staff could be relied on to channel foreign trade through Hull, but there was no means of safeguarding the coastal trade, in which Hull merchants occupied a far less commanding position. Lead shipments in the first quarter of the century were often accounted for by inland merchants (particularly the two firms of Wigfall and Leadbetter of Stockwith and Gainsborough).

[1] *WH* Court Cases Box.

[2] The greatest clash came in 1737, and is fully recorded in Hadley, pp. 310–13 and in the Bench Books, *passim.*

[3] *GH* Minutes of Committee of Trade, 20 Aug 1784.

Sheffield ironmongery was usually ordered by post in the second half of the century, even when a traveller was employed; Newton Chambers, for example, always despatched their goods direct to the customer without the participation of Hull merchants, and the Walkers of Rotherham shipped cannon to the Royal arsenals under their own name. The same is true of some coastwise imports. 'The wool brought to this port', wrote the Hull Customs officers to the Board of Commissioners, in July 1789,[1]

> is very considerable it being consigned to persons residing at Leeds, Wakefield, Halifax and other principal Woollen Manufacturing Towns to which the River Humber has navigable connexions and is delivered from the Vessels which bring the same coastwise into smaller Vessels provided for the purpose in the presence of the Coastwaiter Inwards who attends the delivery thereof after which the same is taken to the place of its consignment without being put on shore until its arrival there.

Crawshay & Company of London were among those who regularly shipped iron coastwise into Hull, and Deponthieu & Company of London entered linen yarn.[2] While Hull merchants still figure among the leading coastal merchants, many of the names appearing in the Coastal Port Books do not appear in the Foreign ones. Some of them were wharfingers, or men—like Robert Standidge—who concentrated on coastal trade, but many were probably not Hull people.

3. OVERSEAS AGENTS

Foreign correspondents were essential for the development of international trade, and Hull merchants had contact with their fellows in many parts of Europe and America. Unfortunately it was not easy at the beginning of the century to find agents in the relatively undeveloped northern and eastern Baltic, where it was left to Dutch, German and British merchants to open up trade. They had to encourage suppliers of raw materials, and make their own markets, by sending representatives abroad. For several generations the Wilberforces, Maisters, Henworths, Mowlds, Fearnleys and other

[1] HCLB, C–B, 6 Jul 1789.

[2] Deponthieu & Co. had at least one connection with Hull: John Deponthieu married Mary, the niece of Joseph Sykes and sister of Sir Christopher Sykes. Unfortunately it is not clear whether the marriage took place before or after trade began.

leading families had at least one member resident in Scandinavia or Russia. Sometimes the head of the family made a tour of inspection, visiting factories and customers. William Crowle begged the Bench of Aldermen not to make him a nominee for a forthcoming election in 1700 because 'his occasions this year would require his going beyond the Seas for several months. . .'.[1] Visits of this kind were, however, unusual once a merchant had succeeded to the headship of his family business. It was not difficult deciding who should go. 'I'm tyed and nailed down in this hole,' wrote one of the Henworths (of Gothenburg), 'by the fate of a younger brother.'[2] Henworth pined for the pleasurable society of Hull, and soon returned to the arms of his partner's sister, Elizabeth Maister. Others, more patient perhaps, built up large businesses and secured a position and income which did not involve eating into the Hull house's profits.

Factors were not entirely dependent on their Principals in Hull. It was usual for them to act in partnerships bearing little relationship to the family concerns they represented. Henworth, for example, went to join a Maister, and when he sold his position after eight years, for £750, it was to a Grundy nominated by Thomas Broadley (his brother- or father-in-law). The Hull Maisters also held a large share in the partnership. 'Agreed with William Maister', noted the Hull house in its Day Book, *c.* 1733, 'to accept for the net produce of the co-partnership Acct with the late William Henworth . . . the sum of C.200,000'[3] (roughly £5,000). The Mowlds and Wilberforces were also in partnership—and Grundy was originally with them before joining Maister—but it was not a happy union, and there was a good deal of bickering between Wilberforce and Samuel Mowld: 'we have never had a good opinion of Mr. W., having ever found him very unsteady . . .', was Maister's comment on one occasion.[4]

These factory partnerships were not based exclusively on Sweden. Indeed, the value of partnership lay in the fact that the partners resided in different countries and maintained a network of com-

[1] BB viii, 465 (18 Jul 1700).

[2] William Henworth, Gothenburg, to Thomas Broadley, Hull, 26 Apr 1725; *WH* Broadley MSS. Extensive use has been made here of this collection of letters from Broadley's Baltic Factors.

[3] *WH* Maister Accounts. William Maister was virtually in exile, owing money to various members of his family, with no prospect of repaying them. He died abroad.

[4] *WM* Broadley MSS, 9 Jun 1729.

munications throughout the Baltic. Thomas Mowld was based on Gothenburg, Samuel Mowld and Wilberforce on Narva. Henworth appears to have remained in Gothenburg, but Grundy had experience of both Gothenburg and Narva. Every important trading centre had at least one Hull man in residence. William Hobman was operating in Danzig in the forties, doing business with his brother-in-law, Richard Sykes, and his brother, Randolph Hobman.[1] Thomas Fearnley represented the Hull firm of Haworth & Stephenson—later Stephenson & Fearnley—in Norway for many years;[2] and a bankrupt cousin, Joseph Turner, was sent off to represent the Peases in Bremen.[3] St. Petersburg, as yet undeveloped, presented the greatest challenge in the first half of the century and, ultimately, the greatest rewards. There was apparently no Hull Factory there in 1725, when Grundy advised Thomas Broadley to consider establishing one. Unfortunately no details at all have survived to illustrate the growth of Hull's interest in St. Petersburg, but we may assume from Hull's predominant position in St. Petersburg's trade that Hull men must have been there from an early date. Certainly at the end of the century the Thorntons were the greatest merchant house in St. Petersburg if the figures quoted by J. J. Oddy are to be relied on.[4]

The various Factors did not work closely together, even when they knew each other personally. There was, in fact, considerable rivalry between the two groups—Maister & Henworth and Wilberforce & Mowld—about which we have information. In 1725, for instance, Maister & Henworth were being overbid for iron by other merchants, and the price was being forced up. On several occasions their thoughts turned to an amalgamation of interest among Hull merchants to thwart the Swedes. 'Very probably in time', Maister wrote in 1729, 'the differences that have been amongst the Contoirs [Factors] dealing your way may be made up and the trade brought under one direction, which will be the only ready way to make a stay in this country worth while. . . .'[5] Whatever the outcome of the ensuing negotiations—in which the Mowlds objected to Grundy because he had deserted them—the fact remained that by 1730

[1] Details from will of William Hobman, Danzig; *GH* MS D944 (L).

[2] See H. S. K. Kent, *passim.*

[3] J. Pease, Hull, to J. R. Pease, 12 Sep 1770; *WH* 59/58/138.

[4] J. J. Oddy, *European Commerce*, p. 131.

[5] Maister to Broadley, 5 Feb 1729, *WH* Broadley MSS.

Maister, Grundy and Mowld were between them exporting almost 40 per cent of the iron leaving Gothenburg.[1]

In the middle of the century Hull men were prominent in the English Factory at Gothenburg. The papers of the Annual Meeting in March 1756 were signed by Robert Hall, John Hall, Senior and Junior, Robert McFarland and William Williamson, and there were others not present.[2] In 1763 English firms mentioned in the Factory accounts included [John] Scott & Robert McFarland, [John] Wilson & [..] Hall, Robert & Benjamin Hall and William Williamson.[3] Williamson, of Joseph & William Williamson, the greatest iron importers in Hull, remained (in partnership with George Carnegie) until the seventies, when he returned to run the family business in Hull. By then there were only Halls left. In many ways the most enterprising of the Hull men, they had their own iron-works which they showed to young Thomas Butler in 1789.[4] The firms—like Carnegie's—which remained at the end of the century were mostly Scottish. They were increasingly naturalised—some of them still exist—and can no longer be described as mere representatives of British interests.[5]

Just as the Factors were semi-independent of the Hull houses, so also they did business with a number of 'Principals' in England. The Maister & Henworth Factory supplied Joseph Pease and several other merchants in Hull, 'the only Gent in Newcastle that imports any iron' (a Mr. Moncaster), Messrs. Ferrand & Meet and Mr. Sly in Stockton, 'one Prankard of Bristol', and probably many others of whom we have no record. To obtain new customers in England, and in their attempt to dominate the Swedish market, the Factors relied on their English connexions. 'As long as you and my brother resolve to push the trade', Maister wrote to Thomas Broadley, 'and we can keep in with our friends in the outports and have Mr. Henworth to push for us in London I no ways fear enjoying a large share of business. . . .'[6]

[1] I am deeply indebted for this, and other information about the Swedish end of the trade, to Mrs. Elsa Britta-Grage.

[2] See A. A. Cormack, *Susan Carnegie* (Aberdeen, 1966), p. 163.

[3] ibid., p. 167.

[4] R. Butler, *Kirkstall Forge*, p. 26.

[5] George Carnegie sent two of his sons to learn the business with Williamsons in Hull, but they were unable to find places on their return to Sweden and eventually went to India; Cormack, pp. 194–6.

[6] *WH* Broadley MSS, 25 Aug 1729.

The majority of firms never had their own related Factors abroad, for a private Factory was a sign of greatness to which only the principal firms aspired. The rest either made do with the existing Factories, or made contact with other firms already established in the Baltic. Colletts & Leuch of Christiania served Andrew Perrott and Samuel Dawson just as well—to judge from their letters—as a related firm would have done, perhaps better in the absence of family jealousy and inter-family rivalry. Even the Maisters made use of an independent man—Hans Ström—in Gothenburg in the thirties, although this may be due to the duties introduced on foreign Factors exporting from Sweden.

The related Factory was a temporary feature of Hull's international relations, adopted out of necessity to deal with primitive economies. The stimulation of those economies by the Factors led to the development of a native commercial system which made them superfluous. They died out at different times in different places. Those in Sweden were the first to go. Penal duties in Sweden on foreign Factors coincided with expanding opportunities in Hull itself to encourage younger sons to stay at home, and the close personal and financial link between Hull and Sweden was dissolved. It was in Russia that the English Factors remained the longest. Firms such as Thorley, Bolton, Ouchterloney & Co. of Narva and Thornton, Cayley & Co. of St. Petersburg continued to dominate Russian trade and finance into the nineteenth century, but they too had ceased to be greatly interested in Hull, although the junior branch of the Thorleys maintained their business until Christopher Thorley went bankrupt, and Robert Thorley of Narva was the largest single shareholder in the Hull Dock Company.[1]

While overseas connexions were necessary for the normal run of business, it was possible on some occasions to deal with intermediaries in England. This was particularly true towards the end of the century as Swedish and Russian houses opened branches in London. Wray & Hollingsworth, for example, bought Swedish iron through Claes Grill, and iron and steel through Wahrendorff & Co. (a Stockholm house).[2] From Stippins & Co. they secured Archangel masts, and logs from John Warburton. Messrs. M. & T.

[1] As late as 1797 Thorley & Co. were acting for Wilberforce & Smiths and William Osbourne, according to their account with Smiths & Thompson's Bank.

[2] These examples are from Wray & Hollingsworth's Letter Books, *passim*.

Yeldhams regularly supplied feathers, old iron and deals. 'Some little time ago', they wrote in 1791, 'our House mentioned having secured of Odinzeff an additional quantity of Deals. . . . We will . . . allot you two more cargoes. . . .'[1] Sometimes the London agents of foreign firms also received payments as well as orders. Money due to Messrs. Forsyth, Pillans & Co. of St. Petersburg was claimed from Wray & Hollingsworth by Forsyth, Hamilton & Jouray of London in 1795. It is probably evidence of the intimacy and strength of Hull's connexions with the Baltic that only one such house—Brandström & Küsel—set up in Hull in the eighteenth century.

London agents were also used in the export trade to the south of Europe. The Maisters regularly sent lead to France in the first quarter of the century '. . . for account of Messrs. Renue, Ferriano & Renue, Merchants in London, and by their order consigned to Mr. Behotte, merchant in Rouen'.[2] Similarly, when they took part in the corn trade in the thirties and forties, they were in despair if they could not ship to the order of one of their London contacts, Mr. Bance, with whom Henry Maister, a Member of Parliament, did business in the Chamber of the House of Commons! When lead was in poor demand it simply piled up in the warehouse awaiting a rise in the price, but corn was a serious worry because of deterioration if it was not carefully tended. On one occasion Nathaniel Maister sent off a cargo to Messrs. Chase & Wilson of Lisbon on the off-chance that they might be able to get rid of it: 'By the recommendation of your friend Mr. Ambrose Wilson', he wrote, 'we have taken the liberty to consign to your care a small cargo of wheat . . . which we must desire your putting in the market with all expedition as our inclinations are to have a quick sale. . . .'[3]

Hull made its name as a Baltic port, but we should not forget the trade with the rest of Europe. Much of it—on paper if not in actual goods—was channelled through Holland, and here the situation was quite different. Merchant traded with merchant, and, if anything, it was the Hull man who was regarded as the novice, the newcomer to international trade. When young Joseph Pease was sent to Hull in 1708 it was as one sent into the wilderness, and thirty years later his brother was still sympathising with him, 'stuck over there'.[4] The

[1] ibid., 12 Jul 1791.
[2] Maister Day Book, Feb 1713/14.
[3] Maister Letters, copy in N. Maister to H. Maister, 22 Apr 1738.
[4] W. Pease, Amsterdam, to J. Pease, 7 Jan 1738, *WH* 59/58/44.

Dutch connexion was the most vital one that a merchant could have, for through it he was linked to the international payments centre in Amsterdam. It was here that the Peases came into their own, with their carefully preserved Dutch connexions—with father Robert Pease, brother William, and cousins Simkinson, Clifford, Reynst and Van Schuylenburgh. Joseph sent his son and two grandsons to Holland as apprentices, and his daughter, little Esje, spent so long with her uncle William that she forgot her English. Robert Pease, Joseph's only son, was constantly on the move between England, Ireland and Holland, spending months—perhaps years—in Amsterdam. In return their Dutch correspondents came to Hull to learn English—men like Isaac Valk of West Sann, a sawmiller who spent a year (1727) in Hull, and still remembered Joseph's kindness to him twenty-five years after.[1] Jan Swaan of Amsterdam, to whom Joseph regularly sent linseed cakes, oxen and horses, came to Hull for two or three months in 1747 to learn the language, and sent his daughter over to school in 1748 'that she may Assist him in his Business'.[2] A merchant neglected his language studies at his peril. In 1730, for example, Isacc Clifford sold red lead for Joseph to an Amsterdam merchant, commenting: 'it seems he has another Correspondent at your place, but Speakes no Dutch So he is at a loss. . . .'[3]

Amsterdam was the commercial centre of Europe, and an agent there could most effectively tap the crossflow of international trade. So Isaac Clifford bought linseed from Konigsberg and staves from Danzig; William Pease secured madder for the Thorntons, German iron and steel for the Sykes, and whale-fins for Joseph Turner and Joseph Pease—carefully wrapped, with fraternal greetings, round illicit canisters of Bohea tea.[4] So integrated were the English and Dutch branches of the Peases that their English coastal trade was directed from Amsterdam for fifteen years without any apparent ill effect.

Correspondents, whether Factors or merchants, were expected to place orders to the instructions of the Hull house, and keep it constantly informed of the state of the market abroad. An accurate knowledge of the movement of prices on the continent, and of events

[1] R. Pease, Amsterdam, to J. Pease, 22 Sep 1752, *WH* 59/58/39.

[2] R. Pease to J. Pease, 7 Aug 1747, ibid.

[3] I. Clifford, Amsterdam, to J. Pease, 28 Mar 1730, *WH* 59/58/46.

[4] W. Pease, Amsterdam, to J. Pease, 26 May 1722, *WH* 59/58/44.

likely to affect prices, was essential to a merchant trying to estimate an economic buying or selling price in Hull—or Sheffield or Manchester. The Maister & Henworth Factory wrote post haste when the Swedes were trying to sell inferior iron at inflated prices, when the 'Gentry . . . hold up the prices . . .', or when stocks were low or high. 'You may be assured,' they told Thomas Broadley in 1728, 'that the Leeds men won't have half their usual quantity to Hull this year, and that your import from Stockholm will in all likelyhood be very inconsiderable.'[1] 'There will be a large demand for our iron', they added, needlessly. William Pease was a mine of general intelligence for his brother. He reported price movements by every post, and gave advice about possible shipments: corn samples should be sent to Hamburg, a 'tryall' of rape oil to Bordeaux, corn to Amsterdam, shot to Hamburg, and so on. News of Utrecht was sent by express to beat the London mails, preceding by a century the famous Rothschild packet after Waterloo.[2] 'I think this News may make Lead rise with you', wrote William, and suggested a joint purchase before the news broke. Occasionally Joseph overdid things. When Cliffords expressed an interest in Linseed cakes he decided to send them a whole year's production—23,000 cakes—which produced an anguished cry from cousin Isaac: 'we should soon be over Stockt over head and Ears. . . .'[3] On another occasion, when he had credit in Newcastle which he could not conveniently collect, Joseph simply ordered litharge to be sent to William and drew on Amsterdam. 'You'l quite weary me of Your Correspondence . . .', retorted his brother, 'if exercise your Cross & ill natured Temper . . ., being would have me Sell whats a Loss and not feazable. . . .'[4]

In the Baltic trade it was generally best to place orders in advance, often from one year to the next, with ships wintering in the Baltic to save a week or two when the spring thaw started. The process of ordering and shipping deals, for example, is admirably summed up in a long letter from Colletts & Leuch of Christiania to Samuel Dawson:[5]

Since our last the 29 past Captain Jn Dickinson brought us your very acceptable of the 1st ditto with an order to load on board his ship the loading as we had already in course of your order in the

[1] *WH* Broadley MSS, 2 Aug 1728.
[2] W. Pease, Amsterdam, to J. Pease, 12 Apr 1713, *WH* 59/58/44.
[3] I. Clifford, Amsterdam, to J. Pease, 12 Dec 1730, *WH* 59/58/46.
[4] W. Pease, Amsterdam, to J. Pease, 22 Jan 1737, *WH* 59/58/44.
[5] *SCRL* Tibbitts 516—15, 5 Dec 1719.

winter, the which is accomplished as near as possible and as the ship would permit us for conviency of stowage, no doubting but it will give you content both in goodness and price, for you may depend on it had not wanted on our particular care (nor never shall) in observing your interest, whereby you have the advantage of one dollar in each hundred of deals, for they actually pay now a dollar more than you is charged, and most the same our very good friend Mr. Perrott in Hull paid being he had not given order beforehand which did not little trouble us and at the same time his ship (for about 14 days ago) was here, we were not able to obtain so many good deals as we wanted, if would give never so much for you, so was forced to load some uffers. We have according to your order to the master, loaded some ladder poles, which it be to content or not we desire your mind for another time that it may be altered.

You have here inclosed the bill of loading and invoice of all, for the amount of which we've debited your Account Current with 777 Dollars and after having deducted the £100 drawn in the winter, we shall take the freedom to draw the ballance on Mr. Hackshaw as permitted and give you all advantage possible in the Exchange.

If you should incline for sending another ship here this year we desire to know your mind as soon as possible, for goods are very scarce and consequently dear, but as we said in above mentioned our last we expect some in by Waggons (which will come dearer than ordinair being that carriage is more chargeable than in the winter) we hope to find means to furnish you with a good loading about the middle of next month.

Financial advances, as described in Collett's letter, played an important part in trade with Scandinavia, for in order to keep the economy of Norway and Sweden alive English merchants had to pay for at least part of their orders while they were still being assembled from mine or forest. An advance assured delivery, often at a lower price than was paid later. In 1772 Williamsons' agents in Gothenburg, Carnegie & Shepherd, were, they said, 'not a little surprised, indeed, to see our neighbours ship out their iron for less than what could sell same for here; the reason of which we believe is that your neighbour [i.e. Sykes] advanced ours a pretty large sum in the winter for which we presume they now make their acknowledgement to him'.[1] Similarly, according to Kent, 'credits to Norway might have to be advanced for two or three years otherwise a valuable connexion might be lost'.[2] His evidence is drawn from the Fearnley MSS and relates directly to Hull.

When merchant and factor or agent were closely related by family

[1] Carnegie & Shepherd's Letter Book, 10 Jul 1771. I owe this reference to Mrs. Britta-Grage. [2] H. S. K. Kent, p. 69.

or financial ties, it was common for adventures to be undertaken on joint account rather than on a commission basis. In the thirties and forties the Maisters were receiving iron cargoes shared with Maister & Grundy and also with their financial agents, the Cliffords in Amsterdam. Sometimes the division was not even a simple one; on at least one occasion it was three-eighths belonging to Maister & Grundy, three-eighths to Cliffords and only two-eighths to the Hull house.[1] The Peases also made use of shared cargoes in the lead trade, but the difficulties they ran into emphasise the fact that this kind of commercial arrangement was unsatisfactory outside the Baltic, and even there it is unlikely to have outlasted the Factors. A great deal more evidence is, however, necessary before we can pronounce judgement on shared cargoes after the middle of the century.

Apart from goods carried on behalf of various merchants or Factors, it was customary for masters to ship goods on their own accounts. Starting with odds and ends of ballast goods, especially ale and coal, they no doubt hoped eventually to emerge as merchants in their own right. Certainly they were in a position to explore the possibilities of a variety of markets, but the Hull-Baltic trade was not one in which masters or supercargoes figured prominently. Foreign masters were a good deal more important. A considerable number of small ships arrived without prior arrangement for the disposal of their cargoes, which were almost always timber from Norway or fruit from southern Europe. The masters of smaller foreign ships—they were not all that common in eighteenth century Hull—were almost always responsible for at least some part of their cargoes, which were more of a speculation than those of English ships. Nor was the speculation always successful; Anthony Atkinson, the Hull broker, was once called upon to act for the creditors when a Dutch galeot bringing staves from Danzig was auctioned to defray the bankruptcy of George Van der Berge, the sole owner and master.[2]

Occasionally the urge to trade hit the lower decks. Here and there a mate—usually related to the captain or merchant—endeavoured to supplement his income, and in the 1737 Port Book there is the fascinating record that five dozen tubs were entered by 'The Ships company, British, in *Eagle*'. Let the Maisters tremble!

[1] Details from *WH* Maister Accounts, *passim.*

[2] Stray letter in *WH* Chronological MSS.

VI. DEVELOPMENTS IN THE SHIPPING INDUSTRY

1. THE GROWTH OF THE MERCANTILE MARINE

Fluctuations in trade had an immediate effect on the shipping industry. Minor advances were covered by more intensive utilisation of shipping.[1] A slight extension of the season, or faster loading, might add a voyage to the trading year; ships might be better stowed; and they might be switched from one trade to another and from foreign to coastal runs to secure continuous employment. Major advances could not, however, be accommodated in this way. A heavy, sustained demand would force up freight rates unless the shipping interest—which must have had a rough idea of 'normal' demand—invested rapidly in new ships. Hull was subjected to just such a demand. The raw materials that were the mainstay of her import trade were extravagant consumers of shipping space, and Hull owners received far greater encouragement than would appear from a consideration of value alone. A ship-ton of silk cloth might be worth four hundred times as much as iron and four thousand times as much as timber, but it was the cheaper goods, not the luxuries, that filled the ships. This does not, of course, mean that Hull ships carried only low value cargoes (the Norwegian run, involving only timber, was in fact left for the most part to foreigners). Eastern Baltic cargoes were of surprisingly high value. The ships that crowded the harbour at Konigsberg loaded yarn worth—ship-ton for ship-ton—five times as much as tobacco, four times as much as sugar and three times as much as pepper. St. Petersburg flax was worth slightly more than sugar, and Riga hemp only a little less than tobacco.[2]

The response of the shipping interest to increasing demand can be followed in official estimates of tonnage 'belonging' to each port,

[1] Under-utilisation—'various forms of concealed unemployment that were taken for granted in normal times and could be reduced or extended as need arose without painful dislocation'—is dealt with very fully by R. Davis, *The Rise of the English Shipping Industry* (1962), pp. 193–7.

[2] Valuations in force in 1754 are quoted in Davis, p. 177.

available at seven-yearly intervals from 1702 and annually from 1751.[1] Unfortunately their accuracy is less impressive than their preciseness. Until 1786 the ships 'belonging' to a port were English ships that entered or cleared during the year—a reasonable guide to shipping *active* in a port, but at best only a rough indication of the tonnage *owned* there. Since ships were only counted in years in which they passed through Customs, the register fluctuated considerably. It was more immediately responsive to trade recessions and war than a modern register: ships laid up or on government service ceased to exist until trade revived or war ended.

Figures for war periods must therefore be recognised as exceptional, but in any case short term fluctuations had little effect on long term trends. A more important defect was the haphazard method of assessing tonnage. Until 1786, owners' estimates were accepted, and these varied from place to place and trade to trade.[2] Measurement became increasingly common after 1773, when a more careful compilation of statistics began,[3] and after the 1786 Registration Act (26 George III, c. 60) all ships had to be registered at measured tonnage in the port of ownership, whether or not they traded there. It follows, of course, that tonnage after 1788 must not be compared directly with tonnage before 1786.

Since the century began in war, the earliest figures are depressed. In 1702 and 1709 Hull was credited with approximately 7,500 tons of shipping, which is certainly not a true indication of peacetime needs. After the treaty of Utrecht the figure rose to about 12,000 tons, and there it remained until the first expansion of Hull's trade in the late forties. Between 1744 and 1754 tonnage increased by 50 per cent, almost certainly reflecting a sudden expansion of trade after the end of the War of the Austrian Succession. But the

[1] *BM* Add. MS 11255.

[2] The estimated tons burden was a ship's capacity bearing in mind her usual cargo, and this could be smaller—sometimes much smaller—than her theoretical capacity, particularly when bulky goods such as timber were carried. Underestimation may have had the effect of artificially depressing the tonnage figures in the first three-quarters of the century, but there is no reason for supposing that there was very much fluctuation in estimated size from year to year. The general movement of shipping figures fits in very well with the pattern of trade growth available in other sources.

[3] Measured tonnage in official returns was encouraged by 13 George III, c. 74. Ships entering the port were assessed at measured tonnage for the dock dues levied after 1774.

total, though boosted by the newly founded whaling fleet, was already declining when war broke out again in 1756.[1] The Seven Years' War had a more noticeable effect on the shipping figures than any other war of the century, and the fleet was down to 12,000 tons again by 1760. It was not until the return of peace that a rapid and fairly steady rise began which, except for the intervention of the American war, lasted into the nineteenth century.

Wars were always, before 1788, followed by additions to the register as ships were put back into service, but there was no precedent for the flood of new ships after 1783. Between the dark days of 1781 and the ending of the old registration system in 1786 the tonnage index moved from 53 to 100, an increase of 100 ships and 17,720 tons.[2] The arrival of large American ships (especially whalers) and the development of trade with the eastern Baltic helped to swell the register (and the average tonnage), and the change in 1788 added another 52 ships. Under the pressure of trade in the early nineties tonnage grew by approximately 32 per cent, to 611 ships totalling 68,533 tons in 1800, but one can hardly overlook the fact that the trend after 1783 was little different from what might have been expected had pre-war development continued unbroken. Hull acquired its fleet over a long period of time, and the bulk of the shipping required for the great trade expansion in the nineties was already on the register by the middle of the eighties. The tremendous increase in tonnage, by bringing down freight rates, was yet another of the favourable cost factors encouraging trade—and industry—at the end of the eighteenth century.

The total tonnage figures tend to mask the sharper—and sometimes divergent—movement taking place in foreign-going and coastal tonnages. In the first half of the century they both remained steady, making up roughly 55 and 45 per cent respectively of the total tonnage; then foreign-going tonnage drew rapidly ahead,

[1] The decline in foreign-going tonnage coincided with the rise in coastal tonnage, and may represent one phase of the movement in the relative importance of the overseas and British markets (see M. W. Flinn, *The Origins of the Industrial Revolution* (1966), Chap. IV). For Hull particularly, the relationship was determined partly by a greater dependence on the London entrepôt trade to the detriment of direct overseas trade.

[2] Some owners were beginning to declare measured tonnage before 1788, and this may account for some of the rise after 1783, as well as that between 1786 and 1788.

while coastal tonnage remained fairly steady until the mid-seventies. By 1786 coastal tonnage had doubled, to 10,971 tons, whereas foreign-going tonnage had trebled, to 21,265.

The two figures follow a roughly similar pattern except in times of stress. During the trade boom in the late forties, for example, ships were transferred from coastal to foreign trade. In the early years of the Seven Years' War, and more noticeably during the American Revolutionary war, the process was reversed, coastal tonnage increasing considerably as foreign-going tonnage declined. A desire for safety, and the ravages of the press-gang, were probably greater determinants than lack of trade, for the loss of tonnage in foreign trade was at least partially covered by the employment of neutral ships. British ships normally accounted for between 80 and 100 per cent of entries in peace time, but for only 39 per cent in 1709, 59 per cent in 1758, and 57 per cent in 1779.[1] The use of foreign ships was not, however, due entirely to the 'failure' of the English shipping industry; it was not unknown for owners to transfer to flags of convenience in wartime.

Ships 'belonging' to Hull also included whalers, which again were counted separately until 1786. They started with 1,453 tons in 1754, but for many years the total did not greatly exceed this original figure.[2] Expansion began in 1785, and at its height whaling accounted for about one-fifth of total tonnage, a factor which ought to be taken into account when considering growth in the period after 1785. Some at least of the ships added in the late eighties were not for normal trading purposes. We must, however, be cautious about dividing ships into categories. Some might always be used in the coastal, some always in the foreign trade; but it was a matter of personal choice rather than peculiar trade requirements until quite late in the century. Apart from the timber ships, which were often of special construction (and foreign-owned), the main difference was in the size of ships in particular trades. A coastal run or two filled up the winter schedule while the Baltic was frozen,

[1] The rise in foreign ships during the Seven Years' War can be followed in the record of 'Townes Dues of forraigners' (*GH* M.447):

	No.		*No.*
Year ending 8 April 1753	28	1756	32
1754	31	1757	69
1755	18	1758	85

[2] Whalers were counted at measured tonnage for bounty purposes, and 'Fishing' figures are therefore more accurate than other figures before 1788.

and foreign voyages often began or ended in a coastal trip, especially to or from London.

The growth in total tonnage was caused partly by the increase in the number of ships and partly by a rise in their average size. English ships clearing from Hull in the war period 1710–17 (inclusive) had averaged roughly 74 tons, a sorry figure compared with 111 tons for foreign ships.[1] In 1737 the average of English and foreign ships together was even lower—58 tons—and it was just under 100 tons in 1758. The average inwards—77 tons in 1737 and 111 in 1758—was a little larger, but still unimpressive, and must have been pulled down by many tiny vessels. All that can be said with certainty is that there was a tendency for ships to grow slightly—but not much—larger in the first half of the century, and for larger vessels to clear in ballast. It was in the sixties that the English average began to grow noticeably, and foreign ships were soon left behind. Clearances averaged 134 tons by 1770, 174 tons in 1790 and no less than 203 tons in 1798.[2] Entries were about thirty tons larger: 153 tons in 1770, 203 in 1790 and 232 in 1798. Average figures are, however, misleading. There was no average ship, and the general increase which did take place was almost negligible. There were many small vessels in 1800, as there were in 1700, but the proportion of larger ships had increased. The growth in average tonnage clearly coincided with the development of extensive trade with the eastern Baltic.[3] Ships built for the Russian and Prussian trades were much bigger than those employed elsewhere, as can be seen from an analysis of ships entering Hull in 1790:[4]

AVERAGE TONNAGE OF SHIPS ENTERING FROM INDIVIDUAL COUNTRIES, 1790

From	*No.*	*Average Tons*	*From*	*No.*	*Average Tons*
Norway	16	100	Netherlands	15	136
Sweden	37	232	France	39	96
Russia	109	277	Spain	4	149

[1] Calculated from figures in *PRO* CO 388—18 and 390—8.

[2] Figures for 1798 are from HCLB, C–B, 12 Jan 1799. Obviously some of the rise between 1770 and 1790 was caused by re-registration in 1787. The average 'Hull' ship rose by about 20 tons, and if this kind of figure is reasonable for ships trading, there was still a significant rise in average tonnage trading.

[3] 30 per cent of entries came from the eastern Baltic in 1766, 45 per cent in 1790.

[4] *PRO* Customs 17/12.

From	No.	Average Tons	From	No.	Average Tons
Poland	15	149	Portugal	14	179
Prussia	82	256	Italy	6	213
Germany	35	119	Ireland	4	103
Holland	66	110	America	16	213
			Whaling	22	285

The highest average—285 tons—was in the whaling fleet, followed by the far more numerous Russian traders at 277 tons, Prussian traders at 256 tons, and Swedish iron ships at 232 tons. The average for the remaining countries, including a few large ships in the American and Italian trades, was no more than 127·5 tons.

The high proportion of large Baltic traders placed Hull in a leading position among the English ports:

AVERAGE TONNAGE OF SHIPS ENTERING AND LEAVING THE MAJOR PORTS, 1790

	TOTAL				AVERAGE	
	Inwards		*Outwards*		*In*	*Out*
	No.	*Tons*	*No.*	*Tons*	*Tons*	*Tons*
Bristol	545	70,668	487	63,734	129·7	130·9
Hull	484	95,962	302	51,060	198·3	169·1
Liverpool	2063	241,117	1975	237,884	116·9	120·4
London	3378	553,722	1869	322,895	163·9	172·8
Newcastle	248	35,364	570	96,620	142·6	169·5
Sunderland	702	105,314	700	102,393	150·0	146·3
Whitehaven	373	34,838	2185	230,562	93·4	105·5

She had the highest average tonnage for entries in 1790, with 198 tons—35 tons ahead of the nearest rival, London. In clearances, since many of the larger ships went to the Baltic in ballast, she dropped to third place with 169 tons, 3·7 tons behind London and 0·4 tons behind Newcastle. This does not, of course, mean that Hull owned more large ships than other major ports, but it does mean that she used them in a slightly different way. Liverpool and London, for example, had a rapid turn round in *small* ships trading with Ireland and adjacent Europe, while their largest ships were involved in long hauls, thus reducing the average tonnage of entries. In contrast Hull had a rapid turn round in *large* ships carrying raw materials from northern Europe, which increased her average. Hull in fact owned few very large ships, but many coasters, pilot and fishing boats, and Humber Keels.

AVERAGE TONNAGE OF SHIPS REGISTERED AT THE MAJOR PORTS, 30 SEPTEMBER 1790, DISTINGUISHING BRITISH BUILT SHIPS

	BRITISH BUILT SHIPS			ALL SHIPS		
	No.	*Tons*	*Av.*	*No.*	*Tons*	*Av.*
Bristol	246	34,272	139·3	301	43,469	144·4
Hull	406	50,432	124·2	443	54,676	123·4
Liverpool	425	59,940	141·0	523	83,696	160·0
London	1592	321,891	202·2	1842	378,574	205·5
Newcastle	501	107,418	214·4	534	115,426	216·2
Sunderland	375	52,757	140·7	388	53,933	139·0
Whitby	253	47,903	189·3	258	49,326	191·2
Whitehaven	438	51,993	118·7	461	54,525	118·3

Despite the fact that the average size of coasters was increasing, foreign-going, coastal and fishing vessels together averaged only 86 tons as late as 1772 and reached the highest point of the century in 1784 with 119 tons. Thereafter the average steadily declined (allowing for the 'increase' in 1788) as a host of small ships were added to the register. In 1790 no fewer than 212 out of 409 vessels, were under 100 tons, and by 1800 this proportion had increased to 350 out of 611.[1] By far the largest group, containing 228 vessels, fell between 40 and 60 tons (see Appendix 20).

2. THE EFFECTS OF WAR

Wars always created difficulties for the shipping industry which were not adequately offset by the higher freight rates which were charged. The slackening of trade reduced the demand for ships, which were unemployed or underemployed. Owners lost the return on their capital, seamen lost their jobs (and often their liberty), and the whole community suffered from the loss of business. Ships laid up for long periods were, literally and metaphorically, ruinous, and owners tried to keep them in employment. Some became privateers or were hired to the government as transports; others became coasters, and there is slight evidence for the sharing of coastal trade in an attempt to keep as many ships as possible at sea.

Those ships continuing in foreign trade faced increased hazards on the high seas from privateers and, occasionally, enemy battleships, although Hull underwriters were prepared to insure against

[1] For 1800 see *PRO* Customs 17/20.

capture and very few ships were lost in this way.[1] Armed ships sometimes braved capture, and advertised their departure 'with or without convoy', but sailing without convoy was generally disapproved of. After 1757—and probably before—sailings in wartime were regulated by the Hull Committee for Convoys, meeting under the chairmanship of the Mayor. 'At the request of the merchants of this place', he wrote to the Admiralty in April 1757,[2] 'I take the liberty to inform your Lordships, that they expect about 15 ships from Konigsberg, Danzig and Riga, will be at the Sound the first week in May. . . .' He requested 'a Convoy to be at Elsinore of the first May, to wait there a week or ten days and take under her protection such ships as are come down to the Sound in that time, and see them safe into the Humber'. Such requests were not always heeded and convoys were often cancelled or delayed because no escorts were available: the tempo of trade was generally slower in war than in peace time.

The importance of the convoy system was stressed many times by the Convoy Committee. Twenty ships, they said in April 1782, were awaiting escorts; 'their Cargoes consisting of various manufactures of this Kingdom cannot amount to less than £150,000 to £200,000'. A strong line was taken against masters who did not submit to the discipline of the convoy:[3]

Resolved the merchants be desired to ship no goods, nor the Underwriters take any Policy for the *Mars*, or any other ship in which Michael Metcalf shall go in the capacity of Master until he had made proper submission to Andrew Agnew Esq., Captain of *H.M.S. Fury* for misbehaviour and insulting him on his duty when under his convoy to Elsinore.

In the sixties ships straying from convoys were denied insurance,[4] and the position of the convoy was eventually regularised in 1798 when ships sailing alone were liable to a fine of £1,000—or £1,500 if they carried naval stores.[5]

[1] Capture did not necessarily mean total loss. Many privateers found it simpler—and no doubt more profitable in the long run—to hold ships to ransom. In 1778 the *Elbe*, with a cargo worth £2,160, and *Ann*, with a cargo worth £5,819, were ransomed for no more than £800 each; HCLB, C–B, 21 Oct 1778.

[2] *GH* Minutes of Committee of Convoy, 2 Apr 1757.

[3] ibid., 22 Aug 1780.

[4] See p. 153.

[5] 38 George III, c. 76.

Although embargoes and convoys delayed or obstructed trade, far more serious in its immediate effect on shipping was the Press-gang. By taking seamen from the merchant marine it imperilled efficiency and reduced the number of vessels available for trade. The insecurity of crews—which might be 'lost' before ships left port—made it difficult to guarantee charterparties, and those lucky seamen who remained demanded excessive wages which inflated the cost of freight. Those who thought more of freedom than high wages fled inland, but even there they were not entirely safe. 'Last Thursday', the *Leeds Intelligencer* reported on 1 May 1759, '27 volunteers and impressed Seamen were put on board a vessel at our Bridge in order to be conveyed to Hull.'

The effects of a Press could be well-nigh catastrophic. It has been estimated that five-sixths or more of the merchant seamen might be taken to man the navy during a heavy campaign, although they would not necessarily remain in the navy for very long periods.[1] 'All business with us is suddenly swept by an embargo,' one merchant complained in March 1756, 'and the few hands that are left, mostly swept away in one night's press.'[2] The result was that although the Corporation were prepared to give bounties to encourage seamen to enlist, they resolutely opposed pressing on several occasions. 'I arrived on June 23rd by their Lordships order to raise men for H.M. Service,' one Press Officer wrote in 1759.[3] 'According to my instructions I went at once to the Mayor for him to sign my warrant; when he told me that I should not press in the town, nor would he sign my warrant.' The Gang managed to get 'about twenty brave men without the help of the Mayor', but 'As for the town', he said, 'I shall take care and bring no gang in it to press until I have further orders'. A less cautious Press Officer found himself bound over to the Quarter Sessions along with his gang, for assaulting citizens of Hull; and his 'contempt of all civil authority', in threatening 'a certain Alderman whom if he could meet with out of the liberties of this Town, he would wring by the nose, as long as his fingers and thumb could hold together', was reported to the Duke of Newcastle, 'to be laid before his Majesty in Council'.[4]

[1] R. Davis, pp. 320–7.

[2] Plumtree of Gainsborough; C. A. J. Skeel, 'The Letter Books of a Quaker Merchant, 1756–58', in *English Historical Review*, Jan 1916.

[3] Lieutenant Ryder to Thomas Grimston, 30 Jun 1758, *BM* Du Cane MSS.

[4] The episode is recorded in Hadley, pp. 315–19.

Sometimes a press was allowed. 'The sea ports are certainly the places where numbers are to be met with,' Nathaniel Maister wrote in March 1758, 'and the Press gangs let nothing escape them that smells the least of tar.'[1] Almost exactly a year later the *Hull Courant* reported 'a very hot Press for Seamen, which occasioned the Gates of the Town to be shut at 7 o'clock after which search was made in some Publick Houses, and several useful Hands were pickt up'.[2] Although a Press might be 'official' it was still obstructed as much as possible. Various evasions were employed by seamen, and liberal assistance was given by the populace, including the constables who were sometimes called upon to assist the gang. 'I don't wonder', said Maister, 'at the small success of the constables in picking up vagrant seamen. It is natural to suppose that these latter will keep about the place where their friends reside; and there the connections are generally too strong between the constables of the several divisions and the people to make them exert themselves.' Even the Customs officers aided seamen. In 1755 Captain O'Brien of HMS *Peggy* complained to the Commissioners of Customs[3] that the Hull Customs sloop was landing seamen from merchant ships and then assisting the ships into port, and some years later a press ship went so far as to fire on a Customs boat which was thought to be carrying Greenland Protections out to a whaler.

It was the 'vagrant seamen' that were caught first—'such seafaring men as shall lurk about the town'—although the type would naturally depend on the number required. Towards the end of the century, when demand was becoming acute, Pitt introduced the simple plan that every ship leaving port should give up one sailor or two landsmen. The embargo became more than ever an obstacle to trade and the weapon of the press-gang, but with Pitt's plan in operation one wonders how many ships' crews were tempted to do a little press-ganging of their own.[4]

[1] N. Maister to Thomas Grimston, 16 Mar 1758, Du Cane MSS.

[2] *Hull Courant*, 20 Mar 1759. Trinity House do not appear to have regarded the press-gang with quite as much disfavour as the Bench, or perhaps they tried to come to terms with the inevitable in an attempt to mitigate its effects: in 1777 and 1802 they elected officers of the 'Impress' as Honorary Elder Brethren (four in all).

[3] HCLB, C–B, 15 Aug 1755.

[4] Pitt's scheme was not, in fact, original. Five Hull ships were allowed to sail in 1740 after surrendering two men each for naval service; *Calendar of Treasury Books and Papers, 1740*, pp. 355–6.

3. THE EMERGENCE OF THE SHIPOWNER

Shipowning was, for most of the eighteenth century, part of the complex activity of merchanting. There were plenty of shipowning companies, but few men for whom shipowning was an important source of income. Contrary to general commercial practice after the Bubble Act, ships were owned by a form of joint-stock company. From time immemorial ships had been divided into shares, from fourths to sixty-fourths, and they were held as a matter of course by merchants who thereby spread their risks in a sphere where the hazards of nature probably played as great a part as human judgement in balancing profit and loss.[1] Insurance was not an adequate alternative until late in the century, and a quarter of four ships was undoubtedly a better investment than the whole of one.

Commercial hazards were only slightly less than natural ones. A merchant's only long term capital investments were his warehouse and his ships. Warehouses were essential, but he could—in theory—follow his inclination about ships: he did not have to own shares. If at the end of a successful year he invested in shares he might be rewarded for his foresight, or punished for his lack of it. In the merchants' world of infinite variables the all-important investment decision, though based on experienced commercial judgement, was still something of a gamble, and the existence of the small share must have greatly eased the decision to invest in new ships in the early stages of growth after 1775.

This does not, of course, mean that all ships were equally shared. There was usually a principal owner, a leading merchant with a controlling interest. The Sykes were the principal owners of a fleet of at least seven ships—*Triton*, *Victory*, *True Briton*, *Shepherdess*, *Industry*, *Sykes* and *Duke of Cumberland*—in which they imported iron ore from Sweden in 1747;[2] Alderman Perrott presumbly had a controlling interest in the *Perrott*, in which he imported linen yarn; James Hamilton had the *Crowle*, *Bayard*, *Bosville*, *Ann* and *York*; and so on. Occasionally the records reveal a sole owner, usually the master of a coaster, or of the cheapest kind of

[1] It should be noted, however, that shares in a ship were not owned *in partnership*. They were independent properties that could be disposed of without reference to the other owners.

[2] HCLB, C–B, 28 Jan 1749.

small foreign-going vessel used in the short distance runs. Thomas Lambkin, for instance, owned the *Emanuel*, which he took to Norway in 1752 for deals for Alderman Perrott. 'But being unable by some means to proceed on her voyage he bought the Experience of the Burgesses of Christiana which had been sunk on the Coast of Norway four years before: and having got her Weighed up he carried her to Moss where he took in the present Cargo.' The *Experience* was not a good bargain. She was, the Customs men thought, 'so old and Crazy that it was with difficulty he arrived in England, and he cannot pretend to proceed with her to any foreign port'.[1] Only rarely did a sole owner—like Joseph Pease in the early thirties—possess a five hundred tonner.

The shipowning group was founded, and its business directed, by the managing owner. He might be a merchant, providing ships for trades in which he was interested by assembling outside capital, sometimes from non-mercantile sources; or he might be a master. When a mate secured his first command he moved firmly into the ranks of the mercantile middle class. His responsibilities were great, but so were his rewards. The perquisites of command included the right to ship goods in unused space, and a man with connexions at home and abroad, and with first-hand knowledge of local economic conditions, might make his fortune in a relatively short time. Samuel Standidge was reputed to have made enough out of a single voyage to America to buy a 120-acre farm in Preston (Holderness), which he called New York as a memorial to his good fortune.[2] But to be placed in a position to make a fortune, a man needed friends and capital. His chances of promotion by merit alone were slight; he was far more likely to buy his way into a ship. If he had sufficient backing he could organise his own company for which he would be master; or he might invest his savings in an existing company on condition that he became master. Most companies in fact insisted that their masters share in the ship—and often the cargo as well—as a guarantee of good faith. The master, then, was the central figure in many shipowning companies, and it was he, rather than the merchant, who emerged eventually as the specialist shipowner.

The evolution of the shipowner, as distinct from the shipowning merchant or master, is a feature of the second half of the eighteenth century—though not all ships were owned by specialist shipowners.

[1] HCLB, C–B, 29 Jan 1752.

[2] G. Poulson, *History . . . of Holderness*, II, p. 495.

As commerce made greater demands on the shipping fleet, men put a greater proportion of their working capital into shipowning, encouraged, no doubt, by greater profitability as large ships settled down to regular runs, loaded to capital by the brokers and fully protected by the underwriters. In the past the successful master had become a merchant. Now he tended to put his savings into shares, and left the sea as a shipowner. His sons remained masters until they in turn left the sea, and thus there emerged a pattern of shipowning families which was firmly established by the end of the century.

There was, of course, a long transitional period, during which shipowning came to be recognised as a distinct profession, though not necessarily a full-time one. The first direct references to shipowners appear in the Apprenticeship records, where owners began to define their profession in their eagerness to recruit steady, cheap labour. The first man to call himself a shipowner officially was William King, who took apprentices in 1766 as 'merchant & shipowner',[1] and in 1771 Benjamin Blaydes, the merchant and shipbuilder, took apprentices as 'Owner of the British Queen'.[2] John Staniforth, one of the leading figures in Hull at the end of the century, was the first man to use the term 'shipowner' alone, in 1773,[3] and it came into common use in 1775.

The majority of men now describing themselves as shipowners had previously been master mariners. The term was not generally used by merchant shipowners unless they were taking apprentices, and only a handful did. Few landsmen who were not merchants collected shares with the avidity of masters, and then called themselves shipowners, although it was said of Henry Denton that his father kept asses 'and by mere dint of starving himself, saved as much as bought his son a share in a ship . . . and by the success of the share has risen to be a principal owner'.[4] Denton was in all probability an exception. Of the 114 'shipowners' who can be traced between 1766 and 1800, 81 can be cross-checked in other sources, and of these no fewer than 54 prove to have been master mariners.[5]

[1] IIA, 1766–87, No. 64, 4 Jun 1766. [2] ibid., No. 377, 4 Apr 1771.
[3] ibid., No. 469, 14 Jun 1773. [4] Strother, f. 27, 30 Sep 1784.
[5] Some outstanding recent research on the Liverpool Shipping Registers (R. Craig and R. Jarvis, *Liverpool Registry of Merchant Ships* (1967)) has revealed an interesting contrast between shipowning there and in Hull. The overwhelming proportion of Liverpool ship shares were owned by

Of the rest, ten were, among other things, shipbuilders. Forty-five shipowners were listed in *Battle's Directory* for 1791–2, and of these at least twenty-nine were originally masters, including Peter Atkinson, master mariner in 1791 and shipowner in the revised edition of 1792. Further evidence would no doubt increase the number of owners directly concerned with shipping, either as masters or builders.

It is in the whaling fleet that the shipowner can first be recognised. Here for the first time were ships not regularly engaged in trade and therefore owned as a matter of course by merchants. Here, moreover, were heavily subsidised ships. With the bounty at forty shillings per ton, the prime cost of a whaler was recovered in four years; there was no better ship in which a competent master could invest. Samuel Standidge led the way, taking his first ship to Greenland in 1766, forming a company to provide another in 1767 and yet another in 1768, when he appears to have moved ashore. Charles Shipman sailed as a master for Standidge before he also became a shipowner, and at one time or another Robert Gee, Daniel Macpharson, John Staniforth and Daniel Tong were to be found in the Arctic, while Humphrey Foord was for many years the leading captain in the whaling industry. The owners who appear most frequently to be taking apprentices were whaler owners, and the rather sudden appearance of 'shipowner' in the records in 1774–5 coincides with the first considerable expansion in the whaling industry.

merchants as late as the end of the century (Craig, Table 26), and the range of occupations of small shareholders was much narrower than in Hull. The Hull Registers are lost, but there are good grounds for assuming a greater number (proportionally) of small shareholders from more diverse backgrounds. Available evidence suggests that merchants did not dominate Hull shipping in the last quarter of the century to the extent they did in Liverpool. The reason for this probably lies in the nature of the respective trades. Hull ships were fewer, smaller and less valuable than those of Liverpool, thus bringing their shares within reach of less wealthy people; and it is possible that Hull partnerships were larger than those in Liverpool, which appear in general to have been quite small (Craig, Table 25). With shorter voyages, ships were not so deeply involved in the affairs of a small group of merchants, who found it less necessary to own their own ships. But above all, there was a long tradition of master-shipowning which led to the emergence of the shipowner independent of merchanting, though it is certain that the Hull 'shipowners' held nothing like the tonnage attributed to merchants in Liverpool (Craig, Table 20).

By the end of the century the shipowner had made his mark on the economic and social life of Hull. John Staniforth M.P. and Sir Samuel Standidge were leading citizens; William Hammond, who owned the 650-ton *Yorkshire*—'the seventh ship of large tonnage this gentleman has had built at Whitby within the last few years'[1]—was the dominant influence in the Dock Company and Trinity House. Even so the specialist shipowner had not yet completely supplanted the man for whom ownership was an ancillary function. John Voase, sole owner of the *Prince of Brazil* and joint owner of the *Hull Packet*,[2] took apprentices as a shipowner, but described himself in the 1791–2 *Directory* as a wine merchant; and William Watson Bolton, head of the Bolton group of whaler-owning companies, was an oil miller and surgeon. The Terrys, with large shares in at least a dozen vessels, continued to call themselves merchants, brokers, or simply Gentlemen. Moreover, there was still a place for the small shareholder in shipowning, and if anything the diversity of occupation among small shareholders was increasing in the last quarter of the century as the expansion of the shipping fleet provided a field for the investment of relatively small sums of money. Managing owners like John Burstall, who specialised in the organisation of companies in which he was not the major shareholder, were able to draw capital from many sources. The *Hope* and *Actaeon*, for example, were owned by a company consisting of John Terry (described as a shipowner), two master mariners, a merchant, a victualler, a banker's clerk, a Gainsborough wharfinger and merchant—William Etherington—and a firm of cornfactors in Brigg. Shares were regularly owned outside Hull. John Smith, wharfinger, of Gainsborough, was the sole owner of the *Maria*; a Jamaican merchant had shares in the *Kingston*, Riga merchants in the *Woodhouse*, and London merchants in many vessels. Not the least interesting of the outsiders was Benjamin Wilson, the Burton brewer, who had one-sixteenth of a whaler owned principally by William Hammond, and one-third of the *Porter* and *Humber*, of which Thomas Barmby was the managing owner.[3]

[1] R. Weatherill, *The Ancient Port of Whitby and its Shipping* (1908), p. 87.

[2] Ownership details from HCLB, C–B, *passim.*

[3] Benjamin Wilson's Day Book, *passim.* I am indebted to Professor P. Matthias for this reference.

4. FREIGHT ARRANGEMENTS

The participation by some merchants in shipowning may have simplified for them the complicated process of finding the right ship at the right time—a process as vital to merchanting as securing the cargo or market. It was common for firms such as Sykes, Mowlds, Hamiltons and Scotts to employ their own ships in trades which interested them. For cheap bulky goods a whole ship might be taken, but no merchants, not even owners, were keen to take the whole of a valuable cargo. As laste as 1791 a merchant seeking ships for Italy thought that 'as the freight is very high, it is always customary for the owners of such vessels, to take a third or quarter part concern of the cargo on their own account . . .'.[1] Chartering in the early part of the century was in fact simplified by the predilection of merchants for the shared cargo, for which one member of the temporary partnership made all the freight and insurance arrangements.

A merchant wishing to hire a ship contacted the managing owner or master and, if they were willing, signed a 'Charterparty of Affreightment', by which the ship was 'hired and taken to freight'. The master agreed to load goods to the order of the merchant and deliver them at an appointed place within a specified period, and the merchant bound himself to pay a prescribed fee 'for the freight and hire of the ship'. Bonuses were payable if the ship arrived safely before the agreed time, and an additional fee if the merchant wished to retain the ship beyond a fixed date.

Ships which brought iron, timber, flax and other raw materials from the Baltic were usually chartered in Hull and sent out in ballast (not always directly). When Joseph Pease bought linseed in Konigsberg in 1719 he sent out his brother-in-law, Captain Lawrence Hill, specially for it, sending coal as ballast.[2] Similarly he chartered the *Union* in 1712 to sail to Rotterdam where she was to take on ballast for Konigsberg. There she was to load rye, tallow, potash and linseed, and sail to Amsterdam, where part of the cargo was to be delivered to one of Pease's correspondents.[3]

[1] John Peters of Falmouth to Andrew Hollingsworth, 17 Jul 1791; *WH* Autograph Letter Box. Peters, who wanted 2 or 3 ships to take pilchards to Italy, addressed his letter 'To any broker in Hull'.

[2] I. Clifford, Amsterdam, to Joseph Pease, 16 Dec 1719; *WH* 59/58/46.

[3] The Charterparty, dated 31 Jan 1712, is in *WH* 59/58/78.

The chief difficulties in chartering arose when ships were required for an unusual or unpopular run. Since the charterparty was legally binding and subject to bond, masters delayed signing as long as possible in the hope of finding an alternative client; merchants tried to avoid disappointment, with consequent delays, by concluding agreements as quickly as possible. One of them, Nathaniel Maister, confessed to using a little low cunning:[1]

I generally bind the master I agree with here by a note till the Charterparty is drawn up . . . and as it appears to be only by way of Memorandum they seldom scruple to sign it, thinking it of no force in case they would break off the voyage but I believe it would be found as binding as a charterparty if signed before witnesses. . . .

The Maisters, whose trade, to judge from their surviving papers, was generally efficient, ran into trouble when they sent corn to southern Europe in the forties. One master they engaged declined at the last minute to sail to Lisbon until he had a return cargo guaranteed. Another ship was found to be too small, and the next, engaged in London on a simple declaration of tonnage, turned out to be 'so sharp made and so long that [the master] dare not bring her into the haven, that we shall have a troublesome and chargeable piece of business to load her in the road'.[2] Maisters eventually got their corn off safetly, despite storms which delayed loading and a shortage of mats used for lining ships, but their experiences are enough to show that chartering a ship was sometimes almost impossible, and certainly tedious.

Too much should not be made of the instances where a merchant appears to have chartered a whole ship. Even with the bulkiest and cheapest raw materials it was the overwhelming practice for half a dozen or more merchants to freight goods in the same ship. They certainly did not charter a ship for a small quantity of goods on popular runs, such as those to Holland or Germany. There was a significant difference in organisation between the two cases. When a ship was chartered, the master went when and where the merchant required; otherwise the master, in consultation with the owners, decided the route, and merchants had to find a sailing to suit their requirements.[3]

[1] Maister Letters, 29 Apr 1744. [2] ibid.

[3] This was not always easy. 'I believe it will be in my power to serve your ship with several hundred casks of ale', Benjamin Wilson wrote to a master eager to secure ballast, 'provided you are willing to make the time of sailing

Gradually ships began to settle down in particular trades, as 'constant sailers', making the same run time after time. Strother noted the arrival, in December 1784, of the *Olive Branch*: 'this', he wrote, 'is the third voyage this year and the 50th that the ship has been to Riga'. So regular were some ships that owners in the Hamburg run were able to sign an elaborate agreement limiting sailings when trade declined during the Napoleonic occupation of Germany.[1] Eight owners agreed to contribute one ship each to a common pool, to sail by rota. They could load in Hamburg for no more than ten days, or until another Hull ship arrived, whichever was the longer, and poor freights were shared:

> . . . whenever it shall be deemed necessary to imploy two ships in loading at Hull at the same time the quantity of Earthenware or other goods which pay inferior freight to cases and bales and Hardware such goods . . . shall be equally divided between the two ships.

The growing complexity of commerce was soon felt by merchants seeking ships. The number of merchants rose; so, too, did the number and size of ships, the variety of goods and the ports with which Hull traded. The threatened confusion was averted by the emergence of the specialist intermediary—the broker. Merchants who acted for their fellows were already, in a limited way, performing the functions of brokers. In the middle of the century the proliferation of small merchant houses encouraged a number of men to sell their services as both ship and insurance brokers. Unfortunately Battle's *Directory* does not include a list of shipbrokers, so we have no means of checking how many were involved. Terry & Wright and Hall & Robinson, who handled the freight and insurance accounts of Wilberforce & Smiths, preferred to call themselves merchants or Gentlemen in the general section of the *Directory*; and we only know that Wray & Hollingsworth, the timber merchants, were brokers because some of their papers have survived.

The general section of the *Directory* does, however, include a number of people whose only, or chief occupation was providing a service to the merchant community. Seven called themselves shipbroker, and another three simply 'broker'. They came, like the specialist shipowner, from the quarter-deck rather than the count-

agreeable to ME.' Benjamin Wilson Papers. I owe this reference to Professor Mathias.

[1] 21 May 1802; *WH* Stanewell Deeds, Parcel 8(15).

ing house. At least five of them appeared as masters in the 1768 or 1775 Port Books, while only two were recognisably merchants. They would have the wide experience and contacts necessary for shipbroking; perhaps they lacked the capital that was essential for the more lucrative profession of shipowning.

The acquisition and disposal of shipping space was further eased with the rise of the Newspaper. Advertisements of 'Constant Sailers' and 'Ships laid on' (accompanied by the inevitable print of a sailing ship) were inserted in Newspapers in Hull and industrial centres such as Leeds, Sheffield and Birmingham. 'Laid on at Hull, for *Newport* in *Rhode Island*,' read one in the *Leeds Intelligencer* in 1770, 'The good sloop *Recovery*, Stanton Hazard, Master, who sails the 20th Sept. next. For Freight or Passage apply to John Burton Jun. in Hull; the Captain on board; or Mr. Samuel Elam in Leeds.'[1] Merchants and brokers both advertised for shipping space. John and William Hentig advertised in the *Hull Packet* in 1793 for 'Two Ships of 4 or 500 tons each to load Timber, with proper stowage, from the Baltic to Hull',[2] and in 1795 Terry & Wright advertised for 'several large ships to load masts at Riga and Petersburgh for England; and also Freight for 200–300 tons of Iron from Petersburgh per first ships'.[3] Hull commerce had never been so complex as it was in the nineties, but the process of finding a ship had never been so simple.

5. THE DEVELOPMENT OF LOCAL MARINE INSURANCE

The ever present desire to spread losses led to the development of marine insurance: owners bought safety for a premium determined by the degree of risk. Insurance was still very much in its infancy at the beginning of the eighteenth century.[4] It was already flourishing in London, but Hull had as yet no underwriters of her own. In their absence, use was made of facilities offered by London and Amsterdam agents. Cargoes imported from the Baltic by Maisters in the first quarter of the century were insured through Peter Baxter and Henry Lyell of London or Henry Chitty & Son of Amsterdam, and

[1] *Leeds Intelligencer*, 28 Aug 1770.

[2] *Hull Packet*, 5 Mar 1793.

[3] ibid., 9 Feb 1795.

[4] The insurance of goods was old, but insurance of ships did not become common until the French wars, *c.* 1700. See R. Davis, p. 87.

lead sent to France was insured by Renue, Ferriano & Renue of London, on whose orders shipments were made.[1] Robert Pease in Amsterdam arranged insurance there for his son and for their friends—from Hull to Memel and back, Hull to Stockholm, and so on.[2]

The spread of insurance to the outports, and the origins of local underwriting, are obscured by lack of evidence. Much of our information comes from Maister accounts and they, regrettably, are not available for the crucial years in the late twenties. By the thirties, when they are again available, insurance was handled exclusively in England, and the lists of names appearing in the accounts strengthen the belief that the underwriters were local men.[3] By the forties local underwriters were well established. 'I may write to London or get insured here . . .', Nathaniel Maister told his brother in 1744.[4] It transpired that London underwriters would not insure against French capture whereas Hull underwriters would, so he insured locally. 'The underwriters here', he said, 'agree to take 6 gns., in the Swede from Stockholm and are to return one guinea p.c. in case she lay till Spring therefore I have given G. Maddison orders to get a policy filled up and to get £600 insured.'[5] When whaling started, in 1754, ships were insured locally as a matter of course,[6] and men like Thomas Broadley were already writing into their trading partnerships clauses saving their right to act as underwriters.[7]

Maddison was the first insurance broker to appear in contemporary records, but the man who was later reputed to have started insurance in Hull was Edward Codd, whose son was for many years the Town Clerk. Fortunately for us, he died in the year in which Strother kept his Hull Journal, and the local gossip was duly recorded:[8]

[1] Maister Day Book, *passim.*

[2] See, for e.g., Robert Pease to J. Pease, 23 May 1713, and 23 Aug 1715, *WH* 59/58/43.

[3] The Day Book did on one occasion (25 Jun 1724) note that insurance was underwritten for '£500 by several'. It is possible that the several were Hull men.

[4] Maister Letters, 12 Nov 1744.

[5] ibid., 21 Nov 1744.

[6] Insurance accounts appear in several places in the Pease Bank Ledgers, with Pease himself as one of the underwriters.

[7] See Broadley's Partnerships Agreement with R. Thorley, 1749, DDHB/60/3.

[8] Strother, fol. 51, 17 Nov 1784.

When he first came to Hull he was Foot boy to Mr. Mountain Town Clerk after which he was taken into the closet as a writer from which he undertook the Business of Policy Broker and Underwriter and as there was no one of that Trade in Town at that time of his commencing business he made a considerable advantage. But other men seeing the Profits to be obtained by underwriting and Policy broking pushed into the trade and as every man has some friends so Mr. Codd's trade would naturally be dwindled from him that at length he had little trade left.

He nevertheless managed to leave a fortune of £5,000 at his death.

When Codd died, in 1784, insurance was both flourishing and highly organised. Battle's *Directory* listed no fewer than twenty-nine underwriters in 1791–2, all but five of them resident in Hull (Appendix 27). All of them were, or had been, engaged in trade. None of them took to underwriting as a specialised occupation; it was merely one facet of their many sided business and financial interests. Eight of them were members of families engaged in banking as well as trade;[1] three of them were recorded simply as 'Gents'; and the rest were 'considerable merchants'. By 1803 there were forty underwriters, of whom at least eleven resided outside Hull (Appendix 28).

The participation of underwriters who were not local men illustrates Hull's position as a centre of marine insurance. In 1791 John Saunders and William Jackson belonged to Whitby shipping interests, and William Hornby was a banker, merchant and shipowner of Gainsborough. Further afield lived John Wood of Beadnell, Northumberland, and Patrick Crighton, manager of the Dundee and Perth Shipping Company, who may also have had an interest in the coastal trade to Hull. In 1803 there were two men resident in Halifax (John Rhodes and Rowdon Briggs), one in Leeds (John Hebblethwaite), one in Barnsley (James Hindle) and one in Pocklington (John Bell).

Underwriters worked alone in the eighteenth century, prevented from forming partnerships by the Bubble Act of 1720.[2] For convenience sake, however, they associated closely together, and on 7

[1] Henry, Isaac, Robert and Charles Broadley, Thomas Harrison, George Knowsley, Richard Moxon and R. C. Pease.

[2] The Act prohibited all corporations except the Royal Exchange and the London Assurance Company, and also 'all such Societies and Partnerships as now are, or hereafter shall or may be entered into by any Person or Persons, for assuring Ships or Merchandizes at Sea . . .'. See C. Wright and C. E. Fayle, *A History of Lloyd's* (1928), pp. 61 and 250.

January 1794 those who 'for some time past signed and underwrote and still continue to sign and underwrite at Kingston-upon-Hull . . .' joined in formal agreement 'in order to promote dispatch and regularity in Underwriting Policies of Assurance and punctuality in the Payment of Losses and Averages'.[1] The seventeen clauses most probably codified the tradition of half a century. A number were aimed at protecting the interests of underwriters. Fraudulent over-insurance was countered by a demand for precise valuations, and the deliberate loss of small packages by a refusal to accept liability for parcels worth less than fifty pounds. Excessive risks were avoided by a refusal to accept liability for 'Boats or Whale lines that shall be lost in the Act of Fishing', and the dangerous part of the Baltic run was excluded by a strange clause that was sufficiently vague to mean almost anything: 'we will not . . . underwrite . . . ships or goods from the Baltic until 10 days after the Ships departure from her sailing port outwards.'

Other clauses protected the insured. Losses were to be 'immediately paid by a Bill on London not exceeding two months date', and premiums remained, as security, in the hands of the brokers until settlement day, the first of March. Finally, both sides gained from the declaration of a common premium rate, to be fixed (as nearly as possible to correspond with Lloyd's) at weekly meeting of the Committee of the Underwriters' Society. Hull had, indeed, secured its own version of Lloyd's; an underwriter who executed the agreement of the Underwriters' Society was a man to be trusted.

Every underwriter drew up his accounts in March and assessed his profit and loss for the previous year, but only two of these accounts have survived: Robert Ramsey's for 1799[2] and Robert C. Broadley's for 1807.[3] Ramsey simply pinned together the accounts sent to him by seven brokers or owners with whom he had regular dealings. Fifty policies on thirty-three ships are recorded, but only four of the accounts contain details of both liability and premium. In these he underwrote £4,252, for which he received premiums amounting to £184. 4*s.* 10*d.*, an average of 4·3 per cent.

Broadley's activities were on a more exalted plane. He had accounts with thirty-nine brokers or owners, ranging from £50 for a single master-owner to £7,400 for the most important of his brokers.

[1] The Agreement is *HUL* MS DA690 H9.

[2] *WH* Chronological MSS, 1799.

[3] DDHB/60/3.

Altogether he signed for approximately £33,000, his premiums amounting to no less than £2,485. This was not, of course, all profit.[1] In normal years Broadley would expect to make a profit, but in 1807 he was to be disappointed—the only reason why he preserved this single account. This was the year of the 'Danish Captures', when Hull ships were caught unawares at the Sound. Broadley had to pay out on twelve losses and five averages, which cost him over £2,100. Even so, he ended the most disastrous year which Hull underwriters had ever known, with a deficit of only £644.[2]

Insurance was an essential service, but it was not a charity. Underwriters were intent on making money, and premiums were very carefully calculated to make sure they did. On the other hand underwriting was not an investment in the normal sense, and a very small profit was acceptable. Insurance in the eighteenth century was, in general, cheap. Even in the midst of the troubles of 1807, Broadley was receiving premiums of one per cent, and the near-European and Baltic runs regularly cost only two, or at most three per cent. Allowing for seasonal fluctuations, there was no rise in premium rates on the Baltic run throughout the eighteenth century. Elsinore to Hull cost the same—two per cent—in 1799 as the Sound to Hull had done in 1714 and, if anything, rates for an uncomplicated Baltic run were fractionally lower in the last decade than they were in the second. The major fluctuations in the rate were the result of war, when many dangers were added to the normal life of the sea. Some of Broadley's policies were paying thirteen per cent for dangerous runs, and twenty per cent was not unknown for West Indies runs when the Atlantic seethed with privateers practising legalised piracy. In 1718, the height of the Northern war, Gothenburg to Hull cost fifteen per cent, whereas the same voyage in 1715 and 1719 cost only three. Similarly Hull to St. Petersburg cost two per cent in July and August 1799, but war and bad weather combined to send it up to ten in September. Even so, insurance accounted

[1] The tax on a policy was 5*s.* per cent for foreign and 2*s.* 6*d* per cent for coastal voyages. Brokerage was originally 5 per cent, but was thought in the early nineteenth century to take as much as a quarter of the underwriter's profit. See Wright & Fayle, pp. 255–89.

[2] The account is a little confused, and contains no details. Broadley endorsed it 'Loss by Danish capture—£1,200', but total losses were £2,100. Whether he was in error, or suffered £900 in other losses is not clear.

for only a fraction of the increased cost of transport in wartime. Freight rates always rose more than insurance rates.

Cheap insurance depended on the avoidance of stupid or unnecessary risks. Occasionally underwriters refused to insure ships going to danger zones; Maisters were unable to insure ships bound for Spain almost a year before the outbreak of war in 1739.[1] Attempts were also made to force ships into convoys. It was generally agreed that convoys reduced risks, but they also reduced speed, and the more impatient masters endeavoured to avoid them. Eventually a case in 1764 (when the Lord Chief Justice denied insurance to a Liverpool ship which had deliberately strayed from convoy) became a useful precedent for bringing pressure to bear on reluctant masters.[2] The Hull Committee for Convoys recommended the withdrawal of insurance facilities in cases of masters' indiscipline, and the status of the convoy was settled once and for all in 1798 when underwriters were subject to a £200 penalty if they knowingly insured ships sailing without convoy.[3] Wars were not good to merchants and shipowners, but if they behaved themselves they had, by the middle of the eighteenth century, little to fear from loss.

Sir Henry Etherington is said to have sat in his attic with a telescope watching for the safe arrival of the ships in which he had an interest. A fanciful tale, perhaps, but one which pinpoints the days of suspense before profit sailed over the horizon. Sometimes the sails did not appear. Claims were then put in to the brokers, who called together the underwriters to pay—or fight. 'Sirs,' wrote one broker in 1801,[4]

> I am directed by the Insured to give you notice, that he abandons to you the ship Catherine Capt Willm Russell seized and detained at St. Petersburgh as far as concerns your subscription of £100 . . . and I call upon you for the payment of that Sum as a Total Loss.

General sympathy was felt for people who lost ships, especially through enemy action, but underwriters were unhappy when the 'enemy' could not be legally identified. In 1799 Robert Ramsey was threatened by a Manchester firm if he did not pay:[5]

[1] Maister Letters, Henry to Nathaniel, 22 Apr 1738.

[2] See Macpherson, *Annals*, III, p. 401.

[3] 38 George III, c. 76.

[4] C. Briggs to Robert Ramsey, 20 Mar 1801. *WH* Autograph Letters Box.

[5] Sharpe & Eccles, Attornies, Manchester, to Robert Ramsey, 25 Mar 1799. *WH* Autograph Letter Box.

In consequence of the Detention at Palermo of the Ship Minerva bound to Leghorne, we sometime since desired Mr. E. F. Coulson as Broker to give notice to the Underwriters that Messrs. C. T. & I. Marriott of this place had abandoned the Goods insured to them on board of that ship—Having received for answer from Mr. Coulson that the Underwriters refuse to comply with the wishes of our clients, and that answer not being satisfactory—we think it necessary now to repeat such notice to you and the other Underwriters individually—And we now demand of you the amount of your Subscription on the Policy.

By the last advice, the Goods are on board the Ship Minerva detained by order of Admiral Lord Nelson. . . .

Not all accidents at sea were as disastrous as total loss—or 'capture' by Lord Nelson. Ships were often beached and their cargoes and fittings partly saved; and ships in difficulties might be helped to safety by other ships, occasionally after being abandoned by their crews. In both cases it had become customary for salvage money to be paid. When the *Alexander*, a Russian ship, was wrecked in the Humber, its remains were auctioned and one-third granted to the rescuers, and five hundred pounds was paid to two fortunate smack-owners of Gravesend who brought in the *Active*, laden with grain, which they had found drifting without its crew.

Such cases raised important questions for the underwriters in the early days: who should receive benefit from salvage, and who should pay for it? In the thirties complicated agreements about salvage were written into policies. A typical Maister cargo, for instance, was insured for £1,200 'without benefit of salvage' at 7 per cent, £200 'without benefit of salvage' at 6 per cent, and £300 'on Interest with benefit of salvage' at 7 per cent.[1] The salvage clause was eventually dropped and the cost of salvage treated as General Average. There was no English law relating to General Average, but the common practice was stated by Mr. Justice Lawrence in 1801:[2]

[1] *WH* Maister Accounts.

[2] A. J. Hodgson & G. R. Rudolf, *Law of General Average* (7th ed., London, 1948), p. 16. There was, in fact, a provision for Average in the Charge to the Admiral (the Mayor) in the Hull Court of Admiralty, given in the reign of Henry VIII: 'If any ship be overladen in a great tempest with merchandise, or with grain, the master for the safeguard of his life, and his mariners, may cast over most of the said merchandise or grain, and every man that hath any goods, shall bear their shares in the loss'; quoted by Hadley, p. 470.

All loss which arises in consequence of extraordinary sacrifices made or expenses incurred for the preservation of the ship and cargo comes within general average, and must be borne proportionately by all who are interested.

At an early stage underwriters began to assume responsibility for Averages and they appear more frequently than losses in insurance accounts.

Since underwriters bore the cost of saving the ship, they also received the benefit of salvage when a ship was too badly damaged to be saved. It was common, in fact, for damaged ships to be abandoned as a total loss to the underwriters, who then recovered what they could. When the *Valiant* ran aground at Saltfleet in 1792, for instance, 10,000 St. Petersburg deals, 100 loads of timber and 2,000 pieces of lathwood were recovered and auctioned for the benefit of the underwriters.[1]

Earlier policies also contained reservations about the amount to be paid in case of total loss. One argument used in favour of insurance companies before the Bubble Act was that 'the present Insurers, over and above the ten per cent mentioned in the Common Policies to be abated, will not pay, without a Suit, unless a further Abatement of six Pounds per cent be made.'[2] 'To pay 84 per cent in case of loss' was a regular clause in the policies of the thirties, although the percentage actually varies from 84 to 98 depending on the premium. A policy to pay 84 per cent demanded a premium of between 2 and 4½ per cent and one to pay 98 per cent demanded 6 or 7 per cent. The disappearance of this rebate clause in the forties represents a very important hidden reduction in the real cost of insurance and was another of the many factors encouraging the growth of trade.

In the complicated work of insurance the broker was almost as necessary as the underwriter. Even in the early informal days there had never been universal contact between underwriters and their customers. Maisters had arranged insurance for master mariners and merchants sharing cargoes with them. In the thirties they were contracting for insurance on behalf of inland and overseas agents and receiving a half per cent commission for their trouble.[3] As with shipbroking, merchants used to arranging insurance for themselves

[1] *Hull Packet*, 12 Mar 1793.
[2] Wright & Fayle, p. 53.
[3] This payment may represent the 'premium' for the broker's guarantee of the underwriters, which was fairly common in the early part of the century. It soon disappeared. See Wright & Fayle, p. 53.

and their partners began to sell the benefit of their long experience and wide connexions. All they had to do was set aside one of their clerks to specialise in insurance on behalf of customers as well as themselves, for it was as easy to knock on every other door in High street with six policies as with one.

The relationship between brokers and underwriters is best seen in the context of Hull's closely-knit business community. Their occupations were variations on a common theme. Underwriters were substantial citizens—semi-retired merchants or 'gentlemen' whose interest in trade was more or less nominal; brokers were juniors, still actively engaged in merchanting. There were only three exceptions among the twenty-four insurance brokers listed in the *Directory* for 1791–2: Robert Stainton, the only professional broker; Hanwith Hordan, a mustard manufacturer; and Heneage Lupton, a brewer (see Appendix 29).

The broker emerged before the local underwriter; he assisted at his birth; but he was still not indispensable. Hull had not yet developed a business organisation based on complete specialisation. The Smiths & Thompson Bank ledgers show clearly that direct contact existed between merchants, shipowners and underwriters, although such contacts were most probably decreasing as business became more voluminous and therefore more complex. One of the most valuable results of the brokers' work was the geographical extension of the insurance business. They called upon underwriters who were not resident in Hull, and they provided a service for merchants and shipowners in a number of British ports. Andrew Hollingsworth regularly arranged insurance for Ralph Forster of Berwick-on-Tweed, on one occasion 'on Goods by a Vessel under American Colours with an American Pass etc. from Gottenburgh to Berwick'.[1] He also acted for Gourock Rope Works, and for at least two Liverpool firms—John Montgomery & Co. and Titherington, Smith & Co. The former insured cargoes of timber from the Baltic; the latter dealt in more exciting things: 'We wrote you of 10th inst.', they said,[2] 'ordering £500 Insurance on the Alexander and the present is to say you may make it £1,500 if convenient, the sums as before. She mounts 24 guns 9 & 6 pounders and will have 50 to 60 People the Voyage to Angola. . . .' It would seem that Hull's underwriters were, as a body, more adventurous than her merchants.

[1] Ralph Forster to Andrew Hollingsworth, 27 May 1797; *WH* Autograph Letter Box. [2] 12 Sep 1798; ibid.

VII. THE WHALING INDUSTRY

1. THE ORIGIN AND GROWTH OF WHALING IN HULL

Of the many branches of 'trade', whaling has always attracted the greatest attention in Hull. A romantic picture of hardship, bravery, adventure and novelty emerges from the log-books that have survived, and many a book has told the harrowing tale of the Arctic. We shall endeavour here to redress the balance a little by attempting to disentangle the motives behind the adventures.

Hull never had an extensive transatlantic trade, yet it was this trade—or rather fluctuations in it—that provided the stimulus for the creation of the local whaling industry. Although whale oil had been highly prized since Tudor times as a superior lighting oil, all attempts at establishing a British industry failed. The Dutch were more successful and for well over a century Holland was the principal source of oil. Eventually, in the seventeen-thirties, whaling developed in British North America, particularly in Nantucket, Rhode Island.[1] The oil merchants turned their attention to America and were soon joined by the small group of American trade specialists, eager to extend the scope of their activities.

The American industry was theoretically admirable: mercantilists loved it. But Anglo-French rivalry threatened it. In 1752 the French in Canada penetrated the American hinterland; war began in earnest in 1754, and the failure of the English colonists to federate made the future of New England seem at least uncertain. In such circumstances the industry virtually ceased. Many whalers were conscripted into government service, Amherst using no fewer than ninety in his 1760 St. Lawrence campaign. Hull merchants were now forced back on their own devices. James Hamilton took the only course open to him, and sent his *York* to Greenland in 1754.[2]

[1] The American whaling industry is dealt with in detail by E. A. Stackpole, *The Sea Hunters: The New England Whalemen During Two Centuries, 1635–1835* (Philadelphia, 1953), from which the information about American whaling in this chapter is chiefly derived.

[2] The only sources of information for early Hull whaling are the Port Books, which record ships and their catches, and the Customs Letter Books, *passim.*

Others took the same line. 'We are likely to fit out at least 2 ships for Greenland', Joseph Pease told his son-in-law;[1] 'my Son R[obert] P[ease] and Bro. W[illiam] T[urner] are like to be Concerned at least £500 Each & Cousn. S. Dewitt the Same.' The result was the Hull Whale Fishery Company, which equipped not two but three ships in 1754: the *Berry*, *Pool* and *Leviathan*. The adventures were successful. Fourteen whales—236 tons of oil and 230 cwt. of bone—and five seal-skins were brought home, the first to reach Hull direct from the Arctic in the eighteenth century. Emboldened by good fortune, Hamilton sent the *Bosville* with the *York* in 1755, and the Hull Whale Fishery Company also sent another ship, the *Ann & Elizabeth*; a seventh, the *Mary & Jane*, was fitted out by the tobacco merchant, William Welfitt.[2]

Little is known of the Hull Whale Fishery Company, the only company active between 1758 and the lapse of whaling after the 1762 season. Its leaders were almost certainly merchants with interests in American and Dutch oil. Peases imported whale oil and bone from Holland, Samuel Dewitt was a Dutch sea captain and merchant, and William Turner was the largest importer of whale-bone in Hull, probably in the whole of Britain. Nor is it without significance that one of their ships was the *Berry*—the name of yet another oil merchant. Every attempt was made, however, to attract support from other sources. The company was divided into eighty transferable shares of £250, a total nominal capital of £20,000—more than enough to cover the cost of putting four whalers to sea. A small profit was made in the first season and a dividend of £9. 7*s*. 6*d*. was declared. The following season was better, and £25 per share was paid—ten per cent on the nominal subscription.[3]

The initial success did not last. By 1758 shares were selling for £200 and returns continued to fall. In 1762 the two remaining ships—the *Berry* and *Leviathan*—brought home only 1½ tons of oil, 22 seal skins and 9 sea-horse skins between them, and they did not return to Greenland.[4] Failure was caused partly by the war in

[1] Joseph Pease to Robert Robinson, 24 Aug 1753; *WH* 59/58/48.

[2] The 7 ships were, on average, less successful than the 4 in 1754. Their total catch amounted to 304 tons of oil and 207 cwt. of bone.

[3] Details from Pease Bank Ledgers, Haldenby Dixon's account. Dixon, a ropemaker, owned one share in the Company, which was sold by his assignees to Isaac Broadley in May 1758 for £203.

[4] The last reference to the Company was in March 1764, when Pease paid

1. Hull Whalers in the Arctic 1769 (*Ferens Art Gallery*)

A West View of the NEW DOCK at KINGSTON upon HULL.
REPRESENTATIVES in PARLIAMENT for the TOWN and COUNTY of KINGSTON upon HULL,

2. The First Dock, looking eastwards: a view in the eighties, by R. Thew (*Ferens Art Gallery*)

Europe which brought a general decline in trade (and a brief financial crisis in 1758–9) and partly by the ending of hostilities in America which enabled whaling to be revived there. This first phase of Hull whaling was an expedient; America was still the best permanent source of whale oil, and Greenland a troublesome alternative in emergencies.[1] In the year following the establishment of the industry in Hull, and in spite of the trouble in America, Christopher Scott had managed to import forty tons of oil from Rhode Island, and as early as 1757 Hamilton had sent his *Bosville* back on the American run after her brief life as a whaler. Thereafter oil was once more imported regularly from America; Pead & Co. brought sixty tons in the *Ann* from Boston, New England, in March 1765, and William Hornby and Christopher Scott were both importing oil from Boston in 1768.

Hull whaling received a fresh impetus in the late sixties, when the oppressive Act of 1766 placed a duty on oil and bone from the colonies. The old Hull Whale Fishery vessel *Berry* was fitted out by Samuel Standidge in 1766 and returned with one whale and several hundred seal-skins, the latter worth, it is said, five shillings each. In the following year Standidge also equipped the *British Queen*, and the *Britannia* in 1768. In 1769 he was joined by another three owners, encouraged by his success; in 1770 there were seven ships, nine in 1772 and twelve in 1775, just before the general depression of the Revolutionary War period reduced the numbers to three or four per annum.[2]

There was, in truth, nothing remarkable or exceptional in the early development of Hull whaling. Until 1785 it accounted for only a relatively small—and steady—proportion of the national industry: 11·1 per cent of the English ships in 1754, none in 1764, 12·3 per cent in 1774 and 10·1 in 1784. Hull attained its leading position with the third great collapse of the American industry, in 1784.

them £11 for some unspecified reason, probably connected with winding up. Pease Bank Ledgers, Joseph Pease's Account.

[1] The rise and fall of the English industry is reflected to some extent in the amount of whale oil imported from America:

1725–32	2544 tons	*1749–55*	3331
1733–9	2871	*1756–62*	2675
1740–8	2430	*1763–9*	6094

(*PRO* CO 390–9).

[2] For full statistical details, see Appendices 30–3.

English ships took at least fifty ships from Nantucket during the war, and many of the remainder fled because of their equivocal position: they needed the English market, but to sail from America they had to satisfy the General Court of Massachusetts Bay that they were rebels. Caught between their fellow New Englanders who regarded them as 'rank Tories who ordered their oil to be carried to the London Market . . .',[1] and the English who regarded them as rebels, the Nantucket fleet alone lost over £200,000 worth of ships. In despair the owners looked to Europe as a likely base, so that on this occasion dwindling American supplies coincided with the arrival of American ships and crews at almost all the principal English ports. They all benefited to some extent from the boom conditions after 1784, when the total whaling fleet rose from 89 in 1784 to 222 in 1788. But whale oil, like other goods, required easy access to its market, and the industry gravitated towards the major trading and shipowning ports. When the boom ended, in the early nineties, the decline was therefore less marked in Hull than in the nation as a whole. Her percentage of the total English ships rose dramatically from 10·6 in 1788 to 44·4 in 1800, when she was, without doubt, the leading outport in the trade.[2]

The amount of oil brought into Hull remained fairly steady for ten years after 1785 (*c.* 800 tons), although the number of ships fluctuated from fourteen to thirty-six. The volume of oil was, in fact, more closely related to the total number of whalers in the Arctic than to the number fitting out from Hull. Between 1790 and 1800 the national tonnage almost exactly halved from 30,819 tons to 15,405, while the tonnage of oil increased very slightly, from 11,364 tons to 11,484. Those ports which persevered found their average cargoes doubled without any effort on their part, and their profits grew accordingly. Thirty-six Hull ships had brought home 958 tons of oil in 1788; in 1798 only 23 ships were able to bring home 2,162 tons (see Appendix 32). The volume of oil continued to grow until by 1805 it reached 5,200 tons and Hull was rapidly catching up to London. She had improved her position from an average of 7·4 per cent of the national importation of oil in 1790–2 to 24 per cent for 1805–7:

[1] Quoted by Stackpole, p. 82.

[2] For general lists of ships, and comparisons, see B. Lubbock, *The Arctic Whalers* (Glasgow, 1937).

TRAIN OIL IMPORTS, MAJOR WHALING PORTS, 1790–1807[1]

(*Italics represent each port's percentage of national tonnage*)

	1790		*1791*		*1792*	
Hull	1041	*9·2*	533	*5·1*	864	*7·8*
Liverpool	229	*2·0*	781	*7·5*	1584	*14·3*
London	5976	*52·6*	5554	*53·0*	5133	*46·2*
Newcastle	673	*5·9*	820	*7·8*	146	*1·3*
Poole	1796	*15·8*	1272	*12·1*	1677	*15·1*
England	11,364		10,480		11,101	

	1800		*1801*		*1802*	
Hull	1756	*15·3*	2118	*14·7*	3726	*20·4*
Liverpool	285	*2·5*	404	*2·8*	681	*3·7*
London	4806	*41·9*	6610	*45·9*	8729	*47·7*
Newcastle	368	*3·2*	663	*4·6*	1564	*8·6*
Poole	1402	*12·2*	2377	*16·5*	1623	*8·9*
England	11,484		14,408		18,283	

	1805		*1806*		*1807*	
Hull	5199	*28·1*	3398	*19·9*	4251	*23·9*
Liverpool	826	*4·5*	682	*4·0*	1367	*7·7*
London	6083	*32·9*	6147	*36·0*	4597	*25·8*
Newcastle	2345	*12·7*	1210	*7·1*	1265	*7·1*
Poole	1415	*7·7*	2791	*16·3*	3550	*20·0*
England	18,485		17,087		17,787	

Oil was not the only consideration in whaling: 'The Whale being dead, the first business is to go with a boat into its jaws, and cut out the whalebone.'[2] The unit of measurement used in whaling was the 'foot of bone'—the length of the plates of bone which in a good sized animal measured fifteen feet by fifteen inches. There were a hundred large pieces and four hundred smaller pieces to a whale, a ton of good bone if the captors were lucky, worth £250 or more in the eighties.[3] Hull had always been interested in whalebone, and there were long traditions of whalebone-cutting and stay making.[4]

[1] Abstracted from *Accounts Presented to the House of Commons of the Quantities of . . . articles Imported . . . and Exported, in the 3 years ending 5 Jan 1793 and 4 years ending 5 Jan 1803 . . ., printed* 2 July 1803; and *Accounts Presented . . . for . . . 5 years ending 5 Jan 1808 . . .* printed 29 Jun 1808; copies in King's Beam House.

[2] Hadley, p. 398.

[3] *BM* Add. MS 38,347, f. 366.

[4] There was a considerable coastwise importation of bone—17,472 lb. in 1775—chiefly from Whitby and Scarborough (see Appendix 15).

One of the most interesting features of whaling in Hull was the way in which the port began to dominate the whalebone trade in the nineties. In the early nineties she had a tenth of the national trade; a third at the turn of the century, and a half by 1805. Bristol, Liverpool and London were on the way down, and Newcastle was the only other port showing a pattern similar to Hull's:[1]

AVERAGE WHALEFIN IMPORTS (cwt.)

	1790–2	*1800–2*	*1805–7*
Total England	5155	7610	7502
Bristol	120	5	0
Hull	704	2881	3914
Liverpool	818	265	212
London	2227	2953	1496
Newcastle	483	982	956
Whitby	481	315	567

It may be that the bright young things of the Metropolis followed the dictates of fashion and put their faith in muslin and little else; but the matrons of the North kept their stays. We need to know a good deal more about the distribution of staymaking and the industrial use of whalebone before we can pass a final verdict on the peculiar distribution of the trade. Why, for example, did Poole not import whalebone? Did Hull captains buy it from Poole captains and import it direct to Hull?

Finally there were the seal-skins, a valuable side-product of whaling. Seals were much easier to catch than whales, and ships that fared badly in whaling endeavoured to make up their cargo with skins. The first ship to do so on a large scale was Standidge's *Berry*, which returned in 1766 with four hundred. Two years later his *British Queen* brought back seven hundred, and after that most ships brought a few hundred. Eventually seven or eight small vessels were fitted out for sealing alone, but no record of their activities has survived. Some of them appear to have spent their time in the Southern Fishery; in April 1793 a ship arrived in Falmouth with the news that when it left the fishery nine weeks earlier the *Minerva* of Hull had already caught 12,000 seals and was still going strong.[2] With the appearance of these sealers Hull took about a third of the

[1] Sources as for Note 1, p. 161.

[2] *Hull Packet*, 12 Mar 1793. The ship which brought the news had 25,000 skins on board.

national importation in the early nineties, and well over half in 1800. But it was not long before Hull withdrew all available men and ships to the oil and bone trade, leaving the skin trade momentarily to Liverpool, Bristol, London and Poole.

Whaler owners, not without a touch of self-interest, maintained that whaling was the creation of the Government bounty, introduced in 1733 to encourage the industry and, by so doing, to produce seamen for naval service in time of war. At the rate of forty shillings per ship-ton after 1750, the bounty was an impressive five or six hundred pounds on the average sized whaler, and statistics in the middle of the century give superficial support to the owners' case.[1] The bounty was obviously of great interest to them, a free gift at the end of a successful voyage, or a means of reducing the loss if a ship returned clean. But once the industry was established, the fluctuation in the value of the bounty did not, in fact, greatly affect the number of ships fitting out, and it is doubtful if the bounty did anything more than maintain an atmosphere favourable to whaling. The early Bounty Acts—1733 (twenty shillings per ton) and 1740 (thirty shillings per ton)—had no noticeable effect on whaling statistics. The 1749 Act, on the other hand, appears to have met with immediate success by increasing the bounty to forty shillings, although it is far from clear why an increase of, say, £150 on a ship should have tipped the balance when profits on whale oil were thought to be so high. The success of the Act may have been partly emotional rather than economic, and it may owe a great deal to its propitious timing, immediately before the American troubles. The fluctuations in whaling in the second half of the century are less

[1] The Bounty Returns, *PRO* CO 390–9 show the following relationships:

	Year	*No.*	*Tons*
20s. bounty	1733	2	613
	4	3	921
	5	3	921
	6	2	613
	7	4	1148
	8	5	1432
	9	6	1781
30s.	1740	2	632
	1	2	632
	2	2	632
	3	1	349

	Year	*No.*	*Tons*
	1744	5	1648
	5	5	1648
	6	5	1648
	7	2	683
	8	2	683
	9	2	683
40s.	1750	17	5569
	1	20	6253
	2	26	8551
	3	27	8954
	4	36	11663

easily related to the bounty. After an Act in 1771 threatened its future, the number of ships almost doubled, and it declined not in 1776, when the bounty was reduced by ten shillings, but in 1779, when the American war became serious. It revived not when the bounty was restored to forty shillings in 1782, but when war ended in 1783, and the reduction of the bounty again in 1786 is unlikely to have been the incentive for the vast increase in whaling between 1784 and 1788.

Hull owners, like those of other ports, overstated their case when they claimed, in December 1785, that 'if the present bounty falls short as it certainly does of defraying the expences attending the outfit etc. of these precarious and hazardous voyages, it cannot be supposed that the shipowners can continue such a trade without a continuation of the encouragement. . . .'[1] The Commissioners of Customs and the Committee for Trade were convinced that the industry was no longer an infant requiring special care, and that bounties, already (1786) standing at £84,000 per annum, were likely to increase owners' profits against the public interest.[2] The whaler owners were a powerful lobby, and the bounty was allowed to remain at thirty shillings into the nineteenth century, but when the time came to encourage the Southern Fishery the Government seized the opportunity of changing the system, and gave prizes for the best catches instead of the blanket subsidy of the Northern Fishery.

We must look to other factors to explain the fluctuations in whaling: to war, and to normal economic motivation. Growing industries cried out for lubricants and a growing population for light. Towns as far away as Birmingham relied for their public lighting on Hull's oil merchants, and each new middle class family put a tile on the bone merchant's mansion. As industry began to boom after 1783 the demand for oil increased—and with it the price.

[1] Letter from the whaler owners to the Bench, *GH* MS L.1386 (234). The Bench petitioned the Treasury for an extension of the bounty in 1781 and 1785; see, for e.g., *PRO* BT 5/3, p. 335f.

[2] At the same time the industry's rôle as a nursery for seamen was seriously questioned. 'The Greenland Fishery', Pitt told the Commons in April 1786, 'was by no means to be regarded as a source for increasing the number of seamen for the navy' (*Parliamentary History*, XXV, 1381–4). Although only specialist whaling men had protection for the whole year, all of them had protection from 1 February till their return, which effectively carried them over the usual pressing season.

The ships flocking from America found the market ready for them:[1]

	1783	*1784*	*1785*	*1786*
Value of oil	£22½–23½	22–26	25–27	—
English Whalers	—	89	140	168
Hull Whalers	—	9	14	21

An increase of five pounds per ton was worth more to a ship with an average cargo than the bounty, but alas, as the number of ships went up, the average cargo went down. In short, rising prices and bounty encouraged the over-capitalisation of the industry; the result was a reduction of profits, a cry that the bounty alone made the profit, and a rapid withdrawal by three-quarters of the owners. Those who remained were able to increase their profits out of the same volume of oil and bone, and to absorb some at least of the rising costs of wartime trade.

2. THE SHIPS

The early whalers were not specially constructed ships. Apart from the gear required to raise and lower the boats, and to haul in the catch, they were normal merchantmen with reinforced hulls to withstand the pack-ice. Most of them were of the transatlantic class, between eighty and a hundred feet long (much the same as a reasonable whale), with two or three masts; for the forty for which a figure is available the average tonnage (excluding the small seal catchers) was 290.[2] The largest ship fitting out from Hull was the 428-ton *Alliance*, the smallest the 83-ton seal catcher *Young Richard*.

In the early days of whaling the ships were acquired in the normal course of business rather than as whalers. B. B. Thompson bought the *Molly* in 1773, two years before he fitted her out, and Robert Gee bought the *Caroline* from Thompson in 1773, four years before he sent her to Greenland.[3] The ships were withdrawn as required from merchant runs. Hamilton's *Bosville* was one of his regular American traders before he sent her to Greenland in 1755,

[1] Prices from *BM* Add. MS 38,347, f. 366. Price alone was not a satisfactory stimulent; it depended on the volume of oil produced, not the number of whalers. High prices one year might encourage owners, but there was no guarantee that the price would hold up.

[2] The tonnages (in the absence of the Shipping Registers) are to be found in HCLB, C–B, *passim*. See Appendix 33.

[3] HCLB, C–B, 23 Feb 1787.

and she returned to the American run when whaling temporarily declined. His 267-ton *Manchester*—Hull's champion whaler in the seventies and eighties—was also an American trader, and was not sent to Greenland until whaling was firmly re-established, in 1770. As we might expect from the American origins of the trade, and from the influx of American whalers after 1783, a large number of Hull whalers were American built—no fewer than thirteen in 1787.[1] In the absence of a large transatlantic trade in Hull, many of them were obtained from other ports. The *Manchester* was originally a Liverpool ship, the *Molly* came via Glasgow and London, and the *Greenland*, *Enterprize*, *Lady Jane* and *Mayflower* were originally registered in London.[2]

The costs of whaling are not easily discovered. An average sized ship could be had for anything between two and four thousand pounds depending on the quality of the hull. Some may have cost less, since age was no obstacle so long as they had better than average soundness. An estimate of £2,434 for one fitted out from Liverpool was given in evidence before the Committee of Trade in 1786,[3] but it would be unwise to make any generalisations on details. The *Enterprize* cost approximately £2,088 when Sparks & Company fitted her out in 1788,[4] while the *Sarah & Elizabeth* had cost Pease & Company £3,744 in 1784.[5] Outfitting accounted for about £500 of the prime cost.

Eighteenth century shipowners were not sophisticated enough to trouble themselves with depreciation charges, but they were well aware of the very heavy running costs of a whaler. Each year she had to be refitted, the damage of the previous season repaired, and provisions for five months or more stored on board; the costs could be anything up to a quarter of the value of the unfitted ship. On top of these expenses were the wages of the crew—about £500 for a 300-ton ship—and such incidentals as insurance and dock dues.

Owners were always faced with the risk of a ship being lost or returning 'clean',[6] but damage was a more common and sometimes

[1] There is a list in HCLB, C–B, 7 Apr 1787.

[2] ibid., 24 Jan 1789. [3] *BM* Add. MS 38,347, f. 366.

[4] Smiths & Thompson's Bank ledgers, Sparks & Company's Account.

[5] 'Account of the Ship *Sarah & Elizabeth*', *WH* 59/58/78.

[6] The risks involved in whaling were not as great as might be expected. Of the 546 voyages between 1754 and 1800, 2·9 per cent ended in loss and 4·8 per cent of the ships returned clean. The probability of a ship being lost or clean was thus only ·077, which is hardly a desperate gamble!

more serious problem. It handicapped the fishing and, by forcing a ship to remain in dry-dock, it could prejudice the chance of out-of-season work. No record of whaling would be complete without some account of the hazards facing owners and, of course, their courageous crews. Sixteen ships, like the *Whalefisher* with a piece of ice pushed clean through her, never returned to Hull.[1] Others, like the *Greenland* were more fortunate.

There was nothing unusual about either the *Greenland* or her damage. She was a 200-ton ship making her maiden voyage in 1788 as one of Samuel Standidge's four whalers.[2] With one of the best captains, John Anderson, in command, she sailed from Hull on 11 March 1788, 'in all respects well and sufficiently fitted furnished fortified manned and provided with all things needful and necessary for a voyage to Davis Streights or the Greenland Seas'.[3] The master intended making for Davis Strait, and after sheltering from gales in the Shetlands for four days they set out across the Atlantic on 19 March. For a month they sailed north-westwards, but 'apprehending from the wind being set in the contrary that they might not reach those seas in time for the Fishery . . .', they altered course and headed for Greenland on 22 April. They reached the ice at latitude 75° North on 8 May and began fishing immediately. On the fourteenth, however, a gale forced the ship on to the ice and the mainpiece of the rudder was broken and the ironwork greatly damaged. On the following day the starboard bow was damaged and one pump had to be set constantly at work, but they continued chasing whales until the twenty-fourth when, as they were trying to dock the ship in ice, she struck with such force that the whole ship was shaken and the cut-water so badly damaged that timbers floated to the surface. Two days later the larboard bow was struck, and the next day a cable had to be cut in fenders 'to prevent the ship being Stove by the ice'. When at last the gale and fog died away the captain, mate, carpenter and harpooners held a conference and decided that it would be suicidal to remain in the Arctic.

[1] For the *Whalefisher* disaster, see Hadley, pp. 406–8.

[2] She was forced to return to Hull before the expiry of the legal period required to secure the bounty, and a Customs Enquiry was held to determine the right to bounty. See HCLB, C–B, Aug 1788 *et seq*. The proceedings were started by an annonymous letter (2 Aug 1788) alleging that the *Greenland* was not equipped for a whaling season (16 weeks) and had been despatched simply for the Bounty.

[3] The Master's affidavit, dated 24 Jun 1788.

They sailed for home and arrived back in Hull on 24 June 1788.

The costs of whaling were heavy, but the profits were sometimes immense, though always unpredictable. A ship had to bring home at least thirty tons of oil and one and a half tons of bone (at £21 and £245 per ton respectively) to make a saving voyage. Since a small whale yielded about 19 tons of oil and a middling one about 22 tons, a whaler began to show a profit with two whales.[1] In the instances recorded, the number of whales was usually between one and five, although higher numbers were common, seventeen being the highest, for the *Caroline* in 1780. The amount of oil naturally varied with the size of the whales—which was going down as indiscriminate slaughter proceeded—but was generally much more than was required for a 'saving voyage'. A good catch may well be 140 tons, and for several years (1780–3 and after 1795) the average cargo was over seventy tons of oil and four tons of bone. With oil at a little over £30 per ton and bone at £250 the average ship in the late nineties could expect to earn £3,000 per annum plus seal skins, saved provisions and bountry. A lucky ship, like the *Manchester* in 1786, could make £3,750 in a single voyage; an unlucky ship made nothing. Fate struck indiscriminately. The *Berry* brought home 114 tons of oil from fifteen whales in 1758, and two seal-skins in 1760. The size of the catch depended on the skill of the master and crew, the weather, the number of whalers in a particular area, and good luck. Average cargoes are therefore of little practical value in assessing the income of any single whaler, and, in particular tell us nothing about a ship's total earning capacity over the whole of its life span.

There was another important source of income. Between seasons many—perhaps all—whalers reverted to the merchant service. In 1771, for example, the *Manchester* and *King of Prussia* both brought deals and iron from St. Petersburg, and the *Berry* brought deals from Narva; in 1789 the *Scarthingwell* and *Bithiah & Mary* turned round so quickly—to Stockholm and Archangel respectively—that they had left the port before bounty formalities were completed. Standidge preferred to use the *Berry* on 'official' service during the winter. In 1770 he offered her to the Customs as a Lazarette for 7*s*. 6*d*. per ton (*c*. £120) per month but the offer was refused, and she entered Russian service as a naval transport. In 1772 she became a 'Brigantine' (presumably in the British navy) and in the following year fitted out from London to save the journey back to Hull. In

[1] *BM* Add. MS 38,347, ff. 14–58 and 366.

1776 she was once more in Government service, carrying coal to Boston, New England, for Government use. As if the dangers of the Arctic were not enough, another of Standidge's ships, the *Britannia*, ran aground off the Suffolk coast in January 1772 while on her way to Oporto with pipe staves.

It is not easy to assess the profitability of whaling. That it was profitable is beyond doubt, but it must be admitted that we cannot cast the accounts of a single ship with certainty. J. R. Pease's account for the 272-ton *Sarah & Elizabeth* is a good example of the confusion which exists even where figures survive.[1] Pease advanced £936. 2*s*. 4*d*. for his quarter share of the fitting out in 1784. Thereafter he made annual subscriptions amounting to approximately £1,000 in ten years, which is unlikely to have covered running costs. On the other hand, no mention is made of bounty or out-of-season earnings, which may have been put into a general expenses fund. Over eleven years Pease was credited with dividends amounting to £1,822. 1*s*. 3*d*. If we deduct the prime cost of the ship, which still remained, he received £1,822 for an investment of £1,000: £822 (less depreciation of the ship), which on the face of it is approximately eight per cent per annum simple interest, and a good deal more if we could disentangle the complicated pattern of investment and withdrawal. In fairness it should be pointed out that the *Sarah & Elizabeth* was an unfortunate ship. She had three clean years in eleven, the highest proportion for any long-serving Hull whaler in the eighteenth century.

We know a little more about William Sparks & Company, founded at the end of 1786 when five partners contributed a total of £3,000 to fit out the *Gibraltar*. The venture was a success, and in March 1788 they invested a further £1,750 which was augmented by £1,000 from the previous year's profit to fit out a second ship, the *Enterprize*. But this was the period of maximum ships and minimum individual returns, and Sparks & Company suffered with the rest. They followed the general trend and withdrew part of their capital, selling the *Enterprize* (for £588 less than they paid for it) in February 1793. The *Gibraltar* continued whaling until, in March 1796, she was sent to Archangel, fell victim to the enemy, and was never seen again. Dividends on the £4,750 investment amounted to £5,815 between 1787 and 1796, a little over 10 per cent per annum. Out of season earnings and expenses are included in these figures; so, too,

[1] *WH* 59/58/78.

is the bounty, amounting to £6,257. 4*s.* (costs paid) in the ten years. Such a huge sum—more or less equal to the total profit—would appear to contradict our earlier conclusion that bounty was of little significance in the development of whaling. We must, however, bear in mind the period covered by the account. These were the bleakest years for whaling. Average cargoes declined because there were too many ships and prices declined because there was too much oil. In such circumstances the bounty appeared more important than in earlier or later years. Pease & Company were not affected to the same extent because they started earlier, when profit was still high, but their account clearly illustrates the declining profitability after 1788:

PEASE & COMPANY'S OIL SALES, 1784–9

Year	*Oil (tons)*	*Value (£)*	*Year*	*Oil (tons)*	*Value (£)*
1784	34	850	*1790*	24	551
1785	65	1495	*1791*	0	0
1786	56	952	*1792*	0	0
1787	48	921½	*1793*	0	0
1788	48	816	*1794*	83	1286
1789	21	376½			

Far from easing the situation the bounty—insofar as it encouraged over-capitalisation—helped to cause it. By upsetting the equilibrium between true profitability and the number of ships, it delayed for a few years the emergence of a healthy whaling industry.[1]

It is clear, then, that whaling made no real profit when over-encouraged, but the small profits plus the bounty were sufficient to return at least eight or ten per cent over a period of time including the bad years. We may justifiably assume higher profits before and after the bleak years—especially as average cargoes doubled and prices rose after 1795. Firms with a long trading history, ample capital or a specific interest in oil, managed to weather the storm; those seeking a large and quick profit after 1786 were disappointed.

3. THE OWNERS

Pease & Company was typical of the newly emergent whaling firms. A quarter belonged to J. R. Pease, and the rest was divided between R. C. Pease (banker), James Dewitt (their cousin, merchant), John

[1] The number of ships increased in the nineteenth century, but this was due to increasing demand rather than bounty. The unfortunate results of over-expansion remained the same, however (see p. 178).

Terrington (glover), John Brooke (merchant) and Elizabeth Nelson of Beverley (widow of Nelson, the tanner).[1] The last whalers belonging to individual merchant houses disappeared in the seventies, the famous *Manchester* leading the way in 1771 when it was sold by James Hamilton, merchant, to John Staniforth, shipowner. In the eighties the whaling firms were independent of the private merchanting business of their owners, existing solely for the exploitation of the whale fishery.

The majority of principal owners were specialist shipowners (who first appear as whaler owners) and oil merchants. Many of the former were originally masters who became managing owners and then principal or even sole owners. Samuel Standidge started in the American trade as mate, bought shares in ships, and at one time or another owned at least the *Berry*, *Britannia*, *British Queen*, *Greenland*, *Ranger* and *Samuel*. Humphrey Foord first went to Greenland as the master of the *Jenny* in 1769. As master of the *Manchester* after 1770 he was the most successful in Hull. Eventually he acquired a half share in the *Manchester*, and in 1799 joined with Henry Coates the oil merchant to buy the *Minerva*. How many principal owners were specialist shipowners cannot be accurately determined, but perhaps half-a-dozen names could be added to those we have already noted: Thomas Locke had interests in the *Diana* and *Truelove*, Daniel Macpharson in the *Chance*, William Sparks in the *Enterprize* and *Gibraltar*, and Daniel Tong in the *Friends* and *Molly*.[2]

Towards the end of the century the oil merchants began to take a greater share in the industry. William Watson Bolton and Christopher Bolton, oil millers, were principals of two companies owning the *Symmetry* and *Minerva* and the *Lottery* and *Ariel*, and W. W. Bolton was also a principal member of Eggintons & Company. Widow Elizabeth Eggington & Sons (Joseph and Gardiner) were the principals in a company owning the *Elizabeth*, *Fanny*, *Mary* and *Oak Hall*, and they presumably also owned the *Eggington*.[3]

Whaler shares—expensive, but offering a good return—were eagerly bought by the growing investing middle class. Master

[1] The original register is recited in Deed of Transfer, Trustees of J. R. Pease, dec'd, to J. R. Pease, Junior, *WH* 59/58/78.

[2] All details of ownerships are taken from HCLB, C–B, *passim*.

[3] Joseph Eggington, 'shipowner', received more apprentices—usually of poor background—than any other person in the eighteenth century, presumably for cheap labour on the family whalers; IIA, *passim*.

mariners, victuallers, ropemakers, wharfingers, merchants, bankers and their clerks all sought the easily transferable shares which were constantly being advertised. 'TO BE SOLD', ran an advertisement in the *Hull Packet* in 1795:[1] 'One fourth part of the good ship or vessel called the *Brothers*, of Hull, of the burthen of between five and six hundred tons; and of her boats Fishing Tackle and Stores.' An analysis of Eggingtons & Company illustrates the variety of people involved in whaling. Supporting Elizabeth Eggington and her two sons were thirteen secondary owners: W. W. Bolton; John Kiero, ropemaker and part owner of the *Enterprize*; John Sykes of Joseph Sykes & Son; John Wray & Andrew Hollingsworth, timber merchants; Robert Kinder & William Lee, tar merchants; Ralph Turner, merchant; Daniel Macpharson, shipowner; John Overend & William Thompson, among the most important wharfingers in Hull; Henry Coates, of Jarratt & Coates, oil merchants and millers and part owner of the *Minerva*; and finally Peter Middleton, another ropemaker.

Not all the shareholders in whaling firms were Hull men. John Smith of Gainsborough was listed as the sole owner of the *Maria* in 1798, and the *London* was owned by a company which included Edmund Taylor, wharfinger of Halifax, and several merchants and Emanuel Silva, 'Insurance Broker' of London. A quarter of the *Kingston* was owned by John Finley, merchant in Jamaica (Edward Finley of Hull was also a shareholder), and a fifth of the *Enterprize* (in 1799) by Joseph Horncastle of London. Benjamin Wilson, the Burton brewer, included shipowning among his many activities, and in February 1790 his Day Book was credited with £18. 15*s*. for '1/16 profits of 2 Voyages of Greenlandman (Henry Hammond)'.[2] This is, incidentally, the only known reference to a distribution of profits for a definite period. Although the ship must have been doing badly to be paying out only £300 for two voyages, the profit represents a dividend of approximately seven per cent of the value of the share if the whaler was worth £2,000.

4. THE GREENLANDMEN

When the South Sea Company commenced whaling in 1725 there were, according to Macpherson, no Englishmen who knew anything

[1] *Hull Packet*, 13 January 1795. Whoever bought this share would make a bad bargain; the official tonnage for bounty purposes was only 378.

[2] I owe this reference to Professor Matthias.

about it, and 'all their commanders, harponeers, boatsteerers, line veerers and blubber-cutters' had to be brought over from Fohrde in Holstein.[1] By the time Hull sent its first whalers to Greenland English seamen were employed exclusively, and the trade had come to be regarded as one of the chief nurseries for seamen. There is, however, little doubt that the men received their training from foreigners, and it may be more than a coincidence that the best whaler captain in Hull was Humphrey *Foord*.[2]

The masters, at least in the early days, were drawn like their ships from the American trade. On the whole they tended to remain with one ship and acquire a share in it, but in the case of the larger companies they often changed about. So far as is known they were all Englishmen. When the industry expanded the mates of the original ships were given commands, and new men brought in were helped by the custom for ships to hunt in packs.

The total crew, including the master, mate, cook, surgeon and one or two carpenters, was usually between thirty and forty-five. By the 1771 Bounty Act all ships of 200 tons were compelled to carry at least four boats and six men for each of them, and one boat and six men for every additional fifty tons. It was these six-man boats, not the whalers, which did the actual catching. The ships cut themselves a dock in the ice and then sent out the boats, three or four together; if boats from more than one ship made a kill, the whale was shared. The dead whale was towed back to the parent ship, dismembered by the flensers, and the blubber or oil stowed away in casks to be processed in the factories in Hull. The process was vividly described by George Hadley:[3]

When a Whale is seen or heard, a long boat with six men in it, (there being always five or six boats ready) makes up to it, and endeavours to approach its side near the head; the Whale finding itself pursued

[1] Macpherson, III, p. 131. It was said of Whitby whalers in the fifties that 'harpooners and other officers were procured from Holland, as our sailors were then unacquainted with whale fishing'. George Young, *A History of Whitby* (Whitby, 1817), Vol. II, p. 563.

[2] It is interesting to note that in the painting of Standidge's ships in the Arctic in 1769 (see Plate 1), one at least of the boats is shown being steered by means of an oar and containing men wearing caps. Ten years earlier Captain Mitchell of the *Humber* sloop arrested a boatload of escaped French prisoners at Cleethorpes, having discovered them because *they steered their boat with an oar and wore caps*, both things foreign to Hull men. HCLB, C–B, 9 Jun 1759.

[3] Hadley, p. 397.

dives, but rising again to breath, which it is obliged to do, the men watch the opportunity, row up to its side, and the harpooner strikes him usually near the fin with the harpoon (a triangular barbed iron, about a foot long, and fastened to a stem) the fish no sooner feels the smart, than it darts down into the deep with the harpoon sticking fast in it; to the harpoon is fastened a line twenty yards long, and as thick as one's finger, which runs with such rapidity after the Whale, that if entangled, it must either snap short, or overset the boat; it is therefore one man's business to attend to this line, and wet the place on the boat's edge on which it runs, least it should take fire. The boat with the line follows the Whale as far as it can, and if the fish be not mortally wounded, he will flounce about in the water for an hour, and draw a line of four hundred yards after him, in which case fresh line is added by other boats. If the fish comes up again alive, they strike it with fresh harpoons, and then kill it with lances; when dead it rises with its belly upwards; should it retreat under the ice, they either pull away the harpoon, or cut the line, in which case they lose the fish, a loss amounting to five hundred pounds, that being its average value.

For the men who chased giant whales in small rowing boats in icy waters the conditions of labour were not good. The cold and danger drove out of the industry all but the toughest, and occasionally a master would add his own brutality to that of nature. Fights were common, and mutinies not unknown. William Allen, master of the ill-fated *Whalefisher*, was beaten up on the maiden voyage by his mate, who took control of the ship in musical-comedy style: 'Now my Lads I am Master of the ship and I wish to be Master.'[1] Several of the crew thought differently, and led by the surgeon they brought the master back from the neighbouring *Young Maria*, where he had taken refuge. The mate came home in chains.

Although conditions were often bad, provision for the crew was good. As part of his evidence in the *Greenland* case in 1788, Samuel Standidge submitted to the Customs a list of stores remaining on board when she arrived home fifty-seven days before she was due.[2] The daily ration for forty-two men was calculated, and the surplus shown:

		Ration	*Surplus*	*Total*
Beef:	1 lb. for 17 days	614	422	1036
Pork:	1 lb. for 17 days	614	394	1008
Fish:	½ lb. for 23 days	483	189	672
Bread:	1 lb. for 57 days	2394	1190	3584
Flour:	½ lb. for 18 days	428	132	560

[1] Details from Brief in *WH* Court Cases Box.

[2] HCLB, C–B, 13 Sep 1788.

3. The Dock Gates and Dock Office, looking westward: a view in the eighties, by R. Thew (showing, incidentally, the whale-oil street lamps that were to be found in the town as well as in the dock estate) (*Ferens Art Gallery*)

4. Samuel Standidge, 1775: Master Mariner, Merchant, Shipowner and Shipbuilder (*Hull Museums*)

The crew shared 16 pints of white peas when flour was not served, four pounds of butter on fish days, and eight pounds of barley every day.

Two great attractions drew seamen to whaling: wages were good, and Greenlandmen were exempt from naval service. About wages little can be said except that they were higher than those paid elsewhere. From a reference in the Customs Letter Books[1] it may be assumed that they were between fifteen and twenty shillings a week, and there may have been bonuses.[2] On the other hand they were employed for not much more than four months in the year, and had to fend for themselves between seasons.

The 'Greenland Protection' may have had a greater influence, for all seamen were loath to serve His Majesty. Even the Protection was not a complete safeguard. Since non-specialist Greenlandmen might be pressed at the end of their voyage, press-ships often waited for the whalers to arrive and boarded them before they docked. In 1757 the crews of the *York*, *Berry*, *Pool* and *Ann & Elizabeth* took no chances, and the *Berry* was the only ship to arrive in Hull with its full crew. The crew of the *Ann & Elizabeth* confined the captain to his cabin—presumably with his connivance—and landed in Lincolnshire; the crew of the *Pool* landed at Paull. Four years later when the Customs boat 'together with Robert Pease Esq. a Proprietor of the Fishery' went out to meet the *Berry* to muster the men and check the cargo, they were actually fired on by the *Mermaid* man-o'-war.[3] When they reached the ship,

> Mr. Storey, a Lieutenant of the *Mermaid* came on board the *Berry* in a Swearing dissolute manner with his Boats crew armed with Carbines, Pistols, and Cutlasses and being asked the reason why he fired on the Customshouse Boat he gave for answer that he thought they were carrying protections off to the Greenlandmen.

[1] HCLB, C–B, 9 Feb 1790.

[2] There is no specific reference to bonuses in Hull, but they certainly operated in Whitby; Young, II, p. 567.

[3] The matter was reported to the Commissioners of Customs on 15 Aug 1761. Protections were valuable documents. They guaranteed freedom, a good wage and immunity from the risks which beset a naval seaman at action stations. As a result the Customs were constantly being asked for new ones, the old having jumped out of its owner's pocket as he happened to be leaning over the side of a ship. . . . One wonders how much these lost protections fetched in Hull (Lloyd's Coffee House traded in them for a time). During the Napoleonic war the more enterprising seamen forged them; *Hull Advertiser*, 11 Oct 1804.

The correct procedure would have been for Pease to challenge the legality of the Press, but Greenlandmen could usually look after themselves. They did not come home from the Arctic to rot in a Press ship; flensing knives were vicious weapons, and boarders were repulsed with an appropriate loss of fingers.[1]

The need for Protections during the many years of conflict determined the conditions of employment for most of the eighteenth century. Crews entered into contracts with owners, and bonds with the Government, to return to their ships when recalled for the next season. In 1783 the owners of the *Manchester* complained to the Customs that two of their line managers had not returned to the ship because the war had ended, and claimed that they should forfeit their £250 bonds because they had caused inconvenience and delay to the ships.[2] During peace time the crews were not legally bound to their ships, but the competition for places was such that they may still have contracted from one season to the next.

Whaling seamen were no more idle than their ships between seasons. Some were retained as skeleton crews when their ship went on merchant runs, and some took jobs in other ships, like Thomas Oliver, who lost his Protection while 'engaged as a Seaman on board the *Mary of Sunderland* employed in the Coast Trade'.[3] The most popular occupation—if it can be called that—was being retained as 'Evidences' by the Customs in the never-ending disputes over bounty, or by underwriters in insurance disputes. The Collector at Hull informed the Commissioners in February 1790 that

> Several of the Greenland Sailors to whom the Collector pays ten shillings per week each by your orders have lately been with us; and the Greenland Ships for the ensuing season are now fitting out, they alledge that if they are not soon dismissed they shall lose the opportunity of shipping themselves, as the owners of such ships are now engaging their Hands.

It was thought they would all disappear soon in any case, 'the wages and allowances at Sea being more than what the Collector pays them, although during the winter all were striving to be on the list of Evidences'. On this occasion their three months idleness cost them dear, for they all missed their ships in the end.

[1] For an account of a pitched battle between press-gang and whaler crew (of the *Blenheim*), see *Hull Advertiser*, 4 & 25 Oct 1798.

[2] HCLB, C–B, 2 Mar 1783.

[3] ibid., 8 Dec 1795.

5. CONCLUSION

The influence of whaling on the general economy of Hull was both deep and far-reaching. Ships and men were employed on a magnificent scale; the oil-merchants grew richer; and people totally unconnected with the trade were encouraged as the wealth which it brought into the town filtered through the retail trades.

The shipping industry soon responded to tales of unimaginable wealth. The ventures of merchants cut off from their normal supplies were supplemented, and then replaced, by the adventures of speculators who bought ships for the purpose of exploiting the fishery. By the late fifties whalers were already 15 per cent of the total ships engaged in foreign trade, and, although the percentage never again reached these heights, whaling accounted for something between five and eight thousand tons of shipping between 1786 and 1800. At its greatest, in 1788, the capital value of the whaling fleet could hardly have been less than £150,000, and, as we have seen, the need to organise and finance whaling companies encouraged the emergence of the specialist shipowner in Hull.

A whaler which performed only its annual trip to the Arctic would have been grossly under-utilised. The liberation of whalers between seasons in fact provided a reservoir of shipping for use during the expansion of trade in the eighties, and it may well have helped to keep down freight rates. At the same time the whalers, by their very existence (independent of normal economic considerations) brought money into the town. Between 1754 and 1800 bounty payments on Hull whalers amounted to no less than £241,000.

At the same time whale oil was the sole property of the owners who brought it into the port, and the full value remained to be distributed in the town, whereas merchants and other shipowners received only a commission on goods carried. Processing was also done in Hull, in the half-dozen Greenland Houses to be found to the north of the town. Thus whaling meant employment and income for a large number of seamen (fluctuating from about a thousand to fifteen hundred in the last quarter of the century), and for their land-based fellows, the blubber refiners, whalebone-cutters, staymakers, and tanners.

Hull whaling was fifty years old in 1804, when 40 ships brought 4,018 tons of oil into the port, but its hey-day was yet to come.

Although the price of bone declined during the Napoleonic war, the demand for oil was insatiable, and the number of ships increased gradually until 1819, when 65 were fitted out. The following year was the best ever, with 60 ships bringing home 7,978 tons of oil and 360 tons of bone, and then began a long period of decline. As in the eighties, the increasing number of ships simply reduced the average cargo, and drove ships out of the business. Again there was prosperity for those that remained, but coal gas and over-fishing spelled the eventual doom of the industry. It lasted, from start to finish, for 105 years. It provided one of the most exciting chapters in Hull's history, but it was, inevitably, a passing phase in the town's economic life.

VIII. INDUSTRY IN HULL

Hull was, above all, the servant of industrial towns. In general she remained aloof from the newer industrial experiments on which her wealth was partly based. She would not appear in a list of industrialised towns, yet she was a hive of industrial activity. It is inevitable, perhaps, that the industries of ports should be underrated by contemporaries and by historians. Commerce, after all, was the key to a port's economy. Towns had industrialists and mills, and ports had merchants and ships; there was no need to look further. While they cannot bear comparison with Manchester, Leeds or Sheffield for singleness of purpose, the ports of Liverpool, Newcastle and Hull nevertheless had a considerable spread of industries, some shared with inland towns, and some native to ports.[1]

The industries flourishing in Hull break down into three main groups, each with extensive ramifications. Firstly, there were those concerned directly with the mechanics of trade: the building, repairing and fitting of ships. Secondly, there were those concerned with the processing of imported raw materials such as oil-seeds and sugar, and the production of derivatives, such as spirits, snuff and soap. Finally, there was a host of smaller ventures—sometimes adventures—providing miscellaneous consumer and luxury goods for the local people and, in some cases, for exportation: perukes, mantuas, stays, hose and slops, candles and sealing-wax, jewellery and plate, ship-biscuits and beer.

1. SHIPBUILDING AND RELATED TRADES

Shipbuilding and repairing was the oldest and most important local industries. For centuries ships had been built along the banks of the

[1] According to F. Eden (*The State of the Poor* (1797), Vol. III, p. 829) there were 'no woollen nor cotton manufacturies in or near Hull; sail-cloth and sacking are manufactured, but the quantity is not very considerable. There are also rope-makers, mast-makers, block-makers; six or seven yards for building, and as many dry docks for repairing ships; two sugar-houses, a soap-house, a paper-mill, several mills for bruising rape-seed and lint-seed, grinding flour, &c., some of which are worked by steam engines and the rest by wind.'

Hull and the Humber, taking full advantage of plentiful and cheap supplies of hinterland oak and Baltic masts, spars and sail cloth. Most were for local owners, some for other ports, and a few, during the major wars, for the Royal Navy. They ranged from the great thousand-tonners for the navy to the small coasters, and the equally necessary keels for the Humber and lighters for the Hull.

It was not difficult to open a shipyard in the days before steam and iron ships. Fixed equipment was minimal, and most of the ships were small and unsophisticated, avoiding the complications accompanying the launching of larger vessels. The major considerations were finance to cover the building costs, skilled labour, and trusting owners. Consequently shipbuilding was carried on in the most unlikely of inland waterways until well into the nineteenth century, and the smallest of independent shipwrights could, with good luck and good friends, call himself a shipbuilder.

Although Armin, Selby, Knottingly and Gainsborough had their flourishing sloop-builders, Hull produced most—but not all—of the larger vessels, if only because that was where the majority of the ship-using merchants lived. The leading shipbuilders, at least until the last quarter of the eighteenth century, were the Blaydes. One of the great aldermanic families, they traded, built and owned ships, made rope, and intermarried with a multitude of merchant families. As early as 1667 William was described as a shipwright;[1] Hugh was practising before 1693, when he was granted a lease of the Corporation's land outside the north gate;[2] and William and Benjamin were both taking apprentices in 1700.[3] In 1720 Joseph agreed with the Corporation to take over the lease of the shipyard, now in the name of his father, Benjamin, but it was another Hugh who eventually secured it in 1721, for a rent of nine pounds per annum.[4] In 1749, after a long period of prosperity in shipbuilding, the Bench gave notice 'That the Shipyard and Premises belonging to the Corporation of Hull, now in the tenure of Mr. Hugh Blaydes, will be lett at the Town Hall, on the first day of May next . . .',[5] and the Blaydes were forced to offer an advanced rent of thirty-one pounds.[6] The

[1] T. Blashill, *Evidences Relating to East Hull* (Hull, 1903), p. 72.

[2] BB viii, 338. [3] BB viii, 469.

[4] BB viii, 695, 700. The low rent was no doubt another cost factor favouring building in Hull.

[5] *Hull Courant*, 14 Apr 1749.

[6] The lease is in *GH* MS M.798.

yard was sold to the Dock Company in 1775, when the Bench asked that Blaydes should remain in possession 'whilst the Spring Ships of the year were fitting out . . .',[1] but its eventual loss (possibly in 1787) did not come as a great blow. Since the forties Blaydes had had a yard at Hessle, where most of their large ships were constructed.

Blaydes' turned out most of the big ships built in Hull, particularly those for the Admiralty (see Appendix 35). They began their contract work with the 436–ton sixth-rate HMS *Success* in 1740, and built a further sixth-rate, five fifth-rates, a fourth-rate and a 271-ton sloop before 1748 brought peace and an end to naval building.[2] The renewal of war in 1756 brought another eight contracts, including two third-rates—the 1,376 ton H.M.S. *Ardent* and the ill-fated H.M.S. *Temple*. The *Temple* was of great moment for Hull shipbuilding: she sank.[3] The *Ardent* was found to be rotten. London builders grasped this wonderful opportunity to denigrate their northern rivals, and Hull's Members of Parliament had to plead for further contracts to be given to the town by a reluctant Admiralty. What effect this incident had on civil building is unknown, but the publicity was unlikely to encourage purchasers from other ports. Hull owners such as the Hammonds had their larger ships built in Whitby, and extensive use was made of cheap and sturdy American ships in the second half of the century, until their acquisition was prohibited by the Navigation Act of 1786.[4]

Three other firms can be traced in the first quarter of the century. John Shields was taking many apprentices until the forties,[5] but is otherwise unknown. John Frame was a Wapping builder who came to Hull for a few years at the end of the seventeenth century because

[1] HDCLB, 10 Jun 1775.

[2] Ships built at Hull are noted by J. A. Rupert-Jones, 'King's Ships Built at Hull', *Notes and Queries*, Vol. 156 (1929), pp. 23–4. His list is incomplete, and may be supplemented by HCLB, *passim*. All the ships between 1740 and 1764 are included in a list (obviously from HCLB) in the Corporation's interleaved copy of Tickell's *History*.

[3] The case of the *Temple* and *Ardent* is discussed by Bernard Pool, *Navy Board Contracts, 1660–1832* (London 1966), pp. 93–4.

[4] This Act tried to stop American vessels from participating in imperial trade (using false or 'double' registration) by denying to recently acquired American vessels the privileges attaching to British built vessels. The British shipbuilding industry was immediately stimulated, as its authors had intended.

[5] IIA, 1720–65, Nos. 62, 98, 730.

it was a convenient place for him to undertake Navy contracts.[1] The third man, John Reed, was second only to Blaydes in importance. He also secured Navy contracts, and was building his fourth sixth-rate battleship when he ran into financial difficulties in 1757.[2] The ship was finished by Hodgson & Bryan in their 'Charlestown' yard, so called to commemorate Bryan's American origin and Hodgson's family's deep interest in American trades.[3] Their partnership was short lived. Between 1763 and 1774 Blaydes & Hodgson were building together in the Charlestown yard, so it looks as if Blaydes had fallen heirs to the Reed business.

Thomas Hodgson is only one of the new names appearing in the middle of the century. Francis Ombler, an important wharfinger,[4] Thomas Walton,[5] Thomas Gleadow[6] and John Barnes[7] were all building in the sixties. Walton was an old Blaydes apprentice (1743–51)[8] who had set up his yard in Armin.[9] He eventually returned to Hull, and no doubt made good use of the capital which came to him through his marriage to Margaret Porter, an heiress of the great merchant house of that name. For a time in the eighties Thomas's son, Nicholas, was joined by Francis Bine, shipowner, merchant and industrialist.[10] Nicholas added to the family fortune and prestige by marrying Samuel Standidge's grand-daughter, and it was their son, Samuel Standidge Walton, who eventually received much of the old man's property.[11] Standidge himself was taking apprentices as a shipbuilder in the nineties[12]—an indication of the

[1] B. Pool, p. 93. A silver tankard presented to him by the Admiralty to mark the launching of the eighty-gun *Humber* (3 Mar 1693) mentions the location of the yard at Hessle. (The tankard is now in Trinity House.)

[2] *London Gazette*, No. 9890, 24 Apr 1758. Reed was discharged, but does not appear to have reopened his yard.

[3] Hodgson was the most vociferous merchant pleading in favour of bounties on Naval Stores in 1771, when their abandonment was considered.

[4] IIA, 1720–65, No. 1835/B (1763).

[5] ibid., No. 1909/B (1765). [6] ibid., No. 1922/B (1765).

[7] IIA, 1766–87, No. 117 (1767).

[8] The Apprenticeship Agreement is in *WH* Chronological MSS.

[9] He was taking apprentices, as of Armin, in 1761. IIA, 1720–65, No. 1757/B.

[10] IIA, 1766–87, No. 1477 (1785). William Walton moved to Gainsborough and set up a yard there in the nineties; IIA, 1788–99, No. 664 (1793).

[11] G. Poulson, *Holderness*, II, p. 495.

[12] IIA, 1788–99, Nos. 982–4 (1796).

ease with which men could move from one aspect of shipping to another (although one presumes that Standidge did little more than direct and finance operations).

Thomas Gleadow was the son of a yeoman of Cowick (Snaith) who came to Hull in 1751 as an apprentice of John Reed.[1] After starting his own business, he specialised in ship-repairing—as important as the original building—and later in the interesting and rewarding work of building, fitting and re-fitting whalers, which were subject to damage on almost every trip to the hazardous waters of the Arctic. The largest single expenditure of William Sparks & Company, owners of the *Gibraltar* and *Enterprise*, was £600 paid to Gleadow for repairs in 1791.[2]

Another man who started in Armin was William Gibson. When the Dock Company offered the old Blaydes yard for renewed lease in 1787 he won it in competition with Alderman Benjamin Blaydes and John Barnes of Hull, John Peel of Itchner (near Chichester) and Thomas Dixon of Sunderland.[3] Thus the Blaydes lost the yard which they had had for at least a century. It mattered little. Benjamin continued to take apprentices almost to his death, in 1805, but his eldest son, Benjamin, was a gentleman, variously of Hull, Beverley, London and Cheltenham; his second son, Hugh, eventually retired to Ranby Hall, Notts, where he climbed the social hill to the castle. Nothing is known about the other Hull man, Barnes, except that he was taking apprentices in the sixties,[4] and, for a time in the nineties, was the partner of Thomas Westerdell, shipowner, broker and Harbour Master.[5]

The shipbuilding industry developed considerably during the last quarter of the century, with expanding trade encouraging new builders and rewarding older ones. Although the output of the yards was great, the ships themselves were not particularly impressive. Large ships could be produced, but they were usually for the Navy. Merchantmen like the 367-ton *Peggy* built for Middleton & Company of Whitby[6] were less common than the smaller ships

[1] IIA, 1720–65, No. 1342 (1751).

[2] Sparks & Co.'s Acct., 1791, Smiths & Thompson's Ledgers.

[3] HDCLB, 16 Oct 1787 (p. 120).

[4] IIA, 1766–87, No. 117 (1767).

[5] IIA, 1788–99, Nos. 641–2 (1793). In 1782 Barnes was threatened with prosecution by the Bench if he did not remove rubbish and materials left outside his yard; BB ix, 564.

[6] R. Weatherill, *Whitby*, p. 72.

which formed the basis of Hull's merchant fleet until well into the nineteenth century—chiefly because of the great coastal trade using small ships. Thus the average tonnage of ships built at Hull during the last thirteen years of the century—127 tons—was small compared with that of the other major shipbuilding ports; but Hull compared very favourably so far as the total number and tonnage of ships was concerned. Hull was building some thirty-five ships per annum between 1787 and 1799, with an average annual tonnage of 4,442, compared with twenty-five ships and 3,766 tons at Liverpool, thirty-two ships and 7,138 tons at Newcastle, twenty-four ships and 4,340 tons at Sunderland, eighteen ships and 4,208 tons at Whitby and forty-four ships and 9,966 tons at London. At the end of the century Hull, not generally recognised as a shipbuilding port, was second only to London and Newcastle in the tonnage, and second only to London in the number of ships built. Moreover, the Hull industry had the distinct advantage of being relatively stable, with none of the great fluctuations which occurred in all the other major ports except Newcastle.

SHIPS BUILT AT THE MAJOR SHIPBUILDING PORTS, 1787–99[1]

	Hull		*L'pool*		*Newc.*		*Sund.*		*Whitby*		*London*	
	No.	*Tons*	*No.*	*Tons*	*No.*	*Tons*	*No.*	*Tons*	*No.*	*Tons*	*No.*	*Tons*
1787	39	5,471	44	5,731	35	5,923	16	2,434	26	2,836	61	16,999
1788	47	5,714	40	5,139	35	6,259	15	2,528	16	2,469	48	8,534
1789	32	3,717	26	3,166	27	5,087	12	1,588	17	4,432	37	8,280
1790	20	1,894	27	4,737	29	6,144	18	2,755	23	4,999	40	9,743
1791	36	4,668	18	2,393	30	6,346	7	1,230	22	5,665	56	6,673
1792	27	3,844	30	3,509	20	4,998	15	2,507	23	5,957	51	11,003
1793	45	5,193	18	2,137	36	8,783	32	5,087	22	5,828	33	4,986
1794	39	4,809	18	2,655	28	7,189	19	3,166	15	4,609	22	1,971
1795	42	4,564	12	1,463	33	7,984	32	6,203	20	5,295	28	7,122
1796	29	4,729	34	5,175	30	7,173	40	8,846	8	1,587	64	22,315
1797	31	4,156	20	4,749	34	7,897	34	5,902	7	1,385	65	20,342
1798	33	4,170	11	2,201	39	8,730	42	6,967	21	5,372	39	6,763
1799	38	4,818	24	5,708	43	10,285	36	7,207	14	4,285	32	4,830
Average	35	4,442	25	3,766	32	7,138	24	4,340	18	4,208	44	9,966

Before leaving shipbuilding we must turn to the enterprise of William Osbourne, the leading timber merchant and saw-miller at the end of the century and founder of Kingston-upon-Spey He turned his timber (good enough for the Royal Dockyards

[1] *PRO* Cust 17, *passim.* Although Hull's average was low, in fact only two outports—Glasgow and Whitby—built larger ships than Hull in 1791, and then only two each; Customs 17/13.

at Deptford and Woolwich) into ships on the Spey rather than bring it down to Hull. Between 1786 and *c.* 1793 his Company had built 23 vessels ranging from 25 to 500 tons, 'the greater number about 200 tons, and amounting in all to about 4000 tons'.[1] They continued building until about 1806. Although built wholly of Scottish fir, the ships were 'thought by good judges to be equal to those of New England oak . . .'. Many of them were registered in Osbourne's own name and used in the Spey trade and the Baltic trade. Some were built under contract. Others were first registered in Osbourne's name and sold later—like the *Sykes*, sold to Stockton in 1795 for £1,800.[2] The majority of the ships were transferred or sold to London *c.* 1814, to a company of which Charles Osbourne was a partner.[3]

A number of smaller, but vital trades served the shipping industry. Sailmaking was as old as sailing itself. The raging elements took a heavy toll in canvas, and every stay in port saw feverish activity with the needle and thread. Many sails were imported coastwise and from Holland in the first half of the century, and there may not have been a very great demand for locally made sails. Only eight sailmakers were recorded in the 1747 Poll Book, although they may have been masters employing workmen. Although the number of freemen sailmakers had risen to twenty-six by 1768, the most important development was not in the number of sailmakers (there is only one in the 1791 *Directory*) but in the rise of the sail-cloth mill. At least by the eighties Hull had begun to convert some of her huge import of linen yarn into cloth, and there were three or four mills making sail-cloth, sacking and tarpauling in the nineties. Robert Spouncer was taking apprentices as a 'Sailcloth and Sacking Manufacturer' in 1798 and as a 'Manufacturer' in 1799;[4] Charles Shipman, master mariner, whaler owner, and ropemaker was making sails in

[1] J. Sinclair (ed.), *Statistical Account of Scotland* (1793), vol. XIV, p. 395.

[2] Wm. Osbourne, Kingston Port, to J. R. Pease, 14 Jun 1795, *WH* 59/58/51.

[3] Hull Custom House, Hull Shipping Register, 1804–16, *passim.* The partners were James Thomson, Charles Osbourne and Isaac Westmoreland, ship agents; ibid., 1812/2.

[4] IIA, 1788–99, Nos. 1157–9 and 1299–1303. One wonders if these were the 'Factory apprentices' to be found in the textile districts. The Corporation were at a loss what to do with pauper children. Spinning was taught in the Charity Hall, and the mills no doubt provided an easy way of disposing of boys.

1797;[1] Whitaker's sail-cloth factory was noted by Turner in 1805, and Joseph Potts may already have opened his factory in Spring Row and his 'Sail-loft' at the Dock. The sailcloth and sacking factory belonging to John Maddison (of Gainsborough) was worth £8,000 when it was offered for sale in 1803.[2]

Ropemaking did not develop in the same way as sailmaking. Weaving lent itself to sophisticated machinery and power, and was concentrated in highly capitalised mills owned by 'manufacturers'. Ropemaking, by contrast, was less capital intensive. Ropers could work where they could 'walk'; but they, too, were beginning to be regimented in the interests of quality control. The first recorded master ropers were landsmen such as Haldenby Dixon, a merchant, who failed *c.* 1757;[3] John Standidge, a leading coastal merchant and tenant of the Corporation's ropery in the forties;[4] and Samuel Wright, merchant.[5] Although a number of landsmen ropemakers persisted till the end of the century (Middleton & Company, Thomas Nicholas, James Cook), the development of ropemaking in the second half of the century placed the industry firmly in the hands of shipowners, who had been for some time concerned about the reliability of ropes supplied to them. Charles Shipman, James Kiero[6] and Horncastle & Foster[7] were all shipowners, and Benjamin Blaydes[8] was both owner and builder.

One of the major difficulties of ropemakers was obtaining spun hemp at a reasonable price. Spinning was an unpleasant task, and wages in Hull were high enough to force costs to a prohibitive level. At the turn of the century Thomas Thompson recorded that ropemakers were sending hemp 'to poor people to spin, at the distance of 50 and 60 miles from Hull'.[9] It may have been for this reason that

[1] IIA, 1788–99, No. 1080.

[2] DDHB/29/106–13. The factory was bought in 1812 by R. C. Broadley.

[3] He was taking apprentices as a Roper in 1746, IIA, 1720–65, No. 1091. He was in partnership as a merchant with Rd. Norcliffe, and it is not known which of his activities led to his bankruptcy. His growing financial embarrassment can be followed in the cases against him in the Hull Court of Record, *GH* Book of Actions 1749–60, Jan–Nov 1756, *passim*. He was sued for at least £520.

[4] He was ordered to leave the Ropery in 1745, BB ix, 81.

[5] IIA, 1720–65, No. 1860/B (1764).

[6] Described always as Ropemaker in his shipowning partnerships.

[7] IIA 1788–99, Nos. 1028–31 (1795/6).

[8] IIA, 1788–99, Nos. 761–4 (1794).

[9] T. Thompson, *A Short Account. . . .*

William Hall, another shipowner, set up what was ultimately the most important and lasting of the roperies in Barton-upon-Humber in 1771. As Hall's Barton Ropery (despite its return to Hull) it gained a reputation for reliability and quality far beyond the Humber.

A third industry involved directly with shipping produced pitch, which was used with oakum (unpicked rope ends) to caulk ships. The best pitch came from Sweden, but people feared for the security of this supply during wars. American pitch, though relatively more secure, was of such poor quality that the Navy Board was reluctant to use it.[1] An acceptable compromise seemed to lie in the conversion of American tar into pitch in British yards, and the chief pitch producers in Hull were the specialists in American trade. Hamilton & Edge imported large quantities of Plantation—and Swedish—tar, which they distilled and mixed with alum, resin and lime in their Wincomblee yard.[2] But whether they were tar merchants who entered the American trade because it was a good source of tar, or American merchants who distilled tar because it was obtainable from America is, unfortunately, unknown. Their place was taken later in the century by Richard Howard (of Howard & Parker) who owned, among other things, tar yards, still houses, boiling houses, brick and tile kilns, and Waltons' dry dock and shipyard.[3] Bourne & Osbourne, the timber and tar merchants, may also have been producing their own pitch.[4]

2. THE PROCESSING INDUSTRIES

The largest consumers of fixed capital were the processing industries, of which the oldest was oil-seed crushing. As far back as the beginning of the fifteenth century Hull had imported seed oil, and the earliest reference to the milling of rape occurs in the early sixteenth century.[5] There is, however, little information about the early history of the industry, and we have only the scantiest knowledge of conditions in 1700. Several mills are known to have been in existence, one of them belonging to the Crown and leased to Francis

[1] J. J. Malone, *Pine Trees and Politics* (London, 1964), p. 31.

[2] HCLB, C–B, 25 Feb 1752.

[3] Richard Howard's Will, 31 Dec 1779, DDHB/45/78.

[4] They appear as tar merchants in the 1791 *Directory*.

[5] H. W. Brace, *History of Seed Crushing in Great Britain* (London, 1960), p. 15.

Wyvill of York in September 1705.[1] Daniel Berry was a prominent 'oilman' from at least the twenties[2] to the middle of the century when he gave his name to the first Hull whaler, and Joseph Berry appeared in his place in the fifties. Thomas Nicholson was an oil-miller in the thirties,[3] and John Richardson had at least two mills when he failed in 1738.[4] Widow Sarah Fearnley had two mills in the thirties, one worked by wind and the other by horse power, and De la Pryme & Company, Daniel Bridges, Christopher Harrison and Pead, Lee & Company had mills flourishing in the middle of the century. Daniel Bridges had reached a degree of experimentation which enabled him to register one of the earliest patents in the oil industry, in 1748. It was, he said, 'A new method to refine, purify and meliorate an oyle extracted from rape oyl', and involved a process of refining using sulphuric acid.[5]

While little can be said about individual firms, the growth of the industry may be roughly gauged from the port's import and export figures. We know, for instance, that the number of cattle cakes exported in 1717 was roughly 150,000 and that by 1737 the number had risen to over 400,000. We also know that the quantity of linseed imported, mainly from the Baltic, rose greatly, from 1,902 bushels in 1728 to 18,880 in 1758 and over 66,000 in 1783. At the same time seed was brought in increasing quantities from various parts of Britain. The East Riding developed its own flax growing, stimulated by government bounties distributed by Smiths & Thompson's bank. The hinterland also responded to the demand, and the Aire & Calder alone carried seed to the value of almost £10,000 in 1792.[6]

In the second half of the century the expansion of milling in Hull was encouraged by the increasing demand for oil for the cloth industry, for soap, paint and putty making, and for lighting. New mills sprang up. The Maisters invested in one (probably two). Mayson Wright, who may have been associated with De la Pryme & Company (he married Sally De la Pryme) earlier in the century,

[1] *WH* Yorkshire Deeds, No. 112.

[2] When his son was apprenticed to Wm. Shields, 'Aromatar'; IIA, 1720–65, No. 252 (1727).

[3] His son was apprenticed to Rewben Gillieat, Translator, in 1737; IIA, 1720–65, No. 617.

[4] He bought £200 of linseed a day or two before he broke, 'which one of his Mills only works on at Daytime'; J. Pease, Hull, to Rbt Pease, 27 Oct 1738, *WH* 59/58/47.

[5] H. W. Brace, p. 161.

[6] Tickell, p. 872.

commissioned John Smeaton in 1776 to construct an oil mill 'to be worked by Water raised by a Fire Engine at Hull'.[1] The result was a ponderous machine incorporating a wheel some twenty-seven feet in diameter, and it seems more than likely that Wright was thinking of making use of the steam engine which he had just installed as lessee of the Corporation water works. Shortly afterwards Jarratt & Coates built a large mill which also employed a steam engine.[2]

Most of the millers so far mentioned had other pursuits. The majority were merchants; Jarratt & Coates were deeply involved in whaling. But in oil-milling, as in other things, the industrialist was beginning to emerge in his own right, unconnected with trade. A handful of millers at the end of the century appear never to have been merchants: Ritchie & Company, Thompson, Rickard & Company, Magginis Fea, George Drant and Richard Tottie. But they lacked the staying power of the more versatile merchants with other things to fall back on, and none of them survived for long.

One firm outshone and outlived all the rest: Joseph Pease & Son. Their surviving letters and papers are the best illustration we have of oil-milling and its related trades. When Robert Pease sent his sons to Britain, he had the oil trade rather than anything else in mind. 'Whilst you are in Ireland', he wrote to them in 1709, 'observe as much as you can what the Country affords, and where such graine & other Commodities are best to bee had & alsoe how the Cropps are of seeds, as of Rapeseed, Linseed, & Hempseed. . . .'[3] George liked what he observed, built a couple of mills with money borrowed from uncle George Clifford, and never left Ireland. Joseph, after a false start in London, settled in Hull, an excellent centre for distributing oil along the east coast and into the interior of England. George and Joseph between them were thus in a position to supply any part of England speedily and efficiently to the order of their father in Amsterdam. Soon their London agent, Richard Hoare, and their English customers wrote direct to Hull, and Joseph became the key figure in the Pease oil business.

Joseph Pease started as an oil merchant, but it was not long before he was building his own mill, and investing heavily in oil seeds, his costs and prices calculated on intelligence received by every letter

[1] Copy of the 'Explanation of the Design for an Oil Mill for Mr. Mayson Wright', *HCRL* L.665.3/12800.

[2] Millers in the last quarter of the century are noted by Tickell, p. 850.

[3] Rbt. Pease, Amsterdam, to 'Sonns', 9 Jul 1709, *WH* 59/58/37.

from London, Ireland and Amsterdam. His father, brother and cousins kept him informed of harvests in the Baltic, frost and thaws in Holland, and ice in the Arctic: the whale fishery, he was told in 1716, 'will have some Influence on price of Rapeseed & that oyle'.[1] By the late thirties oil-milling was his chief concern, to the great annoyance of his brother William, more interested in lead and iron. William complained in 1735 of his ignorance of lead prices: 'you take care to know more of Rapeseed, which you are bragging great matters of'.[2] Three days earlier he had complained about Joseph's dealings with him: 'in such a trade [rapeseed] you delight, tho with other peoples mony & Credit be the loss never so considerable to those you ingage. . . .'[3]

Although much of Pease's seed came from the Baltic, secured by his brother and his cousins Clifford, and shipped by his brother-in-law Captain William Hill, an increasing amount was purchased at home. George Pease sent it over from Ireland, via Bristol and the London coastal trade, and Joseph's son, Robert, went on regular tours of standing seed around Wisbech, Lynn, Spalding and Boston.

By 1736–7, when accounts became available, Pease was processing all but a negligible fraction of the seed he purchased.[4] His sales for that year were impressive: 31,792 gallons of rape oil, 21,958 of 'Green' oil, and 18,825 of linseed oil, together worth £6,100. Over the next twenty years his sales fluctuated, and the last account (1753–4) shows slightly lower sales than the first (though the oil sold was worth about the same). In fact there had been a considerable increase in capacity, with a fourth mill coming into production—for linseed—in 1751, and a very noticeable increase in sales had taken place between 1736–7 and 1743–4.

Pease was eager for technical innovation, and Holland, as we might expect, was his source of inspiration. Pieces of brass equipment of the latest design were brought over, and his son, and later his grandsons, went on tours of inspection of Dutch mills. In 1747 Robert sent over to Hull a book of 'Draughts of all the Mills in the Country',[5] and when they were considering building the fourth

[1] Wm. Pease, Amsterdam, to J. Pease, 11 July 1716, *WH* 59/58/44.
[2] Wm. Pease to J. Pease, 25 Nov 1735, *WH* 59/58/44.
[3] Wm. Pease to J. Pease, 22 Nov 1735, *WH* 59/58/44.
[4] Various accounts, mostly Annual Sales, all in *WH* 59/58/48.
[5] Rbt Pease, Amsterdam, to J. Pease, 31 Jul 1747, *WH* 59/58/39.

JOSEPH PEASE'S OIL SALES, 1736–7 TO 1753–4[1]

(Gallons)

		1737	*1741*	*1744*	*1746*	*1748*	*1749*	*1751*	*1753*
reen Oil	London	21,959	2,176	12,609	9,211	8,802	6,760	9,754	8,402
	Country		15,915	25,176	20,821	23,784	18,151	16,550	13,305
emp Oil		0	0	0	57	1,975	3,614	1,293	837
inseed Oil	London	18,825	1,348	4,322†	8,547†	1,345	772	5,885	3,574
	Country		10,372	9,202	8,410	9,765	10,954	12,105	12,980
ape Oil	London	31,793	807	7,254†	5,172†	8,986	1,478	1,192	4,753
	Country		19,983	28,361	33,678	30,484	33,565	36,585	24,740
rain Oil		146	1,003	0	0	0	0	0	0
OTAL OIL		73,520*	53,197*	86,924	85,897	85,141	75,294	83,363	68,592
ALUE OF OIL		£6,194	£6,788	£9,253	£8,206	£8,134	£7,864	£7,553	£6,183
inseed Cakes (No.)		28,620	21,966	39,550	53,486	28,925	50,577	51,026	82,833
ape Cakes (Tons)		67½	127	99½	171	201	246	152	24

* Includes a small quantity of Olive Oil.
† Includes oil listed as 'Little Book'.

mill Joseph asked friends in Rotterdam to locate the best millwright in Holland to come over to build it.[2] In 1753 they turned to Manchester as a possible source of better rollers: 'I wish you to get Mr Sam Taylor to send me a rough Sketch (in one of his letters) of his Father's Rollers that he uses for Flatning his Organ Mettal Pipes with. I think there is s[ome] difference in the Contrivance from those we use in the Oil Mills.'[3] A year later John Smeaton was drawing up a report on 'A Fire engine and Oyl Mill for Mr Pease'.[4]

Joseph Robinson Pease, with many varied interests to attend to, seems to have divided his oil-milling into two partnerships. The first was with John Wray who was also, after 1795, a partner in the bank. The second, and probably most important, was with John Brooke. The Brooke & Pease mill, complete with steam engine, was insured for no less than £12,000 in the early nineteenth century,[5] but the

[1] *WH* 59/58/48. The dates are not calendar years, but are the years ending Nov 1737, Dec 1741, Jul 1744, Aug 1746, Oct 1748, Oct 1749, Jan 1752 (new style), and Jan 1754.

[2] Draft, n.d., J. Pease, Hull, to Widow John Morgan & Son, Rotterdam, *WH* 59/58/41.

[3] Rbt Pease in postcript to R. Robinson, Manchester, 20 May 1753, *WH* 59/58/47.

[4] No reference to this appears in the surviving letters, but see H. W. Brace, p. 27.

[5] Sun Fire Office Policy Bk, 1804–18, *HUL* DX/43/1.

Pease, Wray & Trigg partnership lasted the longest, into the eighteen-thirties.[1]

The sale of oil was only part of the oil-miller's operations. Pease received a further thousand pounds or more per annum from the sale of the inevitable rape and linseed cakes into which the broken seed was pressed during the last stage of oil extraction. They went at first to Dutch contacts, who had long known their value as cattle and horse food, but as the Agrarian Revolution progressed they were diverted increasingly to the home market.

Oil-milling and refining was the beginning of a complex series of technically related operations. Most of the millers had further interests, some in paint, some in soap. One of the oldest paint firms in Britain, Tudors Mash & Company, trace their ancestry back to Samuel Tudor, who is reputed to have founded the firm in Hull in 1749,[2] but there were paint makers at an earlier date than this. As early as 1703, boxes of painters' colours were sent up to Sunderland, and there are a number of references to paint in later Port Books. Throughout the eighteenth century paint-making seems to have been a side-line of milling, rather than an independent occupation: the contractors supplying paint to the Dock Company in the seventies were Thomas Lee (of Pead & Lee) and Joseph Pease.

The second ingredient of paint was white lead, and it was almost certainly the easy availability of both the raw materials, together with the importation of colours from Holland, that encouraged the paint industry to grow in Hull. It is sometimes said that the existence of firms wishing to make paint encouraged the white lead manufacturers at the end of the eighteenth century.[3] This is not so. Although Pickard's factory, established in 1791, is said to have been the first in England, Hull had, in fact, been exporting white lead for a very long time. Alderman Beilby, married to the daughter of a Chesterfield Alderman, had a white lead mill in the forties,[4] and the ubiquitous Joseph Pease was heavily committed from the beginning.

[1] Mr. Brace traced the Brooke mill to 1811 (pp. 118–19) and the Wray mill to 1831 (p. 128).

[2] Tudors Mash & Co., Ltd., *Pioneers in Paint* (1949). No early records have survived to substantiate the date 1749, and Tudor appears in none of the usual local sources.

[3] See, for example, *Pioneers in Paint*, p. 7.

[4] The existence of the mill did not merit attention in the eighteenth century, but—fortunately for us—one of the workmen was recorded as having hanged himself there in 1743; Hadley, p. 324.

In the forties he was producing red lead, red paint, white lead, white primer and two qualities of white paint:

PEASE'S WHITE LEAD AND PAINT PRODUCTION, 1736–7 TO 1753–4[1]

		1737	*1741*	*1744*	*1746*	*1748*	*1749*	*1751*	*1754*
White Lead	London	439	203	177	181*	62	59	54	1359
	Country		328	424	534	623	828	647	
White Lead Paint	London	632	230	290*	221*	113	170	75	27
	Country		327	362	298	392	413	459	431
White Lead Priming Paint	London	118	52	22	56	0	14	329	264
	Country		214	231	261	297	342		
Read Lead		322	195	0	0	0	0	0	0
Red Lead Paint		62	58	71*	96	92	91	108	104

* Includes small quantities listed as 'Little Book'.

As with everything else, Pease was eager to be pressing on with new things, and constantly strove to improve the quality of his products. In 1738 he wrote to his son in great excitement that he had 'hitt upon something wch I believe will be of advantage to our white Lead trade'.[2] The secret material was, he said,

> exceeding White & with a Bluish Cast & exceeds the Colour of White Lead & is harder than the Sort that wee add in making the 2nd Sort of [. . .] before it bee ground under the Oyle Mill Stones & is heavier than it & will come very low, but not soe low as the former. Will be more Charge in getting it fitt for the use of Paint. The ordering of it in getting it the w Colour I am Certaine of, but havent gott a quantity to make a thorough tryall of it as I hope & endeavour to doe as soon as I can. And to get it fine enough will not bee soe easie as the former & is the better Sign which if I can Compleat as I expect, may bee of great advantage to our Paint Trade, but will be difficult to keep as a Secrett, tho not soe easie to doe by others, few or none has soe good Convenency for doeing it or grinding & washing it etc as wee have. What its made of intend to write at foot hereof which you may cut of after perusall. Such like coal as your Kilkenny Coales that makes the least smoak & Flame is best & such as Mr Rd Thompson dryeth his Malt here with & is your Welch coale I take to be best. . . . I think there is little or noe hazard in it. I never saw anything that cookes more like the nature of the

[1] From Pease Accounts, *WH* 59/58/48. The actual dates are the same as for Pease's oil sales; see p. 191, note 1.

[2] J. Pease, Hull, to R. Pease, 12 Aug 1738; *WH* 59/58/47 (punctuation added).

Whites Chany [sic], but is much Whiter than it & as heavie as. I am apt to think the same or like is made use of in Glasing of Delft ware & such as is made at Liverpool in imitation of China ware. . . .

The postscript with the secret remains:

Black Flint Stone that comes out of Chalk & Lime Stones but the former are as black as Glass Bottles, burnt in a Lime Kiln & of such is our White [. . .]ings made of.

The new material was not an instantaneous success,[1] and Pease did not make his name as a paintmaker, although he continued to make it, no doubt in company with one or two of the other oil millers.

The main development in the paint industry—its partial separation from oil milling—came during the Napoleonic war. There were three or four colour mills by the end of the century (including the Horse Colour Mill of Samuel Thompson, merchant) and they were joined in the early nineteenth century by a developing Tudors and by the great modern firms of Sissons (1803) and Blundells (1811).

Closely associated with the paint 'industry' was the production of whiting. Samuel Lawson had a Whiting House in 1757;[2] and Richard Ross was a whiting manufacturer in 1791, but it was the paint and white lead manufacturers who dominated production without gaining an entry in the *Directory*. Peases made whiting at Hessle, shipping it down to Hull by keel. They had enough awaiting shipment in 1768 'to White Wash all his Majesty's filthy Jails in the Kingdom, as well as his Royal Chapels & Palaces. . . .'[3]

A number of the oil-millers made soap, from tallow and probably also from vegetable oil. Soapmaking was a fine art, only slowly being learned from the Dutch, and huge quantities of both soft and hard soap were imported coastwise from London throughout the century. Peases brought over a Dutch soapboiler, but appear to have concentrated all their soap production in Ireland, since it was easier to move the soap than the oil and tallow of Ireland, and Ireland was also nearer to the kelp supplies of the west of Scotland. Robert & Stephen Gee were making soap in Hull in the forties,[4] but the major step forward came in 1755 when John Thornton induced

[1] Silica, although, as Pease said, extremely white, would have a covering capacity far inferior to white lead which held the field until modern times.

[2] Sculcoats Parish Rate Book, 1757.

[3] Rbt Pease, Hesslewood, to J. Pease, 8 Sep 1768, *WH* 59/58/37.

[4] Rbt Gee, Tallow Chandler and soapboiler took his son Stephen apprentice in 1742; IIA, 1720–65, No. 806.

Benjamin Pead, 'citizen and soapboiler of the city of London' to join with him in a great oil-mill development including a soap-works.[1] As Thornton, Pead & Company, then Pead & Lee and, after *c.* 1795, as Lee & Cross, it survived into the nineteenth century as Hull's major soapworks. Four years after Thornton, Pead & Company were established, a soapboiler called Isaac Steer was advertising in the *Hull Courant* for 'Any person that is willing to join in carrying on the advantageous Art and Mystery of making *Castle Soap* from kelp', and he added the enticement that his soap was selling at 48*s.* per hundred 'which exceeds any that is made in or near that place'.[2] He did not survive until the first *Directory* and, like the Gees, has left no mark. Nor did Christopher Jackson's adventure last for long; a 'Tallow chandler and soap-boiler' in 1774, he was only 'Tallow Chandler' in 1791.

To anyone living in or visiting Hull in the hundred years following 1754 the most obvious of the oilmen were those processing whale blubber. Its appalling stench exceeded even the nauseous aroma of the seed oil mill and the acrid fumes of the tar yard. The blubber was casked and brought back to be rendered down in the 'Greenland' yards which sprang up along the banks of the Hull. The first was opened in the fifties with the beginning of the Hull Whale Fishery Company's adventures. Whether it was owned by one of the whaling firms—the Hull Whale Fishery, Hamilton & Company and Welfitt & Company—or by an oil merchant is a matter for conjecture. The meagre evidence points to Benjamin Pead & Company, the only firm making large payments to the Hull Whale Fishery Company, presumably for blubber.[3] As oil millers and tallow chandlers they would at least have some idea of the technique required for the refining of whale oil, whereas the merchant owners would not. Moreover, whale oil had been processed in Hull long before the native whaling industry developed; blubber as well as oil had been imported from America, and it was the value of the

[1] According to Strother (Oct 1784), Pead had been left £10,000 by his father, who had been cook to the Lord Mayor of London. He died in 1784 worth £40,000. Some of his success may have been due to his marriage to Ann, daughter of Theophilus Somerscales, a leading timber merchant; G. Poulson, II, 338.

[2] *Hull Courant*, 20 Mar 1759.

[3] Pead to Co's Acct, Pease Bank Ledgers. The Sculcoates Rate Bk. refers simply to the 'Greenland Fishery' and gives no owner's name, unless 'Hull Whale Fishery Company' is implied.

refined oil which caused the controversies over the ownership of whales and 'large fish' stranded in the Humber. When whaling revived again after the Seven Years' War, it was merchants rather than owners who had the Greenland Yard in Wincomblee. In 1768 and 1769 the rates were paid by Daniel Williamson, spermaceti chandler, and in 1770 it was once again in the hands of Benjamin Pead.[1]

The expansion of whaling in the eighties encouraged a number of new Greenland yards, but refining was concentrated in a few firms, such as Eggingtons and Boltons, both very important oil merchants and whaler owners. The smaller firms, such as Sparks & Company, confined their activities to the ownership of the whalers, and at the turn of the century the needs of the entire whaling fleet were served by only seven Greenland yards.

Sugar refining began in Hull, as it did in the other major ports, soon after the Dutch introduced planting to the West Indies during the English Civil War.[2] There was already a Sugar House in Hull in the sixteen-sixties, although in 1673 William Smith and William Cattlin entered into a lease of 'One great building of Brick lately called a Sugar House but now occupyed for a Rape Mill'.[3] It was almost sixty years before anyone tried again; with sugar, as with many other things, independence in Hull was hampered by the ease with which supplies could be moved up from London. It was somewhere between 1726 and 1731 that Godfrey Thornton of London, merchant and Director of the Bank of England, and William Thornton of Hull began work on their huge refinery in Lime Street, probably in conjunction with their brother-in-law William Wilberforce, one of the executors of Richard Sykes, who had owned the site. At an unknown date they took into partnership Samuel Watson, and the union was cemented by the marriage of John Thornton, nephew of the founders, to Lucy Watson.[4]

The Lime Street Sugar House was a grand affair. According to Gent, who published an illustration of it in his *History*,[5] it was seventy-four feet high, seventy-nine feet long and forty-six feet wide, and those of the hundred and thirty-six windows which are visible

[1] Sculcoates Rate Bk, *passim.*

[2] See, for an informative comparison, T. C. Smout, 'Early Glasgow Sugar Houses, 1660–1720', *Econ. Hist. Rev.*, Vol. XIV (1961–2), p. 240.

[3] *WH* East Yorks Deeds, No. 24.

[4] See T. Blashill, *Evidences, passim.*

[5] Gent, p. 82 (see Plate 7).

are arranged in nine rows, suggesting the existence of nine separate floors. It was expanded in the middle of the century, possibly when Watson came in and the soap works was added, and by the end of the century its value was considerable. In 1797 the 'Single Refining Sugar House on the South Side of Lime Street Containing 4 pans' and the 'double refining House containing two pans', together with the stock, utensils and warehouse, were insured against fire for £23,000.[1]

Thornton & Watson soon had a rival. Charles Delamotte, son of a London sugar refiner, was sent up to Hull when he returned from his journey with John Wesley to Georgia. He built the New Sugar House in Wincomblee, and was in business from the forties to the seventies, for part of the time in partnership as Delamotte, Beel & Company.[2] Delamotte made—or inherited—enough money to forsake the world of business for the tranquillity of Lincolnshire, spending the last thirty years of his life in retirement in Barrow-upon-Humber.

Delamotte's place was taken in Hull by Francis Bine, master mariner and whaler owner who, it was said, made £20,000 out of the American war, and 'commenced Merchant and Sugar Boiler having bought the New Sugar House on Wincomblee'.[3] He occupied the House for perhaps twenty years, having a turnover, in his bank account for 1785, of a little over £26,000.[4] Some time around 1790 he or his executors sold the House to 'John Bassano, John Carlill, John Boyes and John Levett of Hull Sugar Bakers'; or, to be more accurate, they bought it by running up a huge overdraft with Smiths & Thompson's bank. Their premises were insured for £15,000 until August 1797, when the total was raised to £20,000.[5] We might, without fear of exaggeration, presume that the two Sugar Houses between them had a capital in excess of £50,000.

There were a number of other people connected with sugar, but their importance cannot be gauged. Henry Ecken was described as a sugar baker in 1748 when his son was apprenticed to William Bolton the Surgeon.[6] Since only sons of high ranking merchants

[1] Sun Fire Office Bk.

[2] They are so recorded in the 1758 Port Book as exporting sugar.

[3] Strother, f. 27 (30 Sep 1784).

[4] Smiths & Thompson's Ledgers, Francis Bine's Acct.

[5] Sun Fire Office Bk.

[6] IIA, 1720–65, No. 1160 (1748).

or of gentry were received as surgeon apprentices in Hull, we may assume wealth, but it is likely that he was a continental (his son rejoiced in the name Dodo) brought over to superintend the work of refining by Thorntons or Delamotte. William Cookson, merchant and grocer, was more specific in his claim to be a refiner, but he may have had a rather commercial approach to the truth. He was certainly enterprising enough to insert an advertisement in the *Leeds Intelligencer* (he came originally from Leeds) begging leave 'to acquaint the public, that for the better Accommodation of his friends, he will soon open a Warehouse adjoining the New Inn, in Briggate . . .'.[1] No record of his refinery has survived, although that is far from proving that it did not exist.

As with sugar, Hull had a small direct trade, and a huge coastal trade, in tobacco; and though she could not bear comparison with the western ports she nevertheless had a flourishing tobacco industry. As early as 1728 a tobacco engine and mill had been imported, from Arundell, and the Travis mill was well established by the second half of the century. In 1786, when the Customs drew up an 'Account of the Manufactories for Tobacco and Snuff in the Port and in the Towns up the Rivers',[2] Hull had four mills: William, John and Joseph Travis (one of Hull's few Quaker families), Richard Baker & Company, John Carrick & Company, and Richard Mattson & Company, the latter specialising, according to their advertisements, in the 'Best Virginia'. All four of the mills made both tobacco and snuff, the only manufactories in the Hull area that did, with the exception of Thomas Eastorby and John Capstick of York.

Another, quite different, processing industry was tanning which, like paintmaking, was still in its infancy at the end of the eighteenth century. In the early part of the century leather had been produced in the hinterland, chiefly around Beverley, both for exportation (mainly to Spain and Portugal) and for use in the English shoemaking and leather trades. So long as the hides were obtained locally, Hull tanners had no real advantage over inland tanners, except, perhaps, in possessing a cheaper supply of sumack and other chemicals imported for the tanneries; but when hides produced in the hinterland began to be supplemented by importation, especially from Russia and, to some extent, from the north of England, Hull became important as a tanning centre where raw and salted hides

[1] *Leeds Intelligencer*, 6 May 1760. He was exporting sugar in 1758.

[2] HCLB, C–B, 16 Oct 1786.

and skins were tanned before being sent inland or to London.

We know nothing about the actual details of tanning in Hull. Tanners (or skinners) were causing a nuisance in 1734 by washing skins in the Town ditches,[1] but only one freeman tanner was recorded in the 1747 *Poll Book*, none at all in the 1768 *Poll Book*, and only one—Richard Patrick—in the 1791 *Directory*. There were, however, five curriers in the *Directory* who may also have been tanners, and there may have been some whose names go unrecorded because they worked outside the town. Certainly by the end of the century Hull's two greatest tanneries, Holmes' and Hodgson's (now at Beverley), were flourishing, and the port was well on the way to becoming a major centre of the English tanning industry.

A great quantity of leather was consumed in Hull itself, for the production of belts, boots, shoes, protective clothing and saddlery. Shoemaking, which was doubly important because it supplied a flourishing export trade, occupied some fifty freeman in 1747 and twice that number in 1768. Some were rich master craftsmen employing many journeymen. One of them, William Todd, owned fifteen houses and three tenements in Hull and a house and granary in Patrington in the early nineteenth century,[2] which might be taken to indicate a flourishing business if not actual mass production. Belt making was also becoming very important late in the century with the application of power to machinery and as the coach entered its heyday. Finally, the noble art of saddlemaking was practised by at least eight men in 1791, and many examples of their work found their way to the continent via the trade with Hamburg.

3. MISCELLANEOUS INDUSTRIES

As in most large towns, there were many people in Hull engaged in producing goods for the inhabitants and, occasionally, for a wider market. They multiplied as the town flourished.

The chief purely local industry was building, a fact so obvious that it is often overlooked. Hull, like most places influenced by the Industrial Revolution, was growing fast, and much of the older property was rebuilt in the period of great physical expansion beginning in the eighties.

Small-scale building was carried on by individual craftsmen building to the order of their client and engaging labour as required.

[1] BB viii, 791, 802. [2] Sun Fire Office Bk, *passim*.

When, for instance, the Long Jetty was dropping into decay in 1761, the Mayor was desired 'to Contract with Workmen' and have it rebuilt in brick.[1] Similarly, when a new Council Chamber was needed in 1780, the Town's Husband was instructed 'to procure from different workmen plans and estimates of the expence of rebuilding the Council Chamber with and without a Bow window, to be roofed with slates including the old materials in such Estimate'.[2]

Although the jobbing master still had his place, he was ceasing to have any importance so far as the organisation of large-scale work was concerned, for this side of the business—deliberate planning and speculating—was rapidly passing into the hands of a new race of master builders. It is doubtful, for instance, if major works such as the Sugar Houses could have been built without a fair degree of contracting and sub-contracting.

The earliest known and most important Hull master builder was Joseph Page, who completed his apprenticeship in 1740. In 1748 we hear of him as an architect and at the same time he was moving in the realms of fine art, executing the stucco work in the new Maister House in High Street, and later working for the Grimstons.[3] Besides being an accomplished architect, builder and interior decorator, he was a 'speculator' in the large building schemes necessitated by the development of the port. In 1764 Nathaniel Maister wrote to Thomas Grimston: 'the great number of failures we had among our townsmen 3 or 4 years ago had greatly lowered the rents of houses and occasioned many to stand empty. This is wearing off and I hope our town will flourish again and that Page may be induced to cover your ground with good houses'.[4] Again, in 1771, Grimston was informed that Page had 'lately made a purchase of a row of houses at the west end of the High Church belonging to the Corporation for 600 gns. and had agreed with the Mayor and Burgesses to open a new street to run from the Trinity House Lane into Fish Street. If you know that part of the town you will easily conceive the improvement it will make and I hope be greatly advantageous to Page himself'.[5] Page may not have been a master builder of the Cubitt type, employing all his own men, but his estimate for a

[1] BB ix, 823. [2] BB ix, 520.

[3] Reference in a letter, Henry Maister to John Ingram, quoted in E. Ingram, *Leaves from a Family Tree*, p. 176.

[4] ibid., p. 183. [5] ibid., p. 184.

Customs Lazarette at Skitter Creek (Lincs.) shows the range of activities he took under his control and offered in a single estimate:[1]

The Estimate Room 517 feet long and 40 ft wide	£	s.	d.
To Wharfing 75 ft long with fir timber & plank	112	10	
Crane & fixing	20		
cutting out the haven	80		
embank one acre with sides 126 Roods @ 5/–	31	10	
344 pcs of Sleepers @ 10/–	172		
workmanship & freight upon the same to 6 sq @ 8/–	18	8	
46 sq of Flouring 2 inch deals @ £2 9s.	112	14	
the Quarteren 12 ft high upon the side 4×4 954 ft @ 1/6d.	71	11	
1,485 yds of Weather Boarding @ 1/6	111	7	6
175 sqr Roofing & Tilery @ £2 p Sqr	350		
344 Beams or Jyes 6×6 & 40 ft long is 3415 @ 1/–	170	15	
labour on do & freight	17		
180 Stantions 6×6 & 12 ft long	32		
labour and Sawing	9		
joints, locks & Incidental expences	60		
a Centy Box same as I had for the board of work	2	14	6
	1,371	10	0

Dec 1770 J. Page

There were several master builders besides Page, although they were all less important until the end of the century. One of the early ones was Joseph Scott, who was building Corporation houses in Vicar Lane in 1754 and was appointed 'to pave and repair the Streets Lanes and Alleys of this Town'—at an agreed price of 2½*d.* per square yard—in 1750.[2] Others towards the end of the century included George Pycock, whose plans were used for the alterations to the Charterhouse in 1780,[3] but who refused, apparently, to build St. John's Church at cost price. The importance of the builders is emphasised by the inclusion in the 1791 *Directory* of only one bricklayer; it must have been uncommon for members of the public to deal directly with bricklayers.

The only other extensive industry was brewing. In the 1791 *Directory* there were seventeen breweries catering for locals and the thirsty Baltic, and by the end of the Napoleonic War the number had doubled. Samuel Akam had an 'extensive' brewery in Finkle Street,

[1] HCLB, C–B, Dec 1770. [2] BB ix, 222, 226. [3] BB ix, 527.

which was offered to let in 1795,[1] and Heneage Lupton was sufficiently respectable and wealthy to be a marine underwriter in the last decade of the century. Many of the breweries were no doubt small, serving a very restricted taste. Others, while they cannot be compared with the breweries of London or Burton, were nevertheless reaching respectable size. Richardson & Company was the most important.

John Richardson, of Dobson & Richardson and later of Richardson & Terrington, brewed in Hull for thirty years or more and produced a number of books on his trade.[2] His *Thoughts and Hints on the improved practice of brewing Malt Liquors* was published in 1777, and his *Statistical Estimate of the Materials of Brewing* in 1784. He was also the inventor of the Saccharometer; its effect on the quality of his beer is unrecorded, but it must have been reasonably good, for Richardson's are the first Hull brewers known to have had tied houses. By 1804 they owned the Humber Dock Coffee House, the Spread Eagle in Sutton, the White Horse in Bond Street, a house and shop in Scale Lane, the Angel in Bourne Street, the Marriner in Queen Street, and the Golden Lion in Manor Alley.[3]

Hull also had its share of distillers, hopelessly confused, for most of the century, with merchants. One or two of them seem to have distilled alcohol and oil and traded in both. Laurence Jopson was indentured to Peter Thornton, merchant,[4] but made free by apprenticeship with Peter Thornton, 'Distiller'.[5] Thornton was among the oil merchants supplying the Corporation, and to confuse matters Jopson later practised as a distiller in York[6] and an oil merchant in Stockton![7] A Mr. Horner's distillery was inspected for fire hazard by the Bench in 1741[8] and Thornton & Watson had a 'Distill' house attached to the Sugar House in 1752. Pryme & Fallowfield, distillers, were found to be defrauding the Excise in January 1748 by means of false storage containers.[9] Joseph Berry, from a family of oilmen, was a distiller in 1755 when he took William

[1] *Hull Packet*, 19 Jan 1795.

[2] *DNB*, and C. Frost, *An Address Delivered to the Literary and Philosophical Society, 5 Nov 1830* (Hull, 1830), p. 49.

[3] Sun Fire Office Bk.

[4] IIA, 1720–65, No. 350 (1730).

[5] BB viii, 844.

[6] L. Jopson, York, to J. Pease, 5 May 1752, *WH* 59/58/49.

[7] L. Jopson, Stockton, to J. Pease, 10 Jan 1755, ibid.

[8] BB viii, 913.

[9] HCLB, C–B, Jan 1748.

Huntington as his apprentice.[1] In general however, the Hull distillers were inhibited by the vast importation of liquors from the continent and London.

The industries so far mentioned were all fairly important, employing a large number of men and a great deal of capital. The remainder were for the most part small craftsmen businesses of the kind that one expects to find in any reasonably large town in the eighteenth century. Tallow chandlers were everywhere to be found, and Hull was no exception. Rather less common, perhaps, were the tobacco pipe makers. Huge quantities of pipes were turned out for the Baltic trade by about a dozen men, using clay brought from Poole and East Anglia. Some attempt was also made to make pottery in Hull. Again it was common stuff for the Baltic trade. William Askam, Joseph Mayfield and Richard Eggleston were listed as Potmakers in 1791 and Ridgway, Smith and Hipwood—possibly a branch of Ridgways of Shanley—were functioning at the turn of the century, but there are no connoisseurs of their products. The list of of those working with clay might be extended to include the brick and tile makers, again producing for both the home and Baltic market.

Another group of men worked in wood and metal. The woodworkers ranged from the numerous furniture and cabinet makers (thirteen in 1792) to the coach makers (at least one for most of the century), the gilders and carvers and the saddle tree makers. Spence & King, the leading ironmongers, had already begun to specialise in the making of planes, and by the end of the century had nearly a hundred types and sizes that enabled them to hold the English plane market until the modern steel plane was introduced.

The various metal workers were more important numerically and economically than the woodworkers. The craftsmen producing fine metal luxuries for the upper class of Hull and the East Riding were the elite of the industrial 'workmen', second only to the heads of the shipbuilding and processing firms. Seven watch and clock makers, three silversmiths, one 'working Jeweller' and two gunsmiths were to be found in Hull in the nineties. George Wallis, whose guns were eagerly sought after throughout the Riding, had accumulated a private museum of arms, medals, minerals and other 'curiosities'

[1] IIA, 1720–65, No. 1739 (1755). It was Huntington's unadventurous clerk, Storm, who sold drams and earned Strother's disapproval in 1784 (see p. 101).

which was one of the sights of Hull.[1] At the other end of the scale were the shoeing smiths, the whitesmiths and the braziers. A 'Tin-plait' worker, John Reader, was taking apprentices in the thirties,[2] when much of the tinplate consumed in England was imported from Holland and Germany, and his son Mordecai followed him.[3] Richard Mood was also taking apprentices in the fifties,[4] and four tinners—presumably masters employing others—were recorded in the 1791 *Directory*. To judge from the type of boy taken apprentice, there must have been money in tinplate working, but we have no clear indication whether they were making tinplate or making things with it. It is at least reasonable to assume that some of the vast number of tinplates exported in the second half of the century were made locally.

Although Hull never took a direct interest in the cloth industry from which it drew part of its wealth, there had always been some cloth production. Weavers turn up in the *Poll Books* and the *Directories*, and there were four worsted makers and a wool sheet manufacturer in 1791. There was also a stocking manufacturer and six silk dyers. As early as the thirties the Maisters had organised linen production in Hull or Cottingham,[5] and, as we have noted, many of the sail and rope makers were also involved in the production of linen and sacking. Flax dressing was old established, but the origin of flax spinning cannot be dated. There was a firm in the 1791 *Directory* called Frost & Cross, 'Manufacturers', who may have been the forerunners of R. C. & G. W. Cross who in 1805 were insuring their 'Flax Mill Steam Engine House & Boiling House all communicating, called Hope Mill'.[6]

Finally there was a wide range of miscellaneous manufactures of varying importance. The whale-bone cutters handed their raw materials over to dozens of stay-makers, and when Regency fashions tended to discard stays a variety of experiments turned bone into combs, umbrellas and even brushes. Sealing wax and pens, pins, glue and paper all found their place. Paper had always been imported, usually from Holland, but production in England was beginning towards the end of the eighteenth century. A parchment maker called Gardan appeared in the 1768 *Poll Book*, and some

[1] *Hull Advertiser*, 5 Jul 1794.
[2] IIA, 1720–65, No. 479 (1733).
[3] ibid., No. 1824 (1757).
[4] ibid., No. 1799 (1757).
[5] Nathaniel to Henry Maister, 6 Mar 1737/8, Maister Letters.
[6] Sun Fire Office Bk.

time before 1790 Thomas Lee established a paper mill that was the first in the country to make use of steam power.[1]

Power was always a problem in Hull. Those industries which were imported from Holland were connected with milling and naturally used wind power. But for those industries which were not automatically associated with windmills, Hull could make no provision. There was no fast flowing water to drive looms or hammers. This may have been the most important factor in Hull's industrial development. She had easy access to all raw materials; she could import Sheffield's iron, but she could not drive the grindstones.

Hull was therefore desperately interested in the techniques of windmill construction and in the steam engine. Joseph Pease, and no doubt his rivals too, had thought it necessary to bring millwrights over from Holland. Not until the middle of the century were Englishmen showing the competence in seed crushing that merited recognition, and then it was only in a man of Smeaton's stature. Soon, however, the Dutch engineers and the grand English engineers gave way to the local men. James Norman set himself up as a millwright not long after Smeaton reported on Mayson Wright's mill in the seventies, and he was no doubt responsible for building and maintaining many of the two dozen or more mills grinding and crushing in Hull at the end of the century. He appears to have concentrated on the improvement of seed crushing machinery and his firm, Norman & Smithson, machine makers and engineers, 'where millstones are compounded of French stone', was thriving in the early nineteenth century.

There was an overlap of interests in mill construction, for many bits and pieces in the oil and snuff mills were made of metal. Everywhere metal was finding new uses, in building and in machinery, and there was enough demand to encourage John Todd to open a brass and iron foundry. His background is, alas, obscure. Unsubstantiated tradition in his firm places its foundation in the mid-seventies,[2] but this may be too early. Certainly in 1791 he was taking apprentices as an ironfounder, and before 1805 he had

[1] D. C. Coleman, *The British Paper Industry, 1495–1860* (Oxford, 1958), p. 112, refers to Howard & Houghton's mill having a 10-h.p. engine by Boulton and Watt in 1786. This presumably was the mill which was later owned by Lee.

[2] Rose, Downs & Thompson, Ltd., *At The Tail of Two Centuries* (London, 1949).

formed the partnership of Todd & Campbell that eventually specialised in seed-crushing machinery.

Todd and his fellow citizens must have been aware of the town's dependence on the steam engine as one after another trundled through the gates in bits and pieces and blackened the sky with the smoke of a chalder of coals a day. The waterworks had one or perhaps two, and Mayson Wright *may* had had another for his mill; Joseph Pease and Jarratt & Coates had one each;[1] Frost & Cross had one; one of the flour mills, Casson & Penrose's, modelled on the Albion Mill in London, had one;[2] and Thomas Lee had one in his paper mill. Already before the end of the century Hull men had begun to experiment with steam. Todd joined in 1799 with a local inventor, Richard Witty, to make steam engines,[3] and although the firm does not appear to have lasted for long Witty continued to experiment and take out patents. In 1812 or 1813 he was again in business—Smith, Witty & Company—and one of his engines was installed in the Blundell paint works.[4]

Despite the rise of the various industries noted in this chapter, Hull remained a predominantly commercial town. The amount of capital and labour placed in industry obviously increased dramatically in the last quarter of the century; but so, too, did the energy poured into trade and shipping. There was no major diversion of the labour force or capital from 'trade' to 'industry', and if figures were available they would undoubtedly show no significant increase in the percentage of the population engaged in industrial pursuits before 1800. Both sides drew their extra men from a rapidly increasing population, and there was sufficient surplus capital in the town to back any worthwhile venture, whether at sea or on land.

There was no clear cut distinction between trade and industry. Most of the 'industrialists' were merchants. Many of them, like Francis Bine, Charles Shipman, the Thorntons and the inevitable Peases, had many mercantile and industrial interests. They invested, simply, in anything that made money. So long as importing

[1] Tickell, pp. 850–1, describing industry in Wincomblee.

[2] ibid. 'This is truly a curious piece of mechanism, consumes about a chaldron of coals in twelve hours, works four pair of stones, and throws off a vast quantity of flour in a little time.'

[3] *Hull Advertiser*, 6 Oct 1798 and 9 Oct 1800. On 23 Jan 1802 there appeared an advertisement for 'General Smiths and Millwrights, at the Engine Manufactory, Sculcoates' (i.e. Wincomblee).

[4] ibid., 21 Aug 1813.

whale oil was profitable they imported it. When it was more practical or lucrative to send whalers to the Arctic they invested in whalers. When they found a market for vegetable oil, mills sprang up around the town. But it was not a deliberate withdrawing of money from trade. As we have seen, the development of bank credit, on top of the normal mercantile credit, had relieved many merchants of the obligation to keep large amounts of liquid capital by them, so that they could still trade on a grand scale and have money for 'safe' investments. Land was the safest but it was not lucrative. Our merchant-industrialists were of the same thrusting breed as the normal run of industrialists. Pease would not invest in land when he could get ten per cent in Manchester or Tean, and it was only the incompetence of his son-in-law that stopped him opening a cotton printing works in Hull. Francis Bine preferred a sugar refinery to an estate; it was a calculated risk, a matter of personal inclination rather than capital availability, for there were many men richer than Bine.

Towards the end of the century we find an increasing number of men who had no mercantile background. This was, as one might expect, true of the brewers, although it was not the case with the distillers. The non-mercantile oil-millers were unsuccessful, but the paint industry eventually concentrated in the hands of non-merchants. It was chiefly a matter of money. As mercantile profits were liberated for investment, the 'pure' industrialist found it easier to borrow. Benjamin Pead, in his early twenties when he arrived in Hull, started the oil and soap business with the Thorntons' mercantile capital, and merchants were always ready to lend money on bond. The breakthrough came with the establishment of the banks which made available to the industrialists money from both mercantile and non-mercantile sources on an unprecedented scale.

The absence of statistical information renders it impossible even to guess at the amount of capital invested in industry. Nor is there any indication of the relative yield of industrial capital. Had industrial profits exceeded commercial profits there would doubtless have been a rush to invest in sugar refineries, soap works, and mills. It may be that marginal profits from investments in capital-intensive industries were too low relative to existing investment opportunities in commerce, whaling, shipbuilding and the major processing industries. A certain eagerness to invest in industry may be detected towards the end of the century, but not, it would seem, among merchants. Perhaps it was simply conservatism of action that governed the majority of merchants as it did most other men. It is noticeable, for instance, that industrial growth in nineteenth century Hull coincided with the decline of the great independent merchant house, trading on its own account. It was replaced, in many—but not all—trades, by direct contact between manufacturer and customer, and the enterprising young man in Hull became a lawyer, a shipowner or a brush manufacturer rather than a merchant.

On the other hand it may have been a lack of opportunity. Hull was not well situated for industrial development. It was not geographical obscurity—that myth of modern times which is repeated so often that people tend to believe it. Hull stood at the very heart of the greatest communications network in Britain in the days before the railways—the river and coastal routes, by which all heavy traffic moved. The thing she lacked was not communications with suppliers or customers but a reservoir of skilled labour and cheap motive power. By the time the steam engine was available the pattern of industrial distribution had already been set. Apart from flirtations with cotton spinning—long, and eventually unsuccessful—and the major growth of the fishing industry, Hull developed and intensified her interests in industries which were already flourishing in 1800.

IX. THE REORGANISATION OF THE FINANCIAL SECTOR

1. THE RISE OF THE HULL BANKS

i. THEIR ORIGINS

The great commercial expansion of the last quarter of the century would have been difficult, if not impossible, without the facilities offered by the newly emergent banks. As they came gradually to dominate the financial sector they streamlined the cumbersome procedures of pre-banking days. They provided, for the first time, an adequate and simple system of payments by notes and bills. By specialising in the discount of foreign bills of exchange they acted as efficient intermediaries between Hull merchants and the outside world. And they attracted capital and made it available to their customers on a scale previously unknown.

There was nothing particularly novel about the banker's functions. He did nothing that any reasonably successful merchant could not have done for himself. William Crowle signed his private notes and bills; Nathaniel Maister borrowed money from fellow merchants and from landowners; and the Broadleys had international financial connexions that served them well. The banker's uniqueness lay in his specialisation. By concentrating the several financial functions in one hand, and by channelling a multitude of transactions through one counting house, he introduced speed, efficiency, simplicity of performance and economies of scale that completely overshadowed all but the most versatile of the great merchants. Particularly important were the facilities offered to the industrialists and smaller merchants with no ancestral financial organisation to smooth their path.

Joseph Pease was probably typical of the bankers whose business was an extension of mercantile practice. A wizard at assembling credit, he was never at a loss for money. A master of international payments, he rarely lost on the exchange. Always he drew as early are practicable and paid as late as prudent. 'We never did nor could approve your way of drawing and redrawing as being a very loosing account . . .', was the verdict of his cousin, Isaac Clifford of

Amsterdam,[1] and his brother in Amsterdam referred caustically to 'those damned bills of yours'.[2] A firm believer in stocking to the limit on credit, he practised a nicely judged financial brinkmanship that horrified his staid Dutch relations: 'Your Engaging so deep with other peoples monny who can demand their Capitals together at one moment would cause your Entire ruin and shame of your Family.'[3]

The assessment of risk was something at which Pease excelled. Every penny was sent a-breeding: 'we know your temper to be Such that not the least monny lys idel with you', said cousin Isaac in 1736.[4] In 1753 he was spreading his net in a growing Manchester, buying property, investing in cotton (which returned an average of eighteen per cent) and offering loans at 4½ per cent.[5] Logic demanded that he sell his talents and connexions. In January 1754 Joseph Pease & Son opened their doors as Hull's first bankers, at a time when there were no more than a dozen country banks in the whole of England.[6] They met, they told Wilberforce & Watson, with 'greater Encouragement than we expected'.[7] Son-in-law Robert Robinson expressed his 'pleasure to see that you & Brother are now Jointly concerned in the Banking way, I think the Scheme is a good one & likely to answer much better than purchasing Lands'.[8] He little knew that his infant son Joseph would eventually control a banking and business empire with assets exceeding half a million pounds.

Joseph Pease was not merely a first class banker. He was an excellent teacher, and in his book-keeper, Thomas Harrison, he had the makings of a banker of national repute—or, as it was later alleged, a semi-crooked manipulator of equally great potential. But that was forty years on. For a generation the Peases and Harrison worked amicably together, and the tragic death of Robert Pease in 1770 opened the way for Harrison's partnership. The bank became Pease & Harrison's when J. R. Pease succeeded his grandfather in 1778. Harrison ran the bank, leaving Pease to concentrate

[1] I. Clifford, Amsterdam, to J. Pease, 5 Jun 1736; *WH* 59/58/46.

[2] W. Pease, Amsterdam, to J. Pease, 7 Jan 1738; *WH* 59/58/44.

[3] I. Clifford to J. Pease, 22 Nov 1735; *WH* 59/58/46.

[4] I. Clifford to J. Pease, 5 Jun 1736; *WH* 59/58/46.

[5] J. Pease to Robert Robinson, 8 Oct 1753; *WH* 59/58/47.

[6] L. S. Pressnell, *Country Banking in the Industrial Revolution* (1956), p. 4.

[7] J. Pease & Son to Wilberforce, Watson & Company, 31 Jan 1754; *WH* 59/58/47.

[8] R. Robinson, Manchester, to J. Pease, 9 Feb 1754; *WH* 59/58/45.

on his other, more lucrative, interests. Harrison, too, had his outside interests. To simplify the business of London correspondency he appointed his brother Robert as the London agent with the title Robert & Thomas Harrison & Company. When Robert required a transfusion of credit, Thomas simply bled the Peases; and nobody suspected what they were doing until 1793 or 1794.

Joseph Pease succeeded in trade, in industry, and finally in banking. Less fortunate were Hull's other two early bankers: Sill, Bridges & Blunt and Foster, Adams & Holmes. Thomas Bridges and Joseph Sill were of old and respectable Hull merchant stock. Bridges' father had been Chamberlain and Sheriff, and he was himself Chamberlain in 1745. Sill held the same office in 1757. Both acted as Captain of Volunteers during the '45, a sure sign of high standing in the merchant community. In 1757 they were recorded as merchants in partnership,[1] but at an unknown date they had commenced banking. They broke in the 1759 crisis in partnership with Roger Blount as 'merchants, dealers and chapmen'.[2] None of their records survives to prove they were banking, but Bridges was described as banker when a dividend was at last declared on his estate in 1798.[3] Cary Elwes, the north Lincolnshire landowner, commiserated with his agent, who lost money in March 1759 by taking bills on an unnamed Hull banker. He required his agent to play safe and never trust a merchant who engaged in banking. 'Get me Bills on Merchants of the first credit that do not Bank', he wrote, but he was already behind the times.[4]

The obscurity of Sill, Bridges & Blount is exceeded by that of Foster, Adams & Holmes. No evidence of their activities has survived. Their sole memorial is a notice of their failure in the London Gazette, where they were listed as 'Robert Foster (Myton), William Adams and John Holmes (Southwark) Tanners, Bankers, Dealers, Chapmen and Partners'.[5] That they were operating in Hull rather

[1] Robert Mingay, son of the Collector of Excise, was apprenticed to them, 3 Jan 1757; IIA, 1720–65, No. 1790.

[2] *London Gazette*, Nos. 9863 and 9870. They were similarly described in a Deed of Assignment of part of Blount's property, now in the possession of Mrs Doris Harrison-Broadley.

[3] *Hull Advertiser*, 13 Jan 1798. For a fascinating side-light on Bridges' banking, see his *Adventures of a Bank Note* (4 vols, 1770–1).

[4] C. Elwes to E. Holgate, 28 Apr 1759, *LAO* Elwes MSS, Cary Elwes Letter Book, 1758–76.

[5] London Gazette, No. 9868.

than London is borne out by the location of their creditors' meeting in the King's Head, Hull.

Pease & Son remained the only bank for some time after 1759. Eventually, as the economy began to move again, they were joined by Edmund Bramston, Alderman, merchant and goldsmith, certainly before 1768 when, as 'banker and goldsmith', he took Thomas Brown of Patrington, later a prominent Hull shipowner, as his apprentice.[1] After acting alone for many years, Bramston entered into partnership, in 1791 or 1792, with Richard Moxon, an influential merchant of the firm of Dixon & Moxon, and they moved into new buildings in Whitefriargate as 'Hull Commercial Bank'. The death of Bramston in 1795 left the bank in the hands of the merchants and shipowners Richard, George and John Moxon, who ran it until their liquidation in 1815.[2] Hull Commercial Bank, despite its grand title, was a much smaller concern than Peases, whose assets were eight times greater in 1793.

Pease & Harrison's greatest rivals, attracting much of their official business in the last decade of the century, were Smiths & Thompson's. Opened in 1784, the new bank was the latest venture of the Smiths of Nottingham, the oldest country banking house in England, with branches in Nottingham (1688), London (1758) and Lincoln (1775).[3] Smiths & Thompson's was the logical outcome of the Smiths' close connexion with Hull. As an apprentice of Alderman William Wilberforce, Abel Smith (1717–88) gained first-hand knowledge of the foreign exchange and 'commercial' side of banking, in which he made a great deal of his money. As brother-in-law of Robert Wilberforce, and man-about-town in the fifties and sixties, he gained a number of intimate and sincere friends in Hull.[4] And as the eventual senior partner in Wilberforce & Smiths, he was able to train the promising young clerk, Thomas Thompson, as a future banker. By 1784 Thompson was ready, and he was given charge of a Hull branch of Smiths' bank. From the beginning he was responsible for the private ledger, the note issue and the day to day affairs of the bank. In 1788, when the firm was reorganised after Abel's death, the Smiths lent him the money to buy his partnership

[1] IIA, 1766–87, No. 176.

[2] See notices in *Hull Advertiser*, 18 Nov 1815.

[3] On the Smiths generally, see J. A. S. L. Leighton-Boyce, *Smiths the Bankers* (National Provincial Bank, 1958), *passim*.

[4] He was one of Broadley's social set; see p. 265.

in both the merchant and banking houses, the latter now consisting of four Smiths—Robert (Lord Carrington), Samuel, George and John—and Thompson. William Wilberforce did not become a partner, although the bank had grown out of his ancestral firm and was located in his house.[1]

The East Riding Bank, of Malton and Beverley, was not, strictly speaking, a Hull concern, but had local affinities and a Hull branch that grew in relative importance in the early nineteenth century.[2] It united in partnership two of the greatest merchant families: the Sykes and the Broadleys. Sir Christopher Sykes, Bt., was the head of the senior branch of the Sykes and a leading East Riding landowner. He appears not to have been given a mercantile training and was not offered a partnership in the family business after the death of his elder brother (who had been trained).[3] Instead, he turned to banking in the East Riding, financing agricultural development and collecting surplus agricultural money for lending to the mercantile community. Sykes was joined by Robert Carlile Broadley who had been thoroughly trained—and in an impeccable tradition. He too was deeply involved in East Rising land, but he had maintained his connexion with trade and was an underwriter of considerable standing. In the Hull branch his name was placed before that of Sykes, presumably representing his greater investment and authority in that branch. The other two partners were Ralph Creyke and John Lockwood, about whom little is known.

The last local bank founded in the eighteenth century was Pease & Harrison's—a name deliberately chosen to create confusion and steal the business of the original Pease & Harrison's! The story is a sordid one, of intrigue and dishonesty, but for obvious banking reasons was hushed up and has only recently come to light in the private papers of J. R. Pease.

Disharmony had been growing for some time in Pease & Harrison's as Thomas Harrison, for twenty years its leading figure, grew old and cantankerous. In 1791 he was threatening to join

[1] Smiths & Thompson's (now the Hull office of the National Provincial Bank) are unique among Hull banks in possessing a complete run of ledgers, from which most of the illustrations in this chapter must necessarily be drawn.

[2] The Notes were issued from Malton.

[3] The Rev. Sir Mark Sykes' elder brother and eldest son both died, leaving untrained younger brothers as head of the family.

Broadley & Sykes (who in fact would not have him),[1] but serious trouble was avoided until 1793, when the effects of the national financial crisis, aggravated by his mismanagement, forced Pease & Harrison's to suspend payments, with liabilities exceeding £400,000.[2] The immediate cause of the 'failure' was the failure of Robert & Thomas Harrison in London, which deprived Pease & Harrison's and their related banks of their London agent, their draft acceptances and their gold supply.

Before the doors were closed, a heavy run on the bank had been stimulated by a rumour that 'the private Effects of Bankers are not liable to the payment of notes, and other Debts . . . beyond the amount of . . . their respective capitals . . .'. This interesting belief in bankers' limited liability was immediately contradicted by the Recorder of Hull (who happened to be Pease's nephew),[3] and Pease paid over £100,000 of his personal assets into the Trustees' hands.[4] The crisis was over. In fact the bank's assets were found to exceed liabilities even without this infusion, and the creditors declared themselves satisfied, despite the ill-disguised hostility of Sir Henry Etherington, chairman of the creditors' meetings. He tried to delay cash-raising, insinuated 'that it is next to an impossibility a House going on . . .', and tried to stop payment of drafts by the temporary London agents, Down, Thornton & Company. 'I am fearfull of what I all along told you', wrote R. C. Pease, 'that it is the intention of the Thorntons and Porters to establish a Bank upon the ruins of your House and Sir Henry Etherington's behaviour confirms my suspicions . . .'.[5] They were disappointed if this really was their

[1] Ralph Green, Malton, to J. R. Pease, 15 Nov 1791; *WH* 59/58/51. He added the postscript: 'could say much but dare not'.

[2] Henry Thornton's estimate, quoted by L. S. Pressnell, p. 546. Bramston & Moxon were also forced to close, for the same reasons.

[3] Published in *Hull Advertiser*, 12 Mar 1793.

[4] Report of Creditors' Meeting, 5 Apr 1793; *WH* 59/58/51. Private assets were '£5,550 arising from the joint property' and £116,550 in 'private assets'. Since Harrison could find only £2,000 at Harrison & Co's creditors' meeting on 30 March, it is presumed that the whole £116,550 was Pease's money.

[5] R. C. Pease to J. R. Pease (in London, raising credit), 18 Mar 1793; *WH* 59/58/40. John Thornton's sister married John Porter, whose sister married Sir Henry Etherington. There may have been some truth in R. C. Pease's accusation, but against the unlikelihood of a family compact against Pease's must be set R. C. Pease's known instability and his fine line in flattery which was uninhibited by any respect for the truth.

intention. Pease & Harrison's weathered the storm and secured adequate London correspondents in Boldero, Adey & Company. Bramston & Moxon's also survived the collapse of Harrisons', with their London account transferred to Masterman, Peters, Walker & Mildred.

The importance of all this for Pease's lay not so much in the temporary suspension as in the aftermath. The crisis shocked and angered the Nonconformist Pease, who was not even forewarned by Harrison that the bank was suspending payments. He determined to find the cause of his disgrace. In the past, he told Harrison, 'your system was to keep me as much as possible in the Dark, & instead of making it a pleasure to me to look after my Business, you endeavoured . . . whenever I came into the Bank by looks by Gestures & by Words to make it as uncomfortable to me as possible'.[1] Now Harrison was quietly removed, his partnership surrendered on condition that Pease was responsible for all debts.[2] Harrison's name remained by agreement, but his place was taken by J. R. Pease's son, Robert, and by R. C. Pease (the family reprobate, given a last chance to make good), under the new title of Pease, Harrison & Pease.

The first thing Pease did after taking over was to go through the books. They were confused, and in fact it took him the best part of a year to discover that Robert & Thomas Harrison's had been little more than an unofficial subsidiary of his own firm. Thomas Harrison had secretly and systematically left huge balances in his brother's hands 'sometimes to near the Amount of 100,000£', and this had been the basis for Harrisons' extravagant loans to Hull merchants (behind Pease's back and to his financial loss) and, indeed, for much of their business. It was also the reason for Pease & Harrison's shortage of liquid assets and for the 'want of confidence in the Publick'[3]. Further investigations revealed that interest had not been paid regularly on Pease & Harrison's credit with R. & T. Harrison's —a suspected shortage of at least £14,000 was traced—and that £32,000 had, at some unknown date, been 'lent' permanently to Harrisons'.[4]

[1] Draft, J. R. Pease to T. Harrison, n.d. (but 1795); *WH* 59/58/45.
[2] Draft agreement, 3 Jun 1793, to operate from 1 July; *WH* 59/58/51.
[3] Draft, J. R. Pease to T. Harrison, n.d.; *WH* 59/58/45.
[4] J. R. Pease to T. Harrison, 28 May 1795; *WH* 59/58/51. There is no indication that any of this money was recovered, but the fact that Pease let the matter drop may, perhaps, signify that it was.

Thomas Harrison did not take kindly to his dismissal. While Pease was discovering—but not daring to publish—his malpractices, Harrison was busy perfecting another underhand scheme. Early in 1795 Pease had decided to reorganise and strengthen the partnership by bringing in two prominent merchants (George Knowsley and John Wray) and the chief clerk, Henry Bedford. R. C. Pease, 'a person highly improper to be introduced into a Bank',[1] a spendthrift and gambler owing almost all he had to the generosity of his cousin, was at last to be cast adrift. Unfortunately, Bedford's profit-sharing partnership was opposed by Wray and Knowsley, who suggested £300 per annum (plus £100 salary) instead,[2] and he immediately joined with R. C. Pease to force concessions. At this point Harrison acted. In April 1795 he gave notice that his name must no longer be used by Pease, Harrison & Pease,[3] and three weeks later—ignoring the agreed six months notice period—he published a Circular announcing the dissolution of Pease, Harrison & Pease (of which he was not legally a partner!).[4] At the same time he announced his intention 'to continue the Banking Business at this place, in conjunction with Robert Harrison, Esq., Samuel Nicholson, Esq., of London, and Mr Henry Bedford, under the Firm of PEASE, HARRISON and COMPANY.' On the following day J. R. Pease paid £2,500 to his cousin to dissolve their partnership,[5] and the latter promptly joined Harrison to produce the legal basis for the new title of Pease & Harrison's.

Thus was born the only Hull bank not linked directly with a major merchanting house.[6] It attracted business from men ignorant of the background and remembering only the accommodations they had received in the past from Harrisons', and it lasted until its failure in the mid-nineteenth century. Pease, Knowsley & Wray (and, eventually, Liddell)—more generally known as the 'Old Bank'—continued to flourish until, by a process of amalgamation, it stands today as the Hull office of Barclay's.

[1] J. R. Pease, T. Harrison, n.d.; *WH* 59/58/45.

[2] G. Knowsley to J. Wray, 3 Apr 1795, and J. Wray to J. R. Pease, 13 Apr 1795; *WH* 59/58/51.

[3] T. Harrison to J. R. & R. C. Pease, Bankers, 14 Apr 1795; *WH* 59/58/51.

[4] Copy in J. R. Pease to Robert Harrison, 10 May 1795; *WH* 59/58/51.

[5] Recorded in J. R. Pease's Account Book, 1783–1806, 13 May 1795; *WH* 59/58/114.

[6] All the other bankers continued to trade, even the Smiths, who might be regarded as fully-fledged bankers of national importance.

ii. COUNTRY AGENTS

The activities and influence of the Hull banks ranged throughout Lindsey and the East Riding. In an age when branch banking was unusual, Pease's had 'branches' in Brigg, Barton-on-Humber (the North Lincolnshire Bank), Beverley, Malton and Whitby. Sykes and Broadley's East Riding Bank had offices in Hull, Malton and Beverley, and Smiths & Thompson's had agencies in various strategic places, particularly Howden.

The Hull banks followed the usual practice of establishing a branch by entering into partnership with local men of repute who were expected to deal with the business of the branch. The North Lincolnshire Bank, for instance, consisted of J. R. Pease, Thomas Harrison and Josiah Prickett from Hull and London, and Thomas Marris and William Graburn of Barton-on-Humber. Marris had extensive interests in Lindsey. He lent money to landowners, invested in turnpikes and the Grimsby Haven Company, and eventually went bankrupt in 1814 trying to build a ferry port at New Holland. Graburn, who ran the bank, was the second largest landowner in the huge parish of Barton. The Whitby branch was Pease, Richardson & Company, and the Malton bank was run by Ralph Green, again a local man.[1]

The existence of local partnerships, technically independent, tended to complicate the banker's life. London correspondencies had to be negotiated separately for each of the Pease banks after the failure of Robert & Thomas Harrison's, and for a time after 1795 the Pease cousins were rivals in Hull and partners in Malton and Whitby, a fact which did not encourage public confidence in those places.[2] How much capital was involved in this kind of banking is unknown, but it was probably not very much. J. R. Pease received only £443 for 'Barton Bank Profit & Loss' between July 1797 and January 1803.[3] The 'branches' were truly 'country banks', without the vast commercial business of the Hull offices.

Smiths & Thompson's, unlike Pease & Harrison's, had no related branches. Business was all done through the one office, and even the

[1] The northern branches are referred to in R. Green, Malton, to J. R. Pease, 1 May 1795; *WH* 59/58/51. They were incorrectly assigned to the Darlington Peases by P. W. Matthews, *History of Barclay's Bank* (1926), p. 208.

[2] ibid. [3] J. R. Pease's Account Bk, 19 Feb 1803.

most distant customers were entered in the general ledgers. They did, however, employ an agent, John Barker, who represented the bank in the Howden area and occasionally did business for them in Weighton and York.[1] His account (with a turnover of £61,000 in 1789 and a final balance of £3,100) was composed chiefly of regular monthly supplies of cash 'per Mr Thompson', ranging from 1,000 guineas a month in 1789 to 3,000 a month in 1792, with various sums between the regular deliveries. In return came large numbers of bills and interest on loans made in Barker's area. Similar, but smaller, accounts appeared from time to time in the general ledgers in the names of Henry Priestman of Scarborough[2] and Isaac Cook of Bridlington, confidential clerk of Woodall, Tindall & Company.[3] Most of Smiths & Thompson's country business was done by tours undertaken by Thomas Thompson and Cockerill, the chief clerk. There are many records of journeys to York, Beverley, Bridlington, Wassand, Hessle, Coniston, Stilton, Cottingham, Waltham Cross, Barton-on-Humber, Brigg and Lincoln. Moreover, the bankers were in attendance at country fairs just as they are today: in June 1784, for instance, Terry & Wright were credited 'By cash paid us at York Fair'.

iii. LONDON AGENTS

For success the Hull banks required a first class agent in the capital, through whom they were linked with the outside world. London correspondents arranged the exchange of foreign and inland bills and bank notes, especially after the London Banks' Clearing House was opened in 1773. They printed notes, and despatched bullion for their Hull clients. They invested money by power of attorney, and drew interest and bounties. They were the channel through which Excise, Custom and Tax money was transmitted to the Treasury.

Pease & Harrison's agents were originally Henton, Brown & Company, but, as we have seen, Thomas Harrison replaced them by his brother's firm after the death of Joseph Pease. Bramston also was persuaded to trust Harrisons'. Sykes & Company drew on

[1] On 1 Mar 1792 he was 'allowed for his sign painting' and debited in September 'to stamping and Printing his Draft checks'.

[2] He received huge quantities of cash and notes, and paid interest on various advances.

[3] See P. W. Matthews, p. 212. He has the name of the bank wrong, for this period. In Ledger 'C' they were transmitting tax money from the Scarborough area to Smiths & Thompson's Tax Account.

Joseph Denison & Company who, like the Sykes, originated in Leeds. Smiths & Thompson's agents were, of course, the Smiths' London branch, Smith, Payne & Smiths. Their huge corresponding account is to be found in the General Ledgers and provides an interesting commentary on the growth of Smiths & Thompson's. The total turnover rose from £277,179 in the bank's first year to an average of almost £850,000 for the last decade of the century. The account fluctuated with the rise and fall of trade, stocks bought and sold, and taxes and customs paid into the Treasury. In order to avoid excessive debits or credits, resulting in heavy book debts or long-distance transfer of bullion, the Hull and London offices used as their intermediary Robert Smith, senior partner of both. He was responsible for putting into or taking out of the London bank sufficient cash to keep the balances at a reasonable level as, for instance, in the first year, when he paid £21,000 into Smith, Payne & Smiths to reduce the amount owing to them to £24,105. His own account, however, fluctuated wildly. There was £110,000 difference between his highest and lowest January balances (1793 and 1800).

In 'normal' years it was usual for the Hull bank to have credit in London. The exceptional years for Smiths & Thompson's were the first, when credit was pumped in to get the bank going, and the crisis years of 1793 and 1796–8, when large sums were owed in London to Robert Smith as well as to Smith, Payne & Smiths.[1] A credit balance with the London agent was, indeed, part of his reward for acting for the Hull bank, and an assurance of their good faith when he accepted their drafts. After their disastrous experience with Robert & Thomas Harrison, Pease & Company had to leave at least £12,000 credit permanently in their account with Boldero's and for this acceptances were to be limited to £50,000 at any one time, excluding Customs and Excise money.[2] Two years later this 'lodgement' was 'beaten down' to £10,000, with an extra £4,000 for the Brigg and Barton branches.[3] So long as interest was paid, and the London house was secure, there was little against reasonable credit in London. It was good liquid capital and allowed a greater freedom in drawing on London. On the other hand, it reduced the

[1] Thus, Smiths & Thompson's survived in 1793 because money flowed from London to Hull. Pease & Harrison's were in trouble because money had flowed from Hull to London and stayed there.

[2] G. Knowsley to J. R. Pease, 13 Apr 1793; *WH* 59/58/114.

[3] R. C. Pease to J. R. Pease, 5 & 9 Feb 1795; *WH* 59/58/40.

amount available for local loans, and too much locked up in London might reduce the popularity of the Hull house by making it appear short of money. If the London house failed the consequences could be very serious, as J. R. Pease discovered, and in general the London balance was kept to the minimum. The assessment of the optiumum sum was, of course, part of the art of banking.

2. THE MEANS OF PAYMENT: BILLS OF EXCHANGE

The Bill of Exchange was the life blood of trade. Drawn by a creditor on his debtor, and payable at a specified future date, it circulated from hand to hand, eliminating debts in its passage, until the time came for the original debtor to settle with the last holder. Alternatively a debtor could draw, by arrangement, on a third party, and send the bill to his creditor:[1]

£21 2s. 6d. Hull, 27 April 1793
At Seven days sight pay Mr John Trebbutt or order Twenty One Pounds 2/6d which place to account with or without Advice for value received.
To Messrs J & J Allen,
Furnivals Inn, London Edward Codd.

All merchants needed a commissioned agent in London on whom bills could be drawn, and who would pay bills drawn on Hull. William Maister, for example, 'Accepted Mr Henry Maister's bill the 3 December 1715 payable in London @ 1 month sight, to Mr Matthias Schildt or order: to pay at the house of Mr H. Lyell £150, due 9/12 June.'[2]

The use of agents as a source of credit was of greater importance in the overseas trade. Since there was a permanent adverse trade balance with the northern and eastern Baltic, it was necessary, as well as convenient, for merchants to employ an Amsterdam intermediary, with credit in the Baltic and good financial connexions with England.[3] The Baltic suppliers drew on the Amsterdam

[1] Recorded in *GH* Edward Codd's Letter Books. There are many examples in the Letter Books, arising from Codd's legal practice.

[2] Maister Day Book. The general pattern of payments is outlined in J. Sperling, 'The International Payments Mechanism in the Seventeenth and Eighteenth Centuries', *Econ. Hist. Rev.*, XIV (1961–2).

[3] There was, for example, no exchange rate quoted between London and St. Petersburg until 1763; C. Wilson, *Anglo-Dutch Finance*, pp. 65–6.

houses, which in turn drew on the London agents of the Hull merchants. Alternatively Hull merchants sent to the Baltic bills drawn on Amsterdam. The system is amply illustrated in the surviving accounts of the Maister firm. In the early years of the century their payments abroad, even to their own factors, were made through the Amsterdam house of Chitty & Son, who in turn drew by arrangement on Henry Lyell & Sons in London. A very typical entry in the Day Book reads: '16 September 1718 Sundry Accounts: Dr to H. Lyell for £200 drawn on him this day by Chitty & Son @ 2/usa.'[1] In the thirties Maisters were still paying for Baltic goods in the same way, although the agents were now Knight & Jackson in London and George Clifford, Sons & Archer in Amsterdam.[2] Joseph Pease, as we have seen, drew on his brother William, and on his cousin Isaac Clifford.

The opening of the banks confirmed the growing tendency to draw bills on London.[3] Their correspondents, specialist acceptance houses, became the common agents of their customers, who relinquished their own private agents. Creditors of Hull merchants now drew on Henton, Brown & Company, Robert & Thomas Harrison, or Smith, Payne & Smiths, just as Chitty had once drawn on Lyell for Maisters' debts. The bills were charged against the Hull banks, which in turn debited the accounts of their customers. In reverse, bills payable to Hull merchants were credited in their accounts and sent to London to be forwarded to the drawee's agent. At the same time the banks made it easier for their non-mercantile customers to draw or obtain bills. Besides allowing bills to be drawn on themselves or their London agents, the bankers sold bills which they themselves had drawn on London, and most people without trading credit found it easier to make payments with these. Edward Codd, Town Clerk, and a leading Hull attorney at the end of the century, regularly used bankers' bills to transmit rents to absentee landlords, and the Dock Company used them to pay for the building of the first dock.[4]

Merchants' bill accounts, besides simplifying their financial business at a time when trade was becoming more complex, offered facilities for credit. Bills and drafts were now accepted as a matter

[1] i.e. 2 months' usance.

[2] There are many examples in *WH* Maister Accounts.

[3] For the national picture, see L. S. Pressnell, *Country Banking*, pp. 77–8.

[4] See HDC Letter Book 'A', 1774, *passim*.

of course, whether or not they had sufficient money in hand to pay for them, and they became indebted to their banker instead of to their overseas contacts. At the same time the usance period, so prominent in bills of exchange, declined in value. The Hull bankers appear to have debited drafts when they were received, not when they became due. Smiths & Thompson's were debiting accounts in the nineties after only a week of usance had expired.

Just as the English end of foreign payments passed into the hands of a few London acceptance houses, so the Baltic end was centred almost entirely on the activities of about a dozen Baltic and Dutch financial houses, chiefly in Amsterdam.[1] They drew on Hull firms through Smith, Payne & Smiths nine or ten times a year in the last twenty years of the century, usually in the first four months of the year, when the cargoes amassed during the winter were despatched by the early ships. Out of £31,392 drawn on Wilberforce & Smiths in 1788, no less than £23,233 was drawn in the months February to May. But not all payments were made through Amsterdam. Smiths & Thompson's, and perhaps other banks, had their own financial contacts in the eastern Baltic: Thorley, Ouchterloney & Company in Narva,[2] and Cattleys, Prestcotts & Company and Thornton, Cayley & Company in St. Petersburg.[3] They had a special 'Charges of Money in Russia' account, and left fairly large amounts of cash with their agents. Cattleys & Company had between £9,000 and £11,000 in the early nineties; Thornton & Company had £14,000; and the balance of Thorley & Company in Narva ranged from £6,788 in January 1790 to £16,592 in January 1792. Although these agencies occasionally received payments on behalf of Hull merchants, the bulk of their funds came from London via the usual channels. Cattleys drew over £9,000 from Muilmans' and Smith, Payne & Smiths, in 1790, and Thorley & Company drew over £6,000 through the same agencies in 1789.

By 1780, in time for the Industrial Revolution, something like a modern system of international payments had emerged. Credit could be obtained for the asking in almost any corner of the world.

[1] The chief (for Hull) for most of the century were Muilmans', closely followed by Cliffords, De Haan and Cummings.

[2] Robert Thorley was the head of a prominent Hull family, and lately partner of Thomas Broadley. He was the largest shareholder in the Hull Dock Company, and owned extensive property in Hull.

[3] The Russian branch of Thorntons of Hull and London, and the most important merchant house in St. Petersburg at the end of the century.

No merchant, however small, need worry about paying his suppliers in Archangel or Memel, or receiving payments from Viborg or Galicia. Indeed, considering the crisis of confidence in 1797, and the number of small timber merchants who failed during the Napoleonic War, one might be forgiven for supposing that credit was too easily available to men without sound international trading experience.

3. THE MEANS OF PAYMENT: BANK NOTES

For much of the eighteenth century it was easier to make payments in a distant country than in a neighbouring village. The one was a paper transfer; the other involved coin in an age when coin was not abundant. Outside the commercial community the banker was more important in local than in foreign payments—as a note issuer rather than as a bill discounter.

The bank note evolved directly out of the private notes given to cover debts. In the early days of banking the bankers themselves took Promissory Notes, bearing interest, to cover overdrafts. John Ross, the Hull Court of Record was told,[1]

> on the 16th day July, 1793, to wit at Beverley . . . made his certain Note in writing commonly called a Prommissory Note his own proper hand being thereunto subscribed . . . and then and there delivered the said Note to . . . Sir Christopher Sykes . . . & Company . . . and thereby on demand promised to pay to . . . Sir Christopher Sykes . . . or order, fifty pounds with lawful interest for value received. . . .

Pease's early bank notes were all of this type. They were individually written and signed, and bore their own number, date and value, ranging—in the case of the largest customer, Wilberforce & Company—from £80 to £1,000 in 1757–8. Notes were entered in the Promissory Note Account as credit when issued, and as debit when cashed. They were not at first numerous. In the period May to November 1757 only seventeen were cashed by seven firms, with a total value of £4,838. Pease's Notes grew in popularity in the early sixties. The total 'taken out of the chest' rose from £7,984 for the year 1758 to £45,868 for 1764, while the credit balance (i.e. Notes issued less Notes cashed) rose from £3,310 in April 1759 to an average of £8,783 for the period June 1763 to January 1766.

Although payable on demand, the early bank notes were not

[1] Brief in *WH* Court Cases Box.

expected to circulate in the same way as the later printed Notes. They were looked on, and recorded, as Notes to individuals rather than the world in general. When they returned to the bank they were cancelled. A Note obtained to pay a debt might exist for a brief period only; one accepted against a deposit with a banker might exist for years. Some people hoarded Notes as investments, preferring them to deposit accounts. The Bench, for instance, held £3,030 in Pease Notes from January to December 1776, when it ordered 'that one of Mr Pease's Notes for £500 be taken out of the cash and left with the Treasurer to Discharge Workmen's Notes etc'.[1] Notes issued to Wilberforces' in 1757–8 took between seven days and nine months to return to the chest.

It is not known when the printed 'Bearer' Notes of fixed value were introduced into Hull. Although Pease & Harrison's were certainly using them in the seventies, the earliest surviving record of a printed issue is in Thomas Thompson's 'Note Account' in his General Ledger for 1784. During that year, five and nine guinea notes valued at £15,330 were issued, and the total had reached £17,372 in February 1785 when the account was transferred to Thompson's Private Ledger, which has not survived. The appearance of a 'Bills & Notes in the Chest' account in Ledger 'D' makes it possible to calculate roughly the value of Notes issued and cashed in the last five years of the century. While giving no indication of the volume in circulation, the account shows the tremendous increase in issue since 1784, an increase that fits in well with the national boom in notes taking place in this period. It shows, too, the effect of the crisis in 1797, when the over-issue of Notes and over-liberal credit undermined confidence more severely than in 1793 and caused the Bank of England to suspend payment:[2]

SMITHS & THOMPSON'S NOTE ISSUE, 1795–1800

Year	*Taken out of the chest* (Cr)	*Put into the chest* (Dr)	*Balance*
1795	79,800	90,300	10,500 Dr
1796	90,825	123,900	33,075 Dr
1797	11,025	39,375	28,350 Dr
1798	41,265	111,655	29,610 Cr
1799	148,995	125,790	23,205 Cr

[1] BB ix, 462.

[2] The suspension applied, in law, only to the Bank of England, but other banks also stopped payment.

If this account really is of the number of Notes put into and taken out of circulation, then declining confidence in Notes may, perhaps, be detected in the fairly heavy cashing in 1796, which apparently took £33,000 out of circulation. The first two months of 1797 saw a heavy run which cost the bank almost £30,000 before the suspension of payments put a stop to the account. On the other hand, the volume in circulation had been running down for several years. Thomas Thompson told the 'Committee of Secrecy' of the House of Commons that local Note issues had contracted by more than a third—more than the national average—between the crisis of 1793 and 1797.[1] Confidence was quickly restored in Hull Notes. A document signed by 235 leading citizens and published in the local newspapers,[2] declared it to be 'the duty and Interest of all ranks of Persons to unite in support of the Credit of the respectable PAPER CURRENCY'. They promised to receive Notes of all the Hull banks 'in all payments whatever'. The people were satisfied. Smiths & Thompson's Note issue began to expand again in 1798, and a very encouraging number of Notes were brought out of the chest in 1799. Pease's circulation, the only one for which we have a figure, is reputed to have topped the hundred thousand pounds mark at the end of the century.[3] When Notes came into their own, they did so with the full support of the town. Backed by the merchants, prized by the gentry, they spread through Lincolnshire and the East Riding bearing the glad tidings that money could be printed. The social responsibility of the bankers increased with the popularity of their Notes; those in Hull did not betray the trust placed in them.

4. LOANS AND DEPOSITS: THE ORGANISATION OF CREDIT

An abundance of capital was essential for an expanding trade, rising industries and a growing town. While merchants had always been able to raise credit, from private resources or deferred payments, the system was cumbersome. Now they turned to the banks as the easiest and best source of credit. They paid their debts promptly by overdrawing their bank accounts. Joseph Sykes & Company, who used

[1] Third Report from the Committee of Secrecy on the Outstanding Demands of the Bank; Evidence of Thomas Thompson. *BPP* 1826, Vol. III, pp. 57–8.

[2] *Hull Advertiser*, 4 Mar 1797.

[3] P. W. Matthews, p. 239.

their account with Smiths & Thompson's originally for the payment of Customs duties, had overdrawn by £7,310 before they made any attempt to repay. Many merchants kept little or no cash in their accounts, regularly overdrawing for any heavy or extraordinary expenditure, and using the capital thus liberated for investment in ships or villas. Several of the larger merchant houses had almost permanent overdrafts. The Sykes' stood at £15,914 in May 1790, while the largest recorded in Smiths & Thompson's ledgers, that of the related firm of Wilberforce & Smiths, was no less than £35,468 in July 1792; the partners were clearly using their bank to finance their trade.

Sykes & Company and Wilberforce & Smiths were in a specially favourable position for borrowing money, but they were by no means the only firms borrowing extensively. At Smiths & Thompson's January balance, 1793, Howard & Parker had an overdraft of £2,601, Thompson & Baxter had £5,088, Henry Hammond had £5,970, Carlill, Kirkbride & Company had £8,004 and Marmaduke Constable had £5,815. Bassano, Carlill, Boyes & Levett, the sugar refiners, borrowed heavily to build or buy their £20,000 sugar house.[1] In January 1792 they owed £8,474 to the bank, and £10,686 a year later. Not until 1800 did their account show credit, and then only because £2,250 of debit had been transferred to the account of Boyes & Carlill (as merchants) alone.

Overdrafts of this kind were paid for in the same way as any other loans, since interest was entered on both sides of the account. Wilberforce & Smiths paid at least £1,875 interest in 1792, and the total income of the banks from interest must have been very considerable by the last decade of the century. The overdraft was generally secured by a Promissory Note or bond, which was recorded as credit in the debtor's account.[2] Thus Francis Bine, merchant, whaler-owner and sugar refiner, ended the year 1784 with a credit balance of £1,312 only because he had handed in three notes, each worth £2,000. The notes were outstanding until he sold £6,608 of 5 per cent stock in August 1785. An excellent illustration of the use

[1] It was insured for £20,100; Bassano & Co's Acct, Sun Fire Office Policy Bk, 1804–18.

[2] Mortgages were not usually accepted by the bankers. Pease had less than £7,000 worth in 1765 when they were transferred to his private bank account, and there are no obvious mortgages in the Smiths & Thompson ledgers.

made of notes is contained in the relatively unimportant account of Edmund Riddell & Sons:[1]

	Dr		*Cr*	
17 Mar '84	Cash lent them on Int	£300		
19 Oct			By their Note	£300
26 Oct	Note ret'd them	£300	Bills	£300
22 Jan '85	1 Draft	£300	By their Note	£300
27 Dec	Note ret'd them	£300	Cash	£300
3 Mar '86	Cash Draft	£400	By their Bond	£400
10 Jun	Bond ret'd	£400	Cash	£400

Important as the banks were in providing loans to merchants and industrialists, their activities outside the town must not be overlooked. Sykes & Company's East Riding Bank, and Pease's Barton, Brigg, Malton and Whitby branches were obviously important in country finance, although again our information must come chiefly from Smiths & Thompson's. Despite their lack of formal branches, they made many loans, some of them large. Francis Otter of Coleby, agent to John Julius Angerstein, had an overdraft of £10,750 at the end of 1792; John Bell of Elsternwick had a more modest £200 in 1784 and John Ellis & Others of Barrow-on-Humber had £110 in 1784. Semi-public bodies also borrowed in Hull. The Anlaby Turnpike Trust was paying Pease's £100 per annum interest in the middle of the century. Thirty years later Market Weighton Drainage was paying Smiths & Thompson's £400 per annum, and various enclosures appear to have been partly financed by them.[2]

The banks' assets were not limited to loans to people in and around Hull. As we have seen, money was left in the hands of London and foreign agents and, in the case of Smiths & Thompson's, in the hands of one of the partners. The banks also made their own investments in Government and other funds. In the period covered by Ledger 'E', Pease held or bought Bank Annuities, stocks, 'Subscription 1760' and Navy and Victualling Bills to the value of about £50,000, of which he later sold about £16,000 worth. At the same time there is a record of existing stocks worth £20,000 and mortgages worth £6,500, so that his total known assets in investment must have

[1] Smiths & Thompson's ledgers.

[2] The sums involved in enclosure accounts were small, and may represent the fluctuations of the accounts rather than deliberate financing of enclosures. Thomas Clark & Others of Spaldington had £400 in 1787; The Commissioners of Walkington Inclosure had an account (with £164 credit in 1796); and there was another called, simply, 'Coniston Inclosure'.

been at least £60,000. The only record of Smiths & Thompson's buying securities is contained in their Navy Bills Account for 1793. These Bills amounted to £18,980 when, like so much of interest, they were 'taken by Mr Thompson into his Private Ledger'. On the other hand, part of the money held by Robert Smith was invested by him in government stocks and India Bills—£10,000 in 1791. He was regularly debited with large and varying sums for 'Interest on money in His hands'. Finally, the Peases, Smiths, Thompson, Bramston, the Moxons and Broadley were all whaler- and ship-owners, but how far their ventures were private, and how far official bank investments, is unknown.

After the initial subscription of capital required to launch them, only a fraction of the banks' loanable funds was drawn from the capital invested in them by their owners. The early bankers were beginners, and their book-keeping unfortunately obscures as much as it reveals. It is, for instance, impossible to tell from Pease's ledgers how much capital the bank had, independent of his private account. From his private bank book it appears that he deposited £5,000 worth of securities in the bank on 5 March 1754,[1] but apart from this he simply built up funds in his own account. When the balance reached the limit he had in mind, as in May 1770, he transferred cash 'to Stock Account in the Banking Office',[2] but he presumably also transferred money back to his private funds or to other investments such as the stock he purchased in the names of his two grandsons. As late as 1775 he was lending money independently of the bank, with the transactions going through his private account rather than any special account of the bank. Over £18,000 was involved in that year.[3] The expansion of business did not result from, or encourage, a great capital investment. During the 1793 crisis, with liabilities of £400,000, the only reference to capital was 'joint property' amounting to £5,550.[4]

Smiths & Thompson's, like the related Smith, Payne & Smiths', appear to have opened without independent capital.[5] In this respect

[1] J. Pease's Bank Bk, 1754–5, *WH* 59/58/104.

[2] J. Pease's Bank Bk, 1767–72, *WH* 59/58/107.

[3] £7,000 was lent to John Lee, merchant; £10,000 to Henry Etherington, possibly for land purchase; £500 to Ann Bateman, merchant; and £350 to Thomas Westerdell, the Harbourmaster and shipowner; J. Pease's Bank Bk, 1774–83, *WH* 59/58/109.

[4] Report of Meeting of Creditors, 5 Apr 1793, *WH* 59/58/51.

[5] See L. S. Pressnell, pp. 129 and 234.

it was like a standard joint-stock bank branch, receiving an initial subsidy of over £40,000 of Smith money. Thompson is unlikely to have brought much into the bank in return for his partnership, since the bank had to lend him the money to buy his partnerships in Sykes & Company and Wilberforce & Smiths. Nor would Thomas Harrison, Henry Bedford or Richard Nicholson be great financial assets to Peases, and R. C. Pease was reputed to have had no money of his own. Harrison resigned without payment in 1793, and it cost J. R. Pease only £2,500 to be rid of R. C. Pease and Henry Bedford in 1795. The conclusion is that after the initial input of capital, the banks carried themselves forward and, as often happens, book capital ceased to have any real meaning. Public confidence was assured by the private resources and standing of the partners rather than their capital contributions. With the exception of Harrison—and possibly the Smiths—no important banking figure in eighteenth century Hull put more than a fraction of his total wealth into banking partnerships although the whole was, of course, at risk. The banks were specialists in the financial world, but the bankers were not yet devoting their time and energy completely to the new discipline. J. R. Pease, the greatest of them all, drew just under a quarter of his income from the bank in 1796–7,[1] although these were, admittedly, bad years for banking, and for Pease in particular.

Alderman Bramston, goldsmith, may have followed the traditional pattern of making advances out of money deposited with him, but this was not the case with the other bankers. Neither Pease nor Smiths & Thompson's opened with worthwhile deposit accounts. There were none at all in Pease's early ledgers, and few in Smiths & Thompson's. Not until the late eighties did they begin to multiply, and at the end of the century they were still mostly small. A few ran into several hundreds of pounds, but most were less than a hundred, deposited for short periods only.

Money made available by the growth of the saving habit among the striving lower middle classes—soon to blossom into the Savings Bank Movement[2]—was small compared with the two major sources of credit: the Note Issue and the Current Account. About the Note Issue little can be said, simply because there is no information about the volume of the fiduciary issue of any of the banks. Suffice it to say that bankers preferred to make loans to customers by giving

[1] J. R. Pease's Rents and Interest, 1796 and 1797, *WH* 59/58/45.

[2] The Hull Savings Bank was opened in 1818.

them Notes, which were eventually credited in someone else's account. With luck an endless series of paper transactions deferred indefinitely the obligation to pay cash. So long as the banker kept reasonable reserves to cover normal cashing he was safe.

The current accounts, alternately depleted and replenished by the normal process of trade, were both the chief field for investment and the chief source of loanable funds. Many of the merchants had credit balances of several thousands of pounds. John Staniforth, the shipowner, had £5,253 with Smiths & Thompson's in January 1786, the largest private balance at that time, and slightly over a quarter of their funds from this source. By 1800 the number and value of credit balances had increased enormously. In January 1786 it stood at £18,456; in 1796 it was £144,136; and in 1800 it had soared to £277,119. Of this, the Sykes accounted for £2,235; Overend & Thompson, wharfingers and merchants, for £4,769; John Burstall, shipowner, for £3,420; William Wilberforce for £1,548; Obison Kirkbride, merchant, shipowner and industrialist, for £3,256; and William Hill, once a sea captain, for £6,259.

More reliable, but less valuable, than the fluctuating merchants' accounts, were the credit balances of the Benevolent Societies and charities, Trinity House, the Corporation and the Dock Company. The Benevolent Societies generally had a hundred pounds or more in their accounts, and the largest, the Sailors' Society, had £300 in January 1793. Coggan's Charity had £417 and the Sunday & Spinning Schools had £571. The Corporation banked first with Pease and then, as might be expected, with Alderman Bramston, who endeavoured to keep small sums without paying interest. In December 1789 he complained to the Bench that it was not worth his while to keep their account if he paid interest on less than £500, the benefit being 'inadequate to the trouble of paying and receiving'. The Bench threatened to change their banker and he gave in. The Corporation of neighbouring Hedon banked with Smiths & Thompson's. All the Dock Company business passed through the hands of Pease & Harrison's, and later Smiths & Thompson's (who controlled over twenty shares). Unlike the merchants' accounts, which ran down during the winter months and showed credits or debits lower than a few months earlier, the Dock Company's account reached its maximum in January, prior to dividend distribution in February. Its value, depending on the state of trade, was usually between £5,000 and £9,000 by the end of January.

Smiths & Thompson's soon showed the value of partners in Parliament by capturing from Pease & Harrison's the accounts of the Collector of Customs and the Commissioners of Taxes. Altogether, Customs and Tax money accounted for £137,375 of the money in hand in January 1800. Although these accounts were periodically emptied, there was always a clear £10,000, sometimes very much more; and tax money tended to remain in the account for a very long time, before transmission to London.

The Hull banks had many customers outside the town, and from these came thousands of pounds of surplus 'agricultural' money. Country deposits tended to be more permanent than town ones, and were often quite valuable. In January 1793 the total credit balances of country customers of Smiths & Thompson's (almost 40 per cent of the total customers) amounted to no less than £40,466, compared with the total debit balances of £22,585. The largest deposits came from Lincolnshire: Robert Cropper of Laceby had £8,000, William Cropper of Sixhills had £9,569, Sir John Nelthorpe of Scawby had £5,493 and Walter Nunwick of Saxby had £1,300. Smiths & Thompson's country balances declined noticeably towards the end of the century (country customers were now only 18 per cent of the total), almost certainly the result of renewed pressure from Pease & Harrison's as they organised their branches in the East Riding and Lindsey.

We have no accurate knowledge of the total amount of money deposited with and advanced by Smiths & Thompson's, but a very rough attempt can be made to show the total credit and debit balances on the fifth of January for a number of sample years by simply adding together all the balances in the General ledgers:

TOTAL CREDIT AND DEBIT BALANCES, SMITHS & THOMPSON'S BANK

5 Jan		*Town*	*Country*	*London Agents*	*Russian Agents*	*Total*	*Balance*
1786	*Cr*	26,963	1,737	6,568	0	35,268	13,337 *Cr*
	Dr	4,927	4	17,000	0	21,931	
1793	*Cr*	122,743	40,466	76,551	0	239,760	54,810 *Cr*
	Dr	119,119	22,585	0	43,246	184,950	
1796	*Cr*	120,801	9,269	23,335	0	154,405	102,310 *Cr*
	Dr	37,018	4,098	0	9,979	51,095	
1800	*Cr*	264,890	14,785	12,229	0	291,904	162,666 *Cr*
	Dr	48,048	5,142	69,250	6,798	129,238	

So far as town accounts are concerned, loans (i.e. debtor balances) reached their peak during the boom year of 1792, when the banks made very heavy advances. When the financial crisis came in 1793 they cut back drastically on their loans to customers, and total debtor balances went down from £184,950 in January 1793 to only £51,095 in January 1796. The amount of money left in the hands of the Russian agents was reduced, and at the same time the bank reduced its debts to its London agents. The normal deposits (i.e. excluding the huge tax account) remained fairly steady for the rest of the century, increasing slightly before 1800, but little attempt was made to extend liberal credit again to the mercantile community.

The excessive liabilities appearing in the general ledger accounts need a word of explanation. The bank *may* have kept money behind the great iron door they purchased from Spence & King, but it is unlikely to have been £162,666 in January 1800. The simple truth is that much of this surplus was held in investment appearing in the Private ledger, no doubt backing the Note issue. The January balance was in any case likely to show a reduction in advances because money which merchants borrowed during the months of intense activity had often been repaid by the end of the year.

Banking in Hull was almost half a century old in 1800. It was no longer a novelty. The bankers were now the unchallenged arbiters of the town's finances, accepted and respected by great merchants and small depositors alike. They assembled the surplus capital around Hull, and did much to accelerate its movement into productive enterprise. Money once kept in the chest or the chimney was advanced to men who could use it. The small, and previously unavailable, savings of the not-so-rich were concentrated. The seaman's twenty pounds, of no value to a merchant seeking thousands, now helped to finance a timber shipment, build a sugar house, or pave a street or two. A far greater proportion of the town's aggregate wealth was available for investment than ever before.

Added to the natural accumulation of capital was the banker's special contribution, the fiduciary Note issue, which pushed credit into an already expanding economy. British banks as a whole, still insecure in their new-found power, may have acted recklessly in over-issuing and over-lending, thus creating—or at least aggravating—the crises of 1793 and 1796–7. The Hull banks, after the earlier crisis of 1759, did not suffer from the weakness apparent elsewhere.

The banks did not lose the support of their customers, and the temporary failure of Pease & Harrison's and Bramston & Moxon's was not directly attributable to conditions in Hull. Hull had, after all, been dealing with paper finance for centuries, and her bankers were experienced men, used, perhaps more than many, to the vicissitudes of trade and the vagaries of international finance.

It is difficult to visualise the developments that took place after 1750, without the banks. In handling all the foreign exchange business they met an obvious need for speed and simplicity. The banker, like the mill owner, was a man of the new world—a man of mass production and economies of scale. He was a specialist who could sell his services because it was so much simpler to employ him than do without him.

X. THE PROVISION OF MODERN PORT FACILITIES

Sooner or later in the eighteenth century there came a time when the natural facilities of the great ports were no longer adequate for the traffic flowing through them. First London, then Liverpool, then Hull found art and artifice necessary to avoid strangulation by the very sinews of trade that gave them life. Their dock building was thus a vital part of the great 'Transport Revolution' that accompanied intensive industrialisation. Canals have always received the emphasis they deserve—perhaps more. They have, in decay as in life, a romantic attraction with which the living docks cannot compete. Yet the docks, though neglected by the historian, were equally important, for the volume of traffic flowing along the canals was limited by the capacity of the ports. The multitude of navigations draining into the Humber, for instance, would have been meaningless had they not been accompanied at the right moment by the construction of improved port facilities at Hull.

1. THE BREAKDOWN OF THE PRIMITIVE PORT

Hull was able to cope easily with the ships frequenting the port during the first quarter of the eighteenth century. As its full name implies, Kingston had grown up on the west bank of the tidal mouth of the river Hull, which formed a good natural habour nearly three-quarters of a mile long. From time immemorial the merchants had concentrated in High Street, which ran parallel with the river from the North Bridge to the South End. Here they built their houses, with their private staiths at the end of their 'gardens'.[1] Here, for centuries, was done the business of the port.

The private staiths of High Street gave a uniqueness to Hull's commercial organisation that was jealously preserved by those who enjoyed them and strenuously attacked by those who did not.

[1] The Hull *staith* (occasionally *staithing*) was synonymous with wharf. *Staith* was always used to describe the place; but a man who owned a staith and handled other people's goods was a *wharfinger*.

Since no great merchant could function efficiently without one, there was a simple physical obstacle to the proliferation of important merchant firms.[1] Admittedly there were a few common staiths, built and maintained by the Corporation at points along the river where the streets terminated, but they accounted for only 130 feet out of a total of approximately 3,400 feet of staith between North Bridge and South End. There was nowhere else to trade. The river north of the bridge was generally closed to trade (though it might be used for laying up empty ships), and the Humber banks were unsuitable. The east bank of the Hull was occupied by the Garrison fortress and was therefore not available for commercial development.[2]

The private staith was not valued merely for its prestige, its convenience, or the limited protection it gave from competition. The merchants were naturally pleased about these things, but they took pride, above all, in their special relationship with His Majesty's Customs. Because there was no public quay there could be no Legal Quay, and Hull had been specifically exempted from the 1559 Act establishing Legal Quays in England.[3] It was not that the Hull merchants were inveterate smugglers eager to preserve the means of defrauding the Crown—as their jealous rivals along the east coast invariably alleged. It was a matter of principle. Any attempt to deprive them of their private staiths and ancient privileges was an attack on the liberties—and property—of Englishmen, no more tolerable to the aldermen of Hull than to the aldermen of London.

Unfortunately, what was convenient for the merchants was an

[1] It was possible to trade without a private staith because some were owned by wharfingers; Joseph Pease, for instance, was in business for nearly thirty years before he bought the family staith—eventually the biggest. But *extensive* trade was impossible. For staith-owners *c.* 1770 see Appendix 22.

[2] Ships did in fact tie up on occasions, and land timber and ballast on Garrison Side, 'allowed and connived at by those concerned in the Garrison whose care and business it is to obstruct it if they please' (Town Clerk to the Town's M.P.s, 11 Jan 1716, *GH* MS L. 1244). But since Water Bailiff dues could not be levied beyond the Hull (i.e. outside the Town), the Bench ordered in 1737 that no ships should tie up on the east side except at South End Jetty (BB viii, 846).

[3] The Act (1 Elizabeth, c. 11) declared that loading and unloading should take place only in daylight, 'and in some . . . open place quay, or wharf . . . where a customer, controller, and searcher . . . or the servants of any of them have by the space of ten years last past been accustomably resident or hereafter shall be resident. . . .' Hull had no 'open place'.

increasingly heavy burden for the Customs officers, who checked goods on board ship, in the lighter, or on the merchant's own staith using his own weights. By the middle of the century they had had more than enough, and a series of complaints went up to the Commissioners, usually on the same theme: 'as we have no lawful Key to make examination of any goods upon, so neither have we any Porters, Weighers or Packers to open and make up the same after inspection. . . .'[1] Overwhelmed by the number of ships they were expected to visit, the Customs officers were unable to carry on their work either with the speed required by the merchants or the accuracy demanded by the Commissioners. In 1764 the peculiar position of Hull was again stressed. The merchants, it was said, were 'exceedingly clamorous to have their Goods discharged . . .', but 'having only Seven acting Landwaiters it is impossible for them to give that Dispatch which the merchants expect and require, and at the same time to pay due obedience to the orders which . . . your Honours' late Inspectors at this port have left for the Waterside Officers . . .'.[2] The Inspectors' impossible orders about the method of gauging free goods had been 'in great measure dispensed with in regard the Merchants claim and always have enjoyed the liberty of landing such goods as are for themselves at their own staith and of sending such goods as are on Commission up the Rivers, directly by Keel to the places of their destination . . . and will not now assist the Officers in anything contrary to it. . . .' 'We do not know', they concluded, 'what to do upon this occasion and therefore state the Difficultys the officers labour under at this Port, where the Ship is the Key, and where consequently the Business cannot be done as at other Ports. . . .'

Hard as life was for the Customs officers, the merchants felt they had every right to be clamorous. The Customs Letter Books contain many lists of ships whose unloading was delayed by Customs procedure. On 15 November 1749, for instance, there were thirty-three ships awaiting attention, some of which had been in the Haven for over a month.[3] The Haven, with its warehouses alongside, had been admirable in the leisurely days of the seventeenth century, when a merchant's ships really did tie up at the bottom of his garden. But increasing trade and delays in clearing ships produced, by the middle of the century, a state of virtual chaos that seriously impaired

[1] HCLB, C–B, 3 Jan 1759. [2] ibid., 31 Oct 1764.
[3] ibid., 17 Jan 1749.

the ability of the port to cope with any further expansion of trade. The Haven had always been too small during embargoes and bad winters,[1] but it was generally satisfactory so long as the tonnage of foreign-going shipping remained steady at about 11,000 tons, as it did until *c.* 1740. A steady rise to 24,000 tons by 1751 resulted in a more or less permanent crush in the Haven, with ships experiencing difficulty in manœuvring and sometimes suffering damage. 'The King's Boats', the Collector wrote in 1754,[2] 'of late received considerable damage whilst laying at the Staiths—chiefly by having passage made over them to & from Ships in the harbour when it is low water. . . .' Some time before they had reported the fears of Holgate, 'the most considerable exporter of corn in these parts', that he would arrive in the harbour one morning to find his lighters 'hung up between two Ships which is often the Case in a Crowded Haven . . .'.[3]

There were thus two distinct problems by the middle of the century: the lack of a Legal Quay, and the growing congestion in the Haven. The former was of interest only to the Commissioners of Customs. The merchants in general objected to a Legal Quay, some going so far as to reject any dock building that might include one. Congestion was of greater interest, but there was no agreed solution. The High Street interest insisted that no quays or landing places should be built independent of the High Street side of the Haven, while the remaining merchants insisted that any further quays must be public and separate from High Street. That some change was required was obvious to most people, but opinion in the town split over what actually should be done. Controversy raged for twenty years before a final compromise was reached.[4]

2. PRELUDE TO DOCK BUILDING: THE BATTLE OF THE LEGAL QUAY

Serious agitation for improvements began in the fifties. In January 1756 Thomas Broadley, Edmund Popple and Andrew Perrott,

[1] Shipowners and masters had complained of the crush as early as 1676 (BB vii, 11 May) and similar complaints were made during the embargo of 1739, when many ships could not get into the Haven (BB viii, 872).

[2] HCLB, C–B, 17 May 1754. [3] ibid., 27 Nov 1751.

[4] For a more detailed consideration of the earlier pressure for a dock, see Gordon Jackson, 'The Struggle for the First Hull Dock', *Transport History*, Vol. I, No. 1 (1968).

three of the leading merchants, organised a Town Meeting which resolved that 'by the Increase of Trade the Present Harbour for Ships at this Port is become not near large enough for the shipping and the want of sufficient room therein is found to be very detrimental and hazardous'.[1] Five men were appointed to meet five from the Corporation and five from Trinity House to form a 'Committee for the whole Town', to consider 'an application to Parliament in order to make an additional Harbour or some further Accommodation for the shipping . . .'. In March the committee reported that 'the Harbour . . is sufficient for the Loading and Delivering Ships provided the Light Ships be removed to some convenient place or places'. After considering the Hull above North Bridge they came down firmly in favour of a harbour for light ships on the Humber bank, to be paid for out of duties levied by Act of Parliament. They may have had in mind a full wet dock on land reclaimed from the foreshore, for a plan of the new (1753) Liverpool dock was obtained, specially designed, it was said, 'to be useful and a guide to you in making yours at Hull'.[2] Whatever the plans, they came to nothing, for the matter was shelved when war broke out in 1756.

The intervention of war hides the fact that these proposals for a harbour for light ships stood little chance of becoming law. While pleasing to the High Street interest, they were anathema to the Customs, for they ignored the vexed question of the Legal Quay. As soon as the war was over the Hull Customs officers began a campaign of their own, using the simple argument, to their superiors in London, that 'we believe that the weight or guage of every species of Goods could be more certainly Assertained upon a Legal Quay'.[3] At the same time the town formed another Harbour Committee, which rejected the earlier scheme for a Humber bank dock.[4] In July 1766 the Bench ordered the Mayor to seal 'any Petition or Bill which shall be judged necessary . . . for making a wet Dock or Bason for ships . . . on the East Side of the Haven',[5] and a Bill was duly prepared 'for making Docks and other Conveniences for the use and accommodation of Ships, lengthening the South End Jetty,

[1] The Minutes of the various meetings are in *GH* Box 9(i).

[2] Edward White, Liverpool, to William Harrison, Hull, n.d., a stray letter in *WH* Chronological MSS, 1756. The new Liverpool dock was constructed on land reclaimed from the Mersey. See J. H. Bird, *The Major Seaports of the United Kingdom* (London, 1963), Chapter 11.

[3] HCLB, C–B, 16 May 1765.

[4] BB ix, 362–3. [5] BB ix, 365.

erecting Dolphins and other works in the Haven and Port of Kingston upon Hull; and for appropriating certain Lands belonging to His Majesty, to those uses'.[1] Again it was to be a harbour for light ships. No one might

> upon any Account or Pretence whatsoever, load . . . or unload . . . any Goods . . . into . . . or . . . out of any ship . . . lying in any of the said Docks . . .; but all Goods . . . brought into and carried from the said Port shall . . . at all times hereafter be shipped and . . . unshipped . . . in the said Haven or River of Hull, or at the Staiths or Warehouses adjoining thereto, in such manner as hath been used and accustomed before the passing of this Act. . . .[2]

Matters came to a head in April 1767, when the Commissioners of Customs at last responded to the pleas from Hull and sent a couple of surveyors to report on conditions in the Haven and suggest a location for a Legal Quay. Their Report stressed the need to keep the Haven as free as possible and ruled out the possibility of a quay there. The Committee sponsoring the Hull Bill reconsidered the position and then agreed with the surveyors, thinking it 'impracticable that a Quay could be effected on the West side of the Haven'.[3] The High Street interest were not slow to see the implication here: that a Legal Quay, now excluded from the Haven, might be built in the dock planned for the east side of the Hull. The principal merchants immediately withdrew their support, and the scheme was shelved. The situation had reached stalemate. The merchants objected to a Legal Quay; but the Treasury would secure the rejection of any Dock Bill excluding one. If there *had* to be a Legal Quay, it was imperative for the High Street interest that it should be on the west bank of the Hull; but the west bank had just been declared unsuitable. Here the matter rested for three years while merchants and Commissioners alike surveyed their law books and less reputable weapons for the inevitable conflict.

[1] An annotated copy is in *LAO* Td'E/6, among the papers of George Tennyson who owned (but did not occupy) a High Street staith. The wording of the Bill implies that the Government had already promised the Garrison site for building a dock on the east side (p. 18).

[2] It was not simply a concern for site values that caused hostility to a dock on the east side. The east side was outside Hull, and therefore beyond the Bench's powers to raise Water Bailiff Dues; and communications other than by water were very poor indeed.

[3] The surveyors were Robert Mylne and Joseph Robson. Part of their Report and the decisions of the committee are noted in John Grundy's Report on the river Hull, 1772.

It was the Commissioners who forced the issue. In 1770 the amount of foreign-going shipping topped 46,000 tons, a fourfold increase in thirty years, and the work of the Customs ground almost to a halt. The Commissioners therefore ordered the removal of the Custom House from High Street, where a public quay could not be built, to vacant ground on the Humber bank where it could. The order was ridiculous, as the Commissioners probably knew, but its very enormity stung the merchants into action. The Bench, describing the proposal as 'highly inconvenient to the trade of the place and hurtful to the private property of many of the inhabitants . . .', offered to rent to the Customs the staiths adjoining the Custom House on any terms they thought fit.[1] As a final capitulation to the inevitable the Bench added that 'if by erecting a Custom House here a Quay could be made to follow it . . .' such a quay 'will be very agreeable to the merchants'. The Collector was now ordered to begin negotiations for the lease or purchase of staiths, keeping the Commissioners informed so that they could cancel the plans for South End as soon as possible. Although he might hold out South End as a threat, he was 'to consider the Obtaining a Lawfull Quay as the principal object of the Board . . .'.[2] On 31 May 1771 he was able to inform the Board 'that the Corporation, Merchants, Traders and others at this Place had consented to Your Hons' proposals signified to them by us for building a Free and Legal Quay in the Front of the Stathings on the West Side of the River Hull . . .'.[3]

In fact such a quay was by no means agreeable to the merchants. When a draft of the proposed Bill for creating the Legal Quay was presented to the Bench on 4 November 1771, a Memorial from a large group of merchants pleaded for its rejection.[4] They argued, rather perversely, that the letters they had seen from the Board 'do not appear to contain any proof that Government has absolutely determined to establish a Quay at this Port', and they hoped that 'the reasons arising from our natural situation which have hitherto prevented it will always have their due weight unless the Town shall concur in depriving itself of the valuable exemption we now enjoy on the security of Parliament'. The signatories were too important to be ignored. The Bench deferred the presentation of the Bill and the Customs were thwarted yet again.

The only proposals so far made public were for the building of

[1] HCLB, C–B, 8 Sep 1770. [2] HCLB, B–C, 10 May 1771.
[3] HCLB, C–B, 31 May 1771. [4] BB ix, 412.

a short Legal Quay along fifteen frontages in the Haven adjacent to the existing Customs House. But the merchants were again considering the extension of harbour room. Late in 1771 the Bench appointed a Committee to 'conduct and carry on the business of the Custom House and Quay proposed to be erected and also concerning *the walls and Ditches* . . .'.[1] This is the first indication of interest in the walls as a possible site for a dock, and appears to be the compromise between the High Street interest and other merchant interests that had been sought for so long. An added incentive, no doubt, was the petition to the Customs in March 1772 of 'Merchants, Traders and Manufacturers residing in the Counties of Lincoln, Nottingham, Leicester, Derby, Warwick and Stafford . . .', who demanded that a port be established at Gainsborough because of the inadequate facilities at Hull.[2] In May, and again in November, 1772, the Customs threatened to bring in their own Bill if the Town did not soon produce a Dock Bill.[3] A final decision was at last made, and on 4 December 1772 the Bench recorded that they 'did lately petition for the military works surrounding the Town and have received a very favourable answer and propose to form part of those military works, viz. the ramparts and Both Ditches into a Bason for Light Ships from the North Gates to Beverley Gates'. The Town was to bear all expenses, and recover the cost from Dock Dues.

This new proposal was, in fact, an extremely short-sighted victory for the High Street interest, and could have been satisfactory only if the port remained static. The town later had cause to be grateful to the Customs officers, for it was at their instigation that the plan was again changed before it was too late. As soon as the proposals were made public, they pressed the Bench to deepen the dock to admit loaded ships, so that the Legal Quay could be built in it. When the Bench replied that 'they were unwilling the Quay should be placed anywhere else, than in Hull Haven as formerly proposed . . .', the Collector suggested that the Commissioners allow a little blackmail:[4]

had we authority to Signify to them that if they did not agree to make the Wet Dock of a sufficient Depth for Loaded as well as Light

[1] BB ix, 408. In Feb 1772 Trinity House promised 'most ready support in promoting of the Intended Bill for Making a Quay *and Enlarging the Harbour*'; BB ix, 412.

[2] Copy is HCLB, C–B, Mar 1772.

[3] See HCLB, B–C, 8 May 1772 and HCLB, C–B, 5 Nov 1772.

[4] HCLB, C–B, 18 Dec 1772.

Ships, they could not obtain their Grant of the Walls and Ditches, and that the Ditches, if they refused these conditions, would be given to another Body who might be willing to convert the same into such Wet Dock, they would then be under a necessity of being more expedite, and we apprehend would not forgo the expected advantages from making such Wet Dock, *or at least, that other persons would be found that would accept the Ditches on Such Terms.*

The Treasury eventually agreed, and in March 1773 determined 'that they would be trifled with no longer'. Although asserting their desire 'to proceed in the most friendly manner with the town', they would make a port at Gainsborough if a Legal Quay was not soon built at Hull, 'and do such other things in the neighbourhood of Hull as for the trade of the country it appeared to them they ought to do'.[1] The Bench had no option but to accept the Commissioners' terms,[2] and the final Bill was drafted to build a dock for loaded ships, and to empower the King 'to assign and appoint such open places, quays, or wharfs at Kingston-upon-Hull, on the west side of the Harbour, and on the walls adjoining the Town's ditches . . .' to be the only lawful quays for goods in the overseas trade.

The Commissioners of Customs did not gain their point lightly. Not only did the merchants have their private staiths accepted as Suffrance Quays. They also pleaded, successfully, that it was

impossible for the Trade of the Town to raise the money without being too much distressed, and that they must therefore rely on the Assistance of Government, which they think themselves the more entitled to: As it is to oblige Government that they have so readily agreed to tax their trade, and lay themselves under so great an expence, for Erecting and Maintaining those works. . . .[3]

They had a reasonable case, in that a dock for loaded ships would cost more than one for light ships and, in strict law, they were under no obligation to build a Legal Quay. The Commissioners were not inclined to argue, and on 24 April 1773 the Treasury cleared the way for final agreement by granting 'all that piece . . . of ground, being part of the land belonging to his Majesty's military works . . . , called the Town's Ditches . . .', and also 'out of his Majesty's customs at the said port . . ., the full sum of fifteen thousand pounds of lawful money . . .'. A year later the Bill became law (14 George III, c. 56), owing at least as much to the officers of H.M. Customs as it did

[1] Quoted by W. Wright, 'The Hull Docks', *Minutes of Proceedings of the Institution of Civil Engineers*, Vol. XLI (1875), p. 85.

[2] HCLB, C–B, 25 Mar 1773. [3] HCLB, C–B, 16 Apr 1773.

to the merchants of Hull. Wet docks were not yet the common answer to congestion, and without Customs pressure for a Legal Quay, Hull may have built only a very inferior dock for light ships.

3. THE HULL DOCK COMPANY

It had been the intention of the Bench to follow the example of Liverpool, where 'all the Docks . . . were formed under the authority of Acts of Parliament which have invested the Corporation of the borough, as trustees for the public with the sole direction to them. . . .'[1] As late as 1772 the Bench was expecting to bear the cost of the dock, possibly with assistance from Trinity House, and this had been the basis for the Customs' blackmail. Some time in 1772 the Bench changed its mind, and the Act created a private, independent body: 'whereas the several persons, bodies corporate and politic, hereinafter named, are willing to begin, carry on, and complete the said bason or dock, and quay or wharf adjoining thereto,' they 'shall for those purposes be one body politic and corporate, by the name of the Dock Company at Kingston-upon-Hull'.[2]

The Bench, specifically excluded from holding more than ten shares,[3] never said why it changed its mind.[4] The idea of Corporation docks was not new, and it was natural that the Bench should automatically think of building and running the dock itself. It was only when it got down to details that the task seemed less attractive. When the Bench sought precedents among the public utilities, it found them overwhelmingly in the hands of joint stock companies in which local authorities had a considerable voice but no major capital investment.[5] It was money, above all, that created the difficulty. The Corporation had none. Dues, rents and assorted rates brought in just enough to run the town, and the Bench could not afford to mortage them to raise money. It could have sold property

[1] R. C. Jarvis, *Customs Letter Books of the Port of Liverpool, 1711–1813* (Manchester, 1954), entry No. 406, dated 21 Jul 1789.

[2] The Act, s. xvii. [3] s. xxxvi.

[4] We cannot overlook the hostility of some of the Aldermen to both dock and Legal Quay, or the desire of others to avoid involvement in an issue on which the town was openly divided. Five of the Aldermen opposed the Bill, and a further two had been unsure before finally supporting it.

[5] See G. H. Evans, *British Corporation Finance, 1775–1850* (Johns Hopkins Press, 1936) for the finances of other canal and dock companies.

or mortgaged future income from the dock, but there seemed little point when it was so easy to secure offers of contributions to a joint stock. The shares held by the Bench and Trinity House, and by individual members of both, would ensure an adequate voice for the representatives of the town, and the appointment of the Dock Master was to be reserved to Trinity House. The Dock Company was not at first looked on as a private company. It was a 'Corporation': one of the three Corporations that cared for the well-being of the town.

The Dock Company thus established was vested with all the property of the dock and associated works,[1] and 'in consideration of the great charges and expences which the making . . . such . . . dock . . . and the . . . maintaining . . . the same in repair for the future, will amount unto . . .', the rates and duties were 'vested in the said dock company as their own proper monies . . . for their own proper use . . . for the purpose aforesaid . . .'.[2] More ink was to flow in the future over this apparently unobjectionable clause than over any other section of the Act.

The actual building of the dock was handed over to Commissioners consisting of nine members of the Company, six non-subscribing inhabitants, the Mayor and two Aldermen, and the Warden, one Elder Brother and one Assistant of Trinity House.[3] They were empowered to make by-laws (subject to the approval of the Company) for the running of the dock,[4] to erect and maintain lamps,[5] to purchase land, and sell surplus land, 'the money arising by such sale . . . [to] . . . be applied to the use of the sd Company'.[6] But they had no experience of dock building and, as in 1756, advice was sought from Liverpool. Henry Berry, the Chief Dock Engineer, was consulted, and in February 1775 the Mayor of Liverpool was requested that 'Mr Berry may be permitted to direct and superintend the work intended to be carried on here'.[7]

Henry Berry (1720–1812) was eminently suitable. His famous master, Thomas Steers, whom he succeeded at Liverpool, had worked first in London and then on the first Liverpool dock (1709–15),[8] while Berry had continued working in Liverpool and had also

[1] The Act, s. xxv. [2] s. xlii. [3] s. liv. [4] s. lxi.

[5] s. lxiv. [6] ss. lxxvii-lxxxi.

[7] HDC, Letter Bk 'A'; Chairman of Commissioners to Mayor of Liverpool, 3 Feb 1775.

[8] For Steers and early dock work at Liverpool, see H. Peet, 'Thomas Steers, the Engineer of Liverpool's First Dock', *Transactions of the Hist. Soc. of Lancs and Cheshire*, vol. lxxxii, 1930, reprinted 1932.

built the first canal in eighteenth century England: the Sankey Navigation (1755–9).[1] He was the greatest living expert on docks, and it is fitting that the Hull dock should be correctly attributed to him and not, as it usually is, to John Grundy. The obscurity that today surrounds Berry may be due in no small measure to his concentration on Liverpool—or to the lack of interest shown in docks and harbours until very recently. He was not one of the great all-rounders of the late eighteenth century and appears to have had little contact with them. He was, for instance, unable to recommend a suitable assistant 'capable of carrying into execution such plans as you may from time to time direct, and will make it his daily and only employment'.[2] The man eventually chosen, Luke Holt, was recommended by John Smeaton, who was well known in Hull.

Berry may have been a good engineer, but he was a poor employee. He was, perhaps through no fault of his own, exceedingly dilatory over the planning of the dock, and rarely responded to letters requesting his attendance in Hull. In desperation in May 1775 the Dock Commissioners sent Holt to attend him in Liverpool, 'to make his remarks of your Works and what is more material to consult with you to the necessary plan for the immediate progress in our business'.[3] When Holt arrived in Liverpool Berry was nowhere to be found![4] Not until August was William Waller, chairman of the Commissioners, able to tell his friend Smeaton that 'Mr Berry our engineer has been here and settled the plan for our proceeding in the work of the Dock'.[5]

Two months later, on 19 October 1775, the foundation stone was laid by the Mayor, John Outram. The Irish who flocked to the town took possession of the walls, ramparts and ditches that had successfully withstood Charles I,[6] and a fortnight short of three

[1] For Berry see S. A. Harris, 'Henry Berry (1720–1812): Liverpool's Second Dock Engineer', *Transactions of the Hist. Soc. of Lancs and Cheshire*, vol. lxxxix (1937) and xc (1938); and T. C. Barker, 'The beginnings of the Canal Age in the British Isles', in Pressnell, *Studies in the Industrial Revolution.*

[2] HDC, Letter Bk 'A', Chairman of Commissioners to Henry Berry, 3 Feb 1775.

[3] ibid., same to same, 24 May 1775.

[4] ibid., same to same, 14 Jul 1775.

[5] ibid., Chairman to John Smeaton, 20 Aug 1775.

[6] 'Seven large Military Gates, with the Iron Work therein contained' were offered for sale on 4 Sep 1774; Advertisement, copy in HDC Scrap Book, Hull Dock Office.

years later they emerged from a dock into which Holt slowly and cautiously began to admit the water. The walls (specially strengthened with a new-fangled mortar of cement with added Pozzellana stone)[1] held firm, and on 22 September 1778, amid scenes of general rejoicing, Hull's champion whaler, the *Manchester*, was ceremonially admitted to the dock.[2]

At last Hull had its dock, bigger and better than anything anticipated during the wrangles of the last twenty years. At fractionally under ten acres (1,703 by 254 feet) it was the largest dock yet constructed, three acres bigger than the largest Liverpool dock. Capable in theory of holding a hundred sail, in practice it often sheltered more. They tied up at quays that were equal in length to the private staiths of the old Haven. A new Custom House was built alongside the lock and 1,558 feet of quay on the southern side of the dock was set aside as Legal Quay—more than in the Port of London. More important than the length of quay was its area. For the first time the porters had adequate working space, after centuries of cramped conditions. Eighteen thousand square yards was added by the dock estate, and a further five thousand was contained in the new quay built in the Haven. On the other hand, the warehouse space provided by the Dock Company on 2,251 square yards of land was much smaller than the area in High Street, and the pattern emerged of goods being shipped and unshipped in the dock and warehoused in High Street, carried there by lighter—there were sixty-five at work in 1800—or by carts making use of the 'wheeling way made of wood' provided on the quays.

The Dock Company was a resounding financial success. It suffered from none of the troubles besetting contemporary canal and harbour companies, forever chasing fresh capital in a dismal world of underestimated costs and over-estimated profits. Its authorised capital was £80,000 in £500 shares, and in case shares remained unsold or the cost exceeded £80,000, it was further empowered to borrow £20,000 'for completing and perfecting the said works' on

[1] Neither Berry nor Holt were acquainted with the use of Pozzellana stone, which was specially imported from Civita Vecchia in Italy. The Commissioners had to ask Smeaton for details in August 1775; HDC Commissioners' Transactions.

[2] The scene was fully described by Hadley, pp. 568–9.

security of the duties.[1] In the event neither the reserve nor the full share capital was required. Berry had been remarkably good in his estimating—if it was his—and the final cost—£73,330[2]—was comfortably covered by authorised capital. Moreover, the Company was able to raise large sums from other sources. Unlike canal tolls, which could hardly be raised before the completion of the work, the 'dock' duties were payable from 31 December 1774 by all ships entering the port of Hull. By the end of 1780 they amounted to £26,080, and this, together with the £15,000 Treasury grant, accounted for over half the total expenditure. It was found necessary to sell only £60,000 worth of shares, and the shareholders, who according to later apologists of the Company, faced grave risks and the prospect of ruin, had only a 50 per cent call made on them. Their contribution to the cost of the dock was a mere £30,000, and within ten years the Company had sold land to the value of £19,611, which was given back to shareholders.

Since no debts were incurred in the building of the dock, and the Company had no intention of creating a reserve fund, all the increasing surplus revenue was available for dividend distribution. Starting with £50 in 1780, the total dividends paid between 1780 and 1800 amounted to £1,134 per share (including land sales), an average of £54 per annum: 10·8 per cent on the face value, and 21·6 per cent on the price actually paid by the original subscribers (Appendix 34). There is little wonder that shares were selling at well over a thousand pounds in the nineties.

The original promoters of the Dock Company, named in section xvii of the Act, were almost entirely members of the merchant aristocracy. The non-Hull addresses attributed to some of them in the Directories are misleading. There was no infusion of capital from London—or Narva; but there were Hull people living in those places. The Sykes, Wilberforce, Watson and Maister, Williamson, Waller and King, Etherington, Porter, Howard and Broadley, Thorley, Thompson, Dixon and Welfitt, Staniforth, Hammond and Pease: these were the backbone of Hull. What suited them was likely to be in the best interests of the port.

[1] The Act, ss. xxix and xxxii.

[2] Expenditure on the dock amounted to £64,588, and extra land cost £8,741. 'Official' details of the cost and size of the dock, and records of income and expenditure, are contained in a manuscript known as 'Huffam's Book' in the Hull Dock Office.

Unfortunately the Company that came into existence after the passing of the Act contained a number of shareholders who were less interested in the public good, and share transfers in the first twenty-five years resulted in a Company more inclined to preserve the agreeable *status quo* than to develop a dock system. Merchants retired; their sons became 'Gents'; and their daughters took no interest in the dock. Shares were purchased by those who looked on them merely as an investment, and had little interest in the duties of the Dock Company—except, of course, that of paying the highest possible dividend. It would, however, be wrong to over-emphasise this feature. Far more important was the development of a pressure group of public-spirited merchants within the Company who, by the nineties, had acquired the proxies of at least thirty-three shareholders now residing outside Hull and the eleven females who never attended meetings of the Company.[1] As early as 1780, five men were able to control some seventy votes. Henry Maister could usually find seven or eight in his family circle, and the Travises, tobacco merchants and shipowners, a similar number. William Hammond could muster anything up to twenty, closely followed by R. C. Broadley with eighteen. The greatest of them all, the merchant-banker Thomas Thompson, could muster twenty-three, of which four were his own and seven his partners'. Thompson, the representative of a firm that had vigorously opposed the building of the dock, was thus able to outvote the combined strength of the Bench and Trinity House, the guardians of the public interest. The result could have been serious, but the fact is that the great merchants, having decided that a dock was inevitable, determined to make it a success. Thompson's power and connexions, instead of working against the public interest, were one day to save the town from the disastrous effects of a 'popular' decision about the siting of the second dock (see pp. 257–8). It was not democracy; but it was good sense.

4. THE STRUGGLE FOR A SECOND DOCK: A QUESTION OF SUBSIDY

There were many people soon prepared to argue that the financial success of the Dock Company was due to its betrayal of trust.

[1] Details from HDC Transactions, *passim.*

Hull was justifiably proud of its great new dock, which, with the Haven, was fully expected to accommodate the largest amount of shipping ever likely to frequent the port. Its total inadequacy, only two or three years after it was opened, came as a surprise and disappointment to many.

There were two main reasons for this new development. In the first place the Haven was, quite unexpectedly, deserted by foreign-going shipping in favour of the better facilities of the dock. It was devoted increasingly to coastal and river traffic, became ever more crowded, and, in the words of the Dock Master, was 'a place of danger to shipping, without the greatest attention being paid to prevent it . . .'.[1] He quoted the case of the *Empress*, ordered out of the Haven on to the strand by her owners in the winter of 1786–7. On the other hand, the Company was still arguing in February 1787 that extension of the dock 'does not appear to be necessary, if . . . the Haven or Old Harbour is still considered as the PORT OF KINGSTON-UPON-HULL'.[2]

The move to the dock was not entirely voluntary. The Dock Act contained a flaw, not recognised until it was too late: a merchant could only build his Suffrance Quay if his frontage was connected with a 'common' staith;[3] but there was no provision for compelling anyone to build. It had been assumed that the Haven would remain the centre of trade, with merchants racing to finish their quays. They did not. Sufficient of them declined building to jeopardise the whole quay. Wilberforce & Smiths were one of the first firms to realise their plight, and early in 1780 Abel Smith was complaining to the Customs that 'there is a staith between the Common Staith called New Staith and your Memorialist's staith, the owner of which refuses to Erect a Key . . .'.[4] Alderman B. B. Thompson was stuck because his neighbour, Stephenson, built up only one of his two frontages.[5] The Bench tried to rectify the situation by ordering (with dubious legality) that 'no Gent have a Communication with

[1] Thomas Westerdell, *An Address to the Corporation . . . of Hull . . . in answer to a pamphlet called 'The Defence of the Dock Company . . .'* (1787).

[2] William Hammond, *Remarks on a Publication entitled 'The Case of the Merchants'*, Hull Dock Office, 2 Feb 1787.

[3] The quays were to be 'open at all times to the officers of His Majesty's revenue by free and clear communication with the common staiths adjoining'. The Act, s. iii.

[4] HCLB, C–B, 27 Mar 1780.

[5] ibid., 21 Feb 1783.

any Common Staith by building a Wharf unless he build a Wharf the whole extent of his own front into the Harbour'.[1] An amendment to the Act was obtained in 1784, allowing a merchant to compel his neighbour to build if he paid a third of the cost,[2] but for the survival of High Street as anything more than warehouse space, this was four years too late. By 1784 the pattern of shipping through the dock had been set, and all ideas of using it as a parking place had gone.

The second, and most important, reason for the dock's inadequacy was the boom in commerce that took the town by surprise. Estimates for the size of the dock had been based on the tonnage of shipping frequenting the port in the late sixties, assuming the continued use of the Haven. With the volume of shipping entering the port around 90,000 tons in 1779–80 the dock was comfortably filled and worked efficiently, but within ten years the tonnage had doubled and, although it fluctuated considerably, overcrowding impaired both the efficiency and safety of the dock. The movement is best followed in the Company's own record of the measured tonnage of ships paying dock duties: 88,409 tons in 1780, 156,315 in 1790 and 198,173 in 1800. Two hundred thousand tons was passed for the first time in 1792, and in 1796 there were not far short of a quarter of a million tons paying duties.[3] Already by 1786 ships were competing for access, and discussions about dock extension began in January of that year.[4] On 8 February a committee representing merchants and the Dock Company agreed to extend the dock

[1] BB ix, 515.

[2] 23 Geo III, c. 55, ss. li-lviii. On 18 Nov 1784, W. Wilberforce paid £150 to John Voase 'as a consideration for his expence in building a Quay opposite his own warehouse and in order to obtain the priviledge of building a Quay opposite Mr Wilberforce's Warehouse'; W. Wilberforce's account, Smiths & Thompson's Bank Ledgers.

[3] Tonnage figures from *Hull Dock Office*, 'Huffam's Book', *passim*. See Appendix 10.

[4] There had been some discussion about extension as early as 1784, and a Memorial was presented to the Company; nothing came of it. (No record of it has been found, but it is referred to in *Case of the Merchants, Shipowners, etc....*, 1786). On 28 Oct 1784 Strother noted in his Journal that 'A Meeting of the Proprietors of the dock was held, they having some thoughts of making another dock on the north side of the present one, which is insufficient to hold the number of ships that frequent this port. . . .' This probably represents the gossip of the day rather than fact, for a dock to the north of the existing one appears in no other source.

on the surplus land granted by the Treasury, from Beverley Gates to Myton Gates, to accommodate a further fifty sail.[1]

It had taken less than a month for the delegates to agree to build a dock; it was to take them over twenty-three years to build it. While controversy was to rage over the suitability of four different sites, the basic reason for the delay was the clash of interests arising from the difficulty of financing an expensive public utility owned by a private company that believed itself unable to raise the necessary capital. The Town expected the Company to pay for the new dock out of the existing 'taxes on trade', and the Company expected the Town to subsidise a dock that was patently for the benefit of the Town and against the interests of the Company, which would lose capital without a consequent increase in income. The wrangling resulting from the deadlock produced perhaps the most unhappy episode in the modern history of Hull.

The projected dock was expected to cost £25,000, of which the Company offered to find only £6,000.[2] A Town Meeting thereupon rejected the agreement reached by the delegates, and the chairman, Sir Henry Etherington, was instructed to demand 'that the said Company will make on the ground granted them by government, from Beverley Gates to Myton Gates, a reservoir for the more convenient use of the Dock . . .',[3] and the merchants, led by William Osbourne, began a subscription for Parliamentary action should the Company refuse. It did refuse, whereupon the Corporation proxy introduced a motion that the Company should build a dock at its sole expense. The Company retaliated by refusing to allow the Corporation proxy to vote at the meeting, and a smarting Bench considered legal action, subscribing 300 guineas to the merchants' Action Fund, and ordering a preliminary survey of the Dock Company's estate.[4]

[1] Decisions of the Dock Company and the Bench, and agreements between them and with Trinity House, are recorded in the Bench Books and in HDC Transactions, *passim*. No further reference will be made to them when dates are mentioned in the text.

[2] HDC Transactions, 8 Feb 1786.

[3] The meeting is reported in Hadley, p. 572.

[4] BB x, 13, 19, 20. Anthony Bower, the Hull surveyor, was engaged. He had a fight with one of the Company's 'chief servants', and the Company threatened to expel by force any surveyor trespassing on the estate; William Hammond to the Mayor, Oct 1786, *GH* MS L.1386 (264). Although there was much talk, the Collector of Customs, R. A. Harrison, was not clear what plans were in the air, either from the Town Committee or the Merchants' Committee; HCLB, C–B, 10 Mar 1787.

Acrimonious disputes led eventually to a pamphlet war that lasted almost twenty years as 'Mercator', 'Publicola', 'Vigilant', 'A.B.', 'S' and two dozen others addressed the Mayor, the merchants, the burgesses or the Company. The latter replied with a series of weighty pamphlets that convinced its members—but nobody else—of the justice of its case.[1] The position of the Company was succinctly put by one of its pamphleteers right at the beginning: 'nothing remained on the part of the Dock Company to be *performed*, except the *Maintenance* and support of the works which they had *completed*: more therefore cannot be lawfully required of them.'[2] The Town, by contrast, believed that the Company must have been empowered to build further docks since it had been granted land for the purpose.[3] Nor were they disposed to pay for the dock when the Company's profits so far (1785) amounted to almost £30,000.[4] Apparently the only course was to secure the transfer of the Company's estates and duties to 'public' ownership, and this novel solution was formulated in a Bill presented to Parliament in 1787.[5] The committee of Aldermen and merchants who drew up the Bill and canvassed for it in London proposed that the Bench and Trinity House should jointly receive the duties belonging to the Company, 'together with full and sufficient power to make, carry on, manage, and complete the said works and such further accommodation as may be necessary . . .'. If the Company rejected a final chance to

[1] A more or less complete set of pamphlets are in the Scrapbook in Hull Dock Office and in the 'Dock Boxes' in the Guildhall. Many can be found in the City Library and Wilberforce House Library. Hadley printed many of them (see Appendix 38).

[2] *An Address to the Dock Company* . . ., by 'A Proprietor', 13 Feb 1786.

[3] Strother wrote: 'By an Act of Parliament the dock must be carried round the Town to join the Humber, on the South West side of the Town, for which the present king has given all the ramparts.' 29 Oct 1784.

[4] A letter from Sir Henry Etherington, 'Chairman of the Subscribers for a new dock', to the Dock Co., 25 Jan 1787, made the point that 'The Dock Company, by their Dividends, have been very nearly repaid the WHOLE of their original Subscription Money . . .'.

[5] BB x, 35–7. The Common Seal was fixed to the Petition for leave to bring in the Bill on 10 Feb 1787. It was presented to the Commons by Samuel Thornton with the support of many bodies, including the Phoenix Assurance Society, which believed a new dock would 'lessen the Danger of Fire in the said Town & Port'. Phoenix Assurance Co., Trustees and Directors' Minutes, 24 Mar 1787. (I am grateful to the Phoenix Assurance Company for kindly supplying this information.)

build a dock, all its powers were to devolve upon twenty-one Commissioners, seven each from the Bench, Trinity House and the Company. All surplus Company land was to be sold, and the duties mortgaged, to pay for the work. Existing shareholders were to be safeguarded, but their dividends were limited to six per cent. Surplus income was to be used for paying off the debt and reducing duties.

By far the most startling clause of the Bill provided for the gradual transfer of the Company to 'public' ownership. All shares coming on to the market in future were to be bought alternately by the Bench and Trinity House for a price fixed at £550—only half the market value. The Company retaliated in *A Defence of the Rights of the Dock Company* . . ., a huge pamphlet retailing the iniquities of 'a bill of the most alarming nature to private property, and of the most destructive tendency to all future national improvements under Parliamentary authority'. It concluded, rather blindly, 'that no extension of the present work seems to them to be necessary'. Parliament, impressed by the sanctity of private property, but not unmindful of the needs of the port, referred the vetoed Bill to the local members, Samuel Thornton, Walter Spencer-Stanhope and William Wilberforce, who began work on a compromise solution. Their 'Propositions' retained the twenty-one Commissioners, but the completed dock was to be handed over to the Dock Company, whose rights were thus protected.[1] In return the Company was required to pay £10,000 (later raised to £12,000) of the cost, and the remaining £15,000 was to be obtained from a grant of the Garrison site which the Government offered 'provided a wet Dock was made for one hundred sail . . . and a dry Dock that could occasionally receive a 74 gun ship . . .'.[2]

The merchants were pleased by the Propositions because no extra duties were involved, and the Dock Company noted with satisfaction that its contribution had been held down to the figure it was expecting to raise by the sale of surplus land for the new residential streets to the north of the dock. On 10 November William Hammond, Chairman of the Company, informed the Members of Parliament

[1] Samuel Thornton and W. S. Stanhope to the Bench, 22 Mar 1788; *GH* MS L.1387(16).

[2] BB x, 46. The Propositions were accepted by the Dock Co. in June, by the Town Meeting in August, and by the Bench—after thoroughly testing local opinion—in November.

that 'our local differences relative to an extension of the Dock are I hope happily terminated . . . .',[1] and a Bill was sent to London on 2 February 1788 with almost unanimous support.[2] Once again the feeling of goodwill was short-lived. The Master-General of the Ordnance, the Duke of Richmond, announced that the Garrison site would be granted for 'establishing the works on that spot', but not 'as a subsidiary aid for our making the dock to Myton Gates . . .'.[3] This was a completely unforeseen development. With one unimportant exception, all the schemes for a second dock involved an extension of the existing one. While Richmond's offer was in some ways a sensible one, it was received in the town with mixed feelings. The Dock Company's delegates, disappointed, but eager to save money, accepted Garrison Side on these conditions. When the news broke in Hull, however, a hastily summoned Town Meeting formed what one contemporary called a 'Committee of Safety', under the chairmanship of Thomas Westerdell, the Dock and Harbour Master.[4] The Committee denounced the plan for a 'Garrison dock',[5] which, with its entrance into the Haven, would only aggravate the situation, and the Company was forced to suspend negotiations with the Government.

Once it had had the offer of a Government subsidy, the Company was able to present a more tolerable case to the Town. It could not be expected to forgo a considerable sum of money without some recompense, and the Bench, taking the hint, reluctantly pledged itself to raise a sum of money 'sufficient to defray the Interest of the money which will be required for making a dock from Beverley Gates to Myton Gates above the £12,000 to be advanced by the Dock Company'.[6] In other words, if the Myton dock was so much more advantageous than the Garrison dock, the Town must find an estimated £1,000 per annum to pay for it. The Radical members of the Com-

[1] W. Hammond to W. Wilberforce, H. Duncombe, S. Thornton and W. S. Stanhope, 10 Nov 1787; HDC Letter Bk.

[2] ibid. Hammond had himself drafted the Petition. The delegated committee was, he said, unanimous.

[3] Hammond and delegates, London, to Dock Co., 21 Apr 1788; HDC Transactions.

[4] The proceedings of the Committee are adequately described by Hadley, pp. 653–60.

[5] T. Westerdell, *To the Burgesses of Kingston-upon-Hull*, 3 May 1788.

[6] HDC Transactions, 7 Nov 1788, records the official agreement between the Company and the Bench on this offer.

mittee of Safety exploded with anger at the Bench's compromise. They were in no mood for diplomacy, and prepared to belabour the Company with a second Bill.[1] This time the Company was not given the chance to build a dock. Its property was vested in thirty-five permanent Commissioners chosen from the various interests in the town, presided over by the Mayor. None were to be chosen by, or members of, the Company. Dividends were to be limited to the magical six per cent, and surplus revenue was to be used 'in purchasing the stock of the present company . . . so as to sink the same for the benefit of the public'. It was violent stuff, no more calculated to succeed than the first Bill, but the mood of the Town was unmistakable. The Bench withdrew its offer of subsidy, and the Company thereupon announced the termination of all negotiations, the breaking of all agreements, and the distribution to its shareholders of the £11,357 held in reserve as its contribution to the new dock.[2] It had, apparently, burned its boats.

For two years neither side would give way: two years during which the Company viewed Garrison Side as the only site (voting in its favour by 79 votes to 12 during an abortive round of talks in March 1792),[3] and the situation in the port became desperate. In 1792 the tonnage of shipping paying dock duties passed 200,000 for the first time, and in January 1793 the shipowners as a body entered the fray by refusing to pay dock duties on ships not actually accommodated in the dock. They made a novel contribution to the dispute by rejecting *both* the projected sites as unsuitable. They pressed for a larger dock than either side had yet considered, and thought it should be 'between the west end of the Present Dock and the Humber with an Entrance into it from the Humber'.[4] Even when faced with the possibility of a host of law-suits over duties, the

[1] *Heads of a Bill for the better accommodation of the Trade and Shipping of the Town and Port of Kingston-upon-Hull*; quoted in Hadley, pp. 656–60.

[2] W. Hammond to the Mayor, enclosing copy of Minutes of the Meeting of the Dock Co. for 13 Nov 1789; *GH* MS L.1387(70).

[3] Agreement had been reached on 27 Mar 1792 that the Company would build a dock for 120–140 ships provided it received 30 acres of Garrison Side, £1,000 per annum subsidy, and could sell its surplus land; HDC Transactions, Feb–Mar 1792, *passim.*

[4] Copy of the Resolutions in HDC Transactions, Jan 1793. On 4 Jan Trinity House had passed on the complaints of several members, just returned from the Baltic with valuable cargoes, who could find no place in the dock.

Company refused to give in, declaring, in particular, that a Humber dock would be 'in a place highly improper in point of situation . . .' and 'ruinous in its consequences to the Commerce of the port . . .'.[1]

It was ironic that after three years of argument over the merits of Garrison side, the Town Committee should now appeal to the Treasury, which had started the red-herring in the first place, and even more ironic that three surveyors appointed by the Treasury (William Jessop, Thomas Morris and John Huddart) should report that the west side of the town was best, and, furthermore, that 'wherever the New Dock may be made, it should have a communication with the Humber independent of the Old Harbour'.[2] An incensed Company, now supported by the High Street interest, called on John Hudson to 'point out . . . such parts of the said reports as shall appear to him to be founded on erroneous principles . . .', and to draw up a variety of dock plans. Whatever Hudson may have thought—his unhappy experiences at Grimsby soon discounted him anyway—a Town Meeting, presided over by the Mayor, had already asserted its 'most decided opinion' 'that the Dock ought to be extended to the river Humber, with an entrance from the said river forming a direct communication between the Humber and the present Dock & Quay . . .'.[3]

Opinion in favour of the Humber dock was gaining ground. The engineering problems, which at the time of the first dock would have prevented its siting on the Humber, had now been largely solved. Men such as Rennie were already experimenting with sea locks founded on mud. The Company, however, was unimpressed, and refused to communicate with any persons advocating a Humber

[1] HDC Transactions, 28 Jan 1793, in a letter covering a Memorial to the Treasury in answer to a Memorial sent by the Town.

[2] The Reports were published as Fly Sheets, and are to be found in *GH* Docks Box and HDC Transactions, Apr 1793.

[3] HDC Transactions, Nov–Dec 1793. Hudson was asked for estimates (a) for improving the Haven, (b) for widening and lengthening the existing dock using all the Company's estate, and (c) for a dock according to Jessop's scheme (i) from Whitefriargate to Myton Gate, (ii) from Whitefriargate to Hessle Gate, and (iii) from Hessle Gate to low water, with an entrance from the Humber. Hudson came down in favour of an improved Haven (as at Grimsby), and thought Jessop's estimate for £70,148 for a dock too low. It is an interesting indication of the way the Company was thinking, that Hudson was *not* asked to prepare a scheme for the Garrison side dock which the Company was still officially backing.

dock.[1] But time was beginning to run out for the Company. When, in January 1794, it voted £1,000 to fight yet another 'take-over' Bill, both the Bench and Trinity House objected, the latter withdrawing its proxy altogether. Two Bills had failed, but with the Bench and Trinity House both thoroughly antagonised, a third might well succeed. All arguments over sites, and attempts to blame delay on 'jarring local Interests in the town'[2] were abandoned and the Company fell back on its oldest argument: 'receipts . . . are greatly reduced, and the funds of the Company by no means warrant a large expenditure for any purpose whatever'.[3] The fact that its income had risen considerably since 1790 took the wind out of this, its last rallying cry, and the pamphlet *A Direct Attack on the Private Property of the Dock Company* . . . impressed nobody. On 1 July 1794 it capitulated. As a last attempt to placate the High Street interest, it offered to turn the Haven into a dock on Hudson's plan, but when this was flatly rejected it promised to make a dock from Beverley to Myton Gates, on a plan drawn up by William Jessop. Half the cost was to be met by the Company and the other half by the sale of Garrison land, which it still hoped to obtain.

The Bill for the Myton dock was never presented. In our admiration for the work of the early docks engineers we tend to overlook their mistakes. The Myton scheme was one of them. In its ill-considered consequences it threatened to be one of the worst blunders in the history of dock engineering. By moving ships through the Haven and the first dock into the second, it could only have increased the chaos it was meant to alleviate. The town was saved by the Saints of Clapham. Wilberforce & Smiths showed that resilience and far-sightedness that had kept them at the top for so long by objecting to the continued veneration for High Street, and since four of the five partners were in Parliament and the fifth controlled twenty-three Dock shares, they had more than ordinary influence. Wilberforce, Robert, John and Samuel Smith, Samuel Thornton, Henry Duncombe and E. J. Elliot presented the Town with what was, in effect, an ultimatum.[4] To gain their support the Bill must be delayed 'until the determination of Government be

[1] HDC Transactions, 15 Feb 1793.

[2] As in *The Address of the Dock Company . . . to the Merchants, Shipowners and others concerned in the Trade and Shipping of the Port*, 15 Feb 1793.

[3] *Short State of the Case of the Dock Company*, 6 Feb 1794.

[4] W. Wilberforce *et al.* to Dock Co., 6 Feb 1795.

known respecting the Aid they will give . . .'. While they applied to Pitt (with every chance of success),[1] the Town must consider plans for future extensions of the dock system and, above all, build the Humber dock, not the Myton one. On a more mature deliberation their proposals were accepted, but war was now (1795) in full swing, and a more propitious time was awaited.[2]

Trade continued to expand, despite the war, and in June 1800 the Corporation proxy in the Company moved the building of the Humber dock as soon as peace returned. The Bench guaranteed £1,000 apiece for ten shares 'provided the Dock Company think proper to create thirty new shares . . .',[3] and the Bench and Trinity House between them offered to pay half the cost, hoping, of course, to recover some of it from the sale of Garrison Side land. A series of abortive agreements—twice broken by Trinity House, pleading poverty—led up to the final Bill embodying these provisions, which became law on 22 June 1802.[4]

5. THE HUMBER DOCK

John Rennie, the greatest dock engineer of his day, was engaged for the new dock, with William Chapman as his assistant. It was a wise choice. Although smaller than the first dock, the Humber dock presented greater engineering problems, since the entrance must be built on the mud banks of the heavily silted estuary of the Humber. If the gates were not washed away by the Spring tides they would be buried under the silt! No one had as yet tackled this major

[1] Wilberforce was Pitt's closest friend and Elliot was his brother-in-law.

[2] Not everyone was inhibited by such mundane factors as trade recessions. In 1796 a group of enthusiastic landowners proposed to build a rival dock in Grimsby, encouraged by a number of Hull merchants including William Osbourne, who led, for a time, the attack on the Hull Dock Company. 'They have a fine speculation, if they succeed,' wrote Arthur Young, 'of rivalling Hull, as the great entrepôt of the Humber', and J. S. Brandström (merchant, and Swedish consul in Hull) warned them of the hostility to be expected from Hull 'as they now begin to apprehend the consequences of Grimsby being a port may be very fatal to the town of Hull'. Sir Samuel Standidge warned Hull of the danger during his mayoralty in 1795, but he need not have worried. Hull merchants did not move to Grimsby. See Gordon Jackson, *Grimsby and the Haven Company, 1796–1846* (1971), *passim.*

[3] BB x, 328.

[4] 42 George III, c. 91.

obstacle to building docks opening directly from the sea, or from sea-like estuaries. Grundy had been reasonably successful with his tiny Tetney Lock, where the Louth Canal entered the Humber, but the problems were not quite the same, and he had in any case used a very long outfall. The early engineers of Grimsby Haven, with problems similar to those of Hull, met with disaster, although they, too, employed a long outfall. It was Rennie who came to the rescue at Grimsby with his carefully balanced lock walls, which bore great pressure without putting too severe a strain on insecure foundations,[1] and at the same time he had constructed a creditable lock at Ferriby Sluice, where the Ancholme Navigation entered the Humber.

There could be no outfall at Hull, so Rennie protected his lock from the Humber by a massive dock basin, a third of the size of the dock itself. Apart from a liability to heavy silting, the basin did what was expected of it. It was, in fact, soon supplemented by the building up of the Humber bank, which the Corporation had been engaged in ever since the building of the first dock. The Humber dock was a great feat of engineering skill; but such feats tend to be expensive. The final cost of the dock, which took six years to build in a period of great inflation, was no less than £233,087, over three times the cost of the much bigger first dock, and ten times the original estimates of 1786. Of this sum Trinity House and the Bench found £58,517 each, but the Company expressed itself quite unable to raise £116,056 when it was authorised by the Act to sell only thirty new shares. A further Act was therefore necessary because, as the preamble said,[2]

> from the great price paid for the land purchased for the use of the said works and from the great advance in the price of materials and labour necessary for the completion of the same . . ., it is found that the Act cannot be carried into execution, unless a power be given to the said Company to raise money by creating and selling a greater number of new shares. . . .

Things looked black for a Company that had quibbled over £12,000, and, indeed, for the Corporation and Trinity House, which had never before assembled such huge sums of money. For the last two it was indeed a struggle, involving loss of land and future income; but for the Company, despite its many early protests, it was un-

[1] G. Jackson, *Grimsby*, chapter 2.

[2] 45 George III, c. 42.

believably simple.[1] The sixty new £500 shares brought in no less than £82,390 (an average of £1,373) to which was added £34,893 taken from income in 1807, 1808, 1809, 1812 and 1813. The purchasers of the new shares showed a good deal more sense than the panic pamphleteers of the Dock Company, although with dividends averaging twenty per cent in the years 1800–5, and with a constant increase in the tonnage of shipping frequenting the port, they had ample encouragement.

The early history of the Dock Company was not a happy one. It was a time of constant dispute. The Company boasted, quite rightly, of an excellent, pioneering job well done; its opponents cited—again with justification—the inadequacy of the facilities when the great trade boom began in the eighties. The shareholders were not, as was sometimes alleged, greedy and selfish men sacrificing the interests of the port to their own well being. Individually they were as concerned for the future of Hull as their most resolute opponents, and a good deal more than some of the rabble-raisers who attacked them. But they were, from the first, in an impossible position. The Company was a private concern exploiting a valuable asset for the benefit of its shareholders. It was also, by virtue of that asset, a public utility company with a moral, if not strictly legal, obligation to the public from which it drew its income. The situation might have been acceptable had the Company been *primus inter pares*, but it was not: it was the Dock Company of Kingston-upon-Hull, with chartered monopoly rights. The situation was without precedent, and not unnaturally, no one had thought to provide in the Act for a clash of interests because no one had envisaged the need for further docks. A reserve fund had not been created, so that any new dock could be financed only by heavy borrowing or by increasing the number of shares, both courses detrimental to the interests of existing shareholders.

If the Company, rightly or wrongly, believed itself unable to finance a second dock, there were only two courses of action open to

[1] This was the nearest the Company came to the kind of emergency finance common with many similar companies. Although the Company was authorised to create preference shares (ss. xxxvi–xxxviii), it created another thirty ordinary shares which were in every way the same as the original shares—a sure sign of public confidence. See also ss. v–vi and xxxii–xxxiii.

the advocates of extension: they must either subsidise or supersede the Company. Rather than subvert private property (which, as its defenders argued, would have inhibited future money raising), the Town was forced to pay for most of the new dock and allow the Company to remain in charge and ownership of both. Although the Corporation and Trinity House sacrificed future income by subscribing their half share, only the half subscribed by the Company received dividends out of the dock duties. The Company thus gained the enviable (and unique?) distinction of being a publicly subidised private company. The first two docks cost over £353,000, of which the Company found only £136,000, roughly forty per cent of the whole. It was certainly a company to invest in!

XI. SOCIAL LIFE

1. 'THE DUBLIN OF ENGLAND': THE RICH AND THE POOR

How do our Merchants in London, Bristol, Liverpole, Yarmouth, Hull, and other trading Sea-Ports, appear in their Families, with the Splendour of the best Gentlemen, and even grow rich, tho' with the Luxury and Expence of a Count of the Empire! so true it is, that *an Estate* is but *a Pont*, but *Trade is a Spring*.[1]

DANIEL DEFOE

Everyone, from Daniel Defoe to George III, envied the wealth of the mercantile community. Merchants were, almost by definition, rich men. They were the mainspring of the eighteenth century economy; they drew their commission on everything. It would, of course, be unwise to generalise too far. Not all merchants were successful, and many who were had started with very little before making their fortune. Nor were the various trades equally rewarding. Those flourishing in Hull did not produce merchant princes, and Hull's social life, unlike that of Liverpool or Bristol, lacked the stimulating splendour of the very rich. But if her merchants were not the richest in the land, Hull nevertheless had an abundance of moderately wealthy men who were generally indistinguishable from 'county society', which readily accepted them.

The principal merchant families had long had their territorial interests, celebrating their 'arrival' by buying estates and taking arms. But Hull, with its own Members of Parliament and its own county authority and prestige, remained their centre of gravity. There was as little incentive for them to seek honours in Yorkshire as there was for Yorkshire gentry to seek honours in Derbyshire. This must be borne in mind when considering the county honours system which might elsewhere be used to evaluate the social and political standing of merchants. We cannot judge Hull men by what they did in Yorkshire. One or two families like the Maisters—Deputy Lieutenants, and Colonels of the East Riding Militia—and the Sledmere Sykes, were of obvious influence in Yorkshire, es-

[1] Defoe, *A Plan of the English Commerce*, p. 100.

pecially after the foundation of the Yorkshire Association which helped the last of the Hull Wilberforces to carry the Yorkshire seat in 1784 in the face of the magnates of the West Riding. They were, however, atypical. In retrospect Wilberforce considered his 'Mercantile origin' and 'want of connexion or acquaintance with any of the nobility or gentry of Yorkshire . . .', and ascribed his election—'so utterly improbable'—to providence.[1] Whatever their origins and connexions, Wilberforce and his Thornton cousins amply illustrate the social acceptability of merchants to the leaders of British society, if not, perhaps, to its novelists.

It is often thought, and not infrequently written, that merchants lived for the day when they could retire as country gentry. Such a view is, at best, a simplification of the facts. It is a subjective evaluation of the rôle of merchant and landowner, and owes more to nineteenth-century writers than eighteenth-century merchants. We must not infer from the small minority who reached the House of Lords that this was the purpose of trade. The vast majority of merchants, great and small, did not follow them. It was not simply a matter of wealth, or political influence. It was also a matter of personal choice and local tradition. No Hull merchant in the eighteenth century voluntarily exchanged the counting house for the country house. Many of them owned land, but they continued to trade, and some, of equal wealth and influence, chose to buy no land. The Maisters, Sykes and Broadleys created useful estates; the Mowlds, Williamsons, Wilberforces and Peases did not.

As the eighteenth century drew to a close, the mercantile world began to change. The day of the merchant was over. He was now one of many factors in a booming economy of which he had previously been the leader and prime mover. In Hull as elsewhere the flood of business encouraged the growth of the smaller specialist firm, and the manufacturer began to assume an importance hitherto unknown. The merchant's relative decline coincided with the intellectual revulsion against industry and trade that was part of the gothic revival. The nineteenth-century historians tended to think of merchants as lesser creatures in the evolutionary chain leading to gentility. The merchants themselves were aware of this changing attitude, and increasingly came to terms with it. Many of the richer families left Hull in the early nineteenth century, and the old

[1] R. I. and S. Wilberforce, *The Life of William Wilberforce* (London, 1838), vol. i, p. 57.

merchant dynasties gradually ceased to trade. Even before they left, they were showing their awareness of the gradations of 'society'. Early in the eighteenth century only retired merchants of the first rank called themselves—or were called—gentlemen, and many a prominent man lived and died a 'merchant'. But their grandsons were 'gentlemen', even while actively engaged in trade. In the seventies men like Samuel Standidge might be unconcerned with their status, but already merchant and gentleman were virtually synonymous terms. By 1803 there were a hundred and fifty men listed as gentlemen in the *Directory*, excluding the richer merchants, bankers and shipowners residing outside the town. Just over fifty of these appeared as 'Esquires' in the various specialist sections of the *Directory*.

Social distinctions, though never fully crystallised in this period, became more apparent as the fine new streets were developed beyond the walls. George Street, Charlotte Street and Bond Street replaced Blanket Row and Dagger Lane as 'respectable' residences.[1] A clearer distinction of the elite came when the more opulent merchants began to vie with each other for the possession of country villas, large and small, along all the roads out of Hull. There they repaired when the smell of whale oil and boiling sugar became overpowering during the summer months. In the summer, said Tate Wilkinson at the end of the century,[2] 'a theatre could not afford to open the doors, for the families do not reside there at that season of the year'; and the vicar of St. John's complained of empty pews owned by people 'who have locked them up, and gone into the country'.[3] Some began to live out of Hull all the time, travelling in for business—or pleasure. Any important event in the eighties, for instance, would bring the Halls and Beans from Hessle; J. R. Pease from Hesslewood; Sir Henry Etherington, R. C. Broadley and Samuel Hall from North Ferriby; John Porter from Swanland;

[1] The Rev. Thomas Dikes eloquently compared local streets (in the early nineteenth century) in his sermon on John viii, 7: 'suppose that, instead of being brought up in a decent and virtuous neighbourhood, you had lived from your infancy in those lanes of moral turpitude, from which are emitted fumes of pollution that might almost corrupt an angel of light—can you say what, under these circumstances, you might have been?' J. King, *Memoir of Rev. Thomas Dykes* (London, 1849), pp. 451–2.

[2] Tate Wilkinson, *The Wandering Patentee, or a History of the Yorkshire Theatre* (York, 1795), vol. iii, p. 84.

[3] J. King, *Memoir*, pp. 29–20.

Benjamin Blaydes and B. B. Thompson from Melton; William Williamson from Melton Hill; William Kirkby, Nicholas Sykes, Thomas Haworth and R. C. Pease from Kirk Ella; Joseph Sykes from West Ella; John Boyes and John Voase from Anlaby; and George Knowsley, William Travis, Richard Moxon, Samuel Watson and Thomas Thompson from Cottingham.[1] The list could be extended without difficulty.

The social life of the richer merchants was the same as that of their country cousins. Indeed, Doctor Johnson thought that merchants were better spenders than landowners.[2] Hunting, shooting and—at the end of the century—fishing, played a far larger part in their lives than might be imagined. 'Hold, I almost think myself upon the Scent already and running away with it', an excited Nathaniel Maister wrote to Thomas Broadley when planning a hunting expedition in 1725: 'I wish with all my Soul wee could have had your Company with us for wee propose to ourselves a great deal of Pleasure.'[3]

A merchant's 'great deal of pleasure' is amply illustrated in Robert Broadley's Private Journal for 1768–73.[4] Much of his leisure was spent gambling with his small group of intimate friends: Arthur Maister, Joseph Williamson (the great iron importer) and his partner Samuel Waller, Captain George Thompson, Abel Smith and Benjamin Blaydes. They were as formidable an array of wealth and power as ever assembled in Hull, but no fortunes were at stake in their card games and their many miscellaneous bets rarely exceeded ten guineas. Within this limit they were prepared to wager on anything, from the matrimonial prospects of their friends to their favourites for the next races.

Gambling apart, Broadley's principal interests were hunting and racing, and the social round of Assemblies, concerts and plays that went with them. His year began with hunting at Caistor, organised by Joseph Williamson. In February or March he was hunting at Driffield Park. In May or June he was off to Beverley for the races, and to York for the races in August. November found him hunting with Maisters at Winestead or Patrington and racing at Driffield.

[1] Merchant residences from Tickell, pp. 897–8.

[2] *Boswell's Life of Johnson*, ed. G. B. Hill (1934), vol. iv, p. 4.

[3] 24 Jan 1724–5. Letter in the possession of Mrs Doris Harrison-Broadley, to whom I am grateful for this and other information about the Broadley family.

[4] *HUL* DP/146.

The year ended as it began, with hunting in Lincolnshire, this time at Barton.

Between racing and hunting—taken very seriously, with elaborate uniforms—came the Militia Ball at Beverley in June, a momentous occasion consuming a whole week in 1771, when he took 'Miss Bourryan and Miss Suky B'. Then there was his annual recuperation, a fortnight drinking the water and bathing at Scarborough. His record of his stay was brief: 'It is usual to give the Musick who play to you the morning after your arrival 2/6. I paid 4/- for bathing 8 times & gave the bathing Man 2/-. I gave the Chambermaid 5/-.' On his many ramblings the chambermaids were always the chief recipients of his largesse. Retribution overtook him, but failed to overcome him: one of the last entries records three guineas 'paid Mr Melling for curing me of a venereal disorder'. It is typical of the man that such an entry should appear in the profit and loss account of his diary of pleasure.

Broadley's love of excitement and gaiety was only part of his character. One could just as easily draw attention to his pursuit of culture, to his refreshingly modern criticism of the stuffiness of his age. His business trips were organised to take in country houses, which were surveyed with critical eye. Duncombe Park he thought 'a clumsy heavy building', and Castle Howard 'fell infinitely short of my expectations'. It was 'far from handsome without, and not a good room within', but it was worth going miles to see the magnicent beech trees there. He was honest enough to admit that the endless statuary bored him, and his taste in painting was equally deflating: Titian's *Venus and Adonis* at Duncombe Park pleased him, but he thought the faces poor. In deference to the great man, however, he conceded that his objections 'may rather arise from a desire to criticise than from any defect in the piece'.

When he was not travelling, Broadley was an indefatigable reader of the learned tomes that circulated among his friends. Classics, histories and trivia all attracted him. Undaunted by the lengthy works published to fill elegant libraries, he spent '2 or 3 years or more' reading twenty-two volumes of Lords' and Commons' Debates before confessing: 'I scarce think they are worth the time spent in a thorough perusal of them.'

Broadley's activities were in no way unique. The Crowles hunted, the Wilberforces went racing, the Peases loved shooting, the Osbournes fished the Spey. Joseph Williamson died in 1738 'of a jaundice at his house at West Ella occasioned by his 'tippling';[1] R. C. Pease was thought to be unsuited to banking because of his addiction to gambling; and young Wilberforce, who never learned to shoot properly, very nearly deprived the country of the services of the younger Pitt.[2] Nor was the excitement confined to the men: 'thare was a deal of very good Company at hull in the Race weak', the nonconformist Mary Robinson told her husband,[3] '& very a brilent Assemblys[.] Miss & me was thare 2 nights & one morning at the Concert & 3 days upon the feald.' 'Very good company' was, by common report, the key to Hull social life. 'Everything at this place goes on as usuall,' Andrew Perrott wrote in 1754, 'and we have a very Gay Town with diversions of some kind or other.'[4] William Wilberforce recalled in similar vein the town of his youth (*c.* 1770–80):[5]

It was then as gay a place as could be found out of London. The theatre, balls, great suppers, and card-parties were the delight of the principal families in the town. . . . As grandson to one of the principal inhabitants, I was every where invited and caressed: my voice and love of music made me still more acceptable.

Tate Wilkinson, the Actor-manager, with experience of every fashionable town in Britain, was lavish in his praise:[6]

Hull for hospitality and plenty of good cheer, with too much welcome, intitles that town, in my opinion, to the appelation of 'The Dublin of England'—The many acts of kindness I received in that friendly seat, occasioned my being oftener in bad health in Hull than at any other place in my yearly round.

He said much the same thing on many other occasions. He recalled, for instance, October 1790, with[7]

[1] Nathaniel to Henry Maister, 26 Apr 1738; Maister Letters. Henry replied that he was surprised only that Williamson had lived so long.

[2] 'So at least my companions affirmed, with a roguish wish, perhaps, to make the most of my short-sightedness and inexperience in field sports.' R. I. & S. Wilberforce, i, 34.

[3] Mary Robinson, Hull, to Robert Robinson, 14 Jul 1754; *WH* 59/58/32. She was Joseph Pease's daughter and, like her sister Esjie, never learned English thoroughly. One suspects that Dutch was spoken at home to keep the children in practice.

[4] Andrew Perrot to David Atkinson, 18 Nov 1754; *LAO* Emeris 20/24.

[5] Wilberforce, i, 8.

[6] T. Wilkinson, *Memoirs of His Own Life* (York, 4 vols, 1790), iv, 50.

[7] T. Wilkinson, *Wandering Pantentee*, iv, 54–5.

the company in full march for Hull quarters, full of thought as to good benefits, hot punch, and the roasted duck for supper . . . for they receive more invitations at that port, than during all the rest of the year: therefore whenever Hull is named, each actor smacks his lips, and *ideally* tastes good eating *gratis*.

In contrast to the private parties were the official Corporation dinners, given that touch of zest by the presence of the officers of the garrison and of visiting warships. They were held regularly to celebrate national and local events, the coming of the judges, the election of aldermen—when the new man provided the feast—and any other excuse that came to mind. Trinity House also entertained 'society':[1]

> This is the room where store of meat
> By *Elder Brethren* is eat;
> Tho by the bye, you must not think,
> They eat it all without—much drink.
> No faith those Sons of Neptune must
> Moisten their clay, or turn to dust.

The Dock Company added its dinner to those of the other Corporations after 1774, especially their annual celebration of the 'Royal Munificence'—the granting of the walls and £15,000.

Unofficial, but no less formal occasions, were the meetings of the Hull Assembly, doubtless modelled on the famous York Assembly that had so much influence on the social life of Yorkshire. For thirty years or more, Assemblies were held in the upper room of the Grammar School until the Assembly Rooms were built in Dagger Lane in 1750 by a company of shareholders led by Andrew Perrott and John Porter. Here the young people, London-clad in the latest fashion, danced away the night while their elders gambled and argued about the Baltic blockade, the war in America, the slave trade, or the iniquities of the East India Company. The *Gentleman's Magazine* printed a sharp attack on the Assembly in 1734 in 'A Letter from Hull to a Leeds Merchant'.[2] It poured scorn on the town, though how far it was vicious and how far humorous we cannot tell.

> No sooner entered in the room,
> But whispers fly—whence does he come?
> Who or what is he? can you guess?
> Or what estate may he possess?

[1] *Gentleman's Magazine*, December 1734. [2] ibid.

Who introduced or brought him here?
Observe his clownish awkward air.
'Tis thus a general buz goes round,
And words are lost in empty sound.
Confounded and amaz'd I viewed
From side to side the ill bred crowd;
Where'er I look'd were two or three
Who whispered first—then gaz'd on me.
In several places I have been,
And several meetings I have seen
But never in my life till now,
Saw such a wretched senseless crew.

There may have been a modicum of truth here, though the Assemblies were not in general lacking in social niceties, and their organisers were far from being a 'wretched senseless crew'. They may, perhaps, have been a little too conscious of their commanding position in Hull society. 'The Hull Assembly', Spencer-Stanhope was warned when he canvassed the town during the 1784 by-election, 'is composed of a set of partial proud people . . . you must . . . be all things to *all* the women'.[1]

A little of the gaiety and splendour of these proud Assemblies is caught by the *Hull Packet*'s account of the Ball of the century, the 1788 Centenary Assembly:[2]

That the ladies might also participate in the commemoration of this illustrious event, a ball was given at the assembly rooms . . .; at which near three hundred of the principal inhabitants of the town and neighbourhood were present. The dresses of the ladies were universally decorated with ribbons, and trimmings of orange and blue, agreeably diversified according to the taste of the fair wearers, and while characteristic of the occasion, did not offend the eye with too much uniformity. In the disposition of the two favourite colours, they exhibited a great variety of elegant ornaments, illustrative of their happy invention and creative fancy. The effect was enchanting: such an assemblage of beauty and brilliancy had never before shone forth in those rooms. The same fashion was adopted by the gentlemen. They all wore orange cockades and had universally some part of their dress of the same colour.

When several minuets had been danced, on a signal given, the doors of the card-room were thrown open, and displayed a spectacle equally novel, brilliant, and attractive. On the centre of a set of

[1] John Stephenson, Hull, to W. S. Stanhope, WSS 1784.

[2] *Hull Packet*, 11 Nov 1788 (reprinted in Tickell, pp. 642–4 and Hadley, pp. 387–8).

tables, were placed a most superb, ornamental Portico and Colonnade, extending near twelve feet in length, and of a proportional height. The centre resembled a triumphal arch, surmounted with a refulgent dome: under which, on an elevated pedestal, was a group of figures of the most beautiful sculpture, that represented two nymphs finding cupid asleep, and attempting to steal his arrows. The Colonnade on each side of the Portico was decorated with images, and richly ornamented with medallions of the most exquisite cast. From the entablature were suspended light wreaths of artificial flowers in varied festoons; and on its extremities, above, were perched two golden pheasants, of the richest variegated plumage, supporting in their beaks the ends of the wreaths. This fairy pile, composed of the most transparent and delicate materials, was decorated with a profusion of beautiful devices sparkling with gold and party coloured foil, and illuminated with numerous wax tapers. The symmetry, splendour, and brilliancy of the whole, like the descriptive stories of Arabian authors, filled the minds of the spectators with the delightful reveries of enchantment. . . .

When the curiosity in examining the elegant superstructure had partly subsided, the country dances began in three different sets, and continued with unremitting gaiety to a late hour; yet the succession of exercise to refreshment, and refreshment to exercise, dissipated all languor and ennui, and gave such a zest to hilarity, that numbers were left at four o'clock in the morning enjoying the united pleasures of the enlivening dance, and elegant festivity. At the conclusion of the Ball, a chorus song, suitable to the occasion, was sung by several gentlemen, accompanied by a full band of music, and received with great applause. The company retired with every appearance of satisfaction from the entertainments of the night, concluding the celebration of this remarkable festival with mirth, vivacity and harmony.

The attention paid to clothing by both women and men at the Assembly is characteristic of the eighteenth century, and fine clothes were as necessary for the rich merchant as for any other rich man. Clothes, fine cloth, lace, paper patterns and wigs were all sent up from London, while the ladies were, in the last edecade of the century, treated to an occasional fashion plate in the 'Olla Podrida' column of the *Hull Advertiser*.[1] The burgesses had grown accustomed to seeing fine clothes: 'let me recommend it to you to have a laced coat on', Stanhope's agent wrote in 1784:[2] 'your numerous friends the Cobblers, Shipwrights etc—Do not think a man a Gentleman unless he is well dressed.' Levi, the Hull goldsmith, proved the value

[1] See, for e.g., *Hull Advertiser*, 10 Feb 1798.
[2] John Smith to Stanhope, 31 May 1784, WSS 1784.

5. The Merchant at Home: John Lee and his family, by John Russell (*Ferens Art Gallery*)

6. The Merchant at Play: Sir Henry Etherington in Hunting Regalia (*Ferens Art Gallery*)

of dressing well. His fiancée, it was said, 'was almost crazed for him, attracted by his fine cloaths. . . .'[1]

The second major attraction was the theatre. In the first half of the century an assortment of travelling entertainers (including John Wignell, 'Tragical Comedian', Lambertus Vandersluys, 'Stage Dancer', and Henry Watson, 'Pyrobolist vel Ignis Fatuus') visited the town, presumably to play in the unlicensed theatre in Lowgate that became a chapel for a time in 1771.[2] By then Hull had the brand-new Theatre Royal,[3] built in 1769–70 as the winter base for the travelling company of Tate Wilkinson, 'the pompous one and indivisible, the comprehensive, incomprehensive, Mr. Manager of three patent theatres, the royal trio of Edinburgh, York and Hull'.[4] It was a good company, supplemented on occasions by the best in the land, and the town responded well. 'No actor', wrote Wilkinson, 'will ever be found starved to death at Hull for lack of food or moistening of the clay.'[5] He rated Hull very highly indeed:[6] 'a London, and Edinburgh, a Bath, or a Dublin theatre, from their superior consequence (and after these in the theatrical catalogue, York and Hull), are superior as yearly theatres for assurance of a comfortable constant income, to any other theatrical spots in the kingdom.' Hull he ranked higher than Manchester, which then enjoyed a very great reputation among players.

The company had an extensive and constantly changing repertoire, ranging from Shakespeare to the lowest of eighteenth century plays, with members playing a variety of parts on a fixed salary of £42 a week (£84 in race weeks). Comic operas alternated with the *Merchant of Venice*, *Pious Orgies* and *Father in Heaven* with *Love in a Village*, from which Whitefield—'Why should the devil's house have all the good tunes?'[7]—is said to have taken tunes for his 'songs and

[1] Strother, 9 Aug 1784.

[2] They, or their children, were buried in St. Mary's, Lowgate; E. Ingram, *Our Lady of Hull* (Hull, 1948), *passim.*

[3] Built by Royal licence, 9 George III, c. 17. The Act repealed, for York and Hull, the restrictions placed on travelling players by the vagrancy laws; see Woolley, *Statutes*, p. 197.

[4] The description is his own, as for 1779; *Wandering Patentee*, ii, 76. He had the Edinburgh theatre for a short time only, before extending his Yorkshire tour to Beverley, Wakefield, Doncaster, Sheffield and Leeds.

[5] Ibid., iv, 210. [6] ibid., iv, 45.

[7] Attributed by Wilkinson to Whitefield '*when Love in a Village*, and *The Maid of the Mill* were the rage. . . .' ibid., i, 111–13.

full choruses'. On one occasion there might be an unforgettable performance by Mrs Siddons (who cleared £1,100 for a seventeen nights tour of Yorkshire in 1786);[1] on another, dancers, jugglers, or performing dogs. Christmas was already the occasion for the pantomime—*Harlequin Sorcerer* in 1773, with several hundred pounds worth of scenery, painted by Dahll of Covent Garden, who painted the Great Hall of Harewood.[2]

A night at the theatre was something of a marathon. Proceedings commenced at six or six-thirty with a reputable play, followed by an 'entertainment', usually musical, and finally a farce; although, to Wilkinson's annoyance, Yorkshire people tended to turn up after the third act of the play and pay only half-price.[3] They showed their uncultivated taste in other ways, too. When the war against Revolutionary France broke out, the more vulgar patrons began calling for 'the *popular* tune of "God save the King" '. Wilkinson was asked to do something about it, and so free 'the most respectable part of the audience . . . from what is, at present, very tiresome'. If the Upper Gallery objected, then he should put the song at the end of the farce, 'which will give such persons as do not choose to hear it, an opportunity of leaving the theatre'.[4]

The tiresome behaviour of the Upper Gallery was symptomatic of a change slowly taking place in the theatre. Although the receipts for 1793 were the highest on record,[5] the theatre was entering a period of crisis, and Wilkinson's eight volumes are full of bitter comments on it. Times were changing. 'Middle class values' were beginning to appear. Society, already 'polite', was fast becoming prudish: *Short legg'd ladies, thick legg'd ladies* was no longer funny to those fleeing from the wrath to come. Wilkinson was caught between two camps, neither of which he liked. He relied for his audience partly on the richer box patrons and partly on 'the seafaring persons' who spent the summer 'over-spreading the ocean, and like industrious bees, toiling to procure honey, for a supply for their winter's comfort and diversions'.[6] Eager to pot some of that honey, Wilkinson had always auditioned the more decorative starlets in their 'small-clothes', and not a few had reached the stage by

[1] *Wandering Patentee*, iii, 6.
[2] ibid., i, 186–7.
[3] ibid., ii, 95. Wilkinson tried to discourage the habit.
[4] ibid., iv, 109–10. [5] ibid., iv, 59.
[6] ibid., iv, 84.

undressing gracefully.[1] Now, as fashions changed, nothing was left to the imagination. 'At present', wrote Wilkinson, 'all beholders need not want a peep but look full and be perfectly satisfied whether the view will cause many bidders.'[2]

The 'Methodists' were less than satisfied: they were horrified! Opposition to the theatre, the perverting instrument of the Devil, had been growing among them for some time, and an implacable and mutual hatred had developed by the nineties.[3] In 1792 Garwood of Low Church proclaimed (according to Wilkinson) that 'no player or any of his children ought to be entitled to a Christian burial or even to lie in a churchyard', and that 'Everyone who entered a playhouse was, with the players, equally certain of *eternal* damnation'.[4] When the company arrived in Hull in the following year, Garwood, Milner of High Church, Dikes of St. John's and Lambert of Fish Street Congregational Church pronounced a weighty condemnation,[5] and in 1794 Dikes (again according to Wilkinson) announced the 'banishment from his chapel

[1] Wilkinson's books are full of comments on his actresses. Mrs. Jarman, engaged in 1790, was an actress 'rather uncommon for a young beginner, added to this, her figure was and is excellent, and gave promise, with being familiarised to the stage, she would acquire elegance: And though she had not arrived at that, yet her form being truly a good one, will bear scrutiny, when in small-clothes, beyond that of many actresses who value themselves on their symmetry. She was well received; indeed her figure must have secured partiality in her favour.' ibid., iii, 102.

Neither Miss Waudby nor Miss Mingay of Hull could act. The former was 'a pretty young woman, but wanted power and talents for the stage'; ibid., i, 202–4. The latter, daughter of a Comptroller of Customs, was a pretty, scheming trollop, who became an actress to get a rich husband. She boasted too much of her great expectations and married a man on the same game before they both discovered their error. Their conjugal bliss was brief; ibid., i, 68–9.

[2] Only one actress, to Wilkinson's annoyance, stuck to her old-fashioned stays. Hannah Brand 'would not unveil her beauties even to the chaste Diana; therefore she, with well-bound bone, forbid all access. Her breast-works, and all her works were well defended against all assailants; she might enter the lists with a sisterhood of nuns, or a Methodist love-feast, fearless and undismayed.' ibid., iv, 157.

[3] The conflict between Methodism and the stage is surveyed in T. B. Shepherd, *Methodism and the Literature of the Eighteenth Century* (London, 1940), chapter 9. Dr. Shepherd may be excused for overlooking the fact that the 'Methodists' so roundly condemned by Wilkinson were for the most part 'Evangelicals'.

[4] Wilkinson, *Patentee*, i, 111–13. [5] ibid., iv, 98–9.

of all those who went to plays in 1794–5'.[1] A vicious circle had already begun: as the religious people stopped going the audience—and, one suspects, the performances—sank lower; the lesser-straight-laced then stopped going, and so on. Wilkinson noted in despair that the women were ceasing to come in 1792, and the rich young fops, uninhibited by the presence of their elders, were no longer gentlemen. Indeed, they were rapidly turning the place into a bear-garden. Several times in 1792 the performances were halted and Wilkinson directed his wrath against '*Gentlemen* . . . lower than the *meanest* person at that time in the threatre . . .'; gentlemen, 'as when sick from a load of wine discharging it in a stage box—jumping on the stage, because a bet had been laid over a bottle that it should be done, and singing "God save the King", during the *time* of a *principal scene* of a play. . . .'[2] The air began to resound with 'such language as would be indecent in a brothel'. As part of 'society' entertainment the threatre was, by 1795, dead. Perhaps those with no souls enjoyed it the more.

The troubles were all blamed on to the Methodists. It was easier than reviewing the failings of the theatre or the mistakes of Tate Wilkinson. He was full of misgivings about the change gradually coming over society with the onward march of the new-fangled, stifling, hypocritical religion, which left him cold. Conversion only worked in one direction, to his financial loss: 'It would be easier I believe to make a convert of a violent democrat to an aristocrat, than to make a Methodist like the playhouse.'[3] Full of confidence, they destroyed what they did not like. In vain did Wilkinson pronounce his own version of Christianity and deny a monopoly of the truth:[4]

> Whenever a preacher permits his rancour to pronounce damnation too freely, it is surely being too familiar with the *assumed* knowledge of God's holy purposes.
>
> Methodism retains all the Birds of Paradise itself, and crams Kings, Peers, Peeresses, Knights, Ladies, Lawyers and Actors into the pit. . . .

The stage was at least in good, if not exactly holy, company. If the richer merchants lived as gentlemen, with their fine houses, clothes, paintings and silver, they also gave their children a gentle-

[1] Wilkinson *Patentee*, iv, 201. This brought the cutting remark that 'if all his congregation were as pure and unsullied as himself, there would be no occasion for such pious exhortations and exhibitions of his animal magnetism.'

[2] ibid., iv, 211. [3] ibid., ii, 122. [4] ibid., ii, 120.

man's education. For the majority there is no record of formal education, although it is implied in the literary interests of many of the merchants.[1] Many men no doubt passed through the Corporation's ancient Grammar School.[2] Here the junior Perrotts, Sykes, Wilberforces, Thompsons and the rest learned their dead languages and dusty history from a succession of able masters: from John Clarke (1716–32), moralist and educationalist of national repute, who, concerned with real knowledge rather than languages, introduced the teaching of history, geography, divinity and English; from Henry Therond (1762–6), Fellow of Trinity, always more at home in his college, to which he speedily returned; and from the saintly Joseph Milner, whose methodistical influence was felt in Hull for generations to come. The school was never well organised and always small, but a succession of pupils made their way to Cambridge. William Mason (whose family retired from trade early in the century), Andrew Perrott, William Wilberforce and Charles Pool went to St. John's; and Richard Sykes, George King and John Jarratt to Trinity. Septimus Stainton and a group of clergymen's sons went to Magdalene and the three sons of Thomas Thompson went to Queens', of which Isaac Milner was President.

Occasional references show boys at private schools in the country. None of the Peases, for instance, appear to have been educated in Hull. Joseph Pease sent his son, Robert, to Kirkstead in Lincolnshire, where he received both classical and commercial instruction. 'I endeavour', he wrote home in 1731,[3] 'to improve in learning as much as I can in the mornings. I wright and read Justin & betwixt noons & at nights I get my Confirming Catechism and in the Afternoons I cast up Accompts and am gott into practise.' Robert's own son, R. C. Pease, was sent to Pocklington (though admittedly he was illegitimate, and 'hidden away' till he was eleven), and his nephew, J. R. Pease, went to Usslemonde. Benjamin, son of Benjamin Blaydes Thompson, was sent at the age of fifteen to Germany, where he came under the influence of Kotzebue, and Alderman John Wray had also spent five years of his youth on the continent.[4]

[1] For the extensive literary activities of Hull merchants, see C. Frost, *Address . . . to the Literary and Philosophical Society, 5 November 1830* (Hull, 1830).

[2] See J. Lawson, *A Town Grammar School* (Hull University Press, 1963), for for excellent account of this school. Unfortunately the records do not contain a full list of pupils.

[3] R. Pease, Kirkstead, to J. Pease, 3 Apr 1731; *WH* 59/58/37.

[4] C. Frost, *Address*, pp. 23–4.

To many in the eighteenth century—and not only to the materialistically minded—orthodox education seemed a waste of time. Tickell thought it necessary in his history of a mercantile community to spring to the defence of the old system:[1]

Grammatical and classical merit are not, indeed, so highly esteemed as they once were. The age we live in is rather fond of making experiments, than of profitting by the experience of past times. Had an appeal to experience its due force upon men's minds, the utility of this sort of knowledge might be safely rested thereon. Till men, however, can point out some better method of employing youth in practice, the old grammatical and classical mode will deserve the preference to all mere theories. It is the philosophy of children; it teaches them to reason on the easiest subjects, the use and connexion of words, and gives perhaps the best exercise of the young understanding. If it be asked, what is its use in after life? it should be considered what is meant by use. If the idea be entirely mercantile, the benefit of Grammar is not so evident. But how absurd to measure everything by money. The improvement of the mind, and the more solid feast of the understanding are ends surely worthy the attention of rational beings.

Hull merchants were certainly interested in money, but it should not be inferred from Tickell that they were rejecting the old education and accepting some inferior system. He was obviously unsympathetic to the new trends that led to a revival of education in the eighteenth century by adding to, rather than replacing, the classics. Certainly in the last quarter of the century new schools such as the Mercantile Academy, Bond Street Academy, Brigham's Academy and Hull Academy were providing an excellent education along modern lines for boys, in some cases to the age of eighteen. They were good, especially for the middle rank of the mercantile world, and for boys hoping to thrust themselves into a counting house. But the truth is that 'the solid feast of the understanding' continued to appeal to those in search of gentility, and mercantile vocational training followed rather than replaced a classical education in an age when the witty epigram and apt quotation were the accepted evidence of a cultivated mind. Moreover, not all the sons of merchants followed in father's footsteps, and for these in particular some kind of formal education was required. There was little doubt about the eldest son—or a couple of sons in the case of the Wilberforces, Maisters, Mowlds or Sykes. But the rest were encouraged to follow

[1] Tickell, p. 829n.

an assortment of genteel careers. It was as essential for the merchant as for the landowner to place his younger sons in the professions or in sinecures. Some, like Cornelius Cayley, William Maister and Daniel Sykes took to the law, knowing that business would be pushed their way. Others, but not many, entered the navy or the army, like Commodore Edward Thompson, Lieutenant-General John Maister and General Thomas Peronnet Thompson. William Hammond's son, George, chose a diplomatic career, was Hartley's secretary in Paris in 1783, and later became the first British ambassador to the United States; and Charles Mace, son of a leading Hull surgeon, was able to combine the living of Houghton with the unlikely post of British Consul in Algiers.[1] One or two, like Professor De la Pryme of Cambridge, chose academic careers, and Benjamin Thompson became a professional writer for the London stage after running for a time the Nottingham subsidiary of his father's timber business. A few more became surgeons. But by far the largest number of boys passing through the Grammar School and Cambridge entered the Church. The classical based education, for all its grand theory, was in effect little more than vocational training: ordination was its usual, though not necessarily its logical, conclusion. Particularly under Milner's evangelical influence a host of Clapham-bound clergy were prepared in Hull; and a number of great merchant houses—led by Crowles and the senior branch of the Sykes—ceased to trade when the firm devolved, by chance, on a son in Holy Orders.

We have been dealing for the most part with a select group of Hull's upper class, perhaps a hundred families at the end of the century and certainly less before then. We cannot easily delineate the group. There was a great deal of social mobility and no precise social division. The richer merchants merge imperceptibly with the less rich, the middle rank with the 'poor' merchants and victuallers, and they with the better-off shopkeepers, and so down the scale.

The Poll Books and Directories reveal many of these lesser merchants, master mariners, industrialists, victuallers, brokers, surgeons, brewers, Customs officers and the like who were comfortably situated, with anything from a couple of hundred to a thousand pounds or more per annum. They shared, in so far as their wealth and inclination allowed, the social life of their more opulent neighbours. They tended to congregate in the fine new streets to the

[1] Lawson, p. 158.

north and west of the dock, thus emphasising their difference from the lower orders who remained, for the time being, in the old town. They kept their servants, but made do with a hackney instead of a private carriage, and with prints instead of paintings. They were less likely, perhaps, to accumulate libraries, but they were certainly no more ignorant than their betters. Strother wrote rather contemptuously of those who devoured books from the Subscription Library (founded in 1775) in order to be in fashion.[1] But they were simply doing in a cheaper way what the Broadleys and Sykes did in the more sophisticated atmosphere of their own libraries. It is at least interesting to know that among the lower merchants it was fashionable to read books, and that some of them, like Strother, were intellectual snobs!

It was almost certainly from this class that the supporters of the various short-lived intellectual societies came. Strother was full of the activities of the Sentimental Society, named after Laurence Sterne's famous society of the twenties and thirties. It met every week to discuss such 'Philosophical Problems', as financial corruption in the government, Pitt's failure to fulfil his promise of Parliamentary Reform and to 'inspect the East India affairs which are well known to be most notoriously Villanous in their actions abroad'. Apparently such societies did not always concern themselves with philosophical problems, for there was a special rule forbidding obscene talk. The Sentimental Society eventually died out. 'There never was a Society of this kind subsisted long in Hull', thought Strother, 'owing either to the Great love of money or to the ignorance of some of the members which made the more sensible part think it not worth their while spending their time where no improvement is to be had.'[2] His disillusionment was a little premature. The Society for the Purpose of Literary Information flourished between 1792 and 1797, and managed, among other things, to take a census of the town.[3] The Subscription Library was rebuilt in 1800, and the Lyceum Library was opened in 1807. At the turn of the century a Chemistry Society was organising lectures and experiments, and the town had a stimulating intellectual life in the early nineteenth century.

[1] 17 Aug 1784, folio 9. [2] Strother, fol. 17.

[3] The society was founded by a group of doctors, led by John Alderson, who led the movement to establish an Infirmary. The first two secretaries were John Wray and Andrew Hollingsworth, the timber merchant partners, both of whom were eventually aldermen.

The education of the middle class was reasonably good. The Grammar School probably drew most of its pupils from this source, but the majority of boys went to the innumerable private schools teaching English, writing, mathematics and, sometimes, navigation—one of which was actually held in the upper room of the Grammar School after 1757.[1]

For the promising boy a university education was not impossible, whatever his background. Despite carelessness in administration, and occasional favouritism in selection, a number of 'poor scholars'—usually of the tradesman class—made their way to Cambridge on the Corporation's Bury and Ferries scholarships (awarded together) and the Metcalfe scholarship (to Clare College).[2] John Blyth, master of the Grammar School from 1732 to 1762 and the first Metcalfe scholar, was the orphan son of a grocer, and the second Metcalfe scholar was also an orphan; Thomas Ellis, 'a boy of an extraordinary genius and capacity', was the son of a shipwright. But even without formal education at a high level some boys picked up an astonishing amount of learning. Again Strother may serve as an example: he did exercises in his Journal in Hebrew, Greek, shorthand, Latin and French, besides working on specifically commercial things such as bills of lading and forms of insurance.

It is one of the tragedies of social history that we know most about the smallest social group and least about the largest. The poor left their mark only when they sank below subsistence level or died in a newsworthy manner. About their wages, their diet and their general standard of living we know very little, and we cannot, at the moment, prove either an upward or downward movement in any of these things. However, a rapid increase in employment and an influx of people from all parts of the country would suggest that wages were not so depressed as in less flourishing places, and certainly were better than in purely agricultural regions; flax, for instance, was always sent out of town for spinning because wages were too high to allow it to be done economically in Hull.

There were, of course, many cases of hardship and abject poverty. (For the working of the Poor Law, see pp. 321f.). Old people, the sick and the injured were specially hard pressed, and if a man was incapacitated his family was reduced virtually to beggary before they could receive aid from the rates. What, one wonders, was the lot of the man to whom Smiths & Thompson gave five shillings

[1] Lawson, p. 155.

[2] Details of scholars from Lawson, *passim.*

when his 'house' was blown down,[1] or of the many people who committed suicide? What of Judith Grant, transported for stealing linen, or of Eleanor Fielding who, 'tried on suspicion of murdering her bastard child, was acquitted, sold herself for a slave, and went with them', rather than face life in Hull?[2] One side of Hull's social life is a pleasant picture of decent, orderly luxury. The other extreme is an unhappy, tragic world, where normal existence, never very good at the best of times, was bedevilled by insecurity. Except during emergencies, the bulk of the population probably lived somewhere between the two.

It was insecurity, rather than low annual income, that caused most of the hardship in Hull. Wars and bad weather disrupted trade, and brought a crop of empty houses as people moved to cheaper houses or lodgings; and food was often dearest when people could least afford it. In the difficult winter of 1788–9, for instance, about 1,700 families received assistance, having been found on investigation to exist almost without fire or food.[3] Some 6,000 people were involved—something like a quarter of the entire population. Again, in June 1796, 900 families, containing about 2,600 persons, were receiving outdoor relief.[4] Significantly, perhaps, they were not said to have lacked shelter.

Those who needed money, but were not yet at the end of their tether, had recourse to the money-lenders and pawnshops, which were always busiest during the winter months. Occasionally the Bench acted to prevent the worst abuses of the system. In 1741, for instance, a woman was brought before the Bench for charging a farthing a week interest on a loan of four shillings, which, at twenty per cent, was four times the legally permitted maximum. She argued that the borrowers was aware of the conditions, and was consequently dismissed. Later, in 1790, the Bench instructed the Members of Parliament to try to obtain a government regulation of pawnbroking, which provided a useful service, but was again subject to abuse.[5]

The life of the seaman was notoriously dangerous; but he was not badly paid, and a measure of self-help appeared among seamen

[1] Smiths & Thompson's Ledgers, Petty Cash Account, 21 Jun 1791.

[2] Hadley, p. 327. The slavery referred to was presumably white indentured labour in the colonial plantations.

[3] Hadley, p. 320. [4] F. M. Eden, *State of the Poor*, iii, 837.

[5] 6 Feb 1790; *GH* MS L.1387 (66).

at a very early date. The first Seamen's Friendly Society appears to have been founded in 1726,[1] and the Sailors' Society four years later,[2] but no record of their activities has survived. There was a Marine Society in 1776 which may have been either—or both—of them. The Second Friendly Society was founded in 1771 and the Ropers'—obviously not for seamen—in 1772, but the great increase in societies came with the growth of trade in the eighties. By 1788 there were a dozen or more, and fifteen hundred members, with banners flying and music playing, took part in the centenary celebrations in 1788.[3] There were twenty-eight societies—some now catering for women—in 1796, forty in 1803 and seventy-two in 1810.[4] In 1796 they had about 2,500 members, and by the end of the century between a third and a half of the families in Hull were protected by Benevolent Societies. They were regarded with favour by all sections of the community. Merchants and bankers subscribed to them, and many built up sizeable assets. The Unanimous and the Provident each lent the Corporation £300 in 1795, and the Old Amicable and the Benevolent lent £200 and £260 respectively in 1796.[5]

The Benevolent Societies guarded against the sickness which accompanied—and accelerated—poverty. For those who could pay for attention, Hull was well provided with doctors, many of whom, towards the end of the century, acted as whaler-surgeons for part of the year.[6] Those who could not afford treatment were thrown on the mercy of their betters. In the early years of the century treatment was provided by Charity Hall. In 1731 it was reported that 'we are at a great charge, by people without doors falling ill, which (by the application of the apothecary, at the physician's direction, and some other assistance we allow them), has often kept families from us, and has occasioned the Apothecary's notes to run so high, that about one-third part has been for people not in the house'.[7] The only

[1] Hadley, p. 305. [2] Gent, p. 196. [3] Hadley, p. 384.

[4] Tickell (pp. 853–4) lists the societies flourishing in 1796; figures for 1803 and 1810 are from Battle's *Directories*. [5] BB x, 233, 262, 265.

[6] There were at least nineteen surgeons in 1792. Many of them took apprentices, usually the sons of gentlemen or merchants. Medical training was well established; there was a minor scandal in 1746 over the discovery of a dissected body: 'it was generally accounted a murder', said Hadley, but 'there was some suspicion of the truth, that it was a medical *Resurrection* by the faculty'; Hadley, p. 328.

[7] Report on the Hull Workhouse, 1731, in *An Account of Several Workhouses* (1732), quoted in Eden, iii, 832.

specialised facilities of which there is record were a 'Hospital' for sick and wounded seamen which was functioning in the late fifties; who owned it, and what eventually became of it, is unknown.[1]

A number of leading doctors in the town—there was usually one on the Bench—began to campaign for an Infirmary in the seventies, inspired by the dissenter Dr. John Alderson, whose statue still adorns the (altered) forecourt. On 26 September 1782 the new seventy-bed Infirmary was opened. It was planned, constructed and run on principles that sound, at least to the layman, as advanced as those popularly attributed to a later age.[2] 'This excellent establishment', wrote Tickell,[3]

> is conducted on principles the most liberal and humane; extending its useful charity for the relief of the sick and lame poor, to all proper objects without distinction; not only to those within the town and county . . . of Hull; but to such as disease and poverty may induce to apply for relief, from whatever county they may come, if their cases be found to be such as fall within the nature and design of the institution; provided they can obtain the recommendation of a trustee. Such recommendation, however, in cases of sudden accident is not required; and for accidents, and other cases admitting no delay, a proper number of beds are always kept in reserve.

People residing in Hull could usually be recommended by any of the benefactors who had given more than ten guineas, or by any person subscribing more than two guineas per annum, and townships outside Hull which subscribed three guineas annually could recommend one in-patient and two out-patients at any one time.

So far as contemporary medical knowledge would allow, the Infirmary was a success. The average number of in-patients was about 160 per annum—not many, perhaps, but good for the times, especially as it was all free. The number of cures claimed was fairly high: 2,319 of the 3,536 patients treated before the close of 1792 were

[1] The only known reference to this hospital occurs in a letter from Sir George Savile (Governor of Hull) to the Marquis of Rockingham: 'The Hospital for sick and wounded Seamen not being near full we shall now make use of spare rooms and beds for our sick. It is a private property and we hire what we want as the surgeon for sick and wounded does what he has occasion for. . . .' WWM F.49(a), 17 Nov 1759.

[2] The wards and corridors, for instance, were large, well lit and 'airy'. Particular attention was paid to ventilation; floors were regularly scrubbed; walls periodically whitewashed; and beds changed and taken down at regular intervals.

[3] Tickell, pp. 778f.

'cured', and a further 601 'greatly relieved'. The subscribers might well be proud of their achievement.

One of the major problems of the lower class—aggravated as the population grew rapidly in the late eighteenth century—was bad housing. Low wages, preventing an adequate outlay in rent, combined with population pressure to encourage the division and subdivision of houses in the southern part of the town. A general scarcity of houses in the early part of the century[1] was to some extent relieved by speculative building in the fifties and sixties, although trade recessions usually increased the pressure on poorer quality housing at the expense of the better. As often happens, the movement of the richer people out of the old town into the new suburbs left old houses to degenerate into slums, with the result that the total units of occupation increased faster than the number of houses.

Overcrowding was getting worse in the last decade of the century. The population grew by over 7,000 between 1792 and 1801, when there were 29,516 persons living in 4,649 houses.[2] In 1796 Eden had estimated 4½ persons to the house;[3] in 1801 it was slightly over six. As we might expect, these figures were higher than the national average (and we do not know how many seamen were ignored), and it is tempting to see overcrowding as one of the inherent hardships of the urban working class. It is, however, noticeable that house building between 1801 and 1811 was proportionately greater than population increase,[4] and it may well be that some at least of the overcrowding was caused simply by the inability of the building industry to cope immediately with the demands of a rapidly expanding population. The Napoleonic war, with galloping inflation, wildly fluctuating trade and heavy pressure from the press-gang, was no time for investment in house building in a port concentrating heavily on the northern European trades! No final verdict is possible on slum conditions in the eighteenth century because we have no indication of the number of people per room, a vital factor in assessing overcrowding. Since the largest houses were those of the

[1] Comment in R. Pease, Amsterdam, to J. Pease, 16 Feb 1717, *WH* 59/58/43.

[2] The population in 1792 was 22,286, in 5,256 families, according to the Society for Literary Information; quoted in Tickell, pp. 854–6.

[3] Eden, iii, 844.

[4] I am indebted to Dr. Joyce Bellamy for drawing my attention to this point.

rich,[1] the 1801 census average of 1·6 families per house may well hide a crop of tenements with much higher than average occupancy. On the other hand, the influence of the total environment may have been slightly more benevolent in Hull than in other northern towns. Tickell thought Hull one of the healthiest towns in the country. The birth rate exceeded the death rate, and the latter (at 1 in 33½) compared very favourably with that of Liverpool (1 in 27).[2]

One thing separated the poor from the rest: they were almost—though not completely—without formal education. In the first quarter of the century the only public school in Hull was the Grammar School, but the ideal of free education was not entirely lost. In 1754 the vicar, William Mason, established the Vicar's School—where tuition was entirely free—'in commemoration of the blessings of the revolution'. Sixty pupils were nominated by the vicar at the age of eight, and provided with books, pens and paper. The only conditions were 'That they attend divine service twice every Sunday at Trinity Church, and in the evening be all catechised', and 'That the parents of the children live orderly lives, attend divine worship, and give their children good examples at home'.[3] By the custom of the period, their education was highly concentrated. For three years the boys were in school from seven in the morning to five in the evening in summer and from eight to four in winter, with one hour allowed for lunch. There were no holidays.

The Grammar School and Vicar's School were chiefly for classical education, though what became of boys from the latter is completely unknown. A more practical venture was the Marine School established by Trinity House in 1786, in a combined attempt to train ships' officers for the rapidly expanding fleet and provide charity for its poorer members. Thirty-six deserving sons of members (two nominated by each of the Elder Brethren and Assistants) were taught writing, arithmetic, and navigation. Each boy was provided with one sailor-type uniform, two pairs of shoes and two hats per annum. Tuition was free, and was given on the express understanding that boys should become apprentices to master mariners when they left the school. Indeed, an annual Feast—a kind of open day—was held on 25 March each year 'that they may the more easily find

[1] The Henry Maister household consisted of 5 Maisters and 6 servants when the house was destroyed by fire in 1743; Hadley, p. 324.

[2] See Tickell, pp. 854–6. Conditions became rapidly worse after 1815.

[3] Tickell, p. 832.

masters to get to sea, being about the time of ships going on their first voyages'.[1]

Girls were not entirely forgotten. The rudiments of domestic service were taught in the Charity school for twenty poor girls (more if funds allowed) established in 1753 by William Coggan, one of the town's apothecary aldermen. After three years in the school the girls were put to service, and after seven years' good conduct were to receive six pounds on their marriage. Towards the end of the century there were also three Spinning schools maintained by subscription, each for thirty-four girls, who were clothed and educated, again to fit them for service.

Several attempts were made to establish schools connected with religious congregations. In the sixties John Wesley told the Methodists to stop teaching in the Manor Alley Chapel because of resulting damage;[2] and Fish Street Congregational Church had a school and master in the eighties, though it is not clear what was involved.[3] Apparently there was no attempt by the religious bodies to establish Sabbath Schools. These came after 1786, when the Spinning Schools Committee decided to open eight in various parts of the town. They were a failure. Only four were established, and only one survived when the Committee presented its report in 1788.

A few stray letters, couched in appalling grammar, indicate that literacy of a sort was filtering down to the base of society, and the existence of a Sailors' Evening School in the nineties is evidence of a desire for social improvement for which education was the necessary first step. The historian Hadley was filled with misgivings: 'The working poor are by far the most numerous class of people, and *when kept in due subordination*, they compose the riches of the nation. But there is a degree of ignorance necessary to keep them so, and to make them either useful to others or happy in themselves.'[4] He may, perhaps, have been right in his judgement, but he failed to see that a commercial community requires a greater than average degree of literacy, rather than ignorance.

[1] ibid., p. 833. For an account of the school in the eighteenth century see Gordon Jackson, 'The Foundation of Trinity House School, Kingston-upon-Hull: An Experiment in Marine Education', in *Durham Research Review*, Vol. VI, No. 21, 1968.

[2] F. Baker, *A Charge to Keep* (London, 1947), p. 166.

[3] C. E. Darwent, *The Story of Fish Street Church* (Hull, 1899), p. 159.

[4] Hadley, p. 380. The Sabbath School was particularly objectionable: 'a preposterous institution, replete with folly, indolence, fanaticism and mischief'.

The entertainments of the poor were mundane, but none the less an essential part of the life of the town. The men of Hull, unlike those of most towns, had a considerable amount of free time. Seamen, labourers, coopers and many of the industrial workers were seasonably employed, or, as Hadley put it in his supercilious way, 'left at leisure to exercise their dissolute manners on the inoffensive passenger in the public streets'.

While the upper and middle classes had their hunting and shooting, their Assemblies and clubs, the lower orders made do with the cock-pit, the billiard halls, the public houses and the dram shops (the former selling ale and the latter spirits). The number of licensed premises was large, rising from 103 in 1740 to 187 in 1794.[1] They were the commonest meeting places for the majority of the male population, the place where a man could find his friends. They were used for meetings of the various societies of working men, ranging from the Benevolent Societies to the formidable association of shipwrights; and they were the political headquarters during election campaigns. Dram shops were less convivial. 'Several of the poor people came into his shop', Strother wrote of Storm's Dram Shop, 'as I stood at a little distance from the door yesterday night, called for a Dram which they paid for and drank of immediately and that is the manner in which his trade runs.'[2]

Apart from the social life of the public house, which in any case mainly concerned adult men and could on occasions be rather rough, the chief entertainments of the working class were to be found in the streets. The best regular exuse for three or four days jollity was the annual Fair, still at that time a fair for livestock, but always accompanied by the pleasures of the Fairground. Strother honoured the occasion in 1784 with a rather painful verse:[3]

Here Lads and Lasses all together stare,
Pleased with the thoughts of Kingston Fair;
Then show their Teeth in distorting their chins
And gaping wide with all ludicrous grins.
Some fallal'd out in gaudy ribbands shew
Whilst having by their sides a Country beau
Whose head hangs forward shews just come from plough
Silk handkerchief around his neck to shine
Green Strings on Leather Breeches, Lord how fine.

[1] For 1740 see Hadley, p. 315; for 1794 see *GH* Town's Husband's Cash Book, 26 Nov 1794.

[2] Strother, ff. 49–50.

[3] ibid., f. 41.

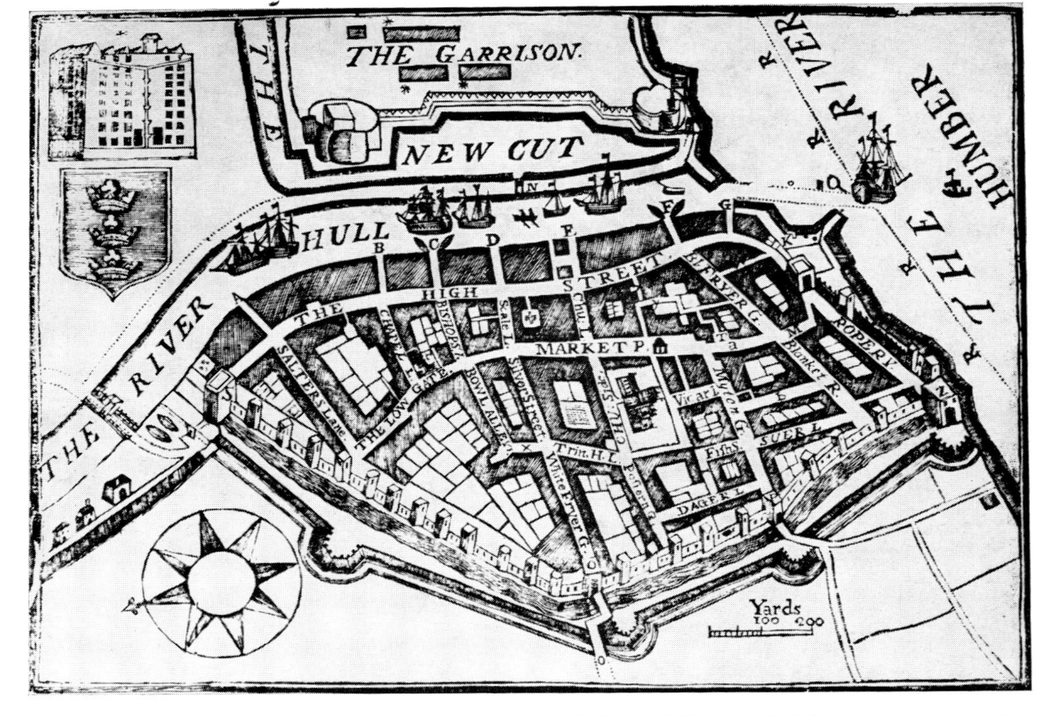

7. Hull *c.* 1730, showing the Sugar House, top left, and Blaydes' Shipyard, centre left. From T. Gent's *The History of the Royal and Beautiful Town of . . . Hull*, 1735

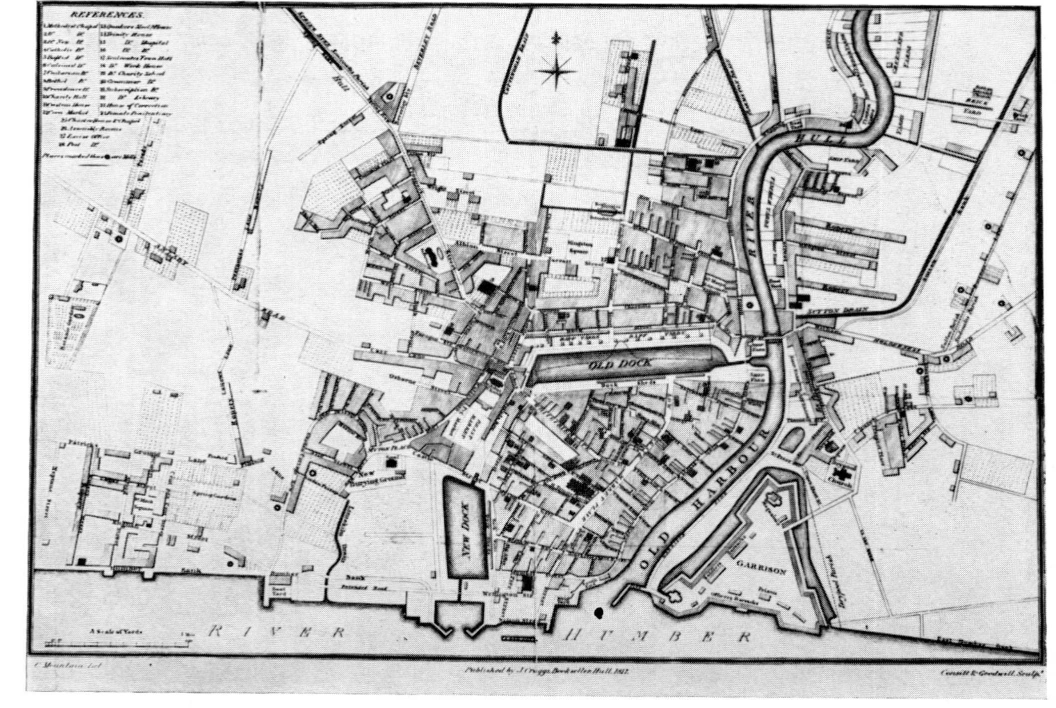

8. Hull in 1817, showing the development beyond the walls and the 'Old' and 'New' docks (C. Mountain). The boundary with Sculcoates is clearly visible running through the middle of the 'Old' dock

Crook'd stick in hand or perhaps a staff,
Which leaning on he grins the Idiot's laugh,
These ruddy country dames, Complexion fair
Caused by good Exercise or wholesome air,
Or something better being free from care;
Who handsome Corps and little else display
Are sauntering up and down to spend the day
Thus careless idling all the time away.

Similarly the national and local elections were recurring excuses for general festivity—in this case at the expense of the candidates. Less laudable, perhaps, was the excitement caused by public punishments such as whipping, pillorying and the occasional ducking. Finally, entertainment was to be found in special events, such as the elaborate and spectacular opening of the dock, and the Centenary celebrations in 1788. For several days in November 1788 the entire population was in a state of great excitement. The Members of Parliament 'were met at some distance from the Town by a great multitude of the inhabitants, and were drawn in their carriages through the principal streets to the noble and beautiful equestrian Statue of our Great Deliverer, where they were saluted by reiterated acclamations of joy. . . .'[1] On Wednesday, 5 November, the whole population turned out to watch or take part in the many orange-bedecked processions that thronged the streets all day. The Marine School boys entertained the crowds with 'God save the King, Rule Britannia, and several other Constitutional songs; in choruses of which they were joined by thousands of the spectators'. The celebrations were, in fact, summed up by 'a gentleman of the town' in the *Hull Packet*'s account:

. . . The service o'er; in solemn pace, and slow,
The Grand Procession moves—the French Horns blow—
Whilst various Instruments in concert play,
And every Tongue proclaims the Welcome Day.
And thrice it moves around the STATUE fair,
And thrice a volly thunders in the air!
Ten thousand hats at once are whirl'd on high,
And loud Huzzas pierce the sky!
Full from the fort the thund'ring Cannons roar!
Whilst ECHO spoke the Joy from shore to shore.
Pass we the hours the Multitudes employ
In hospitable rites, and social Joy.
As Night descended, sparkling Rockets fly,
Blaze thro' the Void, and beautifully die.

[1] *Hull Packet*, 11 Nov 1788.

Then, (following close the well-digested plan)
A Grand illumination straight began—
Gay splendid lights th'imagination seize,
Here curious Emblems, there Transparencies;
Myriads of Lamps their vivid pow'rs display,
Glitter afar, and cause a doubtful Day!
Thro' all the Day, its sacred honours bright,
Thro' all the dangerous Glories of the Night,
No noisy clamour did the Bliss annoy,
Nor accident disturb the General Joy;
But REASON did the Great Occasion crown,
And Harmony preserved thro' all the Town.
Hail KINGSTON, hail! the Jubilee is past!
Yet THY fair Fame thro' ages long shall last....

2. RELIGION: 'AN INFORMAL EVANGELICAL ALLIANCE'

No account of social life would be complete without some consideration of religion, for religion helped to determine the nature of social life, and was itself the reflection of the hopes and fears of the people.

Roman Catholicism had been dealt a near-mortal blow by the troubles of the seventeenth century, culminating in the military occupation of Hull by the Catholic Lord Langdale on the orders of James II. Only two Aldermen and fifteen citizens were classed as disaffected persons after 1689, and Catholicism was too deeply associated with tyranny for it to be acceptable in the eighteenth century.[1] Catholics were not persecuted, but numbers did not increase noticeably at the chapel in Postern Gate. When it was wrecked during the Gordon riots in 1780, the priest sold it to the Jews for a Synagogue, and built a new chapel in Leadenhall Square. It was, like the old one, 'but thinly attended'.[2] Hull did not have the

[1] In 1745, for instance, the 'Humble Address' of the Corporation spoke of miseries 'when last under the Government of a Popish head, and the iminent danger to which our religion, laws, liberty and property were then exposed'. (Quoted in Hadley, pp. 324–5, and Tickell, p. 609.) 'Friends of the Church of England', objecting to the repeal of the Test Acts in 1790, spoke of 'a system of religion, as was best calculated to promote . . . peace, safety, and happiness. . .'. (Hadley, pp. 429–31.)

[2] Tickell, p. 824. There were 40 Roman Catholic communicants in Hull in 1785; H. Aveling, *Post Reformation Catholicism in E. Yorkshire, 1558–1790* (E. Yorks Local Hist. Soc., 1960), p. 53. Halifax and Leeds both received strength from an influx of émigrés during the French Revolution, but Hull did not.

leaven of Catholic gentry that kept the old religion alive in the East Riding.

Protestant dissenters, on the other hand, were both numerous and influential. If the numbers given by Tickell (in his chapter on churches) is anything like accurate, there must have been at least fifteen hundred practising dissenters in the eighties. The oldest congregations were two bodies of Puritans that had played a notable rôle in the seventeenth century and had settled down to a period of respectable and prosperous tranquillity in their chapels in Dagger Lane and Bowlalley Lane. Both underwent doctrinal changes in the middle of the century. The Presbyterians in Bowlalley Lane came under the influence of Socinianism—leading to Unitarianism—which was spreading throughout the neighbourhood in the second quarter of the century. The Reverend John Beverley's ordination service in July 1758 was conducted by Unitarians and thereafter Bowlalley Lane was the seed-ground of Unitarianism in Hull. In the first quarter of the century there were three ministers and about five hundred 'hearers',[1] and throughout the century the members included many leading citizens. Ralph Peacock (a prominent merchant and member of Trinity House) and Alderman Benjamin Blaydes were trustees, and Joseph Pease and his family were members.[2] At the end of the century Hadley thought the congregation 'the genteelest in the town',[3] a description that seems to be typical of Unitarian churches at a slightly later date, and in Liverpool as well as Hull. Their close-knit communities tended to attract—or perhaps produce—the man who was 'going places'.[4] Through-

[1] W. Whitaker, *One Line of the Puritan Tradition in Hull: Bowl Alley Lane Chapel* (London, 1910), p. 95.

[2] ibid., pp. 100–1, 108–9 and 130.

[3] Hadley, p. 801.

[4] The idea that Dissenters unconsciously exerted themselves and showed greater than average initiative in order to gain status in a society that refused to recognise them, is not wholly valid in the case of Hull, where Dissenters *were* respected. But their attitude to child rearing may well have produced children with initiative and self-reliance. (This aspect of Dissent is emphasised, for instance, by D. C. McClelland, *The Achieving Society*, Princeton, 1961, *passim.*) On the other hand, it still seems reasonable to argue that people were attracted to forms of religious expression that were in tune with their existing attitude to life; in other words, that self-reliant, entrepreneurial types had little time for the type of orthodox religion found in eighteenth-century England. In fact by the end of the century it had disappeared altogether from Hull, rejected by nominal Anglicans as well as by Dissenters.

out the century the chapel's library was a centre of social and intellectual life that helped to hold the society together.[1]

The Dagger Lane Church was originally Congregational, but was moving towards Presbyterianism at the same time that the Presbyterians were experimenting with Unitarianism.[2] Eleven members (including Daniel Tong, eventually a leading whaler-owner) objected to the change and built themselves a new chapel in Blanket Row in 1769. Their first minister was George Lambert, a young student from Heckmondwike Academy, under whose energetic and popular guidance the new church grew from strength to strength. In 1773 a couple of galleries were added, and nine years later a bigger church was built in Fish Street where, according to Tickell, more children were baptised than in any other Dissenting church. Fish Street chapel was in turn enlarged in 1802, and a thousand people attended the reopening ceremony.

Little is known of the other Dissenting bodies. Alderman John Beilby, whose family played a great part in civic life, had a house licensed for occasional Independent worship in 1705, and several others were licensed between 1712 and 1717, one of them for Baptists.[3] The Baptists were, in fact, slow to establish themselves, and it was not until 1735 that a Meeting House was opened in Manor Alley. By 1757 they were numerous enough for a new chapel to be build in Salthouse Lane and this in turn became too small and had to be extended in 1790 for a congregation that numbered about four hundred.[4] Their minister for twenty-eight years (1770–98), the Rev. John Beatson, was one of the leaders of cultural society in Hull, and was President of the Subscription Library, 1788–91.[5]

The Baptists also experienced a period of doctrinal ferment in the middle of the century. In 1769 their minister, Rutherford, was dismissed, took his faithful followers with him and, after sheltering for a while in the old theatre, moved into a new chapel in Dagger Lane. Rutherford's doctrine must have changed considerably, for the new chapel appears to have been associated with Lady Huntingdon's

[1] Whitaker, pp. 127–8, records expenditure on 'wine at library thanksgiving' after the Peace of Paris, and on other occasions tobacco, cork screws, punch ladles, lemon strainers and 'waiters'—all for the library!

[2] The Dagger Lane Church is dealt with by C. E. Darwent, *The Story of Fish Street*. The official change to Presbyterianism took place with the arrival of the Rev. John Burnett in 1767.

[3] The licences are noted in Whitaker, p. 104.

[4] Tickell, pp. 820–1.

[5] Frost, *Address*, pp. 42–3.

Connexion, a body of Calvinistic Anglicans who owed their origin mainly to the preaching of George Whitefield. A mixture of Anglicans and Dissenters, they used part of the Anglican ritual and held no services during church hours. One of their ministers, a man called Harris, had received episcopal ordination at some stage, and was a close friend of Dikes of St. John's.[1]

Despite the obvious vitality of the Dissenting churches, and the enthusiasm of their ministers, the shift of emphasis in the late eighteenth century was back to the Church of England—or, more accurately, to a changed and revitalised Church of England. After the middle of the century the Church was slowly infused with that spirit of 'personal religion' that Wesley and his followers had themselves learned from Dissenters. Salvation, they were convinced, came to fallen man only when he was 'born again', when he turned in faith from a life of sin to a life 'in Christ'. It was fairly orthodox theology, but to be reminded of sin was embarrassing, and a life in Christ was inconvenient for the man-about-town. So the concept of Salvation and personal religion arrived in Hull with faltering steps, strongly opposed for many years, as it was elsewhere.

The movement later called Methodism reached Hull, from Grimsby, in 1746. Wesley first visited the town in 1752 and, after initial hostility, was better received than in most places.[2] His audience, he said, was 'a large multitude, rich and poor, horse and foot, with several coaches'. During his next visit, in 1759, the congregation was again a 'fine' one, 'so for once the rich have the Gospel preached'.[3] Wesley's preachers continued to visit Hull

[1] The Lincolnshire diarist, Rev. Dr. John Parkinson, noted two Lady Huntingdon's Chapels in 1802, but only one Methodist; perhaps the two were confused by his informant. He also noted a 'Kelhamite or Bethel Chapel in Dock Street', two Anabaptist Chapels, the Independent Chapel, the 'Dissenting Chapel in Dagger Lane', the 'Arian Chapel in Lowgate' (i.e. Unitarian), the 'German Meeting House', and 'The Christians of Antioch or the true and perfect Church'. Parkinson's English Diary, 6 Jul 1801; *Scunthorpe Museum Library*.

[2] John Wesley, *Journal* (Standard Edition, 8 vols, 1909), entry for 24 Apr 1752: 'Some thousands of the people seriously attended; but many behaved as if possessed by Moloch. Clods and stone flew about on every side; but they neither touched nor disturbed me.'

[3] Wesley's visits, and the growth of Methodism, can be followed in W. H. Thompson, *Early Chapters in Hull Methodism, 1746–1800* (Hull, 1899), *passim*, and R. Treffry, *Remarks on Revivals of Religion* (Hull, 1827), *passim*.

regularly and the band of followers grew larger. But emphasis on personal religion was more noticeable, if not more widespread, after the conversion of Joseph Milner (actually by followers of Whitefield, not Wesley) shortly after he became master of the Grammar School (1767) and Lecturer of Holy Trinity (1768). The wealthy, particularly, were hostile to his new life. For perhaps ten years, his brother later wrote, Milner's ways were objectionable to 'people of superior rank', and 'few persons who wore a tolerably good coat would take notice of him when they met him in the street'.[1] Alderman Wilberforce withdrew his grandson from the school and threatened that, although he might travel abroad with Milner when he came of age, 'if Billy turns Methodist he shall not have a sixpence of mine'.[2] While Tate Wilkinson, seeing his theatre threatened, came in to the attack with all guns blazing, the Wilberforces used more subtle methods to entice young William back to the fold. 'No pious parent', he said later, 'ever laboured more to impress a beloved child with sentiments of piety, than they did to give me a taste for the world and its diversions.'[3]

It is not difficult to understand why some at least of the Evangelicals met with hostility. Milner 'commended and blamed without reserve, and without much consulting the feelings of those who heard him'.[4] As his brother said:[5]

Mr Milner's company did not continue long to be called for in genteel and convivial meetings. The man, who was grown insupportable in the pulpit, ceased to be a desirable guest at the table; and indeed his own heart was now so much engaged in different branches of practical religion, that he had little time and no taste for trifling company. He was constantly seeking opportunities to say 'a word in season'. He had left off playing at cards; he was no longer seen at the playhouse or the assembly; his presence checked and rebuked indecent conversation, and irregularities of every kind; and when in company, by being less trifling, or by some ill-natured attack on religion, presented an opening for grave conversation, Mr Milner would often express himself with so much seriousness and so much admonition, that 'men of the world' no longer felt themselves at ease in his presence.

Nor, on the other hand, is it difficult to see why serious-minded

[1] W. Richardson (ed.), *Practical Sermons by the Late Rev. Joseph Milner . . . to which is prefixed An Account of the Life . . . of the Author . . . by the Rev. Isaac Milner. . . .* (Cambridge, 1801), p. xxiv.

[2] Wilberforce, i, 7.

[3] ibid.

[4] Milner, p. lxiv.

[5] ibid., p. xxiii.

boys should have come from miles around to sit at the feet of this rough Yorkshire diamond before going on to the further influence of his more polished brother, the President of Queens' College and, with Charles Simeon, the leader of Evangelicalism at Cambridge.

In appearing to attack the good life, the new ideas earned many enemies, but a severe and disciplined life was in fact only part of the whole. It was joyfully accepted by those to whom the new religious experience offered a reason for existence, the promise of perfect and eternal happiness, and absolution for real or imaginary sin. John Spence, of Spence & King, the wholesale ironmongers and Carron Company agents, recalling on his death-bed the good things of his life, dwelt on 'the many spiritual helps they [he and his brother] had received amongst the Methodists'.[1] The chief was 'that we should know that God is merciful to us through the death of his Son!—and blessed be God *we do know it*! They taught us poor ignorant creature what we never knew before:

"Why was I made to hear thy voice,
  And enter while there's room;
While thousands make a wretched choice,
  And rather starve than come?"'

Whatever their worldly opponents might have thought, the early Evangelists and Methodists were, in their own way, supremely happy people,[2] and the first to respond to them were often the lonely, unhappy and bewildered, thrashing around in the hostile and inhuman environment of economic progress. The measure of their faith was seen in the ease with which they transmitted it to others. Methodism was magnetic; in some mysterious way it answered the cry from the heart of its age. By 1771 there were enough Methodists for Hull to become a Circuit town with three (episcopally ordained) ministers and a chapel 'pro bono publico'. But the breakthrough came with the spread of conversions up the social scale. Methodism became socially acceptable. Rich people no longer viewed the movement with suspicion and contempt, and it was they, rather than the sacrificing, self-denying poor, who built the chapels, paid the

[1] R. Burdekin, *Memoir of the Life and Character of Mr Robert Spence* (York, 1827), p. 18.

[2] For a typical local example, see the Memoir of Mrs. Hill, *The Methodist Magazine*, Vol. XXXVI (1813), pp. 372–81. 'I found my mind exceedingly happy', she wrote on the day following her conversion; 'all is well', she said, when she died at the age of thirty-one, in child-bed.

ministers, and generally presented a public image that was likely to be seen. The poor had the light; but the rich placed it on the bushel. Four or five thousand pounds was spent on the new chapel in George Yard in 1784, and another was built in Scott Street in 1793, when the total number of people owing allegiance to the Hull Circuit was 1,280. The Waltham Street chapel, built in the early years of the nineteenth century, was said to be 'the most spacious and elegant that that Society possesses'.

Evangelicalism was making similar strides. The Thorntons, patrons of the living of Low Church (St. Mary's), put in an Evangelical vicar and curate, and in 1783 Holy Trinity fell to the cause when Thomas Clarke, a pupil of Joseph Milner and Wilberforce's brother-in-law, was elected vicar by the Bench. John Wesley now dined at the vicarage and preached from the town pulpit; in June 1788 Clarke 'never saw the church so full before'.[1] Isaac Milner, despite his fraternal interest, was near the truth when he summed up his brother's work:[2]

> Great numbers of the poorer and of the middle classes of society became truly religious in practice; and almost all persons affected to approve Mr. Milner's way of stating the truths of the Gospel. In effect, the sentiments which he defended and explained in the pulpit, became so fashionable, that no Clergyman was well received at Hull, who opposed, or did not support them.

In 1792 another of Joseph's disciples, Thomas Dikes, used a legacy to build an Evangelical church for the growing population outside the walls.[3] A man of saintly character and powerful oratory, he soon had a congregation of a thousand packing St. John's, which had to be enlarged by a couple of hundred sittings in 1803.

Although chapels were built, and people called themselves—or were called—Methodists, there was no deliberate secession from the Church of England. Hull Methodists, no less than Evangelicals, regarded themselves as Anglicans at least until the end of the century. The Kelhamites, Dr. Parkinson noted in 1801, 'are seceders from the Church, differing in that respect from the Westleian

[1] Wesley's *Journal*, 22 Jun 1788. Mr. Clarke, wrote Wesley, was 'a friendly sensible man; and, I believe, truly fearing God. And such, by the peculiar providence of God, are all the three stated [i.e. established] Ministers in Hull.' [2] Milner, p. xxxiii.

[3] For a full account, see J. King, *Memoir of the Rev. Thomas Dykes* (London, 1849). With a typical piece of nineteenth-century snobbery, King spelled the name Dykes, though Dikes never used this form.

Methodists. . . . These are disciples of Westley and go to Church.' Whatever the future might bring, and whatever was happening elsewhere, in Hull the terms Methodist and Evangelical were synonymous. Joseph Milner, for example, is now regarded as an Evangelical, but this description was not used in the eighteenth century. Isaac Milner, writing of his brother in 1801, said:

> The name Methodist, when applied to such persons as Mr. Milner, ceased, in a great measure, to be disgraceful with thinking people. . . . In this revival of religion the dissenters were not without a share; but it was principally brought about in the establishment.[1]

Methodism was not, then, a rival church. The chapels were used only for weekday meetings for prayer, Class meetings and, above all, for preaching. They were not open for ritualistic worship on Sundays before the nineteenth century. When Methodists elsewhere pressed for secession after the death of Wesley, those in Hull published a circular prophesying that if Methodism seceded it would 'dwindle away into a dry, dull, separate party'.[2] The Holy Communion continued to be administered by episcopally ordained clergy using the Prayer Book service, and it was still regarded as the duty of Methodists to bring the heathen within the fold of the Anglican Church. There were, for instance, at least two Methodists among the seven prominent men petitioning in favour of Dikes' church in 1788,[3]

[1] Milner, p. xxxii. It is interesting that Richardson, less acquainted with circumstances in Hull, and trying to give Joseph an air of respectability, thought it necessary to qualify Isaac's statement. Methodists, unlike the 'Clergy of the Church of England', held 'wild and dangerous opinions' and incurred reproach 'on account of the Enthusiasm and Schism which disgrace their dispensation . . .'. This reflected on the Anglican clergy, and 'it has proved a stumbling block in the way of some well-disposed young men, who have been hindered from preaching and living as the Gospel requires, for fear of incurring an opprobrious name'. Joseph would have consigned such compromising and obsequious clerical toadies instantly to the pit!

[2] Quoted in Thompson, *Early Chapters*, p. 65.

[3] They were Thomas Thompson and Richard Terry. When Dikes proposed to build, in 1788, the Corporation, as patrons of Hull, withheld permission for a private enterprise venture on the grounds that they intended to build a church themselves. They did nothing, hence the petition (7 Jul 1790) to force a decision one way or the other; King, p. 24. Richard Terry was 'one of the earliest and most intimate of the friends both of Milner and Dykes, in whose house several portions of Milner's Church History was written and who, with his excellent wife, was always "ready to every good work"'; ibid., p. 54n. When Dikes died, in 1847, Avison Terry, another Methodist, was his oldest surviving friend; ibid., p. 183.

and they would have had the greatest difficulty explaining the difference between themselves and Dikes. Many Methodists 'with their preachers' attended St. John's until the end of the Napoleonic war,[1] and Methodists were to be found among the trustees of the new Christ Church in the suburb of Sculcoates in 1814.[2] An eventual divergence was probably inevitable as Methodism assumed a national identity; but the divergence was slower coming in Hull than in most places.

The cordial relations existing between the various denominations was one of the most interesting facets of life in eighteenth-century Hull. The bitterness, hatred and persecution found earlier had almost completely disappeared. There was, in fact, less difference than might be imagined between Anglicanism and Dissent before the Oxford Movement changed the character of the Church of England. In the last quarter of the century, and probably earlier, the various Hull ministers were on the best of terms, visiting each other, losing members to each other, attending each other's ordination and confirmation services, and preaching at each other's funerals. 'I have lost another beloved friend today', Lambert wrote when King, of Low Church, died.[3] It was in Lambert's chapel that Joseph Milner was converted by students from Lady Huntingdon's college at Trevecka,[4] and Lambert himself records in his diary sermons given by 'Mr Barker at Low Church'.[5] Monthly meetings of clergy were organised by Milner and attended by Lambert, Harris of Lady Huntingdon's Connexion, Beatson the Baptist and

[1] King, p. 93. 'The Wesleyans . . . now almost entirely withdrew; and the line of demarcation between them and the members of the Church became more distinct.'

[2] 54 George III, c. 77, s. i, printed in Woolley, pp. 11–19. Avison Terry laid the foundation stone, and Dikes preached the sermon, declaring his love for the Established Church but also the determination that he 'would not, for a moment, interfere with the right of private judgment, or prevent any of my fellow creatures from the liberty which I claim to myself, that of worshipping God according to the dictates of my own conscience'. King, p. 116.

[3] Darwent, p. 107.

[4] ibid., p. 206–7. Isaac Milner did not mention this episode. He simply quoted the text, 'If any man be in Christ he is a new creature' (p. xviii) and *implied* that Joseph became a Methodist (p. xxii). However, Lady Huntingdon claimed him as a convert (*Life of Selina, Countess of Huntingdon* (London, 1844), i, 303–5), and his close friendship with Lambert and Harris makes this seem likely.

[5] Darwent, p. 31.

a number of others whose names are unfortunately unknown.[1]

Whitaker's conclusion[2] that 'the "old Dissent" tended to be a little enclosed lake, not touched by the tidal wave that was driving the world to a new experience of life and religion' is hardly true of Hull at the end of the eighteenth century. With the possible exception of the Unitarians, the old Dissent was far from separate and far from stagnant. As we have seen, the Dissenters were in the forefront of the religious revival, and their growth was, if anything, more spectacular in terms of church-building than that of the Methodists and Evangelicals before 1800. It was not primarily theological discord that separated the two sides—this came later. Nor was it to any great extent the nature of ecclesiastical organisation.[3] It was politics. The Methodists and Evangelicals were mostly Tories; the Dissenters were not. 'At the period of the French Revolution', wrote Dikes' biographer, 'when a large proportion of the dissenting ministers appeared to have drunk deeply into [sic] the spirit of the age, intercourse between them and the evangelical clergy began to be less free and cordial'.[4] Friendship and sympathy remained, however. Dikes attended Lambert's death-bed and preached a funeral sermon for him in St. John's, in which he announced his hatred of Christian division,[5] and, for Lambert's successor, coming to Hull in 1816 was 'like joining an informal Evangelical Alliance'.[6]

We tend to think of the religious revival as a movement embracing the whole of society. Dean Milner certainly implied as much when he spoke of it in Hull in glowing general terms:[7]

The care of the Soul became the topic of common conversation; Great seriousness prevailed: Drunkards and Debauchees were

[1] King, p. 28. [2] Whitaker, p. 104.

[3] Dikes, for instance, 'loved the Episcopal form of government, but did not regard it as indispensable to the existence of a Church'; King, p. 249.

[4] ibid., p. 28. One of the major objections of the Dissenters—and later the Methodists—was to the 'establishment', and this was, in effect, a kind of political rather than religious issue. Dikes 'strenuously maintained the importance of the connection between the Church and State, believing that the advantages far outweigh the disadvantages of such a connection; but he deprecated that pride and arrogance of spirit which tempt some of the younger clergy to anathematize all who are of different religious communions from their own. He lamented the various divisions and subdivisions which exist among us. . . .' ibid., pp. 247–8.

[5] ibid., pp. 92–3. [6] Quoted by Darwent, p. 108.

[7] Milner, p. xxiv.

reformed: The town assumed a new appearance: Great numbers, whose consciences were awakened under his [viz. Joseph Milner's] preaching, earnestly enquired. 'What shall we do to be saved?'

It is, however, by no means clear how generally effective the revival was. 'Great seriousness' prevailed for a century or more if one looks in the right places. The leaders of the community and the middle class were able to give the town an air of respectability, and they were the people who are remembered and quoted. They, and the church- and chapel-goers, may not be representative of the majority of the population in 1780 or 1820. The boys of the Marine School, larking in the dock on Sundays, showed little outward sign of inward light, either in themselves or their set,[1] and the concern of the clergy for the 'Abounding of Open Profligacy and Immorality'[2] shows at least that the 'World' was fighting back.

There is no reason to suppose that the direct influence of religion was spreading rapidly among the working class in the late eighteenth century. Surviving evidence shows a predominantly middle class participation, but this may, of course, be due partly to a nineteenth century eagerness to discover respectable antecedents. The Dissenters in the eighteenth century were notoriously genteel, and one suspects that the same was true of the Evangelicals. When Dikes opened St. John's he sold the pews for an average of a little over

[1] See Jackson, 'An Experiment in Marine Education', pp. 316–18.

[2] The title of a sermon preached by Dikes on 22 Jan 1804 in support of a 'Society for the Suppression of Vice in Hull'; King, pp. 60–1. Like many others, Dikes believed his own time and locality the farthest removed from God. Casting around for an explanation he was inclined, in his pre-Marxian, pre-Freudian innocence, to blame the French Revolution: 'From this mist of Darkness a horrid spirit issued forth, which breathed defiance to the God of Heaven, and subverted the thrones of princes. Terror and dismay preceded him, desolation marked his progress, and death followed in his steps. All laws, human and divine, were trampled under foot. The marriage vow was no longer sacred. Modesty was declared to be an invention of refined voluptuousness; children's regard to their parents a vulgar prejudice of education; and parental authority a cruel bondage not to be endured. Friendship to individuals was considered as a species of narrow selfishness; religion the invention of priestcraft; and death an eternal sleep.' It all sounds familiar to the modern reader; and the tragedy for Dikes was that fifty years of his new, vital religion seems to have made little difference. In 1812 he was still pessimistically asking, of prostitution, 'Is there a town in the kingdom so thoroughly infected with this vice as our own?' (King, p. 77). The clergy of Liverpool could no doubt have provided an acceptable answer.

seventeen pounds each.[1] The result was that 'the Aisles are usually well-filled, but the pews are many of them empty, and many of them have only two or three persons in them'.[2] The pews soon filled with people eager to hear his magnificent sermons, but there can be no doubting their social origin. The depth and sincerity of their faith was a cause for concern to Dikes in the early years: 'I wish they were more spiritual; but we have many that are of the higher class.'[3] Unfortunately he leaves us to speculate on the relationship between these two facts! Faith came gradually, but to how many common people—despite Dean Milner's frequent use of the phrase—we do not know. Probably to fewer in St. John's than in Holy Trinity and the Methodist chapels. Not until the development of Primitive Methodism in the early nineteenth century did the working class have a sect that evolved from the people rather than the Common Room.

Religious revival is usually taken to mean a turning to God of people outside the Church. Here again there is reason for doubt, if we confine our attention to the eighteenth century. There was undeniably a momentous growth in church-going, but there was also a very considerable growth in the population, especially, in Hull, of the commercial, tradesman and small manufacturer classes in which one would expect to find religious observance. Moreover, many people came to Hull from rural communities where church-going was an ingrained habit, and although they would be included in any total of new church members in Hull, they were not the product of revival. Dikes and his curates were well aware that their evangelism was not always as effective as it seemed: 'we have several Meetings, but they only seem to catch people on whom religion has got some former hold.'[4] The history of religion in eighteenth-century Hull is impressive, but it would at least seem probable that the communicants or members, as a percentage of the total population, were declining in the very period that is regarded as the great growth period. Only a great deal of research in church records and census returns can prove or disprove this, but adequate records before 1800 are unlikely to be found.

[1] The total raised by the sale of pews was £4,100 towards the cost of £4,600 (the difference was donated by friends, so Dikes appears to have got his money back); ibid., pp. 29–31.

[2] King, pp. 29–31. [3] ibid., p. 30.

[4] Rev. John Scott, to his father, n.d., quoted in King, p. 53.

3. PARLIAMENTARY POLITICS AND 'CORRUPTION'

You know that I am a man of might, that I have Tar barrels, and Whale-blubber, and that all riches in the land are within my grasp, therefore hear me.

The anonymous local wit whose 'Fragment on Election Time'[1] circulated in the eighties does not appear to have aimed his barb at any particular candidate for parliamentary election; but there could be no doubting the accuracy of his observation. The great merchants were indisputably the masters of parliamentary politics in Hull. They had to be. Effective representation was vital when commercial interests were so often affected by government policy, and when London merchants, nearest the seat of power, were regarded, rightly or wrongly, as arrogant monopolists. Whatever their 'political' affiliations, the responsibility of Members for Hull was to the Bench, and their duty was representing Hull's interests in Parliament. Shoals of letters were sent up to them for presentation to the king, the Commons, or Government departments, and they were expected to furnish detailed accounts of everything happening in London that was likely to affect Hull. The Bench no longer paid its M.P.s, but it made them work.

The political atmosphere in Hull was influenced to a great extent by the same factors that determined religious life. The seventeenth century had been the most troubled period in the history of the town, which staunchly supported the Parliamentary cause in the Civil War and the Protestant cause under James II. In 1688 the Members of Parliament were elected in defiance of the King's instructions, and consequently the town was placed under martial law until the Bench ordered a 'revolt' on 3 December 1688, later celebrated as 'Town-taking' Day. Hull was therefore a keen supporter of William III, whose gilded statue in the market place became the focus of much patriotic fervour; and the Hanoverian dynasty, with all its faults, was eventually welcomed as Divine deliverance from the loathsome Stuarts. Throughout the century Hull was passionately loyal to 'King and Constitution' and could be counted on as a Government borough. But Members of Parliament

[1] Quoted in Hadley, p. 502.

were selected—or emerged—as individuals rather than as members of any particular 'party' grouping. They were first representatives of Hull, and secondly friends of Rockingham or Pitt. In 1765 Rockingham told an applicant for his support that he was bound 'to take no steps whatever in relation to candidates for Hull, but entirely to make it my object to be guided by the Inclination of many respectable and considerable persons in Hull, who are and have been our kind and valuable friends'.[1]

There were, of course, rival groups of political managers in the town, but, as elsewhere, they do not appear to have divided over political issues until 1784. William Wilberforce declared himself an independent in 1780, and voted in Parliament both for the 'fat old fellow' (Lord North) and for Pitt, who was his intimate, according to the dictates of conscience.[2] But by 1784 politics were beginning to be important, as the junior Fox–Pitt drama developed. Philip Green, merchant and shipowner, 'returned to Hull a red hot Foxite and much prejudiced against you', W. S. Stanhope was told in 1784,[3] and the Sykes wrote 'most pressing invitations' to Lord John Cavendish to come to Hull to oppose Stanhope, a supporter—with Wilberforce, his sponsor in Hull—of Pitt.[4] The Pitt faction won the day, with both Stanhope and Samuel Thornton returned for Hull, and the Sykes (soon to become Wilberforce's business partners) rethought their attitude to politics—and, incidentally, to religion. The tremendous prestige and following of Wilberforce helped to determine political affiliations in Hull for many years to come.

Political leadership was a matter of social prestige for the great merchants—or, rather, for those interested in social aggrandisement. 'Very few of the voters', it was said in 1792,[5] 'are independent of the higher ranks of people in the town.' The Crowles and Maisters exercised a great deal of influence in the early part of the century, William Hammond and John Stephenson in the middle, and the Sykes, Broadleys, Hammonds and Stephensons towards the end.

[1] Quoted in Rockingham to William Weddell, 8 Dec 1767, *SCRL* WMM 49.

[2] See W. Wilberforce, London, to B. B. Thompson, 9 Jun 1781, quoted in R. I. & S. Wilberforce, i, 21–2.

[3] J. Smith, Hull, to W. S. Stanhope, 2 May 1784; WSS 1784.

[4] Smith to Stanhope, 6 May 1784.

[5] Oldfield, quoted in L. Namier and J. Brooke, *The House of Commons, 1754–90* (London, 1964), i, p. 435.

But it was not so much a permanent political as a permanent social influence, which occasionally had political content.

The chief influence lay with the Bench, which supported acceptable candidates, though not always successfully. In 1724, for instance, they agreed to 'accept and encourage' the candidature of Sir Henry Houghton rather than that of George Crowle, son of Hull's greatest merchant at the time, but Crowle won the day through his tremendous personal following.[1] In general, however, the Bench spoke for the politically influential. When David Hartley dedicated his attack on the American War to the Corporation of Hull (which supported it), they promptly disowned him, and he lost his seat. Later, forgiven, and supported by William Hammond, he regained his seat, and was M.P. for Hull when he unsuccessfully attempted to draw up the Definitive Peace treaty with the United States of America.[2] Hammond's son, George, was taken along as a reward for support, and this was no doubt one of the factors leading to his eventual appointment as Britain's first ambassador to the U.S.A.

Members for Hull generally had local connexions; exactly half of them were local men. The great merchant families were represented by Alderman Sir William St. Quentin (1695–1724), William Maister (1700–16), Nathaniel Rogers (1716–27), George Crowle (1724–47), Richard Crowle (unsuccessful in 1747; 1754–7), Henry Maister (1732–41), William Wilberforce (1780–4) and Samuel Thornton (1784–1806). Sir George Montgomery Meatham (1757–66) was a local landowner from North Cave, and the Carters of Redbourne, Lincolnshire (William, 1741–4 and Thomas, 1747–54) were friends and distant relations of the Crowles. The remainder were, for the most part, recommended by Rockingham or Sir George Savile, respectively High Steward and Governor of Hull, honorary posts to which they were nominated by the Bench as a mark of esteem. William Weddell was a relation of Rockingham who upset the poorer voters by neglecting the races and the richer by his 'want of activity'.[3] The intolerably boring David Hartley was a

[1] Despite the opposition of the Aldermen, most of whom voted against him; Poll Book, 23 Jan 1723/4 (copy in BM Landsowne 891, ff. 182f.).

[2] Namier & Brooke, ii, 592–3.

[3] ibid., iii, 617–8. In a letter to William Hammond, Rockingham defended Weddell: his 'ill state of health undoubtedly made him not so active as he could have wished', and 'in everything which relates to Hull' he was still 'active and assiduous'. Hammond was not persuaded, and Weddell saw fit to stand down in 1774.

nominee of Savile. Walter Spencer Stanhope was a friend and fellow-traveller of Wilberforce and Thornton, and was more or less nominated by Wilberforce to succeed himself when he won both a Hull and Yorkshire seat in 1784 and chose to sit for Yorkshire.

The electorate was numerous, and could never be permanently or completely 'controlled'. Since there was no restriction placed on freedom (except for a brief period before an election, to prevent the unseemly race that took place in some boroughs),[1] each election saw anything up to seven years' new freemen to be canvassed, as well as the old ones. The most that the political leaders could hope for was willing support, for meaningful bribery was out of the question. And because support could not, in most cases, be demanded, it could be withheld. In 1784 the supporters of the 'tory' Stanhope gleefully reported that 'The lower class of Burgesses who had entered into a written contract to support any Gentlemen Mr H. Broadley or the Sykes should set up in opposition to you are now deserting the Party every day'.[2] Wilberforce's influence had apparently prevailed, but there was no bitterness or open hostility: 'Fine weather, no opposition, cheerfulness and goodwill', was Stanhope's comment on Election Day.[3] (The defeated candidate was Hartley, fighting Hull for the fourth and last time.)

If by bribery we mean the use of an unfair advantage to gain a vote, it is possible to see bribery in the actions of all candidates who had government backing.[4] Obviously a job might be threatened, or an account cancelled by a candidate's friends, but the direct offer of good things to come could only come from the source of all power and influence. In Hull the chief favours at the candidate's disposal were jobs in the Customs, which were usually applied for around election time. One such application, forwarded to Stanhope by his supporters William Thompson & Company, bore the cryptic endorsement: 'Poor, he has several of his relations who are burgesses.'[5] Other favours involved mediation with government

[1] See, for e.g., an order of the Bench on 2 Apr 1741; BB viii, 911.

[2] A series of illuminating letters from various supporters (chiefly from his agent, J. Smith) to W. S. Stanhope is in WSS 1784.

[3] Quoted in Namier & Brooke, iii, 466.

[4] It might be argued that 'patriotic' Hull would have returned government supporters even without places in Excise or Customs to be distributed.

[5] W. Thompson to Stanhope, 28 Jun 1784, WSS 1784. One freeman refused his vote unless his nominee was appointed a tidewaiter; John Cox to Stanhope, 12 May 1784.

departments. Elizabeth Smart, supported by Henry Etherington, John Stephenson, Thomas Wood (a shipowner) and William Osbourne, pleaded for the release of her son, now serving in the army in Ireland. On 19 May 1784 Stephenson sent her petition to Stanhope; on 23 May Lord Harrington wrote to Stanhope from Ireland saying the lad was on his way home. Eighteenth-century administrators could move with lightning speed when the need arose! Stephenson thought his action required a word of explanation, for he added the note: 'I wish the poor Woman's Petition may meet with Success—I know her not, but it has always been customary to Sign every petition that has presented to the Candidate or Member who are my friends that no offence may be taken to them.'

The rich also expected favours in return for support in electioneering. Stephenson himself was constantly pressing Stanhope to find a government post for his nephew Mace, who in the meantime was touring his customers as a traveller and not making much of it.[1] Henry Etherington expected the Stanhopes to take his niece, Miss Moses, into London society, 'tho can assure you, would not trust with any but such as I know would take care to keep her from improper connections'.[2]

One of the easiest ways of bringing pressure to bear on the lesser merchants was to secure political recommendations from their inland contacts. Stanhope and his agents between them wrote to every inland merchant and manufacturer with the least connexion with Hull. Walmsleys of Rochdale were persuaded to recommend Stanhope to Williamsons, Bells and William Thompson & Company; and Walkers of Rotherham sent their best wishes and added: 'Please to write to Mr Richard Fishwick and Mr Archer Ward, both of Newcastle on Tyne, and mention my name. I think they have votes for Hull.'[3] Such were the devious ways in which votes were secured.

Votes were not auctioned to the highest bidder; in this respect no voter was bribed to vote for one side rather than another. But voters expected to be paid a standard rate, usually two guineas per vote. Agreements were reached before election day; votes were registered by the agents; and payments made if the 'contracts' were honoured. Occasionally things went wrong. Poor old Francis Arey, a sail-

[1] J. Stephenson to Stanhope, 16 Mar 1785; WSS 1785.
[2] Etherington to Stanhope, 22 Mar 1785.
[3] Walker to Stanhope, 16 Apr 1784.

maker, complained to Stanhope in 1784:[1] 'I take this Earley Opertuenety to Enfurm you mr Smith Gives his Complements to you and should be Glad for A horder from you to pay Me the Same as the rest of the free Burgises he havin Not My Name in the Books at Hull. . . .' He had given his promise at Stanhope's London house and neglected to contact Smith in Hull. There is no record that he was ever paid, and ten months later John Stephenson thought proper to advise Stanhope that 'Entre Nous, your Agent loves money too well, and is much too long in settling Election Matters'.[2]

With a growing number of burgesses towards the end of the century a seat at Hull would cost its lucky holder something in the region of five or six thousand pounds. The local merchants earlier in the century may well have got by with much less; the outsiders may have had to pay more, depending on the price paid for votes and the amount of free drink and entertainment the agents thought necessary to introduce the new man. Elections were eagerly anticipated, and never were the free burgesses more disgusted than when an undisputed election threatened. Hadley, writing shortly after Stanhope withdrew from the 1790 campaign, leaving only two candidates in the field, said:[3]

Never perhaps did the clouds of disappointment, more suddenly and universally prevail to obscure the sunshine of approaching joy, than on this occasion. The desertion of Mr Stanhope was in every mouth; the plump jocund risibility, that an hour before enlightened all countenances, was gradually drawn down into a longitudinal dejection, which pervaded every face, even the friends of *opposition*, shrunk with the consciousness of their own approaching unimportance, sensible that their consequence was then (for want of a protracted canvass) sunk to nought, and that nothing could restore it but a THIRD MAN; the cry of which resounded in all parts, while scoured through the streets of HULL the disappointed crowds; and a Bell was sent forth to the adjacent towns, to ring out an invitation to a third CANDIDATE FOR HULL.

Hadley should not be taken too literally, but Stanhope himself was aware of the value of an uncontested election. In 1784, when Hartley was his opponent, he had been advised to 'prevail on the Minister in whose service Hartley is now employed to prevent his coming home[.] it will be a great saving of expence to you. His opposition

[1] F. Arey to Stanhope, 7 Jul 1784.
[2] Stephenson to Stanhope, 22 May 1785.
[3] Hadley, p. 491.

to you cannot do you any injury except in the article of expence.'

However the Members were elected, they generally served the town well. William Weddell did not, and soon paid the penalty. Lord Robert Manners, on the other hand, was exceedingly popular, and grew old and venerable in the service of the town, which he represented for no less than thirty-five years (1747–82). We may doubt the legality of Henry Maister's gift of bushels of corn to those who voted for him, but there is no doubting his ability to represent the interests of the port, and indirectly the people, of Hull. The same might be said of most of his successors in the eighteenth century.

XII. LOCAL GOVERNMENT

The quality of social life, for rich and poor alike, depended in large measure on the local administrative authority. The eighteenth century is generally regarded as an age devoid of efficient local government. The spontaneous concentration of industrial society took place for the most part outside the historic boroughs, and such public services as existed were the product of a proliferation of unco-ordinated *ad hoc* commissions. Where new population and ancient borough coincided the problems were, if anything, aggravated, since there was an immediate need for urban renewal. Nor were corrupt and incompetent aldermen always able to control the environment developing around them; in the eighteen-thirties the Municipal Reformers thought them almost worse than no government. Not all boroughs fall into this category. There were some where the ancient government succeeded, to some extent, in controlling the developing community. Even among the best boroughs, Hull stands out as an example of what things might have been. The small size of the town and the religious atmosphere there may have had some effect, but undoubtedly the chief reason for Hull's efficient local government was the continuing unity of political and economic power in the hands of competent and public spirited men.

Hull was governed by her merchant oligarchy. The Charter stated that 'the Mayor, Aldermen and Burgesses . . . assembled, shall elect or nominate one of the Aldermen of the town . . . to be Mayor . . . for the year following . . .',[1] but in practice the aldermen nominated two Lights (candidates) and the burgesses elected one of them.[2]

[1] J. R. Boyle, *Charters and Letters Patent Granted to Kingston-upon-Hull* (Hull, 1905), p. 160. The effective Charter was granted by Charles II, 1661.

[2] The process was recorded annually in the Bench Books, as, for example, on 30 Sep 1772 (BB ix, 421):

> This day came on the Election of Officers for this Corporation for the ensuing year and after the Act of Parliament for preventing Bribery and Corruption in the Election of Members to serve in Parliament had been openly read, The Right Worshipful Benjamin Blaydes Esq., Mayor, According to Custom acquainted the Burgesses that the Lights for

Aldermen were elected—or selected—in the same way: two Lights were presented to the burgesses by the aldermen. Alderman Daniel Hoare, who went bankrupt in 1712, made an unconscious appraisal of local government democracy in his letter of resignation: 'I desire your worships will please to elect another Aldermen in my room.'[1] Naturally the burgesses did not always take kindly to the Bench's nominee. During an election in 1741:[2]

. . . the Burgesses would not disperse, but stood crowding round the place, tho' they had been often asked if any wanted to vote. The books being shut, some persons dissatisfied with the election, cried out *Have you all polled?* An answer was made *No*, and they demanded a fresh poll; which being denied as illegal, a riot ensued, and they threatened to pull down the Hall, and abused and hissed the Aldermen, but the Constables having secured seven or eight of the ringleaders, and carried them to prison, the rest were dismayed, and those who were taken were kept in confinement and fined.

Hull was, then, a politically 'corrupt' borough, in so far as the aldermen more or less nominated their successors. There was, however, no political issue involved and, moreover, there was no deliberate policy of exclusion. Any man could become a burgess, by paternity, apprenticeship or purchase (with the price recouped at the next Parliamentary election in bribes), and any man could, given the required qualifications, become an alderman. He had, simply, to have made good, with influence in the town and a knowledge of its affairs meriting formal recognition. That is why aldermen were usually (but not always) merchants, and the service of several generations of the same family indicates not their ability to 'corrupt', but their ability to remain in the first rank of merchant houses. They began as Chamberlains (who collected the Corporation's rents and dues), two of whom were chosen each year 'from the body of the younger tradesmen, who appear to be rising in the world, and fit to fill the said office'.[3] More than usual ability was 'rewarded'—perhaps to the annoyance of the candidate—by a year as Sheriff, and success in this office would almost certainly mean an eventual place on the Bench. The public career of Joseph Sykes

Mayor were Alderman Bell and Alderman Mace upon which Alderman Mace was duly Elected Mayor for the ensuing year by a Great Majority of the voices of the Burgesses present and was so declared by Mr Mayor for the time being.

[1] Quoted in Hadley, p. 300. [2] ibid., p. 320. [3] Tickell, p. 667.

illustrates the normal sequence: he was Chamberlain in 1751, Sheriff in 1754, and Mayor in 1761 and 1777.

The truth is that membership of the Bench was regarded as a necessary burden rather than a desirable sinecure. Tickell thought the mayoralty 'an office more honourable than lucrative, and attended with a great deal of trouble',[1] and many men paid the £300 fine rather than become aldermen. In 1724 three of the most promising men in Hull—Nathaniel Maister, Richard Sykes and Samuel Mowld—declined even to take up their freedoms and were ordered to pay water bailiff dues,[2] and some years later the Horners and Broadleys were prosecuted for the same reason.[3] On the other hand, it was expected that the great merchant houses would pay periodic fines: this was one of the sources of Corporation income.

Those who assumed the onerous task of government did so because they thought it their duty so to do. They may have represented the commercial community, but in Hull little else mattered. Their interests were a distillation of the town's interests and the Dock Company summed up the position with reasonable accuracy when it described the aldermen as 'ye official Parents of the Town'.[4] The extent to which the Bench was fully representative was, in the context of eighteenth-century Hull, largely irrelevant. The important question is: What did they do? The answer is simple: they maintained an environment in which trade and industry could flourish; in which a reasonably healthy people could live and work with the minimum of discomfort.

The charter gave them 'full power and authority to . . . make . . . so many and such reasonable laws . . . as, according to their wise discretions, shall be seen by them to be . . . necessary, for the good rule and government of the Burgesses, artificers, and inhabitants of the town. . . .'[5] Backed by 'reasonable pains, penalties and punishments, by imprisonment of body or by fines . . .', and by general confirmatory Acts of Parliament in 1755, 1761, 1763 and 1783,[6] they regulated everything from hackney cabs to party walls.

[1] ibid., p. 668.

[2] BB viii, 789. Water bailiff dues were paid by 'Unfreemen of this Town' on goods passing through the port. They were not abolished till 1853.

[3] In 1774, BB ix, 432. This was a test case, taken to appeal by the Horners. Lord Chief Justice Mansfield and three appeal Judges upheld the Town's right to levy the dues.

[4] HDC, Letter Book 'A', 24 Nov 1774.

[5] Boyle, pp. 156–7.

[6] The Acts may be found in Woolley, *Statutes*, pp. 77–108 and 199–236.

There is little evidence of conscious town planning outside the capitals and spa towns in the eighteenth century, and it would be wrong to apply this grandiose term to the Bench's activities, but their careful supervision of the building and rebuilding of houses and streets appears to have prevented the type of urban growth found in most industrial towns of the period. As early as 1732 they ordered that 'no persons do presume to erect any building in the highways or streets of this town, without first acquainting the Mayor for the time being therewith, and having obtained his consent thereto'.[1] With the leading builders—such as Joseph Page—and the merchant-landowners, they planned rows of houses or streets on closes or razed ground—a redevelopment made easier by the large amount of property owned by the Corporation. There was usually harmony between the interested parties, although in 1772 a dispute broke out 'relating to the Agreement concerning the Houses at the West End of the High Church and the new Street to be made there'.[2]

A major breakthrough in local 'town-planning' came at the end of the century, when, by a special Act of Parliament (41 George III, c. 65), the Bench acquired powers of compulsory purchase to demolish the oldest property left in the town, between the Market Place and the Humber. (The houses of owners refusing to sell were to be valued by a jury, and the costs of the action deducted.) Thus armed, the Bench demolished the southern side of the Market Place, built Queen Street through to the Humber Bank, and planned a number of new streets on a couple of hundred yards of land reclaimed from the Humber by dumping there the mud excavated and dredged from the docks.[3]

It was common in eighteenth century towns for the genteel streets to be fine and the rest foul. This does not appear to have been the case in Hull. Not until the last quarter of the century did the merchants begin to leave the labyrinth of mediaeval streets and alleys where they rubbed shoulders with their less affluent fellows. For a variety of reasons Hull did not suffer from that urban spread which in some places eased the conscience of the rulers by separating them from the results of their incompetence.

The Bench could at any time order the streets, squares, lanes and alleys to be paved or repaired, and most were paved from a very early date, often with Dutch stones imported as ballast. Occupiers

[1] BB viii, 778. [2] BB ix, 421. See p. 200.

[3] HDC, Transactions, 26 Jan 1781.

were expected to pay the workmen's wages if the Corporation provided the materials, and to prevent argument a clause to this effect was written into the Bench's general Act of 1755 (28 George II, c. 27, ss. xvi-xvii). The Town's Husband was responsible—especially when the town was completely repaved in the eighties[1]—for organising and supervising work which earned from the Webbs the rare compliment of 'an Enlightened Local Authority',[2] and certainly put Hull far ahead of Bristol and Liverpool.

Street lighting was introduced at the beginning of the century. In 1713 the Members of Parliament were instructed to 'procure at London, such number of convenient lights, to be set up and maintained within this town, as might be most useful and beneficial to the inhabitants thereof',[3] but nothing further is heard about lighting until the 1755 Act said that 'many of the principal inhabitants... do propose to set up and maintain lamps against their own houses ...' (s. xxix). These lamps remained private property until the 1762 Act vested lighting firmly in the hands of the Coporation, for a rate not exceeding one shillings and sixpence. The oil lamps thus provided are clearly visible in the many engravings of street scenes in the last quarter of the century.

Cleansing was originally the responsibility of householders, each dealing with his frontage to the middle of the road. The voluntary principle was, however, unsatisfactory and the 1755 Act (s. xx) enabled the Bench to appoint occasional scavengers to clean dirty streets and demand payment from negligent occupiers. The inhabitants probably preferred this course, which at least had the advantage of uniformity, and the 1761 Act (2 George III, c. 70) made the scavengers permanent employees of the Corporation, under the control of the Town's Husband. After a brief spell of direct control, the Bench delegated responsibility for lighting and cleansing to Assessors elected for each ward by occupiers of property valued at three pounds per annum. Their duties were to 'provide

[1] BB ix, 614. The Bench ordered on 3 April 1784 'that in future all the Public Streets within this town be forthwith paved under the direction of Mr Chandler' (the Town's Husband). Three months later a general naming of the streets was ordered; BB ix, 619.

[2] S. and B. Webb, *English Local Government*, Vol. IV: *Statutory Authorities for Special Purposes* (1922, reprinted 1963), p. 301. This is still the best work on local government, dealing with many of the thousands of local Acts such as those concerning Hull.

[3] Quoted in Hadley, p. 300.

and take care that the streets, squares, lanes and alleys within their respective wards be from time to time lighted swept and cleansed in manner as aforesaid, and . . . apply and dispose of the money which shall be raised by the rates. . . .'[1]

The disposal of refuse was never the problem in Hull that it became in some places, for the town was surrounded by running water. While attempts were made—unsuccessfully—to stop the pollution of the moats, 'South End'—or 'Mucky South End' as it was usually known—was recognised as the traditional dumping ground. Human and animal excreta was highly valued as manure by the improving farmers of the East Riding and Lincolnshire, and was speedily removed from the 'Tileries', provided by the Bench for its reception at various points outside the walls.[2] Arthur Young recorded[3] in the sixties that:

About fifty years ago the manuring from Hull was begun by a poor man who hired a close of grass; he had four asses which he employed constantly in carrying away ashes and dung, and spreading them upon his pasture . . . whoever brought away manure, for many years were paid for taking it. Twenty five years ago it was to be had for sixpence to a shilling a load; by the country around by degrees all coming into the practice, the price has arose to five shillings a load.

Liverpool in the nineties was still knee-deep in the stuff.[4]

The removal of liquid sewage—a vital factor determining public health—was by bricked-in common sewers, about which, regrettably, little is known. Underground sewers certainly existed before the 1755 Act declared the Bench to be responsible for maintaining and cleansing 'all the grates and grate heads, and frames thereof and all the common sewers arched, under the pavements of the said town'.[5] They were built in all the new streets, and the insertion of sewers four and a half feet high preceded the building of streets after 1780 on surplus Dock Company land.

The growth of population and trade in a restricted area soon brought problems of congestion, and Hull, like many other places,

[1] The 1763 Act (4 George III, c. 74), s. xii.

[2] In 1775 the Bench ceased to provide the Tilery, and instead made an allowance of £5 per annum to the Scavengers 'to provide a Proper Place for a Tilery to lay the soil of the Town on instead of the Corporation'. BB ix, 451. (This use of the word *Tilery* is obscure; it may be related to the practice of mixing dung with broken tiles and pots, which to this day are to be found in every spadeful of earth for miles around Hull.)

[3] Quoted in Webbs, IV, p. 331. [4] ibid. [5] s. xxii.

had a mass of regulations governing conduct in the public thoroughfares. As early as 1716 the Bench checked irregularities in the market; in 1722 they regulated the parking of carts and coaches; and in the thirties they considered the Heads of a Bill for, among other things, 'better regulating . . . carriages and labourers and porters wages . . .'.[1] The 1755 Act summed up the situation:

whereas the streets and lanes of the said town are, in general, very narrow, and frequently obstructed by carts, waggons, trucks and other wheel carriages, standing or remaining in the same longer than is necessary; be it therefore enacted by the authority aforesaid, THAT no cart, waggon, truck or other wheel carriage, with or without horses or other cattle, shall be permitted to remain in any of the public streets, squares, lanes or passages in the said town, longer than is or shall be necessary for loading or unloading the same . . .; and that no hackney coach shall be permitted to stand, or remain in any of the said public streets, etc. unless whilst in waiting for any person or persons, who hath or have sent for or hired the same. . . .

The parking regulations were capped by a prohibition on speeding with a goods waggon 'faster than a foot pace, to the annoyance of the inhabitants or others being in, or passing along the said streets . . .'.

By 1763 there was very little that the Bench did not in practice control. Only one more Act was needed, and that (dealing principally with a new gaol) did little more than tidy up loose ends: fall-pipes became compulsory and projections (including business signs) illegal; the size of shop stalls was restricted; and lights were required on obstructions at night; and there were penalties for polluting the water supply, dropping rubbish in the streets, lighting bonfires, or letting off 'any squib, serpent, rocket, or other firework whatsoever'.

Of all the things affecting the lives of town-dwellers, sewage and water were probably the most important. The people of Hull were fortunate: the Bench's attitude to sewage was, as we have seen, better than that of most authorities; their attitude to water was almost unique. The nearest fresh water was the Hull, but the part adjacent to the town was tidal, and the various yards and 'factories' for a mile or so along its bank had no small effect on its quality. The streams passing through the town were also polluted. The moats had

[1] Quoted in Hadley, pp. 302, 304, 306.

long ago been found to be 'not so sweet as they should have been', and in 1616, according to Gent:[1]

> This occasioned the Magistrates to make an application to Richard Sharpleigh, . . . William Maltby, . . . and John Cayer, . . . three famous artists and engineers; Who coming to view the place, found practically what they intended; and therefore took a piece of Ground, for one hundred years. . . . On this they erected Water-works; They had the liberty also, to lay Pipes in the Streets. . . . All this . . . to be at their own expense; since the Inhabitants were yearly to allow a profitable Compensation for the Water.

The works were erected 'to the unspeakable satisfaction of the whole town', but little is known of their subsequent history. In 1700 they were owned by a private company of thirty-two shares, eleven of which were bought by the Corporation in that year.[2]

Although they owned only a third of the works, which were leased to a manager, the Bench had absolute control over the water supply. In 1735 they ordered the Town's Husband to write to London 'to some person skilled in water-works, to know what he would have to come to Hull to view the Waterworks here, in order to improve them',[3] and in August 1736 they ordered the laying of new pipes in Silver Street, Scale Lane and High Street without formal reference to the other shareholders. (At least in the forties they were both on the Bench.) The Town Clerk was responsible in the thirties for collecting the water rate, and in 1736 was ordered to 'cutt off the Strings of such persons as refuse to pay'.[4]

The Corporation bought the remaining shares from Alderman Wilberforce and 'Mr Robinson' in 1765 for approximately £4,000.[5] Thereafter the works were controlled by a Committee of the Bench, although in 1773 they were leased to another manager, Mayson Wright, who paid an annual fee in return for the right to levy the water rate. Wright, a merchant and oil-miller, was already acquainted with the mechanics of water supply, and marked his arrival by installing a steam engine, erected by Hendley of York, in 1773 or 1774. Five years later a second engine, by Boulton &

[1] Gent, pp. 130–1. This was not the first waterworks in Hull. The Corporation were empowered to draw water from springs in the County of Hull 'by subterraneous leaden pipes and other necessary and suitable engines whatsoever' by the Charter of 25 Henry VI, 1446/7; Boyle, p. 59.

[2] BB viii, 465–6.

[3] Quoted in Hadley, p. 307.

[4] BB viii, 827.

[5] BB ix, 358.

Watt, was erected when pipes were laid in the 'exterior' streets of the town and in the newly constructed dock, at a cost, to the Corporation, of £400.[1]

Closely allied to the water supply was the Corporation's 'Fire Service', one of the first in the country. The thought of fire haunted the merchants, living in a compact group along the river, with their highly inflammable warehouses adjacent to each other and to their dwellings. The Maisters were not the only merchants forced to blow up a warehouse to prevent a blaze from spreading.[2] Prevention was generally better and easier than cure, and the Bench made a succession of precautionary by-laws. There was a ban on fires and the heating of pitch aboard the highly vulnerable shipping crowded in the Haven, and all lanterns—including those belonging to the Customs—had to be submitted for approval to the Bench (or later, the Dock Company). In the town itself there was a ban on night-work in textile workships and regular fire inspections of all commercial premises. Places reported as insecure received aldermanic visitations: 'Ald. Collings, Cogan and Beilby or any Two of them are desired to Survey the work shop complained of by Captain Bushell as Insecure from Fire and likewise to survey all such other Places . . . as they shall be Informed are Insecure from fire and Report their opinion to the Bench.'[3]

Despite all precautions, disaster occasionally struck. In the early days of the century the aldermen were expected to cope with the early stages of fire, and kept fire buckets and axes at their homes. They very quickly brought up more substantial reinforcements. In 1705 they enquired the cost of 'an engine for playing water up to the highest house', and in the following year Alderman Mowld wrote to

[1] The system was surprisingly modern: 'by preparing a sufficient reservoir for their fresh water upon the top of a high tower, and conveying it to that elevation by the force of a steam engine', the inhabitants 'are now abundantly supplied on all occasions with that necessary article of life, through proper pipes, pure and unadulterated, at their own doors or in their own kitchens. . . .' Tickell, p. 659. It is, unfortunately, not clear when the supply ceased to be intermittent.

[2] Henry Maister, when fined for the office of alderman, pleaded hardship, 'representing the great loss by the late fire which happened in the High Street . . . in a considerable parcel of corn withall the Blowing up the House . . . in favour and for the preservation of the neighbourhood for which he had not received any consideration.' BB viii, 767. Two years later his wife and child died in a fire that destroyed their dwelling house.

[3] BB viii, 7.

his correspondents in London and Amsterdam for a machine costing about £20. It is not clear if one was secured at that price; but there were certainly three bought in 1715, one from Amsterdam at a cost of £74. 14*s.* 11*d.*, and the others from London. They were, at an unknown date, connected into the public water supply by fire hydrants, which at least in the last quarter of the century gave them water under pressure. There is no record of a regular fire-fighting team until 1743, when thirteen men were appointed by the Bench and there was certainly a group of permanent 'firemen' in 1762, when the Corporation was credited with £1. 17*s.* 6*d.* 'By the Engine men at a Fire at the George'.[1] The 1792 *Directory* lists fifteen men in the 'Fire Engine Company', presumably permanent members to be called in an emergency.

To the Bench fell the unenviable task of controlling a potentially turbulent populace. Beneath its veneer of tranquillity, Hanoverian England seethed with manifold disorders stemming from economic, political and religious discontent. A brutal and hysterical mobocracy was never far beneath the surface in most towns, and callousness and cruelty existed on both sides of the law. In the absence of a modern police force there was little that magistrates could do to overcome the baser instincts of man; sometimes, as Wearmouth[2] and others have shown, they did not try. In town and countryside alike, it was the viciousness rather than the certainty of punishment that was expected to preserve an orderly society; and the magistracy, imposed from above, had little sympathy for—or even knowledge of—the aspirations of those on whom they sat in judgement. In Hull, by contrast, the magistrates were elected. However faulty the system, they represented—and felt themselves to represent—the people they governed. They acted leniently, so far as we can tell. The fine was their favourite weapon, since it swelled Corporation income; but they generally returned fines in part or whole to culprits claiming hardship. They were also firm, expecting their authority and the good order of the town to be respected. 'By a proper exertion of the Magisterial power,' wrote Hadley, 'the honour of the civil authority was vindicated, in the commission of the Lieutenant of the Berwick man of war to the House of Correc-

[1] BB ix, 27, and *GH* Town's Husband's Cash Book, 14 May 1762.

[2] R. F. Wearmouth, *Methodism and the Common People of the Eighteenth Century* (London, 1945), *passim.* The standard work is G. Rudé, *The Crowd in History* (New York, 1964).

tion, for abusing one of the Bench with ill language', during a visit of his ship in 1743.[1]

The strength of the Bench came partly from their acceptance by the inhabitants, and partly from the all-pervading presence of the Chief Constable and his twelve assistants. They were far from being the corrupt and ineffectual constables of popular legend. If the Bench were unusual in putting two naval officers in prison, the constables must have been unique in twice arresting press-gangs and their officers. They apprehended vagrants, arrested criminals and disorderly people, broke up mobs before trouble could develop, prevented religious persecution and turned out whenever there was likely to be turmoil. In August 1762, for example, they were paid £3. 3*s*. 6*d*. 'for various attendances, Searching Bawdy Houses and going round the Town on Rejoicing Nights'.[2] Since Hull had a remarkable number of excuses for rejoicing, the constables were never idle for long. For exciting spectacles, such as a pillorying or whipping, they were supplemented by 'extra constables'. Elections were particularly troublesome, since every freeman had money, and free and non-free alike had as much as they could drink: '48 Constables attending 2 Nights in the Streets during the Election of Members of Parliament' cost the town thirteen guineas in September 1780,[3] when young Wilberforce gained his first seat.

The constables did not keep up a regular patrol, but an atmosphere of peace and security emanated from Garrison Side. Hull was still, in the eighteenth century, a Garrison Town, with a military Governor, a decayed fortress and a body of soldiers. Although they played little part in keeping the peace during the daytime—often quite the reverse—they maintained a night watch from the Guard House, which stood next to the gaol in the Market Place until 1791, when it was moved to Garrison Side as part of the replanning of the southern part of the town. The new Guard House was provided with 'a room appropriated to the use of confining disorderly persons apprehended in the night, till they can conveniently be brought before a civil magistrate, to account for their acting in an improper manner'.[4]

Hull was usually a fairly quiet place.[5] There were, for example,

[1] Hadley, p. 323. [2] Town's Husband's Cash Book.
[3] ibid. [4] Tickell, p. 632n.
[5] One visitor in 1717 wrote: 'The town is not large, but very populous and yet as quiet and free from any noise hurry or disturbance as any country

few disturbances over food prices (the main cause of discontent in the eighteenth century) until August 1795 when there was 'great dissatisfaction and an inclination for tumult' caused by a fifty per cent increase in the price of flour.[1] Mobs 'threatened to pull down the Hall' in 1741, pelted Methodists in the fifties, Quakers in the seventies, Catholics in the eighties, and foreign seamen whenever the beer was strong; but on one occasion only did the constables fail to stop the trouble speedily: in 1780 the Bench gave twenty guineas to the Suffolk Militia and three guineas to the Garrison troops 'for the immediate and effectual assistance they gave the civil power, in suppressing certain riots . . . when the riots in London and other parts of the nation excited by Lord George Gordon, spread such a general alarm'.[2]

No one pretended that a seaport should be entirely free from disturbance. Indeed, some of the magistrates, with fortunes based on the toughness of seamen, would have been worried if it had been. Toughness apart, the major problem of the ports was their peculiar pattern of seasonal unemployment, which delivered idle hands into the hands of the devil. 'When we reflect', wrote Hadley,[3]

> that during the evenings of the winter months, the streets are crowded with boys, intended for the sea-service, who spend their time in the open violation of decency, good order and morality—That there are often fifteen hundred seamen and boys, who arrive from the whale fishery, and that often double that number of unimployed sailors, are left at leisure to excercise their dissolute manners on the inoffensive passenger in the public streets—we cannot sufficiently applaud the effort to prevent the increase of such dissoluteness. . . .
>
> Though to the honour of this Town, it may be said, that there are fewer disturbances, than in any other seaport, where such a number of seamen are constantly resorting; yet it is impossible to assimilate such a number of spirits, as must annually be collected here, when unimployed by their avocations, uncivilised by education, or unrestrained by discipline.

Hull had its share of ordinary criminals, whose offences ranged from cursing the king to murder, bank robbery to infanticide. Not

village.' H. Hare, Hull, to John Hare, 23 Dec 1717, *BM* Lansdowne MSS, 891, f. 140.

[1] There were further food riots in 1796; *Hull Advertiser*, 8 Aug 1795 and 2 Mar 1796.

[2] The episode is reported in Hadley, pp. 358 and 804, and Tickell, p. 825.

[3] Hadley, p. 424.

even the gaol was entirely safe: the Sheriff was warned in 1736 that he would be held responsible for 'all locks, keys, bolts, and lead, belonging to the Gaol, that should be broke, stolen or taken away; as a quantity of lead had been lately taken from the covering thereof'.[1] Most criminals were dealt with by the Quarter Sessions, with the more serious cases coming before the rather vague Sheriff's Court that met twice a year. The Hull Assizes, supposed to be held when requested by the Mayor, were in fact held only once in seven years until 1745, when the Bench managed to persuade the Judges to come every three years. The position was still difficult, but nothing came of an attempt in 1779 to try Hull actions at the York Assizes, or of one in the following year to introduce an annual Assize at Hull.

The Assize dealt with criminal cases. Civil actions were held before the Hull Court of Venire, of which the Recorder was permanent judge, sitting with the Mayor and Sheriff. The 'Attornies and advocates' practising before the Court were appointed by the Mayor, Sheriff and Aldermen. Three were sufficient until the seventies, when the number was increased to seven to cope with the increased amount of litigation that accompanied the expansion of trade. Small debts, of less than forty shillings, were recoverable in the Court of Requests, established in 1761 and held before three of the Commissioners—the Mayor, Aldermen and thirty inhabitants—for the Act establishing it. It took over the minor function of the Court of Venire, which was henceforth concerned only with actions involving greater sums than forty shillings, and with such things as damage and trespass.

The most exacting and expensive problem facing local authorities was poverty. For the most part they understood neither its cause nor its cure. Some, following tradition, saw it as a crime to be punished; but others already saw it as a consequence of trade recession or old age. Ports were especially affected by wars and general economic fluctuations; and they had problems of periodic unemployment that prevented any reasonably intelligent merchant from differentiating between his own inactivity and that of his employees. Seasonal unemployment was an accepted part of life. Hull froze with the Baltic, and wages and relief were adjusted accordingly. The problem of periodic unemployment increased with the volume of trade. As a natural growth point, offering employment and fairly good wages, Hull attracted men from the agricultural districts of

[1] ibid., p. 307.

Yorkshire and Lincolnshire, and from all the decayed ports of the east coast. But each new family was a potential burden to the poor rates. They helped to create Hull's prosperity; but events beyond their control might spell their ruin.

It is not possible to generalise about poverty in Hull, or about the method of treatment. The Bench, perhaps unconsciously, recognised a number of different types of pauper, with appropriate treatment for each. The first category were the vagrants, the wanderers on whom so much sympathy has been lavished. They were not newcomers rounded up by a parsimonious Bench because they were, or would be, unemployed for a few weeks. If Hull attracted men willing and eager to work, it also attracted those for whom work was a greater hardship than poverty. They were treated as harshly in Hull as elsewhere. In 1718 the constables were instructed to seek out and report—but not to expel—all strangers who might become chargeable, and in November 1730 the Bench ordered that nobody likely to become chargeable should be admitted as sub-tenants in Corporation-owned houses.[1] But Hull needed an influx of labour, and only in the very serious crisis in the last decade of the century was any drastic action taken against vagrants. Two men were then employed to apprehend them; they were sometimes whipped, and usually sent to their place of legal settlement.[2]

A far greater problem than the occasional scoundrel were the women and children who, for various reasons, accumulated in the town and were tolerated until the poor rates began to soar after 1790. Whatever their origin, they were technically vagrants if they had no legal settlement, and no fewer than 166 families were sent away between January 1794 and December 1795, to places as far apart as Edinburgh in the north and Plymouth in the south. 'Jane Wilson & Child, ret'd to Grimsby, July 31st., 1793', cost the Corporation a shilling, the usual amount paid for a removal. There is no indication whether she was a wife joining her husband in another port, a widow whose husband had worked in Hull without obtaining a settlement, or an unlucky prostitute. Some were loath to go. Mary Nipper and her two children were sent out to Scotland on 14 October and again on 7 November 1794, and they are not the only

[1] BB viii, 763.

[2] Expenditure on vagrants was recorded in the Town's Husband's Cash Book.

cases of double entry. The men in this group were usually seamen stranded in the port, and discharged naval seamen, who were helped on their way to their home: for example, six discharged sailors were sent to Wisbech, London, Yorksford and Yarmouth on 13 September 1794.

Paupers with a legal settlement were in quite a different category. Already by the sixteen-nineties it was obvious that 'the poor in the Town of Kingston-upon-Hull do daily multiply, and through idleness or want of employment and sufficient authority to compel them thereto, become indigent and disorderly . . .'.[1] Following the example set two years earlier by Bristol,[2] it was enacted in 1697–8 that 'from 1st June 1698, there shall be a corporation consisting of the Mayor, Recorder, and Aldermen and twenty four other persons to be elected by the inhabitants, paying two pence per week poor rates'. They were to raise £2,000 for a workhouse, and an annual sum (not exceeding the average of the last three years) by taxation of all land, houses, ships and stocks.[3] It might be argued from the inclusion of elected ratepayers that the Corporation was abdicating its responsibilities to another, *ad hoc* body, but this is not an adequate interpretation: the Bench continued to have the controlling voice in Poor Relief.

Orphans, the old and the infirm were an inevitable and permanent feature of Poor Relief. More troublesome was temporary poverty arising from unemployment, since it tended to assume grave proportions during trade recessions. There was bound, then, to be a steady rise in rates, with occasional emergencies in wartime, and the total money spent on paupers necessarily grew with the population and fluctuated with economic conditions. Unfortunately the Hull Poor Law Act did not permit an increase in rates to meet a growing problem, and as a result Charity Hall—as the workhouse was

[1] Preamble to the first Hull Poor Law, 9–10 William III, c. 47.

[2] For the Bristol experiment and its imitators, see Webb, *English Local Government*, iv, pp. 110f. The Bristol Act said almost the same as the Hull one: 'the poor . . . do daily multiply, and idleness and debauchery amongst the meaner sort doth greatly increase, for want of workhouses to set them to work, and a sufficient authority to compel them thereto. . . .'

[3] The question of rates payable by shipping was a difficult one. Ships were rateable at their 'home', and shipowners appear to have accepted this until 1803, when Collison & Taylor challenged the rate because they did not reside within the town—although their office was there. See G. Chetwynd (ed.), Burns' *The Justice of the Peace* (London, 1820 edition), iv, pp. 88–9.

euphemistically called—was not at first put into operation as intended. No master was appointed, and it became 'no better than a Charity school for children'. Adults were given pensions because it was cheaper, but even this system began to fail, for 'none could receive any pension but upon the death of some other; whence it necessarily followed, that those, who had the best friends, got upon the list; while others, who had the same right, were forced to beg'. In an attempt to deal with poverty as a whole, the Bench decided in 1727 to employ a master, draft the old and infirm into Charity Hall, and, despite petitions, to end outdoor relief. A Report in 1731 looked forward to the end of beggary in Hull, but it was wishful thinking. Temporary unemployment was inevitable, and outdoor relief was resumed for the able-bodied poor. The rates began to move slowly upwards without any recorded objections. Between 1728 and 1742 the Corporation was raising £442 per annum, roughly three times the legally permitted maximum. In 1743 they had the maximum raised to £650, and in 1755 took discretionary powers to raise whatever was needed. A sudden burst of poverty during the Seven Years' War turned out to be only temporary, but after 1767 the poor rate moved steadily upwards with the population, accelerated by the American and French Revolutionary Wars until it stood at £8,320 per annum by 1798.[1] Like the other growing towns, Hull felt the burden of her increasing population when embargoes prevented them from pursuing their wealth-creating activities; and Hull had the further complication that the poorest families could lose their bread-winner to the press-gang at a time when bread was increasing rapidly in price. At the turn of the century poverty was costing a pound per annum for every family resident in the port.

The Charity Hall was not a place of punishment to which able-bodied men were sent. It was more or less a refuge for old people over sixty and children under fourteen. People between these ages, and families, were only admitted in exceptional circumstances requiring a special entry in the 'comments' column of the Workhouse Admissions Register.[2]

[1] For a contemporary account of poverty in Hull, see Thomas Thompson, *Considerations on the Poor Rates and State of the Workhouse in Kingston-upon-Hull* (1800). For the amount of money raised between 1729 and 1800, see Appendix 36.

[2] *GH* Workhouse Admittance and Discharge Book, 1729–56. All the details that follow are taken from this volume. No other volumes have been found.

Children were admitted when their parents could not or would not support them, through illness or temporary trouble. (Orphans, by contrast, were assigned to foster parents who received an allowance for their clothes and education.) George Buntofe, aged thirteen, and his sister, aged four, were admitted in March 1728 and left in April 1730 when 'His father took him' and 'Her mother took her'. There may have been some hidden tragedy in the lives of the Buntofe children; most stayed for much shorter periods. Mary, Thomas and Grace Fox, aged eleven, eight and six, were admitted in April 1728 and left in July when 'Their parents took they 3 home without leave of anybody'. Occasionally a mother and children were admitted pending the husband's return from a long voyage or a winter in the Baltic: Ann Green and her two small children entered in June 1748 and left a year later when 'Her Husband took them out'. For some there is no simple explanation. Elizabeth Daniel brought her two children into the House in December 1751 and remained for eight months; three years later the children—the youngest under four—'Left at the gate by there mother ordered to be taken in'. They remained for ten months.

Single women were often accommodated, and many came into the House to have their babies.[1] Ann Bailey, for instance, arrived on 3 February 1756; her daughter was born on 16 March, and they both left on 31 May. They returned between October 1757 and March 1758, perhaps to see them over a hard winter, perhaps to have another baby. The young men who were admitted were special cases. Some came in for a few months in the winter because their savings were gone; most were ill. At least one wretched lad was mentally deranged and was locked up; twice he broke out and had to be recaptured. William Nickels, aged 24, was perhaps more fortunate: he was admitted on the second and died on 9 June 1741.

[1] Most authorities were eager for illegitimate births to take place under their roof. By ancient custom a bastard was settled in the place of its birth, unless born in the care of the local authorities (in the House of Correction, in prison, or in a lying-in hospital—which was not always such an altruistic establishment as one might think). In this case it took the settlement of its mother, a tradition confirmed by the Acts 20 George III, c. 36 and 13 George III, c. 82, s. 5; see *Burns' Justice*, iv, pp. 220–5. A clause in the 1783 General Hull Act (23 George III, c. 55, s. xxxviii) officially adopted this policy in Hull when the mother's settlement was known, and the number of births in the House rose from about ten a year to an average of twenty-five for the years 1792–5; See Eden, iii, p. 838.

The number of people maintained by Charity Hall increased towards the end of the century. There were 276 inmates in 1792 and about a thousand people receiving outdoor relief.[1] In the hard winter of 1795–6 the number of inmates rose to 345, and there were still 284 in June 1796.[2] By then the number of men, women and children receiving outdoor relief had reached 2,600, and the Corporation had begun its drastic action to get rid of unsettled paupers. The inmates spent most of their time spinning wool and picking oakum, but the conditions, according to one observer, were reasonably good:[3]

> The children are taught to read in the house, by the persons qualified to instruct them. At stated times on the week days, prayers are read to all who are able to attend, and on Sundays they all attend divine service in Trinity Church, forenoon and afternoon. The internal affairs of the house are conducted with the greatest regularity; provisions are more plentiful, and of better quality than in most other poor houses, and care taken that no article is wasted. . . . The bed cloathes are frequently well aired, all the beds taken down once every year; in every room all is neat, and shews the attention of those who superintend the affairs of this house; so that it may be justly affirmed, the poor here live as comfortably as those in any other house of the like description wheresoever.

The inmates, of course, may have had other ideas. The contemporary observers of the Hull scene in the eighteenth century unanimously praised everything they saw; but we cannot be sure that they saw—or wanted to see—everything there was to see!

Next door to the Charity Hall was the House of Correction that fitted the usual description of a workhouse. Vagrants were sent there pending removal, and so were constant offenders who would not work. It was, as its name implies, used for semi-legal punishment of petty criminals and social misfits: '. . . Aundall having had a Second Bastard child be sent to the House of Correction'.[4] (The Bench supported bastards, but strongly objected to more than one per mother.) Since it was a pretty unpleasant place, several prominent citizens were already campaigning for its improvement at the end of the century.

Charity Hall was the official home of Hull's poor, but the Bench also controlled old people's homes, founded by private benefaction, for about a hundred residents in the second half of the century. The

[1] Tickell, p. 776. [2] Eden, iii, 837. [3] Tickell, p. 777.
[4] BB viii, 479.

oldest was the Charterhouse, which had a large income from land in and around Hull, but maintained only thirty people. A rather sordid wrangle between the Bench and the Master to force the latter to admit more people ended in an eleven-year law suit.[1] The next master—the brother-in-law of Alderman Joseph Sykes—rebuilt the House in 1780 for forty-four inmates who were each allowed 3*s.* 6*d.* per week. Smaller 'hospitals' included Gregg's, Harrison's, Weaver's, Ratcliff's, Gee's and Lister's, which between them accommodated forty-eight women and six men. An eighth home, Watson's, with twenty rooms, was in the gift of Trinity House.

Decayed seamen and their widows and children were the concern of Trinity House. Since 1457 they had had a house for pensioners, containing twenty-eight rooms. The present building in Trinity House Lane was erected in 1753 'for the reception and comfort of decayed seamen who have been admitted younger brethren of that fraternity; but principally at present, and for many years past, for the widows of such seamen after they had attained the age of 50 years'.[2] The new building had rooms for thirty-two pensioners —and was extended when the School was built—but outdoor relief was far more important than the alms-house. In 1728 Trinity House agreed to make an allowance of one shilling per person and sixpence or ninepence per child (according to age), 'towards the maintenance of such poor Seamen, their Widows and Children (who have legal settlement in . . . Hull) as should apply to the Governor and Guardians of the . . . Workhouse for admittance into the same'.[3] Trinity House spent no less than £650 on outdoor relief

[1] See J. Cook, *The History of God's House of Hull, Commonly Called the Charterhouse* (Hull, 1882), *passim.* The income of the Charterhouse rose from £249 in 1716 to £422 in 1752 and £850 in 1794. The Master, John Clarke, wished to use the surplus to raise his own salary from £20 to £50, and the inmates' allowance from 1*s.* 4*d.* to 2*s.*; the Bench wished to allow inmates 1*s.* 6*d.* and admit as many as funds would allow. It cost over £1,000 in legal fees before the Bench agreed to 30 inmates receiving 3*s.*, and the master's salary was increased to £100!

[2] Tickell, p. 736. A clause in the Hull Poor Law (9/10 William III, c. 47) ordering all charitable donations in the town to be handed over to the 'Corporation for the Poor', was repealed to save the rights of Trinity House to relieve its own poor (11 William III, c. 18, s. 8). For a general account of the House's charity, see A. Storey, *Trinity House of Kingston-upon-Hull* (Hull, 1967), chapter IV.

[3] The Agreement is *GH* MS D936(B). The Corporation received £18.9*s.* from Trinity House during the period Ladyday 1728–31; Eden, iii, 834.

in 1745,[1] but unfortunately we do not know if this amount was exceptional.

Besides its considerable income from land, donations and shipping dues, Trinity House also collected superannuation money from Hull seamen. As early as 1640 they were authorised 'not only . . . to collect . . . of the seamen, belonging to the port and members of the said Trinity House . . . all such moneys as they are to pay, according to his Majesty's proclamation, but also to distribute the said monies so collected, to the poor, maimed and shipwrecked seamen, their widows and children'.[2] After 1747 the Seamen's Sixpences levied in Hull were used—at least partly—for local relief work,[3] and in 1781 Trinity House opened a Merchant Seamen's Hospital in Whitefriargate 'for the reception of Seamen and their wives, under an act called the Sixpenny Act, which is for the relief and support of maimed and disabled seamen, and the widows and children of such as shall be killed or drowned in the merchant service'.[4] Relief work by Trinity House was, of course, the most obvious recognition of the seasonal nature of employment in Hull: seamen were compelled to save for the rainy days, and their employers were taxed for the same purpose.

The chief obstacle to greater activity by the Bench was lack of money. There was no general rate to cover all aspects of local government. The Bench, like the monarchy of old, was expected to 'live of its own', with supplementary rates for particular purposes such as lighting, cleansing and poor relief. Fortunately the traditional income of the Corporation increased with the prosperity of the port. Water bailiff dues were levied 'from the time of the contrary of which the memory of man does not exist' on all goods landed within the port of Hull. Over the years, however, the dues had come to be levied only on 'Unfreemen of this town', and consequently their value was in no way related to the value of Hull's total trade. The threat of a claim for dues was, in fact, occasionally used to compel reluctant merchants to take up their expensive freedoms. However, the total water bailiff dues rose fairly rapidly in

[1] Tickell, p. 733.

[2] Duke of Northumberland to Trinity House, 22 Apr 1640, quoted in Tickell, pp. 714–15.

[3] See R. Davis, 'Seamen's Sixpences: An Index of Commercial Activity, 1697–1828', in *Economica*, (Nov 1956), pp. 329–30.

[4] Hadley, p. 756.

the second half of the century—having averaged less than 1730 and 1750—until they reached £990 for the years 1785–9 and £1,290 for 1790–4.[1] An assortment of other tolls, about which there is no adequate information, were probably worth no more than £100 per annum.[2]

A second source of income was the Corporation's extensive and varied property. All manner of people lived in Corporation houses, Alderman Perrott paying £44 per annum for his in the forties.[3] Rents were raised as houses and warehouses appreciated in value, especially after repairs or alterations, when the Bench expected an increase of 1*s.* 6*d.* for every pound spent.[4] With the expenses of government growing in the second half of the century, the Bench began raising rents and disposing of property. The rent of the Custom House went up from £36 to £60 in 1757, and the Collector's appeal (made, according to custom, at the Bench's Quarter Sessions) was apparently rejected.[5] To secure speedier payment, and facilitate rebuilding, the Bench ordered in 1782 'that all Corporation tenants give Bonds to quit their tenements at 6 months notice if necessary'.[6] There is no clear indication of the value of Corporation property in the eighteenth century, but it must have been many hundreds of pounds per annum; it was £4,000 per annum in the eighteen-thirties.

A third source of income was fines. The largest were imposed for refusal to serve as alderman, sheriff or chamberlain, and had the force of law following a test case against William Crowle in 1700.[7] There was, however, a limit to the number of men who could pay this primitive wealth tax in any particular year, and a steadier and perhaps more reliable income came from fines for freedoms, which were purchased for a few pounds by a common seaman and a hundred or more by a young merchant. The Bench also had an income from its magisterial activities. Fines were the commonest form of punishment for all manner of offences: ten pounds was paid by Richard Terry when one of his ships damaged North Bridge (repairs cost only £6. 5*s.* 6*d.*), and ten pounds by one Newlove, 'for keeping a Bawdy house'.

[1] Town's Husband's Cash Books, *passim*.

[2] Woolhouse dues were worth up to £50 per annum, but appear to have ceased around 1758; there was a 'coal skep' worth about £30 in the last quarter of the century; and there were small market tolls and sundries.

[3] BB ix, 6. [4] See, for example, BB ix, 128 (12 Jan 1749).

[5] HCLB, C–B, 22 Apr 1757. [6] BB ix, 568. [7] BB viii, 465f.

The normal income of the Corporation ceased to cover its expenditure towards the end of the century, when the Bench spent a great deal of money in its fight for a second dock and in subsidising that dock. Sporadic sales of property had begun (usually connected with redevelopment), but on the whole the Bench preferred to borrow money on the security of dues and rents. After 1780 Corporation Bonds were issued for sums ranging from £200 to £1,500 borrowed from individuals and from semi-public bodies such as Charity Hall and the Benevolent Societies.[1] They also sold Annuities, which were just becoming popular. On 5 January 1785, for example, the Common Seal was affixed to a bond 'for securing the payment of an Annuity of £62. 10*s.* to John Johnson of Kingston-upon-Hull Landwaiter and Ann his wife during their joint lives and the survivor during his or her natural life payable quarterly in consideration of £500 paid by the said John Johnson into the hands of the Treasurer . . .',[2] and in March of that year the Mayor was empowered to contract Annuities at his own discretion 'on behalf of the Corporation a greeable to Price's Calculations not exceeding the amount or the value of £1,000'.[3]

Although the Bench performed many of the functions of modern local government, it did so with a certain degree of reluctance. The age of municipal enterprise had not yet begun and, with no firm precedents, the Aldermen were diffident about assuming new responsibilities. They were caught, like so many authorities before and since, in the crisis when new and pressing needs met entrenched and obsolete administrative procedures. At one time they acquired new powers or made far-reaching plans—such as those for building a municipal dock; at another they delegated their powers and abandoned their plans. They assumed control over many aspects of town life in order to secure uniformity and orderly development; but they had no administrative machinery capable of organising and directing the daily routine of the town. A paid local government service was still a thing of the distant future—although Hull had moved part of the way towards it—and the Bench were compelled to delegate some of their powers to elected or voluntary officials.

There were drawbacks to the system, as the Webbs eloquently

[1] Some of these bonds ran for very long periods. Those for £600 each to the Provident Brotherhood and the Unanimous Society signed in 1795 (BB x, 233) were not cancelled until 1823 (*GH* Box 115, 41(A)).

[2] BB ix, 627.

[3] BB ix, 630.

pointed out. But, at least in Hull, it got things done, and it would be more realistic to consider the total provision of services, by whatever body, than to allow credit only for those directly administered by members of the Bench. By delegating power the Bench actually increased the number of merchants who took part in the government of the town, and we may justifiably assume that the efficiency of local government was increased, rather than diminished, by their action. The total environment thus created was, by the standards of the time, one of which the Bench and all concerned might be reasonably proud—as, indeed, they were.

Appendix 1

THE NUMBER AND TONNAGE OF SHIPS EMPLOYED IN THE INLAND NAVIGATION, *c.* 1805

	From To	*Miles*	*No.*	*Tons*	*Crew*	
ver Humber	Hull–Skitter Ferry	5	2	83	4	(1 Ferry)
	Hull–Stallingborough	12	1	22	2	(Passenger)
	Hull–Grimsby	20	2	72	4	
	Hull–Louth	40	5	238	12	
	Hull–Paull	8	4	120	9	(Lighters)
	Hull–Patrington	18	3	72	6	
	Hull–Spurn	21	25	937	50	(Lighters)
ver Hull	Hull–Beverley	12	2	71	3	
	Hull–Leven	12	1	22	2	
	Hull–Foston Mills	20	3	111	5	
	Hull–Frodingham	20	2	85	4	
	Hull–Driffield	30	3	124	6	
ver Humber	Hull–Barrow-on-Humber	3	1	25	2	(Passenger)
	Hull–Barton-on-Humber	7	5	160	13	(,,)
	Hessle–Barton-on-Humber	2	2	75	5	(,,)
	Hull–Winteringham	13	6	144	11	(1 ,,)
	Hull–Whitton	15	1	25	2	
	Hull–Garthorpe	25	1	34	2	(,,)
ver Trent	Hull–Burton Stather	25	1	30	2	(,,)
	Hull–Stockwith	34	5	250	12	
	Hull–Gainsborough	50	36	1868	79	
	Ferriby–Hull–Gainsborough	50	1	30	2	(,,)
	Hull–Burringham–Gainsborough	50	2	65	4	
ver Humber	Hull–Brough	15	3	62	6	(,,)
	Winteringham–Brough	3	1	13	2	(,,)
arket Weighton Navigation	Hull–New Village	20	2	84	4	
	Hull–Market Weighton	30	5	157	10	
	Hull–Whitgift	22	1	33	2	
ver Don	Hull–Reed Ness	25	3	70	6	(1 ,,)
	Hull–Thorne	50	25	609	55	
	Hull–Doncaster	60	10	478	19	
	Hull–Greasbrough	70	4	191	8	
	Hull–Rotherham	70	18	821	35	
	Hull–Tinsley	70	12	561	25	
	Hull–Sheffield	73	2	91	4	
ivers Aire & Calder & Tributaries	Hull–Howden	24	4	173	9	
	Hull–Rawcliffe	25	3	88	6	
	Hull–Knottingley	80	24	1076	51	
	Hull–Brotherton	80	2	90	5	
	Hull–Castleford	85	3	137	8	

	From To	*Miles*	*No.*	*Tons.*	*Crew*
	Hull–Leeds	100	58	2602	123
	Driffield–Hull–Leeds	130	1	44	2
	Beverley–Hull–Leeds	112	14	615	28
	Grimsby–Hull–Leeds	116	1	46	4
	Brigg–Hull–Leeds	90	1	45	2
	Hull–Bradford	120	3	137	8
	Hull–Skipton	130	1	46	2
	Hull–Wakefield	100	39	1727	88
	Beverley–Hull–Wakefield	112	2	88	4
	Ferriby–Hull–Wakefield	100	1	45	2
	Satmarsh–Wakefield	50	1	46	2
	Hull–Elland	120	1	42	2
	Hull–Halifax	122	10	452	22
	Malton–Hull–Halifax	90	1	42	2
	Hull–Huddersfield	120	2	87	4
River Derwent	Hull–Stamford Bridge	65	8	338	18
	Hull–Malton	80	5	210	12
River Ouse and Tributaries	Hull–Selby	70	17	884	50
	Hull–Tadcaster	100	2	97	4
	Hull–York	100	5	237	11
	Hull–Boroughbridge	114	6	307	14
	Hull–Ripon	100	1	45	2

Note: This manuscript appears to be an extract from the Hull Shipping Registers, which a now lost. It does not represent the number of vessels engaged in inland transpo lighters and barges were not registered unless (like those going to Paull and Spurn f ballast cobbles) they sailed on the Humber estuary. But it does give an indication of t number of larger craft that regularly sailed up-river from Hull. The mileage figures a very approximate, and the grosser errors have been adjusted. That for Malton–Hu Halifax, which is obviously wrong, has been left because it is not clear whether t error is in the voyage or the mileage.

Source: GH MS M445.

Appendix 2

PRINCIPAL IMPORTS AT HULL, SAMPLE YEARS 1702–1807

	1702	*1717*	*1728*	*1737*	*1751*	*1758*	*1768*	*1783*	*Average 1790–2*	*Average 1799–1802*	*Average 1803–7*
Fir Timber (loads)	0	79	17	25	1,343	1,135	8,260	6,928	20,917	17,895	16,860
Deals (hundreds)	1,498	1,070	1,634	2,433	2,293	2,805	2,520	3,224	5,781	4,787	4,513
Battens (hundreds)	0	0	187	215	305	294	310	774	792	347	243
Pipe Staves (hundreds)	1,205	416	184	1,075	1,935	1,050	1,833	863	3,408	3,817	4,058
Pailing Boards (hundreds)	0	0	300	451	284	134	116	211	52	153	200
Single Uffers (hundreds)	0	0	190	258	195	95	100	18	48	26	68
Cork (cwt.)	0	145	60	617	529	0	389	1,410	1,423	2,368	2,245
Iron (tons)	2,356	353	2,581	3,964	5,260	6,058	8,027	7,879	12,525	8,848	7,572
Old Iron (tons)	0	141	17	40	49	429	910	796	n.a.	n.a.	n.a.
Battry (tons)	119	116	112	0	204	0	0	0	n.a.	n.a.	n.a.
Steel (cwt.)	55	138	668	339	193	254	166	99	n.a.	n.a.	n.a.
Copper (cwt.)	0	12	35	51	17	0	0	0	n.a.	n.a.	n.a.
Tinned Plates (No.)	27,450	166,850	57,150	56,700	2,509	0	0	0	n.a.	n.a.	n.a.
Tinned Plates Double (No.)		3,600	2,700	3,150	0	0	0	0	n.a.	n.a.	n.a.
Spinning Wheels	0	786	806	0	2,631	0	1,131	0	n.a.	n.a.	n.a.
Melting Pots	0	3,100	700	1,690	5,335	0	6,424	2,197	n.a.	n.a.	n.a.
Hemp (cwt.)	838	3,435	5,601	18,132	27,685	4,910	15,524	26,974	49,091	49,561	58,545
Tow (cwt.)	0	0	0	0	78	0	1,826	1,826	2,921	9,517	4,042
Flax (cwt.)	1,679	10,168	17,203	29,758	32,938	19,905	39,933	45,739	n.a.	n.a.	n.a.
Raw Dutch Linen Yarn (lb.)	37,544	233,912	48,642	117,428	274,641	839,274	2,058,810	1,842,882	n.a.	n.a.	n.a.
Spruce Linen Yarn (lb.)	0	49,168	8,344	72,180	418,863	1,002,723	1,239,412	3,590,745	n.a.	n.a.	n.a.
Estridge Wool (lb.)	0	13,664	2,156	3,812	1,924	0	10,737	13,264	n.a.	n.a.	n.a.

	1702	1717	1728	1737	1751	1758	1768	1783	Average 1790–2	Average 1799–1802	Average 1803–7
Inkle (lb.)	0	2,065	807	850	7,893	51,798	7,105	41	n.a.	n.a.	n.a.
Narrow Holland & German Linen (hundred ells)	29	341	517	424	705	223	521	23	74	475	147
Narrow Russian Linen (c. ells)	0	17	121	0	1,050	183	253	1,260	212	451	1,664
Vittry Canvas (c. ells)	38	108	117	69	14	5	0	0	0	0	0
Spruce Canvas (c. ells)	99	2,399	1,458	4,479	8,438	5,943	6,658	5,408	2,541	867	703
Hessian Canvas (c. ells)	0	14	40	39	206	182	692	1,914	2,824	315	221
Cotton Wool (lb.)	0	0	0	0	2,452	0	5,196	409,604	827,428	607,801	389,534
Rags for papermaking (cwt.)	0	0	0	0	0	215	2,893	5,127	n.a.	n.a.	n.a.
Tarras (barrels)	0	0	29	0	42	0	420	166	n.a.	n.a.	n.a.
Bristles (doz. lb.)	0	0	0	0	1,350	0		10,151	17,240	34,884	32,189
Tar (lasts)	96	229	80	45	966	100	1,493	585	1,837	899	1,572
Turpentine (cwt.)	0	0	0	76	351	0	7,587	18,943	7,919	14,369	21,731
Linseed (bushels)	0	0	1,902	2,856	29,770	18,880	46,339	66,661	n.a.	n.a.	n.a.
Smalts (lb.)	0	4,879	391	0	24,530	44,579	124,574	226,206	125,616	98,314	140,205
Madder (cwt.)	583	587	532	0	2,096	1,900	3,010	6,095	n.a.	n.a.	n.a.
Sumack (cwt.)	0	759	35	0	200	0	427	413	n.a.	n.a.	n.a.
Potash (lb.)	0	110,598	21,848	12,084	60,107	244,431	10,747	437,920	n.a.	n.a.	n.a.
Arsenic (lb.)	0	576	224	0	472	0	9,586	12,400	n.a.	n.a.	n.a.
Barilla (cwt.)	0	0	0	0	0	0	10	334	1,453	4,235	385
Oranges	29,700	409,600	245,800	0	121,800	0	109,000	131,500	n.a.	n.a.	n.a.
Rice (cwt.)	0	0	0	708	0	0	10	0	893	3,387	6,097
Sugar (cwt.)	0	0	0	753	0	0	0	0	1,031	4,030	2,660
Tobacco (lb.)	42,615				138,603	588,041			596,756	427,728	246,575
Geneva (galls)								12,998	75,069	165,222	100,453
Rum (galls)			0		13,980			0	18,791	22,012	18,071
Brandy (galls)			2,868	3,874	2,677			34,775	86,405	89,457	86,330
Wine: Port			171,852		149,133			261,385			
Spanish			36,790	308,406	41,749			29,640	511,308	646,632	525,765
Rhenish			[illegible]		[illegible]			[illegible]			

Appendix 3

SHIPS ENTERING HULL FROM INDIVIDUAL COUNTRIES,
SAMPLE YEARS, 1699–1804

From	*1699*	*1717*	*1728*	*1737*	*1751*	*1758*	*1766*	*1767*	*1768*	*1769*	*1770*	*1771*	*1772*	*1783*	*1789*	*1790*	*1796*	*1802*	*1803*	*1804*
Norway		33	37	40	54	28	42	40	38	43	33	27	34	6	22	16	7	28	41	55
Sweden		3	32	49	29	47	27	24	38	27	24	29	29	36	38	37	39	83	114	41
Finland		0	0	0	0	0	5	8	6	1	4	4	2	2	0	0	0	12	11	3
Russia	105	11	19	38	51	26	50	66	61	82	95	86	64	67	106	109	165	116	189	61
Poland		4	31	8	5	11	9	20	18	14	11	17	14	7	6	15	15	41	56	29
Prussia		11	6	12	14	9	19	42	44	23	35	31	38	68	65	82	81	153	136	110
Germany	35	14	12	16	23	17	24	29	22	27	32	34	25	35	30	35	74	116	19	6
Holland		29	61	36	29	25	32	38	38	38	41	39	38	10	61	66	3	73	32	42
Flanders	0	4	6	3	2	0	5	3	4	4	2	3	6	0	16	15	0	0	0	0
France	6	0	1	7	7	0	5	5	5	4	9	4	3	1	46	39	0	11	11	3
Spain	10	2	3	14	11	2	13	6	5	5	4	5	2	0	3	4	5	11	17	8
Portugal		12	10	11	14	5	12	11	14	13	11	8	12	0	6	14	3	11	20	12
Italy	0	0	0	1	1	0	4	2	0	1	3	3	4	1	1	6	3	0	0	0
Greece	0	0	0	0	0	0	0	0	0	0	0	0	0	0	0	0	0	4	5	2
Ireland	0	0	0	0	0	0	0	0	0	0	0	0	0	0	0	0	0	8	4	8
America	1	1	1	3	15	14	8	14	23	17	13	13	15	0	11	16	0	27	32	19
Misc.	4	0	5	0	3	0	0	0	0	0	0	0	0	0	0	0	0	0	0	0
TOTAL	161	124	224	239	259	184	257	308	316	299	317	303	286	233	411	454	395	694	687	399

Source: Port Books.

Appendix 4

THE CHIEF FOREIGN PORTS FROM WHICH SHIPS ENTERED HULL, SAMPLE YEARS, 1717–1796

Ports of Origin	*1717*	*1728*	*1737*	*1751*	*1758*	*1768*	*1783*	*1796*
Gothenburg	3	20	27	15	18	9	6	4
Stockholm	0	12	18	8	14	11	6	2
Gefle	0	0	4	4	5	7	16	22
St Petersburg	2	2	7	18	11	28	33	106
Narva	0	6	11	17	4	9	12	8
Riga	9	11	20	12	11	19	11	31
Archangel	1	0	0	0	0	0	2	15
Danzig	4	31	8	5	11	16	6	15
Memel	4	3	2	1	0	22	32	57
Konigsberg	7	3	10	13	9	22	34	14
Hamburg	5	7	11	16	13	14	14	53
Bremen	9	5	5	7	4	8	3	15
Embden	0	0	0	0	0	0	18	46
Amsterdam	14	11	15	13	11	13	6	1
Rotterdam	15	48	17	16	12	8	2	2
Oporto	9	7	10	8	4	9	0	2

Note: Ships from Norway were entered as of 'Norway' at least until the sixties. Tønsberg and Fredrikshald were the chief ports supplying timber, followed by Christiania (Oslo).

Source: Port Books, 1717–83; 1796 from Accounts in *GH* Port Dues Box.

PRINCIPAL EXPORTS FROM HULL, SAMPLE YEARS 1702–83

	1702	*1717*	*1728*	*1737*	*1751*	*1758*	*1768*	*1783*
Dozens (pieces)	45,833	28,990	40,022	76,157	37,838	69,728	122,710	163,710
Kerseys (pieces)	108,267	68,474	40,297	37,083	13,500 +	33,378	33,399	13,340
Bayes (pieces)	46,487	31,114	22,076	52,221	12,000 +	44,040	70,232	134,600
Plains (pieces)	0	4	790	3,105	500	914	1,880	15,520
Shalloons (pieces)	0	0	400	0	4,485 +	18,400	28,956	17,810
Cotton Stuffs (pieces)	130	94	(1330 lb.)	(8052 lb.)	200	45	50,485	57,877
Cotton Velvets (pieces)	0	0	0	0	0	20	8,352	236,834
Hose (doz. pairs)	4,448	30,849	23,100	47,850	3,240	26,200	9,680	45,510
Leather (cwt.)	646	757	374	273	0	88	0	0
Lead (tons)	1,609	2,403	1,923	2,731	2,828	3,347	2,992	2,074
Lead Shot (cwt.)	0	0	0	0	2,435	0	4,854	2,990
Red Lead (cwt.)	1,137	1,848	11,623	19,158	?	24,322	21,910	81,119
White Lead (cwt.)	0	0	0	1,120	75	735	?	12,903
Ironmongery (tons)	1	7	89	203	850 +	904	2,267	4,676
Manufactured Iron (cwt.)	0	9	15	0	900	0	2,877	12,750
Tinplates	0	0	0	0	57,000	3,375	516,528	5,654,000
Earthenware (pieces)	0	0	0	15,850	645,215 +	449,970	1,624,700	13,287,000
Bricks	162,000	12,000	395,000	44,000	?	60,000	?	480,000
Tobacco Pipes (gross)	3,941	0	130	667	0	1,610	0	0
Wheat (quarters)	10,123	977	0	23,080	36,045	0	0	0
Barley (quarters)	1,745	539	0	71	100	0	0	0
Rye (quarters)	2,005	30	0	0	6,386	0	0	0
Malt (quarters)	2,705	1,214	4	834	997	0	0	0
Butter (firkins)	785	2,283	10	0	0	0	0	0
Ale (tuns)	3	4	14	40	?	?	?	4,593
Linseed Cakes	0	145,700	83,000	407,000	154,000	(52 tons)		
Alum (cwt.)	0	0	0	0	0	0	0	649
Copperas (cwt.)	0	0	0	0	0	3,100	?	2,018
Vitriol (cwt.)	0	0	0	0	0	0	0	12,520

Appendix 6

THE OVERSEAS CORN TRADE, SAMPLE YEARS, 1759–99[1]
(*Quarters*)

	EXPORTS					IMPORTS				
	Wheat	*Flour*	*Rye*	*Barley*	*Oats*	*Wheat*	*Flour*	*Rye*	*Barley*	*Oats*
1759	10,258	194	1,895	0	0	0	0	0	0	0
1760	24,065	532	3,451	0	0	0	0	0	0	0
1761	34,269	126	8,184	2,983	0	0	0	0	0	0
1762	10,716	160	3,806	11,745	0	0	0	0	0	0
1763	3,120	298	21	0	0	0	0	0	0	0
1764	10,259	0	272	0	0	0	0	0	0	0
1765	1,626	162	359	26	0	0	0	0	0	0
1766	3,754	0	0	0	0	0	0	0	0	0
1775	10	0	0	0	62	4,842	50	5,034	19,483	734
1776	248	41	30	0	0	0	0	0	1,269	42
1777	540	0	5	5	5	90	0	0	0	202
1778	90	0	0	0	0	0	0	0	0	105
1779	750	31	95	0	0	0	0	0	0	149
1780	548	167	0	0	0	1	0	0	0	83
1781	0	37	0	122	25	0	344	0	0	0
1782	0	0	0	0	319	0	0	0	525	50
1783	0	0	0	0	0	15,671	0	4,887	5,013	2,587
1792	31,090	9,255	0	0	0	0	0	0	0	0
1793	0	0	0	0	0	6,602	0	0	511	665
1794	84	0	0	0	0	n.a.	n.a.	n.a.	n.a.	n.a.
1795	0	0	0	0	0	n.a.	n.a.	n.a.	n.a.	n.a.
1796	0	0	0	0	0	*c.* 22,600	0	*c.* 8,786	*c.* 1,655	*c.* 4,264
1797	0	0	0	0	0	n.a.	n.a.	n.a.	n.a.	n.a.
1798	0	200	0	0	0	n.a.	n.a.	n.a.	n.a.	n.a.
1799	498	1,135	0	0	0	n.a.	n.a.	n.a.	n.a.	n.a.

[1] *Sources:* 1759–66 in HCLB, C–B, passim; 1775–82 in HCLB, C–B, 21 Feb 1783; 1783 in *PRO* E190/385/3; 1792 in HCLB,

Appendix 7

SHIPS CLEARING FROM HULL FOR INDIVIDUAL COUNTRIES, SAMPLE YEARS, 1699–1804

To	*1699*	*1717*	*1728*	*1737*	*1751*	*1758*	*1766*	*1767*	*1768*	*1769*	*1770*	*1771*	*1772*	*1783*	*1789*	*1790*	*1802*	*1803*	*1804*
Norway		19	14	11	8	3	7	3	6	2	1	2	1	1	1	1	3	36	81
Sweden		0	25	4	6	7	5	3	5	5	5	8	5	4	2	3	1	1	0
Russia	60	12	14	9	7	26	22	25	28	32	32	36	27	50	48	49	46	46	47
Poland		2	7	7	6	10	10	13	14	12	7	9	13	0	6	13	12	13	20
Prussia		2	0	1	5	4	16	15	14	7	10	8	8	42	19	20	17	61	82
Germany	0	19	16	19	14	25	19	20	17	21	22	21	15	7	40	45	104	55	31
Holland	56	51	36	38	17	34	28	27	28	29	33	30	32	0	49	49	69	14	17
Flanders	0	12	4	6	4	0	6	8	6	6	6	10	6	0	12	13	0	0	0
France	8	6	0	6	8	0	5	6	2	4	4	0	1	0	39	42	6	0	1
Spain	15	0	0	16	9	0	12	6	6	3	4	3	4	1	12	10	26	11	17
Portugal		5	8	26	14	6	10	9	11	8	7	8	8	0	13	10	24	12	22
Italy	0	0	2	9	12	4	7	3	3	4	9	8	8	0	11	12	0	0	0
Ireland	0	0	0	0	2	0	0	0	0	0	0	0	0	0	2	1	4	1	0
America	3	1	0	1	11	6	7	8	9	9	14	10	10	0	9	9	19	20	13
TOTAL	142	129	126	153	123	125	153	146	149	142	154	153	138	105	263	277	331	270	330

Source: Port Books.

Appendix 8

THE CHIEF PORTS FOR WHICH SHIPS CLEARED FROM HULL, SAMPLE YEARS, 1717–1783

Destination	*1717*	*1728*	*1737*	*1751*	*1758*	*1768*	*1783*
Gothenburg	0	16	3	2	0	1	1
Stockholm	0	9	1	3	5	3	3
St Petersburg	5	6	6	3	13	23	30
Riga	5	7	3	3	13	5	11
Danzig	2	7	7	6	10	13	1
Konigsberg	2	0	1	5	4	13	19
Hamburg	8	8	13	8	18	17	4
Bremen	11	8	6	5	7	5	3
Amsterdam	28	14	17	8	16	14	1
Rotterdam	23	19	18	9	15	11	2
Bruges	10	3	6	1	0	2	0
Ostend	2	1	0	3	0	4	5
Oporto	5	4	4	4	5	5	0
Lisbon	0	4	22	10	1	6	2
Cadiz	0	0	11	1	0	6	0
Leghorn	0	2	9	9	3	3	1

Source: Port Books.

Appendix 9

NNAGE OF FOREIGN-GOING SHIPPING ENTERING AND CLEARING AT HULL, AS AVAILABLE, 1709–1805

(Figures in italics represent British tonnage as a percentage of total tonnage)

	ENTERING			CLEARING			TOTAL		
	British		*Foreign*	*British*		*Foreign*	ENTERING	CLEARING	*Source*
09	3,190	*39*	4,900	3,370	*58*	2,410	8,090	5,780	(a)
10	n.a.		n.a.	5,200		1,960	n.a.	7,160	(b)
11	n.a.		n.a.	5,850		2,670	n.a.	8,520	(b)
12	n.a.		n.a.	6,275		1,840	n.a.	8,115	(b)
13	n.a.		n.a.	11,222		880	n.a.	12,102	(b)
14	n.a.		n.a.	11,750		1,146	n.a.	12,896	(b)
15	n.a.		n.a.	9,600		616	n.a.	10,216	(c)
16	10,335	*98*	230	7,605	*89*	966	10,565	8,571	(a)
				8,165		846		9,011	(c)
17	n.a.		n.a.	7,954		970	n.a.	8,924	(c)
23	10,710	*97*	295	6,990	*99*	60	11,005	7,050	(a)
30	11,750	*94*	690	8,038	*98*	130	12,440	8,168	(a)
37	18,688	*98*	320	9,245	*100*	0	19,008	9,245	(a)
44	8,920	*79*	2,408	8,055	*88*	1,130	11,328	9,185	(a)
51	21,298	*90*	2,300	15,264	*97*	530	23,598	15,794	(a)
58	12,203	*59*	8,510	8,938	*73*	3,320	20,713	12,258	(a)
65	29,321	*86*	4,690	14,526	*91*	1,400	34,011	15,926	(a)
66	27,180	*86*	4,570	15,050		1,560	31,750	16,610	(d)
67	37,096	*88*	4,910	14,707		1,560	42,006	16,267	(d)
68	35,380	*87*	5,410	15,627		1,580	40,790	17,207	(d)
69	34,821	*86*	5,810	16,361		1,830	40,631	18,191	(d)
70	41,233	*89*	5,242	17,835		1,962	46,475	19,795	(d)
71	38,149	*87*	5,842	17,130		1,545	43,991	18,675	(d)
'72	*40,594	*89*	4,840	16,951	*92*	1,410	45,434	18,361	(d)
	*39,099		4,840	n.a.		n.a.	43,939	n.a.	(e)
	*39,379		4,940	16,951		1,410	44,417	18,361	(a)
'73	*42,368		5,810	n.a.		n.a.	48,178	n.a.	(e)
	*43,118	*88*	5,810	n.a.		n.a.	48,928	n.a.	(f)
'74	*43,378		6,490	n.a.		n.a.	49,868	n.a.	(e)
	*43,758	*87*	6,610	n.a.		n.a.	50,368	n.a.	(f)
'75	*46,607		5,290	n.a.		n.a.	51,897	n.a.	(e)
	*46,707	*90*	5,443	n.a.		n.a.	52,150	n.a.	(f)
'76	*37,628		8,705	n.a.		n.a.	46,333	n.a.	(e)
	*38,228	*82*	8,705	n.a.		n.a.	46,933	n.a.	(f)
'77	*36,713		10,975	n.a.		n.a.	47,688	n.a.	(e)
	*35,667	*74*	12,675	n.a.		n.a.	48,342	n.a.	(f)

	ENTERING			CLEARING			TOTAL		
	British		*Foreign*	*British*		*Foreign*	ENTERING	CLEARING	*Sour*
1778	*35,367		12,515	n.a.		n.a.	47,882	n.a.	(e
	*37,633	*77*	11,435	n.a.		n.a.	49,068	n.a.	(f
1779	*22,989	*57*	17,590	14,082	*60*	9,507	40,579	23,589	(a
	*22,689	*56*	17,590	n.a.		n.a.	40,279	n.a.	(e
1780	25,259	*66*	13,165	n.a.		n.a.	38,424	n.a.	(f
1781	27,070	*63*	16,198	n.a.		n.a.	43,268	n.a.	(f
1787	80,429	*87*	11,691	42,832	*93*	3,275	92,120	46,107	(g
1788	n.a.		n.a.	n.a.		n.a.	90,111	n.a.	(h
1789	*76,073	*86*	12,946	45,893	*89*	5,442	*89,019	51,335	(i)
	* n.a.		n.a.	n.a.		n.a.	*91,497	n.a.	(h
1790	*80,705	*84*	15,257	44,100	*86*	6,960	*95,962	51,060	(i)
	* n.a.		n.a.	n.a.		n.a.	*97,158	n.a.	(h
1791	96,176	*84*	18,843	46,237	*87*	6,805	*115,019 *119,840	53,042	(i) (h
1792	n.a.		n.a.	n.a.		n.a.	135,346	n.a.	(h
1800	n.a.		n.a.	n.a.		n.a.	122,492	43,251	(j)
1805	n.a.		n.a.	n.a.		n.a.	119,832	52,010	(j)

Note: These figures are drawn from a number of different sources and are therefore not, strictly speaking, comparable. Although they are based ultimately on Customs' returns (except (h)), they generally differ when two or more sources are available for the same year. One simple explanation of the difference may be errors in transcription (e.g. British ships entering 1775 or 1779) or addition. It is also possible that some clerks included while others excluded fractional parts of a ton. There would seem to be no difference in the criteria involved in the compilations (the differences are too small to involve the whaling fleet), but it is possible that some sources include and others exclude ships that had called first at another British port before arriving in Hull. That *could* explain the fact that figures from Customs source are lower than from Dock Company source. (On the other hand, Dock Duties were charged on *measured tonnage*, whereas masters would report *assessed tonnage* to the Customs at least until 1788.) Whatever the reason for the differences, they are so slight that they do not invalidate general conclusions. A few hundred tons—or even a couple of thousand—make little difference to the clear trend that emerges. It remains true, as always, that the change in tonnage measurement in 1786–8 makes it impossible to make more than general comparisons between figures before and after that date.

Sources: (a) *BM* Add. MS 11256, f. 19.
(b) *PRO* CO 338–18.
(c) *PRO* CO 390–8.
(d) *GH* Port Dues Box, Loose Paper.
(e) HCLB, C–B, Jan 1781.
(f) Add. MS 11255, f. 16.
(g) HCLB, C–B, 2 Sep 1787.

(h) Tickell, p. 872. These figures are extracted from Dock Company returns. The surviving Dock Company papers do not contain details of foreign and coasting vessels.

(i) *PRO* Customs 17/11–13. The other ledgers in this series do not include repeated voyages.

(j) *Report of the Commissioners on Municipal Boroughs, 1835, vol. XXV*, p. 1573.

Appendix 10

THE NUMBER AND TONNAGE OF SHIPS PAYING DOCK DUTIES AT HULL, 1775–1805

	No.	*Tons*		*No.*	*Tons*
1775	1,012	109,491	1790	1,270	156,315
1776	946	102,791	1791	1,437	181,547
1777	889	97,276	1792	1,522	201,789
1778	864	100,772	1793	1,390	183,403
1779	811	88,778	1794	1,246	147,799
1780	833	88,409	1795	1,323	150,536
1781	878	91,138	1796	1,401	237,946
1782	858	86,408	1797	1,264	213,848
1783	956	104,476	1798	1,268	162,576
1784	902	119,454	1799	1,272	152,825
1785	946	117,743	1800	1,678	198,175
1786	1,050	132,108	1801	1,721	191,180
1787	1,124	144,183	1802	1,619	210,249
1788	1,054	139,204	1803	1,578	208,521
1789	1,150	143,331	1804	1,384	170,964
			1805	1,434	174,875

Source: *Hull Dock Office*, 'Huffam's Book', *passim.*

Appendix 11

SEAMEN'S SIXPENCE PAYMENTS IN HULL, 1735–1814 (FIVE-YEARLY AVERAGES)

(Figures in brackets are the number of years for which records are available)

Years		*Average*	*Seamen/Months*
1735–9	(4)	£96·8	3,872
1740–4	(4)	85·5	3,420
1745–9	(2)	123·0	4,920
1750–4	(3)	214·0	8,560
1755–9	(2)	277·0	11,080
1760–4	(3)	164·3	6,572
1765–9	(5)	251·8	10,072
1770–4	(4)	302·3	12,092
1775–9	(5)	278·4	11,136
1780–4	(5)	261·6	10,464
1785–9	(5)	367·4	14,696
1790–4	(5)	404·6	16,184
1795–9	(5)	373·2	14,928
1800–4	(5)	459·4	18,376
1805–9	(5)	452·8	18,112
1810–14	(4)	484·0	19,360

Note: Seamen's Sixpence returns cannot be used to show the true annual employment of seamen in the port, since there was no strict annual account. Five-yearly averages, allowing for inevitable mistakes, provide a useful rough indication of trend. The figures for 1780–94, for instance, are corroborative evidence that the tonnage increase of the eighties was more than simple registration changes.

Source: *PRO* Admiralty 68, *passim*. I owe these figures to Professor Ralph Davis.

Appendix 12

COASTERS ENTERING FROM AND CLEARING FOR INDIVIDUAL PORTS, 1703/4–96

	1703–4		*1706*		*1728*		*1737*		*1758*		*1768*		*1775*		*1783*		*1796*	
ENGLISH OUTPORTS	*From*	*For*	*From*	*For*	*From*	*For*	*From*	*For*	*From*	*For*	*From*	*For*	*Form*	*For*	*From*	*For*	*From*	*For*
Berwick	0	0	1	0	7	0	4	0	2	2	1	0	6	0	3	4	14	8
Alnmouth	0	0	0	0	6	0	0	0	1	1	2	4	3	3	1	0	17	5
Blyth	2	0	0	0	6	0	2	1	1	3	3	2	0	1	1	1	0	2
Seaton	0	0	1	0	0	0	0	0	0	0	0	0	0	0	0	0	0	0
Cullercoats	0	0	1	0	0	0	0	0	0	0	0	0	0	0	0	0	0	0
Shields	0	0	0	0	0	0	0	0	0	0	0	0	0	1	0	0	0	0
Newcastle	59	27	42	22	111	5	94	75	59	86	44	47	51	52	43	85	53	80
Sunderland	58	8	71	1	138	4	129	66	45	61	28	24	26	18	17	40	29	36
Hartlepool	0	0	0	0	0	0	0	0	0	0	0	0	3	2	0	1	0	0
Stockton	3	2	0	0	1	0	1	11	5	16	11	20	10	10	4	6	4	1
Stockton & Sunderland	0	0	0	0	0	0	0	0	0	0	0	0	0	1	0	0	0	0
Whitby	0	14	0	8	0	2	0	18	20	42	15	41	20	76	31	103	50	81
,, & Stockton	0	0	0	0	0	0	0	0	0	0	0	0	0	5	0	0	0	0
,, & Sunderland	0	0	0	0	0	0	0	0	0	0	0	0	0	7	0	0	0	0
,, & Newcastle	0	0	0	0	0	0	0	0	0	0	0	0	0	2	0	0	0	0
Scarborough	0	4	0	3	0	1	1	23	11	15	10	8	9	11	7	11	2	4
,, & Whitby	0	0	0	0	0	0	0	0	0	0	0	0	0	5	0	0	0	0
,, & Stockton	0	0	0	0	0	0	0	0	0	0	0	0	0	3	0	0	0	0
,, & Sunderland	0	0	0	0	0	0	0	0	0	0	0	0	0	5	0	0	0	0
Bridlington	0	1	0	0	1	0	0	0	7	9	11	14	13	16	11	21	5	9
,, & Sunderland	0	0	0	0	0	0	0	0	0	0	0	0	0	1	0	0	0	0

	1703–4		1706		1728		1737		1758		1768		1775		1783		1790	
	From	*For*	*From*	*For*	*From*	*For*	*From*	*For*	*From*	*For*	*From*	*For*	*From*	*For*	*From*	*For*	*From*	*For*
Grimsby	5	1	3	0	13	0	11	0	22	0	33	0	44	0	25	0	24	0
Saltfleet	0	2	0	0	4	0	2	10	12	13	3	16	10	18	6	11	3	4
Mablethorpe	0	0	0	0	0	0	0	3	0	0	0	0	0	0	0	0	0	0
Sutton	0	0	0	0	0	0	0	2	0	0	0	0	0	0	0	0	0	0
Mumby Chapel	0	0	0	0	0	0	0	1	0	0	0	0	0	2	0	0	0	0
Wainfleet	0	0	0	0	0	0	4	1	0	1	0	6	3	11	5	6	6	22
Boston	0	9	0	7	2	6	1	9	4	19	5	16	11	18	14	19	49	59
Spalding	0	9	0	2	3	0	0	4	3	6	3	9	4	10	5	5	1	2
Holbeach	0	0	0	0	0	0	0	0	0	0	1	0	0	0	0	0	0	0
Ely	0	0	0	0	0	0	0	0	0	0	0	0	0	0	1	1	0	0
Wisbech	0	29	0	19	0	2	1	2	8	15	9	17	10	11	24	28	73	89
Lynn	16	35	12	8	72	14	45	39	56	41	74	58	77	62	93	87	136	96
Burnham	0	0	0	0	0	0	0	0	0	2	0	4	0	1	0	2	1	0
Wells	0	3	0	0	30	11	13	11	13	14	20	15	14	12	24	17	34	19
Blakeney	0	0	0	0	12	2	2	1	0	6	2	4	1	4	2	6	21	8
Cromer	0	0	0	0	0	0	0	0	0	0	0	0	0	0	0	0	1	0
Yarmouth	2	7	3	5	26	9	25	12	27	15	35	33	39	34	31	36	79	53
Southwold	0	0	0	0	1	0	1	0	1	0	2	1	0	0	0	0	2	0
Aldeburgh	0	0	0	0	3	0	3	1	2	0	2	2	2	1	0	0	0	0
Woodbridge	0	0	0	0	4	1	1	0	0	0	3	0	0	0	0	1	0	0
Ipswich	3	1	0	0	5	0	11	1	6	0	22	20	37	18	14	15	15	16
Harwich	0	0	0	0	2	0	0	0	0	1	2	2	0	0	0	0	0	0
Manningtree	0	0	0	0	0	0	0	0	0	0	0	0	0	1	0	0	0	0
Colchester	1	0	1	2	0	3	0	1	0	0	1	0	10	10	11	11	13	12
Maldon	0	0	0	0	0	0	0	0	0	0	0	0	0	0	0	0	5	4
Woolwich	0	0	0	0	0	0	0	0	0	5	0	0	0	0	0	0	0	0
Rochester	2	5	3	0	0	0	2	0	1	5	0	0	1	8	8	12	8	9
Chatham	0	0	0	0	0	0	0	0	0	5	0	0	0	0	0	0	0	0
Sandwich	0	0	0	0	0	0	0	0	0	0	0	0	0	0	0	0	3	3
Dover	0	0	0	0	0	0	0	0	1	2	2	2	1	0	0	0	0	0

	1703–4		1706		1728		1737		1758		1768		1775		1783		1796	
	From	*For*	*From*	*For*	*From*	*For*	*From*	*For*	*From*	*For*	*From*	*For*	*From*	*For*	*From*	*For*	*From*	*For*
Rye	0	0	0	0	0	0	2	0	0	0	0	0	1	0	0	0	0	0
Newhaven	0	0	0	0	0	0	0	0	0	2	1	2	1	6	0	2	4	4
Shoreham	0	0	0	0	0	0	0	0	0	0	0	0	0	0	0	0	1	2
Arundel	0	0	0	0	0	1	0	0	0	0	0	0	0	0	0	0	0	0
Chichester	0	0	0	0	0	0	3	0	0	0	0	0	0	0	0	0	0	0
Portsmouth	0	0	0	0	0	0	0	0	0	0	0	0	0	1	0	0	0	2
Southampton	0	0	0	0	0	1	0	0	0	0	0	1	0	0	0	0	0	0
Cowes	0	0	0	0	0	0	0	0	0	0	0	0	1	0	2	1	0	0
Poole	0	0	1	0	2	0	4	0	0	0	3	2	27	2	9	5	9	0
Exeter	0	0	0	0	0	1	1	0	1	0	6	0	3	0	3	0	5	0
Plymouth	0	0	0	0	0	0	0	0	0	0	0	0	1	0	1	0	1	0
Penzance	0	0	0	0	0	0	0	0	0	0	1	0	0	0	0	0	0	0
Guernsey	0	0	0	0	0	0	0	0	0	0	0	0	0	0	3	0	0	0
Bristol	0	0	0	0	1	2	8	0	0	0	0	0	2	0	0	0	1	0
Milford	0	0	0	0	0	0	1	0	0	0	0	0	0	0	0	0	0	0
Liverpool	0	0	0	0	0	0	0	0	0	1	11	7	9	2	1	3	8	0
Lancaster	0	0	0	0	0	0	0	0	0	0	0	0	1	2	0	2	1	0
Ulverston	0	0	0	0	0	0	0	0	0	0	9	2	13	2	15	1	8	0
Whitehaven	0	0	0	0	0	0	0	0	4	0	1	0	2	0	4	1	3	0
ENGLISH TOTAL	*151*	*157*	*139*	*77*	*456*	*65*	*372*	*292*	*312*	*388*	*376*	*379*	*466*	*455*	*419*	*544*	*689*	*630*
SCOTTISH OUTPORTS																		
Campbelltown	0	0	0	0	0	0	0	0	0	0	0	0	2	0	0	0	0	0
Irvine	0	0	0	0	0	0	0	0	0	0	0	0	0	2	0	0	0	0
Greenock	0	0	0	0	0	0	0	0	0	0	0	0	2	0	0	0	1	0
Glasgow	0	0	0	0	0	0	0	0	0	0	0	0	0	0	0	0	1	2
North & South Uist	0	0	0	0	0	0	0	0	0	0	0	0	0	0	1	1	1	0
Stornaway	0	0	0	0	0	0	0	0	0	0	1	0	0	0	0	0	0	0
Faroe	0	0	0	0	0	0	0	0	0	0	0	0	0	0	0	0	2	1

	From	For	From	For	From	For	From	For	From	For	From	For	From	For	From	For	From	For
Kirkwall	0	0	0	0	0	0	0	0	2	0	7	1	6	0	3	3	2	0
Thurso	0	0	0	0	0	0	0	0	0	0	0	0	0	0	1	1	1	0
Inverness	0	0	0	0	0	0	2	0	1	0	0	0	0	0	0	2	5	1
Fraserburgh	0	0	0	0	0	0	0	0	0	0	0	0	0	1	0	0	0	0
Peterhead	0	0	0	0	0	0	0	0	0	0	0	1	0	0	0	1	1	0
Aberdeen	0	0	0	0	0	0	1	0	1	2	3	7	3	3	8	11	13	14
Montrose	0	0	0	0	0	0	1	1	0	0	1	1	5	0	1	5	5	4
Arbroath	0	0	0	0	0	0	0	0	0	0	0	0	0	1	1	2	0	0
Dundee	0	0	0	0	0	0	0	0	1	7	3	4	2	6	0	6	18	16
Perth	0	0	0	0	0	0	0	1	0	0	0	0	0	0	1	3	2	4
Anstruther	0	0	0	0	0	0	0	0	0	0	0	0	0	0	0	1	0	0
Dysart	0	0	0	0	0	0	0	0	0	0	0	0	0	1	0	5	0	0
Kirkaldy	0	0	0	0	0	0	0	0	0	0	1	1	0	3	1	1	0	0
Burntisland	0	0	0	0	0	0	0	0	0	0	0	0	0	1	1	2	0	0
Inverkeithing	0	0	0	0	0	0	0	0	0	0	0	0	0	0	0	1	0	0
Kinkardine	0	0	0	0	0	0	0	0	0	0	0	1	0	3	2	5	0	2
Alloa	0	0	0	0	0	0	0	0	0	0	0	0	1	4	1	7	1	0
Bo'ness	0	0	0	0	0	0	0	0	2	0	11	6	11	{27}	4	13	4	2
Leith/Carron	0	0	0	0	0	0	1	1	7	18	15	19	15		28	43	34	38
Dunbar	0	0	0	0	0	0	0	0	1	0	3	0	1	0	2	0	3	2
SCOTTISH TOTAL	*0*	*0*	*0*	*0*	*0*	*0*	*5*	*3*	*15*	*27*	*45*	*41*	*49*	*53*	*55*	*113*	*98*	*86*
IRISH OUTPORTS																		
Newry	0	0	0	0	0	0	0	0	0	0	0	0	0	0	0	0	1	1
Dublin	0	0	0	0	0	0	0	0	0	0	0	0	0	0	0	0	3	0
Waterford	0	0	0	0	0	0	0	0	0	0	0	0	0	0	2	2	0	0
IRISH TOTAL	*0*	*0*	*0*	*0*	*0*	*0*	*0*	*0*	*0*	*0*	*0*	*0*	*0*	*0*	*2*	*2*	*4*	*1*
LONDON	93	310	80	185	179	150	190	208	226	318	307	327	387	386	327	382	553	578
BRITISH TOTAL	*244*	*467*	*219*	*262*	*635*	*215*	*567*	*503*	*553*	*733*	*729*	*747*	*903**	*895**	*803*	*1041*	*1346**	*1300*

* Including one unidentified voyage

Appendix 13

GOODS EXPORTED COASTWISE FROM HULL, 1706

To:	*Wheat*	*Barley*	*Oats*	*Malt*	*Beans*	*Butter*	*Cheese*	*Ale*	*Red Herrings*	*Cod & Ling*	*Potatoes*
	Qtr	Qtr	Qtr	Qtr	Qtr	F	Ton	Tun	Brl	No.	
Newcastle		940		30	100				22		
Sunderland											
Whitby											
Scarborough											
Boston	100										
Fosdyke			50		160						
Wisbech											
Lynn				1c 1 Brl 12		91	10	1c 3½			
Yarmouth					70		3½	½			
Colchester					130						
London	230		15,530	9120	9810	21,801	849	103	1768	28 Brl 1740	6 Brl 11½ Hhd
TOTAL	330	940	15,580	1c 1 Brl 9162	10,270	21,892	862½	1c 107	1790	28 Brl 1740	6 Br 11½ Hhd

To:	*Honey*	*Liquorice*	*Metheglin*	*Tobacco*	*Rape Seed*	*Rape Oil*	*Linseed Oil*	*Tallow*	*Rosin*	*Beeswax*	*Brown Paper*	*Soap*
			Hhd	lb	Qtr	Tun		Hhd	cwt		bundles	to
Newcastle		2 Brl			8	19					105	
Sunderland												
Whitby				5480		4 Brl						
Scarborough				400					5			
Boston					640							
Fosdyke												
Wisbech					2355							
Lynn					240		1 Brl	5			80	
Yarmouth								1t				
Colchester						6						
London	4t 4F	25 Hhd	½	1568		118 68p. 19 Hhd	4 Hhd	672 43 Brl	60	7 Brl 23 Hhd 30 cwt		
TOTAL	4t 4F	2 Brl 25 Hhd	½ Hhd	7448	3243	143 tun 68p. 19 Hhd 4 Brl	1 Brl 4 Hhd	677 43 Brl 1t	65	7 Brl 23 Hhd 30 cwt	185	1

:	*Starch*	*Glue*	*Potters' Clay*	*Plaster*	*Lampblack*	*Millstones*	*Scythestones*	*Rottenstone*	*Lead*	*Red Lead*
		Hhd		t	cags	pair	No.		Fodder	Brl
wcastle	6 Hhd									
nderland	2c									
itby	2 Brl									
rborough									1½	
ston										
sdyke										
sbech										
nn			16 bags		60	12	41,500		80	
rmouth						2	7000		114	
chester						15				
ndon	8½t 63 Hhd	47	13t 4 Hhd	77			134,000	3½t 1 Brl 11 Hhd	2723½	657
OTAL	69 Hhd 8½t 2c 2 Brl	47	16 bags 13t 4 Hhd	77	60	29	182,500	3½t 1 Brl 11 Hhd	2919	657

):	*White Lead*	*Lead Shot*	*English Steel*	*English Iron*	*Iron Shot*	*Iron Wire*	*Nails*	*Ironmongery*	*Single White Plates*	*Bricks*	*Pantiles*
		cwt	ton	ton	ton	cwt	bag			No.	
ewcastle				63			66		2700		27,000
nderland							50				
hitby				12½						16,200	2100
arborough				5						25,000	
oston											
osdyke											
isbech			½	2							
ynn		26		13			96	1 pack			
armouth			4 Fag ½	22			9½t				
olchester				2							
ondon	6 Brl 66 Hhd		72 Fag 23¾	138	58	171	3t 538	1 Hhd			80,000
Total	6 Brl 66 Hhd	26	24¾t 76 Fag	257	58	171	750 12½t	1 pack 1 Hhd	2700	41,200	109,100

To:	*Earthenware*	*Glasses*	*Oak Timber*	*Deals*	*Coal Waggon Wheels*	*Pitch*	*Tar*	*Hemp*	*Eng. Canvas*	*Northern Cloth*	*Trennells*
	crates	crates	ton	Hun	No.	Brl	Brl	cwt	pcs	pack	No.
Newcastle			191		912			3			
Sunderland			5		50						
Whitby	11		131	24		3	1				
Scarborough	9		34	1½				63			4000
Boston											
Fosdyke											
Wisbech	hamper 4										
Lynn	2 Hhd 69	5				24		105	36	2	14,000
Yarmouth	110	2 Hhd 2 Brl 30		12						2	2200
Colchester											
London	120		199							894	
TOTAL	319 4 Hamp 2 Hhd	35 2 Hhd 2 Brl	560	37½	962	27	1	171	36	898	20,200

Note: Brl = Barrel
c = Cask
F = Firkin
Fag = Faggot
Hhd = Hogshead
Hun = Hundred
p = pipe
pcs = pieces

Appendix 14

GOODS IMPORTED COASTWISE AT HULL, 1706

	Barley	*Malt*	*Rye*	*Red Herring*	*White Herring*	*Codfish*	*Molasses*	*Sugar*	*Raisins*	*Currants*	*Ginger*	*Figs*	*Rice*	*Lemons & Oranges*	*Groceries*	*Vinegar*	*Pepper*	*Coffee*	*Tobacco*	*Tobacco Stalks*	*Tobacco Dust*	*Snuff*	*English Spirits*
From:	Qtr	Qtr	Qtr	Brl	F		cwt	ton	ton	ton	ton	cwt	F	chest	ton	½ Hhd	lb		lb	lb	lb	lb	Galls
Berwick																							
Seaton																							
Cullercoats																							
Newcastle						1149 22 Brl																	
Sunderland																							
Grimsby																							
Lynn	20	70	114	22	8	9 cwt																	
Yarmouth				295	15																		
Colchester																							
Rochester																							
Poole																							
London							95	767½	101	71½	44	4	6	227	248	372	672	2 bag 1 sack	448,469	15,612	1704	224	17,633
TOTAL	20	70	114	317	23		95	767½	101	71½	44	4	6	227	248	372	672	2 bag 1 sack	448,469	15,612	1704	224	17,633

From:	WINE											TOTAL WINE	Calf Skins	Bones	Foreign Iron	'Iron'	Old Iron	Ironmongery	Shot	Steel	Copper	Copper Plates	Copper/Brass ware	Brass wire
	Red Port	White Port	Spanish	Madeira	Canary	Rhenish	French	Claret	'Red'	Budapest	Florentine													
	Galls	G	G	G	G	G	G	G	G	G	G	Gall	dz		t	t	t	cwt	cwt		cwt	No.	cwt	cwt
Berwick																								
Seaton																								
Cullercoats																								
Newcastle	2164							252				2416	10	10,000						4t				
Sunderland																								
Grimsby																								
Lynn	409	5355			126							5890					5½ ½					60		
Yarmouth														40,000										
Colchester																								
Rochester																								
Poole																								
London	5 Hamp 4945	535	220	1821	3 Hamp 7559	1 Hamp 63	1449	1 Hamp 63	1 Hamp 2926	10 Butts	37 chest 1008	11 Hamp 37 chest 20,589			13	241 bars 20		20	163	Bars 59 Fag 12	2¾		7	2
TOTAL	5H 7518	5890	220	1821	3H 7685	1 H 63	1449	1 H 315	1 H 2926	10 Butts	37 ch 1008	11 H 37 ch 28,895	10	50,000	13	bars 241 20	6	20	163	4t 59B 12F	2¾	60	7	2

From:	Pewter	Tin	Tinplates	Litharge	White Lead	Lead Pipes	Alum	Fuller's Earth	Sand	Tobacco Pipe Clay	Whiting	Starch	Woad	Indigo	Potash	Emery	Pitch
	cwt	cwt	Brl	Brl	cwt	cwt	t	t	t	t	Hhd	cwt	t		Hhd	F	Brl
Berwick																	
Seaton																	
Cullercoats																	
Newcastle																	
Sunderland																	
Grimsby																	
Lynn			21					13t	2			330	12	1 box	2		
Yarmouth																	
Colchester																	
Rochester								loads 145									
Poole										77							
London	74	cwt 4 block 6	2	1	12	15	4	5t loads 18			5	12				36	6
TOTAL	74	4 cwt 6 block	23	1	12	15	4	18t loads 163	2	77	5	342	12	1 box	2	36	6

From:	Rosin	Grease	Soap	Oil	Coal	Salt	Glass	Bottles	Raw Hides	Wool	German Linen	Scotch Linen	Russian Linen	Cordage	Horns	Leather
		F			Chald.	t		doz	No.	cwt	ells	yds	ells	t	No.	cwt
Berwick						22										
Seaton					1	32										
Cullercoats					2	31										
Newcastle					503	535 weys 166	cases 150 366 F	1847	618					7	4200	3
Sunderland					1487											
Grimsby										377						
Lynn										962					4000	
Yarmouth										118						
Colchester										17						
Rochester																
Poole																
London	2c 84 F	1065	1362 Brl 30 F 202 Chest	53 pipes 44 Hhd 185 Brl 41 casks 3 punch. 532 Gall.					1220	1479	33,168	10,588	4394			
TOTAL	2c 84F	1065	1362 Brl 30 F 202 chest	53 P, 44 H, 185 B, 41 c, 3 P, 532 G	1993	620t 166w	150c 366F	1847	1838	3353	33,168	10,588	4394	7	8200	3

Appendix 15

GOODS IMPORTED COASTWISE AT HULL, 1775

Region	Port	Sugar	Molasses	Tea	Coffee	Cocoa	Chocolate	Pepper	Nutmeg	Ginger	Spanish Juice	Raisins	Currants	Almonds	Prunes
		t		lb.	lb.	lb.	lb.	lb.	lb.	lb.	lb.		cwt		cw
THE NORTH	Berwick														
	Alnmouth														
	Newcastle														
	Sunderland														
	Hartlepool														
	Stockton														
YORKS	Whitby														
	Scarborough			150											
	Bridlington			138											
LINCS	Grimsby														
	Saltfleet														
	Wainfleet														
	Boston														
	Spalding														
EAST ANGLIA	Wisbech														
	Lynn														
	Wells														
	Yarmouth														
	Blakeney														
	Aldeburgh														
	Ipswich														
	Colchester														
THE SOUTH	Rochester														
	Dover														
	Rye														
	Newhaven														
	Cowes														
	Poole														
	Exeter														
	Plymouth														
WEST COAST	Bristol		Pun 40												
	Liverpool												68		
	Lancaster														
	Ulverston														
	Whitehaven														
	London	9389	Pun 7150 Hhd 860	153986	3794	10251	487	30941	1125	38178	14115	750 cwt 86 Hhd 3187 Brl	5144	3841	274
	TOTAL ENGLISH	9389	Pun 7190 Hhd 860	154274	3794	10251	487	30941	1125	38178	14115	750 cwt 86 Hhd 3187 Brl	5212	3841	274
SCOTLAND	B'o'ness			100											
	Leith			2027											
	TOTAL SCOTTISH			2225											
	TOTAL BRITISH	9389	Pun 7190 Hhd 860	156499	3794	10251	487	30941	1125	38178	14115	750 cwt 86 Hhd 3187 Brl	5212	3841	27 4

Sugar | Molasses | Tea | Coffee | Cocoa | Chocolate | Pepper | Nutmeg | Ginger | Spanish Juice | Raisins | Currants | Almonds | Prunes

Oranges & Lemons	*Wheat*	*Barley*	*Rye*	*Oats*	*Malt*	*Flour*	*Peas*	*Beans*	*Hops*	*Pork*	*Pickled Codfish*	*'Saltfish'*	*'Fish'*	*Herring*	*Cheese*	*Salt*	*Vinegar*	*Bristol Water*
chts	Qtr	Qtr	Qtr	Qtr	Qtr	Qtr	Qtr	Qtr	cwt	cwt		cwt.		Brl	t	bushel	½ H	Hp.
			200											34		609 t		
	60										29 F 78 Brl							
	210			60														
											72 Brl	8	220 Brl					
											13 F		200 Bass					
								100			95 F	20	2 F					
													15 sacks					
	1				610								20 F					
				111 78 840														
								40										
			180					570										
	588	5254	2095	52	52	257	501	1952										
	110	2009	61			512	184											
	67	830	105		21	3256	7	113				20		1837	5		7	
	450	180	512				44	40						1 F	26			
		30					10											
											8½ t							
															2	740 51,200		100
2223	1336	190	260						3920	430	15 t	121 30 Brl		21 cwt 60			1804	
2223	2822	8493	3413	1141	683	4025	818	2815	3920	430	23½ t 137 F 150 Brl	169 30 Brl	22 F 220 Brl 200 Bass 15 sacks	1892 60 cwt 1 F	33	51940 609 t	1811	100
		441									98 Brl			426				
2223	2822	8934	3413	1141	683	4025	818	2815	3920	430	23½ t 137 F 248 Brl	169 30 Brl	22 F 220 Brl 200 Bass 15 sacks	2318 60 cwt 1 F	33	51940 609 t	1811	100
Oranges/Lemons	*Wheat*	*Barley*	*Rye*	*Oats*	*Malt*	*Flour*	*Peas*	*Beans*	*Hops*	*Pork*	*Pickled Codfish*	*'Saltfish'*	*'Fish'*	*Herring*	*Cheese*	*Salt*	*Vinegar*	*Bristol Water*

Region	Port	Cyder	Beer	Spa Water	'British' Spirits	'Compound' Spirits	'Brit. & Comp.' Spirits	Rum	Brandy	G…
		Hamp.	Gal.		Gal.	Gal.	Gal.	Gal.	Gal.	G…
THE NORTH	Berwick									
	Alnmouth									
	Newcastle							210		8…
	Sunderland									
	Hartlepool									
	Stockton									
YORKS	Whitby									
	Scarborough			24 c 4 Hhd 19 Hamp						4…
	Bridlington		c. 3358							
LINCS	Grimsby									
	Saltfleet									
	Wainfleet									
	Boston									
	Spalding									
EAST ANGLIA	Wisbech									
	Lynn							20		7…
	Wells									
	Yarmouth							237	22	4…
	Blakeney									
	Aldeburgh									
	Ipswich									
	Colchester									1…
THE SOUTH	Rochester									
	Dover									
	Rye									
	Newhaven									
	Cowes									
	Poole									
	Exeter									
	Plymouth									
WEST COAST	Bristol	60 200 doz.			9000	13000				
	Liverpool							235		
	Lancaster									
	Ulverston									
	Whitehaven									
	London		c.330,000		50,519	45,249	12,581	110,071	15,987	1,4…
	TOTAL ENGLAND	60 200 doz.	*c.* 333,400	24 c 4 Hhd 19 Hamp	59,519	58,249	12,581	110,773	16,009	28…
SCOTLAND	B'o'ness									
	Leith									
	TOTAL SCOTLAND							597	30	30…
	TOTAL BRITAIN	60 200 doz.	c. 333,400	24 c 4 Hhd 19 Hamp	59,519	58,249	12,581	111,370	16,039	58…

Cyder | *Beer* | *Spa Water* | *'British' Spirits* | *'Compound' Spirits* | *'Brit. & Comp.' Spirits* | *Rum* | *Brandy* | *Geneva*

Sweets	Red Port	White Port	Sherry	Spanish White	Lisbon	Madeira	Canary	Vidonia	French	Burgundy
Gal.	Gal.	Gal.	Gal.	Gal.	Gal.	Gal.	Gal.	Gal.	Gal.	Gal.
	18 10			121	6					
	6 19 doz				63	246				
	3160	378		216						
22	12 doz 3280	1636 64		430	31		618			
				1						
	535 doz. 3737	126 doz. 2632	27 doz. 229	94 doz. 1940	40 doz. 533	260 doz. 1526	57	1681	110 doz. 1019	2 doz. 16
22	566 doz. 8321	126 doz. 4710	27 doz. 229	94 doz. 2707	40 doz. 633	260 doz. 1772	675	1681	110 doz. 1019	2 doz. 16
	26 doz. 879			414		209			479	
22	592 doz. 9200	126 doz. 4710	27 doz. 229	94 doz. 3121	40 doz. 633	260 doz. 1981	675	1681	110 doz. 1498	2 doz. 16
Sweets	Red Port	White Port	Sherry	Spanish White	Lisbon	Madeira	Canary	Vidonia	French	Burgundy

		Champagne	Claret	Arrack	Rhenish	Hock	'Shrub'	Tobacco: Leaf	Tobacco Cut	
		doz.	doz.	Gal.	Gal.	Gal.	Gal.	lb.	lb.	
THE NORTH	Berwick									
	Alnmouth									
	Newcastle									
	Sunderland									
	Hartlepool									
	Stockton									
YORKS	Whitby									
	Scarborough									
	Bridlington									
LINCS	Grimsby									
	Saltfleet									
	Wainfleet									
	Boston									
	Spalding									
EAST ANGLIA	Wisbech									
	Lynn									
	Wells									
	Yarmouth									
	Blakeney									
	Aldeburgh									
	Ipswich									
	Colchester									
THE SOUTH	Rochester									
	Dover									
	Rye									
	Newhaven									
	Cowes									
	Poole									
	Exeter									
	Plymouth									
WEST COAST	Bristol									
	Liverpool						20			
	Lancaster									
	Ulverston									
	Whitehaven									
	London	10	110	43	9 doz. 38	31 doz. 200	408	380,141	335,433	16
	TOTAL ENGLAND	10	110	43	9 doz. 38	31 doz. 200	428	380,141	335,433	16,
SCOTLAND	B'o'ness							416,785		
	Leith							15,354		
	TOTAL SCOTLAND				10			449,639		
	TOTAL BRITAIN	10	110	43	9 doz. 48	31 doz. 200	428	829,780	335,433	16

Champagne | Claret | Arrack | Rhenish | Hock | 'Shrub' | Tobacco Leaf | Tobacco Cut

	Stalks	Snuff	Swedish Iron	Russian Iron	Plantation Iron	English Pig Iron	Bar Iron	Steel	'Cast & Wrought Iron & Steel'	Slit Iron	Ironmongery
	lb.	lb.	cwt.	t	t	t	cwt.	cwt.	cwt.	cwt.	cwt.
	9505		6½						1116		27 casks 15
						2					
			110	10			43	22			11 c 10 1 c
						10		120	20 1 cask		
[illegible]	61,887	73,000	40	440	340	785	1	40	338	7	57
[illegible]	71,392	73,000	156½	450	340	797	44	182	1474	7	39 c 81
		1794						120 25	2940 160		
		1794						145	3700		
[illegible]	71,392	74,794	156½	450	340	797	44	327	1 c 5174	7	39 c 81
	Stalks	Snuff	Swedish Iron	Russian Iron	Plantation Iron	English Pig Iron	Bar Iron	Steel	'Cast & Wrought Iron & Steel'	Slit Iron	Ironmongery

		Old Iron	*Nut Iron*	*Tin*	*Grain Tin*	*Brass*	*Copper*	*Old Pewter*	*Tutenag*
		cwt.	cwt.	cwt.	cwt.	cwt.	cwt.	cwt.	cwt.
THE NORTH	Berwick								
	Alnmouth								
	Newcastle	5				10		2 c	
	Sunderland	4							
	Hartlepool								
	Stockton							2	
YORKS	Whitby	32						8	
	Scarborough	2 c							
		20							
	Bridlington	3c							
LINCS	Grimsby								
	Saltfleet								
	Wainfleet								
	Boston	41							
	Spalding	4 c							
EAST ANGLIA	Wisbech	6 c						2 c	
		20							
	Lynn	6 Hhd							
	Wells	36 c							
	Yarmouth	3 Hhd							
		8 c 120						1 c	
	Blakeney								
	Aldeburgh								
	Ipswich								
	Colchester								
THE SOUTH	Rochester								
	Dover								
	Rye								
	Newhaven								
	Cowes								
	Poole								
	Exeter								
	Plymouth								
WEST COAST	Bristol								
	Liverpool								
	Lancaster								
	Ulverston								
	Whitehaven								
	London	5100	73	1110	20	25	891	16	47
	TOTAL ENGLAND	9 Hhd 59 c 5342	73	1110	20	35	891	5 c, 26	47
SCOTLAND	B'o'ness								
	Leith								
	TOTAL SCOTLAND								
	TOTAL BRITAIN	9 Hhd 59 c 5342	73	1110	20	35	891	5 c 26	47

Old Iron *Nut Iron* *Tin* *Grain Tin* *Brass* *Copper* *Old Pewter* *Tutenag*

White Lead	Hemp	Flax	Tow	Candlewick	Old Rope	British Raw Wool	Combed Wool	Cotton Wool	Cotton Yarn	Linen Yarn
t	cwt.	cwt.	cwt.	cwt.	t	cwt.	cwt.	lb.	lb.	lb.
			1666 6 10 278		57 59	591				3808 matts 10
			475 6	4	1½					
						8232 21	27			
			Matts 29 bags 14			103 5566 1246 3981 211 428 6376 1259	21			
						194 286 365 121				
34										
	2663	50			31	28,479		69,487	2884	6720 Spind 2800
34	2663	50	2441 29 matts 14 bags	4	148½	57,458	48	69,487	2884	10,528 Spind. 2800
			56		10	1721				Spind. 12,000
			56		10	2591				560 Spind. 12,660
34	2663	50	2497 29 matts 14 bags	4	158½	60,049	48	69,487	2884	11,088 Spind. 15,460 10 matts
White Lead	Hemp	Flax	Tow	Candlewick	Old Rope	British Raw Wool	Combed Wool	Cotton Wool	Cotton Yarn	Linen Yarn

Region	Port	Worsted Yarn	Thread	Rags	British & Printed Linen	Printed Linen	Scottish Linen	Scottish Diaper	Lawns	Muslin	Sail Cloth
		cwt	lb	t	yds	yds	yds	yds	yds	yds	
THE NORTH	Berwick										
	Alnmouth										
	Newcastle			20							
	Sunderland			10							
	Hartlepool										
	Stockton										
YORKS	Whitby										Bolts 453
	Scarborough										
	Bridlington										
LINCS	Grimsby	3									
	Saltfleet			1							
	Wainfleet										
	Boston										
	Spalding										
EAST ANGLIA	Wisbech										
	Lynn	16									
	Wells										
	Yarmouth	26									
	Blakeney										
	Aldeburgh										
	Ipswich										
	Colchester										
THE SOUTH	Rochester										
	Dover										
	Rye										
	Newhaven										
	Cowes										
	Poole										
	Exeter										
	Plymouth										
WEST COAST	Bristol										
	Liverpool										
	Lancaster										
	Ulverston										
	Whitehaven										
	London				130,107	18,596	946				
	TOTAL ENGLAND	45		31	130,107	18,596	946				
SCOTLAND	B'o'ness		3031		3,200	16,292	9000	20,300	10,810	5000	
	Leith		40		22,985						yd 8[illegible]
	TOTAL SCOTLAND		3471		36,785	16,292	9000	20,300	10,810	5000	yd 12[illegible]
	TOTAL BRITAIN	45	3471	31	166,892	34,888	9946	20,300	10,810	5000	Bolt[illegible] 453 1200 y[illegible]

Worsted Yarn | Thread | Rags | British & Printed Linen | Printed Linen | Scottish Linen | Scottish Diaper | Lawns | Muslin | Sail Cloth

Norwich Stuffs	Teazles	Fuller's Earth	Starch	Archil	Blue	Copperas	Indigo	Madder	Ochre	Smalts	Umber
		cwt	cwt	cwt	cwt	cwt	cwt	cwt	cwt	lb.	lb.
					2 c, 37			223		392 1485	
30 truss 22 pack 4 bale	crates 60 bag 28	217									
		6260	4691	252 7 Hhd	85	1474 4 F	342	278	5	2105	112
	crates 60 bag 28	6477	4691	cwt 252 Hhd 7	2 c, 112	4 F 1474	342	501	5	3982	112
	crates 60 28 Bag	6477	4691	cwt 252 Hhd 7	2 c, 112	4 F 1474	342	501	5	3982	112
Norwich Stuffs	*Teazles*	*Fuller's Earth*	*Starch*	*Archil*	*Blue*	*Copperas*	*Indigo*	*Madder*	*Ochre*	*Smalts*	*Umber*

Region	Port	Bar Wood	Brazil Wood	Fustic	Nicaragua & Peach Wood	Red Wood	Sanders Wood	Woad	Alum	Aqua Fortis
		cwt	cwt	cwt	cwt	cwt	cwt	cwt	cwt	b
THE NORTH	Berwick									
	Alnmouth									
	Newcastle									
	Sunderland									
	Hartlepool									
	Stockton								100	
YORKS	Whitby								729	
	Scarborough									
	Bridlington									
LINCS	Grimsby									
	Saltfleet							1165		
	Wainfleet									
	Boston									
	Spalding									
EAST ANGLIA	Wisbech							Hhd 40		
	Lynn							Hhd 3		
	Wells									
	Yarmouth									
	Blakeney									
	Aldeburgh									
	Ipswich									
	Colchester									
THE SOUTH	Rochester									
	Dover									
	Rye									
	Newhaven									
	Cowes									
	Poole									
	Exeter									
	Plymouth									
WEST COAST	Bristol									
	Liverpool			840	80					
	Lancaster									
	Ulverston									
	Whitehaven			20						
	London	322	665	1762½	1285	265	3592	17	1382	7
	TOTAL ENGLAND	322	665	2622½	1365	265	3592	Hhd 43 1182	2211	7
SCOTLAND	B'o'ness									
	Leith									
	TOTAL SCOTLAND									
	TOTAL BRITAIN	322	665	2622½	1365	265	3592	Hhd 43 1182	2211	7

Bar Wood | Brazil Wood | Fustic | Nicaragua & Peach Wood | Red Wood | Sanders Wood | Woad | Alum | Aqua Fortis

Cream of Tartar	*Barilla*	*Pearl Ash*	*Potash*	*'Soza' Ash*	*Kelp*	*Emery*	*Saltpetre*	*Gunpowder*	*Sulphur*	*Sumach*
cwt	t	t	t	cwt	t		cwt	Brl	cwt	cwt
24										
									3 c	
			Hhd 10 1 Hhd 19							
395	559	44½	198½	59	2	7 F 754 cwt	1123	496	Brl 3 334	635
419	559	44½	Hhd 29 199½	59	2	7 F 754 cwt	1123	496	Brl 3 3 c, 334	635
					500		300			
					500		300			
419	559	44½	Hhd 29 199½	59	502	7 F 754 cwt	1423	496	Brl 3 3 c, 334	635
Cream of Tartar	*Barilla*	*Pearl Ash*	*Potash*	*'Soza' Ash*	*Kelp*	*Emery*	*Saltpetre*	*Gunpowder*	*Sulphur*	*Sumach*

Region	Port	*Valonia*	*Valerian*	*Vitriol*	*Tar*	*Pitch*	*Turps*	*Rosin*	*Grease*
		cwt	cwt	bott.	Brl.		cwt	cwt	F
THE NORTH	Berwick								
	Alnmouth								
	Newcastle								
	Sunderland								
	Hartlepool								
	Stockton								
YORKS	Whitby								
	Scarborough								22
	Bridlington								
LINCS	Grimsby								
	Saltfleet								
	Wainfleet								
	Boston								
	Spalding								
EAST ANGLIA	Wisbech								
	Lynn								
	Wells								
	Yarmouth								
	Blakeney								
	Aldeburgh								
	Ipswich								
	Colchester					5			20
THE SOUTH	Rochester								
	Dover								
	Rye								
	Newhaven								
	Cowes								
	Poole								
	Exeter								
	Plymouth								
WEST COAST	Bristol								
	Liverpool				80	5	236 Brl.		
	Lancaster								
	Ulverston								
	Whitehaven								
	London	426	164	333	2053		9240	920 31 c 4 F	866
	TOTAL ENGLAND	426	164	333	2133	10	9240	920 31 c 4 F	908
SCOTLAND	B'o'ness			8					
	Leith				904				
	TOTAL SCOTLAND			868	1677		54		
	TOTAL BRITAIN	426	164	1201	3810	10	9294 236 Brl	920 31 c 4 F	908

Valonia *Valerian* *Vitriol* *Tar* *Pitch* *Turps* *Rosin* *Grease*

Whale Bone	*Oil*	*Oilman's Ware*	*Linseed Oil*	*Rape Oil*	*Linseed*	*Rapeseed*	*Hemp Seed*	*Rape Dust*
lb.					Qtr	Qtr	Qtr	Qtr
36								120
13130 3332								62 bag 20
						106 438 260	25	
			Hhd 60 6 c.	Hhd 55 43 c 1 Brl.	30	154 424		
974 truss 4	Pipe Hhd Butt 346 483 23 Brl c Pun Jar 1619 84 41 82	Hhd Brl c 14 242 118 F Hamp Pcls 232 203 28						
17472 truss 4	Pipe Hhd Butt. 346 483 23 Brl c Pun Jar 1619 84 41 82	Hhd Brl c 14 242 118 F Hamp Pcls 232 203 28	Hhd 60 6 c	Hhd 55 43 c 1 Brl	30	1382	25	182 bag 20
17472 truss 4	Pipe Hhd Butt. 346 483 23 Brl c Pun Jar 1619 54 41 82	Hhd Brl c 14 242 118 F Hamp Pcls 232 203 28	Hhd 60 6 c	55 Hhd 43 c 1 Brl	30	1382	25	182 bag 20
Whale Bone	*Oil*	*Oilman's Ware*	*Linseed Oil*	*Rape Oil*	*Linseed*	*Rapeseed*	*Hemp Seed*	*Rape Dust*

		Hard Soap	Soft Soap	Tallow	Bones	Horns	Raw Hides	Skins: Buck	Calf	
		cwt		cwt	Hhd	No.	No.	No.	No.	
THE NORTH	Berwick									
	Alnmouth									
	Newcastle					24,400	210			
	Sunderland				4/No. 20,000	10,200				
	Hartlepool				No. 7100					
	Stockton				8					
YORKS	Whitby				3 No. 3019	3900 4 c				
	Scarborough				5	2 Hhd				
	Bridlington				2	2 Hhd				
LINCS	Grimsby									
	Saltfleet									
	Wainfleet									
	Boston			15	3, 1 c					
	Spalding				4	2 Hhd				
EAST ANGLIA	Wisbech				3					
	Lynn				38	9076 2 c				
	Wells				9, 1 c					
	Yarmouth				92 No. 17,200	19,932 1 Hhd				
	Blakeney									
	Aldeburgh									
	Ipswich				13	cwt 32				
	Colchester				No. 5000	5000				
THE SOUTH	Rochester									
	Dover									
	Rye									
	Newhaven									
	Cowes				No. 3000	2000				
	Poole									
	Exeter									
	Plymouth									
WEST COAST	Bristol									
	Liverpool									
	Lancaster									
	Ulverston									
	Whitehaven									
	London	5467	4289×F 1278×½F 62×Brl 2364×½ Brl	656		52,353 59 Hhd 10 c	5862	450	1990	20
	TOTAL ENGLAND	5467	4289×F 1278×½F 62×Brl 2364×½ Brl	671	194, 3 c No. 50,319	126,861 66 Hhd 16 c 32 cwt	6072	450	1990	20
SCOTLAND	B'o'ness									
	Leith									
	TOTAL SCOTLAND					cwt 58 4 c			144	
	TOTAL BRITAIN	5467	4289×F 1278×½F 62×Brl 2364×½ Brl	671	194, 3 c No. 50,319	126,861 66 Hhd 20 c 90 cwt	6072	450	2134	20

Hard Soap | Soft Soap | Tallow | Bones | Horns | Raw Hides | Skins: Buck | Calf

	Lamb	*Rabbit*	*Sheep*	*Spetches*	*Glue*	*Chalk*	*Potter's Clay*	*Tobacco Pipe Clay*	*Plaster of Paris*	*Flints*	*Slate*
	No.		No.		cwt	t	cwt	t	t	t	t
			15 Hhd								
				1 t							
			1000								
			48 Hhd	Pack 8		15				40 70	
								2530 270		25	
											172 100
6	31,980	cwt 386 bag 20	2167		96	601	82		1	1060	
6	31,980	cwt 386 bag 20	3167 63 Hhd	1 t pack 8	96	616	82	2800	1	1195	272
										2	
			3360							2	
6	31,980	cwt 386 bag 20	6527 63 Hhd	1 t pack 8	96	616	82	2800	1	1197	272
	Lamb	*Rabbit*	*Sheep*	*Spetches*	*Glue*	*Chalk*	*Potter's Clay*	*Tobacco Pipe Clay*	*Plaster of Paris*	*Flints*	*Slate*

		Blue Slates	*Tiling Stones*	*Paving Stones*	*Dressed Freestone*	*Iron Ore*	*Coal*	*Cinders*	*Glass*	*Bottles*	
			t	t	t	t	Chald.	Ch.	crates	doz	
THE NORTH	Berwick										
	Alnmouth										
	Newcastle						615	16	1647 61 Hhd	6236	25
	Sunderland						584			3	
	Hartlepool										
	Stockton						60				
YORKS	Whitby				71						
	Scarborough										
	Bridlington										
LINCS	Grimsby										
	Saltfleet										
	Wainfleet										
	Boston										
	Spalding										
EAST ANGLIA	Wisbech										
	Lynn										
	Wells										
	Yarmouth										
	Blakeney										
	Aldeburgh										
	Ipswich										
	Colchester										
THE SOUTH	Rochester										
	Dover										
	Rye										
	Newhaven										
	Cowes										
	Poole										
	Exeter										
	Plymouth		120								
WEST COAST	Bristol										
	Liverpool										
	Lancaster	50 t									
	Ulverston					581					
	Whitehaven										
	London										
	TOTAL ENGLAND	25,200 50 t	120	0	71	581	1239	16	1647 61 Hhd	6239	b
SCOTLAND	B'o'ness						19 t				
	Leith										
	TOTAL SCOTLAND	7000		156		110	19 t				
	TOTAL BRITAIN	32,200 50 t	120	156	71	691	1239 19 t	16	1647 61 Hhd	6239	b
		Blue Slates	*Tiling Stones*	*Paving Stones*	*Dressed Freestone*	*Iron Ore*	*Coal*	*Cinders*	*Glass*	*Bottles*	

	Box	Caco	Cedar	Ebony	Logwood	Ironwood	Mahogany	Oak	Hogshead Staves	Pipe Staves	Wood Hoops	Cork
.d	cwt	cwt		cwt	cwt	cwt	cwt	load	No.	No.	No.	cwt
							20					
								40				10
								15				
			Logs 11 3 t	60	270		500 216plank 118 log					
	814	310		481	1907	100	1442		4000	4810	115,000	
	814	310	Log 11 3 t	541	2177	100	1962 216plank 118 Log	55	4000	4810	115,000	10
											115,000	
	814	310	11 Log 3 t	541	2177	100	1962 216 plank 118 Log	55	4000	4810	115,000	10
	Box	Caco	Cedar	Ebony	Logwood	Ironwood	Mahogany	Oak	Hogshead Staves	Pipe Staves	Wood Hoops	Cork

Appendix 16

GOODS EXPORTED COASTWISE FROM HULL, 1775

Region	Port	*Sugar*	*Tea*	*Ginger*	*Mushrooms*	*Ketchup*	*Mustard*	*Nutmeg*	*Pepper*	
		cwt	lb.	lb.		c		lb.	lb.	
THE NORTH	Alnmouth									
	Blyth									
	Shields									
	Newcastle	24								
	Sunderland									
	Hartlepool									
	Stockton	22								
	Stock/Sund'd									
YORKS	Whitby	45							4	
	,, /Stockton	4								
	,, /Sunderland									
	,, /Newcastle									
	Scarborough	87								
	,, /Whitby									
	,, /Stockton									
	,, /Sunderland									
	Bridlington	18		12				2	8	
	,, /Scarborough	2 Hhd								
LINCS	Saltfleet	215	717	14				4	29	
	Mumby	29	218					2	12	
	Wainfleet	15	218					9		
	Boston	29					1 F			
	Spalding	63								
EAST ANGLIA	Wisbech	3 Hhd		336			2 F			
	Lynn	21		3			25 F		6	
	Burnham									
	Wells									
	Blakeney									
	Yarmouth						98 c			
	Aldeburgh									
	Ipswich						31 c			
	Maintree									
	Colchester									
THE SOUTH	Rochester									
	Newhaven									
	Portsmouth									
	Poole									
WEST COAST	Liverpool									
	Lancaster									
	Ulverston	5								
	London	46			Hamp 2 bottles 1248	21	9 F 2 Hhd			14
	ENGLISH TOTAL	623	1153	365	2 Hamp bottles 1248	21	37 F 129 c 2 Hhd	17	59	14
SCOTLAND	B'o'ness									
	SCOTTISH TOTAL									
	BRITISH TOTAL	623	1153	365	Hamp 2 bottles 1248	21	37 F 129 c 2 Hhd	17	59	14

Sugar *Tea* *Ginger* *Mushrooms* *Ketchup* *Mustard* *Nutmeg* *Pepper*

Spanish Juice	Treacle	Vinegar	Salt	Codfish	Herring	Sprag Fish	Sturgeon	Bacon	Pork	Tongue	Cheese
b.	cwt	Galls	bushel		Brl	Brl	Keg		c	c	t
							3				326 10 1½
41		92	81 2								3 1 2 1½ 1 6½ 2
22	10	144 30	367 80 200 180	cwt 3 13 Brl 6 F	78	12 F 26					1 1 1 8
	1 c		40 840	14 Brl	12	11					185 54 492 344
											60
30 d 22			1 c		34		1	Hhd 1216 12c, 6 Brl 34 Pcls	237	4	1723
93 d 22	10 1 c	266	1790 1 c	27 Brl 3 cwt 6 F	124	37 12 F	4	Hhd 1216 12c, 6 Brl 34 Pcls	237	4	3223½
								2 Hhd 5 c			
								2 Hhd 5 c			½
93 d 22	10 1 c	266	1790 1 c	27 Brl 3 cwt 6 F	124	37 12 F	4	Hhd 1218 17c, 6 Brl 34 Pcls	237	4	3224
Spanish Juice	Treacle	Vinegar	Salt	Codfish	Herring	Sprag Fish	Sturgeon	Bacon	Pork	Tongue	Cheese

		Butter	*Wheat*	*Barley*	*Rye*	*Oats*	*Malt*	*Peas*	*Beans*	*Potatoes*
		F	Qtr	Qtr	Qtr	Qtr	Qtr	Qtr	Qtr	Bush & sa
THE NORTH	Alnmouth									
	Blyth									
	Shields									1000
	Newcastle				10					5700 4400 35
	Sunderland	83								20 B
	Hartlepool									660
	Stockton									
	Stock/Sunderland									
YORKS	Whitby									4 s. 60 B
	,, /Stockton									
	,, /Sunderland									
	,, /Newcastle									
	Scarborough	20								
	,, /Whitby									
	,, /Stockton									
	,, /Sunderland									30 B
	Bridlington					1000				
	,, /Scarborough									
LINCS	Saltfleet			30	109					
	Mumby									
	Wainfleet									
	Boston				100					
	Spalding									
EAST ANGLIA	Wisbech									
	Lynn			5						4 t
	Burnham			15						
	Wells					20				
	Blakeney									
	Yarmouth	8								
	Aldeburgh									
	Ipswich									400 B 160 s
	Maintree			390						
	Colchester									
THE SOUTH	Rochester									100 s
	Newhaven							6		
	Portsmouth									200 s
	Poole									21 t
WEST COAST	Liverpool									
	Lancaster									
	Ulverston									
	London	59,976	1940	1538		30,943	279	1259	53	62,271 44772B 408
	ENGLISH TOTAL	60,087	1940	1978	219	31,963	279	1265	53	67,795 52,00 Bu. 468
SCOTLAND	B'o'ness							37		
	SCOTTISH TOTAL							211		
	BRITISH TOTAL	60,087	1940	1978	219	31,963	279	1476	53	67,795 52,00 Bush 468 to
		Butter	*Wheat*	*Barley*	*Rye*	*Oats*	*Malt*	*Peas*	*Beans*	*Potatoes*

[T]obacco	Tobacco Sand	Tobacco Dust	Snuff	Hops	Ale	Port Wine	White Port	Madeira	Spanish White	British Compound	Rum
[l]b.	lb.	lb.	lb.	cwt	c	Gal	Gal	Gal	Gal	Gal	Gal
						413					112
[.]37				5	17 342 gall	748	11,362	28		10	187
[.]311			463		10 552 gall	1557			2100		250
[.]37			712		38 gall	749	2800	38	462		349
[.]644					7	396	162		385		219
[.]391			157				194				47
[.]52					2	1529					
47			73		1 30 gall	723	31		190		256
[.]045			335			1113	641	147	390		143
									161		10
[.]008			245		2	1299	158		161		434
[.]04					1						
[.]07			87			152	12		43	59	333
[.]14				3							17
[.]54						253	32		60		18
[.]72			248		36 120 bott	207	120		31	39	635
[.]24				9		31	30				
[.]69				2	16						13
[.]362			222		7 40 gall	1411	1733		886		215
			1056				1027	58	377		10
[.]80			1152		49 310 gall		433				607
[.]001			11,900			138					
[.]892			7800		2						
						286					
	3316	4787	12,607	341	478 Galls 16941	1683	66	7	67		
,571	3316	4787	37,066	360	593 Gall 18,253	12,690	18,801	278	5313	108	3835
											109
											109
,571	3316	4787	37,066	360	593 18253 galls	12,690	18,801	278	5313	108	3944
[T]obacco	Tobacco Sand	Tobacco Dust	Snuff	Hops	Ale	Port Wine	White Port	Madeira	Spanish White	British Compound	Rum

		Brandy	*Geneva*	*Spa Water*	*Camomile*	*Cassia*	*Flowers of Sulpher*	*British Linen*		
		Gal.	Gal.			lb.	cwt	truss	bale	trus
THE NORTH	Alnmouth									
	Blyth									
	Shields									
	Newcastle	1891		bott. 48			44	1		
	Sunderland	23	10							
	Hartlepool									
	Stockton	587					17			
	Stock/Sund'd									
YORKS	Whitby	23								
	,, /Stockton	180						pack 2		
	,, /Sunderland	135								
	,, /Newcastle									
	Scarborough	46	30							
	,, /Whitby									
	,, /Stockton	243	32							
	,, /Sunderland	10								
	Bridlington	114	10							
	,, /Scarborough									
LINCS	Saltfleet	94	42				½			2
	Mumby									
	Wainfleet	37	10							
	Boston	161	154	1 Hamp	bag 1		1 c 56		1	7
	Spalding		19				1½			3
EAST ANGLIA	Wisbech	65	363				¼	3		6
	Lynn	352	368				1			
	Burnham									
	Wells	125								
	Blakeney									9
	Yarmouth						2 c			
	Aldeburgh									
	Ipswich							16		67
	Maintree									
	Colchester									26
THE SOUTH	Rochester									
	Newhaven									
	Portsmouth									
	Poole									
WEST COAST	Liverpool	30								
	Lancaster									
	Ulverston									
	London	8		Hhd 8 1 Brl 5 Hamp		28	780	bale 1 12	76	132
	ENGLISH TOTAL	4114	1038	Hhd 8 48 bott. 5 Hamp 1 Brl	1	28	4 c 900	32 bale 1 2 pack	77	252
SCOTLAND	B'o'ness	981								
	SCOTTISH TOTAL	981								
	BRITISH TOTAL	5095	1038	8 Hhd 48 bott. 5 Hamp 1 Brl	1	28	4 c 900	32 bale 1 2 pack	77	252

Brandy | *Geneva* | *Spa Water* | *Camomile* | *Cassia* | *Flowers of Sulpher* | *British Linen*

		Manchester and Woollen Drapery				*Woollen Drapery*			*Narrow German Linen*	*Narrow Russian Linen*
ck	case	pack	truss	box	bales	bales	truss	pack	hundred ells	hundred ells
0										
									2·2·0	2·0·10
							6			1·0·10
2										
		7	26	5						
		9	2							
							3			
							21			
						1	2	2		
2		4	10							
		168	350							3·1·20
		50	110							
		823	622	58	26					
2							91	55		13·3·10
0							24	25		
							1			
1	1					1879	8	261	17·2·0	234·0·18
7	1	1061	1120	63	26	1880	156	343	20·0·0	597·2·8
						105	9	3		
						105	9	6		
7	1	1061	1120	63	26	1985	165	349	20·0·0	597·2·8
		Manchester and Woollen Drapery				*Woollen Drapery*			*Narrow German Linen*	*Narrow Russian Linen*

		Russian Diaper	*Hessian Canvas*	*Spruce Canvas*	*Undressed Flax*	*Dressed Flax*	*Tow*	*English Linen Yarn*	*Raw Dutch Linen Yarn*	*Spruce Linen Yarn*
		hundred ells	hundred ells	hundred ells	cwt	cwt	cwt	pack	lb.	lb.
THE NORTH	Alnmouth				40					
	Blyth									
	Shields									
	Newcastle		4·0·21	31·3·12	53	matts 15	33			
	Sunderland					766	matts 14			
	Hartlepool		2·3·6	3·0·10	408				950	500
	Stockton		6·2·28	21·0·7	1178	12	6		10,600	
	Stock/Sunderland									
YORKS	Whitby		1·1·18		819		3		600	6272
	,, /Stockton				82					
	,, /Sunderland				230					
	,, /Newcastle									
	Scarborough				5			1	400	
	,, /Whitby									
	,, /Stockton			8·1·7	392		1			
	,, /Sunderland									
	Bridlington			5·1·0	450					
	,, /Scarborough									
LINCS	Saltfleet		0·1·0	1·0·24		78½				
	Mumby					15				
	Wainfleet		2·1·0	11·1·14		47½				
	Boston		30·0·24	12·3·10	24					
	Spalding		3·1·12	83·1·12						
EAST ANGLIA	Wisbech			67·0·10						
	Lynn		43·2·6	279·1·15	13¾					
	Burnham									
	Wells			17·2·15	4½					
	Blakeney									
	Yarmouth		2·2·0	570·2·0	121					
	Aldeburgh									
	Ipswich			220·0·6						
	Maintree									
	Colchester		3·2·9	125·3·11						
THE SOUTH	Rochester									
	Newhaven									
	Portsmouth									
	Poole									
WEST COAST	Liverpool				1609					
	Lancaster									
	Ulverston				72					
	London	14·0·0	91·1·20	776·1·2	165		42 Matts 21			
	ENGLISH TOTAL	14·0·0	192·0·18	2234·3·25	5626¼ 75 Matts	919 15 Matts	85 Matts 35	1	12,550	677
SCOTLAND	B'o'ness				80				18,056	
	SCOTTISH TOTAL				80				18,056	
	BRITISH TOTAL	14·0·0	192·0·18	2234·3·25	5706¼	919 15 Matts	85 Matts 35	1	30,606	677
		Russian Diaper	*Hessian Canvas*	*Spruce Canvas*	*Undressed Flax*	*Dressed Flax*	*Tow*	*English Linen Yarn*	*Raw Dutch Linen Yarn*	*Spruce Linen Yarn*

	Wool Flocks	Estrige Wool	Tanned Leather	English Dressed Italian Kidskins	English Dressed Italian Lambskins	Bristles	Hemp	Cordage	Old Rope	Candlewick	Fuller's Earth
	cwt	cwt	cwt	No.	No.	Doz . lb.	cwt	cwt	t	bag	cwt
						280	860				
12						103	736	400		13	
							299			8	
							686			1	
						103					
							164				
			2				92	4		11	
							12½				
							89½	45			
									1	3	5
								30			
							54		6	6	
			2				104			2	
			14			483	160			6	
							35			1	
·6						208	364	145		60	
						94					
	171·3·0	44·3·6	1256 bun. 40	14,300	44,390	745 5 c 3 Hhd		761			
·18	171·3·0	44·3·6	1274 bun. 40	14,300	44,390	2016 5 c 3 Hhd	3655	1385	7	111	5
·2 ·2											
·20	171·3·0	44·3·6	1274 bun. 40	14,300	44,390	2016 5 c 3 Hhd	3655	1385	7	111	5
	Wool Flocks	Estrige Wool	Tanned Leather	English Dressed Italian Kidskins	English Dressed Italian Lambskins	Bristles	Hemp	Cordage	Old Rope	Candlewick	Fuller's Earth

		Starch	Archil	Arsenic	Copperas	Ivory Black	Lamp Black	Logwood	Orchre	Rud
		lb.	brl	cwt	cwt			cwt	c	c
THE NORTH	Alnmouth									
	Blyth									
	Shields									
	Newcastle						12 Brl 4 c, 6 F	6	2 1 Hhd	
	Sunderland				2					
	Hartlepool									
	Stockton				1		5 c 2 Brl	24		
	Stock/Sunderland									
YORKS	Whitby	28			5		3 c 1120 lb.	2		
	,, /Stockton									
	,, /Sunderland									
	,, /Newcastle									
	Scarborough					1 c	2 c 500 lb.			
	,, /Whitby									
	,, /Stockton						1 c		1	
	,, /Sunderland									
	Bridlington				1	2 c	5 c	4	1	1
	,, /Scarborough									
LINCS	Saltfleet	538		4¼	¼		cag 50			
	Mumby					2 c				
	Wainfleet									2
	Boston				1, 1 F	1 c	6 c	2 bags 5		
	Spalding				2		5 c 1 Brl	8 1 bag	2	
EAST ANGLIA	Wisbech				3	1 F		8		
	Lynn				10		1 Brl 1 c			
	Burnham									
	Wells				3 1 c		2 c	3		
	Blakeney									
	Yarmouth				106 1 Hhd	1 F	7 c		1	
	Aldeburgh									
	Ipswich									
	Maintree									
	Colchester									
THE SOUTH	Rochester									
	Newhaven									
	Portsmouth									
	Poole									
WEST COAST	Liverpool									
	Lancaster									
	Ulverston									
	London		1			6 Hhd 15 c	6 Brl	30		Hhd 10
	ENGLISH TOTAL	566	1	4¼	134¼ 1 c, 1 F 1 Hhd	6 Hhd 2 F 21 c	22 Brl 91 c 1620 lb.	90 3 bags	8 1 Hhd	3 c 10 Hhd
SCOTLAND	B'o'ness									
	SCOTTISH TOTAL									
	BRITISH TOTAL	566	1	4¼	134¼ 1 c, 1 F 1 Hhd	6 Hhd 2 F 21 c	22 Brl 91 c 1620 lb.	90 3 bag	8 1 Hhd	3 c 10 Hhd

Starch Archil Arsenic Copperas Ivory Black Lamp Black Logwood Orchre Rud

Woad	*Aqua Fortis*	*Brimstone*	*Emery*	*Kelp*	*'Soap Ashes'*	*'Lapis Calaminaris'*	*Pearl Ash*	*Potash*	*Tarras*	*Vitriol*
c	bottles	cwt	brl	t	t	t	lb.	Hhd	c	bottles
3		3		1 F	140		2500 1008			20
		4 1		29				3		1
	1	¼ 10								
3		2 3 c					1120		1	
23	230	1920	5			8 5 c	5 Hhd 120 Brl			Hhd 3
29	231	1939 3 c	5	29 1 F	140	8 5 c	4628 5 Hhd 120 Brl	3	1	21 3 Hhd
							Brl 67			
8							Brl 67			
37	231	1939 3 c	5	29 1 F	140	8 5 c	4628 5 Hhd 187 Brl	3	1	21 3 Hhd
Woad	*Aqua Fortis*	*Brimstone*	*Emery*	*Kelp*	*'Soap Ashes'*	*'Lapis Calaminaris'*	*Pearl Ash*	*Potash*	*Tarras*	*Vitriol*

		Braziery						Brass Wire	Copper
		basket	box	bundle	c	Hamper	Hhd	rings	t
THE NORTH	Alnmouth								
	Blyth								
	Shields								
	Newcastle	2		46	8	2			
	Sunderland	2		10	1	3			
	Hartlepool								
	Stockton	2		5	3				
	Stock/Sunderland								
YORKS	Whitby	2	2	21	3				
	,, /Stockton			2					
	,, /Sunderland	8		11					
	,, /Newcastle								
	Scarborough								
	,, /Whitby								
	,, /Stockton			2					
	,, /Sunderland								
	Bridlington					1			
	,, /Scarborough			2	2				
LINCS	Saltfleet								
	Mumby								
	Wainfleet								
	Boston	4	1	29	2				
	Spalding	4		12	1		1		
EAST ANGLIA	Wisbech	3		48	1				
	Lynn	2		28	6				
	Burnham								
	Wells	8		4	1		1		
	Blakeney								
	Yarmouth	8		47	8		4		
	Aldeburgh								
	Ipswich								
	Maintree								
	Colchester								
THE SOUTH	Rochester								
	Newhaven								
	Portsmouth								
	Poole								
WEST COAST	Liverpool								
	Lancaster								
	Ulverston								
	London		2		21	1	1	120	39
	ENGLISH TOTAL	47	5	267	57	7	7	120	39
SCOTLAND	B'o'ness			41	9	2			
	SCOTTISH TOTAL			42	9	2			
	BRITISH TOTAL	47	5	309	66	9	7	120	39

Braziery Brass Wire Copper

Old Copper	Russian Iron	Swedish Iron	English Iron	Pig Iron	Long German Steel	Steel	Steel Filings	Iron Hoops	Iron Plates
cwt	cwt	cwt	t	t	lb.	bundles	c	bundles	bundles
		558		15					
	140	45	20 bars						
	1340	186				40 bars 5 cwt			
	76	186						34	
		7¾				1 cwt			
	640	35½							
		200	5					4	
	110	105	9						
		4		2		1 cwt			
	36	313							
								2	
	12	69			20				
	210								
	249	337	4 bund 10 bars			1 bar		1	No. 41
	102	156	2		59	3 pcs			No. 10
	408	1802		3		2		19	
			2¼						
	622	898							
	20	693							
	1010	2816							
			3					30	
			4					25	
	125	790	½ 7 bund 35 bars			19 cwt			
						10			
						5			
				50					
	20	80							
108		70	3½ bund 61			729 102½ t	4		257
108	5120	9351¼	30½ 65 bars 72 bund	70	79	757 41 bars 104 t 3 cwt	4	115	257 No. 51
		1035							
	3	1035							
108	5123	10,386¼	30½ 65 bars 72 bund	70	79	757 41 bars 104 t 3 cwt	4	115	257 No. 51
Old Copper	Russian Iron	Swedish Iron	English Iron	Pig Iron	Long German Steel	Steel	Steel Filings	Iron Hoops	Iron Plates

		Rod Iron	Rolled Iron	Slit Iron	Iron Wire	English Manufactured Iron	Wrought & Cast Iron			
		bundles	bundle	bundles		t	t	c	box	T
THE NORTH	Alnmouth									
	Blyth									
	Shields									
	Newcastle					22	23	134	21	3
	Sunderland				rolls 5	17	7	5		
	Hartlepool									
	Stockton				rings 2		36	5	7	
	Stock/Sunderland									
YORKS	Whitby					5¾	13½	6	3	
	,, /Stockton					7		2		
	,, /Sunderland					5	4			
	,, /Newcastle									
	Scarborough					8				
	,, /Whitby									
	,, /Stockton							6	4	
	,, /Sunderland					2				
	Bridlington	2				3¼	7¼			
	,, /Scarborough	2	1			1½				
LINCS	Saltfleet			114		bund 8	1½	2	8	
	Mumby						3			
	Wainfleet	5				½			1	
	Boston					bund 25 3¼ t	2¼	9	8	
	Spalding					14½	½	37	6	
EAST ANGLIA	Wisbech				bund 1	½	9	21	10	
	Lynn					8	120	246	108	
	Burnham									
	Wells		2		bund 2	3¼	9¾	50	27	
	Blakeney									
	Yarmouth					6	133	331	126	
	Aldeburgh									
	Ipswich		10					34	16	
	Maintree									
	Colchester					1	2½	35	1	
THE SOUTH	Rochester									
	Newhaven		34					7	1	
	Portsmouth							}31		
	Poole									
WEST COAST	Liverpool					5		3		
	Lancaster									
	Ulverston									
	London		208		840 rings 560 bund 9t, 1 Hhd 20 c	274 bund 321		1077	46	3
	ENGLISH TOTAL	9	255	114	847 rings 563 bund 9t, 1 Hhd 20 c	388 bund 354	336¼	5020	392	4
SCOTLAND	B'o'ness					16	14			
	SCOTTISH TOTAL					19 bund 37	14	234	40	6
	BRITISH TOTAL	9	255	114	847 rings 563 bund 9 t, 20 c 1 Hhd	407 bund 391	350¼	5252	432	4

Rod Iron | Rolled Iron | Slit Iron | Iron Wire | English Manufactured Iron | Wrought & Cast Iron

		Ironmongery						Anvils	Files	Guns 9 lb.
le	case	Parcel & bag	Pack	Hamp	Hhd	basket	Tierce	No.		
		13		19	3	2				
		22		1		3				
		9	3	5						
		85		5				6		
		40								
		4				3				
		5								
				4						
		30								
		14	6	2		2			2 bag	
		8		1		8	3			
		4								
		1				1				
						10		2		
			2	9	2			1		
		1	5	8				4		
		1084				98				
			3	17		3				
			46			123				
			8	13	2	7				
		6		2		4				
		3								
	5		1	4	6		1	16	14 c	62
5	5	1329	74	90	13	265	4	29	14 c 2 bag	62
								8		
	8	200	22	14		19		8		
5	13	1529	96	104	13	284	4	37	14 c 2 bag	62

Ironmongery Anvils Files Guns 9 lb.

		Guns 18 lb.	Nails	Iron Pots	Saws	Scythes	Sickles	Shovels & Spades	Old Iron	Lead
		No.	bags	No.	bundles	bundles	truss		cwt	c
THE NORTH	Alnmouth									
	Blyth									
	Shields									
	Newcastle		296		1	45	12		63	
	Sunderland				4				70	
	Hartlepool									
	Stockton								40	
	Stock/Sunderland									
YORKS	Whitby				6		1	bund. 6	20	
	,, /Stockton									
	,, /Sunderland					4 doz.				
	,, /Newcastle									
	Scarborough							bund. 4	68	
	,, /Whitby									
	,, /Stockton					5 doz.		2 doz.	120	
	,, /Sunderland								200	
	Bridlington		20							
	,, /Scarborough		4							
LINCS	Saltfleet							bund 3 2 doz.		
	Mumby							bundle 1		
	Wainfleet			26						1
	Boston		52	64	4			bund. 27		2
	Spalding				4			bund. 8		6
EAST ANGLIA	Wisbech					9				
	Lynn		5282		3	60				11
	Burnham									
	Wells				2	40 30 doz.		bund. 12 20 doz.		
	Blakeney		11							1
	Yarmouth					270 doz.		125 doz.		1
	Aldeburgh									
	Ipswich		909	26	6	7 26 doz.	3			
	Maintree									
	Colchester		909			8 doz.				1
THE SOUTH	Rochester									
	Newhaven		246	70		50		bund. 9		5
	Portsmouth					14 doz.				
	Poole				1					
WEST COAST	Liverpool									
	Lancaster									
	Ulverston									
	London	124	sacks 292 20,571		93	337	10	bund. 188 254 doz.		24,
	ENGLISH TOTAL	124	28,300 sacks 298	186	124	548 357 doz.	26	bun. 258 403 doz.	581	28,
SCOTLAND	B'o'ness		5		18					
	SCOTTISH TOTAL		5		18				40	4
	BRITISH TOTAL	124	28,305 sacks 298	186	142	548 357 doz.	26	bund. 258 403 doz.	621	28,

Guns 18 lb. | Nails | Iron Pots | Saws | Scythes | Sickles | Shovels & Spades | Old Iron | Lead

Lead (pieces)	Lead Sheets	Lead Shot	Red Lead		White Lead		Pewter	Old Pewter	Tin Plates	Tinware
No.	cwt.	No.	brl	c	brl	c	cwt	cwt	boxes	basket
	3		10	5		12			98	
									16	
		3½							6	
30		5				3			6	
	2									
	5					5			4	
									18	
						2			6	
	3	3								
						2			4	
		2		1½	14½					
		2c								
										1
		5								
20		12				1			4	
100		10			4	9				
			1	4					9	
668	14	46	1	1		2			16	
15		13½		1					10	
						1				
242	46	160	2	14		22			14	
60	10	158								
120	9	110		2						
		1 c								
	3 12 cwt	40							13	
1,225	659	110	1374	609	19	72	10	16	965	
2,480	754 12 cwt	678 3 c	1388	637½	37½	131	10	16	1189	1
	78	50	2	27		10			205	
	78	100	2	27		10			232	
2,480	832 12 cwt	778 3 c	1390	664½	37½	141	10	16	1421	1
Lead (pieces)	Lead Sheets	Lead Shot	Red Lead		White Lead		Pewter	Old Pewter	Tin Plates	Tinware

		Cod Oil	*Linseed Oil*	*Rape Oil*	*Sperm Oil*	*Whale Oil*	*Paint*	*Pitch*	*Rosin*
		Gall.	c	c	Gall.	Gall.	c	Brl	cwt
THE NORTH	Alnmouth		1 Hhd	4				6	
	Blyth								
	Shields								
	Newcastle	44	46 4 Hhd	15	42	1808 3 c	54	192	117 3 Brl 1 F
	Sunderland		4	4	30	770		45	20 Brl 3 c
	Hartlepool								
	Stockton		4 5 Hhd	1 2 Brl	32	2 c	2	58	55 21 Brl
	Stock/Sunderland								
YORKS	Whitby	44	6	2			3	41	7 Brl
	,, /Stockton								
	,, /Sunderland		1			654		31	5
	,, /Newcastle								
	Scarborough	45	1	1				16	3 Brl
	,, /Whitby								
	,, /Stockton		6 2 Hhd	1 Brl			1	2	
	,, /Sunderland		1			1 Brl		2	
	Bridlington		3	3		73	3 1 F	10	
	,, /Scarborough		2			1 Brl			1 Brl
LINCS	Saltfleet			1 Brl	15	117		½	¾
	Mumby		1					2	
	Wainfleet		3				3	2	
	Boston	60	1	4		364	40	49	3 Brl 2 F
	Spalding	44	2	7 3 Brl		705 3 Brl	11 3 F	79	10½ 6 Brl
EAST ANGLIA	Wisbech		6			316 3 c	18 4 F	71	5
	Lynn	33	2 4 Hhd			320	12	431	15 6 Brl
	Burnham								
	Wells		16 4 Hhd	1	45		7 1 F	14	7
	Blakeney		1					2	2
	Yarmouth		99 8 Hhd	19 2 Hhd		70		344	23 13 Brl
	Aldeburgh								
	Ipswich								
	Maintree								
	Colchester							20	9 Brl
THE SOUTH	Rochester								
	Newhaven							9	
	Portsmouth								
	Poole								
WEST COAST	Liverpool		55	2 Hhd					
	Lancaster								
	Ulverston								
	London		100 38 Hhd 6 pun	5 33 Hhd 1 Brl	2217	74		1772	320
	ENGLISH TOTAL	270	360 66 Hhd 6 pun	66 8 Brl 37 Hhd	2381	5271 8 c 5 Brl	154 9 F	3198½	559 92 Brl
SCOTLAND	B'o'ness		13	88 2 Brl	2 c	554			
	SCOTTISH TOTAL		13	88 2 Brl	2 c	554	6		
	BRITISH TOTAL	270	373 66 Hhd 6 pun	154 10 Brl 37 Hhd	2381 2 c	5825 8 c 5 Brl	9 F 160	3198½	559 92 Brl

Tallow	*Tar*	*Tar Varnish*	*Turps*	*Refined Turps*	*Varnish*	*Hard Soap*	*Soft Soap*		
cwt	brl	c	bottles		c	lb.	F	½F	½ Brl
	100					630			
	108		6 43 Brl 24 c	22 F 6 Brl 1 c		36,920	597	961	164
	568				2	17,374	139	360	
	144		300 Gall 1 Hhd 2 cwt	12 cwt 1 Brl	2	7052 1 F	53	186	
	134		3, 5 Brl 1 c			10,507	4	16	
			1			2232	38	100	20
	64		4 Brl 3 c	10 c		2604	15	66	3
	178		4 Brl 1 F		1	10,525	4	8	
	60		3			3,806	44	72	
	31					2 Hhd 8 c	122	226	1
	41			8½ cwt 2 F, 3 c		2726	1	1	
	21		10, 1 c			6674 1 F	4	6	
	3					1120	1		
	14		3, 2 c			1120	3	2	
	171	1	3, 7 c 1 Brl	3 F		26,590	48	108	
	237	2	22 15 c	1 F 1 Brl		9940	58	68	
	199		12, 4 c 2 Hhd	5 cwt	1	7,816	4	24	
	863		4 3 cwt 4 c	5 cwt 3 F		130	21	30	
	44		2						
	14			½ cwt					
406	111		6 Brl 9 ch	7 F 6 Brl	6				
	30								
20	20								
	9								
1687 3080	405		cwt 800 30 bott.						
2113 308 c	3569	3	99 63 Brl 70 c 3 Hhd 805 cwt	38 F 14 Brl 31 cwt 14 c	12	147,766	1156	2234	188
2113 308 c	3569	3	99, 4 Brl 63 Brl 70c,3Hd 805 cwt	38 F 14 Brl 31 cwt 14 c	12	147,766	1156	2234	188

		Sperm Candles	Tallow Candles	Linseed	Rape Seed	Linseed Cakes	Rape Cakes	Ash Timber	Fir Timber
		lb.	lb.	Qtr	Qtr	t	t	t	loads
THE NORTH	Alnmouth			½					
	Blyth								
	Shields								
	Newcastle	1660		100	100			40	
	Sunderland	178 2 box				4		4	
	Hartlepool								
	Stockton	618		1		28½			3
	,, /Sunderland								
YORKS	Whitby					3		8	5
	,, /Stockton	50				5			
	,, /Sunderland								
	,, /Newcastle								
	Scarborough								
	,, /Whitby								
	,, /Stockton	290							
	,, /Sunderland	6 box							
	Bridlington					2			
	,, /Scarborough					1			
LINCS	Saltfleet		984 7 box			7			183
	Mumby								
	Wainfleet								46
	Boston	36							21
	Spalding					1			
EAST ANGLIA	Wisbech			6 Brl					
	Lynn	1 box		210					40
	Burnham		280						
	Wells						50		12½
	Blakeney								4
	Yarmouth	963 4 box		200					
	Aldeburgh								
	Ipswich	117							
	Maintree								
	Colchester								
THE SOUTH	Rochester								
	Newhaven								
	Portsmouth								
	Poole								
WEST COAST	Liverpool	72							
	Lancaster								40
	Ulverston								20
	London	16,297 32 chest 127 box	5174						
	ENGLISH TOTAL	20,281 140 box 32 chest	6438 7 box	511½ 6 Brl	100	51	50	52	374½
SCOTLAND	B'o'ness	404		50					
	SCOTTISH TOTAL	404		50					
	BRITISH TOTAL	20,685 140 box 32 chest	6438 7 box	561½ 6 Brl	100	51	50	52	374½
		Sperm Candles	Tallow Candles	Linseed	Rape Seed	Linseed Cakes	Rape Cakes	Ash Timber	Fir Timber

Battens	Deals	Laths	Barrel Staves	Butt Staves	Hogshead Staves	Pipe Staves	Pailing Boards	Double Uffers	Single Uffers
hundreds	hundreds	bundles	hundreds	hundreds	hundreds	hundreds	hundreds	No.	No.
	2·9·20								
3·0·0	2·0·0								
	0·1·10	50				3·0·0			
7·3·0	3·3·0	80			1·1·0				
									78
3·0·0	6·0·0								
30·0·26	73·3·16					1·2·0	6·0·0	10	180
2·0·0			3·0·0	16·0·0	5·2·8	7·0·10			
						11·0·0			
			6·0·0			1·0·0			
		1230							
		20							180
									16
7·0·0	10·0·10	500							
		627							
	4·0·0								
2·0·0	7·0·0								
54·3·26	111·1·16	2507	9·0·0	16·0·0	6·3·8	23·2·10	6·0·0	10	454
			230·0·0		15·0·0				
			349·0·0		65·0·0				
54·3·26	111·1·16	2507	558·0·0	16·0·0	71·3·8	23·2·10	6·0·0	10	454
Battens	Deals	Laths	Barrel Staves	Butt Staves	Hogshead Staves	Pipe Staves	Pailing Boards	Double Uffers	Single Uffers

		Oak Timber	*Oak Bark*	*Oak Stoops*	*Cork Machines*	*Spinning Wheels*	*Stocking Frames*	*Ploughs*	*Corks*
		t	t		No.	No.	No.		bag
THE NORTH	Alnmouth	16	18						
	Blyth	17							
	Shields								
	Newcastle	263	188						10 cw
	Sunderland	167	16						6
	Hartlepool								
	Stockton	2	32						43 c
	,, /Sunderland								
YORKS	Whitby	1226	107						
	,, /Stockton								
	,, /Sunderland								
	,, /Newcastle								
	Scarborough	52	42						
	,, /Whitby								
	,, /Stockton								
	,, /Sunderland								8
	Bridlington	38	38						
	,, /Scarborough								
LINCS	Saltfleet			7 doz		30			
	Mumby					12			
	Wainfleet								
	Boston	18				24			5
	Spalding								4
EAST ANGLIA	Wisbech								
	Lynn			6 t	1				
	Burnham								
	Wells				1				
	Blakeney								
	Yarmouth								
	Aldeburgh								
	Ipswich				1				
	Maintree								
	Colchester								
THE SOUTH	Rochester	243							
	Newhaven								
	Portsmouth								
	Poole								
WEST COAST	Liverpool								
	Lancaster								
	Ulverston								
	London	822	144		4			12	
	ENGLISH TOTAL	2864	585	6 t 7 doz	7	66		12	68 11 cw
SCOTLAND	B'o'ness	69	157				21		
	SCOTTISH TOTAL	317	286				21		
	BRITISH TOTAL	3181	871	6 t 7 doz	7	66	21	12	68 11 cw

Oak Timber | *Oak Bark* | *Oak Stoops* | *Cork Machines* | *Spinning Wheels* | *Stocking Frames* | *Ploughs* | *Corks*

	Earthenware			Glass				Paper	Glue
ates	Hhd	pieces	c	crates	box	Hhd	crates	bundles R(eams)	cwt
94	8							130	8
20			2						
51	1								1¼
24									
10									
10									
22									
23	1								
47		480		1	1			1½ R	2
5									
21		720						9, 41 R	½
2								7	
							12 doz	10, 24 R	
8		1140							
27	1	840	3	5	2		7	50	
10	1		3						2
510	6						7		7
								1	
02	15			1		3			1
1		72							
20	66			2		6		334, 10 Hhd 69 truss 18 bales	3
80	43								
04						1			
39	1								
90									
633	117		17	106	43			4446 22 Hhd	
753	260	3252	25	115	46	10	14 12 doz	4986 66½ R 69 truss 18 bales 32 Hhd	24¾
95	5		28						
04	5		28						
957	265	3252	53	115	46	10	14 12 doz	4986 66½ R 69 truss 13 bales 32 Hhd	24¾
	Earthenware			Glass				Paper	Glue

		Bricks	*Flagstones*	*Freestone*	*Limestone*	*Marble*	*Pantiles*
		No.	t	t	t	t	No.
THE NORTH	Alnmouth						
	Blyth						
	Shields						
	Newcastle						
	Sunderland	23,000	6				9000
	Hartlepool						
	Stockton	1400	7				5500
	,, /Sunderland						
YORKS	Whitby						
	,, /Stockton						
	,, /Sunderland	30,000					
	,, /Newcastle						
	Scarborough	3000	40				6000
	,, /Whitby						
	,, /Stockton		6				
	,, /Sunderland						
	Bridlington	2000	29½	3			49,000
	,, /Scarborough						
LINCS	Saltfleet						7000
	Mumby						1500
	Wainfleet	3000					7000
	Boston	5000			20		56,000
	Spalding	3000					26,000
EAST ANGLIA	Wisbech		10		70		48,000
	Lynn		69				251,000
	Burnham						
	Wells	39,000					45,000
	Blakeney						65,000
	Yarmouth		24				257,500
	Aldeburgh						
	Ipswich	44,000	39				1000
	Maintree						
	Colchester						
THE SOUTH	Rochester						
	Newhaven						
	Portsmouth						
	Poole					4	
WEST COAST	Liverpool						
	Lancaster						
	Ulverston	2000					
	London	1000	3832				91,800
	ENGLISH TOTAL	156,000	4059½	3	90	4	926,300
SCOTLAND	B'o'ness				60		
	SCOTTISH TOTAL				150		
	BRITISH TOTAL	156,000	4059½	3	240	4	926,300
		Bricks	*Flagstones*	*Freestone*	*Limestone*	*Marble*	*Pantiles*

Plaster	*Quarry Stones*	*Slate*	*Steps*	*Whiting*	*Grindstones*	*Millstones*	*Scythestones*	*Inland Coal*
t	t	t	t	c	No.	pair	No.	chaldron
10		3						
				1 Hhd				
5				1, 1 Brl		7		
1								
							1000	
1				1 1 Hhd 1 Brl				50
		12		2 6 Brl				
							1000	83
				1 Hhd	20		2 t 3000	
							3t, 1500	22
5							39½ t	155
				1			15,000 2 Hhd	45
19 c	30							
71				3			44,000	
								50
8							13 t	
							1 c	
						8	2 t	
				1				
516 167 Hhd			2	17	4 2 t	7	121½ t	299
617 167 Hhd 19 c	30	15	2	26 3 Hhd 8 Brl	24 2 t	22	181 t 51,000 1 c	704
20								
20								8
637 167 Hhd 19 c	30	15	2	26 3 Hhd 8 Brl	24 2 t	22	181 t 51,000 1 c	712

Plaster *Quarry Stones* *Slate* *Steps* *Whiting* *Grindstones* *Millstones* *Scythestones* *Inland Coal*

Appendix 17

SHIPPING 'BELONGING' TO HULL: FOREIGN-GOING, COASTAL AND FISHING VESSELS WHICH HAVE TRADED, COUNTING EACH SHIP ONCE ONLY, 1709–82

	Foreign	*Coastal*	*Fishing*	*Total*
1709	3,000	4,467		7,467
1716	6,315	5,340		11,655
1723	5,040	5,384		10,424
1730	6,500	5,400		11,900
1737	6,709	5,704		12,413
1744	6,815	5,650		12,465
1751	10,986	4,950		15,936
1752	12,491	4,967		17,458
1753	12,024	5,166		17,190
1754	11,487	5,723	1,453	18,663
1755	9,350	5,194	2,208	16,752
1756	9,870	5,614	2,210	17,694
1757	8,390	5,990	1,227	15,607
1758	6,750	6,384	1,168	14,302
1759	6,060	5,498	1,015	12,573
1760	5,670	5,474	1,015	12,159
1761	6,746	4,894	656	12,296
1762	6,630	4,756	656	12,042
1763	7,266	5,090	0	12,356
1764	8,256	5,486	0	13,742
1765	9,071	6,760	0	15,831
1766	10,630	6,105	315	17,050
1767	9,485	5,743	662	15,890
1768	9,785	6,116	1,054	16,955
1769	9,108	6,272	1,816	17,196
1770	9,552	6,249	1,598	17,399
1771	10,172	5,982	1,934	18,088
1772	10,205	5,844	2,355	18,404
1773	10,908	6,458	2,669	20,035
1774	12,505	6,153	2,703	21,361
1775	10,975	6,420	3,548	20,943
1776	13,770	6,864	2,846	23,480
1177	12,998	7,137	2,533	22,668
1778	13,732	7,312	2,231	23,275
1779	10,470	8,664	982	20,116

	Foreign	*Coastal*	*Fishing*	*Total*
1780	9,820	8,916	1,059	19,795
1781	8,880	9,276	764	18,917
1782	8,410	11,294	761	20,465

Note: In view of later developments, it should be emphasized that 'Fishing' here means, for the most part, whaling.

Source: BM Add. MS 11255–6.

Appendix 18

SHIPPING 'BELONGING' TO HULL: FOREIGN-GOING, COASTAL AND FISHING VESSELS, WHICH HAVE TRADED, 1772–86

	Foreign		*Coastal*		*Fishing*		*Total*			
	No.	*Tons*	*No.*	*Tons*	*No.*	*Tons*	*No.*	*Tons*	*Average*	*Index*
1772	84	10,635	130	6,384	11	2,379	225	19,398	86	52
1773	79	11,158	138	6,947	12	2,693	229	20,798	91	55
1774	91	12,945	135	6,820	12	2,727	238	22,492	95	60
1775	83	11,275	143	6,800	16	3,588	242	21,663	90	58
1776	95	13,970	147	7,479	14	2,872	256	24,321	95	65
1777	87	13,408	151	7,677	14	2,581	252	23,666	94	63
1778	90	14,812	147	7,972	11	2,279	248	25,063	101	67
1779	61	10,770	149	9,282	9	1,030	219	21,082	96	56
1780	66	10,100	162	9,349	9	1,107	237	20,556	87	55
1781	62	9,175	170	9,801	8	809	240	19,785	82	53
1782	56	8,530	171	11,785	6	785	233	21,099	91	56
1783	82	13,290	162	10,107	7	1,090	251	24,487	98	65
1784	114	21,551	172	11,199	10	2,501	296	35,251	119	94
1785	128	21,992	185	11,723	31	4,036	344	37,751	110	101
1786	121	21,265	180	10,971	39	5,279	340	37,515	110	100

Source: PRO Customs 17.

Appendix 19

SHIPS REGISTERED AT HULL, ON 30 SEPTEMBER 1788–1800

	No.	*Tons*	*Average*	*Index*
1788	392	52,101	133	100
1789	397	53,025	134	102
1790	417	53,890	129	103
1791	443	54,677	123	105
1792	467	58,039	124	111
1793	472	57,891	123	111
1794	512	60,749	119	117
1795	531	61,494	116	118
1796	542	64,643	119	124
1797	545	64,477	118	124
1798	546	65,021	119	125
1799	553	65,337	118	125
1800	611	68,533	112	132

Source: PRO Customs 17.

Appendix 20

THE NUMBER AND TONNAGE OF SHIPS REGISTERED AT HULL ON 30 SEPTEMBER 1790, 1795 AND 1800, GROUPED BY SIZE

Group	*1–20 tons*		*20–40*		*40–60*		*60–80*		*80–100*		*100–20*	
	No.	*Tons*	*No.*	*Tons*	*No.*	*Tons*	*No.*	*Tons*	*No.*	*Tons*	*No.*	*Tons*
1790	33	303	8	268	96	4503	56	3900	41	3625	33	3605
1795	40	371	10	305	174	8039	54	3699	34	2975	38	4117
1800	45	488	11	320	228	10518	39	2665	27	2405	33	3626
Group	*120–40*		*140–60*		*160–80*		*180–200*		*200–20*		*220–40*	
	No.	*Tons*	*No.*	*Tons*	*No.*	*Tons*	*No.*	*Tons*	*No.*	*Tons*	*No.*	*Tons*
1790	30	3890	21	3137	14	2376	28	5320	12	2520	11	2531
1795	34	4383	17	2341	11	1879	23	4359	10	2106	13	2986
1800	49	6345	27	3988	11	1862	25	2711	17	3579	19	4372
Group	*240–60*		*260–80*		*280–300*		*300–20*		*320–40*		*340–60*	
	No.	*Tons*	*No.*	*Tons*	*No.*	*Tons*	*No.*	*Tons*	*No.*	*Tons*	*No.*	*Tons*
1790	14	3491	8	2183	7	2036	6	1851	7	2297	6	2100
1795	12	2939	4	1080	7	2034	10	3106	13	4273	6	2090
1800	11	2732	12	3255	9	2601	7	2177	17	5591	8	2773
Group	*360–80*		*380–400*		*400–20*		*420–40*		*440–60*		*460–80*	
	No.	*Tons*	*No.*	*Tons*	*No.*	*Tons*	*No.*	*Tons*	*No.*	*Tons*	*No.*	*Tons*
1790	6	2220	2	777	2	810	1	423	0		0	
1795	13	4791	3	1167	2	810	1	431	1	445	0	
1800	6	2209	3	1161	2	826	3	1288	0		1	465
Group	*480–500*		*500–20*		*520–40*		*540–60*		*650–80* tons			
	No.	*Tons*	*No.*	*Tons*	*No.*	*Tons*	*No.*	*Tons*	*No.*	*Tons*	*No.*	*Tons*
1790	0		1	505	0		0		0			
1795	0		1	505	0		0		0			
1800	0		0		0		0		1	573		

Source: PRO Customs 17/13, 17 & 22.

Appendix 21

THE BACKGROUND OF MERCHANT APPRENTICES IN HULL, 1720–1800

	Hull Merchant Stock	*'Hull Gentry'*	*'Alien' Merchant Stock*	*'Alien' Gentry*	*Others*	TOTAL		*Hull Merchant Stock*	*Hull 'Gentry'*	*'Alien' Merchant Stock*	*'Alien' Gentry*	*Others*	TOTAL		*Hull Merchant Stock*	*Hull 'Gentry'*	*'Alien' Merchant Stock*	*'Alien' Gentry*	*Others*	TOTAL
1720							1750							1780				1		1
1721			1			1	1751							1781						
1722	1			1		2	1752							1782						
1723							1753				1	1	2	1783						
1724			1			1	1754							1784						
1725							1755			1		1	2	1785		1				1
1726			1			1	1756				1		1	1786						
1727				1	1	2	1757	2	2			1	5	1787						
1728							1758			1		2	3	1788						
1729							1759		1			1	2	1789						
1730				2	1	3	1760					1	1	1790		1				1
1731	1				1	2	1761							1791					2	2
1732				1		1	1762	1				1	2	1792				1		1
1733							1763				1	2	3	1793				1	1	2
1734				1		1	1764			1	1	3	5	1794	1	2				3
1735				2		2	1765					1	1	1795	1			1		2
1736				1		1	1766		1				1	1796		1				1
1737		1		3		4	1767					1	1	1797						
1738			3	2		5	1768							1798						
1739				3		3	1769							1799						
1740				3	2	5	1770		1				1	1800						
1741	2					2	1771													
1742							1772							TOTAL	11	11	13	32	26	93
1743			2		1	3	1773													
1744			1	1		2	1774													
1745			1			1	1775													
1746							1776													
1747				1		1	1777													
1748	1			1	2	4	1778													
1749							1779	1					1							

Sources: GH IIA, *passim.*

Appendix 22

'THE HIGH STREET STAITHS: THE WIDTH OF THE DIFFERENT STAITHS AND FRONT-STEADS NEXT THE RIVER HULL'

(*c.* 1770. From Hadley, p. 688)

Working from north to south. The figures show:

(a) the depth from street to river
(*b*) the width of the street front
(*c*) the width of the river front

	(*a*)	(*b*)	(*c*)
'At the Stone Chair	31	8	8
Mr. Maister's Ground	31	425	447
Alderman Blayde's front	31	73	66
Mr. Walton's	31	87	83
Kirkman's & Holgate's	31	70	83
Road to the Bridge	141	40	14
Mr. Blayde's Yard	140	183	250
Mr. Walton's Yard	140	100	96
Mrs. Fernley's	140	25	21
Mr. Bower's	140	42	54
Mr. Thompson's (Brick)	140	70	36
Mr. Blayde's (B)	140	46	77
New Staith	161	13	15
Mrs. Thompson's	161	25	49
Denton's late Lawson's (B)	161	25	44
Test's	161	37	0
Alderman Porter's	161	28	63
Mingay's now Porter's	161	20	0
Mingay's now Porter's (B)	186	17	18
Standage's & Stockdale's	186	47	65
Mr. Rennard's	186	42	48
Mr. Pease's (B)	186	51	119
Mr. Dixon's (B)	205	45	51
Alderman Perrot's & Collector's (B)	205	82	90
New Staith	224	9	12
Mr. Hambledon's (B)	224	50	67
Alderman Wilberforce's (B)	224	62	46
Mr. Kirkby's	224	23	50
Mr. Horner's (B)	224	29	50
Mr. Howard's	251	51	23
Mr. Bealby's	251	28	22

	(a)	(b)	(c)
Alderman Thompson's (B)	251	66	66
Chapel Lane Staith	233	13	13
Mr. Travis's (B)	233	22	19
Alderman Mould's	233	24	20
Custom House	233	46	49
Mr. Ray's	233	26	27
Mr. Isaac Broadley's	233	40	32
Mr. Pease's	233	27	21
The Hawck	233	28	26
Bishop Lane Staith	190	9	10
Captain Keld's	190	18	0
Alderman Cookson's	190	24	43
King's	190	38	28
Mr. Sykes's (B)	188	57	58
Captain Coat's (B)	188	37	37
Mr. Williamson's (B)	188	32	31
Scale Lane Staith	192	10	11
Andrew's (B)	192	26	37
Lambert's	192	29	34
Alderman Etherington's	192	49	48
Mr. Prime's (B)	192	22	19
Mr. Kirkman's	192	20	19
Mr. Taylor's	192	18	16
Mr. Kickson's (B)	194	15	16
Charterhouse (B)	194	34	34
Mr. Bell's	194	44	33
Mr. Lee's Sailmaker	194	23	20
Mr. Master's (B)	194	42	35
Church Lane Staith	185	16	13
Mr. Neave's (B)	185	44	18
Corporation's	185	19	10
Mr. Lee's Cork Merchant	185	13	8
Thomas Broadley's Esq. (B)	185	56	49
Mr. Horner's	185	24	20
Mr. Burrel's (B)	185	19	18
Mr. Wilson's	152	19	14
Mr. Watson's	152	43	41
Mr. Shield's	150	21	11
Mr. Christian Bell's	150	20	16
Mr. Barroby's (B)	150	21	19
Mr. Ward's (B)	150	49	40
Mr. Hickson	150	33	29
Mr. Prymes' (B)	150	15	18
Mr. Etherington's	150	42	37

	(a)	(b)	(c)
Rottenherring Staith	81	12	21
Charterhouse	54	67	68
Crompton's	54	29	43
Ellworth's (B)	49	33	00
Horse Staith	45	8	0
Corporation House and South End	42	197	0'

Note (B) = Brick built

aniel S.

Mark Kirkby

chards. = [1] Mary K
[2] Mary Donkin

Christopher K

thy Twigg = *Ald. Joseph S.*

e

Richd S. *Ald. John S.* Mary Anne = *Henry Thornton*

SYKES

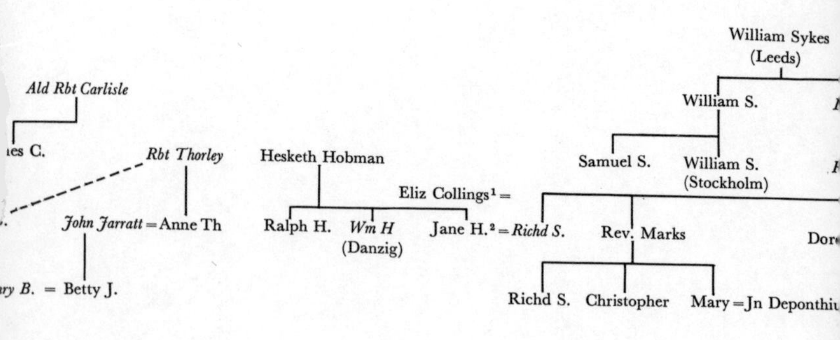

as B.

Rev. J. Bourne = Anne T.
(Charterhouse)

Jn. Twigg

MAISTER

Ald. Jn. Rogers (M.P.)

Henry Maister (1632–99)

[H]ealey = Eliz R. Lucy R. = *William M.* (M.P.)

Sarah M = *Josh Fernley*

Henry M. (M.P.)

Wm. Henworth = Eliz M.

William M. (Stockholm & St. Petersburg)

Nathaniel M.

[Wil]liam M. ([Sto]ckholm)

Arthur M.

Eliz. H. = Jn Moses (Tronjheim)

John Maister

Sarah Twigg = Ald *Wm. Osbourne*

Anne Eliz. O. = John B.

Nicholas Twigg

Nicholas Twigg

BROADLEY

Thomas Broadley

Thomas B. = Ag[...]

Anne Grundy = *Thomas B*[...]

R.C.B. *Ald. He*[...]

Thom[...]

SMITH

Abel Smith (Nottingham)

[...]n. Bird ([Lo]ndon)

Mary Bird = *Abel Smith*

[2] *Robert S.* (M.P.) [1] *Abel S.* =

CROWLE

William Crowle

George C. (M.P.)

Rev. T. C.

John Uppleby = Dorothy C.

Elizabeth U

Geo U – G. Knowsley – J.R. Pease

PEASE

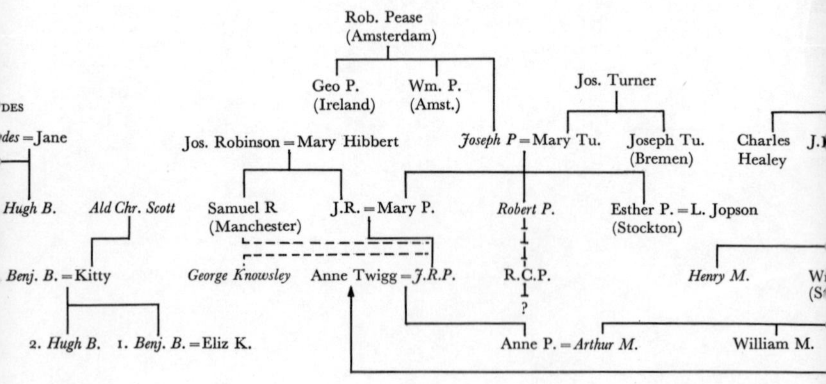
DES
des = Jane
Hugh B.
Ald Chr. Scott
Benj. B. = Kitty
2. Hugh B.
1. Benj. B. = Eliz K.
Rob. Pease
(Amsterdam)
Geo P.
(Ireland)
Wm. P.
(Amst.)
Jos. Turner
Jos. Robinson = Mary Hibbert
Joseph P = Mary Tu.
Joseph Tu.
(Bremen)
Charles
Healey
Samuel R
(Manchester)
J.R. = Mary P.
Robert P.
Esther P. = L. Jopson
(Stockton)
George Knowsley
Anne Twigg = J.R.P.
R.C.P.
?
Henry M.
Anne P. = Arthur M.
William M.

WILBERFORCE

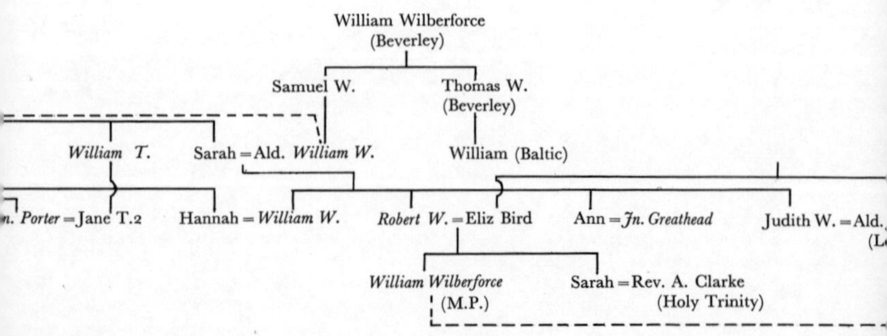
William Wilberforce
(Beverley)
Samuel W.
Thomas W.
(Beverley)
William T.
Sarah = Ald. William W.
William (Baltic)
n. Porter = Jane T.2
Hannah = William W.
Robert W. = Eliz Bird
Ann = Jn. Greathead
Judith W. = Ald.
William Wilberforce
(M.P.)
Sarah = Rev. A. Clarke
(Holy Trinity)

= Thos Slater

. Slater

Appendix 23

SOME MERCHANT RELATIONSHIPS

Note: Partnerships (other than between brothers) indicated thus: ------
Not all children are noted.
Not all children are in order of seniority, in which case they are numbered in order.
Leading merchants thus: *Ald. Francis Pryme.*
[There is some doubt about the connexion between Sir Samuel Standidge and Samuel Thornton; his daughter married Samuel Thornton Esq., but there may have been two Samuel Thorntons.]

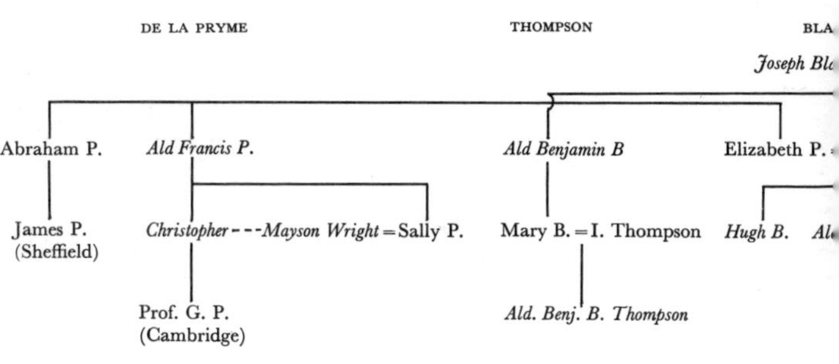

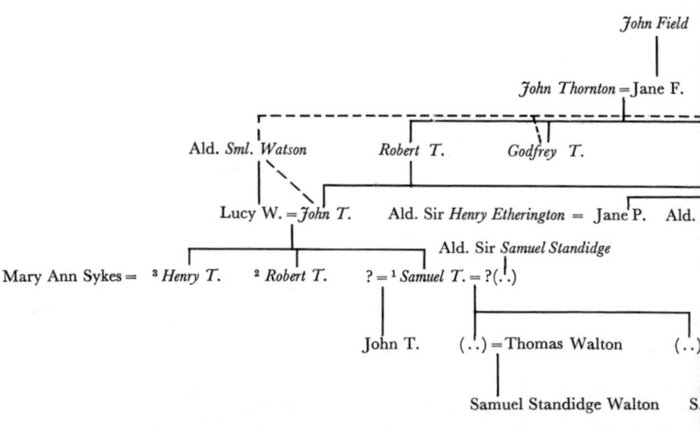

Appendix 24

SHERIFFS OF HULL, 1700–1805

1700 John Somerscales
1701 Andrew Perrott
1702 Benjamin Blaydes
1703 Thomas Clark
1704 Benjamin Ward
1705 John Porter
1706 Laurence Robinson
1707 George Green
1708 John Beatniffe
1709 Richard Beaumont
1710 Joseph Green
1711 John Maddison
1712 Philip Wilkinson
1713 Thomas Scott
1714 William Coggan
1715 John Wood
1716 William Winspear
1717 Christopher Bailes
1718 William Ashmole
1719 John Monckton
1720 Josiah Robinson
1721 Thomas Bridges
1722 William Mantle[1]
1723 George Healey
1724 John Wright
1725 Tristram Carlill
1726 Thomas Ryles
1727 Joseph Lazenby
1728 John Froggett
1729 Henry Maister
1730 James Milne
1731 William Mowld
1732 Christopher Heron
1733 James Bee
1734 John Ferrand
1735 Henry Lee
1736 Andrew Perrott
1737 John Porter
1738 David Field
1739 James Shaw
1740 Richard Sykes
1741 William Cookson
1742 Henry Etherington
1743 John Wood
1744 Charles Pool
1745 Francis De la Pryme
1746 John Fallowfield
1747 Walter Edge
1748 John Booth
1749 George Thompson
1750 Christopher Scott
1751 Francis Beilby
1752 Thomas Mowld
1753 William Hall
1754 Joseph Sykes
1755 Joseph Thompson
1756 John Stephenson
1757 Richard Bell
1758 Henry Etherington (jun.)
1759 John Porter
1760 John Mace
1761 Joseph Williamson
1762 Marmaduke Nelson
1763 John Melling
1764 William Bolton
1765 Joshua Berry
1766 Thomas Williamson
1767 Benjamin Blaydes Thompson
1768 Benjamin Blaydes
1769 John Banks
1770 Stephen Bramston
1771 Joseph Outram
1772 William King
1773 Caius Thompson
1774 Henry Horner
1775 Samuel Standidge

[1] Died; Richard Williamson served.

1776	Edward Coulson	1791	Samuel Bean
1777	Henry Broadley	1792	William Watson Bolton
1778	Edmund Bramston	1793	Joseph Eggington
1779	William Osbourne	1794	John Bateman
1780	Joshua Haworth	1795	Francis Hall
1781	Richard Moxon	1796	Thomas Walton
1782	John Bromby	1797	Andrew Hollingsworth
1783	Thomas Walton	1798	Benjamin Blaydes (jun.)
1784	John Voase	1799	William Jarratt
1785	James Smith[1]	1800	Edward F. Coulson
1786	Francis Bine	1801	Thomas Osbourne
1787	Robert Schonswar	1802	Benjamin Blaydes Haworth
1788	John Harneis	1803	Nicholas Sykes
1789	John Sykes	1804	Richard W. Moxon
1790	John Wray	1805	Thomas Thompson

[1] Died; William Hammond served.

Appendix 25

MAYORS OF HULL, 1700–1800

1700 Daniel Hoare (2)
1701 Philip Wilkinson (2)
1702 Robert Carlisle (2)
1703 William Hydes
1704 Samuel Boyes
1705 Robert Trippet (2)
1706 Richard Gray (2)
1707 Erasmus Darwin
1708 Andrew Perrott
1709 William Fenwick
1710 Towers Wallis
1711 John Somerscales
1712 Benjamin Ward
1713 John Collings
1714 William Mowld (2)
1715 Sir William St Quentin (2)
1716 Leonard Collings
1717 William Coggan
1718 Samuel Boyes (2)
1719 Johanan Beilby
1720 Erasmus Darwin (2)
1721 Andrew Perrott (2)
1722 William Wilberforce
1723 George Green
1724 William Ashmole
1725 John Somerscales (2)
1726 John Collings (2)
1727 William Fenwick (2)
1728 Thomas Scott
1729 Leonard Collings
1730 Richard Williamson
1731 Samuel Watson
1732 John Monckton
1733 Joseph Lazenby
1734 William Mowld
1735 William Cornwall
1736 William Coggan (2)
1737 Christopher Heron
1738 Andrew Perrott
1739 Johanan Beilby
1740 William Wilberforce (2)
1741 John Porter
1742 James Shaw
1743 William Ashmole[1] (2)
1744 John Froggatt
1745 William Cookson
1746 Josiah Robinson
1747 Henry Etherington
1748 John Wood
1749 Francis De la Pryme
1750 Thomas Scott (2)
1751 Samuel Watson (2)
1752 Christopher Heron (2)
1753 George Thompson
1754 Andrew Perrott (3)
1755 John Porter[2] (2)
1756 William Hall
1757 William Cookson (2)
1758 Henry Etherington (2)
1759 John Wood (2)
1760 Richard Bell
1761 Joseph Sykes
1762 Charles Pool
1763 Christopher Scott
1764 Thomas Mowld
1765 John Booth
1766 Francis De la Pryme (2)
1767 George Thompson[3] (2)
1768 John Melling
1769 Henry Etherington (jun.)
1770 John Porter (jun.)
1771 Benjamin Blaydes

[1] Died; Andrew Perrott served.
[2] Died; James Shaw served.
[3] Died; Richard Bell served.

1772 John Mace
1773 Richard Bell (2)
1774 Ralph Darling
1775 Joseph Outram
1776 Charles Pool (2)
1777 Joseph Sykes (2)
1778 Christopher Scott (2)
1779 Benjamin Blaydes Thompson
1780 Edmund Bramston
1781 Edward Coulson
1782 John Booth (2)
1783 John Melling (2)
1784 Henry Broadley
1785 Henry Etherington[1] (2)
1786 William Osbourne
1787 John Porter (2)
1788 Benjamin Blaydes (2)
1789 John Banks
1790 Ralph Darling (2)
1791 Benjamin Blaydes Thompson (2)
1792 John Sykes
1793 John Wray
1794 William Watson Bolton
1795 Samuel Standidge[2]
1796 William Osbourne (2)
1797 John Banks[3] (2)
1798 Joseph Eggington
1799 John Bateman
1800 William Jarratt

[1] Created baronet during his year of office.
[2] Knighted during his year of office.
[3] Died; John Sykes served.

Appendix 26

WARDENS OF TRINITY HOUSE, 1700–1800

1700	Marmaduke Smith	Joseph Lyndall
1701	John Lyndall	Ralph Johnson
1702	Lionel Ripley	John Scott
1703	Michael Watson	Jaques Dewitt
1704	William Cornwall	John Waite
1705	William Robinson	Thomas Seaman
1706	William Hunter	Joseph Lyndall
1707	Ralph Johnson	Marmaduke Smith
1708	Jaques Dewitt	John Waite
1709	Laurence Jopson	Thomas Seaman
1710	William Hunter	Lionel Ripley
1711	William Cornwall	Ralph Johnson
1712	Ralph Sotheron	William Robinson
1713	Peter Thornton	Joseph Lyndall
1714	David Hesslewood	Jaques Dewitt
1715	Robert Young	Laurence Jopson
1716	William Mantle	William Hunter
1717	Stephen Wood	John Barker
1718	Joshua Wilkinson	William Draper
1719	Abraham Thompson	Joseph Lyndall
1720	Simon Richardson	William Robinson
1721	Robert Binks	Robert Young
1722	Jonathan Bagwell	Laurence Jopson
1723	James Seaman	George Beilby
1724	Thomas Wright	Joshua Wilkinson
1725	Thomas Haworth	Samuel Hall
1726	Roger Hall	Abraham Thompson
1727	John Graves	Robert Young
1728	David Crosby	Laurence Jopson
1729	Henry Lee	James Seaman
1730	Thomas Wright	Thomas Haworth
1731	Roger Hall	Samuel Hall
1732	Abraham Thompson	John Graves
1733	Henry Etherington	David Crosby
1734	James Seaman	Henry Lee
1735	Richard Jopson	Thomas Wright
1736	Thomas Haworth	Roger Hall
1737	Abraham Thompson	John Graves
1738	George Woodhouse	David Crosby
1739	Thomas Bell	Richard Lawson
1740	James Seaman	Henry Etherington
1741	Richard Jopson	Henry Lee
1742	Thomas Haworth	Roger Hall
1743	John Haworth	John Graves
1744	George Woodhouse	David Crosby
1745	John Wilkinson	William Purver
1746	Richard Lawson	Thomas Bell
1747	William Draper	Richard Jopson
1748	Joshua Haworth	Thomas Haworth
1749	Richard Cottam	Richard Hill
1750	Roger Hall	Mark Thompson
1751	Samuel Jopson	George Woodhouse
1752	William Purver	John Wilkinson
1753	Thomas Bell	William Draper
1754	Thomas Haworth	Joshua Haworth
1755	Richard Hill	Richard Cottam
1756	John Crispin	Samuel Jopson
1757	William Purver	John Wilkinson
1758	John Green	William Draper
1759	Joshua Haworth	Richard Cottam
1760	Mark Thompson	John Huntington
1761	Baker Hebdon	Laurence Hill
1762	William King	William Purver
1763	Thomas Chambers	Thomas Haworth
1764	Thomas Macfarland	John Staniforth
1765	Thomas Bell	Joshua Haworth
1766	John Huntington	Richard Cottam
1767	John Meggitt	Joel Foster
1768	William King	Thomas Chambers
1769	Thomas Haworth	Thomas Macfarland
1770	John Staniforth	Thomas Bell
1771	John Huntington	John Meggitt
1772	John Woolf	Joel Foster
1773	William Thompson	William King
1774	Thomas Chambers	Thomas Haworth
1775	Thomas Macfarland	John Staniforth
1776	John Huntington	John Woolf
1777	Samuel Standidge	Richard Thorley
1778	Thomas Brown	Joel Foster
1779	William Hammond	William Thompson
1780	William King	Thomas Haworth
1781	Robert Schonswar	John Staniforth
1782	John Huntington	Samuel Standidge
1783	Richard Thorley	Joel Foster
1784	William Sparks	William Thompson
1785	William Hammond	John Woolf
1786	Thomas Haworth	John Staniforth
1787	John Harneis	Robert Schonswar
1788	John Huntington	Samuel Standidge
1789	William Burstall	Richard Thorley
1790	Thomas Jackson	Francis Hall
1791	Thomas Brown	William Sparks
1792	William Hammond	Thomas Haworth
1793	John Green	Benjamin Metcalf
1794	John Staniforth	Robert Schonswar
1795	Samuel Standidge	John Harneis
1796	Charles Shipman	Richard Thorley
1797	Thomas Lundie	Thomas Jackson
1798	Henry Denton	Thomas Locke
1799	Francis Hall	Benjamin Metcalf
1800	John Woolf	Sir Samuel Standidge

Appendix 27

HULL UNDERWRITERS AND THEIR OCCUPATIONS, 1791–2

Name	Occupation
John Bateman, George Street	Merchant
John Bolton (for J. Saunders & W. Jackson, Whitby)	
William Watson Bolton, Lowgate	Surgeon & Shipowner
John Boyes, Market Place	Tea Dealer
Henry Broadley, Esq., Bowlalley Lane	Banker
Isaac Broadley, High Street	Merchant
Robert Carlill Broadley, High Street	Merchant & Gentleman
C. E. Broadley, Esq., High Street	Merchant
John Carrick, Ropery	Snuff manufacturer
Sir Henry Etherington, Bt., High Street	Gentleman
George Fowler, Mytongate	Gentleman
Thomas Harrison, Esq., High Street	Banker
Joseph Hickson, High Street	Merchant
John Horner, High Street	Merchant
Simon Horner, High Street	Merchant
George Knowlsey, High Street	Merchant & Banker
G. Knox (for J. Wood, Esq., Beadnell, Northumberland)	
John Levett (for T. Hinderwell)	
Richard Moxon, High Street	Merchant & Banker
Benjamin Mancklin, Bishop Lane	Gentleman
Edward Miller, King Street	?
Robert Coupland Pease, High Street	Merchant & Banker
Joseph Rhodes (for Patrick Crighton, Dundee)	
Thomas Scratcherd, Market Place	Tea Dealer
John Voase, High Street	Wine & Brandy Merchant
Edward Webster (for W. Hornby, Gainsborough)	
Robert Wharrie, Lowgate	?
Samuel Wright, Esq., Mytongate	Gentleman

Source: Battle's *Directory*, 1791 & 1792.

Appendix 28

HULL UNDERWRITERS, 1803

John Bateman, Esq. (for John Bell, Pocklington)
Benjamin Blaydes, Esq., North Street
William Watson Bolton, Esq., Charlotte St. (for J. McDough, Esq., Renwick)
William Bourne, Exchange Alley
Harrison Briggs (for John Rhodes & Rowdon Briggs, Halifax)
Robert Carlill Broadley, Esq., High Street
John Burstall, junior, Whitefriargate
John Carlill (for John Greenwood)
John Clarkson, George Street
William Corlass, Lowgate
Edward F. Coulson, Esq., Albion Street
John Dutchman, Osbourne Street
Joseph Eggington, Esq., George Street
Anthony Emmett (for C. Smith, W. Smithson, J. Hall & J. H. Yallop)
Thomas Fea, Esq., Paull
John Fearn (for James Hindle, Barnsley)
William Fowler, Esq., Albion Street
William Henry, Bowlalley Lane
Andrew Hollingsworth, Lowgate
George Hopwood, Prospect Street
Edward Kerr, Whitefriargate
George Knowsley, York Street
Benjamin Blaydes Lambert, Quay Street
John Levett (for Thomas Hinderwell, junior)
Thomas Moxon, High Street
D. Nelson, Bowlalley Lane
William Parker, Dock Street (for J. Hebblethwaite, Leeds)
Thomas Rodmell (for Joseph Wilkinson, Esq.)
Thomas Scratcherd, Esq., Market Place
Thomas Shackles, Lowgate
Francis Taylor, Dock Street
Richard Terry, Esq., High Street
Ralph Turner, Dock Street
John Voase, Esq., High Street
John Wilson, Princes Street
Thomas Wood (for Thomas Middleton)

Source: Battle's *Directory*, 1803.

Appendix 29

HULL INSURANCE BROKERS AND THEIR OTHER OCCUPATIONS, 1791–2

Anthony Atkinson, Beverley Gate	Merchant
Atkinson, Hall & Godmund, High Street	Wine & Spirit Merchants
Robert Bell, Wincomblea	Merchant & Candle-maker
Widow Bine & Company	Merchants
Christopher Briggs, Bowlalley Lane	Merchant
Carlill, Gilder, Kirkbride & Company	Merchants
Edward F. Coulson, High Street	Merchant
Joseph Eggington	Oil Merchant & Shipowner
Hall & Robinson, High Street	Merchants & Shipowners
Joshua Haworth, Northend	Brandy Merchant
Henry Hammond, Blanket Row	Merchant & Shipowner
William Holden, High Street	Merchant & Wharfinger
Hanwith Hordan, Dock Side	Mustard Manufacturer
Knowsley & Ewbank, High Street	Wine Merchants
Heneage Lupton, High Street	Brewer
Overend & Thompson, Dock Side	Merchants
Richard Rennards, Northside	Merchant
Robert Stainton, High Street	?
Taylor & Markham, Northside	Merchants
Terry & Wright, High Street	Merchants & Shipowners
John Thompson, Albion Street	?
William Thompson, Storey Street	?
Christopher Thorley, High Street	Merchant
John Wilson, High Street	Merchant & Shipowner

Source: Battle's *Directory*, 1791 & 1792.

Appendix 30

THE GROWTH OF THE WHALING INDUSTRY: ENGLISH AND HULL SHIPS, 1750–1800

Year	*English Ships*	*Hull Ships*	*Bounty*	*Year*	*English Ships*	*Hull Ships*	*Bounty*
1750	17	0		1776	n.a.	9	
1751	20	0		1777	77	9	
1752	26	0		1778	71	8	
1753	27	0		1779	59	4	30*s.*
1754	36	4		1780	52	4	
1755	65	7		1781	34	3	
1756	67	7		1782	38	4	
1757	55	4		1783	47	4	
1758	52	4		1784	89	9	40*s.*
1759	34	3		1785	140	15	
1760	40	3		1786	168	22 (2)	
1761	31	2		1787	217	31 (4)	
1762	28	2		1788	222	34 (2)	
1763	30	0	40*s.*	1789	151	29 (1)	
1764	32	0		1790	103	23 (2)	
1765	33	0		1791	93	21 (1)	
1766	35	1		1792	87	20	
1767	39	2		1793	73	17 (1)	
1768	41	3		1794	53	17	30*s.*
1769	44	6		1795	40	15 (1)	
1770	50	7		1796	44	17 (1)	
1771	n.a.	7		1797	57	21	
1772	50	9		1798	59	23	
1773	55	9		1799	60	27	
1774	65	9		1800	54	24	
1775	96	12					

(Southern Fishery in Brackets)

Sources: National figures 1750–70—*PRO* CO 390–9; 1772–85—*BM* Add. MS 38,347, ff. 14–58; 1781–1800—*PRO* BT 6–230.
Hull figures 1754–72—Port Books and HCLB, C–B, *passim*; 1772–1800—*HCRL* MS L.281, corrected.

Appendix 31

HULL WHALING VOYAGES, 1754–1800

	1754	1755	1756	1757	1758	1759	1760	1761	1762	1763	1764	1765	1766	1767	1768	1769
Berry	×	×	×	×	×	×	×	×	×				×	×	×	×
*Leviathan**	×	×	×			×	×	×	×							×
Pool	×	×	×	×	×	×	×									
York	×	×	×	×												
Ann & Elizabeth		×	×	c												
Bosville		×	×													
Mary & Jane		×	×													
British Queen														×	×	×
Britannia															×	×
Humber																×
Jenny																×
King of Prussia																
Manchester																
Benjamin																
Southampton																
Triton																
Freedom																
Hillstone																
Kingston																
Molly																
Leeds Industry																
Caroline																
Benjamin																
Chance																
Elizabeth																

	1770	1771	1772	1773	1774	1775	1776	1777	1778	1779	1780	1781	1782	1783	1784	1785
Berry	×	×	×	c	×	c										
*Leviathan**																
Pool																
York																
Ann & Elizabeth	×	c	×	c	×	L										
Bosville																
Mary & Jane																
British Queen	×	×	×	×	×	L										
Britannia			×	×	L											
Humber	×	×	×	×	×	×	×	+	×	L						
Jenny	×															
King of Prussia	×	×	×	×	×	L										
Manchester	×	×	+	×	+	×	+	×	+	+	+	×	+	+	×	+
Benjamin		×	×	+	×	+	×	×	×							
Southampton			×	×												
Triton					×	c	×	×	×							
Freedom						c	×	×								
Hillstone						×	×				×					
Kingston						c	×	×	c	×						
Molly						c	×	×	×		×	+	×	×	+	×
Leeds Industry							×	×	c							
Caroline								×	×	×	×	×	×	×	×	×
Benjamin													×	×	×	×
Chance															×	×
Elizabeth															×	×

	1786	1787	1788	1789	1790	1791	1792	1793	1794	1795	1796	1797	1798	1799	1800
Berry															
*Leviathan**															
Pool															
York															
Ann & Elizabeth															
Bosville															
Mary & Jane															
British Queen															
Britannia															
Humber															
Jenny															
King of Prussia															
Manchester	+	×	+	×	×	c	×	×	×	×	×	×	×	×	×
Benjamin															
Southampton															
Triton															
Freedom															
Hillstone															
Kingston															
Molly	×	×	×	×	×	×	×	×	×	×	×	×	×	×	×
Leeds Industry															
Caroline	×	×	×	×	×	×	×	×	×	×	×	×	×	×	
Benjamin	×	c	×												
Chance	×	×	×	×											
Elizabeth	×	×	×	×	×	×	×	×	×	×	×	×	×	×	×

* *BM* Add. MS 11255 has 4 ships for 1758; they cannot be traced. The *Leviathan* fitted out from Whitby in [illegible] and 1758

Mary						× ×	× × ×		
Sarah & Elizabeth						× ×	× × × × ×	c × × × ×	× × × × L
Truelove						× ×	× × × × ×	× × × × ×	× × × × ×
Castle						×	× × × × ×	c ×	
Charlotte						×	×		
Diana						×	× × × × ×	× × × ×	
Endeavour						c	× × × L		
Samuel						×	× × × × ×	× × × × ×	× × × × ×
Whalefisher						×	L		
Fanny							× × × × ×	× × × × ×	× × × × ×
John & Mary							× c ×		
Isabella							× ×		
Mary of Sutton							× L		
Palliser							× × × c		
Ranger							× × × ×	c × × ×	
Young Maria							× × c c ×		
Young Richard							× ×		
Alliance							+ × + ×	× c ×	
Benediction							× × × L		
Brothers							× × × ×	+ × × + +	+ × × × +
Barthia & Mary							× × ×		
Eggington							× × × +	× × + × ×	× × + × ×
Ellison							× ×		× + × × ×
Friends							× × × L		
Gibraltar							× × × ×	× × × × ×	T
Hope							× × c ×		
Selby							× × × ×	× × × ×	
Cave							×		
Enterprize							× × ×	c × × × ×	× × × × ×
Gainsborough							× × c	L	

	1754	1755	1756	1757	1758	1759	1760	1761	1762	1763	1764	1765	1766	1767	1768	1769	1770	1771	1772	1773	1774	1775	1776	1777	1778	1779	1780	1781	1782	1783	1784	1785	1786	1787	1788	1789	1790	1791	1792	1793	1794	1795	1796	1797	1798	1799	1800
Greenland																																			c	L											
Lady Jane																																			×			c									
Scarthingwell																																			×	×	×	×	×	×	×	×	×				
Eliz. of Sutton																																				×	×										
Minerva																																					×		×					×	×	×	
Symmetry																																					×	×	×						×	×	×
Maria																																									×	×	×	×	×	×	×
John																																										×		×	×	×	×
North Briton																																											×	×	×	×	×
Traveller																																											×	×	×	×	×
Blenheim																																												×	×	×	
Countess Hopetoun																																												×	×	L	
London																																												×	×		
Lynx																																												×	×	×	×
Oak Hall																																													×	×	×
Anna Maria																																														×	
Ariel																																														×	×
Catherine																																														×	
Hunter																																														×	×
Lottery																																														×	×
Adventure																																															×
Jane																																															L
Vestal																																															×
SOUTHERN WHALE FISHERY																																															
Albion																																	×	×													
Phoenix																																	×	×													
Edward																																		×	×												
*Minerva**																																		×	×	×		×		×		×	×				

* For the *Minerva*, see notes to Appendix 32.

Key × – voyage with cargo + – champion whaler c – clean voyage L – lost T – taken by the French

Appendix 32

HULL WHALING STATISTICS, 1772–1800
(Based on *HCRL* L.281, with corrections from Customs sources)[1]

Bounty	Year	L.281 Total	Lost	Clean	Corrected Total North	Corrected Total South	Total Oil	Total Bone	Average Oil	Average Bone
	1772	9			9		391	19	43·4	2·1
	1773	9		2	9		365	14	29·4	1·6
40*s*.	1774	8	1		9		466	23	51·8	2·6
	1775	10[2]	3	5	12		68	3	5·7	0·3
	1776	9			9		276	13	30·7	1·4
	1777	9			9		333	15	37·0	1·7
	1778	8		2	8		171	9	21·4	1·1
30*s*.	1779	3	1		4		142	7	35·5	1·8
	1780	4			4		309	15	77·3	3·8
	1781	3			3		263	13	87·7	4·3
	1782	4			4		270	11	67·5	2·8
	1783	4			4		290	15	72·5	3·8
40*s*.	1784	9			9		432	22	48·0	2·4
	1785	14[3]		1	15		722	36	48·1	2·4
	1786	19[4]	1		22	2	856	43	42·8	2·2 (of 20)
	1787	29[5]	1	2	31	4	1,132	56	37·7	1·9 (of 30)
	1788	34[6]		2	34	2	958	47	28·2	1·4
	1789	27	2	3	29	1	854	43	29·4	1·5

1 There are a number of mistakes in L.281 (although it is generally accurate). Several ships are overlooked completely, and ships going to the Southern Fishery are sometimes included as from Greenland, and sometimes ignored.

2 L.281 has 10, implying 2 lost. In fact 3 were lost, and the total was 12.

3 L.281 appears to have overlooked the *Charlotte*.

4 L.281 omits the *Palliser* and *Charlotte*, recorded in the Port Books and in HCLB, C–B, 10 Mar 1786 as fitting out from Hull.

5 L.281 omits one ship, possibly the *Mary*. The Port Book also has the *Cadiz Packet*, Eggington, which does not appear at all in L.281, but it is possible she was not a Hull ship, despite her entry in the name of Eggington.

6 Another place in L.281 has 35 (and 1,042½ tons of oil), but HCLB, C–B has 34.

Bounty	Year	L.281 Total	Lost	Clean	Corrected Total North	Corrected Total South	Total Oil	Total Bone	Average Oil	Average Bone
	1790	23[1]	2	1	23	2	832	42	33·3	1·7
	1791	18[2]	1	6	21	1	345	17	18·2	0·9 (of 19)
	1792	20		1	20		896	45	44·8	2·3
30*s.*	1793	18[3]		1	17	1	835	41	46·4	2·3 (of 18)
	1794	16[4]	1		17		709	35	41·7	2·1
	1795	14[5]		1	15	1	1,148	57	82·0	4·1 (of 14)
	1796	17[6]	1		17	1	1,578	77	92·8	4·5 (of 17)
	1797	21			21		1,741	87	82·9	4·2
	1798	23			23		2,162	100	94·0	4·3
	1799	26	1		27		2,244	110	83·1	4·0
	1800	22	2		24		1,818	90	75·8	3·8

[1] PRO Customs 17/12 has 23 ships (6,509 tons) fitting out for Greenland and 22 (6,265 tons) returning. One of those returning may not have been a Hull ship, or may have fitted out in another port. L.281's total of 23 ships returning must include the *Minerva* and the *Edward*, which in fact went to the Southern Fishery.

[2] L.281 again omits two ships.

[3] L.281 mistakenly includes the *Minerva* as coming from Greenland.

[4] L.281 has 1 ship lost in one place, and none in another. At least 1 loss seems likely, since the *Ranger*, *Diana* and *Selby* made their last voyage that year.

[5] L.281 has 16 in another place. The confusion may again be over the *Minerva*.

[6] L.281 has 18 in one place and 17 in another. Since there were 17 from Greenland and one from the Southern Fishery, the ship in question was no doubt the *Minerva* again.

Appendix 33

HULL WHALERS, WITH KNOWN TONNAGE AND OWNERS, 1754–1800

	Tons	Date of First Voyage	Owners[1]
Adventure	n.a.	1800	n.a.
Albion	128[a]	1786	n.a.
Alliance	428[a]	1787	Richard Moxon (PB).
Ann & Elizabeth	220[d]	1755	Hull Whale Fishery (PB). Lost, 1775.
Anna Maria	n.a.	1799	n.a.
Ariel	n.a.	1799	Bolton & Co. (25:2:98)[2]
Barthia & Mary	152[a]	1787	n.a.
Benediction	177[a]	1787	Wilson & Co. (7:4:87) Blt. Eddington, No. Carolina 1771.[3]
Benjamin	221[d]	1771	n.a.
Benjamin	306[d]	1782	n.a.
Berry	315[d]	1754	Hull Whale Fishery (PB). Samuel Standidge, 1768 (PB).
Blenheim	n.a.	1797	n.a.
Bosville	n.a.	1755	Hamilton & Co. (PB).
Britannia	394[d]	1768	S. Standidge (PB). Lost 1774.
British Queen	350[d]	1767	S. Standidge (PB).[4] Lost 1775.
Brothers	377[a]	1787	R. Hodson (PB).
Caroline	206[a]	1777	R. Gee (7:4:87). Blt. Salisbury, Mass. Bay, 1767.
Castle	344[a]	1785	W. Horncastle (PB).
Catherine	n.a.	1799	n.a.
Cave	n.a.	1788	C. Shipman
Chance	279[a]	1784	D. Macpherson 1782 (7:4:87). Blt. Kent County, Maryland, 1775.
Charlotte	n.a.	1785	n.a. (Not included in *HCRL* L.281.)
Countess Hopetoun	n.a.	1797	n.a.
Diana	306[a]	1785	T. Locke (7:4:87) Blt. Newbury, Mass. Bay, 1774.
Edward	230[a]	1787	n.a.
Eggington	304[a]	1787	? Eggington & Co.
Elizabeth	322[a]	1784	Eggington & Co. (PB).
Elizabeth of Sutton	n.a.	1788	n.a.
Ellison	349[a]	1787	R. & A. Ellison (PB).
Endeavour	255[a]	1785	J. Cullum (PB).

	Tons	Date of First Voyage	Owners[1]
Enterprize	n.a.	1788	W. Sparks & Co., 1788–93. Horncastle & Co., 1793–?.
Fanny	259[a]	1786	Eggington & Co. (7:4:87). Blt. Newbury, Mass. Bay, 1772.
Freedom	303[a]	1775	n.a.
Friends	256[a]	1787	D. Tony (7:4:87). Blt. Portsmouth, New Hampshire, 1771.
Gainsborough	n.a.	1788	n.a.
Gibraltar	307[a]	1787	Sparks & Co. Taken by French, 1796.
Greenland	200[e]	1788	S. Standidge. Lost 1789.
Hillstone	c. 295[h]	1775	n.a.
Hope	289[a]	1787	J. Eggleston (7:4:87), Terry & Co. (26:2:98) Blt. Boston, New England, 1785.
Humber	221[d]	1769	G. Eggington & Philip Green (15:3:77).
Hunter	247[g]	1799	Bolton & Co., 1804.[5]
Isabella	91[a]	1786	n.a.
Jane	n.a.	1800	n.a.
Jenny	n.a.	1769	n.a.
John	n.a.	1795	n.a.
John & Mary	200[a]	1786	n.a.
King of Prussia	334[d]	1770	n.a. Lost 1775.
Kingston	c. 228[h]	1775	Fowler & Co., 1799 (28:2:99).
Lady Jane	n.a.	1788	n.a.
Leeds Industry	303[b]	1776	n.a.
Leviathan	n.a.	1754	Hull Whale Fishery (PB).
London	n.a.	1797	Barmby & Co. (29:8:97).
Lottery	334[g]	1799	Bolton & Co. (25:2:99).
Lynx[6]	n.a.	1797	n.a.
Manchester	267[a]	1770	J. Hamilton, 1770–71; J. Staniforth & H. Foord, 1771–? (7:4:87). Blt. New York, 1762.
Maria	n.a.	1794	J. Smith (of Gainsborough) (28:3:98).
Mary	371[a]	1784	Eggington & Co. (24:2:98).
Mary of Sutton	330[a]	1786	n.a.
Mary & Jane	n.a.	1755	William Welfitt (PB).
Minerva	175[a]	1786	Bolton & Co. (6:2:98); Burstall & Co. (13:10:98); Coates & Foord, 1799.
Molly	291[a]	1775	Gilder & Co., 1786 (PB); D. Tong (7:4:87). Blt. Boston, New England, 1759 (23:2:87).
North Briton	n.a.	1796	n.a.
Oak Hall	256	1798	Eggington & Co. (24:2:98).

	Tons	Date of First Voyage	Owners[1]
Palliser	348[a]	1786	W. Kirkhouse, 1786 (PB); James Thornton, 1787 (PB).
Phoenix	275[a]	1786	n.a.
Pool	n.a.	1754	Hull Whale Fishery (PB).
Ranger	309[a]	1786	S. Standidge, 1786 (PB). Blt. Norfolk, Virginia, 1775.
Samuel	244[a]	1785	S. Standidge (7:4:87). Blt. Saco, Mass. Bay, 1774.
Sarah & Elizabeth	267[a]	1784	J. R. Pease & Co. Blt. Swan Creek, Maryland, 1775.
Scarthingwell	n.a.	1788	n.a.
Selby	199[a]	1787	n.a.
Southampton	345[d]	1772	n.a.
Symmetry	342[g]	1790	Bolton & Co., 1804.[5]
Traveller	n.a.	1796	n.a.
Triton	*c.* 434[h]	1774	n.a.
Truelove	195[a]	1784	T. Locke & J. Voase (7:4:87). Blt. Philadelphia, 1764.
Vestal	n.a.	1800	n.a.
Whalefisher	232[f]	1785	n.a.
Young Maria	98[a]	1786	C. Shipman.
Young Richard	83[a]	1786	n.a.
York	338	1754	J. Hamilton & Co. (PB).

Sources for tonnage:
- a HCLB, C–B, 25 Sep 1787.
- b ibid., Feb 1776.
- c ibid., 5 Mar 1775.
- d ibid., 22 Mar 1772.
- e ibid., Aug 1788.
- f ibid., 10 Mar 1786.
- g Sun Fire Office Policy Book, *passim.*
- h By simple calculation from tables in which the other ships' tonnages and the aggregate are known.

Notes:
1. Individuals listed are managing owners making returns to the Customs Authorities, rather than sole owners.
2. Dates in brackets refer to HCLB, C–B. PB = Port Book.
3. American built ships from HCLB, C–B, 7 Aug 1787.
4. Benjamin Blaydes took an apprentice in April 1771 as 'Owner of the Brittish Queen'; ILA 1766–87, No. 377.
5. Sun Fire Office Policy Book, Bolton's Account.
6. Possibly of Whitby; see G. Young, *History of Whitby*, ii, p. 565.

Appendix 34

THE HULL DOCK COMPANY: INCOME, EXPENDITURE AND DIVIDENDS, 1775–1805

	Gross Income	*Expenditure*	*Net Income*	*Dividends Total*	*Dividends per Share*	*Surplus*	*Deficit*
1775	4,663	443	4,220	0	0	4,220	0
1776	4,668	657	4,011	0	0	4,011	0
1777	4,535	681	3,853	0	0	3,853	0
1778	4,957	1,614	3,343	0	0	3,343	0
1779	4,472	1,771	2,701	0	0	2,701	0
1780	4,806	5,131	0	6,269	52	0	6,269
1781	6,181	3,821	2, 360	10,600	88	11	0
1782	5,590	4,900	690	1,443	12	0	753
1783	7,040	4,002	3,038	3,124	26	0	86
1784	8,217	3,622	4,595	3,909	33	686	0
1785	8,077	4,394	3,683	3,684	31	0	1
1786	8,480	5,078	3,402	2,496	21	906	0
1787	9,307	5,581	3,725	4,726	39	0	1,000
1788	9,269	5,216	4,053	4,053	34	0	0
1789	9,280	4,372	4,908	4,908	41	0	0
1790	9,812	4,758	5,054	5,054	42	0	0
1791	12,698	4,853	7,845	7,845	65	0	0
1792	14,649	4,778	9,870	9,870	82	0	0
1793	13,700	5,816	7,884	6,885	57	1,000	0
1794	11,462	6,437	5,025	5,025	42	0	0
1795	11,149	5,877	5,273	6,272	52	0	1,000
1796	14,858	5,946	8,912	6,512	54	2,400	0
1797	11,703	5,022	6,681	5,481	46	1,200	0
1798	12,754	5,839	6,915	6,916	58	0	0
1799	13,415	5,729	7,685	7,685	64	0	0
1800	17,734	5,762	11,972	11,972	100	0	0
1801	18,496	5,566	12,931	12,931	108	0	0
1802	19,913	6,644	13,269	13,269	111	0	0
1803	23,311	7,803	15,508	14,902	110	606	0
1804	21,434	7,305	14,128	14,734	98	0	606
1805	18,415	7,133	11,282	11,282	73	0	0

Source: Hull Dock Office, 'Huffman's Book', *passim.*

Appendix 35

SHIPS BUILT IN HULL FOR THE ROYAL NAVY, 1690–1810

	Ship	Class	Tons	Guns	Builder	Yard	Source
1	*Etna*	fire-ship	258	n.a.	John Frame	'Hull'	(a)
3	*Humber*	3rd rate	1,223	n.a.	John Frame	'Hull'	(a,c)
5	*Newark*	3rd rate	1,217	n.a.	John Frame	'Hull'	(a,c)
7	*Kingston*	4th rate	924	n.a.	John Frame	'Hull'	(a)
0	*Success*	6th rate	436	20	Hugh Blaydes	'Hull'	(a,b)
1	*Adventure*	5th rate	683	40	Hugh Blaydes	'Hull'	(a,b)
2	*Anglesea*	5th rate	n.a.	40	Hugh Blaydes	'Hull'	(b,d)
2	*Alderney*	6th rate	504	20	John Read	'Hull'	(a,b,d)
3	*Hector*	5th rate	720	40	Hugh Blaydes	'Hull'	(a,b,d)
4	*Shoreham*	6th rate	514	20	John Read	'Hull'	(a,b,d)
4	*Foway*	5th rate	709	40	Hugh Blaydes	'Hull'	(a, b)
5	*Raven*	sloop	273	16	Hugh Blaydes	'Hull'	(a,b,d)
5	*Glasgow*	6th rate	504	20	John Read	'Hull'	(a,b,d)
6	*Pool*	5th rate	706	40	Hugh Blaydes	'Hull'	(a,b,d)
6	*Centum*	6th rate	504	20	Hugh Blaydes	'Hull'	(a,b)
6	*Grampus*	sloop	271	16	John Read	'Hull'	(a,b,d)
7	*Tavistock*	4th rate	1,061	50	Hugh Blaydes	Hessle Cliff	(a,b,d)
6	*Scarborough*	6th rate	n.a.	20	Hugh Blaydes	'Hull'	(b,d)
7	*Rose*	6th rate	n.a.	20	Hugh Blaydes	'Hull'	(b,d)
7	*Glasgow*	6th rate	452	20	John Read*	'Hull'	(a,b,d)
7	*Temple*	3rd rate	n.a.	70	Hugh Blaydes	Hessle	(b,d)
0	*Tweed*	6th rate	n.a.	34	Hugh Blaydes	Hessle	(b,d)
1	*Mermaid*	6th rate	n.a.	28	Hugh Blaydes	Hessle	(a,b,d)
2	*Nautilus*	sloop	n.a.	16	Hodgson & Bryan	'Charlestown'	(b,d)
2	*Emerald*	6th rate	681	32	H. & Benj. Blaydes	Hessle	(a,b,d)
3	*Glory*	6th rate	679	32	Blaydes & Hodgson	'Charlestown'	(a,b,d)
4	*Ardent*	3rd rate	1,376	70	H. & Benj. Blaydes	Hessle	(a,b,d)
4	*Boreas*	6th rate	627	32	Blaydes & Hodgson	'Charlestown'	(a,d)
4	*Diamond*	6th rate	710	36	Blaydes & Hodgson	'Charlestown'	(a,d)
4	*Shark*	sloop	n.a.	16	Thomas Walton	'Hull'	(d)
3	*Otter*	sloop	n.a.	18	Thomas Steemson	Paull	(d)
4	*Combatant*	6th rate	n.a.	24	Peter Atkinson	'Hull'	(d)
4	*Dauntless*	6th rate	n.a.	24	William Gibson	'Hull'	(d)
4	*Valorous*	6th rate	n.a.	24	James Shepherd	'Hull'	(d)
5	*Oberon*	sloop	n.a.	16	James Shepherd	'Hull'	(d)
7	*Porcupine*	('small')	n.a.	n.a.	Owen's Yard	'Hull'	(a)
7	*Hyperion*	5th rate	978	n.a.	William Gibson	'Hull'	(a)
7	*Proserpine*	6th rate	n.a.	32	Thomas Steemson	Paull	(a,d)
8	*Owen Glendower*	5th rate	951	36	Sir William Rule	Paull	(a,d)
0	*Anson*	3rd rate	n.a.	74	Thomas Steemson	Paull	(d)

'inished by Hodgson & Bryan following Read's bankruptcy.

rces: (a) J. A. Rupert-Jones, 'King's Ships Built at Hull', *Notes & Queries*, Vol 156 (1929).
(b) HCLB, C–B, *passim.*
(c) Gent, *passim.*
(d) Sheahan, *passim.* Incorrect in a number of details.

Appendix 36

POOR RATE ASSESSMENTS, 1729–1800; TOTAL OF MONEY RAISED, SHOWING ONLY THOSE YEARS IN WHICH THE SUM CHANGED

	£		£		£
1728	416	1767	702	1785	2080
1729	442	1768	728	1786	2288
1742	650	1769	832	1787	2652
1743	643½	1772	988	1788	3275
1745	650	1773	1144	1791	2457
1749	546	1778	1248	1793	3276
1755	975	1779	1404	1794	4095
1758	1300	1780	1456	1795	5616
1763	988	1781	1664	1797	6760
1766	832	1783	1976	1798	8320

Source: Thomas Thompson's pamphlet *Considerations on the Poor Rates and State of the Workhouse in Kingston-upon-Hull* (1800).

Appendix 37

MEMBERS OF PARLIAMENT FOR HULL, 1690–1806

Elected		
1690	*Charles Osbourne	*John Ramsden
1695	*Charles Osbourne	*Sir William St. Quentin
1700	*William Maister	*Sir William St. Quentin
1716	*Nathaniel Rogers	*Sir William St. Quentin
1724	*Nathaniel Rogers	*George Crowle
1727	Lord Micklethwaite	*George Crowle
1732	*Henry Maister	*George Crowle
1741	William Carter	*George Crowle
1744	Henry Pulteney	*George Crowle
1747	Thomas Carter	Lord Robert Manners
1754	*Richard Crowle	Lord Robert Manners
1757	*Sir George M. Metham	Lord Robert Manners
1766	William Weddell	Lord Robert Manners
1774	David Hartley	Lord Robert Manners
1780	*William Wilberforce	Lord Robert Manners
1782	*William Wilberforce	David Hartley
1784	*William Wilberforce	*Samuel Thornton
1784	Walter S. Stanhope	*Samuel Thornton
1790	The Earl of Burford	*Samuel Thornton
1796	Sir Charles Turner	*Samuel Thornton

* Local man.

Appendix 38

PAMPHLETS PRINTED DURING THE DISPUTE OVER DOCK EXTENSION, 1786–1795

(The titles are abbreviated. Where no date was printed the chronological order has been determined from internal evidence)

'A Proprietor', *An Address to the Dock Company. . .*, 13 Feb 1786.
'A Non-Proprietor', *Thoughts on the Extension of the Dock. . .*, n.d.
'Mercator', *To the Merchants, Shipowners*, etc. . . ., 9 Mar 1786.
'Civis', *To the Merchants, Shipowners*, etc. . ., — Mar 1786.
'Spectator', *An Address to the Inhabitants. . .*, 24 Mar 1786.
'Vigilant', *To the Merchants . . .*, 31 Mar 1786.
The Committee for Dock Extension, *Case of the Merchants*, etc. . ., n.d.
The Dock Company, *Remarks on the Case of the Merchants. . .*, 2 Mar 1787.
Anonymous, *Charges intended to be Exhibited in Parliament against the Dock Company*, n.d.
The Dock Company, *A Defence of the Rights of the Dock Company . . .*, n.d.
Thomas Westerdell, *An Address to the Corporation in reply to 'A Defence of the Rights of the Dock Company'*, n.d.
The Dock Company, *A Plan for the Further Extension of the Dock*, 20 Aug 1787.
'Publicola', *To the Right Worshipful the Mayor. . .*, 15 Sep 1787.
'An Old Burgess', *To the Burgesses of Kingston-upon-Hull. . .*, n.d.
Anonymous, *Conditions Proposed for a Subscription to a New Dock Company at Kingston-upon-Hull*, n.d.
T. Westerdell, *To the Burgesses of Kingston-upon-Hull*, 3 Jun 1788.
Anonymous, *Heads of a Bill for the Better Accommodation of the Trade and Shipping of . . . Hull*, 13 Nov 1788.
William Bell, *An Accurate Statement of the Proceedings at the Guildhall . . . on 23rd September 1788*, n.d.
The Dock Company, *An Address of the Dock Company . . . to the Merchants . . .*, 15 Feb 1793.
'Observator', An Address, no title, 16 Feb 1793, commenting on the Dock Company's Address of the previous day.
Hugh Ker, *Observations and Remarks on the Address of the Dock Company*, 1 Mar 1793.
'A.B.', *The Address of the Dock Company Answered and Refuted*, 2 Mar 1793.
'S', *To the Public . . .*, n.d.
The Dock Company, *Short State of the Case of the Dock Company . . .*, 3 Feb 1794.
The Dock Company, *The Case of the Dock Company*, 12 Mar 1794.

Anonymous, *The Case of the Public interested in the Navigation and Commerce of . . . Hull*, 14 Mar 1794.

The Dock Company, *A Direct Attack on the Private Property of the Dock Company at . . . Hull*, 7 Apr 1794.

'Reconciler', *A Plan for the Accommodation of Trade and Shipping . . .*, 1 Feb 1795.

Appendix 39

THE HULL PORT BOOKS

The Port Books (*PRO* E 190/337–396) are kept in boxes which include Foreign Books, Coastal Books (two per annum) and Books for the 'Member Ports' of Scarborough, Bridlington and Grimsby. The numbering is haphazard, within the boxes. Survival was largely a matter of chance. For several years all three copies of the Foreign Trade Books have survived; for many years there are none at all. Satisfactory sampling of the Coastal Books is prevented by the loss of one of the two half-yearly books for 27 of the 65 years for which books are available. Nor is mere survival a guide to availability; the condition of the books varies from excellent to useless. The books might be divided into five categories:

(a) Very Good (b) Good
(c) Satisfactory, but sometimes only legible to students with a knowledge of Port Books
(d) Unsatisfactory (e) Useless

A. FOREIGN TRADE BOOKS

Year	*Call Number*	*Condition*	*Year*	*Call Number*	*Condition*	*Year*	*Call Number*	*Condition*
1702	337/3	(b)	1716	349/11	(d)		5	(d)
1704	338/2	(d)		12	(c)	1726	359/3	(d)
1705	339/11	(c)		13	(d)		5	(c)
1706	340/5	(c)	1717	350/1	(b)		6	(d)
	8	(b)		8	(c)	1727	359/11	(b)
	10	(d)	1718	351/7	(d)	1728	360/3	(b)
1707	341/6	(c)		11	(c)		4	(d)
	8	(d)	1719	352/6	(d)		13	(c)
1708	342/9	(c)		8	(c)	1729	360/9	(c)
	14	(d)	1720	353/4	(d)	1730	361/7	(b)
1709	343/7	(c)		6	(e)		8	(d)
1711	344/7	(c)	1721	354/3	(b)	1731	362/4	(b)
	11	(c)		7	(c)	1732	363/3	(c)
1712	345/5	(b)		11	(a)	1733	363/9	(b)
	7	(a)	1722	355/7	(d)	1737	365/1	(a)
	14	(c)		8	(b)	1738	365/7	(a)
1713	346/1	(c)		9	(c)	1740	365/11	(a)
1714	347/2	(d)	1723	356/8	(d)	1750	366/3	(d)
	6	(d)		11	(b)		7	(c)
1715	348/1	(c)	1724	357/9	(c)	1751	367/1	(d)
	6	(d)		10	(c)		3	(e)
	12	(d)	1725	358/3	(c)		6	(d)

Year	*Call Number*	*Condition*
1752	367/5	(b)
	368/1	(c)
	2	(d)
1753	368/3	(d)
1754	369/1	(d)
	2	(c)
	3	(c)
1755	369/4	(c)
	7	(c)
1756	370/1	(c)
	2	(c)
	4	(c)
	5	(d)
	369/6	(c)
1758	371/1	(b)
	3	(b)
	4	(c)
1759	371/8	(c)
	9	(c)
1760	372/1	(b)
	2	(c)
	3	(c)
	4	(b)
1761	373/2	(e)
	3	(c)
	4	(b)

Year	*Call Number*	*Condition*
1762	373/5	(c)
	6	(b)
1763	374/3	(d)
	5	(d)
1764	374/6	(d)
	7	(d)
	8	(d)
1765	375/1	(c)
	5	(e)
1766	375/3	(e)
	7	(c)
1767	376/2	(d)
1768	376/6	(c)
	8	(d)
1769	377/1	(c)
	2	(d)
1770	377/4	(c)
	6	(d)
	8	(d)
1771	378/2	(c)
	3	(c)
1772	378/5	(c)
	6	(c)
1773	379/1	(e)
	2	(d)
1774	379/4	(d)
	5	(c)

Year	*Call Number*	*Condition*
1775	379/6	(d)
	380/3	(d)
	4	(c)
1776	380/6	(d)
	7	(e)
1777	381/3	(d)
	4	(d)
	5	(e)
1778	381/7	(c)
1779	382/1	(c)
	3	(c)
	5	(d)
1780	383/4	(c)
1781	384/1	(c)
	3	(d)
1782	384/2	(e)
	4	(d)
	7	(b)
1783	385/1	(d)
	2	(c)
	3	(b)
1784	385/5	(d)
	6	(c)
1785	385/8	(c)
1786	386/4	(c)
1787	386/6	(c)

B. COASTAL TRADE BOOKS

Half Year		*Call Number*	*Condition*
1701	2	337/1	(c)
1702	1	337/2	(d)
		4	(c)
1703	2	338/7	(c)
1704	1	338/10	(b)
	2	339/7	(c)
1705	1	339/1	(c)
1706	1	340/1	(b)
	2	341/7	(b)
1707	1	341/2	(d)
	2	342/2	(b)
1708	1	342/2	(b)
	2	342/12	(b)
1710	1	343/8	(b)

Half Year		*Call Number*	*Condition*
1712	1	345/10	(c)
		346/4	(c)
	2	346/11	(d)
1714	1	347/9	(c)
1715	1	348/9	(d)
	2	348/13	(e)
		349/1	(c)
1716	1	349/10	(e)
	2	350/2	(d)
1717	1	350/4	(c)
	2	351/1	(d)
1718	1	351/6	(d)
1719	1	352/4	(d)

Half Year		*Call Number*	*Condition*
1720	1	353/8	(e)
	2	354/2	(c)
1721	2	355/3	(c)
1722	1	355/6	(c)
	2	356/3	(c)
1723	1	356/7	(d)
	2	357/1	(c)
1724	1	359/1	(c)
	2	358/10	(c)
1725	1	358/8	(c)
	2	359/2	(c)
1726	1	359/4	(b)
1728	1	360/5	(d)
	2	360/17	(b)

Half Year	*Call Number*	*Condition*
1729 1	360/6	(c)
	361/13	(d)
2	361/9	(d)
1730 2	362/1	(d)
1732 1	363/4	(d)
2	363/8	(c)
1735 1	364/6	(d)
1736 1	364/9	(d)
2	365/5	(d)
1737 1	365/3	(c)
2	365/6	(d)
1748 2	366/1	(d)
1749 1	366/2	(c)
2	366/5	(c)
1750 2	366/6	(c)
1751 2	367/2	(d)
1752 1	367/4	(c)
1755 1	369/5	(e)
2	369/8	(c)
1756 1	370/3	(c)
1757 1	370/6	(c)
2	370/7	(c)
1758 1	371/2	(d)
	5	(c)
1759 1	371/7	(c)
2	371/6	(e)
1761 2	373/2	(e)
1762 2	373/7	(b)
1763 1	374/1	(d)
2	374/2	(c)
1764 1	374/4	(d)
1765 2	375/2	(b)
1766 1	375/8	(c)
2	375/9	(c)
1767 1	376/4	(c)
2	376/1	(c)
1768 1	376/5	(c)
2	376/7	(c)
1769 1	377/3	(c)
2	377/5	(e)
1770 ?	377/7	(e)
1771 1	378/1	(c)
1772 1	378/8	(c)
2	378/7	(c)
1773 1	378/8	(c)
1774 1	379/8	(c)
2	379/7	(c)
1775 1	380/2	(c)
2	380/1	(c)
1776 1	380/8	(d)
2	380/5	(d)
1777 1	381/1	(e)
2	381/2	(e)
1778 1	381/6	(d)
2	381/8	(c)
1779 1	382/4	(c)
2	382/2	(c)
1780 1	383/3	(d)
2	383/1	(d)
1782 1	384/6	(b)
2	384/5	(b)
1783 1	385/4	(c)
1785 1	386/1	(d)
2	386/2	(d)
1786 2	386/3	(c)
1787 2	386/5	(d)

Bibliography

MANUSCRIPT SOURCES

I. TRADE AND SHIPPING

(*a*) National Records

i. *Public Record Office.* The PORT BOOKS (E 190/337–88), whatever their drawbacks, must be the basis for any serious port history in the eighteenth century The OVERSEAS PORT BOOKS list the name and master of all ships entering and clearing the port; the volume, origin or destination of cargoes; and the individual shipments of each merchant. The COASTAL PORT BOOKS list the ships and cargoes, but not the merchants. (The best preserved Books were photocopied and are now available in *HCRL.*) Shipping statistics for the early part of the century are in COLONIAL OFFICE PAPERS (CO 388–9, 388–18, 390–8, 390–9), and for the later period in BOARD OF TRADE PAPERS (BT 6–94, 6–140, 6–185, 6–191 and 6–230). For the period after 1772 comparative shipping statistics are available in the great series 'State of Navigation, Commerce and Revenue of Great Britain' in the CUSTOMS PAPERS (Customs 17). The returns of 'Seamen's Sixpences' are in the ADMIRALTY PAPERS (Adm 68).

ii. *British Museum.* Statistics of ships entering, clearing and 'belonging to' the English ports are in Add. MSS 11255 and 11256. Add. MSS 38344, 38345 and 38347 are concerned with trade and shipping, and have useful material relating to Hull.

iii. *King's Beam House.* The best commentary on Hull's development is in the HULL CUSTOMS LETTER BOOKS. The series BOARD TO COLLECTOR is available from 1744, and COLLECTOR TO BOARD from 1748. They are a mine of invaluable information on every aspect of the town's life. There is, alas, no index. A separate LETTER BOOK 1725–95 contains letters about embargoes, quarantine and illegal trade.

(*b*) Local Records

i. *Hull Dock Office.* The difficulty of handling shipping statistics, because of the change in measurement in 1786–8, is to some extent eased by the existence of a long run of measured tonnages from 1775 in the Dock Dues Accounts compiled in the volume known as HUFFAM'S BIBLE.

ii. *Trinity House.* The WARDEN'S ACCOUNTS refer to income from shipping, but the main accounts were apparently transferred to the Humber Conservancy Board, who claim to have destroyed them.

iii. *Guildhall.* The Corporation's PORT DUES BOX is a disappointment. It contains little of value, apart from a series of shipping figures for the sixties and some scattered accounts of foreign and coastal shipping in the last twenty years of the century. Valuable information is contained in TOWNES DUES OF FORRAIGNERS, which has been separated as MS M.447; MINUTES OF THE CONVOY COMMITTEE, 1757–82; and MINUTES OF THE COMMITTEE FOR TRADE, 1780–1800. Much light is thrown on inland trade by the REGISTER OF INLAND SHIPPING, n.d., which is MS M.445.

2. MERCHANTS, FINANCE AND INDUSTRY

i. *Wilberforce House*. The large collection of PEASE PAPERS is the most valuable source of information on merchanting, finance and industry in Hull. The BROADLEY MSS are a series of letters between the Hull house and their Factors in the Baltic and Scandinavia in the early eighteenth century, and the NUMBERED MSS BOX contains MAISTER ACCOUNTS torn from a ledger or Day Book of the thirties, with some unique details of early marine insurance.

ii. *Hull University Library*. The MAISTER DAY BOOK, 1713–23 (MS DA 690 H9 M2) is the most important source for commerce in the first quarter of the century. The SUN FIRE OFFICE POLICY BOOK, 1804–18 (DX/43/1) has a great deal of incidental information about industry and shipping at the end of the century.

iii. *Hull Central Reference Library*. The WRAY & HOLLINGSWORTH LETTER BOOKS, 1791–5, contain some fifteen hundred letters illustrating the connexion between Hull and the hinterland. There is no index. Details of the whaling industry are to be found in a nineteenth century MS, WHALE FISHERY AT HULL (MS L.281). Unfortunately it is not free from error, and should be used, where possible, in conjunction with other sources.

iv. *Guildhall*. The INROLLMENT OF INDENTURES OF APPRENTICESHIP record most of the apprentices taken during the century; they are particularly valuable for tracing merchant apprentices, and the rise of shipowners. The mass of papers of the HULL COURT OF RECORD and the HULL COURT OF VENIRE illustrate to some extent the rise and fall in the economy as measured in debt suits.

v. *Hull Custom House*. The Customs Papers have all been moved to London, but the SHIPPING REGISTERS are available from 1804. They throw some light on our period, but give no indication of the total number of ships and shipowners in the port.

vi. *East Riding Record Office* (Beverley). The vast collection of HARRISON-BROADLEY DEPOSITED DEEDS (DDHB) are concerned with the Broadleys' land rather than with trade or banking, but they include many miscellaneous papers on Hull. They are particularly valuable as a rough guide to merchant landowning.

vii. *Sheffield Central Reference Library*. SAMUEL DAWSON'S DAY BOOK, 1713–21 (Tibbitts 382) is similar in form to the MAISTER DAY BOOK. He traded through Hull, but lived in Bawtry. LETTERS TO SAMUEL DAWSON, 1715–21 (Tibbitts 516) include interesting items from Factors in the Baltic. BARKERS' ORE ACCOUNTS (Bagshawe 491) give details of lead shipments to Hull, and BARKER LETTER BOOKS (Bagshawe 494) discuss the organisation of the lead trade.

viii. *Manuscripts in Private Hands.* Of the Manuscripts remaining in private hands, the following are the most useful:

1. The Bank Records. These are vital for a study of banking and finance, and provide much general information on merchant and industrial life. PEASE BANK LEDGERS (Barclay's Bank, Trinity House Lane) were once complete from 1754, but only ledgers B and D now survive. SMITHS & THOMPSON'S LEDGERS (National Provincial Bank, Silver Street) were more fortunate, and survive from the foundation of the bank in 1784.

2. Maister Papers. A very important group of MAISTER LETTERS between Nathaniel and Henry Maister are owned by Col. Rupert Alec-Smith of Winestead, and a number of Maister Accounts, chiefly for luxuries supplied by them to the Grimston family, are owned by Edward Ingram, Esq., Sewerby.

3. SCULCOATES PARISH RATE BOOKS provide a useful guide to the ownership of factories and mills springing up along the Hull in the second half of the century.

4. NEWTON CHAMBERS' ARCHIVES (Newton, Chambers & Company, Ltd., Chapeltown, Sheffield) include a number of letters to Hull merchants, and details of shipments of their products through Hull after *c.* 1790.

3. DOCK DEVELOPMENT

i. The Negotiations leading to the building of the first dock are best followed in the BENCH BOOKS and CUSTOMS LETTER BOOKS. Resolutions of Trinity House were invariably transmitted to the Bench or the Customs, and can be seen in these two sources. The Minutes of Meetings held in the fifties are the Guildhall, Box 9, and the only copy I have found of the 1766 Dock Bill is in the Lincolnshire Archives Office, Lincoln (Td'E/6).

ii. *British Transport Archives.* The HULL DOCK COMPANY COMMISSIONERS' TRANSACTIONS, 1777–82, contain all the available information on the building of the first dock. The general running of the dock, and the Company's attitude to dock extension are to be found in HULL DOCK COMPANY LETTER BOOK, 1774–88 and HULL DOCK COMPANY TRANSACTIONS (of which the first volume is missing).

iii. *Hull Dock Office.* All the statistics relating to the first dock and its traffic were compiled by Huffam, Secretary of the Company in the early nineteenth century. His book was continued by his successors into the present century, and is known in the Office as 'HUFFAM'S BIBLE'.

iv. No Archive has a complete set of the pamphlets written during the dispute over the second dock; the best sets are in the Corporation's DOCK BOX, and in the Dock Company's SCRAP BOOKS which are in the Dock Office. There is also a good set in Wilberforce House.

4. SOCIAL LIFE AND GENERAL INFORMATION

i. *British Museum.* A number of volumes relate specifically to Hull. Translations of the Charters are in Add. MS 24834, Papers concerning the Corporation in Stow 796, and Miscellaneous material (including the only known copy of the 1724 *Poll Book*) in Lansdowne 891. The original manuscript of STROTHER'S JOURNAL, 1784, with its perceptive comments on the life and people of the town, is Egerton 2479.

ii. *Guildhall.* The starting point for any history of the town is the BENCH BOOKS, which record all the official pronouncements of the Bench of Aldermen, sitting both as magistrates and as 'local government'. Day-to-day administration can be followed in the TOWN'S HUSBAND'S CASH BOOKS. Brief details of Corporation finances are in BOX 115, and the WORKHOUSE ADMITTANCE AND DISCHARGE BOOK, 1729–56 throws light on the type of people using the Workhouse in the eighteenth century.

iii. *Wilberforce House.* A large collection of miscellaneous papers started by T. T. Wildridge and containing his notes are kept in the ante-room of the Library. They are referred to here as CHRONOLOGICAL MSS. The AUTOGRAPH LETTER BOX contains a number of stray letters, and the COURT CASES BOX has a number of apparently unconnected briefs. References to Hull are scattered throughout STANEWELL DEEDS, YORKSHIRE DEEDS, EAST YORKSHIRE DEEDS and HAWORTH–BOOTH DEEDS. A great deal of social and general information is recorded in the PEASE PAPERS.

iv. *Miscellaneous Archives.* A most valuable source for merchant 'society' life is ROBERT BROADLEY'S JOURNAL, 1768–73, *HUL* DP/146. The chief sources for political life (with much incidental material on social life) are two important groups of papers in *SCRL*: WALTER SPENCER-STANHOPE PAPERS (WSS 1784, 1785, 1786) and WENTWORTH WOODHOUSE MUNIMENTS (WWM 49). A refreshingly human side of history is revealed in the TRINITY HOUSE SCHOOL RECORDS; times may have changed, but schoolboys have not.

UNPUBLISHED WORKS

Barnett, C. H., 'Planning and Architectural Development of Kingston-upon-Hull since 1800' (M.A. thesis, Liverpool, 1953; copy in Wilberforce House Library). Contains a useful introduction.

Davies, W. J., 'The Town and Trade of Hull, 1600–1700' (M.A. thesis, Cardiff, 1937).

Davis, P., 'The Old Friendly Societies of Hull' (MS, n.d., *HCRL*).

Garlick, P. C., 'The Sheffield Cutlery and Allied Trades and their Markets in the Eighteenth and Nineteenth Centuries' (M.A. thesis, Sheffield, 1951).

Goldthorpe, I. N., 'Architecture of the Victorian Era of Kingston-upon-Hull' (R.I.B.A. thesis, 1955; copy in Wilberforce House Library). Contains a useful introduction.

Hall, B., 'The Trade of Newcastle and the North East Coast' (M.A. thesis, London, 1934). Contains much on Mediaeval Hull.

Jones, W. R., 'The History of the Port of Hull to the End of the Fourteenth Century' (M.A. thesis, Wales, 1944).

PRINTED WORKS

Anonymous, *A View of the Advantages of Inland Navigation between the Ports of Liverpool and Hull* (1765). Copy in *BM*, Pamphlet B.504.

Albion, R. G., *Forests and Sea Power* (Cambridge, Mass., 1926).

Allen, T., *Complete History of the County of York* (6 vols, 1929–31).

Andrews, J. H., 'Two Problems in the Interpretation of the Port Books', *Econ. Hist. Rev.*, 2nd Ser., IX (1956).

Aris's Gazette (Birmingham).

Ashton, T. S., *Economic Fluctuations in England, 1700–1800* (1959).

Ashton, T. S., *The Economic History of England: The Eighteenth Century* (1955).

Ashton, T. S., *Iron and Steel in the Industrial Revolution* (1924).

Aveling, H., *Post Reformation Catholicism in East Yorkshire, 1558–1790* (East Yorks Local Hist. Soc., 1960).

Bang, N. & Korst, K., *Tabeller over Skibsfart og Varetransport Gennem Øresund, 1661–1783* (2 vols, Copenhagen, 1930, 1953).

Barker, T. C., 'Lancashire Coal, Cheshire Salt and the Rise of Liverpool', *Transactions of the Hist. Soc. of Lancs and Cheshire*, CIII (1951).

Battle, T., *Directory of . . . Hull*; periodically from 1790.

Beckwith, I. S., 'The River Trade of Gainsborough, 1500–1850', *Lincs History and Archaeology*, No. 2 (1967).

Bird, J. H., *The Major Seaports of the United Kingdom* (1963).

Bischoff, J., *A Comprehensive History of the Woollen and Worsted Manufacturers* (1842).

Blashill, T., *Evidences Relating to East Hull* (Hull, 1903). Mostly concerned with early history, but some references to industry in the eighteenth century.

Boucher, C. T. G., *John Rennie* (1963).

Boyce, J. A. S. L. Leighton-, *Smiths the Bankers* (National Provincial Bank, 1958). Contains a good section on Smiths & Thompson's bank.

Boyle, J. R., *Charters and Letters Patent Granted to Kingston-upon-Hull* (Hull, 1905).

Brace, H. W. C., *History of Seed Crushing in Great Britain* (1960).

Bridges, T., *Adventures of a Bank Note* (4 vols, London, 1770–1).

Brooks, F. W., *The Early Judgements of Trinity House, Hull* (Yorks. Archaeological Soc., 1951).

Brooks, F. W., *Order Book of Trinity House, 1632–65* (Yorks Archaeological Soc., 1942).

Burdekin, R., *Memoir of the Late Mr Robert Spence* (York, 1827).

Butler, R., *The History of Kirkstall Forge* (privately printed, Kirkstall, 1945).

Caine, C. (ed.), *Strother's Journal* (Hull, 1912). A shorter version of the manuscript *BM* Egerton 2479.

Campbell, R. H., *The Carron Company* (1961).

Carus-Wilson, E. M., *Medieval Merchant Venturers* (2nd edition, 1967).

Carus-Wilson, E. M. & Coleman, O., *England's Export Trade, 1275–1547* (1963).

Chalmers, G. *Estimate of the Comparative State of Great Britain* (1782).

Chambers, J. D., *The Vale of Trent, 1670–1800* (*Econ. Hist. Rev.*, Supplement 3).

Chetwynd, G. (ed.), *R. Burn's The Justice of the Peace* (5 vols, London, 1820 edn.)

Clark, G. N., *Guide to English Commercial Statistics, 1696–1782* (1938).

Cole, W. A., 'Trends in Eighteenth Century Smuggling', *Econ. Hist. Rev.*, 2nd Ser., X (1958).

Coleman, D. C., *The British Paper Industry, 1495–1860* (1958).

Cook, J., *The History of God's House of Hull, Commonly called the Charterhouse* (Hull, 1882).

Cormack, A. A., *Susan Carnegie* (privately printed, Aberdeen, 1966). Deals with Carnegies in Sweden, and has many references to Hull Factors there.

Court, W. H. B., *The Rise of the Midland Industries, 1600–1838* (1938).

Craig, R. & Jarvis, R., *Liverpool Registry of Merchant Ships* (Chetham Soc., Manchester, 1967).

Cregean, E. R. (ed.), *Argyle Estate Instructions, 1771–1805* (Scottish History Soc., 1964).

Crump, W. B., *The Leeds Woollen Industry, 1780–1820* (1931).

Crump, W. B. & Ghorbal, G., *History of the Huddersfield Woollen Industry* (1935).

Crutwell, C., *Tour Thro' the Whole Island* (5 vols, 1801).

Darwent, C. E., *The Story of Fish Street Church* (Hull, 1899).

Davis, R., 'English Foreign Trade, 1660–1700', *Econ. Hist. Rev.*, 2nd Ser., VII (1954).

Davis, R., 'English Foreign Trade, 1700–1770' *Econ. Hist. Rev.*, 2nd Ser., XV (1962).

Davis, R., *The Rise of the English Shipping Industry* (1962).

Davis, R., 'Seamen's Sixpences: An Index of Commercial Activity, 1697–1820', *Economica*, n.s., XXIII (1956).

Davis, R., *The Trade and Shipping of Hull, 1500–1700* (East Yorks Local Hist. Soc., 1964).

Defoe, D., *A Plan of the English Commerce* (1730).

Defoe, D., *A Tour Through England and Wales* (2 vols, Everyman edn, 1928).

De la Pryme, *The Diary of Abraham De la Pryme* (Surtees Soc., LIV, 1870).

Dickens, A. G. & MacMahon, K. A., *A Guide to Regional Studies on the East Riding of Yorks and the City of Hull* (Hull, 1956).

Duckham, B. F., 'The Fitzwilliams and the Navigation of the Yorkshire Derwent', *Northern History*, II (1967).

Duckham, B. F., 'Selby and the Aire and Calder Navigation, 1774–1826', *Journal of Transport History*, VII, 2 (1965).

Duckham, B. F., 'John Smeaton and the Calder and Hebble Navigation', *Journal of the Railway and Canal Historical Society*, X (1964).

Duckham, B. F., *The Yorkshire Ouse: The History of a River Navigation* (1967).

East, W. G., 'The Port of Kingston-upon-Hull during the Industrial Revolution', *Economica*, II (1931).

Eden, F., *The State of the Poor* (3 vols, 1797, reprinted 1966).

Ellerby, J. R., *History of the Minerva Lodge of Freemasons, No. 250, Hull, 1783–1933* (Hull, 1935).

Evans, G. H., *British Corporation Finance, 1775–1850* (Johns Hopkins Press, 1936).

Fairfax-Blakeborough, J., *Sykes of Sledmere* (1929).

Fisher, H. E. S., 'Anglo-Portuguese Trade, 1700–70', *Econ. Hist. Rev.*, 2nd Ser., XVI (1963).

Fisher, R., *Hearts of Oak* (1763).
Fitton, R. S. & Wadsworth, A. P., *The Strutts and the Arkwrights, 1794–1858* (1958).
Forster, E. M., *Marianne Thornton* (1956).
Frost, C., *An Address Delivered to the Literary and Philosophical Society, 5 November 1830* (Hull, 1830).
Gee, J., *The Trade and Navigation of Great Britain Considered* (1731).
Gent, T., *History of Kingston-upon-Hull* (Hull, 1735).
Gentleman's Magazine.
Gill, C., *Studies in Midland Industry* (1930).
Gill, C., *History of Birmingham* (1952).
Greenwood, J., *Picture of Hull* (Hull, 1835).
Hadley, G., *A New and Complete History of the Town and County of the Town of Kingston-upon-Hull* (Hull, 1788).
Hamilton, H., *An Economic History of Scotland in the Eighteenth Century* (1963).
Harris, A., *The Rural Landscape of the East Riding of Yorkshire, 1700–1850* (1961).
Harris, S. A., 'Henry Berry (1720–1812): Liverpool's Second Dock Engineer', *Transactions of the Hist. Soc. of Lancs and Cheshire*, LXXXIX (1937) and XC (1938).
Heaton, H., *The Yorkshire Woollen and Worsted Industries* (2nd edn, 1965).
Heaton, H., 'Yorkshire Cloth Traders in the U.S., 1770–1840', *Proceedings of the Thoresby Soc.*, Vol 37 (1941).
Heckscher, E., *An Economic History of Sweden* (Harvard, 1954).
Henderson, W. O., 'The Anglo-French Commercial Treaty of 1786', *Econ. Hist. Rev.*, 2nd Ser., X (1957).
Hildebrand, K. G., 'Foreign Markets for Swedish Iron in the Eighteenth Century', *Scandinavian Econ. Hist. Rev.*, VI, i (1958).
Hodgson, A. J. & Rudolf, G. R., *Law of General Average* (7th edn, 1948).
Hoon, E. E., *The Organization of the English Customs System, 1696–1786* (1938).
Hopkinson, G. G., 'The Development of Inland Navigations in South Yorkshire and North Derbyshire, 1697–1850', *Transactions of the Hunter Soc.*, VII, v (1954).
Hoskins, W. G., *Industry, Trade and People in Exeter, 1688–1800* (1935).
Hughes, E., *North Country Life in the Eighteenth Century* (1952).
Hull Advertiser and Exchange Gazette.
Hull Courant. A few copies, *c.* 1750, are preserved in Hull Central Library.
Hull Packet.
Ingram, E., *Leaves from a Family Tree* (Hull, 1951).
Ingram, E., *Our Lady of Hull* (Hull, 1948). A History of 'Low' Church—St Mary's.
Jackman, W. T., *The Development of Transport in Modern England* (2 vols, 1916).
Jackson, G., 'The Foundation of Trinity House School, Kingston-upon-Hull: An Experiment in Marine Education', *Durham Research Review*, VI, 21 (1968).
Jackson, G., *Grimsby and the Haven Company, 1796–1846* (1971).
Jackson, G., 'The Struggle for the First Hull Dock', *Transport History*, I, i (1968).

Jarvis, R. C., 'The Appointment of Ports', *Econ. Hist. Rev.*, 2nd Ser., XI (1959).

Jarvis, R. C., *Customs Letter Books of the Port of Liverpool, 1711–1813* (1954).

Jarvis, R. C., 'Sources for the History of Ports' and 'Sources for the History of Ships and Shipping', *Journal of Transport History*, III (1957–58).

John, A. H., *The Walker Family, 1741–1893* (1951).

Johnson, L. G., *General Perronet Thompson* (1957).

Jones, J. A. Rupert-, 'King's Ships Built at Hull', *Notes & Queries*, 156 (1929).

Jones, L. R., 'Kingston-upon-Hull: a Study in Port Development', *Scottish Geographical Magazine*, 35 (1919).

Kent, H. S. K., 'Anglo-Norwegian Timber Trade in the Eighteenth Century', *Econ. Hist. Rev.*, 2nd. Ser., VIII (1955).

King & Company, *The Bicentenary of the House of King's* (Hull, 1944).

King, J., *Memoir of the Reverend Thomas Dykes* (London, 1849).

Lambert, G. M., *Two Thousand Years of Guild Life, Together with a Full Account of the Guilds and Trading Companies of Kingston-upon-Hull, from the Fourteenth Century to the Eighteenth Century* (London, 1891).

Lawson, J., *A Town Grammar School* (1963).

Leeds Intelligencer.

Leeds Mercury.

Lindsey, J., *The Canals of Scotland* (1968).

Lloyd, G. I. H., *The Cutlery Trades* (1913).

London Gazette.

Lowe, R., *Agriculture of Nottinghamshire* (1794).

Lubbock, B., *The Arctic Whalers* (1937).

McClelland, D. C., *The Achieving Society* (Princeton, N.J., 1961).

MacMahon, K. A., *Acts of Parliament and Proclamations Relating to the East Riding of Yorkshire and Kingston-upon-Hull, 1529–1800* (Hull, 1961).

MacMahon, K. A. (ed.), *An Index to the Hull Advertiser & Exchange Gazette, 1794–1825*. (Typescript published by the Dept. of Adult Education, University of Hull, 1955.)

MacMahon, K. A., *Roads and Turnpikes in East Yorkshire* (East Yorks Local Hist. Soc., 1964).

Macpherson, D., *Annals of Commerce* (4 vols, 1805).

Malone, J. J., *Pine Trees and Politics* (1964).

Mason, B. B., *A Brief History of the Origin and Progress of the Dock Company at Kingston-upon-Hull* (Hull, 1885).

Matthews, P. W., *History of Barclays Bank* (1926). Contains a very brief account of Pease's Bank.

Mathias, P., *The Brewing Industry in England, 1700–1830* (1959).

Minchinton, W. E., *The British Tinplate Industry* (1957).

Minchinton, W. E., 'The Merchants in England in the Eighteenth Century', in *The Entrepreneur, Papers Presented at the Annual Conference of the Economic History Society, April 1957* (Harvard, 1957).

Minchinton, W. E., *The Trade of Bristol in the Eighteenth Century* (Bristol Record Society, 1957).

Muir, R., *A History of Liverpool* (Liverpool, 1907).

Namier, L. & Brooke, J., *The House of Commons, 1754–90* (3 vols, 1964).

Oddy, J. J., *European Commerce* (1805).

Park, G. R., *Parliamentary Representation of Yorkshire* (Hull, 1886).

Parkinson, C. N., *The Rise of the Port of Liverpool* (Liverpool, 1952).

Peck, W., *Bawtry and Thorne* (1813).

Peet, H., 'Thomas Steers, the Engineer of Liverpool's First Dock', *Transactions of the Hist. Soc. of Lancs and Cheshire*, LXXXII (1930–2).

Pool, B., *Navy Boards Contracts, 1660–1832* (1966).

Postlethwayte, M., *Great Britain's True System . . .* (1752).

Poulson, G., *The History . . . of Holderness* (2 vols, 1840–1).

Power, E. & Postan, M. M., *Studies in English Trade in the Fifteenth Century* (1933, reprinted 1951).

Pressnell, L. S., *Country Banking in the Industrial Revolution* (1956).

Pressnell, L. S. (ed.), *Studies in the Industrial Revolution* (1960).

Raistrick, A., 'The South Yorkshire Iron Industry, 1698–1756', *Transactions of the Newcomen Society*, XIX (1939).

Raistrick, A., 'Lead Mines in Upper Wharfedale', *Yorkshire Bulletin of Economic and Social Research*, V (1953).

Ramsay, G. D., *English Overseas Trade During the Centuries of Emergence* (1957).

Ramsden, G., 'Two Notes on the History of the Aire and Calder Navigation', *Proceedings of the Thoresby Soc.*, XLI (1953).

Reading, D. K., *The Anglo-Russian Commercial Treaty of 1734* (Yale, 1938).

Redford, A., *Manchester Merchants and Foreign Trade, 1794–1858* (1934).

Richardson, W. (ed.), *Practical Sermons by the Late Rev. J. Milner . . . to which is prefixed An Account of the Life . . . of the Author . . . by the Rev. Isaac Milner . . .* (1801).

Rimmer, W. G., *Marshalls of Leeds, Flax Spinners, 1788–1886* (1960).

Rose, Down & Thompson, *At the Tail of Two Centuries.* (A brief firm history, privately printed, London, 1949.)

Schumpeter, E. B., *English Overeas Trade Statistics, 1697–1808* (1960).

Sheahan, J. J., *General and Concise History and Description of the Town and Port of Kingston-upon-Hull* (London, 1864).

Shepherd, T., *Methodism and the Literature of the Eighteenth Century* (1940).

Sheppard, T., *The Evolution of Hull* (Hull, 1911). A collection of local maps.

Shipley, C. E. (ed.), *The Baptists of Yorkshire* (1912).

Skeel, C. A. J., 'The Letter Books of a Quaker Merchant, 1756–58', *English Historical Review*, XXX (1916). Deals with Gainsborough and Trent trade.

Smout, T. C., 'Early Glasgow Sugar Houses, 1660–1720', *Econ. Hist. Rev.*, 2nd Ser, XIV (1961).

Sperling, J., 'The International Payments Mechanism in the Seventeenth and Eighteenth Centuries', *Econ. Hist. Rev.*, 2nd Ser, XIV (1961).

Stackpole, E. A., *The Sea Hunters: The New England Whalemen During Two Centuries, 1635–1835* (Philadelphia, 1953).

Stark, A., *History of Gainsborough* (London, 1843).

Storey, A., *Trinity House of Kingston-upon-Hull.* (Published by Trinity House, Hull, 1967.)

Strickland, H. E., *The Agriculture of the East Riding of Yorkshire* (1812).

Swann, D., 'The Engineers of English Port Improvements, 1660–1830', *Transport History*, I, 2 and 3 (1968).

Symons, J., *High Street Hull* (Hull, 1862). Unreliable.

Tawney, R. H. & Power, E., *Tudor Economic Documents* (3 vols, 1924).

Tickell, J., *The History of the Town and County of Kingston-upon-Hull* (Hull, 1798).

Timperley, J., 'An Account of the Harbour and Docks at Kingston-upon-Hull', *Transactions of the Institution of Civil Engineers*, I (1842).

Thompson, Thomas, *Considerations on the Poor Rates and State of the Workhouse in Kingston-upon-Hull* (1800).

Thompson, W. H., *Early Chapters in Hull Methodism, 1746–1800* (Hull, 1895).

Treffry, R., *Remarks on Revivals of Religion* (Hull, 1827).

Tudors Mash & Company, *Pioneers in Paint*. Brief firm history, privately printed, 1949.

Turner, W., *Modern Delineation of Hull* (Hull, 1805).

Unwin, R. W., 'The Aire and Calder Navigation, Part I: The Beginning of the Navigation', *Bradford Antiquary*, n.s., XLII (1964).

Wadsworth, A. P. & Mann, J de L., *The Cotton Trade and Industrial Lancashire* (1931).

Wearmouth, R. F., *Methodism and the Common People of the Eighteenth Century* (1945).

Weatherill, R., *The Ancient Port of Whitby and its Shipping* (Whitby, 1908).

Webb, S. &. B., *English Local Government* (7 vols, 1922).

Wesley, J., *Journey* (standard Edition, 8 vols, 1909).

Whitaker, W., *One Line of the Puritan Tradition in Hull: Bowl Alley Lane Chapel* (London, 1910).

Whitworth, C., *State of the Trade of Great Britain in its Imports and Exports Progressively from the Year 1697* (1776).

Wilberforce, R. I. & S., *The Life of William Wilberforce* (5 vols, 1838).

Wilkinson, T., *Memoirs of His Own Life* (4 vols, York, 1790).

Wilkinson, T., *The Wandering Patentee, or a History of the Yorkshire Theatre* (4 vols, York, 1795).

Willan, T. S., *The Early History of the Don Navigation* (1965).

Willan, T. S., *The Early History of the Russia Company, 1553–1603* (1956).

Willan, T. S., *The English Coasting Trade, 1600–1750* (1938).

Willan, T. S., *River Navigation in England, 1600–1750* (1936).

Willan, T. S., *Studies in Elizabethan Foreign Trade* (1959).

Williams, J. E., 'Whitehaven in the Eighteenth Century', *Econ. Hist. Rev.*, 2nd Ser., VIII (1956).

Wilson, C., *Anglo-Dutch Commerce and Finance in the Eighteenth Century* (1941).

Wilson, C., *England's Apprenticeship* (1966).

Wilson, R. G., 'Transport Dues as Indices of Economic Growth, 1775–1820', *Econ. Hist. Rev.*, 2nd Ser., XIX (1966).

Wood, A. C., *A History of Nottinghamshire* (1948).

Woods, A. C., 'The History of Trade and Transport on the River Trent', *Thoroton Soc.*, LIV (1950).

Woolley, W. (ed.), *A Collection of Statutes Relating to the Town of Kingston-upon-Hull* (Hull, 1830).
Wright, C. &. Fayle, C. E., *A History of Lloyds* (1928).
Wright, W., 'The Hull Docks', *Minutes of Proceedings of the Institution of Civil Engineers*, XLI (1875).
Young, A., *General View of the Agriculture of Lincolnshire* (1799).
Young, A., *A Six Months Tour Through the North of England* (4 vols, 1770).
Young, G., *A History of Whitby* (2 vols, Whitby, 1817).

Fig. 1. The Hinterland of Hull, showing the chief navigations at the end of the eighteenth century

Fig. 2. The Chief Ports with which Hull traded in the eighteenth century

Fig. 3. British Ports with which Hull traded in 1775 (ports with single shipments are marked but not named)

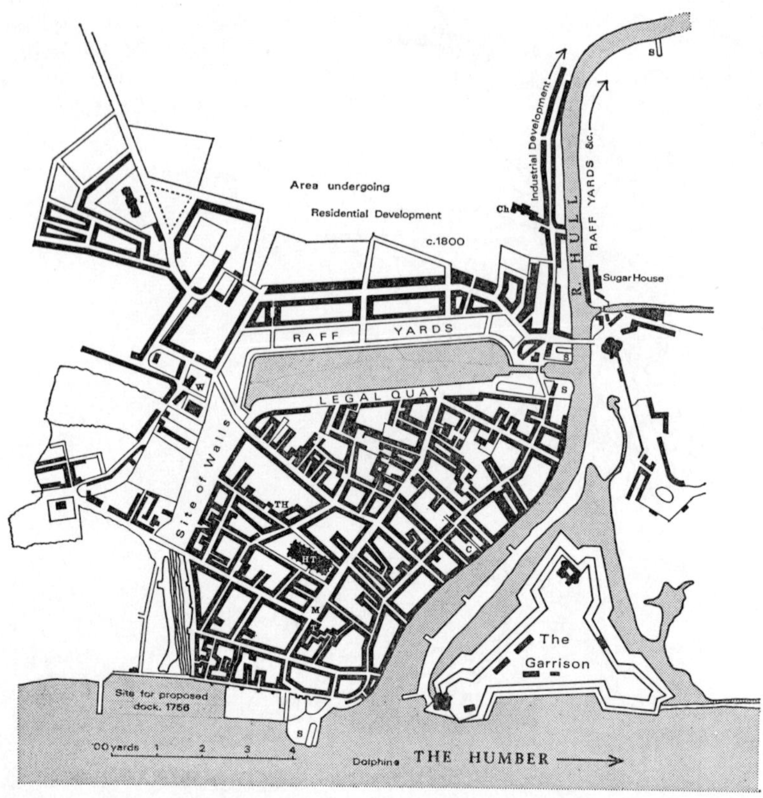

Fig. 4. Hull *c.* 1790, showing the Old Town and the development following the building of the first dock. Based on a plan by Anthony Bower, 1791

KEY

C	=	Custom House	T	=	Old Town Hall
CH	=	Charterhouse	TH	=	Trinity House
HT	=	Holy Trinity	S	=	Shipyards
I	=	Infirmary	W	=	Water works
M	=	Market Place			

INDEX

SHIPS MENTIONED IN THE TEXT